# British Qualifications 2014

# British Qualifications 2014

**44TH EDITION**

**A Complete Guide to Professional, Vocational & Academic Qualifications in the United Kingdom**

LONDON PHILADELPHIA NEW DELHI

**Publisher's note**
Every possible effort has been made to ensure that the information contained in this book is accurate at the time of going to press, and the publishers and authors cannot accept responsibility for any errors or omissions, however caused. No responsibility for loss or damage occasioned to any person acting, or refraining from action, as a result of the material in this publication can be accepted by the editor, the publisher or any of the authors.

First published in Great Britain in 1966

Forty-fourth edition published in Great Britain and the United States in 2014 by Kogan Page Limited



2nd Floor, 45 Gee Street
London EC1V 3RS
United Kingdom
www.koganpage.com

1518 Walnut Street, Suite 1100
Philadelphia PA 19102
USA

4737/23 Ansari Road
Daryaganj
New Delhi 110002
India



**British Library Cataloguing-in-Publication Data**

A CIP record for this book is available from the British Library.

ISBN 978 0 7494 7093 7
E-ISBN 978 0 7494 7094 4
ISSN 0141-5972

Typeset by AMA DataSet Ltd, Preston
Print production managed by Jellyfish
Printed and bound by www.printondemand-worldwide.com

# PUBLISHER'S NOTE

This 44th edition of *British Qualifications* has been considerably revised and updated to reflect the many changes in degree, diploma and certificate courses and to take account of legislative reforms affecting the structure of higher and further education over the past year.

The editor and compilers are most grateful to the academic registrars and the secretaries of the many bodies they have contacted for information and advice. Without their cooperation, the revision and updating of *British Qualifications* would not have been possible.

# CONTENTS

# REFERENCES

Association of MBAs (AMBA) (annual) *AMBA – Financial Times Guide to Business Schools*, AMBA, London

Committee of Vice-Chancellors and Principals (CVCP) (annual) *University Entrance: The official guide*, CVCP, London

Department for Education and Skills (DfES) (2003) *The Future of Higher Education*, The Stationery Office, London [online] http://www.dfes.gov.uk/hegateway/strategy/hestrategy/foreword.shtml

DfES (2004) *Five-Year Strategy for Children and Learners*, DfES, London

Qualifications and Curriculum Authority (QCA) (2004) *New Thinking for Reform: A framework for achievement*, QCA, London (July)

# HOW TO USE THIS BOOK

You may find these notes helpful when using the book.

**Part 1** presents an overview of the further and higher educational systems currently in operation in the United Kingdom, including a discussion of the major reforms that have taken place over the past year and their impact.

**Part 2** takes a look at the teaching establishments whose qualifications are listed in Part 4 of the book, offering an explanation of the different types of institution, their place in the overall system and the levels of qualification that they award.

**Part 3** presents a detailed description of vocational qualifications awarded by many of the professional associations included in Part 5, including an explanation of validating, examining and awarding bodies.

**Part 4** is a directory of qualifications awarded by universities in the United Kingdom (ordered by university name). There is a brief introduction detailing admission to degree courses, degree structure and the various categories of degree available.

**Part 5** is a directory of qualifications awarded by professional, trade and specialist associations in the United Kingdom (ordered by profession / discipline), including certificates, diplomas, NVQs and SVQs. A short introduction explains the functions of professional associations and how to gain membership.

**Part 6** describes various bodies involved in the accreditation of colleges in the independent sector of further and higher education.

**Part 7** is a list of study associations and learned societies.

Also included (at the beginning of the book) is a list of all abbreviations and designatory letters used throughout *British Qualifications*.

# INDEX OF ABBREVIATIONS AND DESIGNATORY LETTERS

| | |
|---|---|
| AAB | Associate of the Association of Book-keepers |
| AACB | Associate of the Association of Certified Bookkeepers |
| AACP | Associate of the Association of Computer Professionals |
| AAFC | Associate of the Association of Financial Controllers and Administrators |
| AAIA | Associate of the Association of International Accountants |
| AAMS | Associate of the Association of Medical Secretaries, Practice Managers, Administrators and Receptionists |
| AASI | Associate of the Ambulance Service Institute |
| AASW | Advanced Award in Social Work |
| AAT | Association of Accounting Technicians |
| ABC | Awarding Body Consortium |
| ABDO | Associate of the British Dispensing Opticians |
| ABE | Association of Business Executives |
| ABEng | Associate Member of the Association of Building Engineers |
| ABHA | Associate of the British Hypnotherapy Association |
| ABIAT | Associate Member of the British Institute of Architectural Technologists |
| ABIPP | Associate of the British Institute of Professional Photography |
| ABMA | Associate of the Business Management Association |
| ABPR | Association of British Picture Restorers |
| ABRSM | Associated Board of the Royal Schools of Music |
| ABS | Association of Business Schools |
| ABSSG | Associate of the British Society of Scientific Glassblowers |
| ACA | Associate of the Institute of Chartered Accountants in England and Wales |
| ACA | Associate of the Institute of Chartered Accountants in Ireland |
| ACB | Association of Certified Bookkeepers |
| ACC | Accredited Clinical Coders |
| ACCA | Associate of the Association of Chartered Certified Accountants |
| ACCA | Association of Chartered Certified Accountants |
| ACE | Association for Conferences and Events |
| ACEA | Associate of the Institute of Cost and Executive Accountants |
| ACertCM | Archbishop of Canterbury's Certificate in Church Music |
| ACGI | Associate of City and Guilds of London Institute |
| ACIArb | Associate of the Chartered Institute of Arbitrators |
| ACIB | Associate of the Chartered Institute of Bankers |
| ACIBS | Associate of the Chartered Institute of Bankers in Scotland |
| ACIBSE | Associate of the Chartered Institution of Building Services Engineers |
| ACIH | Associate of the Chartered Institute of Housing |
| ACII | Associate of the Chartered Insurance Institute |
| ACILA | Associate of the Chartered Institute of Loss Adjusters |
| ACIM | Associate of the Chartered Institute of Marketing |
| ACIOB | Associate of the Chartered Institute of Building |
| ACIS | Associate of the Institute of Chartered Secretaries and Administrators |
| ACIT | Advanced Certificate in International Trade |
| ACLIP | Certified Affiliate of CILIP |
| ACMA | Associate of the Chartered Institute of Management Accountants |
| ACP | Association of Child Psychotherapists |
| ACP | Associate of the College of Preceptors |

| | |
|---|---|
| ACP | Association of Computer Professionals |
| ACPM | Associate of the Confederation of Professional Management |
| ACPP | Associate of the College of Pharmacy Practice |
| ACT | Associate of the College of Teachers |
| ACYW | Associate of the Community and Youth Work Association |
| ADCE | Advanced Diploma in Childcare and Education |
| ADCM | Archbishop of Canterbury's Diploma in Church Music |
| AdDipEd | Advanced Diploma in Education |
| ADI | Approved Driving Instructor |
| AECI | Association Member of the Institute of Employment Consultants |
| AEWVH | Association for the Education and Welfare of the Visually Handicapped |
| AFA | Associate of the Faculty of Actuaries |
| AFA | Associate of the Institute of Financial Accountants |
| AFBPsS | Associate Fellow of the British Psychological Society |
| AFCI | Associate of the Faculty of Commerce and Industry Ltd |
| AffBMA | Affiliate of the Business Management Association |
| AffIManf | Affiliate of the Institute of Manufacturing |
| AffIMI | Affiliate of the Institute of the Motor Industry |
| AffIMS | Affiliate of the Institute of Management Specialists |
| AffInstM | Affiliate of the Meat Training Council |
| AffIP | Affiliate of the Institute of Plumbing |
| AffProfBTM | Affiliate of Professional Business and Technical Management |
| AFIMA | Associate Fellow of the Institute of Mathematics and its Applications |
| AFISOL | Aerodrome Flight Information Service Officer's Licence |
| AFPC | Advanced Financial Planning Certificate |
| AFRCSEd | Associate Fellow of Royal College of Surgeons of Edinburgh |
| AGCL | Associate of the Guild of Cleaners and Launderers |
| AGI | Associate of the Greek Institute |
| AGSM | Associate of the Guildhall School of Music and Drama |
| AHCIMA | Associate of the Hotel and Catering International Management Association |
| AHFS | Associate of the Council of Health Fitness and Sports Therapists |
| AHRIM | Associate of the Institute of Health Record Information and Management |
| AIA | Associate of the Institute of Actuaries |
| AIA | Association of International Accountants |
| AIAgrE | Associate of the Institution of Agricultural Engineers |
| AIAT | Associate of the Institute of Asphalt Technology |
| AIBCM | Associate of the Institute of British Carriage and Automobile Manufacturers |
| AIBMS | Associate of the Institute of Biomedical Science |
| AICB | Associate of the Institute of Certified Book-Keepers |
| AIChor | Associate of the Benesh Institute of Choreology |
| AICHT | Associate of the International Council of Holistic Therapists |
| AICM(Cert) | Associate Member of the Institute of Credit Management |
| AICS | Associate of the Institution of Chartered Shipbrokers |
| AICSc | Associate of the Institute of Consumer Sciences Incorporating Home Economics |
| AIDTA | Associate of the International Dance Teachers' Association |
| AIE | Associate of the Institute of Electrolysis |
| AIEM | Associate of the Institute of Executives and Managers |
| AIExpE | Associate of the Institute of Explosive Engineers |
| AIFA | Associate of the Institute of Field Archaeologists |
| AIFBQ | Associate of the International Faculty of Business Qualifications |
| AIFireE | Associate of the Institution of Fire Engineers |
| AIFP | Associate of the British International Freight Association |

| | |
|---|---|
| AIGD | Associate of the Institute of Grocery Distribution |
| AIHort | Associate Member of the Institute of Horticulture |
| AIIMR | Associate of the Institute of Investment Management and Research |
| AIIRSM | Associate of the International Institute of Risk and Safety Management |
| AIL | Associate of the Institute of Linguists |
| AILAM | Associate of the Institute of Leisure and Amenity Management |
| AIMBM | Associate of the Institute of Maintenance and Building Management |
| AIMC | Associate of the Institute of Management Consultancy |
| AIMgt | Associate of the Institute of Management |
| AIMIS | Associate of the Institute for the Management of Information Systems |
| AIMM | Associate of the Institute of Massage and Movement |
| AInstAM | Associate of the Institute of Administrative Management |
| AInstBA | Associate of the Institute of Business Administration |
| AInstBCA | Associate of the Institute of Burial and Cremation Administration |
| AInstBM | Associate of the Institute of Builders' Merchants |
| AInstCM | Associate of the Institute of Commercial Management |
| AInstM | Associate of the Meat Training Council |
| AInstPkg | Associate of the Institute of Packaging |
| AInstPM | Associate of the Institute of Professional Managers and Administrators |
| AInstSMM | Associate of the Institute of Sales and Marketing Management |
| AInstTA | Associate of the Institute of Transport Administration |
| AInstTT | Associate Member of the Institute of Travel and Tourism |
| AIOC | Associate of the Institute of Carpenters |
| AIOFMS | Associate of the Institute of Financial and Management Studies |
| AIP | Associate of the Institute of Plumbing |
| AIQA | Associate of the Institute of Quality Assurance |
| AIS | Accredited Imaging Scientist |
| AISOB | Associate of the Incorporated Society of Organ Builders |
| AISTD | Associate of the Imperial Society of Teachers of Dancing |
| AISTDDip | Associate Diploma of the Imperial Society of Teachers of Dancing |
| AITSA | Associate of the Institute of Trading Standards Administration |
| AIVehE | Associate of the Institute of Vehicle Engineers |
| AIWSc | Associate Member of the Institute of Wood Science |
| ALCM | Associate of the London College of Music |
| ALI | Associate of the Landscape Institute |
| ALS | Associate of the Linnean Society of London |
| AMA | Associate of the Museums Association |
| AMABE | Associate Member of the Association of Business Executives |
| AMAE | Associate Member of the Academy of Experts |
| AMASI | Associate Member of the Architecture and Surveying Institute |
| AMBA | Association of MBAs |
| AMBA | Non-Teacher Associate Member of the British (Theatrical) Arts |
| AMBCS | Associate Member of the British Computer Society |
| AMBII | Associate Member of the British Institute of Innkeeping |
| AmCAM | Associate of the Communication Advertising and Marketing Education Foundation |
| AMCT | Associate of the Association of Corporate Treasurers |
| AMCTHCM | Associate Member of the Confederation of Tourism, Hotel and Catering Management |
| AMI | Association Montessori Internationale |
| AMIA | Affiliated Member of the Association of International Accountants |
| AMIAgrE | Associate Member of the Institution of Agricultural Engineers |
| AMIAP | Associate Member of the Institution of Analysts and Programmers |

| | |
|---|---|
| AMIAT | Associate Member of the Institute of Asphalt Technology |
| AMIBC | Associate Member of the Institute of Building Control |
| AMIBCM | Associate Member of the Institute of British Carriage and Automobile Manufacturers |
| AMIBE | Associate Member of the Institution of British Engineers |
| AMIBF | Associate Member of the Institute of British Foundrymen |
| AMICE | Associate Member of the Institution of Civil Engineers |
| AMIChemE | Associate Member of the Institution of Chemical Engineers |
| AMIED | Associate Member of the Institution of Engineering Designers |
| AMIEE | Associate Member of the Institution of Electrical Engineers |
| AMIEx | Associate Member of the Institute of Export |
| AMIHIE | Associate Member of the Institute of Highway Incorporated Engineers |
| AMIHT | Associate Member of the Institution of Highways and Transportation |
| AMIIE | Associate Member of the Institution of Incorporated Engineers |
| AMIExE | Associate Member of the Institution of Incorporated Executive Engineers |
| AMIIHTM | Associate Member of the International Institute of Hospitality Tourism & Management |
| AMIISE | Associate Member of the International Institute of Social Economics |
| AMIM | Associate Member of the Institute of Materials |
| AMIManf | Member of the Institute of Manufacturing |
| AMIMechE | Associate Member of the Institution of Mechanical Engineers |
| AMIMechIE | Associate Member of the Institution of Mechanical Incorporated Engineers |
| AMIMI | Associate Member of the Institute of the Motor Industry |
| AMIMinE | Associate of the Institute of Mining Engineers |
| AMIMM | Associate Member of the Institution of Mining and Metallurgy |
| AMIMS | Associate Member of the Institute of Management Specialists |
| AMInstAEA | Associate Member of the Institute of Automotive Engineer Assessors |
| AMInstBE | Associate Member of the Institution of British Engineers |
| AMInstE | Associate Member of the Institute of Energy |
| AMInstR | Associate Member of the Institute of Refrigeration |
| AMInstTA | Associate Member of the Institute of Transport Administration |
| AMIPlantE | Associate Member of the Institution of Plant Engineers |
| AMIPR | Associate Member of the Institute of Public Relations |
| AMIPRE | Associate Member of the Incorporated Practitioners in Radio and Electronics |
| AMIQ | Associate Member of the Institute of Quarrying |
| AMIQA | Associate Member of the Institute of Quality Assurance |
| AMIRTE | Associate Member of the Institute of Road Transport Engineers |
| AMISM | Associate Member of the Institute for Supervision & Management |
| AMIStrutE | Associate Member of the Institution of Structural Engineers |
| AMITD | Associate Member of the Institute of Training and Development |
| AMIVehE | Associate Member of the Institute of Vehicle Engineers |
| AMNI | Associate Member of the Nautical Institute |
| AMPA | Associate Member of the Master Photographers Association |
| AMProfBTM | Associate Member of Professional Business and Technical Management |
| AMRAeS | Associate Member of the Royal Aeronautical Society |
| AMRSH | Associate Member of the Royal Society for the Promotion of Health |
| AMS | Associate of the Institute of Management Services |
| AMS(Aff) | Affiliate of the Association of Medical Secretaries, Practice Managers, Administrators and Receptionists |
| AMSE | Associate Member of the Society of Engineers (Inc) |
| AMSPAR | Association of Medical Secretaries, Practice Managers, Administrators and Receptionists |

| | |
|---|---|
| AMusEd | Associate Diploma in Music Education |
| AMusLCM | Associate in Music of the London College of Music |
| AMusTCL | Associate in Music of Trinity College of Music |
| AMWES | Associate Member of the Women's Engineering Society |
| ANAEA | Associate of the National Association of Estate Agents |
| ANCA | Advanced National Certificate in Agriculture |
| AOP | Association of Photographers |
| AOR | Association of Reflexologists |
| APA | Accreditation of Prior Experience |
| APC | Assessment of Professional Competence |
| APCS | Associate of the Property Consultants Society |
| APMI | Associate of the Pensions Management Institute |
| APMP | Association for Project Management Professional |
| AQA | Assessment & Qualifications Alliance |
| ARAD | Associate of the Royal Academy of Dancing |
| ARAM | Associate of the Royal Academy of Music |
| ARB | Architects Registration Board |
| ARCM | Associate of Royal College of Music |
| ARCO | Associate of the Royal College of Organists |
| ARCS | Associate of the Royal College of Science |
| AREC | Associate of the Recruitment and Employment Confederation |
| ARELS | Association of Recognised English Language Services |
| ARELS-FELCO | Association of Recognised English Language Teaching Establishments in Britain |
| ARIBA | Associate of the Royal Institute of British Architects |
| ARICS | Associate of the Royal Institution of Chartered Surveyors |
| ARIPHH | Associate of the Royal Institute of Public Health and Hygiene |
| ARPS | Associate of the Royal Photographic Society |
| ARSC | Associate of the Royal Society of Chemistry |
| ARSCM | Associate of the Royal School of Church Music |
| ARSM | Associate of the Royal School of Mines |
| AS | Advanced Supplementary level |
| ASCA | Associate of the Institute of Company Accountants |
| ASCT | Associate of the Society of Claims Technicians |
| ASDC | Associate of the Society of Dyers and Colourists |
| ASE | Associate of the Society of Engineers (Inc) |
| ASI | Ambulance Service Institute |
| ASI | Architecture and Surveying Institute |
| ASIAffil | Affiliate of the Ambulance Service Institute |
| ASIS | Accredited Senior Imaging Scientist |
| ASLC | Advanced Secretarial Language Certificate |
| ASMA | Associate of the Society of Sales Management Administrators Ltd |
| ASNN | Associate of the Society of Nursery Nursing |
| AssCI | Associate of the Institute of Commerce |
| AssociateCIPD | Associate of the Chartered Institute of Personnel and Development |
| AssociateIEEE | Associate of the Institution of Electrical and Electronics Engineers Incorporated |
| AssociateIIE | Associate of the Institution of Incorporated Engineers |
| AssocIMechIE | Associate of the Institution of Mechanical Incorporated Engineers |
| AssocIPD | Associate of the Institute of Personnel & Development |
| AssocIPHE | Associate of the Institution of Public Health Engineers |
| AssocMIWM | Associate Member of the Institute of Wastes Management |
| AssocTechIIE | Associate Technician of the Institution of Incorporated Engineers |
| ASTA | Associate of the Swimming Teachers' Association |

| | |
|---|---|
| ASVA | Associate of the Incorporated Society of Valuers and Auctioneers |
| ATC | Art Teacher's Certificate |
| ATCL | Associate of Trinity College of Music |
| ATCLicence | Air Traffic Controller's Licence |
| ATCLTESOL | Associate Diploma in the Teaching of English to Speakers of Other Languages, Trinity College |
| ATD | Art Teacher's Diploma |
| ATI | Associate of the Textile Industry |
| ATII | Associate of the Chartered Institute of Taxation |
| ATPL | Airline Transport Pilot's Licence |
| ATSC | Associate of the Oil and Colour Chemists' Association |
| ATSC | Associate in the Technology of Surface Coatings |
| ATT | Association of Taxation Technicians |
| ATT | Member of the Association of Taxation Technicians |
| ATTA | Association of Therapy Teachers Associate |
| ATTF | Association of Therapy Teachers Fellow |
| ATTM | Association of Therapy Teachers Member |
| AWeldI | Associate of the Welding Institute |
| BA | Bachelor of Arts |
| BA(Econ) | Bachelor of Arts in Economics & Social Studies |
| BA(Ed) | Bachelor of Arts (Education) |
| BA(Lan) | Bachelor of Languages |
| BA(Law) | Bachelor of Arts in Law |
| BA(Music) | Bachelor of Music |
| BABTAC | British Association of Beauty Therapy and Cosmetology Ltd |
| BAC | British Accreditation Council for Independent Further and Higher Education |
| BAC | British Association for Counselling |
| BAcc | Bachelor of Accountancy |
| BACP | British Association for Counselling Psychotherapy |
| BADA | British Antique Dealers' Association |
| BADN | British Association of Dental Nurses |
| BAE | British Association of Electrolysists Ltd |
| BAGMA | British Agricultural and Garden Machinery Association |
| BAgr | Bachelor of Agriculture |
| BAO | Bachelor of Obstetrics |
| BAP | British Association of Psychotherapists |
| BArch | Bachelor of Architecture |
| BASELT | British Association in State English Language Teaching |
| BBO | British Ballet Organisation |
| BChD | Bachelor of Dental Surgery |
| BChir | Bachelor of Surgery |
| BCL | Bachelor of Civil Law |
| BCom | Bachelor of Commerce |
| BCombStuds | Bachelor of Combined Studies |
| BComm | Bachelor of Communications |
| BCS | Bachelor of Combined Studies |
| BCS | British Computer Society |
| BD | Bachelor of Divinity |
| BDA | British Dietetic Association |
| BDes | Bachelor of Design |
| BDS | Bachelor of Dental Surgery |
| BEconSc | Bachelor of Economics |

| | |
|---|---|
| BECTU | Broadcasting, Entertainment, Cinematograph and Theatre Union |
| BEd | Bachelor of Education |
| BEng | Bachelor of Engineering |
| BEng and Man | Bachelor of Mechanical Engineering, Manufacture and Management |
| BER | Board for Engineers' Regulation |
| BFA | Bachelor of Fine Arts |
| BFin | Bachelor of Finance |
| BHA | British Hypnotherapy Association |
| BHI | British Horological Institute Ltd |
| BHS | British Horse Society |
| BHSAI | British Horse Society's Assistant Instructor's Certificate |
| BHSI | British Horse Society's Instructor's Certificate |
| BHSII | British Horse Society's Intermediate Instructor's Certificate |
| BHSIntSM | British Horse Society's Intermediate Stable Manager's Certificate |
| BHSSM | British Horse Society's Stable Manager's Certificate |
| BIA | Beauty Industry Authority |
| BIAT | British Institute of Architectural Technologists |
| BIBA | Bachelor of International Business Administration |
| BIE | British Institute of Embalmers |
| BIFA | British International Freight Association |
| BIPP | British Institute of Professional Photography |
| BIS | British Interplanetary Society |
| BKSTS | British Kinematograph Sound and Television Society |
| BLD | Bachelor of Landscape Design |
| BLE | Bachelor of Land Economy |
| BLEng | Bi-Lingual Engineer |
| BLib | Bachelor of Librarianship |
| BLing | Bachelor of Linguistics |
| BLitt | Bachelor of Letters |
| BLS | Bachelor of Library Studies |
| BM | Bachelor of Medicine |
| BMA | British Medical Association |
| BM, BCh | Conjoint degree of Bachelor of Medicine, Bachelor of Surgery |
| BM, BS | Conjoint degree of Bachelor of Medicine, Bachelor of Surgery |
| BMedBiol | Bachelor of Medical Biology |
| BMedSci | Bachelor of Medical Sciences |
| BMedSci(Speech) | Bachelor of Medical Sciences (Speech) |
| BMet | Bachelor of Metallurgy |
| BMid | Bachelor of Midwifery |
| BMidwif | Bachelor of Midwifery |
| BMSc | Bachelor of Medical Sciences |
| BMus | Bachelor of Music |
| BN | Bachelor of Nursing |
| BNNursing | Bachelor of Nursing, Nursing Studies |
| BNSc | Bachelor of Nursing |
| BNurs | Bachelor of Nursing |
| BOptom | Bachelor of Optometry |
| BPA | Bachelor of Performing Arts |
| BPharm | Bachelor of Pharmacy |
| BPhil | Bachelor of Philosophy |
| BPhil(Ed) | Bachelor of Philosophy (Education) |
| BPL | Bachelor of Planning |

| | |
|---|---|
| BSc | Bachelor of Science |
| BSc(Archit) | Bachelor of Science (Architecture) |
| BSc(DentSci) | Bachelor of Science in Dental Science |
| BSc(Econ) | Bachelor of Science in Economics |
| BSc(MedSci) | Bachelor of Science (Medical Science) |
| BSc(Social Science) | Bachelor of Science (Social Science) |
| BSc(Town & Regional Planning) | Bachelor of Science (Town & Regional Planning) |
| BSc(VetSc) | Bachelor of Science (Veterinary Science) |
| BScAgr | Bachelor of Science in Agriculture |
| BScEng | Bachelor of Science in Engineering |
| BScFor | Bachelor of Science in Forestry |
| BScTech | Bachelor of Technical Science |
| BSocSc | Bachelor of Social Science |
| BSSc | Bachelor of Social Science |
| BSSG | Member of the British Society of Scientific Glassblowers |
| BTEC | Business and Technology Education Council |
| BTech | Bachelor of Technology |
| BTechEd | Bachelor of Technological Education |
| BTEC HC | Business and Technology Education Council Higher Certificate |
| BTEC HD | Business and Technology Education Council Higher Diploma |
| BTEC HNC | Business and Technology Education Council Higher National Certificate |
| BTEC HND | Business and Technology Education Council Higher National Diploma |
| BTechS | Bachelor of Technology Studies |
| BTh | Bachelor of Theology |
| BTheol | Bachelor of Theology |
| BTP | Bachelor of Town Planning |
| BVC | Bar Vocational Course |
| BVetMed | Bachelor of Veterinary Medicine |
| BVMS | Bachelor of Veterinary Medicine |
| BVM&S | Bachelor of Veterinary Medicine |
| BVSc | Bachelor of Veterinary Science |
| C&G | City and Guilds |
| CA | Member of the Institute of Chartered Accountants of Scotland |
| CAA | Civil Aviation Authority |
| CABE | Companion of the Association of Business Executives |
| CACHE | Council for Awards in Children's Care and Education |
| CAE | Certificated Automotive Engineer |
| CAE | Companion of the Academy of Experts |
| CAM | Communication Advertising and Marketing Education Foundation |
| CAS | Certification of Accountancy Studies |
| CASS | Certificate of Applied Social Studies |
| CAT | Certificate for Accounting Technicians |
| CAT | College of Advanced Technology |
| CATS | Postgraduate Qualification by Credit Accumulation and Transfer |
| CBA | Companion of the British (Theatrical) Arts |
| CBAE | Companion of the British Academy of Experts |
| CBIM | Companion of the British Institute of Management |
| CBiol | Chartered Biologist |
| CBLC | Certificate in Business Language Competence |
| CBSSG | Craft Member of the British Society of Scientific Glassblowers |
| CCETSW | Central Council for Education and Training in Social Work |

| | |
|---|---|
| CChem | Chartered Chemist |
| CCol | Chartered Colourist |
| CCST | Certificate of Completion of Specialist Training |
| CDBA | Certified Doctor of Business Administration |
| CDipAF | Certified Diploma in Accounting and Finance |
| CEE | Extended European Command Endorsement |
| CeFA | Certificate for Financial Advisers |
| CEM | Certificate in Executive Management |
| CeMAP | Certificate in Mortgage Advice and Practice |
| CEng | Chartered Engineer |
| CertAMed | Certificate in Aviation Medicine |
| CertArb | Certificate in Arboriculture |
| CertBibKnowl | Certificate of Bible Knowledge |
| CertCIH | Chartered Institute of Housing recognised Housing Qualification |
| CertCM | Certificate of Cash Management |
| CertDesRCA | Certificate of Designer of the Royal College of Art |
| CertEd | Certificate in Education |
| CertEPK | Certificate of Essential Pensions Knowledge |
| CertHE | Certificate of Higher Education |
| CertHSAP | Certificate in Health Services Administration Practice |
| CertHSM | Certificate in Health Services Management |
| CertMFS | Certificate in the Marketing of Financial Services |
| CertOccHyg | Certificate in Operational Competence in Comprehensive Occupational Hygiene |
| CertRP | Certificate in Recruitment Practice |
| CertTEL | Certificate in the Teaching of European Languages |
| CertTESOL | Certificate of Teaching of English to Speakers of Other Languages |
| CertTEYL | Certificate of Teaching of English to Young Learners |
| CertYCW | Certificate in Youth and Community Work |
| CETHV | Certificate of Education in Training as Health Visitor |
| CEYA | Council for Early Years Awards |
| CFS | Certificate in Financial Services |
| CFSP | Certificate in Financial Services Practice |
| CGeol | Chartered Geologist |
| CGLI | City & Guilds of London Institute |
| CHARM | Centre for Hazard and Risk Management |
| ChB | Bachelor of Surgery |
| CHD | Choral-Training Diploma |
| ChM | Master of Surgery |
| CHP | Certificate in Hypnosis and Psychology |
| CHRIM | Certified Member of the Institute of Health Record Information and Management |
| CIAgrE | Companion of the Institution of Agricultural Engineers |
| CIArb | Chartered Institute of Arbitrators |
| CIB | Chartered Institute of Bankers |
| CIBM | Corporate Member of the Institute of Builders' Merchants |
| CIBS | Chartered Institute of Bankers in Scotland |
| CIBSE | Chartered Institution of Building Services Engineers |
| CIC | Construction Industry Council |
| CIEx | Companion of the Institute of Export |
| CIFE | Conference for Independent Further Education |
| CIH | Chartered Institute of Housing |
| CII | Chartered Insurance Institute |
| CILA | Chartered Institute of Loss Adjusters |

| | |
|---|---|
| CILIP | Chartered Institute of Library and Information Professionals |
| CIM | Chartered Institute of Marketing |
| CIMA | Chartered Institute of Management Accountants |
| CIMediE | Companion of the Institution of Mechanical Engineers |
| CIMgt | Companion of the Institute of Management |
| CIOB | Chartered Institute of Building |
| CIP | Certificate of Institute Practice |
| CIPD | Chartered Institute of Personnel and Development |
| CIPFA | Chartered Institute of Public Finance & Accounting |
| CIPS | Chartered Institute of Purchasing and Supply |
| CISOB | Counsellor of the Incorporated Society of Organ Builders |
| CIT | Certificate in Information Technology |
| CIWEM | Chartered Institution of Water and Environmental Management |
| CL(ABDO) | Diploma in Contact Lens Practice of the Association of British Dispensing Opticians |
| CLAC | Commercial Language Assistant Certificate |
| CLAIT | Computer Literacy & Information Technology |
| CLC | Council for Licensed Conveyancers |
| CLE | Limited European Command Endorsement |
| ClinPsyD | Doctorate in Clinical Psychology |
| CMA | Certificate in Management Accountancy |
| CMathFIMA | Fellow of the Institute of Mathematics and its Applications |
| CMBA | Certified Master of Business Administration |
| CMBHI | Craft Member of the British Horological Institute |
| CMC | Certified Management Consultants |
| CMet | Chartered Meteorologist |
| CMIWSc | Certified Member of the Institute of Wood Science |
| CMS | Certificate in Management Studies |
| CNAA | Council for National Academic Awards |
| COA | Certificate of Accreditation |
| COBC | Certificate of Basic Competence |
| CoEA | Certificate of Educational Achievement |
| COES | Certificate of Educational Studies |
| CofE | Church of England |
| CofS | Church of Scotland |
| CompBCS | Companion of the British Computer Society |
| CompIAP | Companion of the Institution of Analysts and Programmers |
| CompIEE | Companion of the Institution of Electrical Engineers |
| CompIGasE | Companion of the Institution of Gas Engineers |
| CompIManf | Companion of the Institute of Manufacturing |
| CompIMS | Companion of the Institute of Management Specialists |
| CompIP | Companion of the Institute of Plumbing |
| CorporateIRRV | Corporate Member of the Institute of Revenues, Rating and Valuation |
| COSCA | Confederation of Scottish Counselling Agencies |
| CPA | Chartered Patent Agents |
| CPC | Certificate of Professional Competence, the Institute of Transport Administration |
| CPD | Continuing Professional Development |
| CPE | Common Professional Exam |
| CPEA | Certificate of Practice in Estate Agency |
| CPFA | Member of Chartered Institute of Public Finance and Accountancy |
| CPhys | Chartered Physicist of the Institute of Physics |
| CPIM | Certificate in Production and Inventory Management |

| | |
|---|---|
| CPL | Commercial Pilot's Licence |
| CPM | Certified Professional Manager |
| CPP | Certificate of Pre-school Practice |
| CPR | Chartered Professional Review |
| CProfBTM | Companion of Professional Business and Technical Management |
| CPS | Certificate in Pastoral Studies and Applied Theology |
| CPSC | Certificate of Proficiency in Survival Craft |
| CPsychol | Chartered Psychologist, British Psychological Society |
| CPT | Continuing Professional Training |
| CPVE | Certificate of Pre-Vocational Training |
| CRAeS | Companion of the Royal Aeronautical Society |
| CRAH | Central Register of Advanced Hypnotherapists |
| CRCW | Church Related Community Workers |
| CRNCM | Companion of the Royal Northern College of Music |
| CSCT | Central School for Counselling Training |
| CSD | Chartered Society of Designers |
| CSE | Certificate of Secondary Education |
| CSM | Certificate in Safety Management |
| CSMGSM | Certificate in Stage Management (Guildhall School of Music and Drama) |
| CStat | Chartered Statistician |
| CSYS | Certificate of Sixth Year Studies |
| CTABRSM | Certificate of Teaching of the Associated Board of the Royal School of Music |
| CTextATI | Associate of the Textile Institute |
| CTextFTI | Fellow of the Textile Institute |
| CTHCM | Confederation of Tourism, Hotel and Catering Management |
| CVA | Certificated Value Analyst |
| CVM | Certificated Value Manager |
| CVT | Certified Vehicle Technologist |
| DA | Diploma in Anaesthetics |
| DAdmin | Doctor of Administration |
| DAES | Diploma in Advanced Educational Studies |
| DArch | Doctor of Architecture |
| DAvMed | Diploma in Aviation Medicine |
| DBA | Doctor of Business Administration |
| DBE | Diploma in Business Engineering |
| DBO | Diploma of the British Orthoptic Society |
| DBS | Diploma in Business Studies |
| DCC | Diploma of Chelsea College |
| DCDH | Diploma in Child Dental Health |
| DCE | Dangerous Cargo Endorsements |
| DCE | Diploma in Childcare and Education |
| DCG | Diploma in Careers Guidance |
| DCH | Diploma in Child Health |
| DChD | Diploma of Dental Surgery |
| DChM | Diploma in Chiropodial Medicine, Institute of Chiropodists and Podiatrists |
| DCHT | Diploma in Community Health in Tropical Countries |
| DCL | Doctor of Civil Law |
| DCLF | Diploma in Contact Lens Fitting |
| DClinPsych | Doctor of Clinical Psychiatry |
| DCLP | Diploma in Contact Lens Practice |
| DCR(R)or(T) | Diploma of the College of Radiographers |
| DD | Doctor of Divinity |

| | |
|---|---|
| DDH(Birm) | Diploma in Dental Health, University of Birmingham |
| DDOrthRCPSGlas | Diploma in Dental Orthopaedics of the Royal College of Physicians and Surgeons of Glasgow |
| DDPHRCS(Eng) | Diploma in Dental Public Health, Royal College of Surgeons of England |
| DDS | Doctor of Dental Surgery |
| DDSc | Doctor of Dental Science |
| DEBA | Diploma in European Business Administration |
| DEdPsy | Doctor of Educational Psychiatry |
| DEM | Diploma in Executive Management |
| DEng | Doctor of Engineering |
| DES | Department of Education and Science (now the Department for Education) |
| DETR | Department of the Environment, Transport and the Regions |
| DFin | Doctor of Finance |
| DFSM | Diploma in Financial Services Management |
| DGA | Diamond Member of the Gemmological Association and Gem Testing Laboratory of Great Britain |
| DGDPRCSEng | Diploma in General Dental Practice, Royal College of Surgeons of England |
| DGM | Diploma in Geriatric Medicine |
| DGO | Diploma in Obstetrics and Gynaecology |
| DHC | Doctorate in Healthcare |
| DHE | Diploma in Horticulture, Royal Botanic Garden, Edinburgh |
| DHMSA | Diploma in the History of Medicine, Society of Apothecaries of London |
| DHP | Diploma in Hypnosis and Psychotherapy |
| DIA | Diploma of Industrial Administration |
| DIB | Diploma in International Business |
| DIC | Diploma of Membership of Imperial College of Science and Technology, University of London |
| DIH | Diploma in Industrial Health |
| DipABRSM | Diploma of the Associated Board of the Royal Schools of Music |
| DipAD | Diploma in Art and Design |
| DipAdvHYP | Diploma in Advanced Hypnotherapy |
| DipAE | Diploma in Adult Education |
| DipAgrComm | Diploma in Agricultural Communication |
| DipArb | Diploma in Arbitration |
| DipArb | Diploma in Arboriculture |
| DipArch | Diploma in Architecture |
| DipASE(CofP) | Graduate Level Specialist Diploma in Advanced Study in Education, College of Preceptors |
| DipASSc | Diploma in Arts and Social Sciences |
| DipAT | Diploma in Accounting Technology |
| DipAvMed | Diploma in Aviation Medicine |
| DipBA | Diploma in Business Administration |
| DipBldgCons | Diploma in Building Conservation |
| DipBMA | Diploma in Business Management |
| DipCAM | Diploma in the Communication Advertising and Marketing Education Foundation |
| DipCD | Diploma in Community Development |
| DipCHM | Diploma in Choir Training, Royal College of Organists |
| DipClinPath | Diploma in Clinical Pathology |
| DipCOT | Diploma of the College of Occupational Therapists |
| DipCP | Diploma of the College of Teachers |
| DipCT | Diploma in Corporate Treasury Management |
| DipDerm | Diploma in Dermatology |

| | |
|---|---|
| DipEd | Diploma in Education |
| DipEF | Diploma in Executive Finance |
| DipEH | Diploma in Environmental Health |
| DipEM | Diploma in Environmental Management |
| DipEMA | Diploma in Executive and Management Accountancy |
| DipEngLit | Diploma in English Literature |
| DipFD | Diploma in Funeral Directing, National Association of Funeral Directors |
| DipFS | Diploma in Financial Services |
| DipGAI | Diploma of the Guild of Architectural Ironmongers |
| DipGrTrans | Diploma in Greek Translation |
| DipGSM | Diploma of the Guildhall School of Music and Drama |
| DipHE | Diploma of Higher Education |
| DipHS | Diploma of the Heraldry Society |
| DipIEB | Diploma of the International Employee Benefits |
| DipISW | Diploma of the Institute of Social Welfare |
| DipLE | Diploma in Land Economy |
| DipLP | Diploma in Legal Practice |
| DipM | Postgraduate Diploma in Marketing |
| DipMedAc | Diploma in Medical Acupuncture |
| DipMetEng | Diploma in Meteorological Engineering |
| DipMFS | Diploma in the Marketing of Financial Services |
| DipMth | Diploma in Music Therapy |
| DipOccH | Diploma in Occupational Health |
| DipOccHyg | Diploma of Professional Competence in Comprehensive Occupational Hygiene |
| DipPDTC | Diploma in Professional Dancers Teaching Course |
| DipPharmMed | Diploma in Pharmaceutical Medicine |
| DipPhil | Diploma in Philosophy |
| DipProjMan | Diploma in Project Management |
| DipPropInv | Diploma in Property Investment |
| DipRAM | Diploma of the Royal Academy of Music |
| DipRCM | Diploma of the Royal College of Music |
| DipRMS | Diploma of the Royal Microscopical Society |
| DipSc | Diploma in Science |
| DipSM | Diploma in Safety Management |
| DipSurv | Diploma in Surveying |
| DipSW | Diploma in Social Work |
| DipTCL | Diploma of the Trinity College of Music, London |
| DipTCR | Diploma in Organ Teaching |
| DipTESOL | Diploma in Teaching of English to Speakers of Other Languages |
| DipTHP | Diploma in Therapeutic Hypnosis and Psychotherapy |
| DipTM | Diploma in Training Management, Institute of Personnel and Development |
| DipTransIoL | Diploma in Translation, Institute of Linguists |
| DipUniv | Diploma of the University |
| DipVen | Diploma in Venereology, Society of Apothecaries of London |
| DipWCF | Diploma of the Worshipful Company of Farriers |
| DIS | Diploma in Industrial Studies |
| DLang | Doctor of Language |
| DLit(t) | Doctor of Letters or Literature |
| DLO | Diploma of Laryngology and Otology |
| DLORCSEng | Diploma in Laryngology and Otology, Royal College of Surgeons of England |
| DLP | Diploma in Legal Practice |
| DM | Doctor of Medicine |

| | |
|---|---|
| DMedRehab | Diploma in Medical Rehabilitation |
| DMedSc | Doctor in Medical Science |
| DMet | Doctor of Metallurgy |
| DMJ(Clin) or DMJ(Path) | Diploma in Medical Jurisprudence (Clinical or Pathological), Society of Apothecaries of London |
| DMRD | Diploma in Medical Radio-Diagnosis |
| DMRT | Diploma in Radiotherapy |
| DMS | Diploma in Management Studies |
| DMU | Diploma in Medical Ultrasound |
| DMus | Doctor of Music |
| DMusCantuar | Archbishop of Canterbury's Doctorate in Music |
| DNSc | Doctor in Nursing Science |
| DO | Diploma in Ophthalmology |
| DO | Diploma in Osteopathy |
| DocEdPsy | Doctorate in Educational Psychology |
| DOpt | Diploma in Ophthalmic Optics |
| DOrth | Diploma in Orthoptics |
| DOrthRCSEdin | Diploma in Orthodontics, Royal College of Surgeons of Edinburgh |
| DOrthRCSEng | Diplomate in Orthodontics, Royal College of Surgeons of England |
| DP | Diploma in Psychotherapy |
| DPA | Diploma in Public Administration |
| DpBact | Diploma in Bacteriology |
| DPD(Dund) | Diploma in Public Dentistry, University of Dundee |
| DPH | Diploma in Public Health |
| DPharm | Diploma in Pharmacy |
| DPhil | Diploma in Philosophy |
| DPHRCSEng | Diploma in Dental Public Health, Royal College of Surgeons of England |
| DPM | Diploma in Psychological Medicine |
| DPodM | Diploma in Podiatric Medicine |
| DProf | Doctor of Professional Studies |
| DPS | Diploma in Professional Studies |
| DPSE | Diploma in Pastoral Studies and Applied Theology |
| DPsychol | Doctor of Psychology |
| DrAc | Doctor of Acupuncture |
| Dr(RCA) | Doctor of the Royal College of Art |
| DRCOG | Diploma of the Royal College of Obstetricians and Gynaecologists |
| DRDRCSEd | Diploma in Restorative Dentistry, Royal College of Surgeons of Edinburgh |
| DRE | Diploma in Remedial Electrolysis, Institute of Electrolysis |
| DRI | Diploma in Radionuclide Imaging |
| DRSAMD | Diploma in the Royal Scottish Academy of Music and Drama |
| DSA | Diploma in Secretarial Administration |
| DSc | Doctor of Science |
| DSc(Econ) | Doctor of Science (Economics) or in Economics |
| DSc(Eng) | Doctor of Science (Engineering) |
| DSc(Social) | Doctor of Science in the Social Sciences |
| DScEcon | Doctor in the Faculty of Economics and Social Studies |
| DSCh(Ox) | Diploma in Surgical Chiropody (Oxon), Oxford School of Chiropody and Podiatry |
| DScTech | Doctor of Technical Science |
| DSocSc | Doctor of Social Science |
| DSSc | Doctor of Social Science |
| DSTA | Diploma Member of the Swimming Teachers' Association |
| DTCD | Diploma in Tuberculosis and Chest Diseases |

| | |
|---|---|
| DTech | Doctor of Technology |
| DTI | Department of Trade and Industry |
| DTMH | Diploma in Tropical Medicine and Hygiene |
| DTM&H | Diploma in Tropical Medicine and Hygiene |
| DTp | Department of Transport |
| DUniv | Doctor of the University |
| DVetMed | Doctor of Veterinary Medicine |
| DVM | Doctor of Veterinary Medicine |
| DVM&S | Doctor of Veterinary Medicine and Surgery |
| DVS | Doctor of Veterinary Surgery |
| DVSc | Doctor of Veterinary Science |
| ECBL | European Certification Board for Logistics |
| ECDL | European Computer Driving Licence |
| ECG | Executive Group Committees (of the Board for Engineers Registration) |
| EDBA | Executive Diploma in Business Accounting |
| EdD | Doctor of Education |
| EDH | Efficient Deck Hand |
| EdPsyD | Doctor of Educational Psychology |
| EEAC | European Executive Assistant Certificate |
| EFB | English for Business |
| EFL | English as a Foreign Language |
| EHO | Environmental Health Officer |
| EIS | Educational Institute of Scotland |
| EITB | Engineering Industry Training Board |
| EMBA | European Master of Business Administration |
| EMBS | European Master of Business Sciences |
| EMFEC | East Midland Further Education Council |
| EN | Enrolled Nurse |
| EN(G) | Enrolled Nurse (General) |
| EN(M) | Enrolled Nurse (Mental) |
| EN(MH) | Enrolled Nurse (Mental Handicap) |
| ENB | English National Board |
| EngC | Engineering Council |
| EngD | Doctor of Engineering |
| EngTech | Engineering Technician |
| ENS | Electronic Navigational System |
| ESD | Executive Secretary's Diploma |
| ESOL | English for Speakers of Other Languages |
| ESSTL | Engineering Services Training Trust Ltd |
| EurIng | European Engineer |
| EuroBiol | European Biologist |
| FABE | Fellow of the Association of Business Executives |
| FACB | Fellow of the Association of Certified Bookkeepers |
| FACP | Fellow of the Association of Computer Professionals |
| FAE | Fellow of the Academy of Experts |
| FAFC | Fellow of the Association of Financial Controllers and Administrators |
| FAIA | Fellow of the Association of International Accountants |
| FAMS | Fellow of the Association of Medical Secretaries, Practice Managers, Administrators and Receptionists |
| FAPM | Fellow of the Association for Project Management |
| FASI | Fellow of the Ambulance Service Institute |
| FASI | Fellow of the Architecture and Surveying Institute |

| | |
|---|---|
| FASP | Fellow of the Association of Sales Personnel |
| FBA | Fellow of the British Academy |
| FBA | Fellow of the British (Theatrical) Arts |
| FBCS | Fellow of the British Computer Society |
| FBDO | Fellow of the Association of British Dispensing Opticians |
| FBDO(Hons) | Fellow of the Association of British Dispensing Opticians with Honours Diploma |
| FBDO(Hons)CL | Fellow of the Association of British Dispensing Opticians with Honours Diploma and Diploma in Contact Lens Practice |
| FBEI | Fellow of the Institution of Body Engineers |
| FBEng | Fellow of the Association of Building Engineers |
| FBHA | Fellow of the British Hypnotherapy Association |
| FBHI | Fellow of the British Horological Institute |
| FBHS | Fellow of the British Horse Society |
| FBID | Fellow of the British Institute of Interior Design |
| FBIDST | Fellow of the British Institute of Dental and Surgical Technologists |
| FBIE | Fellow of the British Institute of Embalmers |
| FBIPP | Fellow of the British Institute of Professional Photography |
| FBIS | Fellow of the British Interplanetary Society |
| FBMA | Fellow of the Business Management Association |
| FBPsS | Fellow of the British Psychological Society |
| FCA | Fellow of the Institute of Chartered Accountants in England and Wales |
| FCAM | Fellow of the Communication Advertising and Marketing Education Foundation |
| FCB | Fellow of the British Association of Communicators in Business Ltd |
| FCBSI | Fellow of the Chartered Building Societies Institute |
| FCCA | Fellow of the Association of Chartered Certified Accountants |
| FCEA | Fellow of the Institute of Cost and Executive Accountants |
| FCGI | Fellowship, City & Guilds |
| FChS | Fellow of the Society of Chiropodists and Podiatrists |
| FCI | Faculty of Commerce and Industry |
| FCI | Fellow of the Institute of Commerce |
| FCIArb | Fellow of the Chartered Institute of Arbitrators |
| FCIB | Fellow of the Chartered Institute of Bankers |
| FCIBS | Fellow of the Chartered Institute of Bankers in Scotland |
| FCIBSE | Fellow of the Chartered Institute of Building Services Engineers |
| FCIH | Fellow of the Chartered Institute of Housing |
| FCII | Fellow of the Chartered Insurance Institute |
| FCIJ | Fellow of the Chartered Institute of Journalists |
| FCILA | Fellow of the Chartered Institute of Loss Adjusters |
| FCIM | Fellow of the Chartered Institute of Marketing |
| FCIOB | Fellow of the Chartered Institute of Building |
| FCIPD | Fellow of the Chartered Institute of Personnel and Development |
| FCIPS | Fellow of the Chartered Institute of Purchasing and Supply |
| FCIS | Fellow of the Institute of Chartered Secretaries and Administrators |
| FCIT | Fellow of the Chartered Institute of Transport |
| FCLIP | Chartered Fellow of CILIP |
| FCLS | First Certificate for Legal Secretaries |
| FCMA | Fellow of the Chartered Institute of Management Accountants |
| FCMA | Fellow of the Institute of Cost and Management Accountants |
| FCMC | Fellow Grade Certified Management Consultants |
| FCOphth | Fellow of the College of Ophthalmology |
| FCOptom | Fellow of the College of Optometrists |
| FCoT | Ordinary Fellow of the College of Teachers |

| | |
|---|---|
| FCPM | Fellow of the Confederation of Professional Management |
| FCPP | Fellow of the College of Pharmacy Practice |
| FCSP | Fellow of the Chartered Society of Physiotherapy |
| FCT | Fellow of the Association of Corporate Treasurers |
| FCoT | Fellow of the College of Teachers |
| FCTHCM | Fellow of the Confederation of Tourism, Hotel and Catering Management |
| FCYW | Fellow of the Community and Youth Work Association |
| FDSRCPSGlas | Fellow in Dental Surgery of the Royal College of Surgeons of Glasgow |
| FDSRCSEd | Fellow in Dental Surgery of the Royal College of Physicians and Surgeons of Edinburgh |
| FDSRCSEng | Fellow in Dental Surgery of the Royal College of Surgeons of England |
| FE | Further Education |
| FEANI | Fédération Europééne d'Associations Nationales d'Ingénieurs |
| FECI | Fellow of the Institute of Employment Consultants |
| FEFC | Further Education Funding Council |
| FEIS | Fellow of the Educational Institute of Scotland |
| FFA | Fellow of the Faculty of Actuaries |
| FFA | Fellow of the Institute of Financial Accountants |
| FFARCSEng | Fellow of the Faculty of Anaesthetists of the Royal College of Surgeons in England |
| FFARCSIrel | Fellow of the Faculty of Anaesthetists of the Royal College of Surgeons in Ireland |
| FFAS | Fellow of the Faculty of Architects and Surveyors (Architects) |
| FFCA | Fellow of the Association of Financial Controllers and Administrators |
| FFCI | Fellow of the Faculty of Commerce and Industry |
| FFCS | Fellow of the Faculty of Secretaries |
| FFHom | Fellow of the Faculty of Homeopathy |
| FFPHM | Fellow of the Faculty of Public Health Medicine, Royal College of Physicians of London and Edinburgh and Royal College of Physicians and Surgeons of Glasgow |
| FFPHMIrel | Fellow of the Faculty of Public Health Medicine, Royal College of Physicians of Ireland |
| FFRRCSIrel | Fellow of the Faculty of Radiologists, Royal College of Surgeons in Ireland |
| FFS | Fellow of the Faculty of Architects and Surveyors (Surveyors) |
| FGA | Fellow of the Gemmological Association and Gem Testing Laboratory of Great Britain |
| FGCL | Fellow of the Guild of Cleaners and Launderers |
| FGI | Fellow of the Greek Institute |
| FGSM | Fellow of the Guildhall School of Music and Drama |
| FHCIMA | Fellow of the Hotel and Catering International Management Association |
| FHFS | Fellow of the Council of Health, Fitness and Sports Therapists |
| FHG | Fellow of the Institute of Heraldic and Genealogical Studies |
| FHRIM | Fellow of the Institute of Health Record Information and Management |
| FHS | Fellow of the Heraldry Society |
| FHSM | Fellow of the Institute of Health Services Management |
| FHT | Federation of Holistic Therapies |
| FIA | Fellow of the Institute of Actuaries |
| FIAB | Fellow of the International Association of Book-keepers |
| FIAEA | Fellow of the Institute of Automotive Engineer Assessors |
| FIAgrE | Fellow of the Institution of Agricultural Engineers |
| FIAP | Fellow of the Institution of Analysts and Programmers |
| FIAT | Fellow of the Institute of Asphalt Technology |
| FIBA | Fellow of the Institution of Business Agents |
| FIBC | Fellow of the Institute of Building Control |

| | |
|---|---|
| FIBCM | Fellow of the Institute of British Carriage and Automobile Manufacturers |
| FIBCO | Fellow of the Institute of Building Control Officers |
| FIBE | Fellow of the Institution of British Engineers |
| FIBF | Fellow of the Institute of British Foundrymen |
| FIBiol | Fellow of the Institute of Biology |
| FIBM | Fellow of the Institute of Builders' Merchants |
| FIBMS | Fellow of the Institute of Biomedical Science |
| FIBMS | Fellow of the Institute of Medical Laboratory Sciences |
| FICA | Fellow of the Institute of Company Accountants |
| FICB | Fellow of the Institute of Certified Book-Keepers |
| FICE | Fellow of the Institution of Civil Engineers |
| FIChemE | Fellow of the Institution of Chemical Engineers |
| FIChor | Fellow of the Benesh Institute of Choreology |
| FICHT | Fellow of the International Council of Holistic Therapies |
| FICM | Fellow of the Institute of Credit Management |
| FICorr | Fellow of the Institute of Corrosion |
| FICS | Fellow of the Institute of Chartered Shipbrokers |
| FICW | Fellow of the Institute of Clerks of Works of Great Britain Incorporated |
| FIDTA | Fellow of the International Dance Teachers' Association |
| FIED | Fellow of the Institution of Engineering Designers |
| FIEE | Fellow of the Institution of Electrical Engineers |
| FIEM | Fellow of the Institute of Executives and Managers |
| FIEx | Fellow of the Institute of Export |
| FIExpE | Fellow of the Institute of Explosives Engineers |
| FIFBQ | Fellow of the International Faculty of Business Qualifications |
| FIFireE | Fellow of the Institution of Fire Engineers |
| FIFM | Fellow of the Institute of Fisheries Management |
| FIFST | Fellow of the Institute of Food Science and Technology |
| FIGasE | Fellow of the Institution of Gas Engineers |
| FIGD | Fellow of the Institute of Grocery Distribution |
| FIGeol | Fellow of the Institute of Geologists |
| FIHEc | Fellow of the Institute of Home Economics Ltd |
| FIHIE | Fellow of the Institute of Highway Incorporated Engineers |
| FIHort | Fellow of the Institute of Horticulture |
| FIHT | Fellow of the Institution of Highways and Transportation |
| FIIE | Fellow of the Institution of Incorporated Engineers |
| FIIHTM | Fellow of the International Institute of Hospitality Tourism & Management |
| FIIM | Fellow of the International Institute of Management |
| FIIMR | Fellow of the Institute of Investment Management and Research |
| FIIRSM | Fellow of the International Institute of Risk and Safety Management |
| FIISE | Fellow of the International Institute of Social Economics |
| FIISec | Fellow of the International Institute of Security |
| FIL | Fellow of the Institute of Linguists |
| FILAM | Fellow of the Institute of Leisure and Amenity Management |
| FILT | Fellow of the Institute of Logistics and Transport |
| FIM | Fellow of the Institute of Materials |
| FIMA | Fellow of the Institute of Mathematics and its Applications |
| FIManf | Fellow of the Institute of Manufacturing |
| FIMarE | Fellow of the Institute of Marine Engineers |
| FIMatM | Fellow of the Institute of Materials Management |
| FIMBM | Fellow of the Institute of Maintenance and Building Management |
| FIMechE | Fellow of the Institute of Mechanical Engineers |

| | |
|---|---|
| FIMechIE | Fellow of the Institute of Mechanical Incorporated Engineers |
| FIMF | Fellow of the Institute of Metal Finishing |
| FIMgt | Fellow of the Institute of Management |
| FIMI | Fellow of the Institute of the Motor Industry |
| FIMIS | Fellow of the Institute for the Management of Information Systems |
| FIMM | Fellow of the Institute of Massage and Movement |
| FIMM | Fellow of the Institution of Mining and Metallurgy |
| FIMM | International Federation of Manual Medicine |
| FIMS | Fellow of the Institute of Management Specialists |
| FIMunE | Fellow of the Institution of Municipal Engineers |
| FInstAEA | Fellow of the Institute of Automotive Engineer Assessors |
| FInstAM | Fellow of the Institute of Administrative Management |
| FInstBA | Fellow of the Institute of Business Administration |
| FInstBCA | Fellow of the Institute of Burial and Cremation Administration |
| FInstBM | Fellow of the Institute of Builders' Merchants |
| FInstBRM | Fellow of the Institute of Baths and Recreation Management |
| FInstCh | Fellow of the Institute of Chiropodists |
| FInstCM | Fellow of the Institute of Commercial Management |
| FInstD | Fellow of the Institute of Directors |
| FInstE | Fellow of the Institute of Energy |
| FInstLEx | Fellow of the Institute of Legal Executives |
| FInstMC | Fellow of the Institute of Measurement and Control |
| FInstNDT | Fellow of the British Institute of Non-Destructive Testing |
| FInstP | Fellow of the Institute of Physics |
| FInstPet | Fellow of the Institute of Petroleum |
| FInstPkg | Fellow of the Institute of Packaging |
| FInstPM | Fellow of the Institute of Professional Managers and Administrators |
| FInstPS | Fellow of the Institute of Purchasing and Supply |
| FInstR | Fellow of the Institute of Refrigeration |
| FInstSMM | Fellow of the Institute of Sales and Marketing Management |
| FInstTA | Fellow of the Institute of Transport Administration |
| FInstTT | Fellow of the Institute of Travel and Tourism |
| FInstWM | Fellow of the Institute of Wastes Management |
| FInstWM | Fellowship of the Institute of Wastes Management |
| FIntMC | Fellow of International Management Centre |
| FIOC | Fellow of the Institute of Carpenters |
| FIOM | Fellow of the Institute of Operations Management |
| FIOP | Fellow of the Institute of Plumbing |
| FIOP | Fellow of the Institute of Printing |
| FIOSH | Fellow of the Institution of Occupational Safety and Health |
| FIPA | Fellow of the Institute of Practitioners in Advertising |
| FIPD | Fellow of the Institute of Personnel Development |
| FIPI | Fellow of the Institute of Professional Investigators |
| FIPlantE | Fellow of the Institution of Plant Engineers |
| FIPR | Fellow of the Institute of Public Relations |
| FIQ | Fellow of the Institute of Quarrying |
| FIQA | Fellow of the Institute of Quality Assurance |
| FIR | Fellow of the Institute of Population Registration |
| FIRSE | Fellow of the Institution of Railway Signal Engineers |
| FIRTE | Fellow of the Institute of Road Transport Engineers |
| FIS | Fellow of the Institute of Statisticians |
| FISM | Fellow of the Institute for Supervision & Management |

| | |
|---|---|
| FISOB | Fellow of the Incorporated Society of Organ Builders |
| FISTC | Fellow of the Institute of Scientific and Technical Communicators |
| FISTD | Fellow of the Imperial Society of Teachers of Dancing |
| FIStrucE | Fellow of the Institution of Structural Engineers |
| FISW | Fellow of the Institute of Social Welfare |
| FIT | Foundation Insurance Test |
| FITD | Fellow of the Institute of Training and Development |
| FITSA | Fellow of the Institute of Trading Standards Administration |
| FIVehE | Fellow of the Institute of Vehicle Engineers |
| FIWM | Fellow of the Institute of Wastes Management |
| FLAW | Foreign Languages at Work |
| FLCM | Fellow of the London College of Music |
| FLCSP | Fellow of the London and Counties Society of Physiologists |
| FLI | Fellow of the Landscape Institute |
| FLIC | Foreign Languages for Industry and Commerce |
| FLS | Fellow of the Linnean Society of London |
| FMA | Fellow of the Museums Association |
| FMAAT | Fellow Member of the Association of Accounting Technicians |
| FMPA | Fellow of the Master Photographers Association |
| FMR | Fellow of the Association of Health Care Information and Medical Records Officers |
| FMS | Fellow of the Institute of Management Services |
| FMusEd | Fellowship in Music Education |
| FN | Fellow of the Nautical Society |
| FNAEA | Fellow of the National Association of Estate Agents |
| FNAEAHon | Honoured Fellow of the National Association of Estate Agents |
| FNCP | Fellow of the National Council of Psychotherapists |
| FNI | Fellow of the Nautical Institute |
| FNIMH | Fellow of the National Institute of Medical Herbalists |
| FPC | Financial Planning Certificate |
| FPC | Foundation for Psychotherapy and Counselling |
| FPCS | Fellow of the Property Consultants Society |
| FPMI | Fellow of the Pensions Management Institute |
| FPodS | Fellow of the Surgical Faculty of the College of Podiatrists |
| FProfBTM | Fellow of Professional Business and Technical Management |
| FRAeS | Fellow of the Royal Aeronautical Society |
| FRAS | Fellow of the Royal Astronomical Society |
| FRCA | Fellow of the Royal College of Anaesthetists |
| FRCGP | Fellow of the Royal College of General Practitioners |
| FRCM | Fellow of the Royal College of Music |
| FRCO | Fellow of the Royal College of Organists |
| FRCO(CHM) | Fellow of the Royal College of Organists (Choir-training Diploma) |
| FRCOG | Fellow of the Royal College of Obstetricians and Gynaecologists |
| FRCP | Fellow of the Royal College of Physicians of London |
| FRCPath | Fellow of the Royal College of Pathologists |
| FRCPEdin | Fellow of the Royal College of Physicians of Edinburgh |
| FRCPsych | Fellow of the Royal College of Psychiatrists |
| FRCR | Fellow of the Royal College of Radiologists |
| FRCS(Irel) | Fellow of the Royal College of Surgeons in Ireland |
| FRCSEd | Fellow of the Royal College of Surgeons of Edinburgh |
| FRCSEd(C/TH) | Fellow of the Royal College of Surgeons of Edinburgh, specialising in Cardiothoracic Surgery |

| | |
|---|---|
| FRCSEd(Orth) | Fellow of the Royal College of Surgeons of Edinburgh, specialising in Orthopaedic Surgery |
| FRCSEd(SN) | Fellow of the Royal College of Surgeons of Edinburgh, specialising in Surgical Neurology |
| FRCSEng | Fellow of the Royal College of Surgeons of England |
| FRCSEng(Oto) | Fellow of the Royal College of Surgeons of England, with Otolaryngology |
| FRCSGlasg | Fellow of the Royal College of Physicians and Surgeons of Glasgow |
| FRCVS | Fellow of the Royal College of Veterinary Surgeons |
| FREC | Fellow of the Recruitment and Employment Confederation |
| FRHS | Fellow of the Royal Horticultural Society |
| FRIBA | Fellow of the Royal Institute of British Architects |
| FRICS | Fellow of the Royal Institution of Chartered Surveyors |
| FRIN | Fellow of the Royal Institute of Navigation |
| FRINA | Fellow of the Royal Institution of Naval Architects |
| FRIPHH | Fellow of the Royal Institution of Public Health and Hygiene |
| FRNCM | Fellow of the Royal Northern College of Music |
| FRPharmS | Fellow of the Royal Pharmaceutical Society of Great Britain |
| FRPS | Fellow of the Royal Photographic Society |
| FRS | Fellow of the Royal Society |
| FRSC | Fellow of the Royal Society of Chemistry |
| FRSCM | Fellow of the Royal School of Church Music |
| FRSH | Fellow of the Royal Society for the Promotion of Health |
| FRTPI | Fellow of the Royal Town Planning Institute |
| FSAPP | Fellow of the Society of Advanced Psychotherapy Practitioners |
| FSBP | Fellow of the Society of Business Practitioners |
| FSBT | Fellow of the Society of Teachers in Business Education |
| FSCT | Fellow of the Society of Claims Technicians |
| FSDC | Fellow of the Society of Dyers and Colourists |
| FSE | Fellow of the Society of Engineers (Inc) |
| FSElec | Fellow of the Society of Electroscience |
| FSG | Fellow of the Society of Genealogists |
| FSG(Hon) | Honorary Fellow of the Society of Genealogists |
| FSGT | Fellow of the Society of Glass Technology |
| FSIAD | Fellow of the Society of Industrial Artists and Designers |
| FSMA | Fellow of the Society of Martial Arts |
| FSMA | Fellow of the Society of Sales Management Administrators Ltd |
| FSNN | Fellow of the Society of Nursery Nursing |
| FSS | Fellow of the Royal Statistical Society |
| FSSCh | Fellow of the British Chiropody and Podiatry Association |
| FSSF | Fellow of the Society of Shoe Fitters |
| FSTA | Fellow of the Swimming Teachers' Association |
| FSVA | Fellow of the Incorporated Society of Valuers and Auctioneers |
| FTCL | Fellow of the Trinity College of Music |
| FTI | Fellow of the Textile Institute |
| FTII | Fellow of the Chartered Institute of Taxation |
| FTSC | Fellow of the Oil and Colour Chemists' Association |
| FTSC | Fellow in the Technology of Surface Coatings |
| FWeldI | Fellow of the Welding Institute |
| FYDA | Associate Fellowship of the Youth Development Association |
| GAGTL | Gemmological Association and Gem Testing Laboratory of Great Britain |
| GAI | Guild of Architectural Ironmongers |
| GASI | Graduate Member of the Ambulance Service Institute |

| | |
|---|---|
| GBSM | Graduate of the Birmingham School of Music |
| GCE | General Certificate of Education |
| GCE A | General Certificate of Education Advanced Level |
| GCE O | General Certificate of Education Ordinary Level |
| GCGI | Graduateship, City & Guilds |
| GCL | Guild of Cleaners and Launderers |
| GCSE | General Certificate of Secondary Education |
| GDC | General Dental Council |
| GIBCM | Graduate of the Institute of British Carriage and Automobile Manufacturers |
| GIBiol | Graduate of the Institute of Biology |
| GIEM | Graduate of the Institute of Executives and Managers |
| GIMA | Graduate of the Institute of Mathematics and its Applications |
| GIMI | Graduate of the Institute of the Motor Industry |
| GInstP | Graduate of the Institute of Physics |
| GIntMC | Graduate of the International Management Centre |
| GIS | Graduate Imaging Scientist |
| GLCM | Graduate Diploma of the London College of Music |
| GMAT | Graduate Management Admissions Test |
| GMC | General Medical Council |
| GMDSS | Global Maritime Distress & Safety System |
| GMInstM | Graduate Member of the Meat Training Council |
| GMus | Graduate Diploma in Music |
| GMusRNCM | Graduate in Music of the Royal Northern College of Music |
| GNSM | Graduate of the Northern School of Music |
| GNVQ | General National Vocational Qualifications |
| GradAES | Graduate of the Royal Aeronautical Society |
| GradBEng | Graduate Member of the Association of Building Engineers |
| GradBHI | Graduate of the British Horological Institute |
| GradDip | Graduate Diploma |
| GradIAP | Graduate of the Institution of Analysts and Programmers |
| GradIBE | Graduate of the Institution of British Engineers |
| GradIElecIE | Graduate of the Institution of Electrical and Electronics Incorporated Engineers |
| GradIIE | Graduate of the Institution of Incorporated Engineers |
| GradIISec | Graduate of the International Institute of Security |
| GradIManf | Graduate of the Institute Manufacturing |
| GradIMF | Graduate of the Institute of Metal Finishing |
| GradIMS | Graduate of the Institute of Management Specialists |
| GradInstNDT | Graduate of the British Institute of Non-Destructive Testing |
| GradInstP | Graduate of the Institute of Physics |
| GradInstPS | Graduate of the Institute of Purchasing and Supply |
| GradIOP | Graduate of the Institute of Printing |
| GradIPD | Graduate of the Institute of Personnel and Development |
| GradIS | Graduate of the Institute of Statisticians |
| GradISCA | Graduate of the Institute of Chartered Secretaries and Administrators |
| GradMechE | Graduate of the Institution of Mechanical Engineers |
| GradMIWM | Graduate Member of the Institute of Wastes Management |
| GradRNCM | Graduate of the Royal Northern College of Music |
| GradRSC | Graduate of the Royal Society of Chemistry |
| GradSMA | Graduate of the Society of Martial Arts |
| GradStat | Graduate Statistician |
| GraduateCIPD | Graduate of the Chartered Institute of Personnel and Development |
| GraduateIEIE | Graduate of the Institution of Electrical and Electronics Incorporated Engineers |

| | |
|---|---|
| GradWeldI | Graduate of the Welding Institute |
| GRC | General Readers Certificate |
| GRC | Grade Related Criteria |
| GRIC | Graduate Membership of the Royal Institute of Chemistry |
| GRSC | Graduate of the Royal Society of Chemistry |
| GRSM | Graduate Diploma of the Royal Manchester School of Music |
| GRSM(Hons) | Graduate of the Royal Schools of Music |
| GSMA | Graduate of the Society of Sales Management Administrators Ltd |
| GSNN | Graduate of the Society of Nursery Nursing |
| GTC | General Teaching Council |
| HABIA | Hairdressing and Beauty Industry Authority |
| HC | Higher Certificate |
| HCIMA | Hotel and Catering International Management Association |
| HD | Higher Diploma |
| HDCR (R) or (T) | Higher Award in Radiodiagnosis or Radiotherapy, College of Radiographers |
| HEFCE | Higher Education Funding Council for England |
| HFInstE | Honorary Fellow of the Institute of Energy |
| HNC | Higher National Certificate |
| HND | Higher National Diploma |
| HonASTA | Honorary Associate of the Swimming Teachers' Association |
| HonDrRCA | Honorary Doctorate of the Royal College of Art |
| HonFAE | Honorary Fellow of the Academy of Experts |
| HonFBID | Honorary Fellow of the British Institute of Interior Design |
| HonFBIPP | Honorary Fellow of the British Institute of Professional Photography |
| HonFCP | Charter Fellow of the College of Preceptors |
| HonFEIS | Honorary Fellow of the Educational Institute of Scotland |
| HonFHCIMA | Honorary Fellow of the Hotel, Catering and Institutional Management Association |
| HonFHS | Honorary Fellow of the Heraldry Society |
| HonFIEE | Honorary Fellow of the Institution of Electrical Engineers |
| HonFIExpE | Honorary Fellow of the Institute of Explosives Engineers |
| HonFIGasE | Honorary Fellow of the Institution of Gas Engineers |
| HonFIMarE | Honorary Fellow of the Institute of Marine Engineers |
| HonFIMechE | Honorary Fellow of the Institution of Mechanical Engineers |
| HonFIMM | Honorary Fellow of the Institution of Mining and Metallurgy |
| HonFInstE | Honorary Fellow of the Institute of Energy |
| HonFInstMC | Honorary Fellow of the Institute of Measurement and Control |
| HonFInstNDT | Honorary Fellow of the British Institute of Non-Destructive Testing |
| HonFIQA | Honorary Fellow of the Institute of Quality Assurance |
| HonFIRSE | Honorary Fellow of the Institution of Railway Signal Engineers |
| HonFIRTE | Honorary Fellow of the Institute of Road Transport Engineers |
| HonFPRI | Honorary Fellow of the Plastics and Rubber Institute |
| HonFRIN | Honorary Fellow of the Royal Institute of Navigation |
| HonFRINA | Honorary Fellow of the Royal Institution of Naval Architects |
| HonFRPS | Honorary Fellow of the Royal Photographic Society |
| HonFSE | Honorary Fellow of the Society of Engineers (Inc) |
| HonFSGT | Honorary Fellow of the Society of Glass Technology |
| HonFWeldI | Honorary Fellow of the Welding Institute |
| HonGSM | Honorary Member of the Guildhall School of Music and Drama |
| HonMIFM | Honorary Member of the Institute of Fisheries Management |
| HonMInstNDT | Honorary Member of the British Institute of Non-Destructive Testing |
| HonMRIN | Honorary Member of the Royal Institute of Navigation |
| HonMWES | Honorary Member of the Women's Engineering Society |

| | |
|---|---|
| HonRAM | Honorary Member of the Royal Academy of Music |
| HonRCM | Honorary Member of the Royal College of Music |
| HonRNCM | Honorary Member of the Royal Northern College of Music |
| HonRSCM | Honorary Member of the Royal School of Church Music |
| HSC | Higher School Certificate |
| HSE | Health & Safety Executive |
| HTB | Hairdressing Training Board |
| HTC | Higher Technical Certificate |
| IAAP | International Association for Analytic Psychology |
| IAB | International Association of Book-Keepers |
| IABC | International Association of Business Computing |
| IAC | Investment Advice Certificate |
| IAgrE | Institution of Agricultural Engineers |
| IAP | Institution of Analysts and Programmers |
| IAQ | Investment Administration Qualification |
| IAT | Institute of Asphalt Technology |
| IBA | Institute of Business Administration |
| IBC | Institute of Building Control |
| IBE | Institution of British Engineers |
| IBF | Institute of British Foundrymen |
| IBMS | Institute of Biomedical Science |
| ICAEW | Institute of Chartered Accountants in England and Wales |
| ICAI | Institute of Chartered Accountants in Ireland |
| ICAS | Institute of Chartered Accountants of Scotland |
| ICB | Institute of Certified Book-Keepers |
| ICE | Institution of Civil Engineers |
| ICEA | Institute of Cost and Executive Accountants |
| ICG | Institute of Careers Guidance |
| IChemE | Institution of Chemical Engineers |
| ICIOB | Incorporated Member of the Chartered Institute of Building |
| ICM | Institute of Commercial Management |
| ICM | Institute of Complementary Medicine |
| ICM | Institute of Credit Management |
| ICMQ | International Capital Markets Qualification |
| ICSA | Institute of Chartered Secretaries and Administrators |
| ICSF | Intermediate Certificate of the Society of Floristry |
| IDA | Improvement and Development Agency |
| IDTA | International Dance Teachers' Association Ltd |
| IED | Institution of Engineering Designers |
| IEE | Institution of Electrical Engineers |
| IEM | Institute of Executives and Managers |
| IEng | Incorporated Engineer |
| IETTL | Insulation and Environmental Training Trust Ltd |
| IEx | Institute of Export |
| IExpE | Institute of Explosives Engineers |
| IFA | Institute of Field Archaeologists |
| IFA | Institute of Financial Accountants |
| IFA | Insurance Foundation Certificate |
| IFBQ | International Faculty of Business Qualifications |
| IFM | Institute of Fisheries Management |
| IFST | Institute of Food Science and Technology (UK) |
| IHBC | International Health & Beauty Council |

| | |
|---|---|
| IHIE | Institute of Highway Incorporated Engineers |
| IHort | Institute of Horticulture |
| IHT | Institute of Highways and Transportation |
| IIA | Institute of Internal Auditors |
| IIE | Institution of Incorporated Engineers |
| IIExE | Institution of Incorporated Executive Engineers |
| IIHHT | International Institute of Health & Holistic Therapies |
| IIHTM | International Institute of Hospitality Tourism & Management |
| IIRSM | International Institute of Risk and Safety Management |
| ILAM | Institute of Leisure and Amenity Management |
| ILE | Institution of Lighting Engineers |
| ILEX | Institute of Legal Executives |
| ILT | Institute of Logistics and Transport |
| IMarE | Institute of Marine Engineers |
| IMBM | Institute of Maintenance and Building Management |
| IMC | Institute of Management Consultancy |
| IMechE | Institution of Mechanical Engineers |
| IMF | Institute of Metal Finishing |
| IMI | Institute of the Motor Industry |
| IMIBC | Incorporated Member of the Institute of Building Control |
| IMInstAEA | Incorporated Member of the Institute of Automotive Engineer Assessors |
| IMIS | Institute for the Management of Information Systems |
| IMM | Institution of Mining and Metallurgy |
| IMS | Institute of Management Specialists |
| IncMWeldI | Incorporated Member of the Welding Institute |
| InstAEA | Institute of Automotive Engineer Assessors |
| InstAM | Institute of Administrative Management |
| InstBCA | Institute of Burial and Cremation Administration |
| InstE | Institute of Energy |
| InstPet | Institute of Petroleum |
| IOB | Institute of Brewing |
| IOC | Institute of Carpenters |
| IoD | Institute of Directors |
| IOM | Institute of Operations Management |
| IOP | Institute of Packaging |
| IOSH | Institution of Occupational Safety and Health |
| IOTA | Institute of Transport Administration |
| IPA | Institute of Practitioners in Advertising |
| IPD | Initial Professional Development |
| IPD | Institute of Personnel and Development |
| IPFA | Member of the Chartered Institute of Public Finance and Accountancy |
| IPlantE | Institution of Plant Engineers |
| IPR | Incorporated Professional Review |
| IPR | Institute of Public Relations |
| IPSM | Institute of Public Service Management |
| IQ | Institute of Quarrying |
| IQA | Institute of Quality Assurance |
| IRMT | International Register of Massage Therapists |
| IRRV | Corporate Member of the Institute of Revenues, Rating and Valuation |
| IRRV | Institute of Revenues, Rating and Valuation |
| IRSE | Institution of Railway Signal Engineers |
| IRTE | Institute of Road Transport Engineers |

| | |
|---|---|
| ISEB | Information Systems Examinations Board |
| ISM | Incorporated Society of Musicians |
| ISM | Institute for Supervision & Management |
| ISMM | Institute of Sales and Marketing Management |
| ISRM | Institute of Sport and Recreation Management |
| ISTD | Imperial Society of Teachers of Dancing |
| IStructE | Institution of Structural Engineers |
| ITEC | International Therapy Examination Council |
| ITIL | IT Infrastructure Library |
| ITSA | Institute of Trading Standards Administration |
| IVehE | Institute of the Vehicle Engineers |
| IVM | Institute of Value Management |
| IWSc | Institute of Wood Science |
| JEB | Joint Examination Board |
| JET | Jewellery, Education and Training |
| JP | Justice of the Peace |
| LA | Library Association |
| LABAC | Licentiate Member of the Association of Business and Administrative Computing |
| LAE | Licentiate Automotive Engineer |
| LAEx | Legal Accounts Executive |
| LAMDA | London Academy of Music and Dramatic Art |
| LAMRTPI | Legal Associate Member of the Royal Town Planning Institute |
| LASI | Licentiate of the Ambulance Service Institute |
| LASI | Licentiate of the Architecture and Surveying Institute |
| LBEI | Licentiate of the Institution of Body Engineers |
| LBIDST | Licentiate of the British Institute of Dental and Surgical Technologists |
| LBIPP | Licentiate of the British Institute of Professional Photography |
| LCCI | London Chamber of Commerce and Industry |
| LCCIEB | London Chamber of Commerce and Industry Examinations Board |
| LCEA | Licentiate of the Association of Cost and Executive Accountants |
| LCFI | Licentiate of CFI International (Clothing and Footwear Institute) |
| LCGI | Licentiate, City & Guilds |
| LCIBSE | Licentiate of the Chartered Institution of Building Services Engineers |
| LCP | Licentiate of the College of Preceptors |
| LCSP | London and Counties Society of Physiologists |
| LCSP(Assoc) | Associate of the London and Counties Society of Physiologists |
| LCSP(BTh) | Member of the London and Counties Society of Physiologists (Beauty Therapy) |
| LCSP(Chir) | Member of the London and Counties Society of Physiologists (Chiropody) |
| LCSP(Phys) | Member of the London and Counties Society of Physiologists (Physical and Manipulative Therapy) |
| LCT | Licentiate of the College of Teachers |
| LDS | Licentiate in Dental Surgery |
| LDSRCPSGlas | Licentiate in Dental Surgery of the Royal College of Physicians and Surgeons of Glasgow |
| LDSRCSEd | Licentiate in Dental Surgery of the Royal College of Surgeons of Edinburgh |
| LDSRCSEng | Licentiate in Dental Surgery of the Royal College of Surgeons of England |
| LFA | Licentiate of the Institute of Financial Accountants |
| LFCI | Licentiate of the Faculty of Commerce and Industry |
| LFCS | Licentiate of the Faculty of Secretaries |
| LFS | Licentiate of the Faculty of Architects and Surveyors (Surveyors) |
| LGCL | Licentiate of the Guild of Cleaners and Launderers |
| LGSM | Licentiate of the Guildhall School of Music and Drama |

| | |
|---|---|
| LHCIMA | Licentiate of the Hotel and Catering International Management Association |
| LHG | Licentiate of the Institute of Heraldic and Genealogical Studies |
| LI | Landscape Institute |
| LicentiateCIPD | Licentiate of the Chartered Institute of Personnel and Development |
| LicIPD | Licentiate of the Institute of Personnel & Development |
| LicIQA | Licentiate of the Institute of Quality Assurance |
| LICW | Licentiate of the Institute of Clerks of Works of Great Britain Incorporated |
| LIDPM | Licentiate of the Institute of Data Processing Management |
| LIEM | Licentiate of the Institute of Executives and Managers |
| LIIST | Licentiate of the International Institute of Sports Therapy |
| LILAM | Licentiate of the Institute of Leisure and Amenity Management |
| LIM | Licentiate of the Institute of Materials |
| LIMA | Licentiate of the Institute of Mathematics and its Applications |
| LIMF | Licentiate of the Institute of Metal Finishing |
| LIMIS | Licentiate of the Institute for the Management of Information Systems |
| LInstBCA | Licentiate of the Institute of Burial and Cremation Administration |
| LInstBM | Licentiate of the Institute of Builders' Merchants |
| LIOC | Licentiate of the Institute of Carpenters |
| LIR | Licentiate of the Institute of Population Registration |
| LISTD | Licentiate of the Imperial Society of Teachers of Dancing |
| LISTD(Dip) | Licentiate Diploma of the Imperial Society of Teachers of Dancing |
| LittD | Doctor of Letters |
| LIWM | Licentiate of the Institute of Wastes Management |
| LLB | Bachelor of Law |
| LLCM | Performers Diploma of Licentiateship in Speech, Drama and Public Speaking |
| LLCM(TD) | Licentiate of the London College of Music and Media (Teachers' Diploma) |
| LLD | Doctor of Law |
| LLM | Master of Law |
| LM | Licentiate in Midwifery |
| LMIFM | Licentiate Member of the Institute of Fisheries Management |
| LMInstE | Licentiate Member of the Institute of Energy |
| LMPA | Licentiate Member of the Master Photographers Association |
| LMRTPI | Legal Member of the Royal Town Planning Institute |
| LMSSALond | Licentiate in Medicine, Surgery and Obstetrics & Gynaecology, Society of Apothecaries of London |
| LMusEd | Licentiate Diploma in Music Education |
| LMusLCM | Licentiate in Music of the London College of Music |
| LMusTCL | Licentiate in Music, Trinity College of Music |
| LNCP | Licentiate of the National Council of Psychotherapists |
| LPC | Legal Practice Course |
| LRAD | Licentiate of the Royal Academy of Dancing |
| LRAM | Licentiate of the Royal Academy of Music |
| LRCPEdin | Conjoint Diplomas Licentiate of the Royal College of Physicians of Edinburgh |
| LRCPSGlasg | Conjoint Diplomas Licentiate of the Royal College of Physicians and Surgeons of Glasgow |
| LRCSEdin | Conjoint Diplomas Licentiate of the Royal College of Surgeons of Edinburgh |
| LRCSEng | Licentiate of the Royal College of Surgeons in England |
| LRPS | Licentiate of the Royal Photographic Society |
| LRSC | Licentiate of the Royal Society of Chemistry |
| LRSM | Licentiate Diploma of the Royal Schools of Music |
| LSBP | Licentiate of the Society of Business Practitioners |
| LSCP(Assoc) | Associate of the London and Counties Society of Physiologists |

| | |
|---|---|
| LTCL | Licentiate of Trinity College of Music |
| LTh | Licentiate in Theology |
| LTI | Licentiate of the Textile Industry |
| LTSC | Licentiate of the Oil and Colour Chemists' Association |
| LVT | Licentiate Vehicle Technologist |
| MA | Master of Arts |
| MA(Architectural) | Master of Arts (Architectural Studies) |
| MA(Econ) | Master of Arts in Economic and Social Studies |
| MA(Ed) | Master of Arts in Education |
| MA(LD) | Master of Arts (Landscape Design) |
| MA(MUS) | Master of Arts (Music) |
| MA(RCA) | Master of Arts, Royal College of Art |
| MA(SocSci) | Master of Arts (Social Science) |
| MA(Theol) | Master of Arts in Theology |
| MAAT | Member of the Association of Accounting Technicians |
| MABAC | Member of the Association of Business and Administrative Computing |
| MABE | Member of the Association of Business Executives |
| MAcc | Master of Accountancy |
| MACP | Member of the Association of Computer Professionals |
| MAE | Member of the Academy of Experts |
| MAgr | Master of Agriculture |
| MAgrSc | Master of Agricultural Science |
| MAMS | Member of the Association of Medical Secretaries, Practice Managers, Administrators and Receptionists |
| MAMSA | Managing & Marketing Sales Association Examination Board |
| MAnimSc | Master of Animal Science |
| MAO | Master of Obstetrics |
| MAP | Membership by Assessment of Performance |
| MAPM | Member of the Association for Project Management |
| MAppSci | Master of Applied Science |
| MAQ | Mortgage Advice Qualification |
| MArAd | Master of Archive Administration |
| MArb | Master of Arboriculture |
| MArch | Master of Architecture |
| MArt/RCA | Master of Arts, Royal College of Art |
| MasFCI | Master of the Faculty of Commerce and Industry |
| MASHAM | Management and Administration of Safety and Health at Mines |
| MASI | Member of the Architecture and Surveying Institute |
| MBA | Master of Business Administration |
| MBAE | Member of the British Association of Electrolysists |
| MB, BCh | Conjoint Degree of Bachelor of Medicine, Bachelor of Surgery |
| MB, BChir | Conjoint Degree of Bachelor of Medicine, Bachelor of Surgery |
| MB, BS | Conjoint Degree of Bachelor of Medicine, Bachelor of Surgery |
| MB, ChB | Conjoint Degree of Bachelor of Medicine, Bachelor of Surgery |
| MBChA | Member of the British Chiropody and Podiatry Association |
| MBCO | Member of the British College of Ophthalmic Opticians |
| MBCS | Member of the British Computer Society |
| MBEng | Member of the Association of Building Engineers |
| MBHA | Member of the British Hypnotherapy Association |
| MBHI | Member of the British Horological Institute |
| MBIAT | Member of the British Institute of Architectural Technologists |
| MBID | Member of the British Institute of Interior Design |

| | |
|---|---|
| MBIE | Member of the British Institute of Embalmers |
| MBII | Member of the British Institute of Innkeeping |
| MBioc | Master of Biochemistry |
| MBKS | Member of the British Kinematograph, Sound and Television Society |
| MBM | Master of Business Management |
| MBMA | Member of the Business Management Association |
| MBSc | Master in Business Science |
| MBSSG | Master of the British Society of Scientific Glassblowers |
| MCAM | Member of the Communication Advertising and Marketing Education Foundation |
| MCB | Mastership in Clinical Biochemistry |
| MCB | Member of the British Association of Communicators in Business |
| MCBDip | Member of the British Association of Communicators in Business who hold the Association's Certificate and Diploma |
| MCC | Master of Community Care |
| MCCDRCS(Eng) | Member of the Royal College of Surgeons of England, Clinical Community Dentistry |
| MCD | Master of Civic Design |
| MCDH | Master of Community Dental Health |
| MCGI | Membership, City & Guilds |
| MCGPIrel | Member of the Irish College of General Practitioners |
| MCh | Master of Surgery |
| MChD | Master of Dental Surgery |
| MChem | Master of Chemistry |
| MChemA | Master of Chemical Analysis |
| MChemPhys | Master of Chemical Physics |
| MChemPST | Master of Chemistry Polymer Science and Technology |
| MChir | Master of Surgery |
| MChOrth | Master of Orthopaedic Surgery |
| MChS | Member of the Society of Chiropodists and Podiatrists |
| MCIArb | Member of the Chartered Institute of Arbitrators |
| MCIBS | Member of the Chartered Institute of Bankers in Scotland |
| MCIBSE | Member of the Chartered Institution of Building Services Engineers |
| MCIH | Corporate Member of the Chartered Institute of Housing |
| MCIJ | Member of the Chartered Institute of Journalists |
| MCIM | Member of the Chartered Institute of Marketing |
| MCIOB | Member of the Chartered Institute of Building |
| MCIPD | Member of the Chartered Institute of Personnel and Development |
| MCIPS | Member of the Chartered Institute of Purchasing and Supply |
| MCIT | Member of the Chartered Institute of Transport |
| MCIWEM | Member of the Chartered Institution of Water and Environmental Management |
| MCLIP | Chartered Member of CILIP |
| MCom | Master of Commerce |
| MCommH | Master of Community Health |
| MComp | Master of Computer Science |
| MCOptom | Member of the College of Optometrists |
| MCoT | Member of the College of Teachers |
| MCPM | Member of the Confederation of Professional Management |
| MCPP | Member of the College of Pharmacy Practice |
| MCQ | Multiple Choice Question paper |
| MCSD | Member of the Chartered Society of Designers |
| MCSP | Member of the Chartered Society of Physiotherapy |
| MCT | Member of the Association of Corporate Treasurers |

| | |
|---|---|
| MCTHCM | Member of the Confederation of Tourism, Hotel and Catering Management |
| MCYW | Member of the Community and Youth Work Association |
| MD | Doctor of Medicine |
| MDA | Master of Defence Administration |
| MD; ChM | Conjoint Doctorate in Medicine, Doctorate in Surgery |
| MDCR | Management Diploma of the College of Radiographers |
| MDent | Master of Dental Science |
| MDes | Master of Design |
| MDes(RCA) | Master of Design, Royal College of Art |
| MDORCPSGlas | Membership of Dental Orthopaedics, Royal College of Physicians and Surgeons of Glasgow |
| MDra | Master of Drama |
| MDS | Master of Dental Surgery |
| MDSc | Master of Dental Science |
| MEBA | Master of European Business Administration |
| MECI | Member of the Institute of Employment Consultants |
| MEd | Master of Education |
| MEd(EdPsych) | Master of Education (Educational Psychology) |
| MEdStud | Master of Educational Studies |
| MEng | Master of Engineering |
| MEnv | Master of Environmental Studies |
| MEnvSci | Master of Environmental Science |
| MESc | Master of Earth Sciences |
| MFA | Master of Fine Art |
| MFC | Mastership in Food Control |
| MFCM | Member of the Faculty of Community Medicine |
| MFDO | Member of the Faculty of Dispensing Opticians |
| MFDS | Member of the Faculty of Dental Surgery |
| MFGDPEng | Membership in General Dental Practice, Royal College of Surgeons of England |
| MFHom | Member of the Faculty of Homeopathy |
| MFM | Master of Forensic Medicine |
| MFPHM | Member of the Faculty of Public Health Medicine, Royal College of Physicians of London and Edinburgh and Royal College of Physicians and Surgeons of Glasgow |
| MFPHMIrel | Member of the Faculty of Public Health Medicine, Royal College of Physicians of Ireland |
| MFTCom | Member of the Faculty of Teachers in Commerce |
| MGDSRCSEd | Membership in General Dental Surgery, Royal College of Surgeons of Edinburgh |
| MGDSRCSEng | Membership in General Dental Surgery, Royal College of Surgeons of England |
| MGeog | Master of Geography |
| MGeol | Master of Geology |
| MGeophys | Master of Geophysical Sciences |
| MHCIMA | Member of the Hotel and Catering International Management Association |
| MHM | Master of Health Management |
| MHort(RHS) | Master of Horticulture, Royal Horticultural Society |
| MHSM | Member of the Institute of Health Services Management |
| MIAB | Member of the International Association of Book-keepers |
| MIAEA | Member of the Institute of Automotive Engineer Assessors |
| MIAgrE | Member of the Institution of Agricultural Engineers |
| MIAP | Member of the Institution of Analysts and Programmers |
| MIAT | Member of the Institute of Asphalt Technology |
| MIBC | Member of the Institute of Building Control |

| | |
|---|---|
| MIBCM | Member of the Institute British Carriage and Automobile Manufacturers |
| MIBCO | Member of the Institution of Building Control Officers |
| MIBE | Member of the Institution of British Engineers |
| MIBF | Member of the Institute of British Foundrymen |
| MIBiol | Member of the Institute of Biology |
| MIBM | Member of the Institute of Builders' Merchants |
| MICB | Member of the Institute of Certified Book-Keepers |
| MICE | Member of the Institute of Civil Engineers |
| MIChemE | Member of the Institution of Chemical Engineers |
| MICHT | Member of the International Council for Holistic Therapies |
| MICM | Member of the Institute of Credit Management |
| MICM(Grad) | Graduate Member of the Institute of Credit Management |
| MICorr | Member of the Institute of Corrosion |
| MICS | Member of the Institute of Chartered Shipbrokers |
| MICSc | Corporate Member of the Institute of Consumer Sciences Incorporating Home Economics |
| MICW | Member of the Institute of Clerks of Works of Great Britain Incorporated |
| MIDTA | Member of the International Dance Teachers' Association |
| MIED | Member of the Institution of Engineering Designers |
| MIEE | Member of the Institution of Electrical Engineers |
| MIEM | Member of the Institute of Executives and Managers |
| MIEx | Member of the Institute of Export |
| MIEx(Grad) | Graduate Member of the Institute of Export |
| MIExpE | Member of the Institute of Explosives Engineers |
| MIFA | Member of the Institute of Field Archaeologists |
| MIFireE | Member of the Institution of Fire Engineers |
| MIFM | Registered Member of the Institute of Fisheries Management |
| MIFST | Member of the Institute of Food Science and Technology |
| MIGasE | Member of the Institution of Gas Engineers |
| MIGD | Member of the Institute of Grocery Distribution |
| MIHEc | Member of the Institute of Home Economics |
| MIHIE | Member of the Institute of Highway Incorporated Engineers |
| MIHM | Member of the Institute of Healthcare Management |
| MIHort | Member of the Institute of Horticulture |
| MIHT | Member of the Institution of Highways and Transportation |
| MIIA | Member of the Institute of Internal Auditors |
| MIIE | Member of the Institution of Incorporated Engineers |
| MIIExE | Member of the Institution of Incorporated Executive Engineers |
| MIIHTM | Member of the International Institute of Hospitality Tourism & Management |
| MIIM | Member of the Institute of Industrial Managers |
| MIIM | Member of the International Institute of Management |
| MIIRSM | Member of the International Institute of Risk and Safety Management |
| MIISE | Member of the International Institute of Social Economics |
| MIISec | Member of the International Institute of Security |
| MIL | Member of the Institute of Linguists |
| MILAM | Member of the Institute of Leisure and Amenity Management |
| MILT | Member of the Institute of Logistics and Transport |
| MIM | Professional Member of the Institute of Materials |
| MIMA | Member of the Institute of Mathematics and its Applications |
| MIManf | Member of the Institute of Manufacturing |
| MIMarE | Member of the Institute of Marine Engineers |
| MIMatM | Member of the Institute of Materials Management |

| | |
|---|---|
| MIMBM | Member of the Institute of Maintenance and Building Management |
| MIMC | Member of the Institute of Management Consultancy |
| MIMechE | Member of the Institution of Mechanical Engineers |
| MIMechIE | Member of the Institution of Mechanical Incorporated Engineers |
| MIMF | Member of the Institute of Metal Finishing |
| MIMI | Member of the Institute of the Motor Industry |
| MIMinE | Member of the Institution of Mining Engineers |
| MIMIS | Member of the Institute for the Management of Information Systems |
| MIMM | Member of the Institute of Massage and Movement |
| MIMM | Member of the Institution of Mining and Metallurgy |
| MIMS | Member of the Institute of Management Specialists |
| MInstAEA | Member of the Institute of Automotive Engineer Assessors |
| MInstAM | Member of the Institute of Administrative Management |
| MInstBA | Member of the Institute of Business Administration |
| MInstBCA | Member of the Institute of Burial and Cremation Administration |
| MInstBE | Member of the Institution of British Engineers |
| MInstBM | Member of the Institute of Builders' Merchants |
| MInstCF | Master Fitter of the National Institute of Carpet and Floorlayers |
| MInstChP | Member of the Institute of Chiropodists & Podiatrists |
| MInstCM | Member of the Institute of Commercial Management |
| MInstD | Member of the Institute of Directors |
| MInstE | Member of the Institute of Energy |
| MInstLEx | Member of the Institute of Legal Executives |
| MInstMC | Member of the Institute of Measurement and Control |
| MInstNDT | Member of the British Institute of Non-Destructive Testing |
| MInstP | Member of the Institute of Physics |
| MInstPet | Member of the Institute of Petroleum |
| MInstPkg | Member of the Institute of Packaging |
| MInstPkg(Dip) | Diploma Member of the Institute of Packaging |
| MInstPM | Member of the Institute of Professional Managers and Administrators |
| MInstPS | Corporate Member of the Institute of Purchasing and Supply |
| MInstPSA | Member of the Institute of Public Service Administrators |
| MInstR | Member of the Institute of Refrigeration |
| MInstSMM | Member of the Institute of Sales and Marketing Management |
| MInstTA | Member of the Institute of Transport Administration |
| MInstTT | Full Member of the Institute of Travel and Tourism |
| MInstWM | Member of the Institute of Wastes Management |
| MIOC | Member of the Institute of Carpenters |
| MIOFMS | Member of the Institute of Financial and Management Studies |
| MIOM | Member of the Institute of Operations Management |
| MIOP | Member of the Institute of Printing |
| MIOSH | Member of the Institution of Occupational Safety and Health |
| MIP | Member of the Institute of Plumbing |
| MIPA | Member of the Institute of Practitioners in Advertising |
| MIPD | Member of the Institute of Personnel and Development |
| MIPI | Member of the Institute of Professional Investigators |
| MIPlantE | Member of the Institution of Plant Engineers |
| MIPR | Member of the Institute of Public Relations |
| MIPRE | Member of the Incorporated Practitioners in Radio & Electronics |
| MIQ | Member of the Institute of Quarrying |
| MIQA | Member of the Institute of Quality Assurance |
| MIR | Member of the Institute of Population Registration |

| | |
|---|---|
| MIRRV | Member of the Institute of Revenue, Rating and Valuation |
| MIRSE | Member of the Institution of Railway Signal Engineers |
| MIRTE | Member of the Institute of Road Transport Engineering |
| MISM | Member of the Institute for Supervision & Management |
| MISOB | Member of the Incorporated Society of Organ Builders |
| MISTC | Member of the Institute of Scientific and Technical Communicators |
| MIStrucE | Member of the Institution of Structural Engineers |
| MISW | Member of the Institute of Social Welfare |
| MITAI | Member of the Institute of Traffic Accident Investigators |
| MITSA | Member of the Institute of Trading Standards Administration |
| MIVehE | Member of the Institute of Vehicle Engineers |
| MIWM | Member of the Institute of Wastes Management |
| MIWPC | Member of the Institute of Water Pollution Control |
| MJur | Master of Jurisprudence |
| MLA | Master of Landscape Architecture |
| MLang | Master of Languages |
| MLangEng | Master of Language Engineering |
| MLD | Master of Landscape Design |
| MLE | Master of Land Economy |
| MLI | Member of the Landscape Institute |
| MLing | Master of Languages |
| MLitt | Master of Letters |
| MLPM | Master of Landscape Planning and Management |
| MLS | Master of Library Science |
| MM | Master of Midwifery |
| MMA | Master of Management and Administration |
| MMAS | Master of Minimal Access Surgery |
| MMath | Master of Mathematics |
| MMedE | Master of Medical Education |
| MMedSci | Master of Medical Science |
| MMet | Master of Metallurgy |
| MML | Master of Modern Languages |
| MMS | Member of the Institute of Management Services |
| MMSc | Master of Medical Sciences |
| MMus | Master of Music |
| MMus(Comp) | Master of Music (Composition) |
| MMus(Perf) | Master of Music (Performance) |
| MMus, RCM | Master of Music, Royal College of Music |
| MMusArt | Master of Musical Arts |
| MN | Master of Nursing |
| MNAEA | Member of the National Association of Estate Agents |
| MNatSc | Master of Natural Science |
| MNCP | Member of the National Council of Psychotherapists |
| MNeuro | Master of Neuroscience |
| MNI | Member of the Nautical Institute |
| MNIMH | Member of the National Institute of Medical Herbalists |
| MNRHP | Full Member of the National Register of Hypnotherapists and Psychotherapists |
| MNRHP(Eqv) | Full Member (Equivalent) of the National Register of Hypnotherapists and Psychotherapists |
| MNTB | Merchant Navy Training Board |
| MObstG | Master of Obstetrics and Gynaecology |
| MOptom | Master of Optometry |

| | |
|---|---|
| MOrthRCSEng | Membership in Orthodontics, Royal College of Surgeons of England |
| MPA | Master of Public Administration |
| MPaedDenRCSEng | Membership in Paediatric Dentistry, Royal College of Surgeons of England |
| MPC | Master of Palliative Care |
| MPH | Master of Public Health |
| MPharm | Master of Pharmacy |
| MPharmSci | Master of Pharmaceutical Science |
| MPhil | Master of Philosophy |
| MPhil(Eng) | Master of Philosophy in Engineering |
| MPhys | Master of Physics |
| MPhysGeog | Master of Physical Geography |
| MPlan | Master of Planning |
| MPPS | Master of Public Policy Studies |
| MPRI | Member of the Plastics and Rubber Institute |
| MProf | Master of Professional Studies |
| MProfBTM | Member of the Professional Business and Technical Management |
| MPS | Member of the Pharmaceutical Society of Northern Ireland |
| MPsychMed | Master of Psychological Medicine |
| MPsychol | Master of Psychology |
| MQB | Mining Qualifications Board |
| MRad | Master of Radiology |
| MRad; MRad(D) | Master of Radiology (Radiodiagnosis) or (Radiotherapy) |
| MRAeS | Member of the Royal Aeronautical Society |
| MRCGP | Member of the Royal College of General Practitioners |
| MRCOG | Member of the Royal College of Obstetricians and Gynaecologists |
| MRCP | Member of the Royal College of Physicians of London |
| MRCP(UK) | Member of the Royal College of Physicians of the United Kingdom |
| MRCPath | Member of the Royal College of Pathologists |
| MRCPEdin | Member of the Royal College of Physicians of Edinburgh (superceded by MRCP(UK)) |
| MRCPGlasg | Member of the Royal College of Physicians of Glasgow (superceded by MRCP(UK)) |
| MRCPIrel | Member of the Royal College of Physicians of Ireland |
| MRCPsych | Member of the Royal College of Psychiatrists |
| MRCSEd | Member of the Royal College of Surgeons of Edinburgh |
| MRCSEng | Member of the Royal College of Surgeons of England |
| MRCVS | Member of the Royal College of Veterinary Surgeons |
| MRDRCS | Membership in Restorative Dentistry, Royal College of Surgeons of England |
| MREC | Member of the Recruitment and Employment Confederation |
| MREHIS | Member of the Royal Environmental Health Institute of Scotland |
| MRes | Master of Research |
| MRIN | Member of the Royal Institute of Navigation |
| MRINA | Member of the Royal Institution of Naval Architects |
| MRIPHH | Member of the Royal Institute of Public Health and Hygiene |
| MRPharmS | Member of the Pharmaceutical Society of Great Britain |
| MRSC | Member of the Royal Society of Chemistry |
| MRSH | Member of the Royal Society for the Promotion of Health |
| MRSS | Member of the Royal Statistical Society |
| MRTPI | Member of the Royal Town Planning Institute |
| MS | Master of Surgery |
| MSA | Marine Safety Agency |
| MSAPP | Member of the Society of Advanced Psychotherapy Practitioners |

| | |
|---|---|
| MSBP | Member of the Society of Business Practitioners |
| MSBT | Member of the Society of Teachers in Business Education |
| MSc | Master of Science |
| MSc(Econ) | Master of Science in Economics |
| MSc(Ed) | Master of Science in Education |
| MSc(Eng) | Master of Science in Engineering |
| MSc(Entr) | Master of Entrepreneurship |
| MSc(Mgt) | Master of Science in Management |
| MScD | Master of Dental Science |
| MScEcon | Master in Faculty of Economic and Social Studies |
| MSCi | Master of Natural Sciences |
| MScTech | Master of Technical Science |
| MSE | Member of Society of Engineers (Inc) |
| MSF | Member of the SMAE Institute |
| MSFA | Advanced Financial Planning Certificate |
| MSIAD | Member of the Society of Industrial Artists and Designers |
| MSMA | Member of the Society of Martial Arts |
| MSocSc | Master of Social Science |
| MSSc | Master of Social Science |
| MSSc | Master of Surgical Science |
| MSSCh | Member of the British Chiropody and Podiatry Association |
| MSSF | Member of the Society of Shoe Fitters |
| MSt | Master of Studies |
| MSTA | Member of the Swimming Teachers' Association |
| MSTI | Certificate of Insurance Work |
| MSurgDentRCSEng | Membership in Surgical Dentistry, Royal College of Surgeons of England |
| MSW | Master of Social Work |
| MTCP | Master of Town and Country Planning |
| MTD | Master of Transport Design |
| MTech | Master of Technology |
| MTh | Master of Theology |
| MTheol | Master of Theology |
| MTP | Master of Town Planning |
| MTPI | Master of Town Planning |
| MTropMed | Master of Tropical Medicine |
| MTropPaediatrics | Master of Tropical Paediatrics |
| MUniv | Master of University (Honorary) |
| MURP | Master of Urban and Regional Planning |
| MusB | Bachelor of Music |
| MusD | Doctor of Music |
| MVC | Management Verification Consortium |
| MVM | Master of Veterinary Medicine |
| MVSc | Master of Veterinary Science |
| MWeldI | Member of the Welding Institute |
| MWES | Member of the Women's Engineering Society |
| MYD | Member of the Youth Development Association |
| NACOS | National Approval Council for Security Systems |
| NAEA | National Association of Estate Agents |
| NAG | National Association of Goldsmiths |
| NAMCW | National Association for Maternal and Child Welfare |
| NC | National Certificate |
| NCA | National Certificate in Agriculture |

| | |
|---|---|
| NCC | National Computing Centre |
| NCC | Navigational Control Course |
| NCDT | National Council for Drama Training |
| NCTJ | National Council for the Training of Journalists |
| NCVQ | National Council for Vocational Qualifications |
| ND | Diploma in Naturopathy |
| NDD | National Diploma in Design |
| NDF | National Diploma in Forestry |
| NDH | National Diploma in Horticulture |
| NDSF | National Diploma of the Society of Floristry |
| NDT | National Diploma in the Science and Practice of Turfculture and Sports Ground Management |
| NEBOSH | National Examination Board in Occupational Safety and Health |
| NEBS | National Examining Board for Supervision & Management |
| NFTS | National Film and Television School |
| NICCEA | Northern Ireland Council for the Curriculum, Examinations and Assessment |
| NID | National Intermediate Diploma |
| NIM | Northern Institute of Massage |
| NNEB | National Nursery Examination Board |
| NRHP | National Register of Hypnotherapists and Psychotherapists |
| NRHP(Affil) | Affiliate of the National Register of Hypnotherapists and Psychotherapists |
| NRHP(Assoc) | Associate of the National Register of Hypnotherapists and Psychotherapists |
| N-SHAP | National School of Hypnosis and Psychotherapy |
| NTTG | National Textile Training Group |
| NUJ | National Union of Journalists |
| NVQ | National Vocational Qualifications |
| NWRAC | North Western Regional Advisory Council for Further Education |
| OCR | Oxford, Cambridge & RSA Examinations |
| ODLQC | Open & Distance Learning Quality Council, formerly CACC, Council for Accreditation of Correspondence Colleges |
| ONC | Ordinary National Certificate |
| OND | Ordinary National Diploma |
| OSCE | Objective Structured Clinical Exam |
| PBTM | Professional Business and Technical Management |
| PCN | Personnel Certification in Non-Destructive Testing Ltd |
| PDP | Professional Development Programme |
| PESD | Private and Executive Secretary's Diploma, London Chamber of Commerce and Industry |
| PgC | Postgraduate Certificate |
| PGCE | Postgraduate Certificate in Education |
| PGCert | Postgraduate Certificate |
| PgD | Postgraduate Diploma |
| PGDip | Postgraduate Diploma |
| PGDip(Comp) | Postgraduate Diploma in Composition |
| PGDip(LCM) | Postgraduate Diploma of the London College of Music |
| PGDip(Perf) | Postgraduate Diploma in Performance |
| PGDip(RCM) | Postgraduate Diploma of the Royal College of Music |
| PGDipMin | Postgraduate Diploma in Ministry |
| PGDipMus | Postgraduate Diploma in Music |
| PhD | Doctor of Philosophy |
| PhD(RCA) | Doctor of Philosophy (Royal College of Art) |
| PIC | Professional Investment Certificate |

| | |
|---|---|
| PIFA | Practitioner of the Institute of Field Archaeologists |
| PIIA | Practitioner of the Institute of Internal Auditors |
| PInstNDT | Practitioner of the British Institute of Non-Destructive Testing |
| PJDip | Professional Jewellers' Diploma |
| PJGemDip | Professional Jewellers' Gemstone Diploma |
| PJManDip | Professional Jewellers' Management Diploma |
| PJValDip | Professional Jewellers' Valuation Diploma |
| PPL | Private Pilot's Licence |
| PPRNCM | Professional Performance Diploma of the Royal Northern College of Music |
| PQS | Professional Qualification Structure |
| PQSW | Post-Qualifying Award in Social Work |
| PRCA | Public Relations Consultants Association |
| PSC | Private Secretary's Certificate |
| PSD | Private Secretary's Diploma |
| PTA | Pianoforte Tuners' Association |
| PVM | Professional in Value Management |
| QC | Queen's Counsel |
| QCA | Qualifications and Curriculum Authority |
| QCG | Qualification in Careers Guidance |
| QDR | Qualified Dispute Resolver |
| QICA | Qualification in Computer Auditing |
| QIS | Qualified Imaging Scientist |
| QPA | Qualification in Pensions Administration |
| QPSPA | Qualification in Public Sector Pensions Administration |
| RA | Royal Academician |
| RAD | Royal Academy of Dancing |
| RADA | Royal Academy of Dramatic Art |
| RAM | Royal Academy of Music |
| RANA | Royal Animal Nursing Auxiliary |
| RAS | Royal Astronomical Society |
| RBS | Royal Ballet School |
| RC | Roman Catholic |
| RCM | Royal College of Midwives |
| RCN | Royal College of Nursing |
| RCSLT | Royal College of Speech and Language Therapists |
| RCVS | Royal College of Veterinary Surgeons |
| REA | Regional Examining Body |
| REC | Recruitment and Employment Confederation |
| Ret'dABID | Retired Associate of the British Institute of Interior Design |
| Ret'dFBID | Retired Fellow of the British Institute of Interior Design |
| Ret'dMBID | Retired Member of the British Institute of Interior Design |
| RGN | Registered General Nurse |
| RHS | Royal Horticultural Society |
| RHV | Registered Health Visitor |
| RIBA | Royal Institute of British Architects |
| RICS | Royal Institution of Chartered Surveyors |
| RINA | Royal Institution of Naval Architects |
| RJDip | Diploma for Retail Jewellers |
| RJGemDip | National Association of Goldsmiths Gemstone Diploma |
| RM | Registered Midwife |
| RMN | Registered Mental Nurse |
| RMS | Royal Microscopical Society |

| | |
|---|---|
| RNMH | Registered Nurse for the Mentally Handicapped |
| RP | Registered Plumber |
| RPS | Royal Photographic Society |
| RSA | Royal Society of Arts |
| RSBEI | Registered Student of the Institution of Body Engineers |
| RSC | Royal Society of Chemistry |
| RSCN | Registered Sick Children's Nurse |
| RSP | Registered Safety Practitioner |
| RTO | Recognised Training Organisation |
| RTPI | Royal Town Planning Institute |
| SA | Salvation Army Management |
| SBP | Society of Business Practitioners |
| SCAA | School Curriculum and Assessment Authority |
| ScD | Doctor of Science |
| SCE | Scottish Certificate of Education |
| SCLS | Second Certificate for Legal Secretaries |
| SCMT | Ship Captain's Medical Training |
| SCOTVEC | Scottish Vocational Education Council |
| SCPL | Senior Commercial Pilot's Licence |
| SE | Society of Engineers |
| SEE | Society of Environmental Engineers |
| SEFIC | Spoken English for Industry and Commerce |
| SenAWeldI | Senior Associate of the Welding Institute |
| SEng | Qualified Sales Engineer |
| SenMWeldI | Senior Member of the Welding Institute |
| SF | Society of Floristry Ltd |
| SFA | Securities and Futures Authority |
| SFInstE | Senior Fellow of the Institute of Energy |
| SG | Society of Genealogists |
| SGT | Society of Glass Technology |
| SHNC | Scottish Higher National Certificate |
| SHND | Scottish Higher National Diploma |
| SIEDip | Securities Industry Examination Diploma |
| SInstPet | Student of the Institute of Petroleum |
| SITO | Security Industry Training Organisation Ltd |
| SLC | Secretarial Language Certificate |
| SLD | Secretarial Language Diploma |
| SNC | Scottish National Certificate |
| SND | Scottish National Diploma |
| SNNEB | Scottish Nursery Nurses Examination Board |
| SPA | Screen Printing Association |
| SPRINT | Sport Play and Recreation Industries National Training Executive |
| SQA | Scottish Qualifications Authority |
| SRD | State Registered Dietician |
| SRN | State Registered Nurse |
| SSC | Secretarial Studies Certificate, London Chamber of Commerce and Industry |
| STA | Specialist Teacher Assistant (CACHE) |
| STA | Swimming Teachers' Association |
| STAT | Society of Teachers of the Alexander Technique |
| StudentIEE | Student of the Institution of Electrical Engineers |
| StudentIIE | Student of the Institution of Incorporated Engineers |
| StudentIMechE | Student of the Institution of Mechanical Engineers |

| | |
|---|---|
| StudIAP | Student of the Institution of Analysts and Programmers |
| StudIManf | Student Member of the Institute of Manufacturing |
| StudIMS | Student of the Institute of Management Specialists |
| StudProfBTM | Student of the Professional Business and Technical Management |
| StudSE | Student of the Society of Engineers (Inc) |
| StudSElec | Student of the Society of Electroscience |
| StudWeldI | Student of the Welding Institute |
| SVQ | Scottish Vocational Qualification |
| TC | Technician Certificate |
| TCA | Technician in Costing and Accounting |
| TCA | Technician of the Institute of Cost and Executive Accountants |
| TCert | Teacher's Certificate |
| TD | Technician Diploma |
| TDCR | Teacher's Diploma of the College of Radiographers |
| TechICorr | Technician of the Institute of Corrosion |
| TechMIWM | Technician Member of the Institute of Wastes Management |
| TechRICS | Technical Surveyor of the Royal Institution of Chartered Surveyors |
| TechRMS | Technological Qualification in Microscopy, Royal Microscopical Society |
| TechRTPI | Technical Member of the Royal Town Planning Institute |
| TechSP | Technician Safety Practitioner |
| TechWeldI | Technician of the Welding Institute |
| TEMOL | Training in Energy Management through Open Learning |
| TI | Textile Institute |
| TIMBM | Technician of the Institute of Maintenance and Building Management |
| TMBA | Teacher Member of the British (Theatrical) Arts |
| TnIMBM | Technicians of the Institute of Maintenance and Building Management |
| TOEFL | Test of English as a Foreign Language |
| TPP | Test of Professional Practice |
| TVM | Trainer in Value Management |
| UCAS | Universities and Colleges Admissions Service |
| UCL | University College London |
| UEB | United Examining Board |
| UKCC | United Kingdom Central Council |
| UKCP | United Kingdom Council for Psychotherapy |
| UMIST | University of Manchester Institute of Science and Technology |
| URC | United Reformed Church |
| VetMB | Bachelor of Veterinary Medicine |
| VTCT | Vocational Training Charitable Trust |
| WCMD | Welsh College of Music and Drama |
| WES | Women's Engineering Society |
| WJEC | Welsh Joint Education Committee |
| WMAC | West Midlands Advisory Council for Further Education |
| WSA | West of Scotland Agricultural College |
| YHAFHE | Yorkshire and Humberside Association for Further and Higher Education |
| ZSL | Zoological Society of London |

# Part 1

# Introduction

Since its first publication in 1970, *British Qualifications* has charted a number of fundamental changes in further and higher education provision in the UK. Major advances in technology and more flexible delivery and attendance patterns have created different types of learning opportunity, encouraging an ever more diverse student population to access education at all levels. The range of subjects delivered has grown beyond all recognition. New areas of research have been established and developed into major subject specialisms. Employers and professional bodies have collaborated to develop subject areas aligned to changing industry requirements. Flexibility and choice are the hallmarks of today's system, and anyone new to higher education may well be bewildered by the sheer variety of degree pathways available. The capacity to combine and mix modules and subjects has in fact grown beyond anything that could have been imagined in 1970.

Traditional boundaries between academic and vocational pathways continue to break down, and today most degrees have a vocational slant. Extended industry and professional placements, sponsored research projects, practitioner input and field-based assignments are common features in many degrees, and provide an important link into practice at the early stages of learning. Overall, in 20 years universities have doubled in size and the responsibilities they have taken on have expanded considerably. Collaboration between further education (FE) and higher education (HE) institutions has enabled a substantial amount of HE-level provision to be delivered in FE institutions. Clear progression routes have been established for some time. Considerable breadth of provision is now available in FE: not only has the sector grown to accommodate sub-degree provision, it has also continued to deliver a wide range of pre- and post-18 vocational qualifications, which include technical, occupational and professional awards.

Today, certain types of external qualification cross the boundaries between further and higher education. Several higher education institutions (HEIs) — particularly those that gained university status in the 1990s and in 2005 — deliver advanced professional qualifications and higher national diplomas or certificates from awarding bodies like Edexcel, OCR and SQA. At the same time there has been a significant shift towards FE's involvement in delivery of these types of qualification, and a greater input from private sector colleges.

## EDUCATION REFORM

The Higher Education Act 2004 introduced in 2006/07 brought new student support and tuition fee arrangements. Following the Browne Review of 2010, universities are able to charge full-time UK and EU undergraduate students up to £9,000 a year as part of a reorganization of HE funding and student finance. You will find further authoritative, official information about universities and colleges in the UK at the Unistats website: http://unistats.direct.gov.uk/. Information on student finance can be found at www.direct.gov.uk

As well as implementing reforms, the further and higher education sectors contribute to UK economic performance and the delivery of the government's policies on HE. As part of this shared responsibility a great deal of effort is being made to increase access to and participation in education, particularly among individuals who have not had much involvement in the past. The general availability of modular study programmes and related credit recognition of units, and greater use of ICT and e-learning resources, have done a lot to create more flexible methods of delivery and attendance requirements in further and higher education.

## FOUNDATION DEGREES

Foundation degrees (FDs) were established to give people the intermediate technical and professional skills that are in demand from employers, and to provide more flexible and accessible ways of studying. They are a higher level qualification awarded by universities. The qualification can be 'built up' from a range of relevant learning experiences, to allow for extremely flexible and adaptable qualifications that can be 'tailored' by employers to support their workforce and business development needs. They offer opportunities for employment and career advancement. Progression routes include links with associated professional qualifications and/or direct entry to the final year of a relevant Honours-level degree. FDs are offered by universities, colleges and other providers.

The first FDs in 2001 were studied by 4,000 students. In 2010, there were just over 99,700 enrolled on FDs. There are now hundreds of FD courses available, both full- and part-time. Foundation degree forward (fdf) was established in the 2003 Higher Education White Paper, but closed on 31 July 2011; however:

- details of fdf's Employer Based Training Accreditation (EBTA) can now be accessed at The Higher Education Academy website: www.heacademy.ac.uk/resources/detail/fdf/EBTA-brochure
- fdf's information, advice and guidance resources for work-based learners and their advisers are now hosted by unionlearn at www.higherlearningatwork.org
- fdf e-learning resources that support delivery of work-based higher education in sectors such as retail, travel and low carbon energy remain available at www.workforcedevelopment.fdf.ac.uk
- The Higher Education Academy hosts publications produced by fdf so that they remain available to the higher education community at www.heacademy.ac.uk/fdf

## POLICY AND REGULATION

National priorities for further and higher education are set by the UK and Scottish parliaments and the Welsh and Northern Ireland assemblies. Policy development, planning and implementation rest with the government departments responsible for each national education brief – the Department for Business, Innovation and Skills (BIS) (www.gov.uk/government/organisations/department-for-business-innovation-skills), the Department for Employment and Learning Northern Ireland (DELNI) (www.delni.gov.uk), the Scottish Government (www.scotland.gov.uk), and The Department for Education and Skills (DfES) (www.learning.wales.gov.uk) in Wales.

In England, delivery of FE is subject to external audit and public reporting by the Office for Standards in Education, Children's Services and Schools (Ofsted). In Scotland, the Scottish Funding Council (SFC) (www.sfc.ac.uk) has overall responsibility for planning, funding and quality assurance of FE through its work with Her Majesty's Inspectorate of Education (HMIE).

DfES is responsible for planning, funding and promotion of all post-16 education in Wales. Estyn (the Welsh-language acronym for Her Majesty's Inspectorate for Education and Training in Wales, website: www.estyn.gov.uk) is the appointed authority for audit of the quality of provision and related areas.

The Department for Employment and Learning (DELNI) is responsible for planning and funding of further education provision in Northern Ireland. Inspection and audit are undertaken by the Education and Training Inspectorate (ETI) on behalf of the Department (www.delni.gov.uk, www.etini.gov.uk).

## QUALITY ASSURANCE

A degree of convergence exists in the quality assurance of qualifications at level 3 and below. England, Wales and Northern Ireland share a common qualifications system, and the regulators in each country (listed below) work together in regulating qualifications for use across the three countries. Scotland has a separate qualifications system, although there is close correlation across all four countries, particularly in the area of vocational qualifications.

The following four bodies are responsible for the accreditation and standards of external qualifications and for curriculum and assessment for ages 3–16:

- *England*: Office of the Qualifications and Examinations Regulator (Ofqual);
- *Northern Ireland*: Council for Curriculum, Examinations and Assessment (CCEA*);
- *Scotland*: Scottish Qualifications Authority (SQA*);
- *Wales*: Department for Education and Skills (DfES).

*CCEA is also an Awarding Body for qualifications in Northern Ireland, which include National Qualifications to A level. SQA is also an Awarding Body that develops and validates SQA-branded qualifications including National Qualifications (Access, Intermediate, Higher and Advanced Higher Levels), Higher National Certificates and Diplomas, Scottish Vocational Qualifications and Scottish Professional Development Awards.

In HE the responsibility for standards and quality rests firmly with each institution. All institutions work with the independent Quality Assurance Agency for Higher Education (QAA) for England, Northern Ireland, Scotland and Wales. Institutional audits and subject-level reviews have been undertaken by QAA since 2001. It publishes its findings on its website as publicly accessible information; see www.qaa.ac.uk

Given the current scale and diversity of degree provision in the HE sector, there has been a need to clarify what can reasonably be expected from undergraduate and postgraduate programmes. QAA has responded to this requirement and developed the Quality Code for HE providers, and subject benchmark statements indicating the expected standards of degrees across a range of subjects.

## QUALIFICATION FRAMEWORKS

In further response to the breadth and diversity of qualifications available, a number of national qualification frameworks have been introduced. The framework concept is closely associated with greater transparency and comparability between types of qualification, particularly between those that were traditionally classified as academic or vocational. Common characteristics of all frameworks include universal adoption and understanding of qualification titles, and national tariffs of credits that recognize relevant levels of achievement.

The framework for Higher Education Qualifications in England, Wales and Northern Ireland (FHEQ) applies to degrees, diplomas, certificates and other academic awards by higher education providers (see Figure 1.1). The Scottish Credit and Qualification Framework (SCQF) was

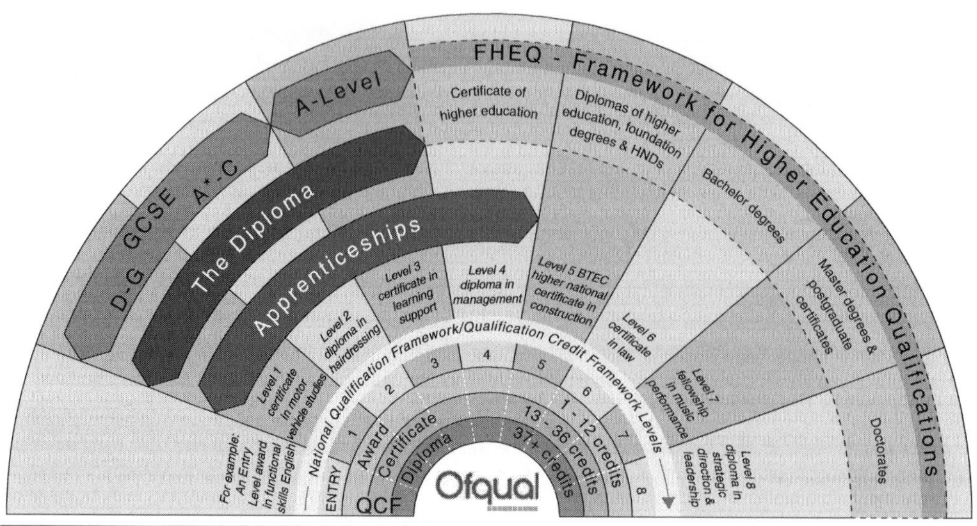


**Figure 1.1** Framework for Higher Education Qualifications in England, Wales and Northern Ireland (*Source*: http://ofqual.gov.uk/help-and-advice/comparing-qualifications)

developed by SQA, the Scottish Executive, QAA (Scottish Office) and Universities for Scotland. It provides an overview of all levels of national and higher qualifications provision in Scotland (see Figure 1.2).

The Qualifications and Credit Framework (QCF) is a new framework for recognizing and accrediting qualifications in England, Wales and Northern Ireland. The intention behind the reform was to make the system and qualifications offered far more relevant to the needs of employers, with more flexibility for learners. Every unit and qualification in the framework has a credit value (where one credit represents 10 hours) and a level between Entry level and level 8. There are three sizes of qualification in the QCF:

Awards: 1–12 credits;
Certificates: 13–36 credits;
Diplomas: 37 credits or more.

This means that each qualification title contains the level (from Entry to level 8), the size (Award/Certificate/Diploma) and the details of the content of the qualification. For a full list of accredited qualifications, see the National Database of Accredited Qualifications at www.accreditedqualifications.org.uk. This is a fully searchable database of qualifications that are accredited by Ofqual, DCELLS and CCEA.

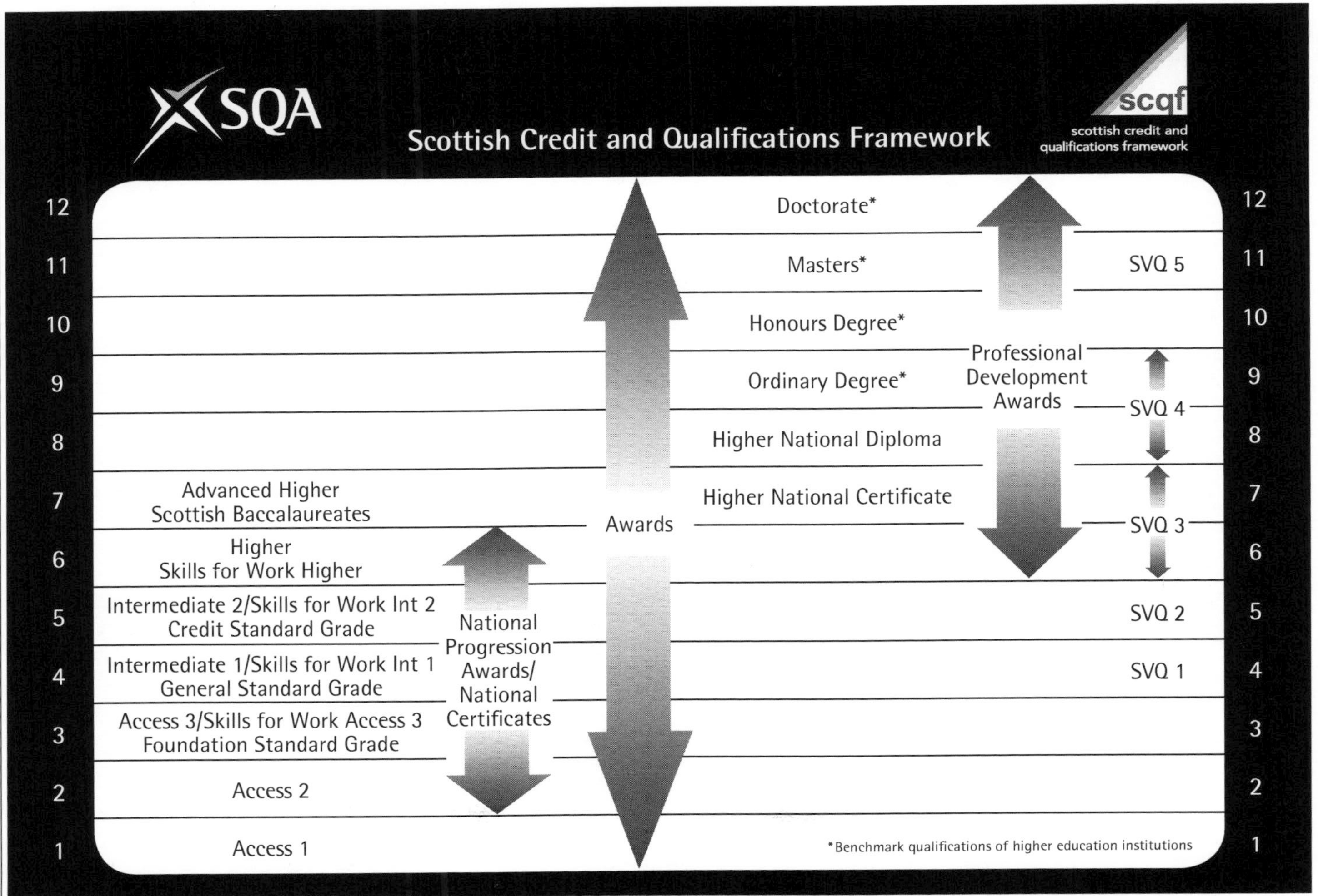


**Figure 1.2** Framework for Higher Education Qualifications in Scotland
(*Source*: www.sqa.org.uk/sqa/4595.html)

# Part 2

# Teaching Establishments

# INTRODUCTION

The statutory responsibility for the provision of education in the United Kingdom lies with the Department for Education and the Department for Business, Innovation and Skills (BIS) in England, the Welsh Assembly Government's Department for Education and Skills (DfES), the Education Department of the Scottish Government and the Department of Education and Department for Employment and Learning in Northern Ireland. In the United Kingdom the statutory system of public education has three progressive stages: primary education (up to the age of 11 or 12), secondary education (up to age 16), and further education (post-16).

This section briefly describes further and higher provision and the main types of institution.

# FURTHER AND HIGHER EDUCATION

'Higher education' (HE) is a term that broadly defines any course of study leading to a qualification at level 4 and above in the Qualifications and Credit Framework (QCF)/National Qualifications Framework (NQF) for England, Wales and Northern Ireland, and level 6 and above in the Scottish Credit and Qualifications Framework.

HE incorporates study towards a wide range of qualifications including Foundation, undergraduate and postgraduate degrees, certificates and diplomas awarded by individual universities and other higher education institutions (HEIs) with degree-awarding powers. It can also include study towards general, technical or occupationally-related diplomas and certificates awarded by the large unitary awarding bodies. Unitary awarding bodies are characterized by their breadth of provision, from GNVQ and A levels through to qualifications at level 5 and above in the national frameworks.

The other category that can be characterized as HE includes post-experience education above level 4 (and level 7 in Scotland). This includes qualifications available from awarding bodies that represent a particular sector, occupation or technical/craft area, and professional institutions that are also approved as awarding bodies.

HE can take place in universities and HE colleges (which continue to provide the majority of undergraduate and postgraduate courses). It can also take place in colleges of further education (FE). A significant number of colleges deliver parts of, and in some cases entire, Foundation and undergraduate degree courses in agreement with a selected university partner that is responsible for quality assurance and final awards.

In general terms, FE is available for students who are over the age of 16 and still in full-time education, and for adults aged 19 and over. FE provision includes GCSEs, A levels and other types of general and vocational qualifications below level 4 (and level 6 in Scotland) in the National Qualifications Frameworks.

All qualifications are awarded by approved external awarding bodies that include AQA, City & Guilds, Edexcel, LCCI, OCR, OCN and SQA in Scotland. This also includes qualifications below level 4 (level 6 in Scotland) that have a craft or technical focus or are related to an occupation/sector. At the time of writing, readers who want to find out more about approved qualifications below level 4 will find The Register of Regulated Qualifications website informative (http://register.ofqual.gov.uk). It contains details of all those qualifications that are accredited by the regulators of external qualifications in England (Ofqual), Wales (DfES) and Northern Ireland (CCEA).

# FURTHER AND HIGHER EDUCATION INSTITUTIONS

## England and Wales

There is a wide range of further and higher education establishments, including colleges with various titles. There are also a number of independent specialist establishments, like secretarial and correspondence colleges.

In 2013 there were 133 universities in the UK. In November 2012, the creation of 10 new universities for England was announced by David Willetts, the universities minister, after the minimum student intake for universities was reduced from 4,000 to 1,000. In 2013, 163 HE institutions were listed in the UK. The 2013 figures show there were 402 FE colleges (304 in England, of which 94 were sixth-form colleges, and 19 in Wales).

Courses include those for first and second degrees, certain graduate-equivalent qualifications, and the examinations of the principal professional associations. These institutions also provide courses leading to important qualifications below degree level, such as Foundation degrees, Higher National Diplomas and Certificates, and Diplomas of Higher Education. Most FE colleges specialize in providing courses that lead to qualifications below degree level, such as A levels and BTEC qualifications. Some offer degree courses, including in many cases Foundation degrees.

Students aged 16–18 who have been ordinarily resident in the UK for three years and European Economic Area nationals normally have the right to attend a full-time course without paying tuition fees. More detailed information on tuition fees can be found at www.ukcisa.org.uk. Colleges are free to determine fee levels for students who do not qualify for 'home fees'.

## Scotland

There are 36 FE colleges in Scotland that provide a broad mix of courses, many awarded by the Scottish Qualifications Authority (SQA). Most HE courses at or near degree level and beyond are provided by the 18 universities/HE institutions and The Open University in Scotland. These institutions offer a range of vocationally-oriented courses ranging from science, engineering and computing to health care, art and design, music and drama, and teacher training, as well as the more traditional 'academic' courses. All the universities and HE institutions are funded by the Scottish Funding Council.

## Northern Ireland

Responsibility for the FE sector in Northern Ireland rests with the Department for Employment and Learning (DELNI) which directly funds colleges. There are six further and higher education colleges, offering a wide range of vocational and non-vocational courses for both full- and part-time students. Details can be found at www.anic.ac.uk

Queen's University Belfast and the University of Ulster receive funding from the Department for Employment and Learning, Northern Ireland. Many of the courses in both universities are designed to suit the needs of industry, commerce and the professions. Agricultural, horticultural and food colleges in Northern Ireland are administered through the Department of Agriculture and Rural Development (DARD), which offers a range of further and higher education courses at the College of Agriculture, Food and Rural Enterprise (CAFRE).

# UNIVERSITIES AND HE COLLEGES

Universities are self-governing bodies, largely financed by the government through the Higher Education Funding Councils in the UK. They generally derive their rights and privileges from Royal Charter or Act of Parliament, and any amendment of their charters or statutes is made by the Crown acting through the Privy Council on the application of the universities themselves. The universities alone decide what degrees they award and the conditions on which they are awarded; they alone decide which students to admit and which staff to appoint. However, government policies have started to influence admission criteria, particularly in terms of widening access and participation in HE. Student fees set by universities are also subject to strict guidelines set by the government.

The Higher Education Funding Council (www.hefce.ac.uk) funds HE, research and related activities in English HE institutions and FE colleges. It funds 130 HE institutions (including University Campus Suffolk, a connected institution of the Universities of East Anglia and Essex) and 122 FE colleges.

## *Institutions receiving funding from Higher Education Funding Council for England*

(*Source*: Higher Education Funding Council for England). The schools and institutes of the University of London which receive funds directly from the HEFCE are marked *.

Anglia Ruskin University; Aston University; University of Bath; Bath Spa University; University of Bedfordshire; Birkbeck, University of London*; University of Birmingham; University College Birmingham; Birmingham City University; Bishop Grosseteste University; University of Bolton; Arts University Bournemouth; Bournemouth University; University of Bradford; University of Brighton; University of Bristol; Brunel University; Buckinghamshire New University; University of Cambridge; Institute of Cancer Research*; Canterbury Christ Church University; University of Central Lancashire; University of Chester; University of Chichester; City University, London; Conservatoire for Dance and Drama; Courtauld Institute of Art*; Coventry University; Cranfield University; University for the Creative Arts; University of Cumbria; De Montfort University; University of Derby; Durham University; University of East Anglia; University of East London; Edge Hill University; Institute of Education*; University of Essex; University of Exeter; Falmouth University; University of Gloucestershire; Goldsmiths, University of London*; University of Greenwich; Guildhall School of Music and Drama; Harper Adams University; University of Hertfordshire; Heythrop College, University of London*; University of Huddersfield; University of Hull; Imperial College London; Keele University; University of Kent; King's College London*; Kingston University; Lancaster University; University of Leeds; Leeds College of Art; Leeds Metropolitan University; Leeds Trinity University; University of Leicester; University of Lincoln; University of Liverpool; Liverpool Hope University; Liverpool Institute for Performing Arts; Liverpool John Moores University; University of London; University of the Arts, London; London Business School*; London School of Economics and Political Science*; London School of Hygiene and Tropical Medicine*; London Metropolitan University; London South Bank University; Loughborough University; University of Manchester; Manchester Metropolitan University; Middlesex University, London; Newcastle University; Newman University College; University of Northampton; Northumbria University; Norwich University of the Arts; University of Nottingham; Nottingham Trent University; The Open University; University of Oxford; Oxford Brookes University; University of Plymouth; University of Portsmouth; Queen Mary, University of London*; Ravensbourne; University of Reading; Roehampton University; Rose Bruford College; Royal Academy of Music*; Royal Agricultural University; Royal Central School of Speech and Drama*; Royal College of Art; Royal College of Music; Royal Holloway, University of London*; Royal Northern College of Music; Royal Veterinary College*; St George's, University of London*; University of St Mark and St John; St Mary's University College; University of Salford; University of Sheffield; Sheffield Hallam University; SOAS, University of London*; University of Southampton; Southampton Solent University; Staffordshire University; University of Sunderland; University of Surrey; University of Sussex; Teesside University; Trinity Laban Conservatoire of Music and Dance; UCL*; University of Warwick; University of the West of England, Bristol; University of West London; University of Westminster; University of Winchester; University of Wolverhampton; University of Worcester; Writtle College; University of York; York St John University.

The Higher Education Funding Council also supports higher education courses in 122 directly funded further education courses.

## *Universities receiving funding from the Department for Employment and Learning in Northern Ireland*

(*Source*: Higher Education Funding Council for England)

Queen's University Belfast; University of Ulster.

## *Higher Education Institutions receiving funding from the Scottish Funding Council*

(*Source*: Scottish Funding Council)

University of Aberdeen; University of Abertay Dundee; University of Dundee; Edinburgh Napier University; University of Edinburgh; Glasgow Caledonian University; Glasgow School of Art; University of Glasgow; Heriot-Watt University; The Open University in Scotland; Queen Margaret University; Robert Gordon University; Royal Conservatoire of Scotland; SRUC; University of St Andrews; University of Stirling; University of Strathclyde; University of the Highlands and Islands; University of the West of Scotland.

## *Institutions receiving funding from the Higher Education Funding Council for Wales*

(*Source*: Higher Education Funding Council for Wales)

Aberystwyth University; Bangor University; Cardiff University; Cardiff Metropolitan University (formerly UWIC); Glyndwr University; The Open University in Wales; Swansea Metropolitan, University of Wales Trinity Saint David; Swansea University; University of South Wales; University of Wales Trinity Saint David.

# OTHER HE ORGANIZATIONS

There are a number of other organizations involved in shaping the HE sector, for example the British Academy, the General Medical Council and Research Councils UK. You can find a full list of these organizations on the Universities UK website: www.universitiesuk.ac.uk

# Part 3

# Qualifications

# INTRODUCTION

## *Definition of Common Terms*

A number of terms are commonly used as synonyms for qualifications, for example 'examinations' and 'courses'. This can hide important differences of meaning and lead to confusion and misunderstanding. In some contexts it may be important to make these differences explicit to guard against exaggerating or diminishing the level of achievement, which is an essential core of the concept of qualification. It is especially important to clarify the difference in meaning between 'examination', 'course' and 'qualification'.

### Examination

An examination is a formal test or assessment. It can focus on one or more of the following: knowledge, understanding, skill or competence. An examination may be set as a written test, an oral test, an aural and oral test (eg a foreign language test) or a practical test. In the past, most forms of external assessment in FE were based on a model of examination dominated by the psychometric model, designed to discriminate between individuals – normative referencing – and took the form of written tests. There was considerable variation in different kinds of written examination, including essays, question and answer, and 'multiple response'. Today, largely as a result of the introduction of National Vocational Qualifications (NVQs), the purpose and format of many examinations have been reappraised, and criterion-referenced examinations that focus on achievement (and in the case of NVQs, competence) are increasingly common. Many forms of assessment are now an integral part of the learning process, with a formative as well as a summative function rather than a separate, terminal, summative function.

### Course

A course implies an ordered sequence of teaching or learning over a period of time. A course is governed by regulations or requirements, frequently imposed by an external awarding body and sometimes by the institution providing the course. An important distinguishing feature between different courses is the length of time allocated to study: it can vary from a few days to several years. Some courses offer a terminal award on the basis of course completion, and these courses are set for a given period of time. Other 'set period' courses may prescribe examinations; these can include continuous assessment, terminal testing or a combination of both. In other courses, the programme of study may be accomplished at a faster or slower rate; such courses normally enjoin continuous assessment or a terminal examination, or both. Many courses require attendance at an institution, while distance learning, correspondence courses, and various forms of flexible-learning courses are usually free of these requirements, although some may require occasional attendance for residential components or face-to-face tutoring. A successful examination result usually confers a qualification or an award.

### Qualification

A qualification is normally a certificated endorsement, from a recognized awarding body, that a level or quality of accomplishment has been achieved by an individual. Qualifications are usually conferred on successful completion of an examination, although not all examinations necessarily offer qualifications. An examination may offer an award that is a part-qualification. For example, an NVQ candidate may acquire a unit of competence that is a part-qualification building towards a full statement of competence – an NVQ. A first-year student on an HND course may be required to pass all first-year examinations to be permitted to continue into the second year: in a sense that student is 'qualified' to continue the course but no qualification is awarded. Some award-bearing examinations may be fully recognized and certificated qualifications in themselves (eg a BTEC HNC) but only part-qualifications for a profession (eg chartered engineer).

Apparent anomalies do exist. Some professional bodies and trade associations award qualifications that are recognized within the profession or association but are not obtained by examination. They are usually awarded on the basis of experience, and payment of a fee, and denote membership or acceptance. When the body also offers an examination route to the same qualification, successful examinees are usually known as 'graduate members'.

There are a number of accreditation authorities that approve qualifications. There are also many specialist and general validating, examining and awarding bodies that are responsible for the design and assessment of qualifications.

# ACCREDITING REGULATORY BODIES

## *England*

### Sector Skills Councils

The Alliance of Sector Skills Councils, launched in April 2008, is an organization that supports the network of licensed UK Sector Skills Councils (SSCs). These are employer-led, independent organizations that cover specific work sectors across the UK (currently accounting for approximately 90 per cent of the UK workforce). With the influence granted by licences from the governments of England, Scotland, Wales and Northern Ireland, and with private and public funding, this independent network engages with the education and training supply-side such as universities, colleges, funders and qualifications bodies to increase productivity at all levels in the workforce. Details are listed in the following table.

**Table 3.1**

**Asset Skills**
***Sector:*** Facilities Management, Housing, Property, Cleaning and Parking
Tel: 01392 423 399
E-mail: enquiries@assetskills.org
Website: www.assetskills.org

**Cogent**
***Sector:*** Chemicals, pharmaceuticals, nuclear, oil and gas, petroleum and polymer industries
Tel: 01925 515 200
E-mail: info@cogent-ssc.com
Website: www.cogent-ssc.com

**CITB**
***Sector:*** Construction
Tel: 0344 994 4133
E-mail: cskillsawards@cskills.org
Website: www.citb.co.uk

**Creative & Cultural Skills**
***Sector:*** Crafts, cultural heritage, design, literature, music, performing and visual arts
Tel: 020 7015 1800
E-mail: info@ccskills.org.uk
Website: www.ccskills.org.uk

**Creative Skillset**
***Sector:*** TV, film, radio, interactive media, animation, computer games, facilities, photo imaging, publishing, advertising and fashion and textiles
Tel: 020 7713 9800
E-mail: info@creativeskillset.org
Website: www.creativeskillset.org

*continued*

**Table 3.1** *Continued*

**e-skills UK**
*Sector:* Software, internet and web, IT services, telecommunications and business change
Tel: 020 7963 8920
E-mail: info@e-skills.com
Website: www.e-skills.com

**Energy & Utility Skills**
*Sector:* Gas, power, waste management and water industries
Tel: 0845 077 9922
E-mail: enquiries@euskills.co.uk
Website: www.euskills.co.uk

**Financial Skills Partnership**
*Sector:* Finance, accountancy and financial services
Tel: 0845 257 3772
E-mail: info@financialskillspartnership.org.uk
Website: www.financialskillspartnership.org.uk

**IMI The Institute of the Motor Industry**
*Sector:* Retail motor industry
Tel: 01992 511 521
E-mail: comms@theimi.org.uk
Website: www.theimi.org.uk

**Improve Ltd**
*Sector:* Food and drink manufacturing and associated supply chains
Tel: 0845 644 0448
E-mail: info@improveltd.co.uk
Website: www.improveltd.co.uk

**Lantra**
*Sector:* Land management and production, animal health and welfare and environmental industries
Tel: 024 7669 6996
E-mail: connect@lantra.co.uk
Website: www.lantra.co.uk

**People 1st**
*Sector:* Hospitality, leisure, passenger transport, travel and tourism
Tel: 01895 817 000
E-mail: info@people1st.co.uk
Website: www.people1st.co.uk

**SEMTA**
*Sector:* Science, engineering and manufacturing technologies
Tel: 0845 643 9001
E-mail: customerservices@semta.org.uk
Website: www.semta.org.uk

**Skills Active**
*Sector:* Sport, fitness, outdoors, playwork, caravans and hair and beauty
Tel: 020 7632 2000
E-mail: skills@skillsactive.com
Website: www.skillsactive.com

**Skills for Care & Development**
*Sector:* Social care, children, early years and young people's workforces in the UK
Tel: 01133 241 1240
E-mail: sscinfo@skillsforcareanddevelopment.org.uk
Website: www.skillsforcareanddevelopment.org.uk

**Skills for Health**
*Sector:* UK Health
Tel: 0117 922 1155
E-mail: office@skillsforhealth.org.uk
Website: www.skillsforhealth.org.uk

**Skills for Justice**
*Sector:* Community justice, courts services, custodial care, fire and rescue, forensic science, policing and law enforcement and prosecution services
Tel: 0114 261 1499
E-mail: info@skillsforjustice.com
Website: www.skillsforjustice.com

*continued*

**Table 3.1** *Continued*

| | |
|---|---|
| **Skills for Logistics**<br>*Sector:* Freight logistics and wholesaling industry<br>Tel: 01908 313 360<br>E-mail: info@skillsforlogistics.org<br>Website: www.skillsforlogistics.org | **The Alliance of Sector Skills Councils (ASSC)**<br>Tel: 0845 072 5600<br>E-mail: info@sscalliance.org<br>Website: www.sscalliance.org |
| **SummitSkills**<br>*Sector:* Building services engineering<br>Tel: 01908 303 960<br>E-mail: enquiries@summitskills.org.uk<br>Website: www.summitskills.org.uk | |

### The Exams Delivery Support Unit

The exams administration function is performed by the Exams Delivery Support Unit (EDSU). The helpline supports exams office staff, helping them to manage and administer exams; Tel: 0300 100 0100; e-mail: edsu@education.gov.uk; website: www.education.gov.uk

### Standards and Testing Agency (STA)

The Standards and Testing Agency is responsible for the development and delivery of all statutory assessments from early years to the end of Key Stage 3; Tel: Public enquiries 0370 000 2288; National Curriculum assessments helpline: 0300 303 3013; e-mail: assessments@education.gov.uk; website: www.education.gov.uk

### Ofqual: Office of Qualifications and Examinations Regulation

Tel: 0300 303 3344; Helpline: 0300 303 3346; e-mail: info@ofqual.gov.uk; website:www.ofqual.gov.uk

In 2009, the government passed the Apprenticeship, Skills, Children and Learning Act, which established Ofqual as the regulator of qualifications, examinations and tests in England. Ofqual commenced work as a fully independent non-ministerial government department on 1 April 2010. Ofqual is accountable to parliament rather than to government ministers.

Ofqual's role is to ensure all learners get the results they deserve, standards are maintained, and qualifications are correctly valued and understood, now and in the future. It regulates exams, qualifications and tests in England and a wide range of vocational qualifications in both England and Northern Ireland. Ofqual also regulates the National Curriculum Assessments in England.

## *Scotland*

### Scottish Qualifications Authority (SQA)

Customer Contact Centre, Tel: 0345 279 1000; Fax: 0345 213 5000; e-mail: customer@sqa.org.uk

The Scottish Qualifications Authority (SQA) is the national accreditation and awarding body in Scotland. It is an executive non-departmental public body (NDPB) sponsored by the Scottish Government's Learning Directorate.

SQA works in partnership with schools, colleges, universities and industry to provide high-quality, flexible and relevant qualifications and assessments, embedding industry standards where appropriate. It strives to ensure that SQA qualifications are inclusive and accessible to all, that they provide clear progression pathways, facilitate lifelong learning and recognize candidate achievement.

People take SQA qualifications at all stages of their lives – at school, at college, at work and in their leisure time. There are qualifications at all levels of attainment. SQA is responsible for three main types of qualification: units, courses and group awards. Most SQA-awarded qualifications are made up of a combination of units, which can also be used in their own right. Each unit represents approximately 40 hours of teaching with additional study. Units are achieved by passing an assessment.

There are seven levels of National Courses – National 1–5, Higher, and Advanced Higher and the Scottish Baccalaureates. There are also Skills for Work Courses from National 3 to Higher. They are mainly taken at school but some colleges may also offer provision at some levels.

National Qualification Group Awards – National Certificates (NCs), Higher National Certificates and Diplomas (HNCs and HNDs) and National Progression Awards (NPAs) – are designed to be taken at college; Scottish Vocational Qualifications (SVQs), Professional Development Awards (PDAs) and Customized Awards are designed for the workplace. A private company or training provider must become an 'approved centre' to deliver SQA qualifications, or work in partnership with a college or training provider.

*National Courses.* National Courses are designed to develop skills and knowledge in a specific subject area as well as skills for learning, skills for life and skills for work. Achieving a National Course shows that a learner has demonstrated the specified knowledge and skills in a particular subject at the defined national standard. Some of the new Awards cover work from across different subject areas, are shorter than traditional Courses and recognize success at different levels of difficulty, meaning they are suitable for young people of all abilities. National 1, 2 and 3 are replacing Access 1, 2 and 3. National Courses 1 and 2 are for students who require additional support for learning, and are assessed internally. There is a comprehensive appeals system for those who do not perform as well as expected.

*Skills for Work.* Skills for Work courses, National 3, 4 and 5 and Higher are designed to develop skills and knowledge in a broad vocational area, as well as an understanding of: the workplace skills and attitudes for employability, Core Skills, and other transferable skills. National 3 is usually made up of three National units at the level of the Course and National 4 and 5 are usually made up of four National units at the level of the Course.

*New Higher National Courses.* New Higher Courses have been designed to meet the aims, purposes and values of Curriculum for Excellence. They provide progression from National 5 and lead on to Advanced Higher and are designed to develop skills and knowledge in a specific subject area.

*New Advanced Higher National Courses.* New Advanced Higher awards are being designed to meet the aims, purposes and values of Curriculum for Excellence, and will provide progression from Higher Courses. These courses are usually made up of three National Units and a Course Assessment and are designed to develop skills and knowledge in a specific subject area.

*Higher Education Qualifications.* Higher National Certificates (HNCs) and Higher National Diplomas (HNDs) are developed by SQA in partnership with FE colleges, universities, and industry and commerce. They are credible, flexible qualifications that are designed to deliver skills and knowledge to meet the needs of today's businesses.

*National Progression Awards (NPAs).* NPAs are designed to assess a defined set of skills and knowledge in specialist vocational areas. They are mainly used by colleges for short programmes of study.

*National Certificates.* National Certificates are primarily aimed at 16–18-year olds and adults in full-time education, normally at a college. They prepare candidates for employment or further study by developing a range of knowledge and skills.

*Scottish Vocational Qualifications (SVQs).* SVQs are based on job competence, and recognize the skills and knowledge people need in employment. SVQs can be attained in most occupations and are available for all types and levels of job. They are primarily delivered to candidates in full-time employment and in the workplace.

*Professional Development Awards (PDAs).* PDAs are qualifications for people who are already in a career and who wish to extend or broaden their skills. In some cases they are designed for people wishing to enter employment. PDAs can be taken at college or the workplace.

*Customized Awards.* Though the above qualifications meet the needs of the majority of organizations, SQA also offers specially designed vocational qualifications at any level to meet an organization's need for skills and expertise and provide recognition and development opportunities for individuals. They can also help a company meet regulatory requirements and demonstrate the competence of its employees to external parties.

### Scottish Credit and Qualifications Framework

The SQA is a partner in a 'credit' system called the Scottish Credit and Qualifications Framework (SCQF), which sets out the Scottish qualifications and how they relate to one another by making clear the credit value of each type of qualification available in Scotland. The framework has 12 levels, from Level 1 for very basic education to Level 12 for doctoral degrees.

More information about SQA and its qualifications can be found at its website: www.sqa.org.uk

## Validating, examining and awarding bodies/organizations

A large number of external bodies provide qualifications recognized by accrediting and regulatory bodies. Not all qualifications are available across the entire FE sector: some colleges specialize in particular vocational areas while others are involved in more general adult education provision.

The Federation of Awarding Bodies (FAB) is a trade federation and membership organization for vocational awarding bodies. At the time of writing there are over 120 Ofqual-recognized awarding bodies that are full members of FAB. It also has associate members. Find more information at www.awarding.org.uk.

It is important to contact the examining or awarding bodies directly to find which colleges deliver the qualifications desired. However, most colleges deliver courses leading to qualifications awarded by the sample selection of organizations listed below.

## ABC Awards

Robins Wood House, Robins Wood Road, Aspley, Nottingham NG8 3NH; Tel: 0115 854 1616; Fax: 0115 854 1617; e-mail: enquiries@abcawards.co.uk; website: www.abcawards.co.uk

ABC Awards is a vocational awarding organization with accredited QCF qualifications in all sectors. Many of ABC's qualifications are included in the Foundation Learning Catalogue and are recognized as being eligible for apprenticeships and additional and specialist learning for diplomas. ABC Awards is dedicated to working with centres to deliver exceptional and flexible qualifications.

## AQA

Stag Hill House, Guildford, Surrey GU2 7XJ; Tel: 01483 506 506 or 0161 953 1180; Fax: 01483 300 152; e-mail: mailbox@aqa.org.uk; website: www.aqa.org.uk

AQA is the largest of the exam boards, currently setting and marking the papers for around half of all GCSEs and A-levels in England, Wales and Northern Ireland. AQA qualifications are internationally recognized and are taught in 30 countries around the world. As an awarding body AQA offers a broad range of academic qualifications for 14–19-year olds including GCEs, GCSEs, AQA iGCSEs, the Extended Project Qualification and the AQA Baccalaureate.

## ASDAN

Wainbrook House, Hudds Vale Road, St George, Bristol BS5 7HY; Tel: 0117 941 1126; e-mail: info@asdan.org.uk; website: www.asdan.org.uk

ASDAN is a curriculum development organization and awarding body, offering programmes and qualifications that explicitly grow skills for learning, for employment and for life. ASDAN is established as a registered charity for the 'advancement of education, by providing opportunities for all learners to develop their personal and social attributes and levels of achievement through ASDAN awards and resources, and the relief of poverty, where poverty inhibits such opportunities for learners'.

The following ASDAN qualifications are available at Entry Level:

- Qualifications in Personal Progress: Entry 1
- Personal and Social Development (PSD): Entry 1–3
- Certificate of Personal Effectiveness (CoPE): Entry 1–3
- Employability: Entry 2 and 3
- Diplomas in Life Skills: Entry 1–3
- Volunteering at an event: Entry 3

The following ASDAN qualifications are available at Levels 1–3:

- Wider Key Skills: Levels 1–3
- Certificate of Personal Effectiveness (CoPE): Levels 1–3
- CoPE Through: Levels 1–3
- Personal and Social Development (PSD): Levels 1–2
- Employability: Levels 1–3
- Community Volunteering Qualifications (CVQ): Levels 1–3
- Award of Personal Effectiveness (AoPE) Levels 1–3

## City & Guilds

1 Giltspur Street, London EC1A 9DD; Tel: 0844 543 0000; e-mail: centresupport@cityandguilds.com; website: www.cityandguilds.com

City & Guilds is a leading vocational educational organization, offering hundreds of work-related qualifications worldwide. City & Guilds' qualifications, which span from basic skills to the highest level of professional achievement, are delivered in more than 10,000 training centres across the world.

With over 130 years of experience, City & Guilds offers a wide range of qualifications from agriculture to engineering; hairdressing to health and social care; IT to tourism; and photography to catering. They are developed with the help of industry experts and are workplace-relevant, so these qualifications equip people for doing a real job – benefiting them and their employer.

City & Guilds qualifications develop both knowledge and practical skills. They are available at nine levels and are suitable for anyone, whether they are beginners or advanced in their career or area of study. Assessment is based on any combination of examination, projects or coursework. The organizations that offer City & Guilds qualifications include schools, colleges, training organizations, companies and adult education institutes. Depending on the organization, it is possible to study full time, part time or through distance learning.

## Edexcel Foundation

190 High Holborn, London WC1V 7BH; Tel. 0845 618 0440; website: www.edexcel.org.uk

Edexcel is the UK's largest awarding organization, offering academic and vocational qualifications and testing to schools, colleges, employers and other places of learning in the UK and internationally. Edexcel academic qualifications include GCSE, GCE (A level) and International GCSE (Edexcel Certificate for UK state schools). Edexcel vocational qualifications include NVQ and BTEC from entry level to Higher National Diplomas.

## EDI plc

International House, Siskin Parkway, Middlemarch Business Park, Coventry CV3 4PE;
Tel: 0844 576 0045; e-mail: wbl@pearson.com; website: www.ediplc.com

Education Development International plc (EDI) is a leading provider of education and training qualifications and assessment services. In the UK, EDI is accredited by the government to award a wide range of vocational qualifications, including apprenticeships and diplomas. EDI's expertise is in quality assuring work-based training programmes working closely with employers and over 1,500 private training providers and FE colleges. Internationally, EDI trades under the London Chamber of Commerce and Industry brand and offers a range of business and English language qualifications that have a history that can be traced back to 1887. LCCI International Qualifications are widely used in South East Asia and over 100 countries around the world.

The EDI website has a search facility: www.ediplc.com/Qualifications_Search.asp

## NCFE

Citygate, St James' Boulevard, Newcastle upon Tyne NE1 4JE; Tel: 0191 239 8000;
Fax: 0191 239 8001; e-mail: service@ncfe.org.uk; website: www.ncfe.org.uk

NCFE is a national awarding organization and registered educational charity. It currently offers over 400 nationally accredited qualifications from Entry level up to and including level 4 as well as NVQs, Functional Skills, Apprenticeships and Key Skills. Further qualifications are constantly in development. The NCFE website has a qualifications finder search facility: www.ncfe.org.uk/QualificationFinder.aspx

## OCR

1 Hills Road, Cambridge CB1 2EU; Fax: 01223 552627;
14–19 qualifications: Tel: 01223 553998; e-mail: general.qualifications@ocr.org.uk;
Post-19 qualifications: Tel: 02476 851 509; e-mail: vocational.qualifications@ocr.org.uk;
website: www.ocr.org.uk

OCR is a leading UK awarding body, committed to providing qualifications that engage learners of all ages at school, college, in work or through part-time learning programmes to achieve their full potential. It offers a wide range of general and vocational qualifications, from GCSEs, A levels and Diplomas to OCR Nationals, NVQs and specialist qualifications. You can find a full index of OCR qualifications at: www.ocr.org.uk/qualifications/index.aspx

## WJEC

245 Western Avenue, Cardiff CF5 2YX; Tel: 029 2026 5000; e-mail: info@wjec.co.uk;
website: www.wjec.co.uk

WJEC is an examining board offering the following major qualifications: GCSE; Entry Level (EL) and Advanced (A)/Advanced Supplementary (AS) levels and the Welsh Baccalaureate, which is available at different levels and incorporates GCSEs, A Levels and NVQs. In addition, WJEC provides Key/Essential Skills, Functional Skills (in England), Project and Extended Project and Principal Learning qualifications.

# Part 4

# Qualifications Awarded or Validated by Universities

# ADMISSION TO DEGREE COURSES

## Higher Education Institutions (HEIs)

Most institutions have a general requirement for admission to a degree course; special requirements may be in force for particular courses. Requirements are usually expressed in terms of subjects passed at GCE A level and the Higher Grade of the SCE. The universities have a clearing house to handle applications for university courses – UCAS: www.ucas.com

All intending students who live in the UK may obtain information on application procedures from their schools or colleges, or directly from UCAS. The scheme covers all universities and all medical schools. UCAS also has specialist services: the Graduate Teacher Training Registry (GTTR), the UK Postgraduate Application and Statistical Service (UKPASS) and the Conservatoires UK Admissions Service (CUKAS). HEIs have specific schemes to encourage access and participation in higher education. These can include partnerships with further education colleges that run access to higher education courses.

## The Open University

For admission to most first-degree courses, no formal educational qualifications are necessary. However, students who have successfully completed one or more years of full-time study at the higher education level (or its equivalent in part-time study) may be eligible for exemption from some credit requirements of the BA degree. The Open University handles its own admissions.

## Business schools

The degrees awarded by the various university business schools are postgraduate and therefore normally require an Honours degree as part of their entrance qualification.

# AWARDS

The awards made by the universities may be separated into the following categories: first degrees; higher degrees; honorary degrees; first diplomas and certificates; higher diplomas and certificates.

## First degrees

### Nomenclature

Various names are given to first degrees at British universities. At most universities the first degree in Arts is the BA (Bachelor of Arts) and the first degree in Science is the BSc (Bachelor of Science), but at the universities of Oxford and Cambridge and at several new universities, the BA is the first degree gained by students in both arts and science. In Scotland the first arts degree at three of the four old universities is Master of Arts (MA). There are numerous variations on the bachelor theme, eg BSc (Econ) (Bachelor of Science in Economics), BCom (Bachelor of Commerce), BSocSc (Bachelor of Social Science), BEng (Bachelor of Engineering) and BTech (Bachelor of Technology). The first award in medicine is the joint degrees of MB, ChB (Bachelor of Medicine, Bachelor of Surgery), the designatory letters of which vary from university to university.

### Structure of courses

First-degree courses vary considerably in structure, not only between one university and another but also between faculties in a single university. The degree examination is usually in two sections, Part I coming after one or two years of the course and Part II, 'finals', at the end of the course. The first-degree system at some Scottish universities differs substantially from that in English and Welsh universities (see below).

## Bachelor degrees

These degrees, sometimes known as 'ordinary' or 'first' degrees, lead to qualifications such as Bachelor of Arts (BA), Bachelor of Science (BSc) or Bachelor of Medicine (MB). Each university decides the form and content of its own degree examinations. These vary from university to university.

The first-degree structure in all British universities is based on the honours degree. Successful candidates in honours degree examinations are placed in different classes according to their performance, first class being the highest. The other classes given vary from university to university, but the classification most often used is: Class I; Class II (Division 1); Class II (Division 2); Class III. Most graduates who go on to higher academic qualifications and those entering, for example, the higher grades in the Civil Service or research, normally have a good class honours degree.

You can find out more about recognized UK degrees at the BIS website: www.bis.gov.uk

## Number of subjects studied

Excluding medicine and dentistry, the broad subject areas are Arts (or Humanities), Social Science, Pure Science and Applied Science. Most students study one main subject selected from one of these areas. It is possible to distinguish many types of degree course according to the number of subjects studied; these types are a variation on three main categories:

1. Honours course in one to three subjects with or without examinable subsidiary subjects.
2. Pass or ordinary courses in one to three subjects with or without examinable subsidiary subjects.
3. Common studies for pass and Honours in one to three subjects, with or without examinable subsidiary subjects.

## Length of degree course

First-degree courses may be preceded by a preliminary year, from which students with the appropriate entry qualifications may be exempted. At most universities Honours and pass courses in arts, social science, pure and applied science last three or four years, but courses in architecture, dentistry and veterinary medicine usually last five years, and complete qualifying courses in medicine up to six years. Courses in fine arts and pharmacy may last four years; four-year courses exist mainly in double Honours schools, especially when they involve foreign languages and a period of study abroad, and in the technological universities where some courses include a period of integrated industrial training (sandwich courses).

## The Scottish first degree

Undergraduate Honours degrees in Scotland are usually four years in duration and are structured to ensure a great deal of flexibility during the first two years of study. Most students only confirm their major in the final two years of study, which usually allows the student to choose a variety of subjects. This is different from the English system of undergraduate education, which is normally three years in duration and is more specialised from the beginning. After three years study students can gain a Bachelor or Ordinary degree or obtain the Honours degree by studying for a further year.

The Medicine and Veterinary Medicine degrees and MA Fine Art degree all take five years. In several science and engineering subjects there are opportunities to study for a five-year MChem, MChemPhys, MEng or MPhys degree. These degrees entail in-depth study, often with a research focus, but are undergraduate degrees and not equivalent to postgraduate Master's.

## Aegrotat degrees

Candidates who have followed a course for a degree but have been prevented from taking the examinations by illness may be awarded a degree certificate indicating that they were likely to have obtained the degree had they taken the examinations.

## Higher degrees

These comprise:

- some Bachelor's degrees: BPhil, BLitt, etc;
- Master's degrees: MA, MSc, etc;
- Doctor of Philosophy: PhD or DPhil;
- Higher Doctorates: DLitt, DSc, etc.

At Oxford and Cambridge the degree of MA is conferred on any BA of the university without any further course of study or examination after a specified number of years and on payment of a fee.

Candidates for a Master's degree at other universities (and at some for the degrees of BPhil, BLitt and BD, which are of equivalent standing) are normally required to have a first degree, although it need not have been obtained in the same university. Master's degrees are taken after one or two years' full-time study. The PhD requires at least two or more – usually three – years of full-time study.

In some universities and faculties students may be selected for a PhD course after an initial year's study or research common to both a PhD and a Master's degree. Candidates for a Master's degree are required either to prepare a thesis for presentation to examiners, who may afterwards question candidates on it orally, or to take written examination papers; they may be required to do both. All PhD students present a thesis; some may be required to take an examination paper as well. MPhil, MSc and similar degrees are usually awarded at the end of a one- or two-year course in a specific topic on the results of a written examination or a thesis. Higher doctorates are designated on a faculty basis, eg DLitt (Doctor of Letters) and DSc (Doctor of Science). Candidates are usually required to have at least a Master's degree of the awarding university. Senior doctorates are conferred on more mature and established people, usually on the basis of published contributions to knowledge.

## Foundation degrees

Foundation degrees were established to give people the intermediate technical and professional skills that are in demand from employers and to provide more flexible and accessible ways of studying. Increasing opportunities for employment and career advancement are priorities; Foundation degree content and assessment are therefore designed in consultation with employers. Additional progression routes include links with associated professional qualifications and/or direct entry to the final year of a relevant Honours-level degree. Provision is available across a range of FE colleges and a number of HEIs.

## Honorary degrees

Most universities confer honorary degrees on people of distinction in academic and public life, and on others who have rendered service to the university or to the local community. Normally degrees awarded are at least Foundation level.

## Diplomas and certificates of higher education

Courses for first diplomas and certificates are relatively simple in structure; they usually reach a level lower than that required for the award of a degree. There is usually a carefully defined course in a specialized or vocational subject, lasting one or two years, followed by all candidates. Most courses are full time.

## Postgraduate diplomas and certificates

Diplomas (eg in public health, social administration, medicine and technology) are awarded either on a full-time or, less often, part-time basis according to the subject and the university. Candidates must usually be graduates or hold equivalent qualifications. Diplomas are awarded after formal courses of instruction and success in written examinations. A Certificate or Diploma in Education is awarded to graduates training to become teachers after one year's full-time study and teaching practice.

## *Postgraduate courses*

A number of courses for graduates or people with equivalent qualifications are offered in FE establishments. They include short specialist courses in management and business studies and secretarial courses for graduates.

## *Business schools*

A Master of Business Administration (MBA) is an internationally recognized postgraduate qualification intended to prepare individuals for middle to senior general managerial positions. Most programmes contain as their core a number of subjects considered essential for understanding the operations of any enterprise. These are: accounting and finance, operations management, business policy, economics, human resource management, marketing, information systems and strategic planning.

Unlike any other Master's programme, the MBA is not only postgraduate, it is also strongly post-experience. A minimum of three years' (often more) work experience at an appropriate level of responsibility is generally expected of applicants. The requirement for a first degree (or equivalent) is sometimes waived for those holding an impressive track record of over five years at managerial level. Approximately one-third of MBA students have an engineering or information technology background. Many undertake the qualification to facilitate change from technical or specialist positions to more general ones.

The MBA was conceived originally in the United States at the beginning of the 20th century. Introduced in the United Kingdom in the late 1960s, it did not grow in popularity until the late 1980s. The popularity of this degree in the United Kingdom can be seen in the rapid expansion in the number of providers.

The Association of MBAs (AMBA) operates a system of accreditation. The accreditation process, which is internationally recognized for all MBA, DBA and Master's in Business and Management (MBM) programmes, measures individual MBA programmes against specific accreditation criteria.

Further information, including a list of accredited MBA programmes, can be obtained from the Association of MBAs, 25 Hosier Lane, London EC1A 9LQ; Tel: 020 7246 2686; e-mail: info@mba-world.com; website: www.mbaworld.com

### The Association of Business Schools (ABS)

137 Euston Road, London NW1 2AA; Tel: 020 7388 0007; Fax: 020 7388 0009; e-mail: abs@the-abs.org.uk; website: www.associationofbusinessschools.org

The ABS is the representative body for management and business education and all the United Kingdom's leading business schools. The ABS works broadly in three main areas: policy development, promotion and representation, and training and development. The ABS is able to provide general information about the wide range of courses and programmes provided by the United Kingdom's business schools.

## *First awards*

- **BA, BEd, BEng, LLB, BSc:** with 1st Class, 2nd Class (Divisions 1 and 2), 3rd Class Honours or Pass; or unclassified with or without Distinction.
- **MEng:** awarded to students who successfully complete a course of study that is longer and more demanding than the BEng first degree course in engineering.
- **GMus (Graduate Diploma in Music):** awarded to those students who complete three years' approved full-time study (or equivalent) in music and who demonstrate competence in musical performance.
- **DipHE (Diploma of Higher Education):** equivalent in standard and often similar in content to the first two years of an Honours degree course.
- **Certificates of Higher Education:** equivalent to the first year of an Honours degree course.

## Higher awards

- **MA, MBA, Med, MSc:** for successful completion of an approved postgraduate course of study of 48 weeks' duration (or the part-time equivalent).
- **MPhil, PhD:** for successful completion of approved programmes of supervised research.
- **DSc, DLitt, DTech:** for original and important contributions to knowledge and/or its applications.
- **Postgraduate Diploma:** awarded for the successful completion of an approved postgraduate course of study of 25 weeks' duration (or the part-time equivalent).
- **Postgraduate Certificate:** awarded for the successful completion of postgraduate/post-experience courses of 15 weeks' duration (or the part-time equivalent).
- **Postgraduate Certificate in Education (PGCE):** awarded on completion of a one-year full-time course; candidates must be British graduates or hold another recognized qualification.
- **Diploma in Professional Studies:** available in the fields of education and nursing, health visiting, midwifery and sports coaching. Students normally hold an initial professional qualification. A minimum of two years' experience is normally expected.

## UNIVERSITY OF ABERDEEN
## www.abdn.ac.uk

### *College of Arts and Social Sciences: www.abdn.ac.uk/about/social-sciences/php*

#### Aberdeen Business School; www.abdn.ac.uk/business

accountancy, coaching, economics, energy/health economics, enterprise, entrepreneurship, finance, management studies, petroleum economics, real estate/management, MBA programmes, petroleum, energy finance, investment management, managing enterprise & innovation; MA(Hons), MBA, MRes, MSc, MPhil, PgCert, PhD

#### School of Divinity, History & Philosophy; www.abdn.ac.uk/sdhp

biblical studies, cultural history, divinity, history, history of art, Jewish studies, pastoral studies, philosophy, history & philosophy of science, science, technology & medicine, philosophical research, religious studies, theoethics, theology, ministry, biblical/practical/systematic theology, church history, medieval studies, early modern studies, modern historical studies, Irish & Scottish studies, cultural history, Scandinavian studies, social anthropology, ethnology & cultural history; BD, BTh, DMin, LicTh, MA(Hons), MLitt, MTh, PgDip, PhD, DPS

#### School of Education; www.abdn.ac.uk/education

childhood practice, community learning & development, advanced educational/professional studies, counselling, early years, plurilingualism, autism & learning, continuous learning & development, enterprise & employability, primary education, professional development, TQFE, secondary education, tertiary education, autism, adult literacy, inclusive practice, social pedagogy; BA(Hons), BEd(Hons), MEd, MPhil, MRes, MSc, Mus(Hons), PGCert, PGDE, PGDip, PhD, EdD

#### School of Language & Literature; www.abdn.ac.uk/sll

Celtic, comparative literature, creative writing, English/literature/language, film & visual culture, French, German & Hispanic studies, Irish–Scottish studies, linguistics the novel, literature in world context, linguistics; MA, MA(Designated), MA(Hons), MLitt, PhD

#### School of Law; www.abdn.ac.uk/law

law, French/Belgian/Spanish/German law, international commercial/business/energy/oil & gas law, private/public international law, criminal justice, human rights, climate change law; LlB(Hons), LlM, MPhil, PhD

#### School of Social Science; www.abdn.ac.uk/socsci

anthropology of religion, gender studies, politics & international relations, international law, social anthropology, cultural/sociology, religion & society, Europolitics & society, globalisation, Latin American studies, sex, gender & violence, sociology, strategic studies, transitional justice, people & the environment; MA(Hons), MA, MLitt, MPhil, MRes, MSc, PGDip, PhD

## College of Life Sciences and Medicine; www.abdn.ac.uk/clsm

### School of Biological Sciences; www.abdn.ac.uk/biologicalsci

biology, zoology, marine biology, conservation biology, ecology, environmental science, animal ecology, wildlife management, forestry, forest sciences, plant & soil science

### School of Medical Science; www.abdn.ac.uk/sms

applied sports science, biochemistry, biomedical sciences, biotechnology, genetics, health economics, human embryology & development, immunology, medical education, microbiology, molecular biology, neuroscience, pharmacology, physiology, sport & exercise science, sports studies

### School of Medicine & Dentistry; www.abdn.ac.uk/medicine-dentistry

dentistry, health science/studies, medicine, primary care, rural health, chronic disability, epidemiology, immunology, psychiatry, respiratory, musculoskeletal, obstetrics & gynaecology, primary care, urology, epidemiology, health economics, health psychology, medical statistics, public health nutrition

### School of Psychology; www.abdn.ac.uk/psychology

psychology, social/cognition, perception & attention

### Rowett Institute of Nutrition and Health Studies; www.abdn.ac.uk/rowett

impacts on human health

### CLSM Graduate School; www.abdn.ac.uk/clsm/graduate

economics of health, global health, health economics/services, public health, human nutrition & metabolism, international health, molecular nutrition, nursing/midwifery/health care, public health, nutrition, applied marine & fisheries ecology, ecology & environmental sustainability, environmental microbiology, environmental science, forestry, soil science, bio-business & medical sciences, cell & molecular systems biology, medical molecular genetics, medical molecular microbiology, molecular biology, molecular & cellular immunology, medical education, paediatric dentistry, physician assistant, clinical pharmacology, drug discovery, medical imaging, medical physics; BDS, BSc(Hons), MA, MBChB, MMedSci, MPhil, MSc, PhD, PGDip/Cert, MD, MRes

## College of Physical Sciences; www.abdn.ac.uk/about/physical-sciences.php

### School of Engineering; www.abdn.ac.uk/engineering

chemical engineering, civil engineering, electrical & electronic engineering, mechanical engineering, project management, safety engineering, renewable energy, subsea engineering, oil & gas engineering/structures, petroleum engineering; BEng(Hons), BScEng, EngD, MEng, MSc

### School of Geosciences; www.abdn.ac.uk/geosciences

### Dept of Archaeology; www.abdn.ac.uk/archaeology

archaeology, with Celtic civilization/history/geography, archaeology of the north; BSc(Hons), MA(Hons), MPhil, PhD, MSc

### Dept of Geography & the Environment; www.abdn.ac.uk/geography

geography, physical/human geography, geospatial information science, marine & coastal resource management, urban/rural planning, rural surveying/change, sustainable rural development, transport geography, environmental management/hydrology; BSc(Hons), MA(Hons), MSc, PgDip/Cert, PhD, MLE, DiplE

### Dept of Geology & Petroleum Geology; www.abdn.ac.uk/geology

oil & gas enterprise management, geology, geoscience, integrated petroleum geoscience; BSc(Hons), MA(Hons), MRes, MSc, PgDip/Cert, PhD, MGeol

## School of Natural & Computing Sciences; www.abdn.ac.uk/ncs

### Chemistry; www.abdn.ac.uk/ncs/chemistry

chemistry, biomedical materials, chemical science, environmental/analytical chemistry, oil & gas chemistry, medicinal chemistry; BSc(Hons), MChem, MSc, PgDip, PhD

### Computing Science; www.abdn.ac.uk/ncs/computing

artificial intelligence, adv information systems, computing, computing science, business computing systems, cloud computing, information systems/technology/science, electronic commerce technology, informatics, software project management; BSc(Hons), MA(Hons), MSc, MSci, PhD, PGDip

### Institute of Mathematics; www.abdn.ac.uk/ncs/mathematics

mathematics, statistics; BSc(Hons), MA(Hons), MSc, PhD, MPhil

### Physics; www.abdn.ac.uk/ncs/physics

physical sciences, physics, physics education, physics with chemistry/geology/philosophy/engineering/mathematics; BSc(Hons), MSc(Hons)

## UNIVERSITY OF ABERTAY, DUNDEE
## www.abertay.ac.uk

### School of Arts, Media & Computer Games www.abertay.ac.uk/studying/schools/amg

computer arts, computer games/technology/design/production/applications, creative sound production, visual communication & media design; BA(Hons), BSc(Hons), DipHE, MProf, MSc/PGDip

### School of Engineering, Computing & Applied Mathematics; www.abertay.ac.uk/studying/schools/secam

computing & networks, digital forensics, ethical hacking & computer security/counter measures, information technology, intelligence & security informatics, web, design & communication; BSc(Hons), MSc, DipHE, PGDip

### Dundee Business School; www.abertay.ac.uk/studying/schools/dbs

accounting, biotechnology, business administration/studies, enterprise, Europe (economy, business law, management), entrepreneurship & consultancy, finance, HRM, international management, law, management, marketing, management accounting, oil & gas accounting/finance, retail marketing, tourism, golf management; BA(Hons), GradCert, LlB, MBA, MSc, PGDip, DipHE

### The School of Contemporary Sciences; www.abertay.ac.uk/studying/schools/cs

bioinformatics, biomedical science, food nutrition & health, medical biotechnology, civil engineering, energy & environmental management, environment & business industrial environment, food biotechnology/product design, food & consumer science, forensic sciences, environmental technology, policing & security, renewable bioenergy, urban water, water pollution control; BSc(Hons), DipHE, MSc, MTech, PGDip

### The School of Social & Health Sciences; www.abertay.ac.uk/studying/schools/shs

cognitive behavioural therapy, counselling, criminological studies, forensic psychobiology, media, culture and society, mental health/nursing, psychology, social & health science, sociology, social science, sports/coaching, performance golf, sport & exercise/science, sports development, strength & conditioning; BA(Hons), BSc(Hons), GradCert, MSc, PGDip, DipHE

## ABERYSTWYTH UNIVERSITY
## www.aber.ac.uk

### School of Art; www.aber.ac.uk/en/art

art, art history, fine art; BA(Hons), MA, MPhil, PhD

### Institute of Biological, Environmental & Rural Sciences; www.aber.ac.uk/en/ibers

agriculture, animal science/zoology, biochemistry, biology, conservation/countryside/environmental management, environmental bioscience & ecology, microbiology, equine science, food & water security, genetics, livestock science, marine & freshwater biology/systems, green biotechnology & innovation management, managing the environment – environmental sustainability/bioenergy & environmental change/habitat restoration & conservation; BSc(Hons), MPhil, MSc, PhD

**Dept of Computer Science; www.aber.ac.uk/en/cs**
business IT, robotics, software engineering, artificial intelligence, ubiquitous computing, computer science, computer graphics vision & games, internet computing & systems administration, internet engineering, 3D imaging, analysis & applications, intelligent autonomous systems, intelligent systems; BEng, BSc(Hons), HND, MEng, MSc, PhD, MRes

**School of Education & Lifelong Learning; www.aber.ac.uk/en/sell**
childhood studies, lifelong learning, education, secondary education (English, drama, geography, ICT & modern languages); BA(Hons), BSc(Hons), MPhil, PGCE, PGDip, PhD

**Dept of English & Creative Writing; www.aber.ac.uk/en/english**
creative writing, English literature, literary/classical studies, English & world literatures; BA(Hons), MA, PhD

**Dept of European Languages; www.aber.ac.uk/en/eurolangs**
French, German, Italian, European culture, Romance languages, Spanish; BA(Hons), MA, PhD

**Institute of Geography & Earth Sciences; www.aber.ac.uk/en/iges**
environmental earth/science, geography, GIS and remote sensing, glaciology, human/physical geography, regional & environmental planning, landscape & territory, practising human geography, environmental monitoring & analysis; BSc(Hons), MPhil, MRes, MSc, PhD

**Dept of History & Welsh History; www.aber.ac.uk/en/history**
economic/social/European/medieval & modern history, Welsh history, history & media, modern & contemporary history, politics & modern history, medieval Britain & Europe, the British Isles c.1536-1801, 18th century Britain, modern British/European history, history & heritage, media history; BA(Hons), MA, PhD

**Dept of Information Studies; www.aber.ac.uk/en/dis**
archive administration, business information, historical & archival/information & library studies, records management, information management; BA(Hons), BSc(Econ), Dip/Cert, MPhil, MSc(Econ), PhD

**Dept of International Politics; www.aber.ac.uk/en/interpol**
European studies/politics, internatioal politics/ & strategic studies/international history/military history/intelligence studies/third world, intelligence & strategic studies, international history/strategic studies/third world/military history, political studies, intelligence studies/ & strategic studies/ international history, international history/relations, postcolonial politics, strategic/security studies, Welsh politics society, food & water security, international politics of the internet, critical international politics, politics, media & performance; BSc(Econ), MA, MSc, MSc(Econ), PhD

**Dept of Law and Criminology; www.aber.ac.uk/en/law-criminology**
business law, criminal law, criminology with applied psychology/law, European law, human rights, law, criminology & criminal/international justice, climate change & human rights, democracy, human security & international law, international law & IT /human rights/criminology of armed conflict, internet commerce & law, human rights & development/humanitarian law, rights, gender & international law; BA(Hons), BSc(Econ), LlB, LlM, PhD

**School of Management and Business; www.aber.ac.uk/en/smb**
accounting & finance, business management, business economics/finance, corporate leadership, economics, entrepreneurship & innovation, international finance & banking/accountancy, management & digital business/finance/marketing/project management/tourism management, marketing; BSc(Econ), MBA, MSc(Econ), PhD

**Institute of Mathematics & Physics; www.aber.ac.uk/en/maps**
applied mathematics, statistics, pure mathematics, physics, planetary and space physics, space science & robotics, mathematics & theoretical physics, astrophysics, robotics; BSc(Hons), MMath, MPhys, PhD

**Dept of Psychology; www.aber.ac.uk/en/psychology**
psychology/ & criminology; BSc(Econ), BSc(Hons), PhD

**Dept of Sport & Exercise Science; www.aber.ac.uk/en/sport-exercise**
sport & exercise science, exercise & health sciences; BSc(Hons), PhD

**Dept of Theatre, Film & Television Studies; www.aber.ac.uk/en/tfts**
drama & theatre, film & television studies, media & communication, practising theatre performance, scenography/theatre design, scriptwriting, Welsh medium courses, politics, media & performance; BA(Hons), MA, MPhil, PhD

**Dept of Welsh; www.aber.ac.uk/en/cymraeg**
Breton, Welsh & Celtic languages, Celtic studies, Irish language & literature, Welsh 1st/2nd language, medieval Welsh literature; BA(Hons), MA

## ANGLIA RUSKIN UNIVERSITY
## www.anglia.ac.uk

### *Faculty of Arts, Law and Social Sciences: www.anglia.ac.uk/en/home/faculties/alss.html*

**Dept of English, Communication, Film & Media; www.anglia.ac.uk/ruskin/en/home/faculties/alss/deps/english_media**
English language/literature, ELT, TESOL, film/media studies, creative writing, applied linguistics, intercultural communication, international business English writing, publishing, sports journalism, writing & film studies; BA(Hons), MPhil, PhD

**Anglia Law School; www.anglia.ac.uk/ruskin/en/home/faculties/alss/deps/law**
international business/ law, law, legal practice; BA(Hons), LlB, LlD, LlM, PGDip, MPhil, PhD

**Cambridge School of Art; www.anglia.ac.uk/ruskin/en/home/faculties/alss/deps/csoa**
animation, children's book illustration, computer games, fashion/interior design, film & TV production, fine art, illustration, photography, professional typography, printmaking, graphic design, typography; BA(Hons), FdA, MA, MFA

**Dept of Humanities & Social Sciences; www.anglia.ac.uk/ruskin/en/home/faculties/alss/deps/hss**
archaeology & landscape history, criminology, forensic science, history, English, philosophy, psychosocial studies, public service, sociology, transnational crime; BA(Hons), FdA, MPhil, PhD

**Dept of Music & Performing Arts; www.anglia.ac.uk/ruskin/en/home/faculties/alss/deps/music**
creative music technology, drama, music/drama therapy, performing arts, pop music, film studies; BA(Hons), FdADip, MA, MPhil, PhD

### *Lord Ashcroft International Business School; www.anglia.ac.uk/ruskin/en/home/faculties/aibs*
accounting & finance/financial management, business economics, business management, enterprise & entrepreneurial management, management, HRM, international business/business strategy/management, marketing, tourism management, charity & social enterprise management, international hospitality & tourism management, management & leadership; BA(Hons), BSc(Hons), MA, MBA, MSc, CertHE, HNC, HND

### *Faculty of Health, Social Care & Education; www.anglia.ac.uk/ruskin/en/home/faculties/fhsce*
acute care, counselling, decontamination sciences, early childhood studies, early years professional practice, early years, playwork & education, education/& childhood studies, health & social care, healthcare science/management, international nursing studies, leadership & management in health & social care, learning through technology, midwifery, nursing (adult/child/mental health), operating department practice, primary community care, primary & community care, public health, social policy, social work, specialist community public health nursing, playwork & education, learning through technology, management of social & affordable housing, mental health, paediatric intensive care nursing, palliative care, adult critical care nursing, advanced midwifery practice, advanced practice, children & young people, hospital management, international nursing studies, international social welfare & social policy, learning & teaching (higher education), magnetic resonance imaging, medical & healthcare education, mental health services, minimally invasive & robotic surgery, physiotherapy, plastic & aesthetic surgery primary PGCE, PGCE

(secondary computer science with ICT/mathematics/ modern languages/biology/chemistry/physics, family therapy & systemic practice), public health, social work; BSc(Hons), FdSc, FdA, Cert HE, Dip HE, MSc, MA, DipPGCE, PGDip/Cert, BA(Hons), Dips, Professional Practice, MBA

## *Faculty of Science and Technology; www.anglia.ac.uk/ruskin/en/home/ faculties/fst*

### Dept of Engineering & Built Environment; www.anglia.ac.uk/ruskin/en/home/ faculties/fst/departments/eng_builtenv

architecture/technology, building surveying, civil engineering, construction/project management, engineering management, integrated/engineering, environmental planning, manufacturing systems, mechanical engineering, motorsport engineering, project management in built environment, quantity surveying, real estate management, structural engineering, sustainable construction, town planning, clear filters; BSc(Hons), BEng, FdSc, MSc, PGCert, PGDip, FSc

### Dept of Computing & Technology; www.anglia.ac.uk/ruskin/en/home/ faculties/fst/departments/comptech

audio music technology, business information systems, computer gaming technology/science, computing & information systems, information security & forensic computing, media & internet technology, mobile telecommunication, multimedia, network infrastructure & security/management/security audio & video technology, electronic & electrical engineering, information & communication technology, mobile telecommunications; BEng(Hons), BSc(Hons), FdSc, MSc

### Dept of Vision and Hearing Sciences; www.anglia.ac.uk/ruskin/en/home/ departments/vision_hearing

ophthalmic dispensing, optometry, hearing aid technology; BOptom(Hons), BSc(Hons), FdSc, UnivCert

### Dept of Psychology; www.anglia.ac.uk/ ruskin/en/home/faculties/fst/ departments/psychology

cognitive neuroscience, abnormal/clinical/child/ applied, cognitive & clonical neuroscience, psychology, criminology; BSc(Hons), MSc

### Dept of Life Sciences; www.anglia.ac.uk/ ruskin/en/home/faculties/fst/ departments/lifesciences

animal behaviour/welfare, biodiversity & conservation, biomedical sciences, conservation, ecology, crimininal & investigative studies, equine science & rehab therapy, forensic science, marine biology, microbiology, sports coaching & PE/science, wildlife conservation, zoology; BSc(Hons), FdSc, MSc, PGDip

## *Degrees validated by Anglia Ruskin University offered at:*

---

# COLCHESTER INSTITUTE
www.colchester.ac.uk

## *Institute for Arts, Science and Technology; www.glyndwr.ac.uk/en/ UniversityInstitutes/ ArtsScience&Technology*

### Creative Industries, Media & Performance; www.glyndwr.ac.uk/en/ UniversityInstitutes/ ArtsScienceandTechnology/ CreativeIndustries

Applied Art; design: applied arts, art practice, design practice
Design Communication & Digital Art; design: animation, visual effects and game art/film and photography/graphic design and multimedia/illustration, graphic novels and children's publishing, creative media, communications & digital art
Fine Art; fine art
Creative Media Technology; music technology, sound technology, television production and technology
Broadcasting & Journalism; broadcasting, journalism and media communications
Creative Writing; creative writing and history/ English
English; English, English and creative writing/history
History; history, creative writing/English and history
Information Management; library and information practice/management;
BEng(Hons), FdEng, MSc, PhD, MPhil, MRes

### Engineering and Applied Physics; www.glyndwr.ac.uk/en/UniversityInstitutes/ArtsScienceandTechnology/Engineering

Electrical and Electronic Engineering; electrical and electronic engineering, digital and radio frequency communication systems, advanced electronic techniques, electrical and electronic systems, renewable energy systems and sustainability/distributed generation
Aeronautical Engineering; aeronautical and mechanical engineering/manufacture, aircraft maintenance, aircraft electronics & control, composites
Performance Car Technology; performance car technology, motorsport design and management
Renewable Energy and Sustainable Technologies; renewable energy and sustainable technologies
Industrial Engineering; industrial engineering
Mechanical Engineering; mechanical engineering, manufacture, manufacturing engineering
Digital and Radio Frequency Communication Systems; advanced electronic techniques, electrical and electronic systems, renewable energy systems and sustainability/distributed generation;
BSc(Hons), MSc, MRes, FdEng, BEng, MEng, MPhil, PhD

### Computing;

www.glyndwr.ac.uk/en/UniversityInstitutes/ArtsScienceandTechnology/Computing
applied computing, computer game development, computer network management and security, creative media computing, app design, IT management for business, information technology support, business management and IT, applied computing, creative media computing, library and information practice, computer networking, computer science, creative audio technology, computing, high performance computing, creative media technology; BSc(Hons), FdSc, MSc, MRes, PhD, MPhil

### Biology & the Environment;

www.glyndwr.ac.uk/en/UniversityInstitutes/ArtsScienceandTechnology/BiologyandEnvironment
Built environment; architectural design technology, building studies (construction/maintenance management), facilities management, housing studies, housing & sustainable communities, supported housing, rural business
Animal Studies & Equine Science; animal studies, equestrian psychology, equine science & welfare
Wildlife & Plant Biology
Science & Environment; formulation science, photovoltaics, polymer & biopolymer science;
BSc(Hons), FdSc, MPhil, PhD

### Chemistry; www.glyndwr.ac.uk/en/UniversityInstitutes/ArtScienceandTechnology/Chemistry

forensic science, polymer & biopolymer science, BSc(Hons), MSc

### Management & Business; www.glyndwr.ac.uk/en/UniversityInstitutes/ArtsScienceandTechnology/BusinessandManagement

accounting and finance, business management/and IT, entrepreneurship, app design, business marketing, business and events management, professional education and training, IT management for business, business management/with accounting/marketing, rural business, HRM, executive/MBA, international business, IT management, marketing, management; BA(Hons), FdA, PhD, MPhil, MA, MBA, MSc, ProfDoc

## *Institute for Health, Medical Sciences & Society; www.glyndwr.ac.uk/en/UniversityInstitutes/HealthMedicalSciencesandSociety*

**Applied Social Sciences**

criminology & criminal justice, therapeutic childcare, health & social care, youth & community work/studies, social work, counselling with children & young people, counselling work

**Education**

post-compulsory education and training, professional education and training; compulsory education sector; learning support: learning and teaching/SEN, education, education (psychology and counselling/additional learning needs/special educational needs), dyslexia, e-learning: theory and practice, professional development in HE, professional development (education), teaching of psychology, professional education, youth and community studies, youth studies

**Health, Psychology & Social Care**

Counselling; person-centred and experiential counselling and psychotherapy, health care studies; health and social care, health and care studies, nursing post-registration
Community Practice; community specialist practice (community children's nursing/district nursing/general practice nursing), health studies, healthcare leadership and management, specialist community

public health nursing (health visiting/school nursing), clinical/community practice
Occupational Health and Safety; environmental health management (environmental and public health/occupational health, safety and environmental management)
Occupational Therapy; occupational therapy
Health and Medical Science; nursing and healthcare studies; advanced clinical practice, leadership in health and social care, professional education, counselling studies with children and young people

**Childhood & Family Studies**

childhood studies, education & childhood studies, early childhood care & education, childhood studies/babies & young children/play/early childhood education

**Psychology**

psychology, psychology of religion, teaching of psychology
BA(Hons), BSc(Hons), FdSc, MSc, MPhil
Environment

**Polymer science & technology**

MRes, MPhil, PhD

**Society & Community**

Counselling: counselling studies, person-centred & experiential counselling & psychotherapy
Criminal Justice: criminology & criminal justice
Social Care: social work, therapeutic childcare, counselling & psychotherapy, counselling studies/with children & young people
Social Science: public & social policy
Youth & Community: youth & community work/studies; Cer/DiptHE, BA(Hons), FdA, MPhil, PhD, MA, ProfDoc

**Social Sciences**

social science; MRes, MPhil, PhD

**Sport & Exercise Sciences; www.glyndwr.ac.uk/en/UniversityInstitutes/HealthMedicalSciencesandSociety/SportandExerciseSciences**

sport & exercise sciences, sport coaching; BSc(Hons), MRes, MPhil, PhD

## ASHRIDGE
## www.ashridge.ac.uk

management, executive/advanced coaching/& organisation development supervision, sustainability & responsibility, organisational change, development supervision; Doc Orgn Change, ExecMBA, MBA, MSc, Masters, PGCert

## ASTON UNIVERSITY
## www.aston.ac.uk

### *Aston Business School: www1.aston.ac.uk/aston-business-school*

accounting for management, business/economics & management, business & marketing analytics, business computing & IT, finance, HRM & business, international business & management/economics, marketing, law/with management, international commercial law, accounting & fnance, business & management/marketing analytics, finance & financial regulation/investments, information systems & business analysis, international business, investment analysis, Islamic banking & finance, marketing management, market research & consultancy, organisational psychology & business, operational research & performance management, organisational behaviour,
social responsibility & sustainability, strategy & international business, supply chain management, work psychology & business; BSc(Hons), DBA, LlB, LlM, MBA, PhD, FD

### *Centre for Learning, Innovation and Professional Practice; www1.aston.ac.uk/clipp/*

curriculum & learning development, professional practice; MA, PG Cert

## *School of Engineering and Applied Science: www1.aston.ac.uk/eas*

### Chemical Engineering & Applied Chemistry; www1.aston.ac.uk/eas/about-eas/academic-groups/ceac

applied/biological chemistry, chemical engineering, chemistry, professional engineering; BEng, MEng, MChem

### Computer Science; www1.aston.ac.uk/eas/about-eas/academic-groups/computer-science

computing science, computing for business, multimedia computing, IT project management, software engineering, professional engineering; BSc, MSc

### Electrical, Electronic & Power Engineering; www1.aston.ac.uk/eas/about-eas/academic-groups/electronic-engineering/

communications engineering/networks, data communications systems, electronic & electrical engineering, sensors & sensing systems, electrical & electronic engineering/computer science, telecommunications technology, professional engineering; BEng, MEng, MSc

### Engineering Systems & Management; www1.aston.ac.uk/eas/about-eas/academic-groups/esm

construction project management, engineering management, industrial enterprise management, supply chain management, professional engineering, logistics management, transport management; BSc, MSc

### Mathematics; www1.aston.ac.uk/eas/about-eas/academic-groups/mathematics

mathematics, mathematics with computing/business/economics, mathematics in complex systems; BSc, MSc

### Mechanical Engineering & Design; www1.aston.ac.uk/eas/about-eas/academic-groups/med

electromechanical engineering, mechanical engineering/modelling, design engineering, transport product design, product design/& management/enterprise/innovation, professional engineering; BEng, MEng, MSc

## *School of Life and Health Sciences: www1.aston.ac.uk/lhs*

human biology, audiology, biological sciences, cell & molecular biology, clinical science, drug delivery, microbiology & immunology, biomedical science, clinical health management/science, health psychology, healthcare science (audiology), medical bioscience, molecular toxic drug design, psychiatric pharmacy/ therapeutics, hearing aid audiology, optometry, pharmacy, psychiatric pharmacy/ therapeutics, psychology, molecular pharmaceutics, occupational toxicology, pharmaceutical sciences, pharmacokinetics, pharmacology, cognitive neurosciences, psychology of health & illness; BSc(Hons), GradDip, FD, MPharm, MRes, MSc, PGCert/Dip, PhD, M/DOptom

## *School of Languages and Social Sciences: www1.aston.ac.uk/lss*

### Languages & Translation Studies

French, German, Spanish, translation studies, international business & modern languages studies, TESOL, applied linguistics, forensic/corpus linguistics, literary linguistics, sociolinguistics

### English Language

English language, number of joint honours degrees with English language, ELT, TESP, TEYL, EMT, applied linguistics, international business

### Politics & International Relations

sociology, politics, global governance, international relations & business/politics/policy/sociology, social change, public policy & management/sociology

### Sociology & Public Policy

sociology & business/social policy/international relations/politics/psychology/social change, social policy, politics, international relations/policy, public policy, business & management

### Taught postgraduate

TESOL, translation studies, translation in a European context, applied linguistics, sociolinguistics, forensic linguistics, corpus linguistics, the EU/multilevel governance & international relations/global governance, Europe & the world, governance & international politics, social research/public policy & social change, TESOL, TESP, TEYL, applied linguistics, forensic linguistics

BA(Hons), BSc(Hons), MA, MPhil, MRes, MSc, PhD

# BANGOR UNIVERSITY
# www.bangor.ac.uk

## College of Arts and Humanities; www.bangor.ac.uk/cah

### Creative Studies & Media; www.bangor.ac.uk/creative_industries

creative/film studies/practice, digital media, film-making, international media management, consumer psychology, film & visual culture, journalism, media studies, theatre, professional writing, creative writing, digital media, film; BA (Hons), MA, MRes, MSc, PhD/MPhil

### English; www.bangor.ac.uk/english

creative writing, English literature/language, journalism, publishing, theatre & performance, Arthurian legend, medieval & early modern literature, song-writing; BA (Hons), MA/Diploma, PhD/MPhil

### History, Welsh History & Archaeology; www.bangor.ac.uk/history

archaeology, contemporary/medieval & early modern/Welsh history, heritage, history, Celtic archaeology, the Celts, medieval studies, political & social sciences; BA (Hons), MA/Diploma, PhD/MPhil

### School of Linguistics & English Language; www.bangor.ac.uk/linguistics

creative writing, English language/literature, applied/ cognitive/forensic linguistics, bilingualism, media studies, film studies, language development; BA (Hons), MA, MSc, PhD/MPhil

### School of Modern Languages; www.bangor.ac.uk/ml

French, German, Italian, Spanish, European languages & cultures, translation studies; BA (Hons), MA, PhD/MPhil

### School of Music; www.bangor.ac.uk/music

music/technology/electronics, composition, electroacoustics, early music, 20/21st century music, performance; BA, BMus, BSc, MA/Diploma/Certificate, MMus/Dip

### School of Philosophy & Religion; www.bangor.ac.uk/spar

philiosophy & religion, study of religion; BA, MA

### School of Welsh; www.bangor.ac.uk/ ysgolygymraeg

details of courses provided in Welsh language, Welsh, Celtic studies, the Celts, Welsh for beginners; BA(Hons), BD, BMus, Dip, MA, MMus, MPhil, MTh, PgDip, PhD, MSc

## College of Business, Social Sciences & Law: www.bangor.ac.uk/cbss

### Bangor Business School; www.bangor.ac.uk/business

accounting, banking, business/studies, consumer psychology, international banking & development finance, economics, environmental management, finance, financial economics, law, marketing, administration, ICT, management, social authority law, Islamic banking, information management; BA, BSc(Hons), MA, MSc, MBA

### School of Social Sciences; www.bangor.ac.uk/so

comparative/criminology & criminal justice/law/ sociology, health & social care, language policy & planning, social policy/work/studies/research, sociology, international social work, policy research & evaluation; BA(Hons), MA/Dip/Cert, PhD, MPhil, MARes

### School of Law; www.bangor.ac.uk/law

law, criminology, public procurement, international UIP law, European law, global trade, international crime/human rights, criminal justice, law & devolved government, company/commercial/family & welfare/ media, international law/ intellectual property, international law (European/global trade/criminal law/ human rights law) law & banking/criminology, international commercial & business law; BA(Hons), MBA, DBA, HND, LlB, LlM(Res/Dip), MA, MSc, MPhil, PGDip, PhD

### School of Education and Lifelong Learning: www.bangor.ac.uk/cell

childhood studies, design & technology secondary education, education studies, product design, secondary education, early childhood & learning support studies, primary education, PGCE primary/ secondary, preparing to teach; BA Cert, Dipl, FdA, HNC/HND, MA, MEd

### Academic Development Unit; www.bangor.ac.uk/adu

Welsh for adults; PGCertHE, BSc(Hons), EdMed, FdA, MA, MEd, MMusD, MPhil, MTh, PGCE, PhD

## *College of Natural Sciences; www.bangor.ac.uk/cns*

### CNS School of Biological Sciences; www.bangor.ac.uk/biology

medical biology, biology, biomedical science, biotechnology, ecology, zoology with animal behaviour/ conservation/marine genetics, medical biology, molecular zoology, ecology, natural sciences; BSc(Hons), Dipl, MA, MBiol, MPhil, MRes, MSc, MZool, PhD

### School of Environment, Natural Resources, & Geography; www.bangor.ac.uk/senrgy

agriculture, conservation & environment/land management, applied terrestrial & marine ecology, conservation & forest ecosystems, environmental conservation/management/science, geography, agroforestry, environmental/forestry, sustainable forest & nature management, sustainable tropical forestry, forestry, tropical forestry; BA(Hons), BSc(Hons), MA, MBA, MPhil, MSc, PhD, MEnvSci

### School of Ocean Sciences; www.bangor.ac.uk/sos

applied marine biology, geoscience, coastal geography, geological/physical oceanography, marine biology/& zoology/oceanography/protection, marine science, marine environmental sciences, marine vertebrate zoology, ocean science; BSc(Hons), MMBiol, MMSci, MOcean, MPhil, MSc, PhD

## *Welsh Institute for Natural Resources; www.bangor.ac.uk/winr*

## *College of Health & Behavioural Sciences; www.bangor.ac.uk/cohabs*

### School of Healthcare Sciences; www.bangor.ac.uk/healthcaresciences

adv clinical practice, health studies/science, critical care, health & social care leadership, midwifery, nursing, occupational therapy, pharmacology, operating department practice, public health, diagnostic radiography & imaging, risk management in health & social care; BN(Hons), BSc(Hons), BMidw, DipHE, GradCert/Dip, MPhil, PhD

### School of Medical Sciences; www.bangor.ac.uk/sms

medical education/sciences, exercise physiology, exercise, behavioural change & disease prevention, neuropsychology, sport science; MSc, PGDip/ Cert(HE), BMed Sci, BSc PhD

### School of Psychology; www.bangor.ac.uk/ psychology

psychology, child & language development, clinical psychology, consumer psychology with business/ digital media, mindfulness-based approaches, foundations of clinical neuropsychology/psychology, neuroimaging, psychological research, applied behaviour analysis, behavioural neurology & neuropsychiatry, clinical & functional brain imaging, ageing & cognitive health; BSc(Hons), MSc, PhD, MRes, MA, PGDip/Cert,

### School of Sport, Health & Exercise Science; www.bangor.ac.uk/sport

sport science, sport, health & exercise science/& PE, physical education, applied exercise science, applied sport & exercise physiology/psychology, applied sport science & outdoor activities, exercise rehabilitation; BSc(Hons), MPhil, MSc, PhD, MRes, MA

### Institute of Medical & Social Care Research; www.bangor.ac.uk/imscar

dementia & ageing, health economics, health services research; PhD, MPhil, MSc

## *College of Physical and Applied Sciences; www.bangor.ac.uk/copas*

### School of Chemistry; www.bangor.ac.uk/ chemistry

analytical chemistry, chemistry, environmental/marine chemistry; BSc, MChem, MSc, MRes, PGDip, PhD, MPhil

### School of Electronics; www.bangor.ac.uk/ eng

bioelectronics, critical safety engineering, computer systems engineering, control & instrument engineering, electronic engineering, electronics (hardware systems/sofware programming), micromachining, organic/polymer electronics, microtechnology, microfabrication, microwave dev, music technology, broadband communications, optoelectronics, nanotechnology; BEng(Hons), BSc(Hons), MEng(Hons), MSc, PhD

### School of Computer Science; www.bangor.ac.uk/cs

adv visualisation, AI & intelligent agents, communication networks, computer science for business, creative technologies, information & communications technology, computer systems engineering, electronic engineering, medical visualisation & simulation, computing & oceanography pattern recognition; BA(Hons), BEng(Hons), MEng(Hons), MPhil, MRes, MSc, PhD

## UNIVERSITY CENTRE BARNSLEY
## www.hud.ac.uk/barnsley

interdisciplinary art & design, construction & project management, early years, teacher training, lifelong learning, education & professional development, digital film & visual effects, film, animation, music, music production & sound recording, popular music & promotion, professional development for staff in education; CertEd, PGCE, BA(Hons), BSc(Hons), MA/PGDip/PGCert

## UNIVERSITY OF BATH
## www.bath.ac.uk

### *Faculty of Engineering and Design: www.bath.ac.uk/engineering*

#### Architecture & Civil Engineering; www.bath.ac.uk/ace

architectural engineering: environmental design, architecture, civil engineering, conservation of historic buildings/gardens & cultural landscapes, architectural engineering (facade engineering/innovative structural engineering), international construction management, professional practice; BEng, BSc, EngD, MArch, MEng, MPhil, MSc, PGCert, PhD

#### Chemical Engineering; www.bath.ac.uk/chem-eng

biochemical/chemical/biomedical/bioprocessing engineering; BEng, EngD, MEng, MPhil, MSc, PhD

#### Electronic & Electrical Engineering; www.bath.ac.uk/elec-eng

electronic communication/computer systems engineering, digital communications, electrical & electronic/electrical power engineering, electrical power systems, mechatronics, space science & technology, wireless systems; BEng, EngD, MEng, MPhil, MSc, PhD

#### Mechanical Engineering; www.bath.ac.uk/mech-eng

aerospace/automotive engineering, innovation/& engineering design, mechanical engineering, manufacture & management, mechatronics, technology management, adv design & innovation; EngD, MEng, MPhil, MSc, PhD

### *Faculty of Humanities and Social Science: www.bath.ac.uk/hss*

#### Dept of Economics; www.bath.ac.uk/economics

economics/& finance/politics, international development, international money & banking, economics (development); BSc(Hons), MPhil, MRes, PhD

#### Dept of Education; www.bath.ac.uk/education

childhood, youth & education studies, education, TESOL, sports performance, sport & social sciences; BA(Hons), EdD, FdSc, MA, MPhil, MRes, PGCE, PhD, ProfPGCE

#### Dept of Politics, Languages & International Studies; www.bath.ac.uk/polis

European politics, contemporary European studies, international relations/studies, interpreting, politics/ & economics/international relations, translating, international management/security, international management & modern languages, language & politics, professional language skills, modern languages & European Studies; BA(Hons), BSc(Hons), MA, MPhil, PGDip, PhD

#### Dept of Psychology; www.bath.ac.uk/psychology

psychology, health psychology, clinical psychology, risk & resilience; BSc(Hons), MPhil, MSc, PhD

#### Dept for Health; www.bath.ac.uk/health/

health, primary care, sport & exercise science/ medicine, sports physiotherapy, professional development; BSc, MPhil, MRes, MSc, PhD, Prof Doc

#### Dept of Social & Policy Science; www.bath.ac.uk/sps

sociology, social science, social policy, international development/public policy analysis, wellbeing in public policy & international development, European social policy, global political economy, security, conflict & justice; BSc(Hons), MSc, MRes, MPhil, PhD,

## *Faculty of Science; www.bath.ac.uk/science*

### Dept of Biology & Biochemistry; www.bath.ac.uk/bio-sci

biology, biochemistry, biosciences, molecular & cellular biology, developmental biology, evolution & population biology, medical bioscience, molecular plant science, microbiology; BSc(Hons), MPhil, MRes, PhD

### Dept of Chemistry; www.bath.ac.uk/chemistry

chemistry/for drug discovery, management, education; BSc(Hons), MChem, MSci, PhD

### Dept of Computer Science; www.bath.ac.uk/comp-sci

computer information systems, computer science/with maths/business, software systems, internet systems & security, human-computer interaction; BSc(Hons), EngD, MComp, MSc, PhD

### Dept of Mathematics; www.bath.ac.uk/math-sci

mathematical sciences, mathematics, modern applics of mathematics, statistics; BSc(Hons), MMath, MSc, PhD

### Dept of Natural Sciences; www.bath.ac.uk/nat-sci

multidisciplinary studies include biology, chemistry, pharmacology, physics; BSc(Hons), MSci

### Dept of Pharmacy & Pharmacology; www.bath.ac.uk/pharmacy

advanced & specialist healthcare, clinical pharmaceutical practice & therapeutics, pharmacology, pharmaceutical prescribing, medicinal chemistry, pharmacy; MPharm, MPharmacol, PhD

### Dept of Physics; www.bath.ac.uk/physics

mathematics and physics, physics/with computing, nanoscience, photonics; BSc, MSc, MPhil, MPhys, PhD

## *School of Management: www.bath.ac.uk/management*

accounting & finance, business administration, international management, management, marketing, innovation & technology management, sustainability, advanced management practice, HRM & consulting, finance & banking/risk, HR; BSc(Hons), DBA, EngD, MBA, MPhil, MRes, MSc, PhD

# BATH SPA UNIVERSITY
# www.bathspa.ac.uk

### Bath School of Art & Design: www.artbathspa.com

design ceramics, contemporary arts practice, fine art, creative arts, fashion/textile design, digital/3D design, photography & digital media, visual communication, graphic des, curatorial practice, brand development; BA(Hons), FdA, MFA, MPhil, PhD

### School of Education; www.bathspa.ac.uk/schools/education

early years/education, education/studies, counselling & psychotherapy, professional practice in HE, learning difficulties/dyslexia, initial teacher education, teaching assistants, PGCE (primary (3–11)/middle years (7–14)/ secondary (11–16); range of subjects), TESOL, international education & global citizenship; FD, GradCert, MA/MTeach, PGCE, PGCert/Dip

### School of Humanities & Cultural Industries; www.bathspa.ac.uk/schools/humanities-and-cultural-industries

creative media practice/writing/arts, film & screen studies, media communications, music production, English literature, heritage, publishing, study of religions, philosophy & ethics, history; BA(Hons), MPhil, PhD, MA

### Music & the Performing Arts; www.bathspampa.com

commercial music, creative arts, music technology, dance, drama, acting, music, composition, songwriting, creative & media technology, performance, arts management; BA(Hons), FdA, FdMus, MA, PhD

### School of Society, Enterprise & Environment; www.bathspa.ac.uk/schools/society-enterprise-and-environment;

biology, business & management, global development & sustainability, biology, business & management, geography, development/geography, counselling, HRM, environmental science, food & nutrition, GIS, health studies, human nutrition, marketing, tourism, psychology, sociology; BA(Hons), BSc (Hons), MPhil, MSc, PhD, FDA, DipHE

## UNIVERSITY OF BEDFORDSHIRE
## www.beds.ac.uk

## *Faculty of Creative Arts, Technologies & Science; www.beds.ac.uk/departments/cats*

### Bedfordshire Institute of Media, Arts & Performance; www.beds.ac.uk/departments/bim

**Div of Art & Design**

advertising design, animation, art & design, fine art, advertising/craft/interior/fashion & textile design, graphic design & advertising/print & new media, illustration, interior design, creative & editorial photography, photography & video art, contemporary fine arts practice, art design & internet technologies

**Div of Journalism & Communications**

creative writing/photography, community media, sports/magazine/international broadcast/journalism, international cinema/journalism, mass communication, multimedia journalism, PR, international cinema, professional writing

**Div of Media Arts & Production**

media production (moving image, new media, radio, scriptwriting), creative digital production/technology, documentary, production/technology, media technology & culture

**Div of Performing Arts & English**

dance & professional practice, community dance leadership, dance performance & choreography/science, community dance leadership, education studies, English/& theatre studies/literature, performing arts, theatre & professional practice;
BA(Hons), FdA, MA, MRes, PhD

### Dept of Computer Science & Technology; www.beds.ac.uk/departments/computing

animation technology, computer science & robotics/software engineering, AI & robotics, business/information systems, computer animation technology, applied computing & IT, computer games development, business/information systems, software / development, engineering, network management, building services & sustainability, building technology, computer networking/& systems engineering, computer security & forensics, IT networking & security, mechanical engineering, modern telecommunications, sustainable construction, telecommunications & network engineering, web design, applied computing & information technology, computer applications/forensics & IT security/networking/science/systems, embedded systems, engineering information management & security/systems & egovernment, telecommunications management; BSc(Hons), FdSc, MSc, BEng

**Life Sciences**

biomedical science, biological sciences, bioscience, environmental management, mechanical engineering, forensic science, medical science, nutritional sciences, pharmacology; BSc(Hons), FdSc, MSc, PgCert, PgDip, MPhil, PhD

## *Faculty of Health and Social Sciences; www.beds.ac.uk/departments/healthsciences*

### Dept of Acute Health Care; Dept of Community Services; Dept of Midwifery & Child Health

accident & emergency, antenatal education, applied/psychology, social studies, long-term/temporary care, midwifery, neonatal care, operating dept practice, palliative care, perioperative care, postnatal care, criminology, counselling, respiratory care, social work, sports therapy, surgical care, youth & community/child & adolescent studies, complementary therapies, coronary care, diabetes, environmental health, health and social care, health psychology, intensive care, nursing (adult, children, mental health), learning disabilities, mental health, osteopathy, care management, complementary therapy, management & leadership in health & social care, dental nursing/practice management, clinical science, health studies, leadership, medical education/simulation, public health nursing; BSc(Hons), FdA, FdSc, MSc, PGDip/Cert, Adv/DipHE, FdA/Sc, MOst

### Dept of Applied Social Studies; www.beds.ac.uk/departments/appliedsocialstudies

applied social studies, criminology, early years, child and adolescent studies, counselling health and social care, social work, sociology, children/young people's services, youth & community studies, public policy, children, families & community health,
applied social work practice: children & families/leadership and management/practice education, comparative European perspectives: youth work & social disadvantage, family & systemic psychotherapy, intermediate child focused systemic practice, professional social work practice; BSc(Hons), FdA, FdSc, MSc, ProfDoc, PGCert/Dip

#### Div of Psychology; www.beds.ac.uk/departments/psychology

applied/health psychology, counselling and therapies, criminal behaviour, forensics; BSc(Hons), CertHE, FdA, MSc, PhD

#### Div of Sports Therapy; www.beds.ac.uk/departments/spoth

sports therapy/& exercise rehabilitation; BSc(Hons)

### Bedfordshire & Hertfordshire Postgraduate Medical School; www.beds.ac.uk/departments/bhpms

diabetes, dental/medical education, public health, sexual health, medical simulation; MA, MSc, PGDip, PGCert

### Institute for Health Research; www.beds.ac.uk/research/ihr

psychological approach to health & management, public health, research & evaluation; MSc, PhD

### Institute of Applied Social Research; www.beds.ac.uk/research/iasr

applied social studies, Europerspectives, leadership; ProfDoc, MA

## *University of Bedfordshire Business School; www.beds.ac.uk/departments/ubbs*

### Depts of Accounting & Finance, Marketing, Strategy & HRM, Business Systems, Law (School of), Language & Communication

accounting, advertising & marketing, event management, international tourist management, travel & tourism, travel operations management, engineering management, finance & business management, international/finance, banking investment; advertising/marketing/communications, PR, leadership, innovation, management, business management, international business & management, international tourism/& hospitality management, marketing & business management, marketing communications, hospitality & hotel/information business management, logistics & supply chain management, marketing communications; international/HRM, business administration, business studies, business decision making/strategy, e-business, project management; corporate/international commercial law, Islamic finance and banking; applied linguistics, sport tourism management, tourism & environmental management/events management, brand management, finance, business administration (educational leadership/healthcare/hospital & health services, management/information technology management)/business web analytics, project management, psychology of organisational development & change; BA(Hons), BSc(Hons), MBA, DBA, FdA, LlB, LlM, MA, MSc, PGCert, LLM

## *Faculty of Education, Sport & Tourism; www.beds.ac.uk/departments/es*

primary education/QTS, early years, educational studies/practice primary languages, ESOL, individual development & learning, specialist maths, post-compulsory education, lifelong learning, PGCE secondary education (range of subjects)/Key 2-3, applied/special education, childhood & youth/disability studies, football studies, sport & PE, sports management/studies, event management, sport/international tourism management; PGCE, BA(Hons), BEd(Hons), MA, FdA, PGCSMT

## THE QUEEN'S UNIVERSITY OF BELFAST
## www.qub.ac.uk

### School of Biological Sciences; www.qub.ac.uk/schools/schoolofbiologicalsciences

agricultural technology, adv food safety, animal behaviour, biological sciences, biochemistry & welfare, communication/strategy management/training & development/for rural business, environmental biology, ecological management & conservation biology, food quality, safety & nutrition, genetics, land use & environmental management, land environmental sustainability, marine biology, molecular biology, rural sustainability, sustainable/rural development/aquaculture, zoology; BSc(Hons), MSc, PGDip, PhD

### School of Chemistry and Chemical Engineering; www.ch.qub.ac.uk

chemistry, medicinal chemistry, chemistry with forensic analysis, chemical engineering, chemical biology, process engineering, professional studies; BSc(Hons), MSci, BEng, MEng, MSc, PGDip, PhD

### School of Creative Arts; www.qub.ac.uk/schools/SchoolofCreativeArts

music, music technology, composition, Irish traditional music, English, sonic arts, film studies, film & drama, visual studies, arts management; BA, MA, BMus, BSc, MPhil, PhD

### School of Education; www.qub.ac.uk/schools/schoolofeducation

autism spectrum disorders, coaching & mentoring, education studies, inclusion, counselling, initial teacher education (range of subjects), educational leadership, inclusion/education & special education needs, HE teaching, lifelong learning, professional development, work-based learning, TESOL; AdvCertEd, DASE, EdD, MA, MEd, MSc, MSSc, PGCE, PGDip/Cert, UnivCert, BA(Hons)

### School of Electronics, Electrical Engineering and Computer Science; www.qub.ac.uk/schools/eeecs

business IT, computing and IT, computer games design & development, computer science, creative multimedia, educational multimedia, electrical & electronic engineering, electronics, telecommunications, software/development & electronic systems engineering/engineering, advanced wireless communication, sustainable electrical energy systems; BEng, BSc, MEng, MSc, MPhil, PhD

### School of English; www.qub.ac.uk/schools/SchoolofEnglish

creative writing, English literature & linguistics, Irish writing, linguistics, medieval studies, modern literary studies, modern poetry, reconceiving the Renaissance, broadcast literacy; BA(Hons), MA, PhD

### School of Geography, Archaeology and Palaeoecology; www.qub.ac.uk/schools/gap

archaeology & environment, professional/archaeology/& palaeoecology, dating & chronology, geography, landscape, heritage science, human geography & society, social space & culture, palaeoecology, geography; BA(Hons), BSc(Hons), MSc, PhD

### School of History and Anthropology; www.qub.ac.uk/schools/SchoolofHistoryandAnthropology

ancient history, archaeology, English & history/social anthropology, history/& archaeology/international studies, Irish/local history/studies, modern history, social anthropology, cognition & culture; BA(Hons), GradDip, MA, MPhil, PhD

### School of Modern Languages; www.qub.ac.uk/schools/SchoolofModernLanguages

French/German/Irish & Celtic/ Spanish & Portugese studies, interpreting, translation, Irish translation, Irish – medium film & production, jt degrees offered; BA(Hons), MA, PhD

### School of Law; www.law.qub.ac.uk/

law/with politics, common & civil law, corporate governance, environmental law/& sustainability, criminal justice, legal science, criminology, governance, international commerce, human rights; LlB, LlM, MSSc, MLSc, PGdip, MPhil, PhD, JD

### Queen's University Management School; www.qub.ac.uk/schools/QueensUniversityManagementSchool

accounting, finance, actuarial science & risk, organisation & business economics/management, economics, management, international business, environmental management, financial regulation, sustainabilty & corporate responsibility, HRM, business studies/management, actuarial science & risk management, computational finance & trading marketing, risk management; BSc(Hons), MSc, MScs, MBA, PhD

### School of Mathematics and Physics; www.qub.ac.uk/schools/SchoolofMathematicsandPhysics

applied/pure mathematics, physics, computer science & physics, operational research, statistics, theoretical/plasma physics, vacuum technology; BSc(Hons), GradDip, MSc, MSci, PhD

### School of Mechanical and Aerospace Engineering; www.qub.ac.uk/schools/SchoolofMechanicaland AerospaceEngineering

aerospace engineering, adv/mechanical/manufacturing engineering, product design & development; BEng, MEng, MSc, PhD

### School of Medicine, Dentistry and Biomedical Sciences; www.qub.ac.uk/schools/mdbs

medicine, biomedical science, clinical education, clinical anatomy, dentistry, surgery, human/computational biology, molecular medicine, mental health, obstetrics, public health, translational medicine, health & social care; BCh, BAO, BSc(Hons), BDS, DAO, Diploma, MB, MD, MSc

### School of Nursing and Midwifery; www.qub.ac.uk/schools/SchoolofNursingandMidwifery

nursing – adult/children's/learning disability/mental health, maternal and child health, midwifery, continuing professional development, clinical practice, neonatal studies, non-medical prescribing, health studies; BSc(Hons), Diploma, MPhil, PhD, DNursingPractice

### School of Pharmacy; www.qub.ac.uk/schools/SchoolofPharmacy

clinical pharmacy, community pharmacy, pharmacist prescribing, pharmacy practice; MPharm, MSc, PGCert/Dip

### School of Planning, Architecture and Civil Engineering; www.qub.ac.uk/schools/SchoolofPlanningArchitectureand CivilEngineering

architecture, adv concrete technology, civil engineering, construction & project management, durability of structures, environmental engineering/planning, management, professional practice, spatial regeneration, urban & rural design, structural engineering, sustainable design; BSc(Hons), MSc, MArch, MPhil, PhD, PGDip/Cert

### School of Politics, International Studies and Philosophy; www.qub.ac.uk/schools/SchoolofPoliticsInternationalStudies andPhilosophy

comparative ethnic conflict, gender & society, European Union politics, international relations, Irish politics, politics, legislative studies & practice, philosophy, politics & economics, international politics & conflict studies, violence, terrorism and security; BA(Hons), LlB, MA, MRes, MPhil, PhD

### School of Psychology; www.psych.qub.ac.uk

atypical child development, psychology, educational child & adolescent psychology, political psychology, applied/clinical psychology, psychology of performance in sport & health; BSc(Hons), MSc, DocClinPsych, PhD DocEducational

### School of Sociology, Social Policy and Social Work; www.qub.ac.uk/schools/SchoolofSociologySocialPolicySocialWork

applied social studies, criminology, childhood studies, social work, social policy, social research methods, sociology; BA(Hons), BSW, MA, MSc, DChild

# UNIVERSITY OF BIRMINGHAM
## www.bham.ac.uk

## *College of Arts and Law; www.birmingham.ac.uk/schools/historycultures/departments/caha/index.aspx*

### Classics, Ancient History & Archaeology; www.birmingham.ac.uk/schools/historycultures/departments/caha/index.aspx

antiquity, archaeology (Greek/landscape), archaeology & ancient history/computers/history/anthroplogy, archaeological practice, Egyptology, classics, classical literature & civilization, cuneiform & ancient near eastern studies, Egyptology, professional & applied archaeology, archaeology, heritage and the environment; BA(Hons), MA, MPhil, diploma, PhD

### Birmingham Law School; www.birmingham.ac.uk/schools/law/index.aspx

law, commercial law, criminal law & criminal justice, international commercial law, law with business/French/German; GradDip, LlB, LlM, MPhil/MJur/PhD

### English, Drama and American & Canadian Studies; www.birmingham.ac.uk/schools/edacs/index.aspx

American & Canadian studies, applied linguistics, business & American studies, English & American literature, creative writing, directing & dramaturgy, playwriting studies, drama & theatre arts, English language/literature, gender studies, literary linguistics, medieval studies, modernity, Shakespeare studies & theatre, transatlantic studies, film & TV; BA(Hons), BSc(Hons), MPhil, PhD

### School of History and Cultures; www.birmingham.ac.uk/schools/historycultures/index.aspx

African studies/with development, history (ancient & medieval/economic & social) archaeology & anthropology, Caribbean literature, history of warfare, military history, Renaissance, Reformation & early modern studies, social research (economic & social history), cultural heritage of Shakespeare's England, contemporary British history, early modern history, history of Christianity, modern European history, Reformation & early modern studies, social research (African studies), medieval history, 20th-century British history, war studies, West Midlands history, air power, history, theory & practice, British 1st/2nd world war studies; BA(Hons), MA, MPhil, PGDip, PhD

### School of Languages, Cultures, Art History and Music; www.birmingham.ac.uk/schools/lcahm/index.aspx

modern languages, film studies, cultural enquiry, European studies, French, gender studies, German, Hispanic, Italian, translation studies, Japanese, Mandarin, Russian & E European studies, history of art, music, composition, early music editing/performance, musicology, performance/practice, electroacoustic composition, British music, choral conducting; BA, MA, BMus, MPhil, PhD

### The School of Philosophy, Theology and Religion; www.birmingham.ac.uk/schools/ptr/index.aspx

global ethics, history of Christianity, inter-religious relations, cognitive science, evangelical & charismatic studies, Islamic studies, philosophy, philosophy of language and linguistics/of mind & cognition/of religion and ethics/health & happiness, pentecostal & charismatic studies, human rights & values, Quaker studies, religion & culture, Sikh studies, theology & religion; BA(Hons), BMus, MA, MPhil, PhD, MRes, Dip/Cert

## *College of Engineering and Physical Sciences; www.birmingham.ac.uk/university/colleges/eps/index.aspx*

### School of Chemistry; www.birmingham.ac.uk/schools/chemistry/index.aspx

chemical biology & biochemical imaging, chemistry/with analytical science/bioorganic chemistry/pharmacology, materials chemistry, molecular processes & theory, molecular synthesis, drug discovery & medical chemistry; BSc, MSci, Msc, PhD/MPhil

### School of Chemical Engineering; www.birmingham.ac.uk/schools/chemical-engineering/index.aspx

adv/chemical engineering, biochemical engineering, energy engineering, food safety, hygiene & management, industrial project management, food quality &

health; BEng, MEng, Masters/MSc/Diploma/PG Certificate

### School of Civil Engineering; www.birmingham.ac.uk/schools/civil-engineering/index.aspx

civil engineering, energy engineering, geotechnical engineering, railway systems engineering & integration, road management & engineering, transport technology, construction management, water resources technology & management; BEng, MEng, Masters/MSC/Diploma/Certificate

### School of Computer Science; www.cs.bham.ac.uk/

artificial intelligence, computer science, software engineering, computer security, electronic & software engineering, internet software systems, natural computation, multidisciplinary optimisation, human/computer interaction, cognitive/ & computer engineering, robotics, robotic/cognitive psychology; BSc, MEng, MSc, MRes, PhD

### School of Electronic, Electrical and Computer Engineering; www.birmingham.ac.uk/schools/eece/index.aspx

communications engineering/networks, business management, digital entrepreneurship, electrical & energy/electronic engineering, electromagnetic sensor networks, RF & microwave engineering, computer systems engineering, RF & satellite engineering, electronic & computer engineering, embedded systems, industrial experience; BEng, MEng, MSc, MRes, PhD

### School of Mathematics; www.birmingham.ac.uk/schools/mathematics/index.aspx

pure/applied mathematics, mathematics/with engineering, operational research, statistics, theoretical physics, computer science, management mathematics, mathematic modelling, financial engineering, OR, econometrics; BA, BSc, MSci, MSc, MRes, PhD

### School of Mechanical Engineering; www.birmingham.ac.uk/schools/mechanical-engineering/index.aspx

adv/mechanical/automotive engineering, engineering/project management; BEng, MEng, Masters/MSc, PhD/MSc

### School of Metallurgy and Materials; www.birmingham.ac.uk/schools/metallurgy-materials/index.aspx

materials/for sustainable energy technologies, metallurgy, biomaterials, mechanical & materials engineering, nuclear engineering/science & materials, science & engineering of materials, materials engineering, energy engineering, metallurgy & materials, sports & materials science, engineering materials for applications in aerospace; BSc, BEng, MEng, MRes, PhD/MSc

### School of Physics and Astronomy; www.birmingham.ac.uk/schools/physics/index.aspx

physics, physics & astrophysics/technology of nuclear reactors/nanoscale physics/particle physics & cosmology, nuclear engineering/science & materials, theoretical physics, & applied mathematics, radioactive waste management & decommissioning; BEng, BNatSci, BSc(Hons), DEng, MEng, MPhil, MRes, MSc, MSci, PGDip/Cert, PhD

## *College of Life and Environmental Sciences; www.birmingham.ac.uk/university/colleges/les/index.aspx*

### School of Biosciences; www.birmingham.ac.uk/schools/biosciences/index.aspx

biochemistry, biological sciences, genetics, molecular biotechnology, microbiology, molecular cell biology, environmental/human/medical biology, ornithology, toxicology, plant biology, zoology, human/medical biology, natural sciences; BSc, MSci, MSc

### School of Geography, Earth and Environmental Sciences; www.birmingham.ac.uk/schools/gees/index.aspx

geography (numerous jt degrees), geology, applied & petroleum micropalaeontology, environmental geology/science, air pollution management & control, applied meteorology & climatology, human geography(res), human & environmental impacts of nanoscience & nanotechnology, environmental science/geology/health, nuclear decommissioning & waste management, planning & environment, public & environmental health science, safety & the environment, palaeobiology & palaeoenvironment, planning & social policy, resilience & urban living, science of occupational health, safety & environment, spatial planning & business management, urban & regional planning/studies, urban & regional studies, urban regeneration & renewal; BA, BSc/MSci, MSci, MSc, MRes

### School of Psychology; www.birmingham.ac.uk/schools/psychology/index.aspx

psychology, clinical criminology/psychology, cognitive robotics & computational neuroscience, cognitive behaviour therapy, forensic psychology, neuroscience, psychological practice/res, rational emotional behaviour therapy; BSc, MSci, MSc/Dip/Cert, ForPsyD, PhD

### School of Sport, Exercise and Rehabilitation Sciences; www.birmingham.ac.uk/schools/sport-exercise/index.aspx

sport & exercise sciences, sports science/& materials, sport PE, coaching science, PE & sport pedagogy, sport policy & management, golf coaching, applied golf management technology/mathematics; BSc(Hons), MPhil, MRes, MSc, PhD, PGDip, PGDips

## *College of Medical and Dental Sciences; www.birmingham.ac.uk/university/colleges/mds/index.aspx*

The Five Schools of the College are: Cancer Sciences, Clinical & Experimental Medicine, Dentistry, Health & Population Sciences, Immunity & Infection

biomedical materials science, cancer, clinical & experimental medicine, clinical neuropsychiatry, clinical oncology, dental hygiene & therapy, dental surgery, dentistry, health sciences, healthcare, ethics & the law, history of medicine, international health, forensic mental health, hormones & genes, immunity & infection, medical science, medicine, surgery, neuroscience, nursing, pharmacy, psychological medicine, physiotherapy, public health, translational medicine; BDS, BMedSci, BSc(Hons), BNurs, DDS, MBChB, MD, DPharm, MEd, MSc, MRes, PGDip/Cert, MPH

## *College of Social Sciences; www.birmingham.ac.uk/university/colleges/socsci/index.aspx*

### Birmingham Business School; www.birmingham.ac.uk/schools/business/index.aspx

accounting & finance, banking, business management/with communications, business administration, corporate governance, development economics, economic policy/& international business, economics/finance & business, environmental & natural resource economics, global business & finance, HRM, international accounting & finance, international business/economics/marketing/money & banking, investments, land & regional economic development, management, marketing/communications, mathematical economics & statistics/finance, money, planning with economics, money, banking, finance, political science, public service, social policy, strategy & procurement management; BSc Economics, BSc(Hons), Dip, MSc, MBA, DBA, MPhil, PhD, PGCert, PGDip, UCert

### School of Education;

www.birmingham.ac.uk/schools/education/index.aspx

autism/spectrum disorders/adults/children, bilingualism in education, childhood, culture & education, educational & history/sociology, inclusion & special needs, international studies in education, speech/learning difficulties/ disabilities, multisensory impairment (deafblindness), primary education/early years/mathematics, school improvement & educational leadership, social, emotional and behavioural difficulties, sports coaching, teacher training (early years, primary, secondary subject courses) – (English, geography, history and citizenship, mathematics, modern foreign languages, PE, RE, biology, chemistry, physics), TEFL, visual impairment; AdCert, BA(Hons), BPhil, ChildPsyD, EdD, EdPsychD, MEd, MPhil, PGCE, PGCert/Dip, PhD

### School of Government and Society; www.birmingham.ac.uk/schools/government-society/index.aspx

political science, African studies, anthropology, economics, history, Russian studies, sociology, global cooperation & security, social/& political theory/policy, philosophy, political economy/science/theory, society & economics, contemporary/Russian & East European studies, European studies, international relations (contemporary Asia Pacific/gender/international peacekeeping/political economy/security/terrorism & political violence), international development (conflict/security/development/governance & statebuilding/international political economy/urban development/poverty/inequality), development management (public economic management & finance/aid management/HR), international law, ethics, politics, public administration, public management (criminal justice/local government/social care & well-being), public service commissioning, local policy & politics, integration for health & well-being, local government & public policy, international peace & security, terrorism, public service, poverty reduction, local government; BA(Hons), BSc(Hons), PGDipG-DipGCert, MA, MEd, AdvCert, MPhil, MSc, PhD, MP

**The School of Social Policy (The Health Services Management Centre; Institute of Applied Social Studies); www.birmingham.ac.uk/schools/social-policy/index.aspx**

community justice, health care policy & management, policy into practice, leadership for health service improvement, health service management, leadership & management for social care/social work, managing integrated health & wellbeing, mental health & deafness, new migration & social policy, policy, politics & economics, public service commissioning, management for social care/work/research, social policy: crime, policing & community/health & social care/housing & communities; BA(Hons), MA, MSc, PGDip, SocScD, PhD

## *Degrees validated at the University of Birmingham offered at:*

### SCHOOL OF EDUCATION, SELLY OAK
### www.education.bham.ac.uk

applied golf management studies, autism, bilingualism in education, childhood, culture & education, dyslexia studies, education for health professionals, English language and literature in education, educational psychology, hearing impairment, inclusion & special educational needs, international studies in education, IT & education, leaders & leadership in education, learning & learning contexts, learning difficulties/ multisensory impairment, sports coaching, teacher training – primary courses, early years, general primary/secondary subject courses (English, geography, history & citizenship, mathematics, modern foreign languages, PE, professional development, RE, biology, chemistry, physics), TEFL, visual impairment; AppEd, BA, ChildPsyD, EdPsychD, MPhil, PhD, PGCE

### UNIVERSITY COLLEGE BIRMINGHAM
### www.ucb.ac.uk

business & marketing, childhood & education, cullinary arts, hospitality, events management, sport & tourism, sports therapy, spa management; BA(Hons), BSc(Hons), FdA Dip HE, FdSc, MA, MSc, PGCE, PGDip/Cert

## BIRMINGHAM CITY UNIVERSITY
## www.bcu.ac.uk

### *Birmingham Institute of Art & Design; www.bcu.ac.uk/biad*

architecture/practice, art, health & wellbeing, arts & project management, education, art & design, contemporary curatorial practice, design & vision, design management, fashion design, design for performance/accessories/communication/garment technology/retail management, fine art, gemmology, horology, interior/product design, jewellery & silversmithing, landscape design, product design, textile design, constructed textiles, embroidery, printed textiles/retail management, theatre performance & event design, visual communication (animation & moving image/graphic communication)/illustration/ photography), digital arts in performance, fashion accessory design/promotion/styling, history of art & design, media arts philosophical practice, queer arts, surface/textile design, visual communication, graphic communication – photography; BA(Hons), BTEC, Cert/DipHE, MA, MPhil, PGCert/Dip, PhD

### Birmingham City Business School; www.bcu.ac.uk/business-school

accounting/& business/finance, audit management & consultancy, business administration, business & administration/economics/finance/HRM/management/marketing, economics & finance, internal audit practice/& management, international finance/HRM, leadership & management practice/organisational performance/strategy, management & finance/international finance/marketing, marketing & advertising/PR, risk management; BA(Hons), MBA, DBA, HND, MPhil, MSc, PhD

## *Faculty of Education, Law & Social Sciences; www.bcu.ac.uk/elss*

### School of Education; www.bcu.ac.uk/school-of-education

integrated professional care, education, continuous professional developmemt/teachers, early childhood/education studies, early years, international education, post compulsory education & training, teaching & learning, secondary art & design/drama/education/mathematics/music, primary education with QTS, subject enhancement in mathematics, teaching & learning; BA(Hons), FD, MPhil, PGCert/Dip, PGCE, PhD, MTL

### The School of Law; www.bcu.ac.uk/law

international business/human rights law, law, legal studies, law with American legal studies/business law/criminology, legal practice; Grad Dip, MPhil, PhD, LlB(Hons), LlM, PGDip/Cert

### School of Social Sciences; www.bcu.ac.uk/socialsciences

forensic/social science, criminal investigation, criminology & policing/psychology/security studies, public/sociology; BA(Hons), BSc(Hons), CertHE, FDA, MA, MPhil, MSc, PGCert/Dip, PhD

## *Faculty of Health; www.bcu.ac.uk/health*

adv health care/practice, health & social care/wellbeing (nutrition science/leadership), public health, midwifery, nursing (child/adult/learning disability), operating dept practice, diagnostic radiography, radiotherapy, paramedic science, medical ultrasound, pain management, social work, speech & language therapy, rehabilitation (visual impairment), mental health; BSc(Hons), DipHE, FdA, MPhil, MSc, PGDip/Cert, PQ, PhD

## *Faculty of Performance, Media & English; www.bcu.ac.uk/pme*

### Birmingham Conservatoire; www.bcu.ac.uk/conservatoire

music, performance & pedagogy, composition, conducting, professional performance/specialism, music technology, musicology, orchestral/instrumental performance, pop music, vocal performance; AdvPGDip, BMus(Hons), MA, MMus, MPhil, PhD

### Birmingham School of Media; www.bcu.ac.uk/media

international/broadcast/online journalism, creative industries & cultural policy, freelance photography/media, event & exhibition management, film futures, video games development, media & communication/music industry/new media/PR/radio/TV, TV production, screen studies, social media; BA(Hons), PGDip, MA, MPhil, PhD

### Birmingham School of Acting; www.bsa.bcu.ac.uk

acting/British tradition, physical theatre, professional voice practice, stage management, applied performance (community & education); BA(Hons), MPhil, PhD

### School of English; www.bcu.ac.uk/English

English & media/creative writing, English language/literature/linguistics, writing, philosophy; BA(Hons), Dip, MA, MPhil, PhD

## *Faculty of Technology, Engineering & the Environment; www.bcu.ac.uk/tee*

business information & communication technology/computing, computer networks, computer science/games technology, computing & multimedia technology, integrated construction & design management, data networks & security, enterprise/information systems management, film production & technology, forensic computing, music technology, telecommunication networks, electronic engineering, mechanical engineering, architectural technology, building surveying/services engineering, construction management/quantity surveying, international logistics & supply chain management, automotive engineering/technology/calibration & control, motorsports technology, project quality management, environmental spacial planning/sustainability; BSc(Hons), FdSc, MSc, PGCert/Dip

## BISHOP GROSSETESTE UNIVERSITY COLLEGE
## www.bgc.ac.uk

applied drama & enterprise/music, early childhood/ children & youth work, early childhood studies, drama in the community, English & applied drama/ history & other subjects, education, primary education with QTS, special education & inclusion/numerous subjects, heritage education, sport/& tourism, visual arts, English literature, education studies in art & design/drama/English/geography/history/mathematics/music, PGCE (primary/secondary), community archaeology, theology & ethics in society; BA(Hons), FdA, GradDip, MA, PhD, EdD, PGCE

## BLACKBURN COLLEGE
## www.blackburn.ac.uk

Vocation qualifications (BTEC, City & Guilds etc) accounting, applied psychology(counselling & health), business accounting/studies/administration, care practice, community policing & justice management, complementary therapies, design (contemporary textiles/graphic communication/illustration & animation/interiors/moving image/new media/fashion), disability studies, early childhood, educational studies, history, English language, literary studies, civil/electrical/electronic/mechanical engineering, construction project management, computing (business information, networks, forensic, software), English language & literature, fine art (integrated media), fire & rescue services, hospitality management, criminology, HRM, journalism, law/with psychology, legal studies, leadership, marketing, mechanical engineering, mechatronics, media production, photographic media, politics, public service management, social care, sociology, sports coaching, sustainable construction, teacher training, working with children & young people; BA(Hons, Ord), BEng(Hons, Ord), BSc(Hons, Ord), DMS (validated externally), FD, HNC, HND, LlB (validated by Lancaster), LlM, MBA, MSc

## BOURNEMOUTH UNIVERSITY
## www.bournemouth.ac.uk

### The School of Applied Sciences; www.bournemouth.ac.uk/applied-sciences

prehistoric & Roman archaeology, applied geography, archaeology, anthropology, applied archaeological stonework, archaeological, anthropological & forensic sciences, biological/forensic/environmental science, animal/& landbased studies/behaviour & welfare, biological/forensic anthropology, ecology & wildlife conservation, forensic osteology/science/ investigation/toxicology, anthropology & heritage, geography & environmental science, conservation, ecology & environmental change, marine ecology, tourism park management; BSc(Hons), BA(Hons), MSc, PhD, FD

### The Business School; www.business.bournemouth.ac.uk

accounting/& business/finance/law/taxation, business studies with economics/enterprise/finance/HRM/law/ marketing, law, business/entertainment law, law & corporate governance, operations & project management, economics, finance, HRM, risk management, professional development, international business studies/finance/management/commercial law, international business & management, intellectual property, law and taxation, management, marketing; BA(Hons), LlB(Hons), LlM, MA, MBA, MPhil, MSc, PhD

### School of Design, Engineering & Computing; www.dec.bournemouth.ac.uk

applied data analytics, business/computing, computer networks, design/business management/engineering, engineering project management, sustainable/

product design/management, design engineering, mechanical design, industrial/product design, manufacturing management, business/information technology, engineering, enterprise information systems, computer games/programming/technology, music & audio technology, computer games, psychology, clinical psychology, lifespan neuropsychology, computing, information technology management, software engineering/product design, forensic computing & security, digital media/music & audio production, network systems management; BA(Hons), BSc(Hons), FD, HNC, HND, MA, MPhil, MSc, PhD

### School of Health and Social Care; www.bournemouth.ac.uk/hsc

advance practice/children's & family service/vulnerable adults, nutrition, early years care, operating dept practice, paramedic science, adult/children & young people/mental health/public health nursing, mental health, adv nurse practitioner, midwifery, clinical exercise science, leading & developing services, occupational therapy, professional practitioner, physiotherapy, social work, sociology & social policy/anthropology; AdvDip, BA(Hons), BSc(Hons), DipHE, FdA, FdSc, MPhil, PGDip/Cert, PhD, Dr Prof Practice

### The Media School; www.media.bournemouth.ac.uk

advertising, adaptation. marketing/communications, communication & media, computer/animation arts, 3D computer animation & visual effects, directing, games & effects, English, film production & cinematography, global media practice, media design/production/effects, multimedia/international journalism, journalism & new media, literary media, politics and media, photography, post production editing, PR, radio sound production, software development for animation for effects & games, scriptwriting/for film and TV, digital/TV & film production, politics & media, screenwriting; BA(Hons), BSc(Hons), FdA, MA, MBA, MPhil, MSc, PhD, DProfD

### School of Tourism; www.bournemouth.ac.uk/tourism

events management/marketing, events & leisure marketing, hospitality & food service management, international hospitality & tourism management, managing sports performance, sustainable tourism planning, tourism management & marketing/planning; FDA, FDSc, BA(Hons), BSc(Hons), MA, MSc, PhD

## UNIVERSITY OF BRADFORD
## www.bradford.ac.uk

### School of Computing, Informatics and Media; www.scim.brad.ac.uk

Computing: advanced computer science, AI for games, business computing, computational mathematics, computer science/for games, forensic computing, ICT with business/law/marketing, intelligent systems & robotics, internet computing & systems security, mobile computing applications, networks & performance engineering, software project management, applications/engineering

Media: digital media, digital & creative enterprise, digital arts/media/film-making, film studies, informatics, media production & technology, media studies/with cinematics/computer animation/digital imaging/TV, music video production, photography for digital media, TV production, web design & technology

Mathematics: computational mathematics; informatics

Creative technology: advanced computer animation visual effects, computer animation, graphics for games, informatics, interactive systems & video games design, visual computing effects/production; BA(Hons), BSc(Hons), MA, MSc, FdSc, BEng(Hons)

### School of Engineering, Design and Technology; www.eng.brad.ac.uk

applied physics, automotive design technology/engineering quality improvement, chemical & petroleum engineering, civil & structural engineering, clinical technology, electrical & electronic engineering, health science, telecommunications & internet computing, power electronics, IT management, industrial engineering, manufacturing engineering/management, mechanical/& automotive engineering, medical engineering, personal, mobile & satellite communications, polymer engineering, product design, technology management, wireless sensor & embedded systems; BEng, BSc, FD, MEng, MPhil, MSc, PhD

## School of Health Studies; www.brad.ac.uk/acad/health

acute & critical care, adult/child/mental health, nursing, dementia/studies/& older people, diversity management, health & social care, long term conditions, midwifery, occupational therapy, physiotherapy, public health & well being, diagnostic radiography, sport rehabilitation; AdvDip, BSc(Hons), CertHE, DipHE, FD, MSc, MPhil, PGDip/Cert, PhD

## School of Life Sciences; www.brad.ac.uk/acad/lifesci

### Div of Archaeological & Environmental Sciences

archaeological prospection/sciences, archaeology, environmental management/science, forensic archaeology & crime scene investigation, human osteology & palaeopathology; BA, BSc, CertHE, MA, MSc, MPhil, PhD

### Div of Medical Sciences

analytical science, biomedical science, cancer pharmacology, cancer drug discovery, cellular pathology, chemical & forensic science, drug toxicology & safety pharmacology, medical biochemistry, medical microbiology, pharmacology, medicine development; BSc(Hons), MSC, PgD

### Bradford School of Pharmacy

pharmacy, pharmaceutical services & medicines/management/community/hospital, medicines control, pharmacological technology, prescribing, drug discovery; DPharm, MSC, MPharm

### Dept of Chemical Studies and Forensic Sciences

chemistry/with pharmacy for forensic science, chemistry for analytics/drug discovery/forensic science, forensic science, medical science/development, medical chemistry & anti-cancer drug development; BSc(Hons), MPhil, PhD, MChem

### Div of Optometry & Vision Science

optometry; BSc, MPhil, PhD

## The School of Management (inc Law); www.brad.ac.uk/acad/management

accounting, business management, finance, financial planning, business & management studies, European/ international business management, employee rights, global finance & banking, HRM, law, management, marketing, operational & information management, strategic international marketing sustainable operations & management; BA(Hons), BSc(Hons), DBA, LlB, GradDip(Law), MBA, MRes, PhD

## The School of Social and International Studies; www.brad.ac.uk/acad/ssis

development & project planning, economics & finance for development, human & organisational capacity building, international development management, project planning & management, public administration, African peace studies & conflict studies, international policing & security studies, peace, conflict, & development, counselling, conflict resolution/security, creative writing, applied/criminal justice studies, development & peace studies, economics, English, modern European/history, interdisciplinary human studies, global trading & finance, human trafficking, international development/relations, mental health studies/practice, peace studies, philosophy, politics, law, psychology, sociology, working with children, young people & families; BA(Hons), BSc(Hons), MA, MPhil, PhD, PGDip, MPA

*Degrees validated by University of Bradford offered at:*

## BRADFORD COLLEGE
www.bradfordcollege.ac.uk

accounting, art & design, beauty therapy management, business management, civil/electrical/mechanical engineering, construction management/marketing, counselling & psychology, early years practice/studies, education studies, childhood & youth studies, counselling & psychology, fashion/textile/interior/surface design, film, health & social welfare/nutrition, law/international & comparative/social welfare, lifelong learning, marketing, media & creative writing, ophthalmic dispensing, photography, public service management, social work/care, sport & physical activity, sports coaching, teaching, ESOL, ELTS, EFL, PGCE (primary/secondary/vocational), hospitality & travel/tourism management, visual culture/arts, youth & community development; BSc(Hons), CertHE, DipHE, FD, HNC, HND, BA(Hons), LlB(Hons), MA, MEd, PGDipCert, MSc, PGCE, FD

# UNIVERSITY OF BRIGHTON
# www.brighton.ac.uk

## *Faculty of Arts; www.arts.brighton.ac.uk*

Architecture, Interior Architecture & Urban Studies; architecture/urban studies, interior design

3D Design, Sustainable Design, Materials & Craft; design, future, design & craft, craft, sustainable design

English Langauge Teacher Education; TESOL, English language teaching, media accessible/language teaching

Literature; English literature/& media/English

Fashion Design; fashion with business

Fine Art; fine art, fine art (painting/printmaking/sculpture/cultural practice

Fine Art Performance, Music, Theatre Dance; theatre performance, visual art, music & visual art, performance & visual performance

Graphic Design, Illustration, Digital Arts; graphic design, illustration, sequential design, digital media art, art & design by individual projects, arts & cultural research

History of Art & Design; fashion & dress history, history of decorative arts & culture, history of design/art & design, museum & heritage studies, visual culture

Human History, Philosophy, Culture & Politics; politics, philosophy & ethics, globalisation, history, politics, culture, humanities, war conflict, modernisation, applied ethics, culture & cultural theory, cultural history, memory & identity

Language & Linguistics; linguistics, English literature & language/media, philosophy of language, arts & cultural research

Media; media studies, film & screen studies, English literature & media studies, English language & media/English literature, broadcast journalism/media, environmental & media studies, TV production, radio production, creative media

Photography, Moving Image & Sound; photography, digital music & sound entertainment, moving image

Textile Design; textiles with business, textile design; BA(Hons), FdSA, Grad Dip, MA, MDes, MFA, MPhil, MRes, PGDip/Cert, PhD

## *Faculty of Education and Sport; www.brighton.ac.uk/fes*

### School of Education; www.brighton.ac.uk/education

key stage 2/3 English/mathematics/education primary education with QTS (3–7 /5–11 years), English education/mathematics education (7–14 years)/ science education (chemistry)(with QTS), education, adult learning and development, early years care and education, playwork, professional studies in primary education, working with young people, professional studies in learning & development, youth work, early years professional status, education (higher education/(international education)/leadership & management)

PGCert; chemistry for secondary teachers, developing mathematical practice, education leadership and management: strategies for inspirational leadership, mathematics for secondary teachers, mentoring and coaching: maximising potential, primary mathematics specialist teacher programme, specific learning difficulties: strategies for working with autistic learners, specific learning difficulties: strategies for working with dyslexic learners; BA(Hons), MA, FdA, CertEd, PGCert, QTS, PGCE

### School of Sport & Service Management; www.brighton.ac.uk/sasm

international hospitality management, food services & wellbeing management, hospitality & event management, retail marketing/management, sports coaching/& development, sport & fitness/exercise science/leisure management, sport journalism, sport & society/international development, applied experimental physiology, international tourism/travel management, retail management/enterprise/marketing, tourism & international development/social anthropology, travel & tourism marketing; BA(Hons), FdA, MA, MSc, PhD

### Centre for Learning and Teaching; www.brighton.ac.uk/clt

higher education, learning & teaching in HE; MA, PGCE

## Faculty of Health and Social Science; www.brighton.ac.uk/fhss

### School of Applied Social Science; www.brighton.ac.uk/sass

applied psychology, applied social & community research, social science/sociology/criminology, community psychology, counselling & psychotherapy, criminology, approved mental health practice, politics, psychology, public admin, social policy, sociology, social work, substance misuse, humanistic/psychodynamic therapeutic counselling, public admin; BA(Hons), MA, MPhil, MSc, PGDip/Cert, PhD, MPA, FD, Prof Doc

### School of Health Professions; www.brighton.ac.uk/sohs

clinical education/practice, podiatry & management/education/surgery, diabetes, clinical biomechanics, neuromusculoskeletal physiology, occupational therapy, physiotherapy/& education/management, rheumatology, sports injury management, clinical research; BS(Hons), MSc, PGDip/Cert, PhD, Prof Doc, MRes

### School of Nursing and Midwifery; www.brighton.ac.uk/snm

acute clinical practice, adult/child/mental health nursing, clinical studies, community specialist practice, health & social care/education, health studies, adv/nurse practitioner, midwifery, paramedic practice, professional practice, specialist community public health nursing, community health, health promotion & education, international health promotion; BSc(Hons), FdSc, MPhil, MRes, MSc, PGDip/Cert, PhD

## Brighton Business School; www.brighton.ac.uk/bbs

accounting, business management, business & enterprise, change management, economics, finance, international business, investment, knowledge & innovation management, law with business/criminology, leadership, logistics & supply chain management (enterprise/HR/innovation/public service), marketing (branding, international, social), HRM, international/retail management; ACCA, BA(Hons), LlB, MBA, MSc, PGCert/Dip, CPE

## Faculty of Science and Engineering; www.brighton.ac.uk/scieng

### School of Computing, Engineering & Mathematics; www.brighton.ac.uk/cem

business computer/information systems, computer science/games, computing systems & communication/networking, creative computing, digital media/production, digital games production, European computing, internet/computing, software engineering, computing, information systems, internet & distributed systems, mobile computing engineering, electrical & electronic engineering, computing communications, automotive engineering, mathematics/with business/finance, aeronautical engineering, mechanical engineering, product innovation & design, product design technology, sports/sustainable product design; BSc(Hons), FdSc, MA, MComp, MPhil, MSc, PGDip/Cert, MEng

### School of Environment and Technology; www.brighton.ac.uk/set

architectural technology, building surveying, construction management, environmental assessment & management, facilities management, project management for construction, town planning, civil engineering, environmental engineering, environmental/hazards/management & assessment/sciences/media studies, GIS & sustainability of the built environment, water & environmental management; geography, earth & ocean science, environmental geology, geology; BA/BSc(Hons), BEng(Hons), BSc(Hons), FdSc, FdEng, MEng, MPhil, PGDip/Cert, PhD

### School of Pharmacy and Biomolecular Sciences; www.brighton.ac.uk/pharmacy

biomedical/biological sciences, bioscience, clinical/general pharmacy practice, pharmacology, ecology, industrial pharmaceutical studies, chemical sciences, pharmaceutical & chemical biomedical science; BSc(Hons), MSc, MPharmHons, MPhil, MRes, PGDip, PhD

### Brighton and Sussex Medical School; www.bsms.ac.uk

cardiology, medical education, diabetes, epidemiology, geriatric medicine, education in clinical settings, global health, oncology, infectious disease, primary care, psychiatry, medicine, nephrology, public health, surgery, trauma & orthopaedics; BSMS, MD, MPhil, MSc, PGDip/Cert, PhD

# UNIVERSITY OF BRISTOL
# www.bris.ac.uk

## Faculty of Arts; www.bris.ac.uk/arts

### School of Arts; www.bris.ac.uk/arts

**Dept of Archaeology & Anthropology; www.bris.ac.uk/archanth**

archaeology, evolutionary/medical/social anthropology, landscape & prehistoric archaeology, 20th century archaeology, archaeology for screen media, conflict/landscape/maritime archaeology, historical archaeology of the modern world

**Dept of Drama, Theatre, Film, Television; www.bris.ac.uk/drama**

archaeology for screen media, drama, film & TV studies/production, performance research, composition of music for film & TV

**Dept of Music; www.bris.ac.uk/music**

British music, composition/for film, TV, medieval music, music/theory, musicology, performance, Russian music, music/& modern languages

**Dept of Philosophy; www.bris.ac.uk/philosophy**

philosophy, philosophy & history of science/law/biology & cognitive science, philosophy of mathematics/psychology; BA(Hons), BSc(Hons), MA, Mlitt, MMus, MSci, PGDip, PhD

### School of Humanities; www.bris.ac.uk/humanities

**Dept of Classics & Ancient History; www.bris.ac.uk/classics**

ancient history, ancient history, classical studies, classics, history, classical reception

**Dept of English; www.bris.ac.uk/english**

English, English & philosophy/classical studies/drama, English literature/& community engagement, romantic & Victorian literature, 20th century & contemporary literature, Shakespeare & renaissance literature, late medieval & early modern literature, culture & intellectual history, public history

**Dept of History; www.bris.ac.uk/history**

empires, contemporary history, medieval studies, medieval and early modern history, Russian history, ancient history, medieval studies

**Dept of Art History; www.bris.ac.uk/arthistory**

art histories and interpretations, history of art

**Dept of Theology and Religious Studies; www.bris.ac.uk/thrs**

biblical studies, theology & religious studies, Buddhist studies, philosophy & ethics, reception of the bible: tradition, theology, & culture, medieval studies, Christianity, Chinese religion, Hinduism, Judaism

**School of Modern Languages; www.bris.ac.uk/sml**

French, German, Hispanic, Portuguese & Latin American studies/history, Italian, Russian, Russian studies (includes Czech); European literatures, screen studies, medieval, Renaissance & early modern studies, literary & cultural studies, linguistics; BA(Hons), MA, MLitt, MPhil, PGDip, PhD

## Faculty of Engineering; www.bris.ac.uk/engineering

**Dept of Aerospace Engineering; www.bris.ac.uk/aerospace**

integrated aerospace systems design aeronautical engineering

**Dept of Civil Engineering; www.bris.ac.uk/civilengineering**

civil engineering, water & environmental management

**Dept of Computer Science; www.cs.bris.ac.uk**

computer science/& electronic/mathematics, adv computing (internet technologies with security/machine learning & data mining & high performance computing/creative technologies), adv microelectronic systems engineering

**Dept of Electrical and Electronic Engineering; www.bris.ac.uk/eeng**

optical communications/image & video communications & signals processing, communication networks & signal processing, computer science & electronics, electrical & electronic engineering, wireless communication systems & signal processing

**Dept of Engineering Mathematics; www.enm.bris.ac.uk**

complexity sciences, systems engineering, adv engineering robotics, neurodynamics, engineering mathematics

**Dept of Mechanical Engineering; www.bris.ac.uk/mecheng**

mechanical engineering, adv engineering robotics
BSc(Hons), BEng, EngD, PGCert, MEng, MSc, PhD

## Faculty of Medical and Veterinary Science; www.bris.ac.uk/mvs

**Dept of Biochemistry; www.bris.ac.uk/biochemistry**
biochemistry/with molecular biology & biotechnology, biophysics, molecular life sciences, medical biochemistry, biomedical sciences

**Dept of Cellular and Molecular Medicine; www.bris.ac.uk/cellmolmed**
cancer biology, immunology, medical /microbiology, pathology, transfusion & transplantation science, virology, stem cell biology

**Bristol Veterinary School; www.bris.ac.uk/vetscience**
animal behaviour & welfare, meat science & technology, veterinary nursing & bioveterinary science, veterinary science, global wildlife health & conservation

**Dept of Physiology & Pharmacology; www.bris.ac.uk/phys-pharm**
biomedical science, systems/neuroscience, pharmacology, physiological science; BSc(Hons), BVSc, MD, MSc, MSci, PhD

## Faculty of Medicine and Dentistry; www.bris.ac.uk/fmd

medicine, surgery, dentistry, dental implantology, health care ethics & the law, molecular neuroscience, orthodontics, palliative medicine, reproduction & development, stem cells and regeneration, health professionals; MB, BDS, BSc(Hons), ChB, ChM, DDS, Diploma, DPDS, MClinDent, MD, MMedEd, MSci, PhD

## Faculty of Science; www.bris.ac.uk/science

### School of Biological Sciences; www.bris.ac.uk/biology

biology, botany, geology, zoology, palaeontology & the natural environment, animal behaviour, agricultural ecosystems

### School of Chemistry; www.chm.bris.ac.uk/

chemistry, chemical physics, inorganic & materials chemistry, organic & biological chemistry, physical & theoretical chemistry, chemical synthesis

### School of Earth Sciences; www.bris.ac.uk/earthsciences

earth sciences, biology, environmental geoscience, geology, palaeobiology, science of natural hazards

### Dept of Experimental Psychology; www.psychology.psy.bris.ac.uk/

biological psychology, cognition, computational/clinical/applied neuroscience, clinical/applied neuropsychology, psychology & philosophy/zoology, vision sciences

### School of Geographical Sciences; www.ggy.bris.ac.uk/

geography, human/physical geography, society & space, science of natural hazards, environmental policy, climate change science & policy

### Dept of Mathematics; www.maths.bris.ac.uk/

applied/pure mathematics, mathematics, mathematics & philosophy/physics/statistics, probability studies, statistics & probability of complexity studies, statistics, mathematical science, applied/pure mathematics

### Dept of Physics; www.bris.ac.uk/physics

astrophysics, physics mathematics and physics, nanoscience & functional nanomaterial particle physics, physics/& philosophy, theoretical physics; BSc(Hons), DSc, LlB, MRes, MSci, MSc, PhD, UGCert

## Faculty of Social Science and Law; www.bris.ac.uk/fss

**Graduate School of Education; www.bris.ac.uk/education**
education, psychology of education, secondary education, education management, education, neuroscience & education, technology & society, leadership policy & development, mathematics in/science & education, TESOL, special & inclusive education

### School for Policy Studies; www.bristol.ac.uk/sps

early/childhood studies, international health, social policy & politics/sociology, disability studies, inclusion policy & practice, public policy, social work, sociology

### School of Economics, Finance & Management; www.bristol.ac.uk/efm

accounting, finance, management, econometrics, economics, public policy, investment, strategy, change & leadership, economics & mathematics/politics/philosophy

### School of Law; www.bris.ac.uk/law

law, law and French/ German, socio-legal studies, adv studies legal system

**School of Sociology, Politics & International Studies; www.bristol.ac.uk/spais**

sociology, politics, social policy, philosophy, theology & sociology/& politics/sociology, politics & economics/philosophy/social policy/foreign languages, identities, ethnicity & multiculturalism, social & cultural theory, European governance, gender, international relations, international security, development & security, E Asian development & global economy, international development

**School of Geographical Sciences; www.bris.ac.uk/geography**

geography, human geography; society space, environmental policy & management, climate change science & policy

BA(Hons), BSc(Hons), DSocSci, EdD, LlB, LlD, LlM, MEd, MPhil, MSc, MSci, PGCE, PhD, Dip, MEd, DEdPsY

## UNIVERSITY OF THE WEST OF ENGLAND, BRISTOL
## www.uwe.ac.uk

### *Faculty of Business & Law; www.uwe.ac.uk/bl*

**Bristol Business School; www.uwe.ac.uk/bbs**

accounting & finance, applied economics, financial management, business (team enterprise), business & events management/HRM/law/management; business enterprise, business management (leadership, change & organisations/practice), business studies, business management with accounting & finance/economics/marketing/tourism, economics, events management, international business, professional accounting, banking & finance, family business admin, marketing/communications, social marketing, business & law/management, leadership & management (coaching & mentoring) creativity & change (health & social care), international HRM/management/tourism management, tourism management; BA(Hons), BSc(Hons), MA, MBA, MSc, PhD, MBA

**Bristol Law School; www1.uwe.ac.uk/bl/bls**

adv legal practice, commercial law, criminology, environmental law & sustainability, European & international law, international banking & financial/trade law/economic law, law; LlB, LlM, PhD

### *Faculty of Arts, Creative Industries & Education; www.uwe.ac.uk/cahe*

**Dept of Creative Industries; www.uwe.ac.uk/cahe/creative industries**

animation, art, culture, curating media & design by project, creative practices/media, design, drawing & applied art, craft, fashion design, textile design, documentary & features, film studies, illustration, media culture & practice fine art, graphic arts, journalism, PR, printmaking, wildlife filming, photography, printmaking; BA(Hons), FdA, MA, MPhil, PhD

**Dept of Education; www1.uwe.ac.uk/cahe/edu**

early childhood studies, early years education, education in professional practice, initial teacher education, PGCE primary – early years (3–7)/7–11/secondary/post-16 training, educational support, education, learning & development, inclusive practice, lifelong learning, post-compulsory education, learning & skills; ASR, BA(Hons), CertEd, DipHE, MA, MPhil, MSc, PGCert/Dip, PhD, FD

**Dept of Arts; www.uwe.ac.uk/cahe/arts**

acting, drama, English, creative writing, English language, history, journalism, philosophy, linguistics, film studies, screenwriting, politics, international relations, media & cultural studies, European philosophy, human rights, intercultural conflict; BA(Hons), MA, PhD

### *Faculty of Environment and Technology; www.uwe.ac.uk/et*

**Dept of Computer Science & Creative Technologies; www.uwe.ac.uk/et/cst**

audio music technology, computer science for games & security, computer systems integration, computing, creative music technology, digital media, enterprise/forensic computing, IT management for business, information & library management, information management/technology, network systems, software engineering, web & data analytics; BSc(Hons), MSc, MPhil, PhD, PGDip/Cert

### Dept of Construction & Property; www.uwe.ac.uk/et/cp

building/quantity surveying, building services engineering, commercial/property management, construction/project management/law, housing developments & management, property development & planning/investment & management, real estate/ management, residential property, construction law/ project management, traffic engineering FDA BA(Hons), BSc(Hons) MSc, MPhil, PhD

### Dept of Engineering, Design & Mathematics; www.uwe.ac.uk/et/edm

aerospace engineering/manufacture, automation, machine vision & management, automotive engineering, computer systems, creative product design, design for smart products, electrical & electronic engineering, engineering/management, electronics & communications, manufacturing process improvement, mathematics, mechanical engineering, motor sport engineering, product design technology, adv technology in electronics, adv techniques in robotics engineering, robotics, statistics; BEng, MEng, BSc(Hons), MPhil, PhD

### Dept of Geography & Environmental Management; www.uwe.acf.uk/et/gem

civil & environment engineering, geography, air quality & carbon management, applied GIS, environmental management/engineering, climate change & environment management/planning, professional practice, river & coastal engineering, sustainable development in practice, traffic engineering, uniformed services; BA(Hons), BSc(Hons), GradDip, MPhil, PhD

### Dept of Planning & Architecture; www.uwe.ac.uk/et/pa

architecture & planning, architectural technology & design, environment engineering, geography, interior architecture, town & country planning, spatial/transport planning, urban design/planning; BA(Hons), BSc(Hons), BArch, MA, MSc, MPlan, MPhil, PhD

## *Faculty of Health & Life Sciences; www.uwe.ac.uk/hls*

### Dept of Allied Health Professions; www.uwe.ac.uk/hls/ahp

diagnostic imaging, applied/ paramedic science, veterinary/physiotherapy, health professions, occupational therapy, radiotherapy & oncology, medical ultrasound, music therapy, nuclear medicine; FdSc, BSc(Hons), MSc, PGDip/Cert, MPhil, PhD

### Dept of Applied Sciences; www.uwe.ac.uk/ hls/as

applied/biomedical sciences/(clinical), adv forensic analysis, biological science, cellular pathology, conservation biology, environmental health/science, human biology, forensic science/biology/chemistry/ photography, healthcare science, integrated wildlife conservation, biosensing technologies, paramedic science, science communication, molecular biotechnology; FdSc, BSc(Hons), MSc, MRes, ProfDoc, PGCert/Dip, MPhil, PhD, CertHE

### Dept of Health & Applied Social Sciences; www.uwe.ac.uk/hls/hass

criminology, criminal justice, sociology, environmental health, psychology, integrated professional development, public health, social work/with adults, psychosocial studies, social work with adults, specialist community public health, therapeutic education; FdA, BSc(Hons), BA(Hons), MSc, PGDip/Cert, GradDip, MPhil, PhD

### Dept of Nursing & Midwifery; www.uwe.ac.uk/hls/nm

adult/children's/mental health/learning disability nursing, adv practice, community practice, emergency care, midwifery, healthcare practice, health professions, professional studies, psychosocial interventions, specialist practice; FdSc, BSc(Hons), MSc, PGDip/Cert, ProfDoc, MPhil, PhD

### Dept of Psychology; www.uwe.ac.uk/hls/ psychology

psychology, psychology & criminology/law/sociology, health psychology, psychological therapy (cognitive behaviour/relational psychotherapy), counselling psychology, psychological health, sport & exercise psychology; BA(Hons), BSc(Hons), MSc, DPS, ProfDoc, MPhil, PhD

## *Hartpury College (Associate Faculty); www.hartpury.ac.uk*

agricultural business/conservation & sustainability management, animal behaviour & veterinary science/ welfare, animal science management, bioveterinary science, conservation & countryside management, equine business management/performance/sports science, equine performance & rehabilitation/behaviour & welfare, coaching science, sport management/studies/injury management/business management/coaching performance, equine veterinary nursing, veterinary nursing science; BA(Hons), BSc(Hons), FdSc, FdA, MA, MSc, PGDip/Cert

# BRUNEL UNIVERSITY
# www.brunel.ac.uk

## School of Arts: www.brunel.ac.uk/about/acad/sa

contemporary literature & culture, performance making, composition, creative writing/with English/games design, digital games theory & design, documentary practice, drama, film & TV, English/literature/& contemporary drama, games design, campaigning & journalism, international journalism, media & PR, music, sonic arts, theatre; BA(Hons), BMus, MA, MMus, MPhil, PhD

## Brunel Law School: www.brunel.ac.uk/about/acad/bls

law, legal practice, European & international commercial law/financial regulation/& corporate law, intellectual property/economic/international economic & trade law, property/commercial/economic law, international human rights law, international & comparative criminal justice; CPE, European Masters, GradDip, LlM, LLB, MPhil, PhD

## School of Engineering and Design; www.brunel.ac.uk /about/acad/sed

advanced engineering design, engineering management, design & innovation, industrial design & technology, broadcast media design & technology, multimedia technology, packing technology, product design/engineering, multimedia design & 3D technologies, computer systems engineering, electrical/electronic/computer & communications engineering, renewable energy systems, sustainable electrical power, wireless communication systems, mechanical engineering, aerospace/aviation/engineering, aeronautics, automotive & motorsport engineering, biomedical engineering, building services engineering/management, engineering/management, civil engineering/ with sustainability, pilot studies; BA(Hons), BEng, BSc(Hons), EngD, MEng, MPhil, MSc, PhD

## Brunel Business School;

www.brunel.ac.uk /about/acad/bbs

business & management, business management, business intelligence & social media, accounting, aviation management, marketing, international business, corporate brand management, global supply chain management, healthcare management, HRM, HR and employment relations; BSc, MSc, MBA, PhD

## School of Health Sciences and Social Care; www.brunel.ac.uk/about/acad/health

biomedical sciences, biochemistry/forensics/genetics/human health/immunology, children, youth & international development, occupational therapy, physiotherapy, social work, specialist community social work/adults/children & families, health promotion and public health, neurorehabilitation, public health nursing, molecular medicine, hand therapy; BSc, BA, MSc, MA, PGDip, PGCert

## School of Information Systems, Computing and Mathematics: www.brunel.ac.uk/about/acad/siscm

artificial intelligence, adv business systems integration, adv/business computing, computational mathematics with modelling, computer science (AI/digital media & games/network computing/software engineering), computing, digital media & games, financial maths, information & communication technology in business, information systems management/computing & mathematics, mathematics/with computer science/project management, modelling and management of risk, statistics; BSc, MSc, MTech, PhD

## School of Social Sciences; www.brunel.ac.uk/about/acad/sss

accounting, economics, finance, anthropology/with sociology/professional development/psychology, psychology, sociology, business economics/finance, history globalisation & governance, intelligence & security, psychoanalysis, international money/politics/relations, investment, media & communications/studies, modern political theory, political economy, public affairs & lobbying, war & conflict, politics, anthropology of childhood; BA, BSc, MRes, MSc, PhD

## School of Sport and Education; www.brunel.ac.uk/about/acad/sse

sport sciences (coaching/human performance/sport development/PE & youth sport), sport psychology, contemporary education, PE, education, PGCE (in range of secondary subjects) sport & exercise psychology; BA, BSc, MSc, MA, PGCert, EdD, MPhil, PhD

## University Specialist Research Institutes offer postgraduate degree opportunities

# UNIVERSITY OF BUCKINGHAM
# www.buckingham.ac.uk

### Buckingham School of Business; www.buckingham.ac.uk/business

accounting, applied computing, business, business enterprise/administration, communication studies, finance, financial management, investment, lean entrepreneurship, management/in global service economy, marketing, media communications, psychology; BSc(Econ)(Hons), BSc(Hons), CMS, MBA, MSc/Diploma

## *School of Humanities; www.buckingham.ac.uk/humanities*

### Dept of Education; www.buckingham.ac.uk/education

Teacher's Standards: primary, secondary PGCE with QTS, educational leadership; MEd, BA(Hons), MPhil, DPhil

### Dept of Economics & International Studies; www.buckingham.ac.uk/economics-international

biography, business, business/economics, contemporary art & collecting, economics, English literature, global affairs, heritage management, history, international studies, journalism, law, military history, politics, security, intelligence/international affairs & diplomacy, war studies; BA(Hons), BSc(Econ)Hons, DPhil, MA, MPhil, MSc

### Dept of Modern Foreign Languages; www.buckingham.ac.uk/mfl

range of languages taught for part of joint degrees

### Dept of English; www.buckingham.ac.uk/english

foundation English, English language/literature, communication & media studies, media, journalism, biography, English studies; BA(Hons), MA

### London Programmes; www.buckingham.ac.uk/london

biography, contemporary art & collecting, decorative arts & historic interiors, garden histories, military history, war studies;MA

## *Buckingham Law School; www.buckingham.ac.uk/law*

law, common law, international & commercial law, joint degrees; Cert/Dip, LlB, LlM

## *School of Sciences & Medicine; www.buckingham.ac.uk/sciences*

### School of Medicine & dentistry; www.buckingham.ac.uk/medicine

graduate entry, PG medical school, general internal medicine, clinical science, dental surgery; Clinical MD, MBBS, MSc, BDS

### Dept of Applied Computing; www.buckingham.ac.uk/applied computing

applied computing, computing (with jt degrees), innovative computing; BSc, Cert Comp, MSc, PGDip, DPhil

### Dept of Psychology; www.buckingham.ac.uk/psychology

psychology, adult dyslexia; BSc(Hons), MPhil, MSc, PhD

### Clore Laboratory; www.buckingham.ac.uk/clore

diabetes, obesity & metabolic research, molecular genetics, biochemistry, bioinformatics, nutrition; DPhil, MPhil, MSc

## BUCKINGHAMSHIRE NEW UNIVERSITY
## www.bucks.ac.uk

### Faculty of Design, Media & Management; www.bucks.ac.uk/about/structure/academic/faculties/design-media-management

**School of Applied Management & Law; www.bucks.ac.uk/about/structure/academic-schools/applied-management-law**

business & mangement, law, music & event management, sports management

**School of Design, Craft & Visual Arts; www.bucks.ac.uk/about/structure/academic_schools/design-craft-visual-arts**

art & design, creative & visual communication, design & craft, furniture

**Dept of Security & Resilience; www.bucks.ac.uk/about/structure/academic_schools/security-and-resilience**

business continuity, security, & emergency management

### Faculty of Society and Health; www.bucks.ac.uk/about/structure/faculties/society-and-health

**School of Social Sciences; www.bucks.ac.uk/about/structure/academic_schools/social-science**

psychology, criminology, sport psychology

**School of Advanced and Continuing Practice; www.bucks.ac.uk/about/structure/academic_schools/advanced-continuing-practice**

cancer & palliative care, critical/cardiac/respiratory care, adv practice

**School of Pre-qualifying Nursing; www.bucks.ac.uk/about/structure/academic_schools/pre-registration-nursing**

adult/child/mental health nursing

additional first and postgraduate degrees are offered in the following academic areas of study:

audio music production, children & young people, computing technology & new media, drama & performance, education, furniture, health & nursing, law, media production, social science, social work, sport & fitness, travel & aviation; BA(Hons), BSc(Hons), Certs, DMS, GradDip, FD, HNC, HND, LlB(Hons), LlM, MA, MBA, MCommunMan, MSc, PhD, FD

## UNIVERSITY OF CAMBRIDGE
## www.cam.ac.uk

### *Arts and Humanities; www.csah.cam.ac.uk*

### Faculty of Architecture and History of Art; www.aha.cam.ac.uk

architecture/and urban design/practice, professional practice, interdisciplinary design in the built environment, British architecture, building history, history of art, medieval art & architecture, Renaissance art & architecture, sustainable building, conflict in the city, 20th-century art & theory, western & non-western cultural exchange; BA, MPhil, MSt, PhD

### Faculty of Asian & Middle Eastern Studies; www.ames.cam.ac.uk

Chinese studies, Hebrew and Semitic studies, Japanese studies, Korean studies, Arabic & Persian studies, East Asia, Southern Asia studies, Assyriology, Egyptology; BA, MPhil, PhD

### Faculty of Classics; www.classics.cam.ac.uk

classics & Latin literature, history, philology and linguistics, philosophy; BA, MPhil, PGCE

### Faculty of Divinity; www.divinity.cam.ac.uk

biblical studies, church history, ancient & modern Judaism, historical & systematic theology, religious studies, the philosophy of religion & ethics, religion & natural/social science, the Christian tradition, world religions, New Testament, patristics; BA, MPhil, PhD, PGDip

### Faculty of English; www.english.cam.ac.uk

American literature, Anglo-Saxon, Norse & Celtic, English & applied linguistics, medieval/English literature studies, European languages & literatures, English studies: criticism & culture/18th-century & romantic studies; language for literature, modern & contemporary literature; BA, MLitt, MPhil, PhD

### Faculty of Modern and Medieval Languages; www.mml.cam.ac.uk

Depts of French, German & Dutch, Italian, Spanish & Portuguese, European literature, linguistics, modern Greek, neo-Latin, Polish, Russian studies, screen & media cultures, Slavonic studies, Ukrainian; BA, MPhil, PhD

### Faculty of Music; www.mus.cam.ac.uk

ethnomusicology, music studies, music/with education studies, analysis, jazz & pop music, performance studies, recitals, tonal compositions & analysis & repertoire, musical composition, choral studies; BA, MPhil, PhD, MMusD

### Faculty of Philosophy; www.phil.cam.ac

ethics, experimental psychology, history of philosophy, logic, metaphysics, philosophy of science, political philosophy, aesthetics, mathematical logic, ancient philosophy; BA, MPhil, PhD

## *Humanities & Social Sciences; www.cshss.cam.ac.uk*

### Faculty of Human, Social & Political Science

**Dept of Archaeology and Anthropology; www.hsps.cam.ac.uk**

archaeological heritage & museum/science, Aegean prehistory, archaeology, archaeology of the Americas, biological anthropology, Egyptian archaeology, Egyptology, Assyriology, European prehistory, human evolutionary studies, medieval archaeology/Britain, Mesopotamian studies, palaeolithic & mesolithic archaeology, social anthropology, south Asian archaeology; BA, MPhil, PhD

**Dept of Politics & International Relations; www.hsps.cam.ac.uk**

politics and international relations

**Centre of Latin American Studies; www.latin-america.cam.ac.uk**

economic issues in contemporary Latin America, history of South American external relations, Latin American literary culture/film and visual arts, race & ethnicity/anthropology/sociology & politics in Latin America/studies; MPhil, PhD

**Centre of African Studies; www.africa.cam.ac.uk**

African studies; MPhil

**Centre of South Asian Studies**

modern South Asian studies; MPhil

**Centre of Development Studies; www.devstudies.cam.ac.uk**

development studies; MPhil

**Dept of Social Sciences**

### Sociology; www.sociology.cam.ac.uk

sociology, modern society & global transformations, politics, social anthropology; BA, MPhil, PhD

### Social and Developmental Psychology; www.sdp.cam.ac.uk

psychology, social and developmental psychology

**Centre for Family Research; www.cfr.cam.ac.uk**

bioethics & the family, early social development & the family, genetics, health & families, non-traditional families, parent, children & family relationships; MPhil, PhD

### The Pyschometrics Centre; www.psychometrics.cam.ac.uk

MPhil, PhD

### Faculty of Economics; www.econ.cam.ac.uk

asset pricing, behavioural economics, economic theory, finance, microeconomics, quantitative methods, microeconomics, macroeconomics, macroeconometrics, economics; BA, Diploma, MPhil, PhD

### Faculty of Education; www.educ.cam.ac.uk

arts culture & education, psychotherapeutic counselling, children & literature, early years, education, educational leadership & school improvement, educational diversity & inclusion/special education, language communication & literacy, second language, mathematics education, PGCE primary, secondary education (numerous subjects); BA, MEd, PGCE, PGDip/Cert, PhD

### Faculty of History; www.hist.cam.ac.uk

American history, British/early modern history, economic, social & cultural history, mid/European history, ancient & medieval history, political thought & intellectual history, world history; BA, MPhil, PhD

**History and Philosophy of Science;**

www.hps.cam.ac.uk

philosophy of science, history of ancient & medieval/early modern science, history & ethics of medicine, history, philosophy & sociology of the life sciences/physical & mathematical sciences/social & psychological sciences/medicine, ethics & politics of science, biological & biomedical sciences; BA, MPhil, PhD

### Faculty of Law; www.law.cam.ac.uk

criminological research, criminology, international law, law, legal studies, civil law, communication law, European law, large range of legal topics at

Master level; BA, Diploma, LLD, LLM, MLitt, MPhil, PhD, MCL

**Institute of Criminology; www.crim.cam.ac**
applied/criminology, penology/& management; MPhil, MSt, PhD

**Dept of Land Economy; www.landecon.cam.ac.uk**
land economy, planning, growth & regeneration, real estate finance, environmental policy; BA, MPhil, PhD

## *School of Biological Sciences; www.cam.ac.uk/sbs*

### Faculty of Biology; www.cam.ac.uk

**Biochemistry; www.bio.cam.ac.uk**
biology of cells, bioscience, systems biology, evolution & behaviour, biochemistry & molecular biology

**Psychology; www.psych.cam.ac.uk**
psychology & human behaviour, experimental psychology, social & developmental psychology, neuropsychology

**Genetics; www.gen.cam.ac.uk**
mathematical biology, molecules in medical science, cells & developmental biology, genetics, ecology, systems biology, biology of cells

**Centre for Family Research; www.cfr.cam.ac.uk**
early social developoment & the family, non-traditional families, genetics, health and family, bioethics & the family

**Pathology; www.path.cam.ac.uk**
graduate clinical course in medicine

**Pharmacology; www.pha.ca.ac.uk**
pharmacology, medicinal chemistry

**Physiology, Development & Neuroscience; www.pdn.cam.ac.uk**
biological & biomedical sciences, physiology, neuroscience, neurobiology, developmental biology, stem cell biology

**Plant Science; www/pplant.cam.ac.uk**
plant science, cell & developmental biology, ecology, plant & microbiological science

**Zoology; www.zoo.cam.ac.uk**
animal biology, cell & developmental biology, ecology, zoology, neurobiology/science, molecular biology; BA, MPhil, PhD

### Faculty of Veterinary Medicine

**Department of Veterinary Medicine; www.vet.cam.ac.uk**
Clinical Course: veterinary science, preclinical course; MPhil, VetMB

### Wellcome Trust Centre for Stem Cell Research; www.cscr.cam.ac.uk

stem cell biology, mammalian stem cells; PhD

### Wellcome Trust/Cancer Research UK Gurdon InstituteTechnology; www.gurdon.cam.ac.uk

cellular & molecular biology, developmental, cell & cancer biology; PhD

## *School of Technology; www.tech.ac.uk*

### Faculty of Engineering; www.eng.cam.ac.uk

energy, fluid mechanics & turbomechanics, materials design, civil, structural and environmental engineering, construction engineering, geotechnology & environmental structures, applied mechanics, manufacture & management, information engineering, engineering for life sciences, turbomachines, energy & fluid mechanics, electrical engineering, mechanics, materials & design, manufacture & management, manufacturing engineering, sustainable development, production processes; BA(Hons), MEng, MPhil, PhD

### Faculty of Business & Management (Judge Business School); www.jbs.cam.ac.uk

courses include: finance & accounting, management science, operations, economics & policy, information systems & organisational behaviour, strategy & marketing, international business; MBA, MFin

### Faculty of Computer Science & Technology;

**Computer Laboratory; www.cl.cam.ac.uk**
adv/computer science, AI, computer architecture, digital technology, graphics & integrated action, natural language & information, network architecture, internet user interface, forensic signal analysis, language processing, embedded systems, programming logic etc; BA, MPhil, PhD

### Department of Chemical Engineering & Biotechnology; www.ceb.cam.ac.uk

advanced chemical engineering, biotechnology, measurement, bioscientific enterprise, modelling, processes; BA/MEng, MPhil, PhD, MBE

**Cambridge Programme for Sustainability Leadership; www.cpi.cam.ac.uk**
sustainability, health care services, climate, innovation, extractives; MSt, PGCert

## School of Physical Sciences; www.physci.cam.ac.uk

### Faculty of Earth Sciences & Geography; www.physci.cam.ac.uk

**Dept of Earth Sciences; www.esc.cam.ac.uk**
earth sciences, environmental science, palaeontology, geological sciences, climate change, seismology, geophysics, oceanography, sedimentology, tectonics, minerals physics/science, palaeobiology, volcanology, petrology; BA, MPhil, PhD

**Dept of Geography; www.geog.cam.ac.uk (inc Scott Polar Research Institute)**
geography, earth's atmosphere, glacial environments, volcanology, physical geography, polar studies, environmental science, conservation leadership, environment & development, multidisciplinary gender studies; BA, MPhil, PhD

### Faculty of Mathematics; wwwmaths.cam.ac.uk

**Dept of Applied Mathematics & Theoretical Physics; www.physci.cam.ac.uk/about the school/dampt**
mathematical science, applied mathematics, statistical science, theoretical physics, computational biology, quantum mechanics, relativity, fluid dynamics, numerical analysis

**Dept of Pure Mathematics & Mathematical Statistics**
pure mathematics & mathematical statistics, statistical science; BA, MPhil, PhD, MMath, MAdvStud, MASt

### Faculty of Physics & Chemistry; www.cam.ac.uk/physchemfaculty

**Institute of Astronomy; www.ast.cam.ac.uk**
theoretical & observational astronomy, astrophysics

**Dept of Chemistry; www.ch.cam.ac.uk**
physical, theoretical, organic, inorganic biochemistry, synthesis, materials chemistry, chemistry, theoretical modelling & information

**Dept of Material Science & Metallurgy; www.physci.cam.ac.uk/abouttheschool/materialsscience**
materials science, metals, alloys, ceramics, polymers, semiconducting/magnetic/superconducting/ferroelectric/biomedical materials, composites, micro & nanotechnology enterprises

**Dept of Physics; www.phyi.cam.ac.uk**
experimental & theoretical physics, astrophysics, scientific computing, nanoscience & technology, atomic/high energy/quantum & condensed matter/thin film magnetism, scientific computing
BA, MPhil, MSci, PhD, MASt, MSC, EngD

## School of Clinical Medicine; www.medschl.cam.ac.uk

### Dept of Clinical Biochemistry (Metabolic Research Laboratories); www.clbc.cam.ac.uk

biomedical research, diabetes, molecular cell biology of membrane traffic pathways, obesity & other related endocrine and metabolic disorders; PhD

### Dept of Clinical Neurosciences (Cambridge Centre for Brain Repair; Neurology Unit; Neurosurgery; Wolfson Brain Imaging Centre); www.neurosciences.medschl.am.ac.uk

brain repair, neurology, neurosurgery, brain imaging; MB/PhD

### Dept of Haematology; www.haem.cam.ac.uk

transfusion medicine diagnostics development, structural medicine & thrombosis, haematopoiesis & leukaemia; PhD

### Dept of Medical Genetics; www.cimr.cam.ac.uk/medgen

genetics of inflammatory disorders, juvenile diabetes, autoimmune liver, neurological/Xlinked, renal genetics, cancer disease; BChir, MB, MD, PhD

### Dept of Medicine; www.med.cam.ac.uk

anasthesia, clinical pharmacology

**Obstetrics & Gynaecology**

**Oncology**

**Paediatrics**

**Psychiatry**
brain mapping, developmental psychiatry

**Public Health & Primary Care**
general practice & primary care research, clinical gerentology

**Radiology**

**Surgery**
orthopaedic research

## CAMBRIDGE INTERNATIONAL COLLEGE
## www.cambridgecollege.ac.uk

accounting, finance, business/financial/project/HR/logistics/marketing administration, commerce, hospitality (many courses at non-graduate level); HRM, BA, Diplomas, AMBA

## CANTERBURY CHRIST CHURCH UNIVERSITY
## www.canterbury.ac.uk

### *Faculty of Arts and Humanities; www.canterbury.ac.uk/arts-humanities*

**English & Language Studies; www.canterbury.ac.uk/arts-humanities/english-language-studies/**

English/literature/language & communication, creative/& professional writing, prose fiction, intercultural communication, TESOL, modern languages, French

**History & American Studies; www.canterbury.ac.uk/arts-humanities/history-and-american-studies/Home.aspx**

American studies, Canadian studies, archaeology, history

**Media, Art & Design; www.canterbury.ac.uk/arts-humanities/MediaArtAndDesign/home.aspx**

broadcast & interactive TV, digital media, film, radio & TV, multimedia journalism/design, graphic design, web design, fine & applied arts, film & digital video graphics, media & communication, cultural studies, PR, media marketing, photography, web & motion graphics

**Music & Performing Arts; www.canterbury.ac.uk/arts-humanities/Music/departmenthome/Home.aspx**

commercial/music production, creative arts, creative music technology, dance education, drama, performing arts, church music

**Theology & Religious Studies; www.canterbury.ac.uk/arts-humanities/theology-and-religious-studies/Home.aspx**

theology, religious studies;
BA, BSC, MA, MPhil, PhD, PGDip, FD, MMus

### *Faculty of Education; www.canterbury.ac.uk/education*

early/childhood studies, careers guidance, early years/professional status/studies, educational studies, enabling learning (SEN & inclusion), initial teacher education, leadership & management for learning, lifelong learning, literacy & learning, teaching skills for life – numeracy, literacy/ESOL, PGCE, primary teaching, post-compulsory education & training, teaching & learning, modular (primary/secondary), PE, RE, post-primary education, professional learning & education, qualified teacher status (QTS), supporting children's learning/young people, PE & sport & exercise science; BA(Hons), EdD, EYPS, FDA, MA, MPhil/PhD

### *Faculty of Health and Social Care; www.canterbury.ac.uk/health/home*

**Department of Allied Health Professions; www.canterbury.ac.uk/health/allied-health-professions**

advanced/occupational therapy, clinical reporting/imaging, diagnostic radiography, interprofessional health & social care, medical imaging, musculoskeletal ultrasound, operating dept practice, ophthalmic dispensing, paramedic science, speech & language therapy

**Centre for Health and Social Care Research; www.canterbury.ac.uk/health/health-social-care-research**

**Dementia Services Development Centre South East; www.dementiacentre.canterbury.ac.uk**

mental health, public health

**Dept of Health, Well-being & the Family; www.canterbury.ac.uk/health**

midwifery, advanced practice, child nursing, health studies, health & social care (health promotion, public health, mental health/practice/nursing), interprofessional health & social care, play therapy, dance movement therapy, social work, children & families, volunteering

**Department of Nursing and Applied Clinical Studies; www.canterbury.ac.uk/health/nursing-applied-clinical-studies**
adult nursing, acute care, advanced practice, interprofessional health & social care, leadership & management in public health nursing, public health nursing, return to practice, independent & supplementary prescribing

**Sidney De Haan Research Centre; www.canterbury.ac.uk/research/centre/SDHR**
singing & mental health, singing & dementia projects, arts & health; BA(Hons), BSc(Hons), FD, EdD, MPhil, PhD, MA, MSc

## *Faculty of Social and Applied Sciences; www.canterbury.ac.uk/social-applied-science*

**Dept of Applied Psychology; www.canterbury.ac.uk/social-applied-sciences/aspd**
cognitive behavioural therapy and psychological wellbeing practice, psychology/arts & health, clinical psychology

**Dept of Applied Social Science; www.canterbury.ac.uk/social-applied-sciences**
global politics, politics & global governance/ international relations, sociology & social science, psychology;
BA(Hons), BSc(Hons), BA/BSC, MPhil, PhD

## *Faculty of Business and Management; www.canterbury.ac.uk/business-management*

**The Business School; www.canterbury.ac.uk/business-management/business-school**
accounting & finance, advertising management, business finance/management/studies, education/healthcare leadership & management, economics, entrepreneurship, HRM, digital/marketing, information management & business communication, international business, organisational behaviour, PR, music industry management, management

**Centre for Leadership & Management; www.canterbury.ac.uk/business-management/CLMD**
coaching, leadership development, organizational development, management skills, personal effectiveness, project management, recruitment and selection, team dev, strategic leadership; BSc(Hons), MA, MBA, MPhil/PhD, MSc, PGDip/Cert

**Centre for Entrepreneurship & Innovation; www.canterbury.ac.uk/business-management/CEI**
accounting, finance, environment, HRM & organisational behaviour, marketing, advertsising; MPhil, PhD

**Dept of Computing; www.canterbury.ac.uk/social-applied-sciences/computing**
business computing, computing, cybercrime forensics, forensic computing, internet computing; BSc(Hons), MSc, FD

**The Department of Law and Criminal Justice Studies; www.canterbury.ac.uk/social-applied-sciences/crime-and-policing**
criminology & criminal justice/policing, law & legal studies, applied criminology, crime & policing/policing studies, forensic investigation; BA/BSc, LlB, LPC, MA, MSc

**Dept of Geographical and Life Sciences; www.canterbury.ac.uk/social-applied-sciences/geographical-and-life-sciences**
bioscience, ecology & conservation, animal science, plant science, environmental biology/science, geography, integrated science, urban and regional studies, GIS

**Dept of Sports Science, Tourism and Leisure; www.canterbury.ac.uk/social-applied-sciences/sport-science-tourism-and-leisure**
applied health & fitness, PE & sport exercise science, event management, exercise psychology, leisure management, tourism & leisure studies, tourism management, physical education & sport

**Centre for Sport, Physical Education, www.canterbury.ac.uk/SPEAR**
Olympic & Paralympic research, physical education & activity in schools, sport, physical activity & health; BA/BSc, MBA, MSc, MA, Adv Dip, Grad Cert, PGDip, FD, DipHE, MPhil, PhD

# CARDIFF UNIVERSITY
## www.cardiff.ac.uk

### Welsh School of Architecture; www.cardiff.ac.uk/archi

architectural studies/& urban design, environmental design of buildings, sustainable energy & environment, urban design, sustainable design, professional studies, building, building & performance modelling, vertical studies; BSc, DipProfStudies, MA, MArch, MPhil, MSc, PhD

### School of Biosciences; www.cardiff.ac.uk/bios

biochemistry, biology, biomedical science – anatomy/neuroscience/physiology, biotechnology, ecology, dental hygiene/therapy, medical pharmacy, biophotonics, dentistry, genetics, microbiology, medicine, medical pharmacology, molecular biology, tissue engineering, zoology; BSc(Hons), MRes, MSc, PhD, BDS, MBBCh

### Cardiff Business School; www.cardiff.ac.uk/carbs

accounting, banking, business administration/economics/studies, economics & history/politics/philosophy, business strategy & entrepreneurship, business management – HRM, international/logistics & operations management/marketing, economics, finance, financial economics, HRM, international transport, international economics, banking & finance, marine policy, marketing, port and shipping administration, media management, strategic marketing; BSc, BScEcon, MBA, MBA, MSc, PhD, Dip

### School of Chemistry; www.cardiff.ac.uk/chemy

chemical biology, chemistry, chemistry with physics/industrial experience, catalytic science, chemical biology, inorganic chemistry, organic synthesis, physical organic chemistry, molecular modelling, sustainable chemistry, theoretical and computational chemistry; BSc, MChem, MPhil, PhD

### School of Computer Science & Informatics; www.cardiff.cs.cf.ac.uk

computer science/with high performance/security & forensics, business/information systems, computer systems engineering, software engineering, information security & privacy, strategic information systems, IT management; BSc, MSc, PhD

### School of Dentistry; www.cardiff.ac.uk/denti

dental surgery, conscious sedation, dental therapy & hygiene, implantology, orthodontics, tissue engineering; BDS, BSc(Hons), MClinDent, MD, MPhil, MSc, PhD

### School of Earth and Ocean Sciences; www.cardiff.ac.uk/earth

applied environmental geology, earth sciences, environmental geoscience/hydrogeology, exploration & resource geology, geology, marine geography; BSc, MESc, MPhil, MSc, PhD

### School of Engineering; www.cardiff.ac.uk/engin

architectural/civil/environmental/clinical engineering, computer systems, electrical and electronic / communications engineering, electrical energy systems, electronic and geoenvironmental/integrated engineering, adv/ mechanical engineering, medical/orthopaedic/structural engineering, sustainable energy & environment, hydroenvironmental engineering, wireless & microwave communications engineering; BEng, EngD, MEng, MPhil, MSc, PhD

### School of English, Communication & Philosophy; www.cardiff.ac.uk/encap

applied linguistics, creative writing, critical & cultural theory, analytic & modern mid-European philosophy, English language/literature, ethics & social philosophy, forensic linguistics, language & communication, philosophy; BA, Dip, MA/Dip, MPhil, PhD

### School of European Studies; www.cardiff.ac.uk/euros

French, German, Spanish, Italian, European/European Union studies, European governanace & public policy, international relations, political theory, languages, law, politics, translation studies, politics & public policy, Welsh politics & government; BA, BScEcon, LlB, MA, MScEcon, MPhil, PhD

### School of Healthcare Studies; www.cardiff.ac.uk/sohcs

healthcare science, intra & perioperative practice, medical illustration, image appreciation, neuro-musculoskeletal physiotherapy, managing care in pre-operative practice, neurorehabilitation, occupation &

health, occupational therapy, operating department practice, physiotherapy, radiography & imaging/ reporting, diagnostic/radiotherapy & oncology, sports & exercise physiotherapy, surgical care practice; CertHE, DipHE, MPhil, MSc, PGDip/Cert, PhD

### School of History, Archaeology & Religion; www.cardiff.ac.uk/share

ancient/& medieval history, archaeology, care of collections, professional conservation, history & archaeology of the Greek and Roman world, early Celt studies, Byzantine studies, late antique & history of the Crusades, medieval British studies/history, Welsh history, practical theology, religious & theological studies; Indian religions/religions of late antiquity/myth, narrative & theory, Christian doctrine/ ethics, Islam in contemporary Britain, church history, chaplaincy studies; BA, BSc, MA, MPhil, MSc, PhD

### Journalism, Media and Cultural Studies; www.cardiff.ac.uk/jomec

international/broadcast/magazine/newspaper journalism, PR/political/global communication & science, media & communication, media management, journalism, media & cultural studies; BA, MA, MPhil, MSc, PGDip, PhD

### School of Law; www.law.cf.ac.uk

canon law, commercial law, European legal studies, governance & devolution, law & governance of EU, legal & political aspects of international affairs, human rights, medical practice, international commercial law, law & social care, governance development, law; LlB, LlM, MPhil, PhD

### Centre for Lifelong Learning; www.cardiff.ac.uk/learn/

languages, business & management, computer studies, law, science & environment, social studies, humanities, professional development

### School of Mathematics; www.cardiff.ac.uk/ maths

applied statistics, mathematics/& its applications, operational research & statistics and risk; BSc, MMath, MPhil, MSc, PhD

### School of Medicine; www.cardiff.ac.uk/ medic

advanced surgical practice, clinical neuroscience, geriatric medicine, infection & immunisation, intensive care medicine, public health, genetics, medical pharmacology, medicine, obstetrics & gynaecology, occupational health, oncology, paediatrics, pain management, palliative medicine, pharmacology, primary care & public health, psychiatric medicine, public health, ultrasound, therapeutics & toxology, psychiatry, therapeutics, wound healing; MBBCh, MD, MPH, MPhil, MSc/PGDip/Cert, PhD

### School of Music; www.cardiff.ac.uk/music

composition, ethnomusicology, music, musicology, music, culture & politics, performance studies; BA/ BMus, MA, MMus, PhD

### School of Nursing & Midwifery Studies; www.cardiff.ac.uk/sonims

adult/child/mental health nursing, clinical practice, community health studies & specialist practice, specialist community/public health nursing, advanced/community practice, health studies, midwifery, return to practice; BMid, BN, BSc(Hons), DipHE, DNurs, DocProf, MPhil, MSc, PGDip/Cert, PhD

### School of Optometry & Vision Sciences; www.cardiff.ac.uk/optom

clinical optometry, vision sciences, optometry, visual neuroscience & molecular biology, structural biophysics; BSc, MPhil, PhD

### School of Pharmacy; www.cardiff.ac.uk/ phring

clinical pharmacy, clinical research, clinical (community & primary care practice), community pharmacy, health economics, non-medical prescribing, pharmacology, pharmacist, independent prescribing, international pharmacological economics; Dipl, MPharm, MPhil, MSc, PhD

### School of Physics and Astronomy; www.astro.cardiff.ac.uk

astrophysics, biophotonics, physics, astronomy, gravitational physics, condensed matter & photionics; BSc, MPhil, MPhys, PhD

### Postgraduate Medical and Dental Education; www.cardiff.ac.uk/pgmde

paediatric/emergency medication, paediatric intensive care, obstetrics & gynaecology, psychiatry

### School of Psychology; www.cardiff.ac.uk/ psych

clinical/educational psychology, neuroimaging, cognitive behavioural theory, psychology; BSc, DEdPsych, DClinPsych, GradDip, PhD

**School of Social Sciences; www.cardiff.ac.uk/socsci**
criminology, science, media & communications, social policy/work, sociology; BA, BSc, DHS, DSW, EdD, MED, MA, MSc, PGCE

**School of Welsh; www.cardiff.ac.uk/welsh**
into to/Welsh, Welsh history/literature/second language, early Celtic studies, medieval British studies, Wales & its culture, Welsh & Celtic studies; BA, MA, PhD

## CARDIFF METROPOLITAN UNIVERSITY
## www.cardiffmet.ac.uk

### *Cardiff School of Art & Design; www.csad.cardiffmet.uwic.ac.uk*
advanced/product design, architectural design & technology, artist designer maker, art & design/communication/art & science/death & visual culture, ceramics, design, fine art, textiles, graphic communication, illustration, product design/management; BA, BSc, HNC, HND, MA, MFA, MPhil, MSc, MDes, PGCert, PhD

### *Cardiff School of Education; www3.cardiffmet.ac.uk/English/education*

**Dept of Humanities; www3.cardiffmet.ac.uk/English/education/humanities**
education, educational studies, English & contemporary media/drama/creative writing, post compulsory education & training, prepare to teach, PGCE primary/secondary education, youth and creative writing; BA(Hons), MA, PGCert/Dip, PGCE

**Dept of Professional Development; www3.cardiffmet.ac.uk/English/education/profdevelopment**
education, management in the community professions, youth & community work, prepare to teach, learning support; BA, MA, MPhil, MSc, PhD, CertEd, FdD, PGCE

**Dept of Teacher Education & Training**
PGCE (primary, secondary), secondary music/Welsh; BA(Hons), PGCE

### *Cardiff School of Health Sciences; www3.cardiffmet.ac.uk/English/health*

**Centre for Applied Social Sciences; www3.cardiffmet.ac.uk/English/health/ass**
health & social care, housing: policy & practice/supported housing, youth & community, management in the community professions, health & social science res, postqual/social work; BA, BSc, FdSc, GradCert, GradDip, HNC, HND, MRes, MSc, PGCert, PGDip

**Institute of Biomedical Science; www3.cardiffmet.ac.uk/English/StudyAtUWIC/Courses/Pages/CareerBiomedical**
applied/biomedical sciences, healthcare science, sports biomedicine & nutrition; BSc, FdSc, HNC, HND, MSc, PGCert/Dip

**Centre for Complementary Therapies; www3.cardiffmet.ac.uk/English/health/cct**
complementary therapies, aromatherapy, reflexology, holistic massage, health science, dental technology, podiatry, speech & language therapy, musculoskeletal studies, clinical research methods; BSc, Dip/Cert

**Centre for Dental Technology; www3.cardiffmet.ac.uk/English/health/cdt**
dental technology; BSc, FdSc, MSc, PGCert, PGDip

**Centre for Nutrition, Dietetics & Food Sciences; www3.cardiffmet.ac.uk/English/health/cnfc**
applied public health, dietetics, food science & technology, human nutrition & dietetics, adv dietetic practice, food technology for industry, clinical research methods, public health nutrition, sports biomedicine & management/nutrition, food science & technology/safety management; BSc(Hons) MRes, FdSc, MSc, PGDip

**Dept of Applied Psychology; www3.cardiffmet.ac.uk/English/health/cp**
forensic/health psychology, psychology; BSc, FdSc, MSc, PgDip, MRes

**Centre for Environmental Health & Public Protection; www3.cardiffmet.ac.uk/English/health/cpp**
applied public health, environmental health/risk management, health science, occupational health, safety, & wellbeing, waste management; BSc, FdSc, HNC, MSc, PGDip

**Centre for Speech & Language Therapy; www3.cardiffmet.ac.uk/English/health/cslt**
speech & language therapy; BSc(Hons)

**Wales Centre for Podiatric Studies; www3.cardiffmet.ac.uk/English/health/wcps**
musculoskeletal studies, podiatry, adv/therapeutic footware; BSc, MSc, PGCert, PGDip

### *Cardiff School of Management; www3.cardiffmet.ac.uk/English/management*

**Business & Management; www3.cardiffmet.ac.uk/English/Cardiff-School-of-Management/Business-and-Management/Pages/Home.aspx**
business administration/studies, business & management, management, international business management/administration, marketing management, law, project development management; BA(Hons), LlB, HND, MBA, MSc

**Accounting, Economics & Finance; www3.cardiffmet.ac.uk/English/Cardiff-School-of-Management/Accounting-Economics-Finance/Pages/Home.aspx**
accounting, finance, business economics, economics, financial management, finance & information management, international economics & finance; BA(Hons), BSc(Hons), FdA, MSc, BSc(Econ)

**Information Systems & International Studies**
business information systems/technology, computing, software development, information & communication, project technology management, computing, management & technology, mobile technology, computing & software development, technology project management, international business management/adminstration; BA(Hons), BSc(Hons), HNC, HND, MSc

**Tourism, Hospitality & Events Management; www3.cardiffmet.ac.uk/English/Cardiff-School-of-Management/Tourism-Hospitality-Events-Management/Pages/Home.aspx**
tourism, hospitality/& events management/marketing management, international hospitality/events/marketing/tourism management, sports tourism management; BA(Hons), FdA, HNC, HND, MSc, PGCert, PGDip

### *Cardiff School of Sport; www3.cardiffmet.ac.uk/English/sport*

applied sports coaching, dance, performance analysis, physical activity & health, sports coaching/development, sport & exercise/ medicine/physical education, sport management & leadership, sport psychology, sport conditioning rehabilitation & massage, strengthening & conditioning; BA(Hons), BSc(Hons), MA, MSc, PGDip/Cert

## UNIVERSITY OF CENTRAL LANCASHIRE
## www.uclan.ac.uk

**School of Art, Design & Performance; www.uclan.ac.uk/schools/adp**
acting, animation, antiques, arts health, art & design, brand management/promotion, contemporary theatre & performance/crafts, creative business management/thinking, dance & somatic well-being, performance, & teaching, fine art/studio practice/site & archive, consumer product design, contemporary visual arts, drawing, design enterprise, digital design for fashion/graphics, Eastern/fashion design, drawing & image making, fashion promotion with styling promotion/design, games design, children's books/illustration, interior design, journalism, music production/theatre/practice, performance, photography, product design, textiles, toy design, transdisciplinary design; MA, MBA, MPhil, PGCert/Dip, PhD, UniCert

**School of Built & Natural Environment; www.uclan.ac.uk/schools/built_natural_environment**
architecture/technology, building conservation & regeneration, building services & sustainable engineering, building/quantity surveying, construction law, construction/project management, construction economics/facilities management, environment hazards/management, project management, geography, sustainable energy/waste management; BSc(Hons), BA(Hons), FdSc, PGDip/Cert, MSc

**School of Computing, Engineering & Physical Sciences; www.uclan.ac.uk/schools/computing_engineering_physical**
computing: agile software, computer games/networks/development, computing, database systems, digital signals & imaging, forensic computing, computer network technology, information systems, IT security, mobile interactive technology, multimedia/games development, network computing, renewable/wind energy engineering, software engineering
engineering: electronic computing, robotics & mechatronics, digital computing/signal & image processing, electronic design automation, electronic engineering, engineering development, computer-aided engineering, motorsports/engineering, mechanical maintenance engineering, renewable energy engineering, wind energy engineering, nuclear engineering
physics & mathematics: mathematics, physics, astrophysics, astronomy, mathematical physics; BSc(Hons), BEng(Hons), MPhys, MSc, FdSc, MPhil, PhD

**School of Dentistry, & Institute for Postgraduate Dental Education; www.uclan.ac.uk/health/schools/dentistry_at_uclan/**
dental surgery, dentistry, endodontology, oral surgery, orthodontic therapy, continuous professional development; BDS, CertHE, MSc, PGDip, Adv Cert

**School of Education and Social Sciences; www.uclan.ac.uk/schools/education_social_sciences**
lifelong learning, adult literacy, British sign language, education & political studies/psychology/sociology, ESOL, children, schools & families services, community leadership/safety, criminal justice, criminology, deaf studies, equality & diversity in the workplace, ethnicity & human rights, education studies, history, lifelong learning, museums & heritage, history, Islamic studies, modern world history, philosophy, politics, public services, religion, culture & society, sociology, volunteering & community action/safety management, professional practice in education/children & young people, social policy, criminology & criminal justice, promoting equality & managing diversity; BA(Hons), BSc(Hons), MA, MSc, PGcert/Dip, DipHE, UnivCer, PGCE, Adv Certt

**School of Forensic & investigative Sciences; www.uclan.ac.uk/schools/forensic.investigative**
archaeology/of death, criminal investigation, osteoarchaeology, chemistry, forensic toxicology, documentary analysis, synthorganic chemistry, fire & disaster studies/rescue services, fire & leadership studies/engineering/investigation, safety engineering, forensic science/anthropology/chemistry/science & criminology/investigation, policing & criminal investigation, airport security management, counter-terrorism, DNA profiling; BA(Hons), BEng, BSc(Hons), FdSc, MPhil, PhD

**School of Health; www.uclan.ac.uk/schools/school of health**
nursing, mental/child/adolescent/psychosocial health, counselling, health & social care, caring for dementia, herbal medicine, homeopathy, paramedic practice, neonatal practice, operating dept practice, physiotherapy, primary care, complementary medicine, counselling, health informatics, integrated healthcare, occupational therapy, personality disorder, psychotherapy, sexual health, professional practice, midwifery; BA(Hons), BSc(Hons), MA, MPhil, PGDip/Cert, PhD

**School of Journalism, Media and Communication; www.uclan.ac.uk/schools/journalism_media_communication**
journalism (international, magazine, newspaper, broadcasting), communication, film/production/studies, film & media, web & multimedia, screenwriting, scriptwriting, digital, media management/technology, photography, English language/literature & linguistics, publishing, rhetorics, TV production, web & multimedia, writing for children; BSc(Hons), BA(Hons), MA, MPhil, PGDip, PGCert, PhD

**Lancashire Business School; www.uclan.ac.uk/schools/lbs**
accounting, advertising, finance, business/administration/information systems, management/studies, digital marketing/media, economics, economic management, enterprise, financial management/analysis/

studies, global business, HRM, HR development, international business/communication/management, logistics & supply chain management/operations, PR, professional practice, operations management, marketing management/communications/fashion, strategic marketing, oil & gas operations management, PR & communications, retail management, sports PR, strategic communication/marketing leadership; BA(Hons), DBA, MA, MBA, MSc, PGDip/Cert

### Lancashire Law School; www.uclan.ac.uk/schools/lancashire_law_school

advanced legal practice, employment/European business law, forensic & legal medicine, international business law, law, criminology, senior status, legal practice, medical law & bioethics; BA(Hons), BA/BSc, LlB, LLM, MA, MPhil, PGDip

### School of Languages and International Studies; www.uclan.ac.uk/schools/languages_and_international

business English, Arabic, French, German, Japanese, Asia Pacific studies, business management in China, international business English, modern languages/for international business, interpretation & translation, TESOL; BA(Hons), MPhil, PhD

### School of Pharmacy and Biomedical Sciences; www.uclan.ac.uk/schools/pharmacy

appl biomolecular sciences – biotechnology/clinical sciences/medicinal chemistry, biomedical sciences, pharmaceutics, biological sciences, healthcare science, pharmacy, physiology, cancer biology & therapy, clinical pharmacy practice, industrial pharmaceutics, pharmaceutical biotechnology; BSc(Hons), MPharm, MSc, PGDip/Cert, PhD

### School of Psychology; www.uclan.ac.uk/schools/psychology

applied/psychology, criminology, forensic psychology, child development, social psychology, sport & exercise psychology, health psychology, neuropsychology; BSc(Hons), GradDip, MSc

### School of Social Work; www.uclan.ac.uk/health/schools/school_of_social_work/

child health & welfare/practice, childcare management, community & social care, mental health practice, safeguarding children, social policy/work, policy & practice; BA(Hons), MA, PGCert

### School of Sport, Tourism and the Outdoors; www.uclan.ac.uk/management/ssto

adventure sports/cricket coaching, event management, exercise & fitness management, hospitality/international hospitality management, hospitality & event management, management in events/hospitality/tourism, nutrition & food science, PE & school sport, international tourism, heritage & attraction management, outdoor leadership, physiotherapy, sport & exercise science, sport development/coaching/development/studies/business management/therapy/marketing, strength & conditioning, elite performance, food quality & safety management, hazard analysis, international festivals & tourism management, sport & exercise biomechanics, sport marketing & management, management of long-term conditions; BSc(Hons), FdA, BA(Hons), Cert, MSc, PGDip/Cert, MA

# UNIVERSITY OF CHESTER
# www.chester.ac.uk

## *Faculty of Applied Sciences; www.chester.ac.uk/faculties#A*

### Dept of Biological Sciences; www.chester.ac.uk/biology

animal behaviour/welfare, animal/zoo management, biomedical sciences, biology, conservation & ecology, wildlife conservation, forensic biology; BSc, MSc, PhD

### Computer Science and Information Systems; www.chester.ac.uk/csis

computer science, computing, interactive digital technology/media, games development, internet, business information systems/management, multimedia technology, programming, information systems; BSc(Hons), MPhil, PhD, FD

### Dept of Mathematics; www.chester.ac.uk/maths

mathematics

### Dept of Clinical Science; www.chester.ac.uk/cens

cardiovascular health & rehabilitation, diabetes, exercise & nutrition science, weight management, human nutrition, neuromuscular therapy, nutrition &

dietetics, osteopathy, public health nutrition, MSc, PhD, MPhil

**Centre for Public Health Research; www.chester.ac.uk/cphr**
public health, research methods; MSc

**Centre for Science Communication**

**Centre for Research into Sport & Society; www.chester.ac.uk/scicom**
sociology of sport & exercise; MSc, PhD

**Dept of Sport & Exercise Science; www.chester.ac.uk/sport**
sport science/development, sport coaching/journalism, fitness health, sport & exercise science; BA, BSc, MSc

## Faculty of Arts & Media; www.chester.ac.uk/faculties#B

**Dept of Art & Design; www.chester.ac.uk/ art & design**
fine art, graphic design, design, photography; BA(Hons), MA, MSc

**Dept of Media; www.chester.ac.uk/media**
advertising, commercial music production, digital photography, radio/TV production, film studies, sports/journalism, media studies; BA(Hons)

**Dept of Performing Arts; www.chester.ac.uk/departments/ performing-arts**
drama, dance & music, pop music, performance practice; BA(Hons), MA

**Chester Centre for Arts & Media**
drama, dance & music, pop music, performance practice

## Faculty of Business, Enterprise & Lifelong Learning; www.chester.ac.uk/ faculties#C

**Chester Business School; www.chester.ac.uk/chester-business-school**
business administration/management/studies, business & management development, business enterprise & lifelong learning/management, accounting, entrepreneurship, information systems, international business, finance, HRM, management, marketing/ communications, PR, tourism & events management, tourism management, strategy; BA(Hons), BA/BSc, FdA, MBA, MPhil, PhD, MBA, DBA, DProfStuds

**Centre for Work Related Studies; Professional Development Unit; Work Based Learning Office; www.chester.ac.uk/ pdu**
work-based & integrated studies; FD, BA, MA

## Faculty of Education & Children's Services; www.chester.ac.uk/education

children & young people, coaching, families, early childhood studies, continuing professional development, education/studies, education (leadership & management/teaching & learning), early years practice/early years professional status, graduate teacher programme, PGCE (primary/secondary/early years), QTS, initial teacher education, teaching assistance, teacher training/primary & early years; BA(Hons), BEd, EdD, FdA, MA, MEd, PGCE

## Faculty of Health and Social Care; www.chester.ac.uk/health

midwifery, nursing, health & social care/commissioning, children, non-medical prescribing, social work, young people & families, public health/nursing, community health studies, advanced practice, mental health practice, art therapy, communicable diseases, endodontology, health improvement & well-being, infection prevention, psychotherapy, method therapy, neonatal clinical practice, occupational health, oncology, applied mental health practice, clinical bariatric practice, eating disorders, global health, intercultural psychotherapy, multi-method therapy, professional education/studies, specialist community public health nursing, specialist practice community, paediatrics, sexual & reproductive health, teaching & learning in clinical practice, youth matters
FD, BA(Hons), BSc(Hons), MA, MSc, PGCert, PhD

## Faculty of Humanities; www.chester.ac.uk/faculties#F

**English; www.chester.ac.uk/english**
creative writing, English/ language & literature, 19th-century literature and culture, modern & contemporary fiction; BA, MA, PhD

**History and Archaeology; www.chester.ac.uk/departments/history-archaeology**
American, British, Irish, world history, military history, archaeology; BA(Hons), MA, MPhil, PhD

**Dept of Modern Languages; www.chester.ac.uk/languages**
European languages & cultures, French, German & Spanish, modern languages; BA(Hons), MA, PGCert/Dip

**Theology & Religious Studies; www.chester.ac.uk/trs**
religious studies, theology, faith & public policy, practical & contextual theology, theology, media, & community; BA(Hons), BTh, Dip HE, FdA, MA, MPhil, MTh, PhD

*Faculty of Social Sciences; www.chester.ac.uk/faculties#G*

**Geography and Development Studies; www.chester.ac.uk/geography**
geography, international development studies, natural hazard/environmental management, housing practice, regeneration, sustainability for community & business; BA(Hons), MA, MSc, PhD, PGDip/Cert

**Dept of Psychology; www.chester.ac.uk/psychology**
psychology, cognitive & behavioural approches, cognitive behavioural therapy, family & child psychology, interpersonal psychology; BA(Hons), BSc(Hons), PhD, MPhil, MSc

**Dept of Social Studies & Counselling; www.chester.ac.uk/scc**
criminology, sociology, politics, therapeutic practice/for psychological trauma, clinical/counselling/skills; BA, BSc, MA, MSc

**Law School; www.chester.ac.uk/law**
law/& business/criminology/politics, contemporary legal studies, family law, criminal justice, human rights & discrimination; LlB, LlM

## UNIVERSITY OF CHICHESTER
## www.chiuni.ac.uk

performance/dance, English, creative writing, cultural history, performance, early childhood studies/years, PGCE (primary, secondary), fine art, history, media production/studies, choral studies, digital film production, film & TV studies, media & cultural studies, music (performance/composition/business/theatre), instrumental/vocal teaching, musical theatre, theatre performance, commercial music, performing arts, psychology, counselling, accounting, finance, business studies, enterprise, management & leadership, event management, finance, HRM, IT management for business, marketing, management, tourism management, international business, social work, social care, sport & exercise science/psychology, strength & conditioning, PE & coaching/ science, biomechanics, physiology, sport development/studies, sport & fitness, community sport coaching, theology & religion; BA(Hons), BSc(Hons), FD, GradDip/Cert, MA, PGCE, MSc, MSW, PhD, MEd, BMus

## CITY UNIVERSITY LONDON
## www.city.ac.uk

*School of of Arts & Social Sciences; www.city.ac.uk/arts_and-social_science*

**Dept of Journalism; www.city.ac.uk/journalism**
broadcast/TV/investigative/magazine/newspaper/science/international/financial/interactive/political journalism, creative writing; BA(Hons), MA, MSc, PhD

**Dept of Creative Practice & Enterprise; www.city.ac.uk/creative-practice-and-enterprise**

**Centre for Music Studies; Centre for Cultural Policy & Management; Centre for Creative Writing, Translation & Publishing Studies**
music, music composition (electroacoustic/instrumental and vocal), music performance, musicology/ethnomusicology, culture studies, cultural & creative industries, cultural policy & management, creative writing (non-fiction/novels/playwriting & screenwriting), electronic publishing, international/publishing

studies, audiovisual translation, legal translation, translating popular culture

### Department of Economics; www.city.ac.uk/economics

accountancy, int business economics, economics, economic evaluation in health care, economic regulation & competition, development/financial/health economics; BSc, MSc, PhD

### Department of International Politics; www.city.ac.uk/intpol

international politics/& sociology, human rights, global political economy, diplomacy & foreign policy; BSc, MA, PhD

### Department of Psychology; www.city.ac.uk/psychology

counselling psychology, health psychology, organizational psychology/organizational behaviour, psychology/& health, BSc, MSc, PhD, DPsych

### Dept of Sociology; www.city.ac.uk/sociology

criminology, criminal justice, food policy, global migration, human rights, international communications & development, media studies, international politics, politics, social research methods, sociology, social media, political communication, transnational media & communication; BEng, BSc(Hons), DPsych, GradDip/Cert, MA, MSc, PhD, ProfDoc

## *Cass Business School; www.cass.city.ac.uk*

### Faculty of Actuarial Science and Insurance; www.cass.city.ac.uk/facact

actuarial management, actuarial science, insurance; BSc(Hons), MSc, Dip, PhD, MPhil

### Faculty of Finance; www.cass.city.ac.uk/facfin

accounting, finance, investment & financial risk management, actuarial management/science, banking & international finance, business studies, insurance & risk management, financial mathematics, mathematical trading & finance, quantitative analysis, real estate, shipping, supply chain & energy, charity accounts, charity marketing & fund-raising, NGO management, voluntary sector management; BSc, MSc, PGDip

### Faculty of Management; www.cass.city.ac.uk/facmana

corporate governance, business studies, energy, trade & finance, European business, information & knowledge management, management, marketing, organisational behaviour & HR management, operations & supply chain management, voluntary sector management, strategy, entrepreneurship; BSc(Hons), MBA, MEb, MPhil, MSc, PGDip, PhD

### School of Engineering and Mathematical Sciences; www.city.ac.uk/sems

aeronautical engineering, air safety management/transport engineering/transport operations/management, aircraft maintenance management, architecture, automotive & motorsport engineering, biomedical engineering, civil engineering, computer systems engineering, construction management, bioengineering with healthcare technology management, computer systems engineering, decision sciences, engineering with management & entrepreneurship, electrical/electronic engineering, energy engineering, energy & environmental technology & economics, maritime operations & management, mathematical science with statistics/computer science, mathematics & finance, mechanical engineering, media communication systems, power systems and energy management, project management with finance & risk, renewable energy & power systems management, statistics, signals & sensor systems, systems & control engineering, telecommunications/& networks, transport systems strategy & systems; BEng, BSc(Hons), MEng, MMath, MPhil, MSc, PgDip, PhD

mathematics, finance, mathematical science with statistics/computer science/finance/economics; BSc, MMath, PhD

## *School of Health Sciences; www.city.ac.uk/health*

human communication, clinical/optometry, radiography (diagnostic imaging/oncology), speech & language therapy, health sciences, health services e-learning, primary care (practice nursing), professional practice (child & youth studies, policing of public services), advanced practice in health and social care (adult mental health/child and adolescent mental health/management of chronic conditions and long-term care/midwifery/nursing – adult, child and neonatal/ophthalmic nursing/optometry/radiotherapy/speech, language & communication), clinical optometry, clinical research, health management (in strategic management & leadership), health policy, health services research, professional practice (language and communication), medical ultrasound, public health, radiography, language &

communication, public health (school nursing, health visiting, district nursing), food policy/food & nutrition policy, health management in strategic management & leadership, health policy, health services research, medical ultrasound, nuclear medicine technology, ophthalmic dispensing, public service management, speech & language therapy, working with children & young people; FD, BSc(Hons), MSc, DipHE, PGDip, MPhil, PhD, Grad Dip, Cert

**School of Informatics; www.soi.city.ac.uk**
business computing systems, adv/computer science, artificial intelligence, games technology, information systems, software engineering, business systems analysis & design, computer games technology, e-business systems, electronic publishing, health informatics, information management in culture sector, information science/security & management, information systems & technology, information, creativity & leadership, library science, software engineering; MSc, PhD, MPhil, BSc(Hons), MA, MScMII, MInnov

**City Law School; www.city.ac.uk/law**
law, city litigation & dispute resolution, int banking & finance/commercial/competition law/energy litigation, maritime law, energy law, competition law, criminal litigation, dispute resolution, EU commercial law, innovation, civil litigation & dispute resolution, creativity & leadership, legal practice, professional legal practice/study, public international law; LlB, LlM, MPhil, PhD, MJur, Grad Dip

## *Degrees validated by City University offered at:*

### GUILDHALL SCHOOL OF MUSIC & DRAMA
www.gsmd.ac.uk

acting, training actors, design realisation, music, music composition, music therapy, leadership, performance, singing, electronic music, technical theatre arts, stage management; BA(Hons), BMus, MA, MMA/DMA, MMP, MMus, MPerf, PGDip

### SCHOOL OF PSYCHOTHERAPY & COUNSELLING PSYCHOLOGY AT REGENT'S COLLEGE
www.spc.ac.uk

counselling, psychology, psychotherapy, creative leadership, integrative psychotherapy, existential phenomiological counselling psychology; DCounsPsy, MA, MPhil/PhD, PGDip, DPysch

### THE NORDOFF-ROBBINS MUSIC THERAPY CENTRE
www.nordoff-robbins.org.uk

music therapy, music, health, society, MMusTherapy, PGDip, MPhil, PhD, DPsych

### TRINITY LABAN CONSERVATOIRE OF MUSIC & DANCE
www.laban.org

choreography, dance, dance studies/theatre/performance/science, contemporary dance, dance: the body in performance, music, music theatre, jazz composition, music in education, performance/design, composition, design creative practice, PGCE; BA(Hons), MA, MPhil, MSc, PGDipls, PhD

## COVENTRY UNIVERSITY
## www.coventry.ac.uk

### *Faculty of Business, Environment and Society*

#### Coventry Business School

business & human resource management, human resource management, international human resource management; BA(Hons), MA, MSc

#### Department of English and Languages

English/& creative writing/& journalism/& TEFL, English language teaching (ELT), French/& business/& English/& international relations/& Spanish/& TEFL, languages for business, Spanish/& business/& English/& international relations/& TEFL; BA(Hons), MA

#### Coventry Law School

commercial law, international corporate governance, international law, international business law, law; LLB(Hons), LLM

#### Geography, Environment & Disaster Management; www.coventry.ac.uk/life-on-campus/faculties-and-schools/faculty-of-business-environment-and-society/schools-and-departments/department-of-geography-environment-and-disaster-management

disaster management/& emergency planning, emergency planning & management, environmental management, food security management, geography/& natural hazards, international disaster management, international tourism management, oil & gas management, oil, gas & energy management, petroleum & environmental technology; BA(Hons), BSc(Hons), MSc, PgDip, PgCert

#### International Studies and Social Science

commercial law, conflict resolution skills, diplomacy, law & global change, history, international law, international relations, maritime security, peace & reconciliation studies, peacebuilding, politics/& history, sociology/& criminology/& psychology, terrorism, international crime & global security; BA(Hons), LLB(Hons), MA, PgCert

## CRANFIELD UNIVERSITY
## www.cranfield.ac.uk

#### School of Applied Sciences; www.cranfield.ac.uk/sas

manufacturing, materials & nanotechnology design, motorsport, business & IS, design, economics & management, engineering, environment & water, energy & offshore, ultraprecision techniques, welding; EngD, MPhil, MSc, MTech, PhD

#### Cranfield Defence and Security; www.cranfield.ac.uk/cds

cyberdefence & information assurance, defence acquisition management, defence/leadership/sensors & data/simulation & modelling, explosives ordnance eng, forensic archaeology & anthropology/ballistics/computing/engineering & science/investigation, guided weapons, gun systems design, information capability management/operations, international defence & security/marketing, military aerospace & airworthiness/electronic systems/OR/vehicle technology, programme & project management, resilience, scientific computation, security sector management, systems engineering for defence capability, through-life system sustainment, vehicle & weapons engineering; EngD, MSc, PGDip/Cert, PhD

#### School of Engineering; www.cranfield.ac.uk/soe

advanced lightweight structures and impact, aeronatics/human & safety factors aerospace dynamics, adv mechanical engineering, aerodynamics, flight dynamics, aerospace vehicle design, aircraft design/engineering, airport planning and management, air transport management, executive air transport management, airworthiness, astronautics and space engineering, automotive engineering, autonomous vehicle dynamics and control, computational fluid dynamics/& software techniques, engineering/mechatronics, human factors and safety assessment in aeronautics, thermal power, aerospace propulsion, gas turbine technology, power, propulsion and the environment, rotating machinery design/engineering and management, thermal power; EngD, MSc, PhD, PGCert/Dip

### Cranfield Health; www.cranfield.ac.uk/health

applied bioinformatics, analytical biotechnology, clinical research/information/management, health administration, medical diagnostics/technology, nanomedicine, pharmocovigilance data, translational medicine, environment & health, food chain systems, molecular medicine, quality management, toxicology & epidemiology, quality management; DM, MSc

### Cranfield School of Management; www.cranfield.ac.uk/som

finance & management, international HRM, managing organizational performance, logistics & supply chain management, management development, programme & project management, retail management, strategic marketing; DBA, MBA, MSc, PhD

## UNIVERSITY FOR THE CREATIVE ARTS
## www.ucreative.ac.uk (at Canterbury, Epsom, Farnham, Maidstone and Rochester)

architecture/design, arts & animation, arts management, broadcast media, creative industries management, curatorial practice, design for performance & events, design, innovation & brand management, digital communications/ design, fine art, graphic design, fashion promotion & imaging/design/journalism/textiles/marketing/accessories/atelier/retail management, fashion & lifestyle, music/sports journalism, fine art, contemporary jewellery, illustration, interior architecture & design, textiles, product design, advertising & brand communication, computer games arts, silversmithing, goldsmithing & jewellery, CG arts & animation, photography, creative arts for theatre & film, contemporary arts(ceramics or glass & jewellery), urban design; BA(Hons), FD, Grad Dip, MA, MPhil, PGCert, PhD

## UNIVERSITY OF CUMBRIA
## www.cumbria.ac.uk

### *Faculty of the Arts, Business & Science; www.cumbria.ac.uk/about us/faculties/ABS*

Creative Arts: advertising & media, contemporary fine art, wildlife & media, art of games des, film & TV production, fine art, graphic design, illustration, photography

Business School: accounting & finance, business entrepreneurship and computing innovations, business management and e-commerce/, finance and accounting, computing and IT, international business management, international marketing management, professional practice for business, retail marketing management, diversity and equality management, events leadership and management, innovative technology solutions, international business/management, international marketing management, leadership and management in policing, leadership and sustainability

Humanities: children's ministry, English/& creative writing/Journalism, mass communications, practical theology, religious studies

Law & Social Science: criminology & law/social science, law, youth & community work

Forestry & Outdoor: adventure media, animal conservation science, conservation biology, forest ecosystems management, outdoor & experiential learning, outdoor education/studies, forestry, wildlife & media

Performance: dance/drama/musical theatre performance, drama, event management, performing arts, performance, festivals & events, production

Policing: policing, investigation & criminology

Science & Engineering: applied sciences, forensic science, sustainable energy technology; BA(Hons), BSc(Hons), FdA, MBA, MA, PGDip/Cert

### *Faculty of Education; www.cumbria.ac.uk/about us/faculties/ FacultyEducation*

early years/QTS, early childhood studies, primary ed (QTS), inclusive ed/special needs, teaching, learning support, working with children & families, PGCE, general/lower primary (QTS), secondary with QTS in range of subjects, TESOL, QTS Direct, assessment, academic practice, education, graduate teacher programme; BA(Hons), MA, PGDip/Cert, PGCE

### *Faculty of Health, Wellbeing, Social Work & Sport; www.cumbria.ac.uk/about us/ facultyofHealthWellbeing*

adv nurse practitioner, coaching & sport development, adv practice/cognitive behaviour therapy, community special practice (district nursing/general practice nursing), developing paramedic practice, adv practice in health & social care, early childhood studies, midwifery, mental health practice, non-medical prescribing, nursing (adult/child/learning disabilities/mental health), nursing practice, occupational health/nursing, physiotherapy, occupational therapy, radiology, children's & adolescent mental health, counselling & psychotherapy, evidence-based psychological approaches, higher specialist social work (mental health), managing health & social care, specialist community public health nursing, diagnostic radiography, medical imaging, magnetic resonance, ultrasound, physical activity & health development, sport massage therapy, sport/coaching & sport development, sport & exercise science/ therapy, PE, working with children & families; BA, BSc(Hons), GradDip, MA, MSc, PgC, UC, UAD, DipHE, FdA, MPhil, PhD

## DE MONTFORT UNIVERSITY
## www.dmu.ac.uk

### Leicester Business School; www.dmu.ac.uk/about-dmu/schools-and-departments/leicester-business-school

advertising & PR management, accounting & business management, banking & finance, business man/ studies/information systems, entrepreneurship, finance & investment, forensic accounting, international marketing/business & global enterprise/corporate social responsibility/PR/HRM/management, Islamic banking & finance, lean operations management, management of HR, management studies, project management, public finance, risk management, strategic marketing BA(Hons), BSc(Hons), DipHE, GDL/CPE, HND, MA, MPhil, MBA, MSc, PGDip/ Cert, PhD

### Leicester De Montfort School of Law; www.dmu.ac.uk/about-dmu/schools-and-departments/leicester-de-montfort-law-school/leicester-de-montfort-law-school

law, criminology/law & criminal justice, HR & social justice, business law, environmental law, international business/human rights law, legal practice, sports law, medical law, food law; LlB(Hons), LlM, LPC, DCCJ, MA, PGDip/Cert

### Leicester School of Architecture; www.dmu.ac.uk/about-dmu/schools-and-departments/leicester-school-of-architecture/leicester-school-of-architecture

architecture, architectural design/practice; BA, BArch, PGDip, MA

### School of Arts; www.dmu.ac.uk/about-dmu/schools-and-departments/school-of-arts

art & design, animation, arts & festival management, dance, drama studies, fine art, music, technology & innovation/performance, performing arts, cultural events management, independent study in art & design/humanities; BA(Hons), MA, MSc

### School of Design; www.dmu.ac.uk/about-dmu/schools-and-departments/school-of design

design crafts/production, furniture/interior/product design, multimedia design, design entrepreneurship/innovation/management; BA(Hons), MDes, MA

**School of Fashion & Textiles; www.dmu.ac.uk/about-dmu/schools-and-departments/school-of fashion-and-textiles**
contour fashion, fashion design/buying/fabrics & accessories, footwear design, textile design, fashion & bodywear; BA(Hons), MA

**School of Humanities; www.dmu.ac.uk/about-dmu/schools-and-departments/school-of-humanities**
creative writing, English/language, history, English language teaching, sports history & culture, management, law and humanities of sport; BA(Hons), MA, PGDip

**School of Media & Communication; www.dmu.ac.uk/about-dmu/schools-and-departments/school-of-media-and-communication**
animation design, creative writing, film studies, game art design, graphic design, illustration, e-media, journalism, media & communication, photography & video, creative technologies, independent study/art & design/humanities, international journalism/PR, TV & film production/scriptwriting, visual journalism & documentary photography; BA(Hons), FdA, MA, MSc

**Institute of Creative Technologies; www.ioct.ac.uk**
creative technologies; Masters, PhD

**Dept of Computer Technology; www.dmu.ac.uk/about-dmu/schools-and-departments/department-of-computer-technology**
audio & recording technology, business information systems, computer science/security, computer games programming, computing, information technology, software engineering, forensic computing; BSc(Hons), MSc

**Dept of Engineering; www.dmu.ac.uk/about-dmu/schools-and-departments/department-of-engineering**
mechanical engineering, mechatronics, communications engineering, electrical & electronic engineering, intelligent systems & robotics, microelectronics & nanotechnology, rapid production development; BSc(Hons), BEng(Hons), MSc

**Dept of Informatics; www.dmu.ac.uk/about-dmu/schools-and-departments/department-of-informatics**
business informatics/information systems, computing for business, information & communications technology, artificial intelligence, robotics, computer games programming, communications engineering, data mining, information & computing technology, business intelligent systems; BSc(Hons), MSc

**Dept of Media Technology; www.dmu.ac.uk/about-dmu/schools-and-departments/department-of-media-technology**
audio recording/creative sound/music technology, games technology, multimedia computing, media production/technology, music, technology & innovation/performance; BSc(Hons), MSc

**Institute of Energy & Sustainable Development; www.iesd.dme.ac.uk**
climate change & sustainable development, energy & sustainability management, energy & industrial sustainability; MSc

**School of Allied Health Sciences; www.dmu.ac.uk/about-dmu/schools-and-departments/school-of-allied-health-sciences**
speech & language therapy (human communication), biomedical science, healthcare science (audiology), medical science/education, speech & language therapy; BSc(Hons), PGDip/Cert, MSc

**School of Applied Social Sciences; www.dmu.ac.uk/about-dmu/schools-and-departments/school-of-applied-social-sciences**
children, families & community health, criminology & criminal justice, education studies, health studies, policing studies, psychology, sociology, social work, youth work & community development; BA(Hons), BSc(Hons), FD, MSc, PGDip/Cert

**School of Nursing & Midwifery; www.dmu.ac.uk/about-dmu/schools-and-departments/school-of-nursing-and midwifery**
nursing, midwifery, palliative care; BSc(Hons), RSHDip

#### School of Pharmacy; www.dmu.ac.uk/about-dmu/schools-and-departments/school-of-pharmacy

pharmacy, forensic science, pharmaceutical & cosmetic science, pharmaceutical technology/quality by design; BSc(Hons), MPharm, MSc

## UNIVERSITY OF DERBY
## www.derby.ac.uk

### *Faculty of Art, Design, and Technology; www.derby.ac.uk/adt*

Art & Design: animation, fashion, fine art, film & TV/video production, commercial/photography, textiles, visual communication, graphic design, illustration; Humanities: American studies, creative writing, English, film & TV, horror & transgression, history, media, theatre; Technology: architecture & built environment, sustainable architecture & healthy buildings, control & instrumentation, construction project management, electrical/electronic/mechanical/civil/manufacturing engineering, construction, product design, professional engineering, music/production & media technology, motorsport, sustainable design & innovation; BA(Hons), MDes, PhD, Univ Cert/Dip, BEng, FdSc/Eng

### *Faculty of Business, Computing and Law; www.derby.ac.uk/bcl*

#### Derbyshire Business School; www.derby.ac.uk/dbs

accountancy & finance, business, coaching, enterprise, HRM, leadership, marketing, purchasing & supply, management, strategy

#### Law & Criminology; www.derby.ac.uk/law

law, commercial/corporate & financial law, international/protection of human rights & personal freedom, intellectual property & information technology/comparative law, transnational criminal/oil, gas & energy law, criminology, crime & justice, legal practice

#### Computing & Mathematics; www.derby.ac.uk/computing

computer forensics, computer games modelling & animation/programming, computer science/networks, information technology/security, networks & security, mobile device software development, computer graphics production, investment/mathematics/with education; BA(Hons), BSc(Hons), FD, LlBHons, LlM, MA, MPhil/PhD, MSc, PGDip/Cert

### *Faculty of Education, Health and Sciences; www.derby.ac.uk/ehs*

#### Education & Social Sciences; www.derby.ac.uk/education

applied community & youth work, child & youth work, education studies/guidance, CPD, teacher education, early childhood/years/studies, children's & young people's services, sociology, social studies, leadership, PGCE (primary/secondary education with QTS)

#### Health & Social Care; www.derby.ac.uk/health

advanced practice, applied social work, arts therapy, cognitive behaviour therapy, counselling, creative expression therapy, dance/therapy & movement studies, mentoring, nursing studies (adult/mental health/public health), nursing & healthcare practice, mental health & therapeutic practice/wellbeing, community specialist practitioner, long term conditions, non-medical prescribing, LBR modules, occupational therapy, health & social care practice, radiography, systematic psychotherapy

#### Science; www.derby.ac.uk/science

applied petroleum geoscience, biological science, biology, ergonomics, geography, geology, conservation biology, criminology, environmental science/health/management, forensic science, psychology, sport & exercise science, zoology; Adv Dip, BA(Hons), BEd, BSc(Hons), EdD, FdA, HNC/HND, jtHons, MA, MSC, PGCert/Dip, PGCE, PhD, Univ Cert/Dip, MPhil

## UNIVERSITY CENTRE DONCASTER
## www.don.ac.uk/dbs

animation & games/illustration, applied social science, building services, business management, construction, counselling, criminal justice, dance/practice & theatre, early years/working with children & young people, early childhood studies, education, English, fashion & textiles, fim & TV, fine art, games art, graphic design, integrative technology, moving image production, creative music technology, performance, sport & exercise/fitness/health science, business administration, HRM, relationship therapy, psychosexual therapy, education, innovation & enterprise; BA(Hons), BSc(Hons), MBA, MSc, PGDip/Cert, MA, PGCE, FdA

## UNIVERSITY OF DUNDEE
## www.dundee.ac.uk

### *College of Art, Sciences and Engineering; www.dundee.ac.uk/case*

#### School of Computing; www.computing.dundee.ac.uk

applied computing, business intelligence/computing, computing/science/research, data science, information technology & international business, human-computer interaction, user experience engineering, vision & imaging computing

#### Duncan of Jordanstone College of Art and Design; www.dundee.ac.uk/djcad

animation & visualisation/bivisual art, art & humanities, art philosophy, graphic design, interior/environmental/jewellery & metal/textiles design, digital interaction design, exhibitions, fine art, illustration, media arts & imaging, forensic/media/medical art, product design, time-based art & digital film, design ethnology

#### School of Engineering, Physics and Mathematics; www.dundee.ac.uk/eps

biomedical engineering, civil engineering/& management, concrete engineering & environmental management, construction enterprise management, design for medical technology, electronic & electrical engineering, financial economics, physics, electronic circuit design & manufacture, earthquake & offshore geotechnical engineering, mathematics ( mechatronics, product design, renewable energy & environmental modelling, structural engineering; BEng, BSc, CertHE, DipHE, MArch, MEng, MA, MSc, MSci, PhD, PGDE, PGDip

### *College of Arts and Social Sciences; www.dundee.ac.uk/artsoc*

#### School of Business; www.dundee.ac.uk/business

accountancy, finance, business management/economics, international/accounting/HRM/marketing/finance/business, financial/economics, strategic financial management; BSc, BAcc, BFin, MA, MSc, PGDip

#### Continuing Education; www.dundee.ac.uk/conted

CPD, communication & languages, community outreach; MACert, Dip

#### School of Education, Social Work and Community Education; www.dundee.ac.uk/eswce

childhood practice, community learning & development, education (primary), HE (adult literacies), professional development (community regeneration, leadership & management), healthcare/integrated services, volunteering, social work, adult/child care & protection, applied professional studies: adult/child care & protection, community learning & development/planning, equality & social inclusion, leadership & organisational development, policing studies, practice learning, tertiary education, education, leading learning & teaching, inclusion & learner support, nursery/early education, professional practice, pupil care & support, adult literacies, primary, science (maths/sciences), educational psychology, social work, teaching/(FE)/HE), volunteering management; BA/BA(Hons), Dip, Cert, PGCert, Masters, PGDE, MSc, MA, PhD, MPhil, ProfDoc, DCLD, DEd, DSW, DEdPsych

**Interdisciplinary Disability Research Institute (IDRIS)**
**Institute for Research and Innovation in Social Services (IRISS)**

## School of the Environment; www.dundee.ac.uk/socialsciences

Architecture: architecture, architectural humanity/ practice, technology, communication, environment, renewable energy & sustainable building, adv sustainability of built environment, adv sustainable urbanism
Environmental Science: environmental science, geography
Geography: geography ( welfare geography, remote sensing, catchment, hydrology & hydrology
Town & Regional Planning: city planning & regeneration, environmental sustainability, local & regional economic development, geography & planning, community regeneration, spatial planning, town & country/regional planning, maritime; BSc, MA, BArch, MArch

## School of Humanities; www.dundee.ac.uk/ humanities

**American Studies**
American studies ( www.dundee.ac.uk/cias
archives & records management/information rights, family & local history, digital records keeping, records management & information rights, CPD
**Languages; www.dundee.ac.uk/languagesstudies**
French, German, Spanish, European languages & cultures, European studies
**English; www.dundee.ac.uk/English**
English, English and film studies ( literature, women, comic & graphic novels, comics studies, theatre studies, writing practice, gender, culture & society, creative writing
**European Studies**
interdisciplinary courses, practical languages (French, German, Spanish)
**History; www.dundee.ac.uk/history**
early America, European history, Greater Britain in the twentieth century, history, Scottish/English/ church history, urban and cultural history, global empires, family & local history
**Philosophy; www.dundee.ac.uk/philosophy**
European philosophy, philosophy/& literature, continental/recent analytic philosophy, women, culture & society, continental philosophy
**Politics; www.dundee.ac.uk/politics**
politics, European politics, international relations & politics/geopolitics, international politics & security; MA(Hons), MLitt, MSc

## School of Law; www.dundee.ac.uk/law

commercial & international commercial law, corporate & commercial law, competition & European private international law, international criminal justice & human rights, environmental law & sustainable development, family law, European law, law & governance, public law, Scottish/English law, international dispute resolution; LlB, LlM, PhD
**Graduate School of Natural Resources Law, Policy and Management; www.dundee.ac.uk/postgradschool**
mineral resource management, international oil & gas management
**UNESCO Centre for Water Law, Policy and Science**
water law; PGCert, LlM, PhD
**Centre for Petroleum, & Mineral Law & Policy; www.dundee.ac.uk/cepmlp**
climate change & energy law and policy, international business law & transactions/ dispute resolution & management, mineral law, natural resources law, petroleum law/taxation and finance, energy economics, mineral/natural resources/petroleum law, international mineral resources/oil & gas management, climate change economics & policy, energy studies (energy and the environment/energy economics/ energy finance/energy policy/oil & gas economics); MBA, MSc

## School of Psychology; www.dundee.ac.uk/ psychology

psychology, visual/cognition, eye movements, language & communication, psychological therapy, abnormal & clinical psychology; BA(Hons), MA(Hons), PhD

# *College of Life Sciences; www.lifesci.dundee.ac.uk*

anatomical sciences, anatomy & human identification, biochemistry, biomedical/biological sciences, drug discovery, cancer cell signalling & immunisation, biology, forensic anthropology/facial identification, human anatomy, medical art, microbiology, molecular biology/microbiology, molecular genetics, neuroscience, pharmacology, physiological sciences, plant science, sports biomedicine; BSc(Hons), MRes, MSc, PhD

### Schools of Research

**Biological Chemistry & Drug Discovery (CLS); www.lifesci.dundee.ac.uk/bcdd**
**Div of Cell and Developmental Biology; www.lifesci.dundee.ac.uk/cdb**
**Div of Cell Signalling & Immunology; www.lifesci.dundee.ac.uk/csi**
**Drug Discovery Unit; www.drugdiscovery.ac.uk**
**Gene Regulation & Expression; www.lifescience.dundee.ac.uk/gre**
**Molecular Microbiology; www.lifesci.dundee.ac.uk/mmb**
**Div of Molecular Medicine; www.lifesci.dundee.ac.uk/mm**
**Div of Plant Sciences; www.lifesci.dundee.ac.uk/pl**
**Scottish Institute of Cell signalling**

## *College of Medicine, Dentistry and Nursing; www.dundee.ac.uk/cmdn*

premedical & medical courses, cardiovascular disease & diabetes, health skills, immunology, medical science, medicine, molecular medicine, neuroscience, oncology, trauma surgery, orthopaedic and rehabilitation technology, palliative care, population science, primary care, psychiatry cognitive behavioural psychotherapy, psychological therapy in primary care, public health, skin disease, advanced practice (nursing), clinical audit and research for health care professionals, cognitive behavioural psychotherapy, nursing, medical education, minimal access surgery, motion analysis, cancer biology, health and social care, oral cancer, applied health statistics, global health and wellbeing, orthodontics, psychological therapy in primary care, quality improvement, sports and biomechanical medicine, orthopaedic and rehabilitation technology, orthopaedic surgery, palliative care, prosthodontics, public health (palliative care research)

### School of Dentistry; www.dundee.ac.uk/dentalschool

oral health science, prosthodontics, dental surgery, cancer biology, oral cancer, forensic odontology

### School of Nursing and Midwifery; www.dundee.ac.uk/medden

advanced practice, adult/child/mental health nursing, palliative care, midwifery, global health & well-being, health & social care, infection prevention & control, health studies, community health nursing, mental health, physiotherapeutics, quality management, clinical assessment governance, CPD, numerous Master modules

IMSc, MRes, Masters, Dip, Cert, MCHOrth, MDSc, BDS, BHealthN, BM, BMSc, BN, BSc, DDSc, DipCert, MA, MBChB, MChOrth, MD, MDSc, MFM, MMAS, MMSc, MNurs, MPH, MPhil, MSc, MSSc

### School of Medicine Institutes

Centre for Biomedical Science & Public Health; Centre for Medical Education; Centre for Undergraduate Medicine; Clinical Skills Centre; CLS/MRI Molecular Medicine; Cuschieri Skills Centre; Division of Cancer Research; Division of Cardiovascular & Diabetes Medicine; Division of Neuroscience; Division of Population Health Sciences; Division of Imaging & Technology; Medical Education Institute; Medical Research Institute

# DURHAM UNIVERSITY
# www.dur.ac.uk

## *Faculty of Arts and Humanities; www.dur.ac.uk /arts.humanities*

### Dept of Classics and Ancient History; www.dur.ac.uk/classics

ancient history & archaeology, ancient history, classics, classical past, ancient, medieval & modern history, ancient epic/histiography/philosophy, Greece, Rome & the Near East

### Dept of English Studies; www.dur.ac.uk/english.studies

English literature/history/philosophy, medieval & Renaissance literary studies, poetry, 20th-century literary studies, Victorian & romantic literary studies, educational studies/English literature

### English Language Centre; www.dur.ac.uk/englishlanguage

English past & present, English language teaching, English & its social context, TESOL, applied language studies

### Dept of History; www.dur.ac.uk/history

history, medieval history, early modern/modern history, research methods (economic and social history), ancient history

### Dept of Music; www.dur.ac.uk/music

music, ethnomusicology, composition, performance, musicology

### School of Modern Languages and Cultures; www.dur.ac.uk/mlac

Arabic/English translation & interpreting, arts & social sciences, medieval and Renaissance studies, French, German, Hispanic studies, Italian, Russian, Chinese studies, modern languages & history, Arabic-English translation & interpreting, translation studies, culture & difference

### Dept of Philosophy; www.dur.ac.uk/philosophy

philosophy ( philosophy of science & medicine, metaphysics, ethics, aesthetics

### Dept of Theology and Religion; www.dur.ac.uk/theology.religion

biblical studies, Christian theology (Anglican, Catholic studies), faith & globalisation, historical & systemic theology, study religions, Jewish studies, religion and society, spirituality, theology & religion; BA(Hons), GDip, MA, MLitt, MMus, MTh, PhD

## *Faculty of Science; www.dur.ac.uk/science.faculty*

### School of Biological and Biomedical Sciences; www.dur.ac.uk/biological.sciences

biology, biomedical sciences, biological sciences, biosciences, cell biology, ecology, molecular biology & biochemistry

### Dept of Chemistry; www.dur.ac.uk/chemistry

chemistry ( dynamics, structural chemistry, natural science

### Dept of Engineering and Computer Science; www.dur.ac.uk/ecs/computing.science

advanced software engineering, aeronautical engineering, civil/electronic/mechanical/electrical engineering, communications engineering, computer science, design & operations, general engineering, internet and distributed systems technologies, internet systems and e-business, new and renewable energy, design & operations engineering, software engineering management

### Dept of Earth Sciences; www.dur.ac.uk/earth.sciences

earth sciences, climate & environmental change, geohazards, the solid earth, geology, resources & waste, geology, natural sciences, geophysics, environmental/geosciences

### Dept of Mathematical Sciences; www.dur.ac.uk/mathematical.sciences

mathematics, mathematical sciences, particles, strings & cosmology

### Dept of Physics; www.dur.ac.uk/physics

physics, astronomy, theoretical physics, particles, strings & cosmology, natural sciences

### Dept of Psychology; www.dur.ac.uk/psychology

developmental/cognitive neuroscience, developmental psychopathology, applied/psychology, research methods; BA(Hons), BEng, BSc(Hons), MA, MChem, MEng, MMath, MPhil, MPhys, MSc, MSci, PhD

## *Faculty of Social Science and Health; www.dur.ac.uk/science.health*

### School of Applied Social Sciences; www.dur.ac.uk/sass

criminology & criminal justice, anthropology & sociology, social policy, social work, society & politics, social research, managing community practice/youth work practice, community and youth work, sociology/with law, sport, exercise & physical activity

### Dept of Anthropology; www.dur.ac.uk/anthropology

anthropology/& archaeology/sociology, development/evolutionary anthropology, health and human sciences, medical anthropology, well-being, sustainability, culture & development anthropology, energy & society, sociocultural anthropology

### Dept of Archaeology; www.dur.ac.uk/archaeology

archaeology/& ancient civilizations/history/prehistoric/Roman/Egypt/ancient India/near East/intercultural heritage management, conservation of archaeological & museum objects, museums & artefacts, palaeopathology, archaeological science, natural sciences

### Durham Business School; www.dur.ac.uk/dbs

accounting & finance/management, business finance/economic/& marketing, client management, corporate & international finance, economics, enterprise management, environmental & natural resource economics, experimental economics, entrepreneurship, financial accounting, international business management investment/banking & finance/money, finance & investment, global finance, HRM, Islamic finance, leadership & management, management accounting, sponsorship, strategy and organization, strategic marketing, philosophy, politics & economics

### School of Education; www.dur.ac.uk/education

educational assessment, education studies, initial training, PGCE primary education with QTS, secondary education, intercultural education & internationalism, history of art, maths/science education, practice of education, teaching A levels, technically enhanced education

### Dept of Geography; www.dur.ac.uk/geo

risk & environmental hazards, geography, contemporary human geography, research methods, natural science, risk, health & public policy, risk & security

### School of Government and International Affairs; www.dur.ac.uk/sgia

Arab world studies, defence, development, diplomacy, conflict prevention & security, global politics, international relations/studies, Islamic finance, economics, philosophy/& politics; BA(Hons), DBA, EdD, MA, MA(Ed), MBA, MAnth, MSc, MScW, PGCE, PGCert/Dip, PhD

### Durham Law School; www.dur.ac.uk

European trade/international trade & commercial law, law, society & law, legal studies

### School of Medicine, Pharmacy www.dur.ac.uk/school.health

clinical management, global health, health research methods, philosophy of science, interdisciplinary mental health, medical education, pharmacy, public policy and health, spirituality theology & health; BA(Hons), BA(Ed), BSc(Ed), BSc(Hons), Cert Leg Stud, LlB, LlM, MA, MBBS, MPhil, PGCert, PGCert/Dip, PGCE, PhD, MA, MPharm, MJur

## *Degrees validated by Durham University offered at:*

---

## CRANMER HALL, ST JOHN'S COLLEGE
www.cranmerhall.com

theology and ministry; BA, MA, diploma/certificate, Doc

---

## NEW COLLEGE DURHAM
www.newdur.ac.uk

education, podiatry, applied health & social care, public health, counselling, management & administration in the public sector; BA(Hons), BSc(Hons), FD, numerous non-graduate courses

---

## ROYAL ACADEMY OF DANCE
www.rad.org.uk

ballet education, ballet teaching studies, Benesh, dance education, movement notation; BA(Hons), Dip/CertHE, MTeach(Dance), licenciate

## USHAW COLLEGE
www.ushaw.ac.uk

theology & ministry; BA, Certs, Dipls, MA, PGCert/ Dip

## UNIVERSITY OF EAST ANGLIA
**www.uea.ac.uk**

### *Faculty of Arts and Humanities; www.uea.ac.uk/hum*

**American Studies; www.uea.ac.uk/ams**
American studies/literature, & American history/ English history/politics, & creative writing

**School of World Art & Museum Studies; www.uea.ac.uk/art**
archaeology, anthropology & art history, arts of Africa, Oceana & the Americas, creative entrepreneurship, film studies & art history, history of art & literature, gallery & museum studies, history of art, cultural heritage & international development/ museum studies

**School of Film & Television Studies; www.uea.ac.uk/ftv**
film & TV studies, film & English/American studies, media studies, TV & creative practice, film archives

**School of History; www.uea.ac.uk/his**
modern history, history, modern British history, history & politics/languages/landscape, medieval/ modern European history, environmental science & humanities

**School of Literature, Drama & Creative Writing; www.uea.ac.uk/lit**
biography & creative non-fiction, creative entrepreneurship, creative writing – poetry/prose/scriptwriting, culture & modernity, drama, scriptwriting & performance, English & American literature, critical writing, literary translation, literature & history, medieval & early modern textual cultures, theatre direction, writing the modern world

**School of Language and Communication Studies; www.uea.ac.uk/lcs**
cross-cultural communication/business & management, language studies, international development, film & TV, French, media, Spanish, Japanese, applied translation studies, language & conflict in intercultural communication

**School of Music; www.uea.ac.uk/mus**
music, music & technology, creative entrepreneurship, performance, conducting

**School of Philosophy; www.uea.ac.uk/ philosophy**
philosophy, philosophy & history/film studies/English literature, environmental sciences & humanities

**School of Political, Social and International Studies; www.uea.ac.uk/psi**
culture, literature, broadcast journalism, European studies/politics, international relations & politics/ European politics/modern history, media & cultural/ culture & society, philosophy & politics, politics & economics of public choice, international/public policy & management, social & political theory, society, culture & media; BA(Hons), MA, MMus, MPhil, PGDip, PhD, MRes

### *Faculty of Health; www.uea.ac.uk/foh*

**School of Allied Health Professions; www.uea.ac.uk/ahp**
occupational therapy, physiotherapy, speech & language therapy, clinical education, musculoskeletal research & practice, stroke recovery

**Norwich Medical School; www.uea.ac.uk/ medicine**
medicine, surgery, clinical science/research, cognitive behavioural therapy, coloproctology, health economics/research, onoplastic breast surgery, regional anaesthesia, health economics/research, CPD (numerous topics)

**School of Nursing Sciences; www.uea.ac.uk/nursing sciences**
acute, children's palliative care, critical and emergency practice, midwifery, nursing (adult, children's, learning disabilities), medicine management/mental health, nurse practitioner, operating department practice, HE community healthcare, sport & exercise injuries, advanced practitioner, emergency care

practitioner, midwife, nurse, occupational therapy, pharmacist, physiotherapist, neonatal nurse, mental health, paramedic, innovation for clinical practitioners, dementia care, clinical education, clinical research
BA(Hons), BSc(Hons), ClinPsyD, DipHE, FD, MBBS, MClinEd, MD, MHeaRes, MPhil, MSc, PGDip, PhD

## Faculty of Science; www.uea.ac.uk/sci

### School of Actuarial Science; www.uea.ac.uk/actuarial-science
actuarial science, business statistics

### School of Biological Sciences; www.uea.ac.uk/biological-sciences
biochemistry, biological sciences, biomedicine, ecology, microbiology, genetics, applied ecology & conservation, plant science, molecular medicine, plant genetics & plant improvement

### School of Chemistry Science; www.uea.ac.uk/chemistry
chemistry, adv organic chemistry, biological and medicinal chemistry, chemical & forensic physics, chemical sciences, forensic & investigational chemistry

### School of Computing Science; www.uea.ac.uk/computing
actuarial sciences, applied/advanced computing/ science, business information systems, business statistics, computational biology, computer graphics/systems engineering/science, computing for business, games development, information systems, knowledge discovery & data mining, software engineering, statistics

### School of Environmental Sciences; www.uea.ac.uk/env
applied ecology, environmental sciences, atmospheric sciences, climate change/science, environmental assessment & management/chemistry/earth sciences, environmental geography & international development/climate change/geophysics, environmental science, geophysical sciences, meteorology & oceanography

### School of Natural Science; www. uea.ac.uk/sci/natsci
natural science

### School of Mathematics; www.uea.ac.uk/mathematics
mathematics, mathematics with business, energy engineering & environmental management

### School of Pharmacy; www.uea.ac.uk/pha
pharmacy practice, pharmacy; BSc(Hons), GradDip, MPhil, MSc, MSci, PGDip, PhD, MMath, MChem

## Faculty of Social Sciences; www.uea.ac.uk/ssf

### School of Economics; www.uea.ac.uk/economics
economics/ & accountancy, business economics, business finance & economics, environmental/experimental/industrial economics, international business finance & economics, media economics, philosophy, politics, international relations

### School of Education and Lifelong Learning; www.uea.ac.uk/edu
adult literacy, advanced educational practice, counselling/ focusing-orientated psychotherapy, early childhood studies, education studies, lifelong learning & development, mathematics education, PE, professional studies

### School of International Development; www.uea.ac.uk/dev
agriculture & rural development, international development with economics/overseas experience/social anthropology & politics/environment & society, development economics, education & development, geography/climate change/environment & independent development, gender analysis in independent development, independent development, international relations & development studies, international social development, water security & international development

### Law School; www.uea.ac.uk/law
law, employment law, European legal systems, information technology & intellectual property law, international commercial & business law/competition law & policy/trade law, law with American law/ French law & language, legal studies, media law, policy and practice

### Norwich Business School; www.uea.ac.uk/nbs
accounting & finance/management, brand leadership, business information management, advanced/ international business management, entrepreneurship, HRM, international accounting & business management, investment & finance, management, marketing, supply chain management, sustainable business

**School of Social Work; www.uea.ac.uk/ social work**
social work, advanced professional practice & policy

**School of Psychology; www.uae.ac.uk/ psychology**
psychology, child & family psychology, social science research

BA(Hons), BSc(Hons), CPE/Dip, DEd, GradDip, LlBHons, LLM, MA, MA/DipSW, MBA, MPhil, MRes, MSc, MScEd, PGCert, PGDip, PhD

## *Degrees validated by University of East Anglia offered by:*

### CITY COLLEGE NORWICH
### www.ccn.ac.uk

applied social work, art & design, business computing, business management, care management, creative exercise & practice, culinary arts, early childhood studies/years, engineering (civil, electrical, electronic, mechanical), English, & cultural studies, finance & accountancy, health studies, hospitality, tourism & leisure management, leisure & event management, HRM, leadership & management, media practice, retailing, mental health practice, natural sciences, psychology/& sociology, public sector management, public services, social work, sport, health & exercise; BA(Hons), BSc(Hons), FdA, FdSc, HNC, HND

### OTLEY COLLEGE
### www.otleycollege.ac.uk

agriculture, animal studies, arboriculture, conservation, construction, engineering, fishery studies, floristry, HE, horse studies, horticulture, outdoor activities

## THE UNIVERSITY OF EDINBURGH
## www.ed.ac.uk

### *College of Humanities and Social Sciences; www.hss.ed.ac.uk*

**The Edinburgh College of Art; www.ed.ac.uk/schools-departments/ edinburgh-college-art**

**Undergraduate qualifications;**

School of Art: intermedia art, drawing, video, photography, sound recording object construction, psychogeography

School of Design: animation, fashion, film & TV, glass, graphic design, illustration, interior design, jewellery & silversmithing, performance costume, product design, textiles

Architecture & Landscape: architecture, landscape architecture, architecture in the creative environment, architectural history

History of Art: history of art, architectural history, art in the global middle east, theory & display, Renaissance & early modern studies, modern & contemporary art, Scottish art & visual culture

Reid School of Music: music, music technology

**Taught degrees in Graduate School;**

acoustics & music technology, advanced sustainable design, animation, architectural & urban design, architectural conservation, architectural project management, art in the global middle ages, art, space and nature, composition, composition for screen, contemporary art painting, contemporary art photography/practice/sculpture/theory, cultural studies, design and digital media, digital composition & performance, early keyboard performance studies, fashion, film directing, glass, graphic design, history of art, theory & display, illustration, interior design/ interior architectural design, jewellery, landscape architecture, modern & contemporary art: history, curating & criticism, music in the community, musical instrument research, musicology, performance costume, product design, Renaissance and early modern studies, Scottish art & visual culture, sound design, textiles

### The Business School; www.business-school.ed.ac.uk

business accounting, accounting & finance, banking & risk, business studies, carbon finance/management, economics, finance & investment, international business & emerging markets, management science, marketing, MBA courses

### School of Divinity; www.div.ed.ac.uk

divinity, biblical studies, ethics, ministry, philosophy & theology, religious studies, science & religion, theology/in history, world Christianity

### School of Economics; www.ed.ac.uk/schools-departments/economics

asset pricing, corporate finance, economics, international money & finance, economics analysis, econometrics/finance, macroeconomics, microeconomics, economics of labour markets, adv time econometrics, development economics, personnel economics, economic history, environment & natural resources health & industrial organisations

### School of Health in Social Science; www.ed.ac.uk/schools-departments/health

advancing nursing practice, applied psychology for children & young people, children & young people mental health, clinical psychology, counselling, dementia, integrated service improvement, nursing studies/adult, psychotherapy, social science in health, cancer care, caring & emotional work in nursing, community nursing, ethical, legal & social issues in child health, transplantation nursing

### School of History, Classics and Archaeology; www.shc.ed.ac.uk

American history, classical studies, diaspora & migration studies, ancient philosophy, contemporary/medieval/intellectual/ Scottish history, 18th century culture, 1st millennium history, 2nd world war in Europe, the Hellenic world, Renaissance to enlightenment, landscape, environment & history, modern British & Irish history, social & cultural history, classical art & archaeology, Celtic, Scottish studies, Greek/Latin studies, classics, gender history, late antique, Islamic & Byzantine studies, archaeology (European/forensic/Mediterranean), archaeology & history/GIS, human/osteoarchaeology, social anthropology

### School of Law; www.law.ed.ac.uk

law (English, family, commercial, comparative European private law, criminal, European, global environmental & climate change) law, public health, intellectual property law, international private, competition/innovation, international economic, trusts, international tax law, criminal & global crime, criminology & criminal justice

### School of Literatures, Languages and Cultures; www.ed.ac.uk/schools-departments/literatures-languages-cultures

Asian studies, Celtic & Scottish studies, comparative literature, European languages & cultures, English literature, European theatre, film studies, Islamic & Middle Eastern studies, literature & transatlanticism, material cultures & study of the book, medieval studies, theatre studies, translation, word & music studies

### Moray House School of Education; www.education.ed.ac.uk

academic practice, additional support for learning, childhood practice, applied sport science, community education, dance science & education, digital education, e-learning, leadership, education in context, headship, inclusive & special education, language teaching, outdoor education, performance psychology, physical activity for health, PE, primary education, sport & recreation, sport, PE & health & recreation, sustainability education, TESOL, strength & conditioning, swimming science, training & management, technical education

### School of Philosophy, Psychology and Language Science; www.ppls.ed.ac.uk

ancient philosophy, psychological linguistics, cognitive science, cognition in science & society, developmental linguistics, evolution of language & cognition, English language, epistemology, ethics, history & theory of psychology, human cognitive neuropsychology, individual differences, language & embodied cognition, linguistics, parapsychology, philosophy, psychology of reading, social psychology, aesthetics, knowledge, epistemology, logistics, Hellenistic philosophy, metaethics, psychology/of individual differences, mind & language/cognition, speech & language processing

### School of Social & Political Science; www.sps.ed.ac.uk

politics & international relations, science, innovation & technology, social anthropology, social policy, social work, sociology, adult protection, African studies/international development, comparative public policy, global social change/crime, global health & anthropology/public policy/justice & security/crime, global environment, childhood studies, health inequalities/systems & public policy, international & European politics, international political theory/development, international relations/of the Middle East/with Arabic, S Asian studies, management of bioeconomy, nationalism studies, innovation & governance, medical anthropology, policy studies, science & technology in society/& international development, social anthropology, social research, sustainable development; BA(Arch), BD, BEd(Hons), BMedSci, BMus, BN, BSc(Hons), DD, DLitt, DMus, DClinPsychol, EdD, LlM, MA, MA(Hons), MBA, MLA, MPhil/PhD, MSc, MTeach, MTh/Sc, PGDipCert, PGDE

## *College of Medicine and Veterinary Medicine; www.ed.ac.uk/schools-departments/medicine-vet-medicine*

medicine, medical sciences, veterinary medicine, animal bioscience, public health, regenerative medicine: clinical & industrial delivery, reproductive sciences biosciences, applied animal behaviour & welfare, biomedical sciences, cardiovascular biology, human anatomy, integrative neuroscience, oral surgery/health science

### School of Clinical Sciences; www.ed.ac.uk/schools-departments/clinical-sciences

clinical & surgical sciences, community health sciences, medical and radiological sciences, reproductive and developmental sciences, postgraduate dental education, primary healthcare, oral health

### School of Biomedical Sciences; www.ed.ac.uk/schools-departments/biomedical-sciences

biomedical sciences, human anatomy, global health & infectious/noncommunicable diseases, integrative neuroscience, medical sciences, translational medicine, international animal health, biodiversity, science communication & public engagement, wildlife,

### School of Molecular Genetics & Population Health Sciences

### The Royal (Dick) School of Veterinary Studies; www.ed.ac.uk/schools-departments/vet

animal biology, one health, conservation medicine, international animal welfare, ethics & law, veterinary medicine & surgery, applied animal behaviour & animal welfare, equine science; BSc(Hons), MBChB, MSC, BVMS, DipCert, MPhil, PhD

## *College of Science and Engineering; www.scieng.ed.ac.uk*

### School of Biological Sciences; www.ed.ac.uk/schools-departments/biology

biochemistry, biological science, biotechnology, developmental & cell biology, ecology, evolutionary biology, genetics, immunology, infectious diseases, medical biology, molecular biology, molecular genetics, neuroscience, pharmacology, physiology, plant science, reproductive biology, zoology, biodiversity & taxonomy of plants, bioinformatics, drug discovery & translational biology, next generation drug development, quantitative genetics & genome analysis, systematic & synthetic biology

### School of Chemistry; www.chem.ed.ac.uk

chemical physics, chemistry/with environmental & sustainable chemistry/materials chemistry, medicinal & biological chemistry

### School of Engineering; www.see.ed.ac.uk

Chemical Engineering with environmental engineering/management, materials & processes, energy systems

Civil and Environmental Engineering: civil engineering, civil and environmental engineering/construction management, structural engineering with architecture, structural & fire safety engineering

Electronics and Electrical Engineering: electrical engineering/& management, renewable energy, electronics, computer science, bioelectronics, communications, software engineering, mechanical engineering, energy systems, integrated micro and nano systems, digital communications

Mechanical Engineering: advanced materials applications, electrical & mechanical engineering, fluid and particle dynamics, manufacturing & process optimization, materials & processes, mechanical engineering with management/structural mechanics/renewable energy

Institute for Energy Systems: environmental mitigation, energy delivery, renewable energy, restructuring and regulation

General Engineering

Engineering MSc Programmes

biomechanics, bioelectronics & biosensing, carbon capture & storage, electronic signal processing & storage

**School for Informatics; www.inf.ed.ac.uk**
informatics, artificial intelligence, cognitive science, computer science, software engineering/computer science, analytical & scientific databases, bioinformatics, systems & synthetic biology, intelligent robotics, knowledge management, representation & reasoning, learning from data, natural languages & language engineering, neural computation & neuroinformatics, theoretical computer science, adv design informatics

**School of Geosciences; www.geos.ed.ac.uk**
Ecological Sciences, Geography, Earth Science: geography, physical geography, geology, geophysics, archaeology, GIS, meteorology, environment & development, environmental studies, earth sciences, ecological economics, ecosystem engineering, forestry, ecology & environmental science/geoscience, integrated resource management, environment & development, carbon capture & storage/management, sustainable energy systems, ecological environmental science, meteorological & atmospheric science

**School of Mathematics; www.maths.ed.ac.uk**
pure/applied mathematics, financial mathematics/& modelling mathematical physics, mathematics & statistics/management/physics/artificial intelligence/ computer science/philosophy/music/economics operational research, scientific computing

**School of Physics and Astronomy; www.ph.ed.ac.uk**
astrophysics, physics, chemical physics, computational physics, mathematical physics, theoretical physics, physics and computer sci/mathematics/ meteorology/music, high performance computing, science education; BEng, BSc, MChem, MChemPhys, MEarthSci, MEng, MInf, MPhil, MPhys, MS, MSc, MSci, PGDip, PhD

## EDINBURGH NAPIER UNIVERSITY
## www.napier.ac.uk

### *The Business School; www.napier.ac.uk/business-school*

**School of Accountancy, Financial Services & Law; www.napier.ac.uk/business-school/SchoolsandCentres/Pages/SchoolofAccountingFinancialLaw.aspx**

**School of Management; www.napier.ac.uk/business-school/SchoolsandCentres/Pages/SchoolofManagement.aspx**

**School of Marketing, Tourism & Languages; www.napier.ac.uk/business-school/SchoolsandCentres/Pages/SchoolofMarketingTourismLanguages.aspx**

**Accounting, Economics and Statistics**
accounting/with corporate finance, advertising, advanced networking/leadership, business management/studies, business & entrepreneurship, business information systems, consumer studies, corporate strategy & law/finance, creative advertising, economics, ecotourism, entrepreneurship/leadership, facilities management, finance, financial services, flexible management, global investment banking/languages, HRM, international tourism management, international finance/marketing, investment, law, festival & event management, management, managerial leadership, marketing/digital media, promotion & economic development, property management/ development & valuation/construction management, PR, tourist marketing/management, transport management, marketing management/with consumer studies, wealth management; BA, BA(Hons), MSc, MBA, MPhil, LlB, LlM

### *Faculty of Engineering, Computing and Creative Industries; www.napier.ac.uk/fecci*

**School of Computing; www.napier.ac.uk/soc/Pages/Home.aspx**
advanced networking, applied informatics, business information systems/technology, computer network systems, computing security & forensics, computing/ systems (user experience), digital media/networking, mobile & embedded computer systems, interactive media design/systems, entertainment & games development, adv/security & digital forensics, adv/software engineering, software technology for the web,

web technologies, strategic ITC leadership; BEng, BSc, MPhil, MSc, PhD

### Arts & Creative Industries; www.napier.ac.uk/sci/Pages/SchoolOfArtsCreativeIndustries.aspx

adv film practice, acting for stage & screen, advertising, PR, creative advertising/writing, communication, design & digital arts, design (digital arts/graphic design/lighting products), design (sustainability/urbanism), English/& acting, film, graphic design, interaction/interdisciplinary design, international journalism for media professionals, interior architecture, journalism, music/(pop), photography, product design, magazine/publishing, screen project development, screenwriting, TV; BA/BA(Hons), BDes, BDes(Hons), BMus, BMus(Hons), MDes, MFA, MSc, PGCert/Dip

### Engineering & the Built Environment; www.napier.ac.uk/sebe/Pages/default.aspx

architectural technology & building performance, adv materials engineering, automation & control, building surveying, built environment, timber engineering, civil engineering, communications engineering, computer-aided design, construction project management, electronic/computer/electrical engineering, digital systems, energy & environmental engineering, engineering design, engineering with management, environmental sustainability, facilities management, adv materials engineering, mechanical engineering, mechatronics, polymer engineering, product design engineering, project management, property development & valuation/investment, quantity surveying, adv/structural engineering, timber industry management/engineering, transport management/planning and engineering, transportation engineering; BSc/BSc(Hons), BEng, BEng/Hons, MEng, MSc, MSci, PGCert/Dip

## *Faculty of Health, Life & Social Science; www.napier.ac.uk/fhlss*

### Life, Sport & Social Sciences; www.napier.ac.uk/FHLSS/SLSSS/Pages/Home.aspx

biomedical sciences, biotechnology, career guidance & development, complementary healthcare (aromatherapy/reflexology), criminology, drug design & biomedical science, psychology, sociology, social science, social research; conservation & management of protected areas, ecotourism, environmental biology, forensic biology, pharmaceutical science, sports & exercise science, sport performance enhancement/coaching/conditioning/physiology/psychology, wildlife biology & conservation, youth work; BSc(Hons), MSc, BA(Hons), PGCert/Dip

### School of Nursing, Midwifery and Social Care; www.napier.ac.uk/fhlss/NMSC/Pages/SchoolofNursing.aspx

nursing – child health/adult/mental health/intellectual disabilities, adv/profession practice/child protection, complementary therapy practice, neonatal nursing/child protection/diabetes nursing, counselling, health admin/& social work care, leadership compassionate care, midwifery, social care, veterinary nursing, CPD; BMid, BN, DipHE, MSc, PGDip/Cert

---

## EDINBURGH COLLEGE OF ART
## www.eca.ac.uk

fine art, intermedia art, painting, photography, sculpture, animation, fashion, film & TV, glass, graphic design, illustration, interior design, jewellery & silversmithing, performance costume, product design, textiles, architecture/in creative & cultural environments, landscape architecture, architectural history, music, music technology, sound design, digital composition & media/performance, acoustics, adv sustainable design, architectural & urban design, art in the global middle ages, art, space & nature, composition/for screen, contemporary art painting/photography/practice/sculpture/theory, theory & design, cultural studies, design and digital media, digital composition & performance, early keyboard performance studies, film directing, architectural conservation, interior architectural design, landscape architecture, modern & contemporary art, history of art ( criticism, music in the community, musicology, performance costume, Renaissance early modern studies, Scottish art & visual culture, sound design;-BA(Hons), MA, MSc, MFA, MArch, MLA, MPhil, PhD

# UNIVERSITY OF ESSEX
# www.essex.ac.uk

## *Faculty of Humanities and Comparative Studies; www.essex.ac.uk/hcs*

### History; www.essex.ac.uk/depts/history.aspx

history (modern, social & cultural, American), film studies, joint honours in range of subjects, cultural & social, local & regional history, public history

### Department of Literature, Film, and Theatre Studies; www.essex.ac.uk/depts/lifts.aspx

comparative literature, creative writing, drama/& literature, English language/literature, English & United States literature, literature & film studies/ history of art/sociology/philosophy/history/ myth/ drama, literature and the unconscious, wild writing, literature & the environment, theatre studies

### Dept of Philosophy & Art History; www.essex.ac.uk/depts/spah

philosophy/religion & ethics, continental philosophy, philosophy & psychoanalysis, ethics, politics & public policy, politics, philosophy & economics, theory & practice of human rights, art history: numerous joint hons degrees, art history & visual culture, history of art/with theory, with mod langs/ literature/film studies/history, gallery studies, curating contemporary/Latin American art

### Centre for Interdisciplinary Studies in the Humanities; www.essex.ac.uk/depts/centres-and-institutes/cish

**Latin American Studies**

Latin American studies with human rights or business

**European Studies**

European studies/with politics or modern languages

**American studies**

American (US) studies with politics/criminology

**Humanities**

liberal arts with sociology

BA(Hons), CertHE, Dip/MA, FdA, MA, MFA, MPhil, PGCert, PhD, LlB

## *Faculty of Social Sciences; www.essex.ac.uk/ss*

### Dept of Economics; www.essex.ac.uk/economics

accounting & financial economics, applied economics & data analysis, business/financial economics, econometrics, economics, economics with mathematics/ history, numerous jt courses, financial/international/ management economics, financial markets & policy, political economy

### Dept of Government; www.essex.ac.uk/government

European integration/politics, global & comparative politics, ideology & discourse analysis, international development/relations/& media, philosophy, politics & economics, political behaviour/economy, political science, conflict resolution, public opinion and polling

### Dept of Languages and Linguistics; www.essex.ac.uk/linguistics

applied/experiential/linguistics, analysing language use, applied & intercultural communication, English language/literature, language acquisition, translation, interpretation & subediting, sociolinguistics, syntax, teaching English, language disorders, modern languages & linguistics, psycholinguistics & neurolinguistics, TEFL, phonology, syntax, literature & modern languages

### Dept of Sociology; www.essex.ac.uk/sociology

advertising, culture & the media, media, culture & society, sociology & humanities/politics, criminology & media/social legislation, criminological & socio-legal research, crime & media, human rights, social psychology, social neurology, sociology/& anthropology, psychosocial studies, organized crime, terrorism & security; BA(Hons), BSc(Hons), Diploma, GradDip, MA, MPhil, MRes, MSc, PGDip, PhD, ProcDoc

## Faculty of Law and Management; www.essex.ac.uk/lm

### Essex Business School; www.essex.ac.uk/ebs

**Centre for Global Accountability; Centre for Entrepreneurship Research; Essex Finance Centre; Essex Management Centre**

accounting, economics, entrepreneurship & innovation, finance, financial management, banking/& finance, brand management, business management/administration, marketing/& branding, HRM, financial engineering/economics, international enterprise & entrepreneurship/accounting/finance/management, financial engineering & risk, social enterprise, global project & innovation management, management & organizational dynamics

### Human Rights Centre; www.essex.ac.uk/humanrightscentre

human rights & Latin American studies/law/philosophy/politics/sociology, human rights & cultural diversity/public law, human rights theory & practice, international human rights law

### School of Law; www.essex.ac.uk/law

law/philosophy/politics/human rights, criminology & socio-legal research, English & French laws, European business law/governance, EU law, international law, health care law, human rights law, information technology, international human rights & humanitarian law, international trade law/internet law, public law, environmental governance, philosophy human rights & law, UK human rights & public law; BA(Hons), BSc(Hons), DocProg, LlM, LLB, MPhil, MSc, PhD

## Faculty of Science and Engineering; www.essex.ac.uk/se

### Dept of Biological Sciences; www.essex.ac.uk/bs

biochemistry, biological sciences, biology, biomedical science, biotechnology, cardiac rehabilitation, ecology, environment & society, environmental governance, natural world, environmental resource management, genetics, marine biology, molecular medicine, nature, environment, science & society, sports & exercise science, wild writing

### School of Computer Science and Electronic Engineering; www.essex.ac.uk/csee

computer /systems engineering, computational finance, data communication, electronics engineering, telecommunications engineering, telecommunications & data communications

### School of Health and Human Sciences; www.essex.ac.uk/hss

adult/mental health nursing, muscoloskeletal assessment,, medical & clinical education, health studies, health & organisational research, public health, midwifery, clinical psychology, social speech & language/occupational therapy, physiotherapy, healthcare practice, CPD

### Department of Mathematical Sciences; www.essex.ac.uk/maths

mathematics & computing/economics/finance/accounting/humanities, cryptography & network security, discrete mathematics & its applications, econometrics, human decision-making with applications, operational research & computer science, statistics & data analysis/computer science/econometrics/operational research, mathematics for teaching, mathematics for secondary teaching

### Dept of Psychology; www.essex.ac.uk/psychology

psychology, cognitive psychology/neuropsychology/neuroscience, research methods in psychology; BA(Hons), BEng, BSc(Hons), GradDip, MA, MPhil, MRes, MSc, PGDip, PhD, ProfDoc

## Degrees validated by the University of Essex offered at:

---

## WRITTLE COLLEGE
www.writtle.ac.uk

agriculture, animal science, conservation management/& environment, conservation wild life/management, design, equine, floristry, horticulture, sport & exercise performance; BA(Hons), BSc(Hons), CertMS, Certs, DipMS, FdAs, Higher Certs, MA, MBA, MSc

## UNIVERSITY OF EXETER
## www.exeter.ac.uk

### University of Exeter Business School; www.business-school.exeter.ac.uk

accounting, finance, business, economics, econometrics, management, marketing, leadership, politics, tourism, employability; BA(Hons), MBA, MPhil, MSc, PGDip/Cert, PhD

### College of Engineering, Mathematics & Physical Sciences; www.emps.exeter.ac.uk/engineering

Computer Science: bioinformation & systems biology, IT management for business, computer science, applied artificial intelligence, electronic engineering

Engineering: civil & environmental engineering, electronic engineering & computer science, biosystems/mechanical/materials engineering, engineering and management, water management, international supply chain management, renewable energy, mining engineering

Geology: applied geology, mining geotechnology, engineering geology & geotechnics, mining geology, applied geotechnics

Mathematics: mathematics climate science, mathematical biology, mathematics with computer science/accounting/economics/finance/business/engineering/physics, financial management, natural science, financial mathematics

Medical Imaging: diagnostic radiography

Minerals & Mining Engineering: minerals/mining engineering, mining geology, surveying & land/environmental management, applied geotechnics

Natural Sciences; natural sciences

Physics & Astronomy: physics, astrophysics, medical imaging, biomedical physics, quantum systems, electromagnetic materials, nanomaterials, natural science

Renewable Energy: renewable energy; BSc(Hons), BEng, MEng, MSc, MPhil, PhD, MPhys

### College of Humanities; www.humanities.exeter.ac.uk

Archaeology: archaeology & forensic science, anthropology, ancient history, heritage management, bioarchaeology, experimental/landscape archaeology, alternative histories through art & archaeology, food & culture in antiquity

Classics & Ancient History: ancient history, classical studies, classics, art history/art & archaeology, ancient drama & society, Hellenistic culture, Roman myth & history, food & culture

Drama: drama, theatre practice – appl theatre, directing, physical performance, actor training, playwriting, dramaturgy, staging Shakespeare, drama & visual culture/English

English: English/studies, film, creative writing, criticism & theory, the 20th century, Victorian studies

Film Studies: film studies/with English, modern languages, independent film business

History: history & English/French/philosophy/visual culture/geography/international relations/politics, ancient history, early history, medieval studies, western esotericism, maritime/medical history, war & society

Liberal Arts; liberal arts

Art History & Visual Cultures; art history/drama/English/history/modern languages & visual culture,

Modern Languages: French, German, Italian, Hispanic studies, Russian, modern languages & visual culture, European languages & cultures, literature, linguistics, literary & applied translation

Foreign Language Centre: French German, Spanish, Portuguese, Japanese, Mandarin Chinese

Theology & religion: theology/with classics/philosophy/arabic stied/Islamic studies/Arabic studies/Bible studies, ethics, religion & society

### College of Life & Environmental Sciences; www.lifesciences.exeter.ac.uk

Biosciences: biological sciences (animal biology/microbiology & infectious disease/molecular & cellular biology), biochemistry, biological & medicinal chemistry, human biosciences, sport & health sciences, clinical science, animal behaviour, conservation biology & ecology, environmental science, evolutionary biology, human sciences, zoology, biological sciences, molecular & cellular biology, biochemistry & chemistry

Geography: geography, environmental science/studies, European studies, climate change/& risk management/impacts & feedbacks, conservation science & policy, environment & resilience, critical human geography, sustainable development, energy policy

Psychology: psychology, animal behaviour, applied psychology (clinical), clinical therapy/practice, evidence based psychological practice, psychological

therapies, social & organizational psychology, psychological/cognitive therapies, sports exercise science
Sport and Health Sciences: sport & health science paediatric exercise & health, sport & exercise medicine/science/psychology, exercise, human biosciences, sports science; BSc(Hons), MPhil, BA(Hons), DocCliniPsychology, MSc, PhD, PGCert/Dip, MRes, BClinSci

**College of Social Science & International Studies; www.social sciences.exeter.ac.uk**

Arabic thinking, educational psychology, childhood & youth studies, English & education, sport science, professional studies
PGCE: primary art/music/science/modern foreign languages, early years, secondary sciences/design & technology/English with media/drama/modern foreign languages/geography/information, communication technologies, post compulsory education

**School of Law**

law, European (German/French) law, European studies, international commercial/international & comparative public law, international human rights law
Politics & International Relations: politics, international relations/studies ( political philosophy, public administration, politics, security, conflict & justice
Sociology & Philosophy philosophy of biology, social & political philosophy, science & technology; BA(Hons), MA, PhD, MPhil, MA, PhD, LlB, LlM, MRes, DEdPsych, EdD, MEd

**University of Exeter Medical School;**

www.exeter.ac.uk/medicine
clinical sciences, environmental & human health, medicine, surgery, medical studies; BClinSci, BMBS, MSc, MS, MPhil, PhD, MD, PhD, MSc, PGDip/Cert

## *Degrees validated by University of Exeter offered at:*

## UCP MARJON-UNIVERSITY COLLEGE PLYMOUTH ST MARK & ST JOHN
www.ucpmarjon.ac.uk

acting, business management, children, young people & communities, drama, education & teacher training, English language/literature, creative writing, leadership, live music, media, journalism, speech, language, linguistics, sport, outdoor, coaching & PE; BA(Hons), BA/BSc, BEd, FdA, church college certs; GTP, MA, MEd, MPhil, PGCE

## UNIVERSITY OF FALMOUTH
**www.falmouth.ac.uk**

**Department of Art**

architecture, drawing, fine art, illustration, art & environment: curatorial practice, fine art: contemporary practice

**School of Media & Performance**

acting, animation & visual effects, choreography, creative advertising, creative events management, creative music techniques, creative writing, dance, digital music, English, film, journalism, intermedia broadcasting, marine & natural history photography, music, music theatre, photography, pop, press editorial, performance, professional writing, TV production
BA(Hons), Foundation Dip, MPhil, PhD, FdA, PGDip

## UNIVERSITY OF GLAMORGAN
**www.glam.ac.uk**

*Cardiff School of Creative and Cultural Industries; www.ccc.glam.ac.uk*

computer animation, contemporary music performance, computer games enterprise, culture & journalism, drama, theatre, fashion design/marketing & retail distribution/promotion, film studies/producing/media/visual effects interior design, international/journalism, video, games art, graphic communication, music/sound technology, performance & moving media, pop, photography, music engineering & production, radio, sound technology, scriptwriting, research/social media, TV & film set design, theatre & drama, visual effect & motion graphics; BA(Hons), FdA, MA, MPhil, DDes

## *Faculty of Health, Sport and Science; www.hesas.glam.ac.uk*

Health & Social Care chiropractic, clinical physiology (cardiology/respiratory), counselling & psychotherapy, systemic counselling, diagnostic clinical ultrasound, nursing (children, adult, mental health, learning disability), midwifery, nutrition, pharmacology & prescribing, social work & health & social care
Science: astronomy, chemistry, pharmaceutical science, biology, geology, geography, natural history, forensic & police science, environment & sustainability
Sport & Coaching: coaching sports & exercise science, conditioning, sports coaching/development/management/psychology/studies, youth sport, nutrition, performance coaching, physical activity, coaching rugby/football; BA(Hons), BSc(Hons), BN, FoundCerts, HEDip, HNC, HND, MA, MPhil, MSc/PGDip/Cert, PhD

## *Faculty of Advanced Technology; www.fat.glam.ac.uk*

civil engineering, construction & surveying, quantity surveying & commercial management, construction project management (surveying), structural engineering management, environmental management, safety, health & environment management, computer science, computing/& software engineering, business information modelling & sustainability communications engineering, embedded systems design, mobile & satellite communications, communications engineering, computer games development, intelligent computer systems, electrical & electronic engineering, electronic product design, computer forensics/security/systems security/systems engineering, information technology/mgt in business; energy systems engineering, mechanical/manufacturing engineering, renewable energy, sustainable power technology, professional engineering, total quality; lighting design & tech, live events technology; aeronautical engineering/systems, aircraft maintenance, avionics; mathematics, computing/financial mathematics, mathematical science; BEng(Hons), BSc, BSc(Hons), CertHE, DipHE, HNC, HND, MEng

## *Faculty of Business & Society; fbs.glam.ac.uk*

### Glamorgan Business School; www.bus.glam.ac.uk/business

advertising/retail marketing & management, finance, accounting, business & management, business studies, forensic/international accounting/auditing & accounting, international business, Islamic banking & finance, management & development of international financial systems, HRM, logistics & supply chain management, marketing, international fashion marketing, events management, PR & media communications, sports management/development, psychology

### School of Humanities & Social Sciences; fbs.glam.ac.uk/humanities

art & design, fine art, art practice, art & health, wellbeing, criminology, criminology & law/psychology/sociology, criminal justice, English/literature, creative & professional writing, Gothic studies, language, culture, & society, history, social & cultural history, professional Welsh/TESOL/education/history/law, Welsh courses, public services, public/emergency services, health/& public service management, public leadership, community regeneration, health/& public service management, sociology & criminology/education/history/law/psychology

### School of Law, accountancy & finance; fbs.glam.ac.uk/law

law, accounting, finance, financial planning, forensic/international accounting, business, forensic/audit, Islamic banking & finance, finance & investment, management & development, international financial systems, law, legal practice, international/commercial law, criminology & law, legal practice

### School of Psychology; fbs.glam.ac.uk/psychology

psychology, applied/developmental/sport/health psychology, behavioural analysis, behaviour & therapy, supervisory practice & therapy, play & therapeutic play, play therapy, supervisory practice in sport psychology, clinical & abnormal psychology; BA(Hons), BA/BSc, BSc(Hons), DocPublServ, FCert, FdA, GradDip Law, LlB(Hons), LlM/PhD/PgD, MA/PDip/Cert, MSc, PGD/PGC

# UNIVERSITY OF GLASGOW
# www.gla.ac.uk

## College of Arts; www.gla.ac.uk/colleges/arts

### School of Critical Studies; Culture & Creative Arts; Humanities; Modern Languages & Cultures

American studies, applied linguistics, arts practice (fine art, art, health & wellbeing), battlefield & conflict, Mediterranean/archaeology, archaeological studies, art, style & design, arts of China/Europe, art history (transgression: 20th century avant-garde/dress & textiles history/art world practice/history of collecting/collections/international art nouveau), art & design, Celtic & Viking archaeology, Scottish/& Celtic studies, classics (classical civilisations), comparative literature, French, German, Hispanic studies, Italian, Spanish, composition, computer/forensics & e-discovery, music, creative writing, digital media & information science, electronic music, English/English literature, early modern/modern/medieval history, European studies, film & TV studies, film journalism, Gaelic, Latin, historically informed performance practice, information management & forensics/preservation, international cinemas, modernities: literature-theory/religion/theology & religious studies, landscape, material culture & artefact studies, pop: creative practice/music, theology & culture media management, medieval & renaissance studies, modern & contemporary art, modernities (modernism/modernity & postmodernism), museum studies, musicology, music, philosophy, Scottish literature/history, social & cultural history, sonic arts, textile conservation, theatre studies/history/practice, translation studies, Victorian literature, war studies; BD(Min), BMus, DLitt, MA, MAHons, MLitt, MPhil, MTh, PhD

## College of Medical Veterinary & Life Sciences; www.gla.ac.uk/colleges/mvls

Institutes: Biodiversity, Animal Health & Comparative Medicine; Cancer Sciences; Cardiovascular & Medical Sciences; Health & Wellbeing; Infection, Immunity & Inflammation, Molecular, Cell & Systems Biology, Neuroscience & Psychology

Postgraduate degrees in: ecology & environmental biology, animal welfare science, quantitative methods in biodiversity, conservation & epidemiology, veterinary public health, comparative medicine, immunitity biology, medical microbiology, mental health, global molecular parasitology, virology, environmental biology & systematics, marine & freshwater ecology & environmental management, medical molecular medicine, cardiovascular sciences, clinical pharmacology, sport & exercise science/medicine, translational medicine, clinical/applied neuropsychology, clinical psychology, global health, primary care, public health, health technology

### School of Life Sciences; www.gla.ac.uk/schools/lifesciences

anatomy, biochemistry, bioinformatics, biomedical/biological sciences, biotechnology, computing/& physiology, exercise science, genetics, immunology, marine & freshwater biology/ecology & environmental management, medical visualisation & human anatomy, microbiology, molecular/medicine & cellular biology, molecular/parasitology, pharmacology, physiology, plant science, sports medicine/science, zoology

### School of Medicine; www.gla.ac.uk/medicine,

applied medical sciences, dentistry, evidence based medicine & education, medicine, health care, immunology, nursing (community, adult, surgical, children, public health), cardiovascular, child health, clinical nutrition/physics/neuroscience, evidence-based informatics, fixed & removable prosthodontics, health profession education, human nutrition, forensic toxicology, primary dentistry, paediatric science, medical genetics, molecular medicine, public health, physiology, reproductive & maternal science, radiation physics, sport science & nutrition, sports/& exercise medicine/physiology, surgical oncology, translational medicine

### School of Veterinary Medicine; www.gla.ac.uk/schools/vet

animal welfare science, ethics & law, quantitative methods in diversity, conservation & epidemiology, veterinary biosciences, animal reproduction, veterinary medicine/surgery/public health, biomedical sciences

BSc, BSc(Vet Sci), BVMS, MVPH, PhD B(MedSci), MBChB, MD, MML, MMLE, MPC, MPH, PhD, BDS, BSc(Dent Sc), DDS, MSc

## *College of Science & Engineering; www.gla.ac.uk/colleges/scienceengineering*

### School of Chemistry; www.gla.ac.uk/schools/chemistry

chemistry, chemical physics, medical chemistry

### School of Engineering; www.gla.ac.uk/schools/engineering

aerospace engineering/systems & management, aeronautical engineering, aeronautics, architecture, automotive engineering, biomedical engineering, civil engineering with architecture/management, computer systems engineering, electronics & software engineering/music, electronic design, electronic engineering, embedded electronic systems, engineering & management, mechanical design/engineering, mechatronics, microcomputer systems engineering, nanosystems & nanotechnology, product design engineering, embedded systems engineering, structural engineering & mechanics, sustainable energy, telecommunications electronics

### School of Computing Science; www.gla.ac.uk/schools/computing

computing science, computing forensics & e-discovery, neuroinformatics, electronic & software engineering/development, mobile/software engineering, software development, information retrieval/security/technology, mobile design & engineering, search engine technology

### School of Geographical & Earth Sciences; www.gla.ac.uk/schools/ges

earth science, geography, coastal systems management, freshwater/marine/aquatic systems science, geoinformation technology & cartography, geomatics & management, geospatial & mapping science, human geography/space, politics & power, marine systems science, international development

### School of Mathematics & Statistics; www.gla.ac.uk/schools/mathematicsstatistics

applied/pure mathematics, finance/accounting & mathematics/statistics, biostatistics, adv/statistics, environmental/social statistics, financial modelling/finance

### School of Physics & Astronomy; www.gla.ac.uk/schools/physics

astronomy, physics, chemical/theoretical physics, astrophysics, physics, advanced materials, energy & the environment, global security, life sciences, nuclear technology, physics with mathematics/applied mathematics/computer science

### School of Psychology; www.gla.ac.uk/schools/psychology

psychology, brain imaging/sciences – from molecules to mind, psychological science

BEng, BSc, EngD, MEng, MSc, PGDip, PhD, EngD, PGDip, MRes

## *College of Social Sciences; www.gla.ac.uk/schools/social sciences*

### Adam Smith Business School; www.gla.ac.uk/schools/business

accountancy, economics, banking & financial services, business & management, development studies, economic & financial sector policies, asset pricing & investment, banking & financial services, corporate governance & accountability, development studies, economic & financial sector policies, economic development, economics, environment & sustainable development, Europe & international development (politics & economics), finance & economic development/management, financial economics/forecasting & investment/modelling/risk management; international accounting & financial management/banking & finance/business & economic development/entrepreneurship/corporate finance & banking/development/finance/finance & economic policy/financial analysis/management & design innovation/management & leadership/management for china/strategic marketing/trade & finance, investment banking & finance, investment fund management, management, management with enterprise & business growth/human resources/international finance/ international real estate, master of business administration, public administration, quantitative finance

BA, BSc, MA, MAQ(SocSci), MAcc, MBA, MFin, MSc, PhD, MPA

### School of Education; www.gla.ac.uk/schools/education

academic practice, adult & continuous education, childhood practice, community development, drug & alcohol studies, education (primary, secondary), literature & literacy, community learning/& development, interprofessional science education, music, RE, English language teaching/studies, inclusive education, learning & teaching in HE, leadership drugs & alcohol setting, learning & teaching languages in primary school, middle leadership & management in schools, organizational leadership, PGDE, primary

PE, professional learning & enquiry, psychological studies, religious & philosophical education, religion, education & culture, school strategic leadership & management, teaching adults, technological education, TESOL, young people, social inclusion & change; BA(Hons), BTechEd, BTechS, EdD, MA, MA(Hons), MEd, MLitt, MSc, MusicBEd, PhD

### School of Interdisciplinary Studies; www.gla.ac.uk/schools/interdisciplinary

applied carbon management, environmental stewardship, health & social policies, health & wellbeing, tourism, heritage & development, environment, culture & community, environmental science, technology & society; BSc, MA, MLitt, PGCert/Dip

### *School of Law; www.gla.ac.uk/schools/law*

law, contemporary law & practice, constitutional corporate & financial/medical/family law, European law, intellectual property & digital economy, international competition/commercial/property law, international law, jurisprudence, law & organisations, law & security, professional legal practice, socio-legal studies; MRes, LlB, LlM, MRes, PgDip/Cert, PhD

### School of Social & Political Science; www.ac.uk/schools/socialpolitical

Central & East European studies, Chinese studies, economic & social history, politics, public policy, sociology, city/regional planning & real estate planning, criminology, criminal justice, equality & human rights, Euro politics/law, global health/economy/security, housing studies, human rights & international politics, international politics/relations, international management for China, political communication, public policy, real estate development/regeneration, Russian, Central & East European studies, social science, social & cultural history, sociology, spatial planning, transnational crime, justice & security, urban policy/practice/regeneration; MA, MA(SocSci), MSc, MRes, CPD, MLitt, EdD, PhD

## GLASGOW CALEDONIAN UNIVERSITY
## www.gcu.ac.uk/ebe

### School of Engineering & the Built Environment; www.caledonian.ac.uk/ebe

3D computer animation, 3D design for virtual environments, adv computer networking, applied instrumentation & control, audio technology with electronics/multimedia, building services engineering/surveying, computer aided mechanical engineering, computer games (art & animation/design/software development), computer science, computing (information/web systs development), construction management/economics, cyber security & networks, design practice & methods, digital security/forensics, forensics & ethical hacking, digital systems engineering, engineering, information technology/security, computing or creative industries, electrical power engineering, energy & environmental management, environmental civil engineering/management & planning, fire risk engineering, foundation (built environment/computing/engineering), graphic design for digital media, instrumentation & robotic/systems engineering, interior design, international project design/management, maintenance management, mechanical & power plant systems engineering, mechanical electronic systems engineering, mechanical engineering design/manufacture, network & communication engineering, network security/systems engineering, NET web systems development, particulate solids handling, property management & valuation, quantity surveying, real estate management, robotic & mechatronic systems engineering, sustainable energy technology, telecomunication engineering, waste management, wireless communication technologies/networking; BA/BA(Hons), BEng/BEng(Hons), BSc/BSc(Hons), DipHE, MA/PGD, MSc/PGD, PhD, FD, Dips

### Glasgow School for Business & Sociology; www.caledonian.ac.uk/cbs

accountancy, banking finance & risk management, business, business/studies/management/law, citizenship & human rights, creative & cultural business, economics & statistical analysis, European & international trade/law, fashion buying/business, finance, financial investment & management/services/risk & operations, global supply chain management, health history, history (modern Scottish), HRM, investment, international banking & finance/business/hospitality management/event management/tourism management, international contracting/HRM, international brand management/fashion branding & marketing/retail, international development/trade, international retailing, law, business law, learning contracts, leadership & management in public sector, luxury brand management, management of IT operations, media & communications, occupational health & safety management, operations & business management, management, public sector finance, management, technology & enterprise, marketing, multimedia journalism, railway operations management, risk management, social enterprise, social sciences, TV writing (fiction); BA (Hons), MRes, PhD, LlB, LlM, MSc, PGD/C, PhD

### School of Health & Life Sciences; www.caledonian.ac.uk/hls

adv practice, bimolecular science, biotechnology, cell & molecular biology, clinical nutrition & health, diagnostic imaging sci, clinical ophthalmology & vision, counselling & psychology, diabetes control, health studies, human nutrition & dietetics, human bioscience, life sciences, medical ultrasound, midwifery, musculoskeletal physiotherapy, nursing (adult/child/mental health/learning disabilities), nursing studies, occupational therapy, oncology, operating dept practices, optometry, orthoptics, ophthalmic dispensing, oral health science, podiatry, professional development, psychology in forensic settings, specialist practice, sexual health, physiotherapy, public health, radiography, specialist community public health nursing, social work, biological & biomedical sciences, cell & molecular biology, food bioscience, forensic psychology, human biology, sociology, psychology, microbiology, pharmacology, psychology; BSc, BSc(Hons), DipHE, DPsych, MSc, OphthDisp, PGCert/Dip, PhD, MRes, BSc(Hons), BA(Hons), GradCert, MPhil, MSc, PgCert/Dip, PhD, ProfDoc, BMidwifery, BN

## THE GLASGOW SCHOOL OF ART
## www.gsa.ac.uk

architecture/studies, communication design, creative practices, design innovation & citizenship, digital/design culture, engineering with architecture, environmental/service dseign, graphics illustration photography, interior/silversmithing & jewellery/fashion & textiles/product design engineering, fine art practice, graphics, international management & design/innovation, medical visualisation & human anatomy, painting & printmaking, product design engineering, sculpture & environmental art, serious games design, sound for the moving media; BA(Hons), BEng, BArch, DipArch, MA, MArch, MDes, MEng, MPhil, MRes, PhD

## UNIVERSITY OF GLOUCESTERSHIRE
## www.glos.ac.uk

### School of Accounting & Law; insight.glos.ac.uk/academicschools/dal/Pages/default.aspx

accounting, law, financial management

### School of Art & Design; insight.glos.ac.uk/academicschools/dad/Pages/default.aspx

advertising, advanced graphic design, fine art, photojournalism & documentary philosophy, photography, illustration, landscape architecture, visual communication

### School of Business & Management; insight.glos.ac.uk/academicschools/dbm/Pages/default.aspx

business management/administration/information technology, economics, enterprise, international business studies, strategy, marketing management & branding/advertising, management studies, hospitality management, HRM/strategy, marketing, advertising & communications, tourism management

### School of Media; insight.glos.ac.uk/academicschools/dcmp/Pages/default.aspx

creative media, film/production, journalism, mass communication, media practice, pop music, radio/TV production

### School of Computing & Technology; insight.glos.ac.uk/academicschools/dc/Pages/default.aspx

forensic/computing, computing ebusiness/IT management, dependable software, media production, multimedia web design, music & media management, media, film & communication, interactive games design, information security, information & communication technology, business/information technology

**School of Humanities; insight.glos.ac.uk/academicschools/dh/Pages/default.aspx**
creative writing, English literature/language, history, religion, philosophy, ethics, theology & religious studies

**School of Leisure; insight.glos.ac.uk/academicschools/delth/Pages/default.aspx**
performing arts, strategic events hospitality/management, tourism/hospitality/leisure management, sports management & development, play & playwork

**School of Natural & Social Sciences; insight.glos.ac.uk/academicschools/NSS/Pages/default.aspx**
animal biology, biology, counselling, community engagement & governance, criminology, geography, psychology, sociology, business/criminal/forensic/occupational psychology

**Sport & Exercise; insight.glos.ac.uk/academicschools/dse/Pages/default.aspx**
applied/sport & exercise science, sports science/coaching/development/education/strength & conditioning/therapy, sports chaplaincy/ministry, sport & Christian outreach, psychology of sport & exercise

**Institute of Education & Public Service; insight.glos.ac.uk/academicschools/education/Pages/default.aspx**
applied health study, child care/community practice, early childhood studies, education studies, health, community & social care, nonmedical prescribing, social work/with adults, youth work;
BA/BA(Hons), BSc/BSc(Hons), DipSW, HND, BEd, LlB MA, MPhil, MRes, MSc, PGCert, PGDip, MBA, CMS, DMS

## UNIVERSITY OF GREENWICH
## www.gre.ac.uk

**School of Architecture and Construction; www.gre.ac.uk/schools/arc**
architecture/ & construction, advanced architectural design/practice, building surveying/rehabilitation/engineering, built environment studies, construction surveying/management & economics, design & construction management, 3D digital design & animation, graphic & digital design, housing management & policy, facilities management, project management, real estate/ development & investment, estate management, fine art, garden design/history, landscape architecture/design/planning & assessment, occupational safety/hygiene, health & environment, photography, project management, quantity surveying, web design & content planning; BA(Hons), BSc(Hons), Certs, Dip, HNC, HND, MA, MSc, MPhil, PGDip, PhD

**The Business School; www.gre.ac.uk/schools/business**
accounting, advertising/& marketing/communications, international/banking, business administration/entrepreneurship & innovation/psychology/studies/economics, business technology/law/technology, business & financial economics, business logistics & transport management/purchasing & supply chain management, business management/studies, economics/with banking, e-logistics & supply chain management, events management, finance/& investment, financial information systems, financial management, HRM, investment, international business/banking/finance, international tourism management, marketing, marketing/communications, mathematics with business/economics, multimedia, personnel & development, PR & communication, project management for logistics, public services, purchasing & supply chain management/e-logistics, tourism management, strategic marketing/communications, transport & logistics management; BA(Hons), BSc(Hons), Certs, DBA, FD, HNC, HND, MA, MBA, MSc, PGDip, PhD

**School of Computing & Mathematical Science; www.gre.ac.uk/schools/cms**
applicable mathematics, business computing/information systems/information technology, cinematography & post management, computer science, computer security & forensics/& the law, computer

systems & networking/cyber security/law, computing (with games development, digital multimedia/& finance), computing & information systems, creative digital media, information security & audit, data warehousing & business intelligence, digital media technologies, digital TV & interactive media, film production, film & TV production, enterprise systems & business management, financial mathematics, games/design & development, informatics (ebusiness/security), information systems management, IT with ebusiness/esecurity/systems & digital media, mathematics & computing, mathematics/with financial management, networks & computer systems security, statistics, software engineering systems development, web technologies; BSc(Hons), FDSc, MA, MEng/BEng, MPhil, MSc, PhD

### School of Education; www.gre.ac.uk/education

childhood studies, early years, education studies, ESOL in, lifelong learning sector, primary education with QTS, PGCE, secondary education (numerous subject courses), physical education & sport, primary education, design & technology, lifelong/learning, teaching literacy/English, mathematics, teaching & training with digital technology, youth & community work; BA(Hons), BELT, Cert, DipHE, EdD, FD, MA, MPhil, MSc, PGCert/Dip, PhD, PGCE

### School of Engineering; www.gre.ac.uk/schools/engineering

business admin, accounting & financial management, business studies, civil engineering/project management, communications systems & software engineering, computer networking/& server administration, computing & electronic systems, computer forensics/network security/networking/systems & software engineering, control & instument engineering, electrical & electronic/communications engineering, electrical power engineering, engineering business management, engineering management/projects & programming, embedded systems, extended engineering, games & entertainment systems, information & communication technology, IT management for business, manufacturing systems engineering, mechanical/& sustainable electrical power engineering, mechanical engineering/technology, mechanical & manufacturing engineering, professional engineering, telecommunications systems engineering, waste environmental management engineering, water & environmental management, wireless mobile communications systems engineering; BEng(Hons), BSc(Hons), HNC, HND, MEng, MSc

### Greenwich Maritime Institute; www.gre.ac.uk/schools/gmi

maritime history/security studies, international maritime policy; MA, MBA, MPhil, PhD

### School of Health and Social Care; www.gre.ac.uk/schools/health

health & wellbeing/social care, health visiting & school nursing, nursing (adult, child, mental health, learning disabilities), counselling psychology, criminology/& criminal psychology, mental health/nursing studies, professional practice health & social care, public health, safeguarding children & young people, sexual health, social work & social care, speech & language therapy, special community public health (mental health, school nursing), therapeutic counselling; BA(Hons), BSc(Hons), DipHE, FD, GradDips, MA, MPhil, PGCert, PhD

### School of Humanities and Social Sciences; www.gre.ac.uk/schools/humanities

criminology/& criminal psychology, drama/ & performing arts/ English literature, creative writing/& English literature/philosophy, English language/& literature, forensic science with criminology, history & English/philosophy, politics, sociology, English language teaching ELT), English literary London, finance & ecommerce/international & commercial law, international justice, language learning, media, arts, philosophy & practice, philosophy & creative writing/English literature/ history, politics/& international studies/philosophy, sociology/& philosophy/psychology; BSc(Hons), BA(Hons), FD, LlB, MA, MPhil, MSc, PGCert, PGDip, PhD

### Medway School of Pharmacy; www.gre.ac.uk/schools/study/pa

applied drugs discovery, applied bioscience, medicines management, pharmacy, general/pharmacy practice, independent/supplementary prescribing, pharmacotherapy & services development; BSc(Hons), FdMM, FdPP, MPharm, MSc, PGCert/Dip

### Natural Resources Institute; www.gre.ac.uk/schools/nri

agriculture for sustainable development, sustainable environmental management, rural development dynamic, food safety & quality management; BSc(Hons), MPhil, MSc, PhD

### School of Science; www.gre.ac.uk/schools/science

app/biomedical sciences, biological sciences, biosciences, biotechnology, chemistry, forensic science/

with criminology, formulation science, environmental & earth sciences/conservation, geography, GIS, remote sensing, human nutrition, landscape economics, natural resources, pharmaceutical science/ biology/analysis, coaching, professional football coaching, sport science, strength & conditioning, sustainable futures; BSc(Hons), HNC, HND, MPhil, MSc, PGDip, PhD

## GRIMSBY INSTITUTE/UNIVERSITY CENTRE
## www.grimsby.ac.uk

applied computing, air conditioning engineering, business management with accounting/marketing, business & events management, children/parenting/ community/youth studies/development, counselling studies, creative music, creative & internet design, criminality & youth work, early childhood studies, digital film & TV production, English studies, fine arts, food manufacturing, games design, hair & beauty, health & child care, HE, learning support, marketing, mechanical engineering, mental health studies, operations management, make-up/design, performance, photography, professional writing, psychology, refrigeration, social care, sports coaching, sport & fitness, tourism & business management; BA(Hons), BSc(Hons), FdA, FdEd, FdSc, HEdDip, HNC, HND, MA, MBA, MSc, PGCE

## HARPER ADAMS UNIVERSITY
## www.harper-adams.ac.uk

agriculture, advanced/veterinary nursing/practice management, agricultural engineering/business/food marketing/science, agribusiness, animal health/welfare/wellbeing/management/science, applied mechatronic engineering, bioveterinary science, business management, conservation & forest protection, countryside management/& environment, crop management, dairy business management, entomology, environmental management, farm business management, food marketing/& consumer studies/marketing/management, food, international agricultural business & food chain management, land management, nutrition & wellbeing, meat business management, negotiated studies, off-road vehicle design, poultry business management, production management, real estate & property management, rural affairs estate management, management, marketing, soil & water management, veterinary/nursing, physiotherapy/pharmacy, wildlife conservation & resource management, sustainable agriculture; BSc(Hons), FdSc, MBA, MSc, PGDip/Cert, MRes

## HERIOT-WATT UNIVERSITY
## www.hw.ac.uk

### School of the Built Environment; www.sbe.hw.ac.uk

architectural engineering/project management/ design, carbon management in the built environment, civil & structural engineering, housing & real estate, quantity surveying, construction project management, structural & foundation engineering & water resources, built environment research, real estate & planning/investment & finance/management & development, building conservation, sustainable urban management, community design, urban and regional planning, planning & property development, water resources, safety & risk/reliability management, urban/planning & property development/studies, regional planning; BSc(Hons, Ord), BEng, MEng, MRes, MSc, PGDip/Cert, PhD

### School of Mathematical and Computer Sciences; www.macs.hw.ac.uk

actuarial mathematics/science management, advanced internet applications, applied mathematical sciences, artificial intelligence, computational biology, computer science (interactive design/internet systems technology), computer systems management, creative software systems, financial mathematics/quantitative finance, financial risk management, information systems/technology (business/software systems/interactive design/internet systems/management), mathematics, probabilty & statistics, software engineering, statistical modelling, statistics; BSc(Hons), MEng, MMath, MRes, MSc, PGDip/Cert, PhD

### School of Engineering and Physical Sciences; www.eps.hw.ac.uk

biochemistry, biological & ecological modelling, biomimetic & medicinal chemistry, chemical dynamics, photochemical applied spectra, inorganic chemical synthesis, synthesis and properties of new materials, chemistry/with forensic materials/biology/management/nanoscience/pharmaceutical chemistry, chemical engineering with/energy/oil & gas technology/pharmaceutical chemistry, industrial engineering, climate change impacts, combined science, computational sustainability engineering, energy engineering, electrical power engineering, physics/with electronics/environmental science, applied mathematical science, mathematical statistics & actuarial science, computational mathematics, quantitative finance, mathematical engineering physics, microengineering, nano-technology and photonics, optoelectronic devices, robotics, computing & electronics, electrical & electronic engineering, electrical power & energy, computer & internet engineering/microwaves & electronics information technology (embedded systems/mobile communications, applied systems/software systems), microsystems, nanoscience, photonics & optoelectronic devices, renewable energy, energy & distributed generation, sustainability engineering, mechanical engineering, energy, engineering, renewable energy, energy, science & technology, materials for sustainable & renewable energies, renewable/energy engineering, robotics & cybertronics/vision, robotics, autonomous & interactive systems, industrial engineering, sustainability, energy physics, mathematical physics, nanoscience, combined studies; BEng, BSc(Ord, Hons), EngD, MChem, MEng, MPhil, MPhys, PhD

### School of Life Sciences; www.hw.ac.uk/sls

applied psychology (forensic science), engineering psychology with ergonomics, psychology, biological sciences (cell and molecular biology/human health/microbiology), bioprocesses, biotechnology, brewing and distilling, business psychology, food science/safety & health/nutrition, food & beverage science, applied marine biology, climate change: managing the marine environment/impacts & migration, environmental analysis & assessment, marine biodiversity & biotechnology, marine resource development & protection; BSc(Hons), MSc/Cert/Dip, PGDip, PhD

### School of Management and Languages; www.hw.ac.uk/sml

accountancy & business law/finance, applied language studies, business/adminstration, business management with HRM/marketing/business law/enterprise, economics, finance & management/business languages, international fashion marketing/management, international business management with accountancy/finance/HRM/logistics/sustainable management, international marketing & business communication, investment management, logistics & supply chain management, management with business law/enterprise/HRM/marketing/operations management, maritime logistics & supply chain management, Arabic–English translating & conference interpreting, applied languages & translating (French/German) (French/Spanish) (German/Spanish), Chinese–English translating and conference interpreting/computer-assisted translation tools, interpreting studies & skills, strategic change/project management, social science research; BA(Hons, Ord), GradDip, MA(Hons), MSc

### Heriot-Watt Institute of Petroleum Engineering; www.pet.hw.ac.uk

marine resource management, marine renewable energy, petroleum engineering/geoscience, renewable energy development, reservoir evaluation & management; MPhil, MSc, PhD

### School of Textiles and Design; www.tex.hw.ac.uk

design for textiles/fashion/interior/art, fashion & textile design/management/fashion technology/communication/marketing & retailing/menswear/womenswear, interior design, innovation & new applications, ; BA, BSc(Hons, Ord), MA, MSc, MPhil, PhD

### Edinburgh Business School; www.ebsglobal.net

financial management, HRM, finance, marketing, strategic planning; DBA, MBA, MSc

*Degrees validated by Heriot-Watt University offered at:*

## EDINBURGH COLLEGE OF ART
www.eca.ac.uk

architecture, architectural/conservation/project management, architecture in creative & cultural environments/urban design/action, landscape architecture, adv sustainable development, cultural studies, history of art/theory & display, art, space & nature, Renaissance & early modern studies, modern & contemporary art, art in global middle ages, animation, fashion, film directing, glass, graphic design, illustration, interior design, fine art, jewellery, design & digital media, painting, performance costume, photographic science, product design, sculpture, textiles, urban design; Reid School of Music: acoustics & audiotechnology, composition/for screen, digital composition & performance, music, musicology, music in the community, sound design; BArch, MArch, MLA, MFA, BA(Comb), BSc(Hons, Ord), MA(Hons), MPhil, MSc, PhD, BMus(Hons), MMus

# UNIVERSITY OF HERTFORDSHIRE
**www.herts.ac.uk**

### Business School; www.herts.ac.uk/schools-of-study/courses/business
accounting with financial management/finance, business adminstration/economics/studies/analysis & consultancy, economics, finance & investment management, global business, global economy & business, hospitality, HRM, international business/management/tourism management/tourist & hospitality management, investment management, international/IT management for business, for business, marketing, tourism management, professional studies, project management, proprietary trading, strategic business information systems; BA/BSc, BA(Hons), BSc, DBA, DMan, MA, MBA, MPhil, MSc, PGCert/Dip, PhD

### School of Computer Science; www.herts.ac.uk/courses/schools-of-study/computer-science
advanced computer science, computer science (artificial intelligence/networks/software engineering), artificial intelligence/robotics, information technology (business/entertainment/web-based systems), software engineering, web-based systems; BSc(Hons), MEng, MPhil, MSc, PGCert/Dip, PhD

### School of Creative Arts; www.herts.ac.uk/courses/schools-of-study/creative-arts
animation, applied arts, art therapy, architecture/international/& design, games art, character creation & technical effects, contemporary textiles, composition for film & media, fashion, film & TV, fine art, graphic design, illustration, interactive media software/design, industrial/engineering product/design, interior & spatial design, model design, music composition for film & media, music & sound technology, photography, screen cultures & media production, special/visual effects; BA(Hons), MA, PgCert/Dip, MSc, MPhil, PhD

### School of Education; www.herts.ac.uk/courses/schools-of-study/education
early years, graduate teaching, initial teacher training, PGCE (education: upper, lower, secondary: art & design, business studies, English, mathematics, modern foreign languages), teaching & learning, CPD, primary/secondary education; BA(Hons), BEd, EdD, FdA, MA, MPhil, PGCert/Dip, PGCE, PhD

### School of Engineering & Technology; www.herts.ac.uk/courses/schools-of-study/engineering-and-technology
aerospace engineering/systems/management/with pilot studies, automotive engineering, motorsport technology, broadcast media technology, computer & network technology, data communication & electronics, embedded intelligent systems, film & TV production, mechanical engineering, multimedia systems technology, digital communications & electronics, digital systems & computer engineering, electronics/electrical engineering, adv digital systems, manufacturing management, mobile & smart systems, operations & supply chain management; BSc(Hons), BEng, MEng, MSc, PgDip/Cert, MPhil, PhD

**School of Health and Social Work; www.herts.ac.uk/courses/schools-of-study/health-and-social-work**
diagnostic imaging/radiography, dietetics, interventions, medical imaging & radiation sciences/diagnostic imaging/image interpretation/oncology sciences/radiation science/ultrasound, midwifery/& women's health, nursing(children, adults, mental health, learning disabaility), radiotherapy & oncology, paramedic science, physiotherapy, special community nursing, social work; BSc(Hons), DHRes, FD, MPhil, MSc, PG/Cert/Dip, PhD

**School of Humanities; www.herts.ac.uk/courses/schools-of-study/humanities**
English language & communications or English literature combined with one of the following subjects: acting & screen performance, American studies, creative writing, teaching, ELT, film, French, German, Italian, Spanish, Japanese, history, journalism, media cultures, computing, mass communication, modern literary cultures, new media publishing, philosophy; BA(Hons), MA, MPhil, PGCert/Dip, PhD

**School of Law; www.herts.ac.uk/courses/schools-of-study/law**
law, commercial law, e-commerce law, international law, telecomm law, legal practice, maritime law, corporate practice, government & politics; BSc(Hons), Diploma, LlB(Hons), LlM, MPhil, PGDip, PhD, Univ Cert

**School of Life & Medical Sciences: www.herts.ac.uk/courses/schools-of-study/life-and-medical-sciences**
biochemistry, biological/biomedical/science, biotechnology, counselling, dietetics, dermatological skills & treatment, skin & integrity skills & treatment, medical healthcare simulation, health & medical education, psychiatric/mental health practice, nutrition, therapeutic counselling, business /agriculture with environmental management, environmental management, genetics, geography, medical chemistry, molecular biology, pharmaceutical/& medical science, pharmacology, pharmacovigilance, pharmacy practice, pharmaceutics, psychology (clinical/business/health/occupational), neuropsychology, physiology, sports studies/therapy, sport & exercise science/rehabilitation, water & environmental management, western world acupuncture; BSc/BSc(Hons), MSc, PgCert/Dip

**School of Physics, Astronomy and Mathematics; www.herts.ac.uk/courses/schools-of-study/physics-astronomy-and-mathematics**
astrophysics, financial market analysis, financial maths, mathematics, physics; BSc(Hons), MPhil, MSc, PhD

*Degrees validated by the University of Hertfordshire offered at:*

---

## HERTFORDSHIRE REGIONAL COLLEGE
www.hrc.ac.uk

3D dimensional design, art & design, business, early years, fine art practice, graphic design, community playwork; FD, extension degrees

---

## NORTH HERTFORDSHIRE COLLEGE
www.nhc.ac.uk

Access to HE in a number of subjects

---

## OAKLANDS COLLEGE
www.oaklands.ac.uk

animal management, teacher training, numerous non-degree courses in range of subjects, work-based learning; FD, access to HE in number of subjects

## WEST HERTS COLLEGE
www.westherts.ac.uk

accounting, advertising, art & design, beauty & holistic therapy, business & management, construction, counselling, ESOL, holistic therapies, management studies, marketing, media & photography, teaching; FD, Dip teaching

## THE UNIVERSITY OF HUDDERSFIELD
**www2.hud.ac.uk**

### School of Applied Sciences; www2.hud.ac.uk/sas

Chemical & Biological Sciences: analytical/chemistry, biochemistry, bioscience, chemical engineering/science/biology (molecular & cellular), human biology, nutrition & health, forensic & analytical science, medical biochemistry/biology/genetics/chemical/pharmacy, pharmaceutical chemistry/analytical science, public health

Logistics & Hospitality Management: global/business & logistics management, air/transport & logistics management, logistics & supply chain management, global logistics, hospitality management, events management, travel & tourism; BA(Hons), BSc(Hons), HND, MA, MChem, MPharm, MSc, MSci, PhD

### School of Art, Design and Architecture; www2.hud.ac.uk/ada

3D digital design, animation, architectural technology, architecture, construction/& project management, contemporary arts, construction, costume/with textiles, creative industries, digital media, fashion communication & promotion/design with marketing & production/textiles, fashion and textiles buying, fine art, graphic design, illustration, interdisciplinary art & design, interior design, international design marketing & communication/fashion design/management/promotion/graphic design practice, motion graphics, multimedia design, photography, product design, spatial design, surface design for fashion & interiors; BA(Hons), BSc(Hons), CerHE, DipHE, FdA, FdSc, MA, MArch, MSc

### University of Huddersfield Business School; www2.hud.ac.uk/uhbs

accountancy, advertising/marketing communications, air transport/business economics & logistics management, business administration & management/leadership/operations management, business & journalism/HRM, business administration/studies, entrepreneurship & business, enterprise development, environmental management, European business, events management, financial services, finance, global business/marketing, healthcare management, hospitality management, HRM, international hospitality management/HRM, international business with financial services, legal executive/practice, marketing/communications, logistic & supply chain management, sport promotion & marketing, supply chain management with logistics, transport logistics management, journalism, law, legal practice, management studies, marketing communications/management, international/marketing, media relations, PR, retail, risk, disaster & environmental management, travel & tourism; BA(Hons), FdA, GradDipLaw, HND, LlB(Hons), LlM, MBA, MSc, PGCE, PGDip, PGDip/Cert

### School of Computing and Engineering; www2.hud.ac.uk/ce

automotive design/engineering, motorsport engineering, computer games programming/technology, computing science, computer games production/technology/systems engineering, communications/electronic/electrical engineering, construction & project management, embedded systems engineering, energy engineering, engineering control systems & instrumentation, engineering management, engineering & technical management, information & communication technology, information systems management, mechanical engineering/design, software development/engineering, engineering & technology management, web technologies; BEng(Hons), HNC, HND, MEng, MSc, PhD, UniFdCert

### School of Education and Professional Development; www2.hud.ac.uk/edu

teacher training (PGCE in numerous subjects; primary, secondary, lifelong learning), education, early/childhood studies, early years, enhanced learning, guidance, international education, leadership in education & public service, learning & development management, religion & education, TESOL, vocational education & training; BA(Hons), CertEd, FdA, MA, PGradDip/Cert, PGCE

**Human and Health Sciences; www2.hud.ac.uk/hhs**

childcare welfare & safeguarding, childhood studies, criminology/& international politics, community nursing practice (district nursing), diabetes/end of life palliative care, food nutrition & health, health & social care/community development, health studies (long-term conditions/adv diabetic care/adv practice acute & clinical care/adv midwifery practice), health professional education, teaching healthy lifestyle, health visiting/schools, operating dept practice, public health nursing, sociology, behavioural sciences, district nursing, midwifery, occupational therapy, physiotherapy, podiatry, psychology, social work, nursing (adult, child, learning disability, mental health), perioperative practice, child/welfare, safeguarding, health & community studies, youth & community work; DipHE, MA, MSc, PGDip/Cert, PhD, ProfDoc

**Music, Humanities and Media; www2.hud.ac.uk/mhm**

drama, English/literature/language, creative writing, broadcast/sports journalism, history/& politics, film studies, modern languages, music, music technology/journalism, media & popular culture, pop music; BA(Hons), FdA, MA, PdF, PhD

## UNIVERSITY OF HULL
## www.hull.ac.uk

### *Faculty of Arts and Social Sciences; www.hull.ac.uk/fass*

Drama & Music: drama & theatre practice/history of art, music, jazz /& pop music, creative music technology

English: English, American literature & culture, creative writing, film studies, English in jt dgrees, music & the creative media, music technology

History: regional local history & regional studies & archaeology, history (20th century, cultural, medieval, maritime, military, European, social)

Humanities: American studies, film studies, philosophy, religion

Modern Languages: French/German/Italian studies, modern language studies, combined language degrees

Politics & International Studies: politics, British politics & legal studies, politics & international relations, /history, philosophy, politics, philosophy & economics, war & security studies, civilization, terrorism & dissent, EWU governance, globalisation & governance, global communications & international politics, /political economy, international law & politics, strategy & international security

Social Sciences: criminology, sociology, social work, community & youthwork studies, media studies, applied social research, women & gender studies, restorative justice

### *School of Law*

law (commercial, international, business, human rights, environmental, French, Spanish, German, European public), legislative studies, criminology, international law & restorative justice/politics, senior status; BA(Hons), BMus, BSc(Hons), LIB, LLM, MA, MEd, MMus, MPhil, MR/MRes, PGDip/Cert, PhD

### *The Hull University Business School; www.hull.ac.uk/hubs*

accounting, advertising, business, business/economics/technology management/analytics, economics, energy marketing, finance & investment, financial management/economics/mathematics, HRM, international business, investment, IT/management, logistics, management consultancy, marketing management, money, banking, finance, sport, leisure, tourism, logistics & supply chain management; BA(Hons), BSc(Hons), MBA, MPhil, MRes, MSc, PhD

### *Faculty of Health and Social Care; www.hull.ac.uk/fhsc*

acute mental health/care, advanced practice (neonatal care) autonomous practice, community care, colonoscopy, consultation, clinical leadership, cognitive behaviour therapy, clinical psychology, critical care, dental nursing, family therapy & systemic practice, nursing (adult, children's, knowledge transfer, practice teaching, learning disabilities, acute/mental health, community), gastroenterology, leadership in health & social care, midwifery, non-medical prescribing, operating dept practice, critical/emergency/neonatal care, public health, return to practice, sexual health & well being; Adv Diploma, BSc(Hons), FD, MPhil, MRes, PhD, Univ Cert, PGDip/Cert, D Clin Psy

**The Hull York Medical School; www.hyms.ac.uk**

anatomical science, biomedical science, cancer, cardiovascular medicine, child health, clinical sciences, clinical techniques & skills, cognitive behavioural therapy, dermatology, evidence-based decision making, gastrointestinal medicine, human evolution/science, immunology, medicine, medical education/science, mental health, metabolic & renal medicine, pathology, person-centred care, population health & medicine, reproduction, respiration, sport & exercise education/science, surgery; BSc, MBBS, MPhil, MA, MRes, MSc/Dip/Cert, PGCert/Dip, PhD

## *Faculty of Education; www.2.hull.ac.uk/ifl*

learning support, childhood studies, integrative counselling, education and learning, learning and teaching – primary education with QTS, early childhood education and care, higher education, education and society, education, social inclusion and special needs, education and early learning, children's inter-professional studies, teaching English (literacy/mathematics) in the lifelong learning sector, ESOL, teaching maths (numeracy) in the lifelong learning sector, educational studies, initial teacher training, HE, PGCE primary: 5–11, PGCE secondary (numerous subjects), sustained professional development, early childhood studies, elearning, inclusive education, leadership and learning, mentoring in education, teaching and learning; BA, EdD, FD, GradCert, MA, MEd, MPhil, MSc, PGCE, PhD, PGCert(HE), CertEd, MTL

## *Postgraduate Medical Institute; www2.hull.ac.uk/pgmi*

post-graduate medical education; PGCME, MD, MPhil, PhD

## *Faculty of Science & Engineering; www.hull.ac.uk/science*

Biological Sciences: aquatic zoology, biology, biomedical science, coastal marine biology, ecology, human biology, marine & freshwater biology, molecular medicine, zoology, environmental science

Chemistry: biological chemistry, chemistry, analytical chemistry, forensic science/& criminology, pharmaceutical science, molecular medicine, nanotechnology, toxicology

Computer Science: computer science/engineering, games development/programming, computer software/systems development, information systems, computer graphics/games programming, NET distribution systems/development

Engineering: automatic control & logistics technology, chemical engineering, computer aided engineering, electrical & electronic engineering, electronics product design, mechanical engineering, medical engineering, medical product design, product innovation, embedded systems, automatic control, wireless systems engineering, plant & process /process engineering management

Geography, Environment & Earth Sciences: human/physical geography, environmental management/technology, geology, renewable energy

Physics & Mathematics: applied/physics, astrophysics, nanotechnology, philosophy, mathematics

Sports Science, Health & Exercise Science: coaching & performance, sports & exercise science, sports rehabilitation, performance, sports science

Psychology: psychology, clinical psychology, health psychology; BA, BEng, BSc, BSc/MEng, MPhil, MPhys, MPhysGeog, MRes, MSc, PhD, FdEng

# *Degrees validated by the University of Hull offered at:*

## BISHOP BURTON COLLEGE
www.bishopburton.ac.uk

agriculture, animal management, applied science, art, design & fashion, business & management, countryside, environmental sustainability, equine, floristry, food, garden design & horticulture, public services, sport, teacher training, tourism; BA(Hons), BSc(Hons), HNC, MSc, PGCE

## DONCASTER COLLEGE
## www.don.ac.uk

animation and games art, contemporary performance practice, creative music technology, dance practice, fashion & textiles, fine art, graphic design, illustration & animation, business management, applied social science, criminal justice, early childhood studies, English, sport, exercise & health sciences, sport, fitness & exercise science, working with children and young people, integrated technology, creative pattern cutting, business administration, education, innovation & enterprise, relationship theory; BA(Hons), BSc, BSc(Hons), FD, HND, MA, MSc, PGCE, PGCert/Dip, MBA

## IMPERIAL COLLEGE, LONDON
## www3.imperial.ac.uk

### *Faculty of Engineering; www3.engineering.imperial.ac.uk*

Aeronautics: composites, adv computational methods for aeronautics, flow management & fluid structure interaction
Bioengineering: bioengineering, biomedical engineering, biomedical device design & entrepreneurship
Chemical Engineering: chemical engineering/ with nuclear engineering, adv chemical engineering with biotechnology/process systems engineering
Civil & Environmental Engineering: civil/structural engineering, structural steel design, concrete structures, civil & environmental engineering, earthquake engineering, engineering geology, environmental engineering, geotechnics, hydrology, soil mechanics & engineering geology, transport, systems engineering & innovation
Computing: adv computing, computing & artificial intelligence/biology & medicine/games/vision & interactivity/software engineering, computer science (games, vision, software engineering, biology, medicine), computing (architecture/creative industries/ distributed systems/visual information processing/ artificial intelligence), data science & management, robotics & image intervention
Earth Science & Engineering: geology, geophysics, environmental/petroleum geoscience/geophysics, materials & energy finance, petroleum science engineering/geophysics, metals, remote sensing
Electrical & Electronic Engineering: electronic & electrical engineering, analogue & digital integrated circuit design, information systems engineering, communications & signal processing, control systems
Materials: material science & engineering, aerospace materials, biomaterials & tissue engineering, biomedical engineering & biomaterials, materials & nuclear engineering, advanced materials, composites
Mechanical Engineering: adv/mechanical engineering, nuclear engineering, innovation design engineering, global engineering design; BEng, MA, MEng, MSc, MSci, PhD

### *Faculty of Medicine; www1.medicine.imperial.ac.uk*

medicine, allergy, bioinformation & theoretical systems, biomedical research/science, cancer biology, cardiorespiratory nursing, cellular pathology, clinical research design & management, epidemiology, haematology, experimental neuroscience, health, policy quality & safety in healthcare, human molecular genetics, human nutrition, immunology, infection management for pharmacists, medical ultrasound, molecular biology & pathology of viruses, molecular medicine, neuroscience, paediatrics, preventative cardiology, public health, quality & safety in healthcare, reproductive biology, respiratory, science, surgery & cancer, surgery/technology/science; BSc, CAS, MB BS, MEd, MPH, MRes, MSc, MSci, PhD

### *Imperial College Business School; www3.imperial.ac.uk/business-school*

accounting, actuarial finance, data science & management, economics & strategy for business, finance, global business, innovation management, innovation, entrepreneurship & management, international health management, management, managerial economics, marketing/management, materials & energy finance, people & organisational behaviour, project management, risk management and financial engineering, strategic marketing; BSc, MBA, MSc, PhD

### Faculty of Natural Sciences; www3.imperial.ac.uk/naturalsciences

Chemistry: chemical biology/health & design, bioimaging sciences, chemistry and management/medicinal chemistry/molecular physics, green chemistry, nanomaterials, plant chemical biology, drug discovery & development
Life Sciences: applied biosciences, biology, theoretical systems biology, bioinformatics & theoretical systems biology, biomedical science, biosystematics, biotechnology, biology, ecology & environmental biology, environment & conservation, microbiology, plant science & biotechnics, taxonomy & biomedicine, zoology
biodiversity informatics and genomics, chemical biology of crop sustainability and protection, conservation science, ecology, evolution & conservation, ecology, molecular and cellular biosciences, molecular plant and microbial sciences quantitative biology, structural molecular biology, systems and synthetic biology
Mathematics: applied/pure mathematics, computational statistics/logistics, mathematical sciences, mathematical physics, mathematics & computer science, optimisation & statistics for finance, statistical financial management, statistics
Physics: physics, optics and photonics, controlled quantum dynamics, plastic electronics, plasmonics & metamaterials, quantum fields and fundamental forces, theoretical physics, theory and simulation of materials; BSc, MRes, MSci, PhD

## KEELE UNIVERSITY
## www.keele.ac.uk

### Faculty of Health; www.keele.ac.uk/facs/health

#### School of Medicine; www.keele.ac.uk/depts/schoolofmedicine

anatomical sciences, biomedical engineering, cell and tissue engineering, clinical audit, end of life care, formulative medicine, health professionals education, individual health, primary care, parasitology, vector biology, foundation medical practice/ethics, geriatric medicine, leadership & management, medical education, medical science/practice, medicine, obstetrics & gynaecology, palliative care, stroke treatment, surgery

#### School of Pharmacy; www.keele.ac.uk/schools/pharm

adv professional practice, clinical (hospital) pharmacy, pharmacist, public health/community pharmacist, prescribing adviser, medical/non medical/practice-based prescribing, medicines management

#### School of Nursing and Midwifery; www.keele.ac.uk/depts/ns

acute care, adult/children's nursing/mental health/learning disabilities, adv professional practice, clinical practice, critical care, end of life care, independent practice development, midwifery, operating department practice, pain science & management, physiotherapy (neurology) post-registration rheumatology nursing

#### School of Health and Rehabilitation; www.keele.ac.uk/depts/pt

applied clinical anatomy, health science/social care, individual health, neurological rehabilitation, neuromusculoskeletal healthcare, osteopathy, pain science management, physiotherapy; MBChB, BSc, MSc, MSci, MPharm, PGCert/Dip, MMedSci, MPhil, PhD, MD

### Faculty of Humanities and Social Sciences; www.keele.ac.uk/facs/humass

#### Keele Management School; www.keele.ac.uk/schools/ems

accounting, finance, actuarial science, business management/economics, economics, European industrial relations,, finance & IT/management, HRM, international business, leadership, management, management & IT, marketing; MA, MBA, MSc, PGCert, PGDip, UnivCert

#### School of Humanities; www.keele.ac.uk/schools/hums

American studies/literature and culture, English, creative writing, English and American literatures, humanities, Victorian studies, early modern history, history, local and public history, medieval cultural history, film studies/theory, media communication/global media & culture, medical humanities, music/technology, popular music, performance, composition

**Keele Law School; www.keele.ac.uk/depts/law**
child care law & practice, gender, sexuality & human rights, globalization & justice, medical ethics & law, law, law with politics/criminology, law & society, safeguarding adults, international law, palliative care

**School of Politics, International Relations and Philosophy; www.keele.ac.uk/spire**
diplomatic studies, environmental politics, environment, European politics & culture, global security, international relations, politics & elections, philosophy, politics,

**School of Public Policy and Professional Practice; www.keele.ac.uk/schools/pppp**
Education: ADP, creative and critical practice, developing educational practice, educational leadership/studies/management/learning/international, mathematics development, PGCE (primary, secondary, subject enhancement, pre-teaching training), teaching & learning, social work, education, health executive/systems/policy, public policy, gerontology, health services management, HE teaching & learning, community health, geriatric medicine, mentoring management, professional leadership & management; GradDip Law, EdD, LlB, LLM, MA, MBA, MRes, MSc, PGCE, PGDip/Cert, PhD

### *Faculty of Natural Sciences; www.keele.ac.uk/facs/sci/*

**School of Computing and Mathematics; www.scm.keele.ac.uk**
actuarial science, computer science, creative computing, finance/management and IT, information systems, IT management for business, mathematics (pure, applied, statistics), project management, smart systems, web & internet technologies

**School of Life Sciences; www. keele.ac.uk/depts/bi**
biochemistry, biology, biomedical blood/science, human biology, molecular parasitology and vector biology, neuroscience

**School of Physical and Geographical Sciences; www.keele.ac.uk/schools/dps/**
chemistry, chemical sciences, medicinal chemistry, analytical, materials & surface chemistry, spectroscopy, bioinorganic chemistry, chemical ecology, forensic science, green chemistry and clean energy, organic chemistry, photochemistry, applied environmental science, earth science, environment and sustainability, environmental sustainability & green technology, geography, geology, geoscience, human/physical geography: forensic science, astrophysics, physics

**School of Psychology; www.keele.ac.uk/depts/ps**
psychology, child social development, clinical psychology, counselling psychology/supervision, psychology/of health & wellbeing; BA, BSc, DClinPsy, DSc, MGeoscience, MRes, MSc, PGCert, PGDip, PhD

## UNIVERSITY OF KENT
## www.kent.ac.uk

### *Faculty of Humanities; www.kent.ac.uk/humanities*

**Kent School of Architecture; www.kent.ac.uk/architecture**
architecture, architectural visualisation, architecture & cities/sustainable development

**School of Arts; www.kent.ac.uk/arts**
arts criticism, creative events, curating, drama & theatre studies, European theatre, film studies, fine art, history & philosophy of art/aesthetics, in the contemporay, music technology/composition, event & experience design, music & audio arts, Shakespeare, theatre dramaturgy

**School of English; www.kent.ac.uk/english**
English/American literature, post-colonial studies/literature, creative writing, critical theory, Dickens & Victorian culture, medieval & early modern studies, 18th century studies, jt degrees

**School of European Culture & Languages; www.kent.ac.uk/secl**
ancient history, classical & archaeological studies/history, archaeology of the late transmarche, heritage

management, Hellenic & Hellenic near east, drama, English language & linguistics, English & American literature, history, medical humanities, modern French/German/Hispanic studies & comparative literature, history of archaeology, Italian, language & linguistic studies, modern European literature, philosophy, post-colonial studies, theory & method in the study of religion, mysticism in religious experience, Roman history & architecture, history & philosophy of art

### School of History; www.kent.ac.uk/history

American studies, history, European history, history of science, modern history, technology & medicine, medieval & modern studies, propaganda & war, war studies, war, media & society, science, communication & society, science medicine & society; BA(Hons), BSc(Hons), MA, MArch, MDram, MPhil, PhD

## *Faculty of Science; www.kent.ac.uk/stms*

### Dept of Bioscience; www.kent.ac.uk/bio

biology, biomedical sciences, biochemistry, biotechnology & bioengineering, reproductive medicine/ science & ethics, cancer biology, science, community & society

### School of Computing; www.cs.kent.ac.uk

adv/computer science – artificial intelligence/consultancy/networks, business administration/information science, computing & entrepreneurship, computational intelligence, business information technology, computing security, future computing, IT (consulting, ) information security & biometrics, adv software development, business/IT/information science, web computing

### School of Engineering and Digital Arts; www.eda.kent.ac.uk

advanced/electronic/computer systems engineering, architectural visualisation, broadband & mobile communications, computing systems, digital visual effects/arts, electronic & communications engineering, embedded systems & instrumentation, drama & multimedia, information security/biometrics, mobile communication methods, mobile applications design, multimedia technology & design, web computing, wireless communication & signal processing

### School of Mathematics, Statistics & Actuarial Science; www.kent.ac.uk/Ismsas

applied/actuarial science, bioscience, drug, financial & accounting mathematics, pure/applied maths, statistics, finance, investment, risk, mathematics & applications

### Medway School of Pharmacy; www.msp.kent.ac.uk

medicines management, pharmacy/& physiology, independent supplementary prescribing, drug discovery, applied bioscience technology

### School of Physical Sciences; www.kent.ac.uk/physical-sciences

astrophysics, astronomy, forensic science, chemistry, physics, planetary/space science; BA(Hons), BEng, BSc(Hons), DClinPsych, MD, MRes, MPhil, MSc, MSurg, PCert, PDip, PhD

### School of Sport & Exercise Science; www.kent.ac.uk/sportscience

sport & exercise science/management, sports therapy & rehabilitation, sport for exercise & health, sport science for optimal performance; BSc(Hons), MSc, ProfDoc, MPhil, PhD

## *Faculty of Social Sciences; www.kent.ac.uk/socsci*

### School of Anthropology and Conservation; www.kent.ac.uk/sac

anthropology (social/biological/medical), biodiversity conservation & management, conservation biology, environmental anthropology/studies, conservation & int wildlife trade/tourism, liberal arts, social/visual anthropology, wildlife conservation; BA(Hons), BSc(Hons), MA, MSc, PhD

### Kent Business School; www.kent.ac.uk/kbs

accounting, business administration, business/management studies, finance, financial services/management, HRM, international business/management, logistics, management science, marketing, value chain management; BA(Hons), BBA, BSc(Hons), MBA, MEBA, MPhil, MSc

### School of Economics; www.kent.ac.uk/economics

agricultural economics & policies, applied economics & international development, applied environmental economics, econometrics, economics, finance, financial economics, economic development, international finance/economic development; BSc(Hons), MPhil, PhD, MSc

### Kent Law School; www.kent.ac.uk/law

international/criminal justice, English law, European legal studies/law, numerous joint degrees, French/ German/Spanish/Italian law, international environmental/commercial/economic law, international criminal justice, medical law & ethics, public international law, senior status; BA(Hons), LlB, LlM, MPhil, PhD, GradDip

**Centre for Journalism; www.kent.ac.uk/journalism**
journalism, international multimedia journalism, journalism & the news industry; BA(Hons), MA

**School of Politics and International Relations; www.kent.ac.uk/politics**
comparative politics, conflict peace & security, environmental & global governance, European and global governance, human rights, international conflict analysis/relations, international law, international security and the politics of terror, peace and conflict studies, political theory and practices of resistance, security and terrorism, methods in social research; BA(Hons), MA, MPhil, PhD, PGDip

**Dept of Psychology; www.kent.ac.uk/psychology**
applied psychology, cognitive psychology/neuropsychology, clinical/ developmental psychology, forensic psychology, group processes & intergroup relations, psychology, social psychology; BSc(Hons), MPhil, MSc, PhD

**School of Social Policy, Sociology and Social Research; www.kent.ac.uk/sspssr**
criminal justice studies, criminology, cultural studies, health & social care, intellectual & development disabilities, international/social policy, sociology, social work/sciences, advanced child protection research and practice, autism studies, analysis and intervention in intellectual and developmental disabilities, applied behavioural analysis, civil society, NGO and non-profit studies, criminology, environmental social science, international social policy, methods of social research, political sociology, social and public policy (commissioning/criminal justice/urban regeneration); BA(Hons), BSc(Hons), GradDip/Cert Diplomas, MA, MPhil, MSc, PhD

## KINGSTON UNIVERSITY
## www.kingston.ac.uk

### *Faculty of Art, Design and Architecture; www.kingston.ac.uk/faculties/#design*
architecture/professional practice, aesthetics & art theory, art & design/history/market/space, art market appraisal, building surveying, design, thinking buildings, communication design & the creative economy, computer generated design, curating contemporary design, design for development, design with learning & technology in HE, design & human wellbeing/product & space, European art practice, experimental film, fashion/retailing/& the creative economy, film studies/making, fine art (painting, sculpture, intermedia, games development, print/with learning in creative economy), graphic design, generated image, heritage, historic building conservation, history of art, design & film, illustration & animation, interior design, landscape architecture/urbanism, museum & gallery studies, photography, planning & sustainability, product & furniture design, product design for film & TV, professional practice (design), property planning & development, quantity surveying consultancy, real estate management, residential property, sustainable placemaking & urban design user experience; BA(Hons), FdA, FdSc, MA, MSc, PGCert/Dip

### *Faculty of Arts and Social Sciences; www.fass.kingston.ac.uk*
applied economics, business, business economics, creative music technologies, criminology/with law, dance, drama, economics, English language & communication, English literature, film studies, financial economics, French, history, human rights, international relations, journalism, media and cultural studies, politics/and international relations, psychology, sociology, Spanish, TV and new broadcasting media, aesthetics and art theory, applied econometrics, applied linguistics for language teaching, applied social research methods, business and economic forecasting, business economics/psychology, child psychology, clinical applications of psychology, composing for film and television, contemporary European philosophy, creative writing and pedagogy/publishing/low residency, creative writing & the creative economy, criminological psychology, criminology/with law, criticism, literature, theory,

cybercrime, development and international economics, developmental psychology, economics (political economy), environmental politics, film making/& the creative economy, financial economics, human rights/ and genocide studies, international conflict, international political communication, advocacy and campaigning, international politics and economics, international relations, journalism/ in open societies/& the creative economy, language and society, law with criminology or human rights, magazine journalism, media and communication, modern European philosophy, music/education/performance, music & the creative economy, nationalism, occupational psychology, philosophy and contemporary critical theory/ political economy, playwriting, political communication, advocacy and campaigning, politics, production of popular music, publishing/& the creative economy, sonic arts, terrorism and political violence, translation studies

BA(Hons), MA, PgCert/Dip, EdD, BMus, MMus, MSc, MFA

## Faculty of Law & Business; www.business.kingston.ac.uk

### Kingston Business School:

accounting, banking, finance, business, management, business information technology & perational management, marketing & communications, creative industries, general management, leadership, HRM, professional practice

### Kingston School of Law:

law, criminology, international commercial/corporate & financial/employment/general law, dispute resolution, employment law & mediation, human rights, immigration law, international/commercial law, conflict, international relations, law of international trade, legal studies, senior status, law with business/criminology/human rights; BA(Hons), BSc(Hons), DBA, FdA, GradDip Law, HND, LlM, MA, MBA, MSC, PhD

## Faculty of Science, Engineering & Computing; www.sec.kingston.ac.uk

Aerospace & Aircraft Engineering: aerospace engineering, astronautics & space technology, aircraft engineering/maintenance/repair, aviation studies for commercial pilots

Civil Engineering & Construction: civil engineering, construction management, construction management & law, management in construction structural design, sustainable construction/development

Computing & Information Systems: computer science (computer graphics & digital imaging), electronic commerce, embedded systems, games programming, information systems with management, IT & strategic innovation, network & data communications/& information security, network communications, computing/studies, cyber security & computer forensics, games technology/programming, geology, information systems, internet business, mobile computing, network & data security, networking & data communication, software engineering/communication, TV & video technology, web development, wireless communication

Geography, Geology and the Environment: applied & environmental geology, environmental/hazards & disaster management/& earth resources management, environmental/management/science/systems, GIS & science, geography/human/physical, sustainable development, sustainability environment & change, sustainable environmental development & management studies

Life Sciences: biochemistry, biology, biomedical/ genetics & molecular/human/medical biology), cancer biology, cell & molecular biology, health information management, forensic biology/science, human biology, medical biochemistry, nutrition, pharmacology, sports science/analysis & coaching

Mathematics: actuarial mathematics & statistics, mathematical science, mathematics, statistics, financial mathematics & business, computational mathematics

Mechanical & Automotive Engineering: advanced industrial & manufacturing systems, advanced product design engineering, automotive engineering, commercial vehicle /motorcycle technology/hybrid & electrical vehicles, communication systems, computer graphics technology, creative technology, engineering projects & systems management, mechanical engineering, mechatronic systems, media technology, motorsport engineering, professional engineering, renewable energy engineering

Pharmacy & Chemistry: analytical chemistry, chemistry, forensic analysis, pharmaceutical analysis/ science, pharmaceutical & chemical sciences, pharmacy; BSc(Hons), BEng, FdSc, FdEng, HND, MComp, MPharmSci, MPhil, MSc, PhD, PGCert/ Dip, MEng

## Faculty of Health, Social Care Sciences & Education; www.healthcare.kingston.ac.uk

advanced practice (health care), breast imaging, clinical practice, CPD, English (language teaching), primary/secondary teaching leading to QTS, professional eduaction & training, professional studies in education, child-centred interprofessional practice, children's special needs, early years management & leadership/teaching, exercise for health, health education/healthcare practice & clinical leadership, maternal & child health/social/cultural perspective, midwifery/registered midwife, nursing/registered nurse, paramedic science, physiotherapy, radiography (breast evaluation/medical imaging/mammography/oncology practice) rehabilitation, social work, BSc(Hons), DipHE, FdSc, MREs, MPhil, MSc, MA, MSW, PGCert/Dip, PhD, PGDip, FdA, FdSc

# LANCASTER UNIVERSITY
# www.lancs.ac.uk

## Faculty of Arts and Social Sciences: www.lancs.ac.uk/fass/faculty

### European Languages and Cultures; www.lancs.ac.uk/fass/eurolang

European languages/management & film studies, European legal studies, German, Italian, French, Spanish, modern languages, film studies, European institutions & policy/languages & cultures/legal studies/languages & management studies

### Applied Social Science; www.lancs.ac.uk/fass/appsocsci

criminology, social work

### Educational Research; www.lancs.ac.uk/fass/edres

educational research, education & social justice, HE, Research & evaluation

### English and Creative Writing; www.lancs.ac.uk/fass/english

English language & literature studies/creative writing, film studies, creative writing/art, contemporary literature, English creative writing & practice

### History; www.lancs.ac.uk/fass/history

history, medieval & Renaissance studies, modern European/ social history, locality & regional history, landscape & heritage, digital humanities, early modern history

### Lancaster Institute for the Contemporary Arts; www.lancs.ac.uk/fass/licr

contemporary arts, fine art, marketing & design, music, innovation & design, theatre studies, film studies, design/management & policy

### School of Law; www.lancs.ac.uk/fass/law

law, bioethics, medical law, European legal studies, humanitarian/diplomatic/international law, business & corporate law, international human rights/law, law & criminology, human rights/law & the environment, terrorism law, international relations

### Linguistics & English Language; www.ling.lancs.ac.uk

English language, linguistics & Chinese/philosophy, English language & creative writing/Chinese/French/German/Spanish/the media/linguistics, applied/linguistics, English language & literary studies, teaching English (TESOL/TEFL), discourse studies, language testing

### Politics, Philosophy & Religion; www.lancs.ac.uk/fass/ppr

politics, conflict resolution & peace studies, conflict, development & security, diplomacy & foreign policy, international relations/religion, politics & international relations, history & international relations, philosophy & religious studies, philosophy/history, politics & economics, medical law, religious studies, philosophy, diplomacy, foreign policy, international law, religion, conflict, development & security, conflict resolution & peace studies, religion & conflict

### Sociology; www.lancs.ac.uk/fass/sociology

sociology, environment, culture & society, gender and women's studies, media & cultural studies, sociological research, science studies; BSc(Hons), LlB, LlM, MA, MPhil, MSc, PGDip, PhD

## School of Health and Medicine; www.lancs.ac.uk/shm/faculties

### Biomedical & Life Sciences; www.lancs.ac.uk/shm/bls

biochemistry/with biomedicine or genetics, biomedical (applied), biological science, cell biology, clinical psychology, life sciences, premedical studies, medical biotechnology & leadership

**Lancaster Medical School; www.lancs.ac.uk/shm/med**
basic biomedical research, biomedicine, biomedical & life sciences, environment & biochemical toxicology, health research, medical education/sciences, medical statistics & epidemiology, medicine, surgery, premedical studies, toxicology, clinical psychology/research; BSc(Hons), CertHE, DClinPsych, MBChB, MBiomed, MD, MHospice leadership, MPhil, MRes, MSc, PgDip/Cert, PhD

## *Lancaster University Management School; www.lums.lancs.ac.uk*

accounting/finance & computer science/management, advertising, auditing, banking, business studies/analytics & consultancy/economics, economics, entrepreneurship, European-American management, quantitative/finance, financial management/analysis/mathematics, HR, management & entrepreneurship/IT/organisation/mathematics, management studies & European languages, organisational studies & psychology/sociology, marketing, operational research; BA(Hons), BBA, BSc(Hons), LlM, MBA, MPhil, MRes, MSc, PhD

## *Faculty of Science and Technology; www.lancs.ac.uk/shm/sci-tech/faculties*

**Computing & Communication; www.lancs.ac.uk/sci-tech/departments/computing_and_communication**
business information & information systems, computer science, computer systems & electronics, communications/computer/systems, engineering/& electronics/innovation, cyber security, high wire, software engineering, IT for creative industries, network & internet systems

**Engineering; www.engineering.lancs.ac.uk**
chemical engineering, engineering, electronic/electrical engineering, mechatronics, mechanical engineering/systems engineering, nuclear engineering, sustainable engineering, computer systems engineering, decommissioning & environmental clean-up, safety engineering, smart systems engineering

**Lancaster Environment Centre; www.lec.lancs.ac.uk**
biological/biomedical science, contamination, risk assessment & remediation & conservation, ecology & conservation, environmental/biology/chemistry, environment & development, environment, culture & society, environmental change & sustainable development, environmental management & consultancy/science & technology, environmental & biochemical toxology, earth/& environmental science, geography, plant science, resource & environmental management, sustainable water management, agriculture & food security, volcanology & geological hazard

**Mathematics and Statistics; www.maths.lancs.ac.uk**
applied social statistics, mathematics, computer science and mathematics, statistics, financial mathematics, mathematics & philosophy/statistics/psychology/theoretical physics, quantitative methods for science/social science, statistics & operational research

**Natural Sciences; www.naturalsci.lancs.ac.uk**
combined science, combined technology, natural sciences

**Physics; www.lancs.ac.uk/depts/physics**
astrophysics, cosmology, biomedical physics, physics, space science, theoretical physics/with mathematics, particle physics

**Psychology; www.psych.lancs.ac.uk**
development psychology/disorders, language, organisational studies & psychology, linguistics & psychology/French/German/Spanish, psychology, psychology of advertising, social psychology, psychological research methods; BEng(Hons), BSc(Hons), MChem, MEng (Hons), MPhil, MPhys (Hons), MRes, MSc, MSci(Hons), PGDip, PhD

## *Degrees validated by Lancaster University offered at:*

---

### BLACKPOOL AND THE FYLDE COLLEGE
### www.blackpool.ac.uk

criminology and criminal justice, English language, literature and writing, history and heritage management studies, marine biology and coastal zone management, marine biology and coastal zone management, media writing with production, contemporary media practice, acting, fashion and costume for performance, fine art and professional practice, graphic design, illustration, musical theatre, photography/and digital design, engineering illustration, automotive (autosport) engineering and technology, mechanical and production engineering, mechatronics, information technology, interactive design (game), interactive media development, network engineering security and systems administration, project management, automotive engineering and technology, autosport engineering and technology, interactive media development, network engineering security and systems administration, software engineering, game development, hospitality management (international hotel management, international resort tourism management, sports studies and development, sports coaching, events management, hospitality management (licensed retail), sports studies and development, travel and tourism management; FD, HNC, HND, BEng, BA(Hons), BSc/(Hons)

---

## EDGE HILL UNIVERSITY
## www.edgehill.ac.uk

### *Faculty of Education; www.edgehill.ac.uk/education*

Education with QTS, (PGCE): primary English education/ mathematics/ modern languages/ science secondary computer science and information technology/ design and technology/ English/ mathematics/ modern foreign languages/ religious education/ science (biology)/science (chemistry) education/ science (physics), post-compulsory education and training, children and young people's learning and development, early years professional practice and leadership, international early years education, teaching, learning and mentoring practice, teaching, learning and mentoring practice, early years leadership, early years practice, professional development, teaching in the lifelong learning sector, professional development, clinical education, education, management of international higher education, qualitative educational research, simulation and clinical learning, specialist dyslexia training, specialist primary mathematics practice; BA(Hons), BSc(Hons), CertHE, FD, PGCE, MA, MTL, PGCert

### *Faculty of Health & Social Care; www.edgehill.ac.uk/health*

children's nursing/learning disabilities & social work, health & social care, integrated children's & young people practice, nursing studies (adult, learning disabilities, mental health, children's), midwifery, operating department practice, paramedic practice, children's health & wellbeing, health & social wellbeing, leadership & management in children's services, midwifery, nutrition & health, complementary therapies, counselling & psychotherapy, playwork intervention, psychosocial analysis of offending behaviour, support for families & communities, social work, working with vulnerable adults; BSc(Hons), Dip/CertHE, FdA/Sc, MCh, MPhil, MSc, MPhil, PhD

### *Faculty of Arts and Science*

#### Biology; www.edgehill.ac.uk/biology

biology, also conservation management; BSc{Hons), MSc

#### Business School; www.edgehill.ac.uk/business

accounting, advertising, business, management/administration/development, civil society leadership, HRM, int business, leisure & tourism, management (accounting), marketing/& communications, PR, sustainable production, public administration, voluntary & 3rd sector management

#### Dept of English and History; www.edgehill.ac.uk/history

creative writing, English language/literature, film studies/production, history, pop/culture, humanities

#### Computing; www.edgehill.ac.uk/computing

computing (application development/mobile and embedded systems/games programming/information systems/networking, security and forensics/IT management for business/web systems development, advanced software application development, computing, information security and IT management, IT (computing/multimedia); BSc(Hons), MSc, MRes, FdSc

#### Law & Criminology; www.edgehill.ac.uk/law

criminology & criminal justice, law, international business & commercial/justice & human rights law, law

**Media; www.edgehill.ac.uk/media**
digital SFX/animation, advertising, film & TV production, journalism, media, film & TV or music & sound/enterprise, stop-motion animation, screen production, media/TV production management

**Dept Geography and Geology; www.edgehill.ac.uk/geography**
environmental science, geography, geology, human/physical geography

**Performing Arts; www.edgehill.ac.uk/performingart**
drama & dance, design for performance, physical/visual theatre, music & sound/enterprise/drama, performance & health, making performance, scriptwriting, dance movement psychotherapy

**Dept of Psychology; www.edgehill.ac.uk/psychology**
psychology, educational psychology, sport & exercise psychology

**Dept of Social Science; www.edgehill.ac.uk/social science**
childhood & youth studies, early childhood studies, sociology, youth & community work

**Dept of Sport & Physical Activity; www.edgehill.ac.uk/sport**
applied sport & exercise science, coach education, PE & school sport, sport & exercise psychology/science, sports development/studies/therapy, football rehabilitation;
BA(Hons), BSc(Hons), FDA, FDSc, LlB(Hons), MA, MSc, PhD, MBA, MRes, PGDip

## UNIVERSITY OF LEEDS
## www.leeds.ac.uk

### *Faculty of Arts; www.leeds.ac.uk/arts*

**School of English; www.leeds.ac.uk/english**
American literature & culture, critical & cultural studies, English language/literature, modern & contemporary/English Renaissance literature, post-colonial literary & cultural studies, romantic literature & culture, theatre & global studies, theatre making/studies, Victorian literature

**School of History; www.leeds.ac.uk/history**
history, international history & politics, medieval history, modern history, race & resistance, social & cultural history

**School of Philosophy, Religion & History of Science; www.leeds.ac.uk/religion_philosophy_and_history_of_science**
classical civilization/studies, classics, philosophy, psychology & scientific thought, history and philosophy of science, philosophy of religion, religion/theology and public life, religious studies/theology & global development, theology & religious studies, science communication, theology

**Institute for Colonial and Post-colonial Studies; www.leeds.ac.uk/icps**
post-colonial literary & cultural studies, race & resistance, world cinema, modern languages & cultures

**School of Modern Languages and Cultures; www.leeds.ac.uk/smlc**
Arabic & Middle Eastern/Islamic studies, Asia-Pacific studies, Chinese, Japanese, South/East Asian studies, Thai studies, French, German, Italian, linguistics & phonetics, Russian, Spanish, Portuguese and Latin American studies, translation & interpreting, world cinema; BA(Hons), MA, MPhil, PGDip, PhD

### *Faculty of Biological Studies; www.fbs.leeds.ac.uk*

biochemistry, applied/biology, biological science, bioscience, bioinformatics & computational biology, biotechnology, biodiversity & human disease & therapy, infection/microbiology & immunology, plant science, ecology & environmental biology, biodiversity & conservation, genetics, human physiology, medical biochemistry/microbiology/sciences, microbiology, neuroscience, pharmacology, virology, sport & exercise sciences, sport science & physiology, zoology; BSc(Hons), MRes, MSc, PhD

### *Faculty of Business; www.fbs.leeds.ac.uk*

**Leeds University Business School; www.leeds.ac.uk/lbs**
accounting, advertising & design/marketing, banking & international finance, business economics, computing & management, corporate communications & PR, diversity management, economics, enterprise,

actuarial/finance, financial economics/mathematics/risk management, finance & investment, HRM, international business/finance/marketing management, law & finance, leading in a clinical context, management, organizational psychology, textile innovation & branding, marketing, transport studies; BSc(Hons), ExecMBA, MA, MBA, MPhil, MSc, PhD

## Faculty of Education, Social Sciences & Law; www.essl.leeds.ac.uk

### School of Education; www.education.leeds.ac.uk

childhood studies, clinical education, deaf education, English/as additional/ language & education, mathematics/science education, PGCE primary, secondary (biology/chemistry/mathematics/modern foreign languages/physics), provision for children with learning difficulties/developmental disorders, special educational needs, teaching, teaching education & learning, teaching English (TESOL) for young learners/studies/teacher education, teaching English for academic professional purposes, SEN coordination

### School of Law; www.law.leeds.ac.uk

law, constitutional law, contract law, criminal law, criminal justice & criminology/criminal law, cyber law & IT, English legal system, torts, European law, international & comparative criminal justice, law, policing, European & international business law/corporate law/trade /banking & finance law, intellectual property law, law & finance, security & justice, senior status

### School of Politics and International Studies; www.leeds.ac.uk/polis

economics & policy, global development (Africa, gender, international political economy), politics & parliamentary studies, political theory, global development & political economy of international resources, global development ( security, security, terrorism & insurgency

### School of Sociology and Social Policy; www.sociology.leeds.ac.uk

disability studies & global development/special education/social policy/gender, crime, gender & culture/studies, disability, health & illness, gender, sexuality & queer studies, global genders, geography & science, interdisciplinary social policy & sociology/crime, social & public policy/political thought, international social transformation, politics & society/social policy, racism & ethnicity studies, social science/policy, society & international relations, sociology; BA(Hons), LLM, MA, MEd, MPhil, MSc, PGCert, PGCE, PhD

## Faculty of Engineering; www.engineering.leeds.ac.uk

### School of Civil Engineering; www.engineering.leeds.ac.uk/civil

architectural engineering, civil & environmental engineering/structural engineering, international construction management, environmental engineering, engineering project management, water, sanitation & health engineering, civil/environmental engineering & project management

### School of Computing; www.engineering.leeds.ac.uk/comp

artificial intelligence, adv/computer science/& mathematics/cloud computing/data analytics/intelligent systems, information technology

### School of Electronic and Electrical Engineering; www.engineering.leeds.ac.uk/elec

adv electronic devices, digital communication networks, electrical engineering/& electronic engineering/renewable energy systems, communication systems & signal processing, electronic/& communications engineering/& signal processing, mechatronics & robotics, music, multimedia & electronics, electronics/& nanotechnology, embedded systems engineering

### Mechanical Engineering; www.engineering.leeds.ac.uk/mech

aeronautical & aerospace engineering, automotive engineering, adv/mechanical engineering, mechatronics & robotics, medical engineering, oilfield corrosion engineering, mechanical with nuclear engineering, tribology & engineering interfaces, product design

### School of Process, Environmental and Materials Engineering; www.engineering.leeds.ac.uk/speme

aviation technology/management, pilot studies, chemical & energy/materials/minerals/nuclear engineering, pharmaceutical science & engineering, chemical engineering, computational fluid dynamics, energy & environment, computational fluid mechanics, energy engineering, fire & explosion engineering, nanotechnology, petroleum engineering; BEng, MEng, MSc, MSc(Eng), MPhil, PhD

## Faculty of the Environment; www.leeds.ac.uk/foe

### School of Earth & Environment; www.see.leeds.ac.uk

engineering geology, environment & business/management, climatic/& atmospheric science/conservation, engineering geology, exploration geophysics, geochemistry, geological/geophysical sciences, hydrogeology, meteorology & climate change, physics of the earth & atmosphere, structural geology & geophysics, sustainability (transport/business environment & corporate responsibility/environmental consultancy/environment & development/environmental politics & policy/project management), sustainability & environmental /management

### School of Geography; www.geog.leeds.ac.uk

geography, activism & social change, catchment dynamics & management, geography/with transport planning, geography – geology, GIS, social & cultural geography, river basin dynamics with GIS

### Institute for Transport Studies; www.its.leeds.ac.uk

economics with transport studies, geography with transport planning, planning & the environment/engineering, transport economics, sustainability (transport)

### Earth & Biosphere Institute; www.earth.leeds.ac.uk/ebi

global change & the biosphere; BA(Hons), BSc(Hons), MA, MGeol, MGeophys, MRes, MSc, DGCert/Dip, PhD, MEnv, MGeol

## Faculty of Mathematics and Physical Science; www.maps.leeds.ac.uk

### School of Chemistry; www.chemi.leeds.ac.uk

chemistry, chemical process research & development, colour & imaging science, analytical chemistry, medicinal chemistry, polymers, colorants & fine chemicals, chemical biology & drug design

### School of Food Science and Nutrition; www.food.leeds.ac.uk

food biotechnology, food quality & innovation, nutrition, food studies/& nutrition

### School of Physics and Astronomy; www.physics.leeds.ac.uk

physics/with astrophysics, nanotechnology, physics/with mathematics, quantum technologies, theoretical physics

### School of Mathematics; www.amsta.ac.uk

actuarial/financial mathematics, mathematics/with applications to finance, mathematics with computer science, mathematical studies, statistics, atmosphere ocean dynamics; BSc(Hons), MChem, MMath, MNatSci, MPhil, MPhys, MSc, PhD

## Faculty of Medicine & Health; www.leeds.ac.uk/medhealth

### Leeds Dental Institute; www.leeds.ac.uk/dental

hygiene & dental therapy, clinical dentistry, restorative/implant dentistry, dental nursing/surgery/technology, dental public health, paediatric dentistry, oral science

### School of Healthcare; www.healthcare.leeds.ac.uk

adult/child nursing, adv practice, audiological science, counselling, diagnostic imaging (radiology), innovative healthcare, healthcare sciences (audiology/cardiology), mental health, midwifery, nursing, public health, radiography, social work, leadership management in health & social care

### Leeds School of Medicine; www.leeds.ac.uk/medicine

child health, clinical embryology/psychology/science, family therapy, health informatics/research, hospital management, medical physics/imaging, medicine, molecular medicine, nutrition, obesity & health, patient safety, primary health care, psychiatry, psychoanalytical observation, public health, epidemiology & biostatistics, stroke care, surgery

### Institute of Psychological Sciences; www.psych.leeds.ac.uk

psychology, psychological approach to health; BHSc, BSc(Hons), CPD, DClinPsych, GradDip, MA, MBChB, MD, MMedSci, MPH, MPsycObs, MSc, PGDip/Cert, PhD

## *Faculty of Performance, Visual Arts and Communication: www.leeds.ac.uk/pvac*

**Institute of Communication Studies; www.ics.leeds.ac.uk**
broadcast journalism, cinema & photography, communications studies, international/political communications, journalism, new media, media industries, PR & society

**School of Design; www.design.leeds.ac.uk**
adv/textile design & performance clothing, advertising & design, art & design, design, technology management, fashion design/marketing, fashion, enterprise & society, graphic and communication design, textile innovation & branding

**School of Fine Art, History of Art and Cultural Studies; www.leeds.ac.uk/fine_art**
art history with museum studies, cultural studies, fine art, history of art, art gallery & museum studies

**School of Music; www.leeds.ac.uk/music**
composition, app/psychology of music, music, music technology management

**School of Performance & Cultural Industries; www.leeds.ac.uk/paci**
choreography, culture, creativity & entrepreneurship, dance, managing performance, performance design/ culture & context, theatre & performance, writing for performance and publication; BA(Hons), GradDip, MFA, BMus, BSc(Hons), MA, MMus, MSc, PhD

## *Degrees validated by University of Leeds offered at:*

---

### ASKHAM BRYAN COLLEGE
www.askham-bryan.ac.uk

adventure, sport & public service, agriculture, animal management, countryside & environment, engineering, equine, forestry & arboriculture, horticulture, landscaping & garden management, motorsport & highway, sports & leisure, veterinary nursing, teacher education; BSc, BSc(Hons), Nat Dips, FD

---

### COLLEGE OF THE RESURRECTION
www.mirfield.org.uk

theology & pastoral studies, theological studies, ministry & theology; BA(Hons), DipHE, MA, MPhil, PGDip, PhD

---

### LEEDS COLLEGE OF ART
www.leeds-art.ac.uk

art & design, creative advertising, creative practice, digital film, games & animation, fashion, fine art, furniture making, graphic design, photography, printed textiles & surface pattern design, visual communication; BA(Hons), FD, MA

---

### LEEDS COLLEGE OF MUSIC
www.lcm.ac.uk

music (classical/pop/production), composition, jazz, musicology, performance, composition; BA (Hons), FD, MA, PGDip, MMus

## LEEDS TRINITY UNIVERSITY
www.leedstrinity.ac.uk

**English; www.leedstrinity.ac.uk/departments/English**

English, history, film studies, journalism, media, creative writing, Victorian studies; BA(Hons), BSc(Hons), MA, MSc

**History; www.leedstrinity.ac.uk/departments/history**

history; BA(Hons), MA

**Children, Young People & Families; wwwleedstrinity.ac.uk/cyp**

education studies, early childhood studies, working with/supporting children, young people & families, supporting learning, professional practice, sport PE, education & health; BA(Hons), FD, MA, PGCert, PGCE

**Business, Media & Marketing: www.leedstrinity.ac.uk/departments/business**

accounting, business & management/marketing, business management, management, marketing & media, tourism & leisure; BA(Hons), MA/PGDip, MB

**Secondary Education; www.leedstrinity.ac.uk/departments/secondary**

education, secondary education, PE & sport, PGCE (10 subjects), teacher training (SCiTT); BSc(Hons), PGCE, MA

**Sport Health & Nutrition; www.leedstrinity.ac.uk/departments/shln**

health & wellbeing, primary education PE & sport, sport development & PE, primary/secondary education sport, sport education, exercise, & nutrition/sport nutrition/strength & conditioning; BSc(Hons), BA(Hons), MSc

**Journalism; www.leedstrinity.ac.uk/departments/cfj**

journalism, broadcast/magazine/sport/radio journalism, English & journalism; BA(Hons), BA, PGDip

**Media, Film & Culture; www.leedstrinity.ac.uk/departments/media**

digital & social media, film & TV studies, film studies, media, TV production; BA(Hons)

**Theology & Religious Studies; www.leedstrinity.ac.uk/departments/theology**

philosophy, ethics & religion, theology, religious studies, Catholic studies, literature & spirituality; BA(Hons), MA

**Victorian studies; www.leedstrinity.ac.uk/departments/victorian_studies;**

MPhil, PhD

## NORTHERN SCHOOL OF CONTEMPORARY DANCE
www.nscd.ac.uk

contemporary dance, choreography; BPA(Hons), PgDip, MA, FD

## YORK ST JOHN UNIVERSITY
www.yorksj.ac.uk

*Faculty of Arts; www.yorksj.ac.uk/arts/faculty_of_arts*

film & TV production, music composition/performance/production, computer studies, contemporary literature, American studies, creative writing, dance, documentary/film production, English literature, film/literature studies, fine arts, history, media, product design, applied/theatre, theatre & performance; FD, BA(Hons), PgCert/Dip, MA

*Faculty of Education & Theology; www.yorksj.ac.uk/education-theology*

PGCE, primary/secondary education, education studies, academic practice, religious studies, improving practitioner practice, initial teacher education, foreign modern languages, evangelism supporting learning, theology & ministry/religious studies, religion, philosophy & ethics, religion & education/public life, Christian theology, teacher education, children, school leadership, young people & families, youth & community work; MFL, BA(Hons), GradDip, PgDip, PGCE, PhD

### *Faculty of Health & Life Sciences; www.yorksj.ac.uk/health-and-life-sciences*

counselling, coaching & mentoring/psychotherapy, occupational therapy, physiotherapy, community & clinical social psychology, psychology/of child & adolescent development, PE & sport coaching, sports development, sports science (exercise practice/injury management/performance conditioning); BA(Hons), MA, MSc, PgDip/Cert

### *York St John Business School; www.yorksj.ac.uk/business*

accounting & finance, business management/& HRM/languages/finance, business administration with finance/design management/media management, web technologies, English language & linguistics, design & creativity, international tourism/ business management/business strategy, strategic/HRM, marketing/ management, TESOL, global marketing, languages, leadership & management, innovation & change, international tourism management/& hospitality management, tourism management; BA(Hons), FD, MA, PGDip/Cert, MBA

## LEEDS METROPOLITAN UNIVERSITY
## www.leedsmet.ac.uk

### *Faculty of Arts, Environment & Technology; www.leedsmet.ac.uk/aet*

#### The Leeds School of Architecture, Landscape & Design; www.leedsmet.ac.uk/aet/#art-architecture-design

architecture, architectural professional practice, contemporary art practice, fine art, urban design, garden art & design, design (applied textile/digital/furniture), play production, professional studies, interior architecture, landscape architecture & design, urban design

#### School of Built Environment & Engineering; www. www.leedsmet.ac.uk/aet/#built-environment-engineering

adv engineering management, building/engineering studies, civil engineering, construction/commercial/ management, strategic/project management, facilities management; architectural technology, building/ quantity surveying, housing, housing, regeneration & urban management, human geography/& planning, planning law & practice, project management/ construction, town & regional planning, heritage planning, construction law & dispute resolution

#### School of Computing & Creative technology; www.leedsmet.ac.uk/aet/#computing-creative-technology

advanced engineering management, business information systems, computer forensics, computing, computer security & ethical hacking, information management/systems, systems & networking, green computing, managing software development, web applications development, software development/ engineering, mobile device applications, information & technology, broadcast media technologies, computer animation technology, photographic journalism, computer animation/& special effects, games design, digital animation & creative visualization, digital video & special effects, managing software development, mobile device/applications/development, multimedia/entertainment technology, creative technology

#### School of Film, Music & Performing Arts; www.leedsmet.ac.uk/aet/#film-music-performingarts

music performance/production/technology, audio post-production, music for moving image, sound & music for interactive games, sound design

**Northern Film School**

animation, film and moving image production, film & TV

#### School of Cultural Studies & Humanities; www.lmu.ac.uk/as/cs

English, English literature, history, media, communication & culture, cultural planning & policy, English contemporary literature, screen media cultures, social history; BA(Hons), BSc(Hons), DipHE, FdAA, GradCert, MPhil, MRes, MSc, PGDip

## *Faculty of Business and Law; www.leedsmet.ac.uk/fbl*

### Leeds Business School; www.leedsmet.ac.uk/fbl/leeds_business_school

accounting, advertising management, business studies, business & management, contract management, corporate governance, economics for business, EFL, entertainment management, financial economics, international/ events management, facility management, tourism & hospitality management, applied/ finance, financial services, HRM, tourism management, international business/communications/business law/trade & finance/tourist management, leadership & change management, management, managing cultural & major events, marketing/advertising management, organizational behaviour, PR, purchasing & supply/logistics, strategy & economic analysis

### Leeds Law School; www.leedsmet.ac.uk/lbs/law

law, legal practice, commercial/employment/family/ property/business law, legal practice, paralegal practice, UK planning law & practice; BA(Hons), HND, LlB(Hons), LlM, MA, MSc, PGDip/Cert, MBA

## *Faculty of Health & Social Sciences; www.leedsmet.ac.uk/hss*

biomedical sciences (human biology/microbiology/ molecular biology/physiology/pharmacology), clinical language sciences (speech & language therapy), community specialist practitioner – community children's nursing/district nursing/practice nursing, criminology/& psychology/sociology, dietetics, health & safety regulation, international relations & global/ peace studies, nursing (adult health/mental health), osteopathy, peace studies & international relations/ politics, playwork, politics, psychology/& society, public health – environmental health/nutrition, safety health & environmental management, social work, sociology, sports & exercise therapy, therapeutic counselling, working with young people & young people's services, youth work & community development; BA(Hons), BSc(Hons), CertHE, HNC, MA, MSc, PGDip/Cert, Prof Dip, DipHE, FdAA, Grad-Cert, MPhil, MRes, PGDip

## *Carnegie Faculty; www.leedsmet.ac.uk/carnegie*

English language teaching, business & EFL/marketing/tourism management/event management, language studies, French, German, Spanish, contemporary European studies, childhood & educational studies, early childhood education, primary education, QTS with primary early childhood, PE, learning, teaching, leadership, international tourism & hospitality/business management/leadership & management, international/resort/student hospitality management, managing international hospitality, resort hospitality, consumer/retail marketing, retail business administration, international business administration, sports/events management, sport & exercise physiology, conference & exhibitions management, culture/sports events, international festival management; BA(Hons), BSc(Hons), FSc, PGCE, PGCert/Dip, MA, PhD

# UNIVERSITY OF LEICESTER
**www.le.ac.uk**

## *College of Arts, Humanities and Law; www2.le.ac.uk/colleges/artshumlaw*

### School of Archaeology & Ancient History; www.le.ac.uk/ar

ancient history, archaeology, classical Mediterranean, history, historical archaeology, archaeology of the Roman world

### School of English; www.le.ac.uk/ee

American studies/history, English studies, English, history of art, modern literature & creative writing/ linguistics, Victorian studies

### Dept of History of Art and Film; www.le.ac.uk/ha

the country house in art, history & culture, film & media history, film studies and the visual arts, history of art/& English, humanities, film & film cultures

### School of Historical Studies;

www.le.ac.uk/hi

contemporary history, English local history, history, history and politics/international relations/ancient history/archaeology/American studies, archaeology, urban history/conservation, European urbanization

### School of Law; www.le.ac.uk/law

law, law (international/human rights/commercial/public/employment), general law, law with French law, human rights, legal research, law & criminology/politics/languages

### School of Modern Languages; www.le.ac.uk/ml

European studies, French, German, Italian, modern language studies, modern languages with film studies/history of art, Spanish, humanities, translation studies

### Museum Studies; www.le.ac.uk /ms

art museum/& gallery studies, digital heritage, interpretation, representation, & heritage studies, learning & visitor studies in museums & galleries; BA(Hons), BSc(Hons), LlB, LlM, MSC, MA/GradDip, MPhil, PhD

## *College of Science and Engineering; www2.le.ac.uk/colleges/science*

### Dept of Chemistry; www.le.ac.uk/ch

chemistry, cancer chemistry, biological/physical chemistry, green chemistry

### Dept of Computer Science; www.cs.le.ac.uk

advanced computational methods/distributed systems/software engineering, agile software engineering technology, computer science, computers, computing with management, software engineering for financial services, web applications & services

### Dept of Engineering; www2.le.ac.uk/departments/engineering

advanced control & dynamics, advanced engineering, advanced materials engineering, aerospace engineering, communications & electronic engineering, control & signal processing, adv/electrical & electronic engineering, embedded systems & control engineering, general engineering, information & communication engineering, mechanical engineering, software & electronic engineering

### Dept of Geography; www.le.ac.uk/geography

environmental informatics, geography, geology, GIS, global environmental change, human/physical geography, sustainable management of natural resources

### Dept of Geology; www2.le.ac.uk/departments/geology

applied & environmental geology, crustal processes, geology, borehole/geophysics, geology with geophysics/palaeobiology/geography

### Dept of Mathematics; www2.le.ac.uk/departments/mathematics

actuarial science, data analysis for business intelligence, financial mathematics/& computation, mathematical modelling in biology, mathematics with management/economics

### Dept of Physics and Astronomy; www2.le.ac.uk/departments/physics

astronomy, physics, physics with nanotechnology/astrophysics/space science & technology/planetary science, space exploration & development systems; BA(Hons), BSc(Hons), BEng/MEng, MA, MChem, MComp, MGeol, MMath, MPhil, MPhys, MSc, MSci, PGDip, PhD

## *College of Medicine, Biological Sciences and Psychology; www2.le.ac.uk/colleges/medbiopsych*

### School of Biological Sciences; www2.le.ac.uk/departments/biologicalscience

bioinformatics, biology, biological sciences (biochemistry/genetics/microbiology/physiology with pharmacology/zoology), microbiology, medical genetics, biochemistry/microbiology/physiology, molecular biology/genetics/toxicology, cell physiology & pharmacology, molecular biology/genetics/toxicology, pharmacology, zoology

### School of Medicine, Leicester Medical School; www2.le.ac.uk/departments/msce

medicine, cancer cell studies & molecular medicine/biology, bioinformatics, cardiovascular sciences, clinical science, health sciences, infection & immunisation, medical statistics, medical & social care education, molecular pathology/toxicology, mountain medicine, occupational psychology, operating department practice, pain management, physiotherapy, primary care research, social science applied to health, child & adolescent mental health, integrated provision for children & families, social work

### School of Psychology; www2.le.ac.uk/departments/psychology

psychology/with sociology/cognitive neuroscience/media, clinical/forensic psychology, applied forensic psychology, forensic legal psychology, occupational psychology, psychology of work; DocClinPsych, BSc, MBChB, MBioSci, MD, MSc, PostgradDip/Cert, PhD

## College of the Social Sciences www.le.ac.uk/colleges/socsci

### Dept of Criminology; www2.le.ac.uk/departments/criminology

applied/clinical/criminology, terrorism, security & policing, criminology

### Dept of Economics; www2.le.ac.uk/departments/economics

banking & finance, business/financial economics, economics, business analysis & finance, money & banking

### School of Education; www2.le.ac.uk/departments/education

educational studies, education, learning & teaching, understanding and managing children/mental health problems and children with social, emotional and behavioural difficulties, specialist assessment and teaching of pupils with specific learning difficulties, promoting language development in the early years, issues in mathematics/science/English education, mentoring and coaching, developing leadership in education, teaching mathematics, education and sustainable development, PGCE primary/secondary education, teachfirst, TESOL & applied linguistics

### The Centre for Labour Market Studies; www2.le.ac.uk/departments/clms

HRM, HRM & training, performance management/industrial relations & workplace learning

### Institute of Lifelong Learning; www2.le.ac.uk/departments/lifelong-learning

humanities & arts, cognitive behaviour therapy, counselling psychotherapy, managing political & community orgs, emergency planning, management studies, risk crisis, disaster management

### School of Management; www2.le.ac.ukdepartments/management

accounting, finance, management studies, marketing, finance, organisational studies, economics, politics, business administration, global financial markets, HRM & training

### Dept of Media & Communication; www.le.ac.uk/mc

communications & globalization, media/communications & society/PR/advertising, media & PR/communications/advertising new media & sociology, mass communications, new media governance & democracy

### Dept of Politics and International Relations; www2.le.ac.uk/departments/politics

diplomatic studies, politics, international relations/& history/world order, economics, politics & sociology/history/management studies/economics, human rights & global ethics, international security, political research

### Dept of Sociology; www2.le.ac.uk/departments/sociology

sociology, contemporary society, social research, criminology, politics; BA(Hons), DocSocSci, EdD, FD, MA, MBA, MPhil, MSc, PGCE, PGDip/Cert, PhD

## Degrees validated by the University of Leicester offered at:

---

## NEWMAN UNIVERSITY COLLEGE
www.newman.ac.uk

ancient history, applied psychology, art & design, business (sustainability and ethics), business & media production, classical civilisations, counselling studies, creative writing, criminology, drama, early childhood education and care, education studies, English/language/literature, history, information technology/& technology support, integrative counselling, Islamic studies, local history and heritage, management & business, management studies, media and communication, philosophy and theology, philosophy, religion and ethics, psychology, RE, sports coaching science/science/studies, teaching & learning support, theology/for education, working with children, young people and families, youth and community work; BA/BSc(Hons), FD, MA, MPhil, PGCE, PhD

# UNIVERSITY OF LINCOLN
# www.lincoln.ac.uk

## *Faculty of Agriculture, Animal Science & Food; www.lincoln.ac.uk/afas*

agriculture & environment, bioveterinary science, clinical/animal behaviour & welfare, conservation biology, equine science/sports science, food manufacture, process & business improvement/quality assurance & technology management; BSc, FdSc, MPhil, MSc, PhD

## *Faculty of Art, Architecture & Design; www.lincoln.ac.uk/aad*

animation, architecture, sustainable architectural design, art, architecture/& design, conservation of historic objects/studies/restoration, contemporary curatorial practice, creative advertising, construction project management, contemporary lens media, design, design/exhibition & museums, development & regeneration, fashion studies, fine art, graphic design, interactive design, interior design/architecture/enterprise, jewellery & objects, product design, planning/& urban design; BA(Hons), BArch, GradDip, MA, March, MPhil, PhD

## *Faculty of Business & Law; www.lincoln.ac.uk/bl*

accountancy, advertising, business administration/management/studies, business & marketing/management, engineering management, event management, finance, hospitality & tourism management, HRM, HRD, international business management/tourism, international business law, international law, management studies/development, marketing strategy, tourism, law & business/criminology/finance, legal studies, logistics management, marketing, personal executive & corporate coaching, PR, BA(Hons), BSc(Hons), LlB(Hons), LlM, MA, MBA, MPhil, MRes, MSc, PhD

## *Faculty of Health, Life & Social Sciences; www.lincoln.ac.uk/hlss*

adv professional practice in social work, adv development in social work, clinical/forensic psychology, contemporary culture & communication, criminology/& international relations/politics/forensic investigation/social policy, employment-based social work, health & social care, healthcare in secure environments, politics/& social policy, social policy & management, media & cultural studies, nursing (adult, mental health), clinical/developmental psychology, psychology with criminology/marketing/social policy, sports & exercise science, sports development & coaching, sport & PE, sports coaching/science; BA(Hons), BSc(Hons), CertHE, DClinPsy, MA, MClinRes, MPhil, PGCert, PhD

## *Faculty of Media, Humanities and Performance; www.lincoln.ac.uk/mhp*

21st-century literature, audio production, adv performance practice, choreography, community radio, creative writing, dance, digital imaging/arts, digital media, drama, film & TV, English, games/computing, history/& politics, historical studies, medieval studies, arts/investigative/science & environmental, journalism, war & international human rights, sports/science & environment/ journalism, web technology, media & culture, media, film & TV production, play writing & script development, politics, photography, PR; BA(Hons), MA, MRes, MPhil, PhD

## *Faculty of Science; www.lincoln.ac.uk/science*

### Lincoln School of Engineering

engineering, mechanical engineering; BEng(Hons), MEng(Hons), MSc, MPhil, PhD

### Lincoln School of Computer Science

computer information systems, computer science, games computing, intelligent systems; BSc(Hons), MComp, MSC, MPhil, PhD

### School of Life Science

animal behaviour & welfare/science, biochemistry, biology, biomedical science, bioveterinary science, computer information systems/science, computing, criminological & forensic investigation, intelligence systems, forensic science, games computing, mechanical engineering/control systems/power & energy, pharmaceutical science, signals intelligence, sustainable power & energy engineering, zoology; BA(Hons), BSc(Hons), BEng(Hons), FdSC, MA, MComp, MPhil, MRes, MSc, PhD, EMM

### Lincoln School of Pharmacy; www.lincoln.ac.uk/home/lsp

pharmacy, pharmaceutical science; BSc(Hons), MPharm, MPhil, PhD

**Centre for Educational Research & Development; www.lincoln.ac.uk/cerd**
educational research & development; EdD, PhD

## *Degrees validated by the University of Lincoln offered at:*

## EAST RIDING COLLEGE
www.eastridingcollege.ac.uk

access to higher education, applied digital media, early childhood policy & practice, education & professional development, computing, applied digital media, contemporary media design, lifelong learning, learning support, sport coaching & exercise/health science; BA(Hons), FdA, FdEd, FdSc, PGCE

## HULL COLLEGE
www.hull-college.ac.uk

### *Faculty of Arts*

**Hull School of Art & Design; www.hull-college.ac.uk/hull-school-of-art-and-design**
animation, architecture, architectural design, contemporary fine art practice, creative practice, design (interior/product), fashion, film-making & creative media practice, games/graphic design, illustration, interactive multimedia, journalism & digital media, photography, media & communications, textiles, web design; BA(Hons), FdA, MA, MArch

**School of Performing Arts & Media**
acting, broadcast media, dance, music performance/production/theatre, theatre production, scriptwriting, musical theatre; BA, FdA

### *Faculty of Business & Science*

accounting, automotive technology, business & management, computing, business information technology, computer network management, construction management, criminology with applied social science, education/& professional development, engineering technology, express logistics, education, policing & community safety studies, sports studies, travel & tourism management, young people's learning & development; FdA, FdSc, BSc(Hons), BA(Hons), PGCE

## NORTH LINDSEY COLLEGE
www.northlindsey.ac.uk

business studies, business & HRM, biochemistry, bioscience, leadership & management, children's services, children & youth work, early childhood, computing information systems, education/& training, learning support, electrical/mechanical/electronic engineering, English, history, health & social science, sport performance & exercise development; BA(Hons), Dips, FdA/Sc/Ed/Eng, Grad Cert Ed

# UNIVERSITY OF LIVERPOOL
# www.liv.ac.uk

## *Faculty of Health & Life Sciences; www.liv.ac.uk/health_and_life_sciences*

### Institute of Learning & Teaching; www.liverpool.ac.uk/learning-and-teaching/

**Dentistry; www.liverpool.ac.uk/dentistry/**
dental hygiene/therapy/surgery, orthodontics

**Health Sciences; www.liverpool.ac.uk/health-sciences/**
adv practice in healthcare, diagnostic radiography, health & veterinary studies, medical diagnostic ultrasound, nursing, occupational therapy, orthoptics, physiotherapy, radiotherapy, health sciences

**Medicine; www.liverpool.ac.uk/medicine/**
medicine, surgery, medical science, public health

**Psychology; www.liverpool.ac.uk/psychology/**
psychology, addictive behaviour, critical & major incidents, investigative & forensic psychology, research methods

**Life Sciences; www.liverpool.ac.uk/life-sciences/**
anatomy & human biology, biochemistry, biological sciences, genetics, life sciences/medicine, microbiology, microbial biotechnology, molecular biology, pharmacology, physiology, post genomic science, tropical disease biology, zoology, advanced biological science (numerous subjects)

**Veterinary Science; www.liverpool.ac.uk/veterinary-science/**
veterinary science, bioveterinary science/reproduction, veterinary practice, bovine reproduction

### Institute of Ageing & Chronic Disease; www.liv.ac.uk/ageing-and-chronic-disease

anatomy & human biology, clinical science

### Institute of Infection & Global Health; www.liv.ac.uk/infection-and-global-health

infection biology, clinical infection, microbiology & immunology, epidemiology & population health

### Institute of Integrative Biology; www.liv.ac.uk/integrative-biology

advanced biological sciences

### Institute of Psychology, Health & Society; www.liv.ac.uk/psychology-health-and-society

clinical psychology, health service research, medical education/science, psychology, psychiatry

### Institute of Translational Medicine; www.liv.ac.uk/translational-medicine

physiology, pharmacology, anatomy & human biology, biomedical science & translational medicine; BSc(Hons), BN, BVSc, BDS, MBChB, FD, PGCert/Dip, MRes, MSc, MPhil, PhD, MD, MChOrth, MCommH, D/MClinPsychol, MDS, MPH, MRCPsych, MTCH&CP, MTropMed, MTropPaed

## *Faculty of Humanities & Social Sciences; www.liv.ac.uk/humanities_and_social_sciences/hss*

### School of the Arts; www.liv.ac.uk/arts

**Architecture; www.liv.ac.uk/lsa/index.htm**
architecture, architectural design, sustainable architectural design, design studies

**Communications & Media; www.liv.ac.uk/communication-and-media/index.htm**
communications, business studies, media, pop music, English/politics & communications studies, politics & mass media

**English; www.liv.ac.uk/english/index.htm**
English, medieval, Renaissance, 17th/18th century, Victorian, romantic literature, 20th century poetry, science fiction, applied linguistics & TESOL, modern & contemporary literature, reading in practice

**Music; www.liv.ac.uk/music/index.htm**
music, pop music, music industry, musicology, composition, performance

**Philosophy; www.liv.ac.uk/philosophy/index.htm**
philosophy & maths/politics/English/French/German/Italian/Hispanic studies/law/modern languages studies, art, philosophy as a way of life, metaphysics, language, mind

### School of History, Language & Culture

**History; www.liv.ac.uk/history/index.htm**
history – social & economic, modern Renaissance studies, 18th century world, 20th century history, international slavery studies, archives & records management, English & modern history, Irish studies & history

**Irish Studies; www.liv.ac.uk/irish/index.htm**
Irish studies, English history/politics, understanding conflict

**Politics; www.liv.ac.uk/politics/index.htm**
politics, international politics & policy, politics & international business, international relations & security, politics & Irish studies/modern history/philosophy/communication studies

**Archaeology, Classics & Egyptology; www.liv.ac.uk/sace/index.htm**
ancient history, archaeology/of ancient civilisations, human evolution, Egyptian archaeology, classics & modern languages, Egyptology, palaeoanthropology, Manx studies, 18th century worlds

**Culture, Language & Area studies; www.liv.ac.uk/soclas/index.htm**
French, German, Hispanic studies, Italian, linguistics, Latin American studies, Caribbean & American studies, modern European languages, film studies, classical studies, modern language studies & business/English/history/philosophy, 18th century worlds; BA(Hons), MA, MArch, MPhil, PhD

## School of Law & Social Justice; www.liv.ac.uk/law-and-social-justice/index.htm

**Liverpool Law School; www.liv.ac.uk/law/index.htm**
law, law & business/accounting/finance/business studies/criminology/philosophy/French/German/Italian/Spanish, international human rights/business law, European law, law, medicine & healthcare, technology & intellectual property law

**Dept of Sociology & Social Policy; www.liv.ac.uk/sociology-social-policy-and-criminology/**
sociology, sociology & social policy/criminology, research methodology, cities, criminology & sociology, sociology & social policy

## School of Management; www.liv.ac.uk/management

University of Liverpool Management School: accounting, business economics/studies, consumer marketing, e-business strategy & systems, international business, marketing, business finance & management, economics & finance, football industries, operations & supply chain management, programme & project management, entrepreneurship, HRM, management; BA(Hons), MA, MMus, MPhil, MBA, PhD, MRes, PGDip/Cert

# *Faculty of Science & Engineering; www.liv.ac.uk/science_and_engineering*

## School of Engineering; www.liv.ac.uk/engineering

adv manufacturing systems & technology, adv engineering materials, aerospace engineering/pilot studies, maritime/civil & structural engineering, materials science & engineering, mechanical engineering, aerospace & mechanical systems, adv engineering materials/manufacture, energy generation, engineering applications of lasers, materials engineering, product design & management, simulation in aerospace engineering, sustainable civil/structural/maritime engineering

## Electrical Engineering & Electronics; www.liv.ac.uk/eee

avionic systems, pilot studies, computer science, electronic engineering, electrical engineering, electronics, engineering, communications engineering, mechatronics & robotic systems, medical electronics & instrumentation, micoelectronic systems & telecommunications, information & intelligence engineering, energy & power systems

## Dept of Computer Science; www.csc.liv.ac.uk

adv/computer science, algorithms, artificial intelligence, computing, computer information systems, data mining, e-finance, electronic commerce computing, information systems, internet computing, safety critical systems software development

## School of Environmental Sciences; www.liv.ac.uk/environmental-sciences

applied GIS, ecology, the environment, environmental science, geography, geology, geophysics, ocean science, marine biology, town & regional planning, environmental management & planning, urban regeneration & management, marine planning & management, globalization & development, environmental & climate change, population studies, conservation & resource management, urban regeneration & development

## School of Physical Sciences;

**Chemistry; www.liv.ac.uk/chemistry/index.htm**
chemistry, medicinal chemistry, materials chemistry, pharmacology, adv chemical science (organic with catalysis/chemical synthesis/biomolecular chemistry/nanoscale with materials interfacial chemistry)

**Mathematical Sciences; www.liv.ac.uk/mathematical-sciences/**
mathematics, actuarial mathematics, pure/applied mathematics, mathematical sciences, maths with joint subjects, financial mathematics, mathematical/theoretical physics, statistics & probability, mathematics with economics/computer science/education/physics/European languages

**Physics; www.liv.ac.uk/physics/**
physics, astronomy, astrophysics, mathematical/theoretical physics, nuclear science/& technology, medical applications, advanced science (nanoscale & condensed matter physics/clinical science/medical physics/clinical engineering/particle physics); BSc(Hons), MChem, BEng, MEng, DEng, MPhil, MMath, MPhys, MESci, MRes, MSc, PhD, MSc(Eng)

*Degrees validated at the University of Liverpool offered by:*

## LIVERPOOL HOPE UNIVERSITY
www.hope.ac.uk

### Faculty of Arts & Humanities; www.hope.ac.uk/artsand humanities
drama, dance, performance, English language/literature, fine art, art history & curating, design, music, music since 1900, sacred music, Beatles, pop & sociology, creative performance arts, contemporary popular theatre, popular literatures, theatre studies, art & design studies, politics, history, media & communications, creative practice, theatre studies, philosophy & ethics/religion, Christian theology, international relations, peace studies, Jewish history & literature, messianic studies, theological issues in Judaism, theology & religious education, biblical studies

### Faculty of Education; www.hope.ac.uk/education
teacher education, graduate education, professional development, PGCE courses (primary/secondary education), childhood & youth studies (early childhood studies/special education/mentoring & coaching/teaching & learning), primary education with QTS, the discipline of education (history, philosophy, psychology & sociology), CPD

### Faculty of Science & Social Science; www.hope.ac.uk/scienceandsocialscience
Business School: business, management, marketing management, HRM/D, law, accounting, marketing
Mathematics & Computer Science: computing, computer science, information technology, mathematical informatics, simulation & modelling, mathematics, networks & security
Geography: environmental science/management, tourism management, geography
Health Sciences: health & wellbeing, biology, human biology, nutrition, health nutrition & fitness, sport & exercise science, sport & PE, exercise testing & description, health, exercise & nutrition, management in healthcare
Psychology: psychology, sports psychology
Social Work, Care & Justice: social work, criminology, criminal justice, social policy; BA(Hons), BMin, BSc(Hons), BDes, FdA, FdSc, MA, MBA, MMin, MPhil, MSc, PGCE, PhD

## LIVERPOOL JOHN MOORES UNIVERSITY
**www.ljmu.ac.uk**

*Faculty of Arts, Professional & Social Studies: www.ljmu.ac.uk/APS*

### Liverpool Business School; www.ljmu.ac.uk/lbs
accounting, business/studies/communications/management, business & PR, finance, entrepreneurship, HRM, management, marketing, personnel & development, international accounting/finance, operations management, banking/business/management/administration

### School of Law; www.ljmu.ac.uk/LAW
law, criminal justice, European law, forensic psychology, global crime, justice & security, international business corporate & finance law, legal practice; BA(Hons), BSc(Hons), DBA, HND, LlB, LlM, MA, MBA, MPhil, MRes, MSc, PgDip/Cert

**Liverpool School of Art & Design; www.ljmu.ac.uk/LSA**
architecture, art & design, fashion, graphic design, illustration, history of art, fine art, interior design, spatial design, urban design

**Liverpool Screen School; www.ljmu.ac.uk/LSS**
creative writing, film studies, English, drama, media studies, international news/journalism, writing

**School of Humanities & Social Science; www.ljmu.ac.uk/HSS**
critical social science, criminology, psychology, sociology, English, media & cultural studies, modern/history, mass communications, media/& cultural studies, communication, literature & cultural history, modern literature, policing studies, cultural history, critical & creative arts, social science; BA, BA(Hons), BDes, DipArch, DipHE, MA, MPhil, MRes, PG, PGCE, PhD

## *Faculty of Education, Community and Leisure: www.ljmu.ac.uk/ECL*

CPD, adv educational practice (artist teacher/education & society/dyslexia/leadership & management/mentoring & coaching/SEN), education studies & early years, early childhood studies, education & society, educational studies & PE, PGCE (art & design/design & technology/early years/modern languages/PE/science/secondary/engineering/food & textiles/ICT/mathematics), special and inclusive education, outdoor education, primary & secondary education, learning development, mathematics & science education, coaching development, dance practice, sport development management, event management, hospitality management, tourism & leisure management, food & nutrition, home economics, special educational needs, sport & inclusive needs, teacher training courses (primary, secondary), BA(Hons), BSc(Hons), EdD, FD, MA, MPhil, MRes, PGCert, PgDip, PhD

## *Faculty of Science; www.ljmu.ac.uk/faculties/scs*

**School of Sport & Exercise Science; www.ljmu.ac.uk/sps**
sport science/biomechanics, science & football, exercise sciences, app/sports psychology/physiology, biomechanics of gait & posture, clinical exercise physiology

**School of Pharmacy & Biomolecular Sciences; www.ljmu.ac.uk/PBS**
biomedical sciences, biochemistry, biotechnology, forensic science, applied chemical & pharmaceutical science, clinical/pharmacy, virology

**School of Natural Sciences & Psychology; www.ljmu.ac.uk/NSP**
animal behaviour, applied sports psychology, criminal justice, criminology & psychology, forensic psychology & criminal justice, forensic anthropology, human/forensic/applied psychology, health/occupational psychology, geography, zoology, biology, wildlife conservation, criminal justice; BSc(Hons), MPhil, MPhys, MRes, MSc, PGCE, PhD

**Astrophysics Research Institute www.ljmu.ac.uk/astro**
physics, astronomy, astrophysics

## *Faculty of Technology & the Environment; www.ljmu.ac.uk/faculties/TAE*

**School of Computing & Mathematical Sciences; www.ljmu.ac.uk/cmp**
computer animation & visualization, adv/computer studies/ forensics, computing & information systems, IT & multimedia, computer games technology, computer network security, software engineering, wireless & mobile computing, cyber security, mathematics

**School of Engineering & Technology & Maritime Operations; www.ljmu.ac.uk/ENG**
audio & music technology, computer aided design, product innovation & development, maritime business/management operations/port management, management transport & logistics, product innovation & development, mechanical and marine engineering, marine and offshore, mechanical engineering, manufacturing engineering, automotive engineering, electrical and electronic engineering, computer technology, power and control engineering, telecomunications engineering, microelectronic systems, manufacturing systems engineering, industrial electronics and control, risk and safety management, power asset management

**School of the Built Environment; www.ljmu.ac.uk/BLT**
architectural technology, applied facilities management, commercial/building surveying, building

service project management, civil engineering, commercial property development, construction smart techniques for infrastructure & buildings, practice & commercial management, construction management, quantity surveying/& commercial management, real estate management, environmental planning, building service engineering/construction project management, water, energy & environment; BA(Hons), BSc(Hons), FdSc, MPhil, MSc, PgCert, PGCE, PgDip, PhD

### Faculty of Health & Applied Social Services; www.ljmu.ac.uk/HEA

adv healthcare practice, child nursing, environmental health, health and social care/for families, individuals & communities/practice, health sciences, midwifery, nursing (adult/child/mental health/paramedic practice), neonatal/diabetes care, public health, social work, specialist community practitioner (district nursing/public health nursing, school visiting/health visiting), counselling, psychotherapy, adv paediatric nursing; BA(Hons), BSc, DNurs, DMidw, DPH, DipHE, FD, FdA MPhil, MRes, MSc, PGDip/Cert

## UNIVERSITY OF THE ARTS LONDON
## www.arts.ac.uk

### Camberwell College of Art & Design: www.camberwell.arts.ac.uk

3D design, arts practice/theory, book arts, conservation, curating, art, design & communication, designer–maker, digital theatre, drawing, graphic design/communication, fine art, visual art, illustration, interior & spatial design, painting, photography, printmaking, sculpture, textile design, theatre design; BA(Hons), Dip, FdA, MA, MPhil, PGDip, PhD, MFA

### Central Saint Martins College of Art & Design: www.csm.arts.ac.uk

acting, applied imagination in creative industries, architecture: spaces and objects, art theory & philosophy, art & design/science, art, exhibition studies/moving image/theory & philosophy, ceramic design, character animation, collaborative performance, creative practice for narrative environment, criticism, curation & communication/art & design (ceramics/furniture/jewellery), directing, dramatic writing, fashion design/knitwear/marketing/menswear/womenswear, fashion production/journalism/promotion, fine art, graphic design, industrial design, innovation management, moving image, screen acting/directing/writing, performance design & practice, photography, textile design; BA(Hons), FdA, FD, GradDip, MA, MPhil, PGCert/Dip, PhD

### Chelsea College of Art & Design: www.chelsea.arts.ac.uk

art theory/practice, art & design, curating, fine art, graphic design communication, graphic design, interior & spatial design, textile design; BA(Hons), FdA, Foundation Dip, GradDip, MA, MPhil, PGCert/Dip, PhD

### London College of Communication: www.lcc.arts.ac.uk

advertising, animation, architecture, artefact & spatial design, book arts, curation & criticism, design culture/for graphic communication, collaborative performance, contemporary graphic media, digital arts/media, documentary film, games design, graphic design, graphic brands & identity/moving image/media design, illustration & visual media, interactive media, journalism, practice/TV, photojournalism & documentary, marketing, media & cultural studies, photography, print media & production, printmaking, product design, PR, publishing, production for live events & TV, magazine publishing, screenwriting, service innovation, sound art, spatial development, surface design, theatre design, typography, visual communication; BA(Hons), FdA, ABCDip, MA, MDes, MRes, MSc, PgDip

### London College of Fashion: www.fashion.arts.ac.uk

accessories; product design & development/footwear, beauty therapy & spa management, buying & merchandising, cosmetic science, costume for performance, creative direction, curation, digital arts/media, fashion design, fashion media practice, fashion styling/surface textiles/knitwear, bespoke tailoring, fashion contour/design & development/design & realisation/technology/womens' wear/illustration/jewellery/journalism, international preparation for fashion/management/production, textiles, make-up

& image styling, pattern cutting, PR, theatre design & performing arts, visual merchandising; BA(Hons), BSc(Hons), diplomas, FD, MA, PgDip/Cert

### Wimbledon College of Art; www.wimbledon.arts.ac.uk

digital theatre, drawing, fine art (painting/sculpture), interactive media, painting, print & time-based media, theatre & screen: costume design/interpretation/set design for screen, technical arts & special effects, theatre design, visual language of performance; BA(Hons), FdA, MA

## LONDON CONTEMPORARY DANCE SCHOOL
## www.theplace.org.uk

advanced dance training, choreography, contemporary dance, dance training & education, improvisation, performance studies; BA, PGDip, MA

## LONDON METROPOLITAN UNIVERSITY
## www.londonmet.ac.uk

### Faculty of Social Sciences & Humanities; www.londonmet.ac.uk/faculties/faculty-of-social-sciences-and-humanities

development and leadership, community work, creative writing/& English literature, criminology and community policing/law/psychology/sociology/youth studies, dance, digital media/design, early childhood studies, early years teaching, education studies/& English literature, film & tv studies, health and social care/social policy, journalism/film and television studies, media, communications/journalism, Montessori early childhood practice, public health and social care, social sciences/and humanities, social work, sociology/and social policy, theatre practice, translation, youth studies, youth work, assessment for specific learning difficulties (dyslexia), child abuse, comparative European social studies, conference interpreting, creative industries, creative writing, criminology, digital media/ management, education, health & social care management and policy, housing and inclusion, information management, journalism, international social work, interpreting, labour and trade union studies, learning and teaching in HE, managing equality and diversity, media and communications, mental health and well-being/practice, organising for social and community development, PGCE early years and primary, PGCE secondary (numerous subjects), policing, security and community safety, practice education in social work, professional writing, public health, public service interpreting (health and legal), researching work, screenwriting, specialised translation, sustainable cities, teaching adult dyslexic learners in H & FE, TESOL and applied linguistics, translation/and technology, violence against women, woman and child abuse; BA(Hons), BSc(Hons), MA, MPhil, MRes, MSc, PGCert/Dip, PhD, FdA, PGCE, ProfDoc

### Sir John Cass Faculty of Art, Architecture and Design; www.thecass.

architectural history, theory & interpretation, architecture/& digital design systems, interior architecture, architecture & interior design, architecture, energy & sustainability, spatial planning & urban design, art, media & design, curating the contemporary, film & animation, drawing, film & broadcast production, fine art, furniture/product design, graphic design, illustration, interior design, jewellery & silversmithing, music technology (audio systems/music production/sound for media), musical instruments, painting, photography, product design, sculpture & installation, textile design; BA(Hons), PGCert, FdA, MA, MPhil, MSc, PhD, ProfDip

## Faculty of Life Sciences & Computing; www.londonmet.ac.uk/depts/flsc

### Communications Technology/Science

computer networking/systems engineering/science, computing, electronic & computer/communications engineering, electronics, telecommunications & network engineering, embedded systems, mobile & satellite communication, network management & security, software engineering

### Applied Computing

business computing, business IT/information systems,, computer forensics & IT security/science, computer networking & computer forensics/IT security, computing & business IT, IT security, software engineering

### Mathematics

mathematics & computer science, financial mathematics, mathematical sciences, mathematics, statistics

### Multimedia

computer animation, computer games modelling & design/programming, interactive media & technology; BSc(Hons), FdSc, MEng, MRes, MSc, PhD

### School of Human Sciences; www.londonmet.ac.uk/depts/fls/hhs

biochemistry, bioethics, biological sciences, biology, biotechnology, appl/biomedical science, blood science, chemistry, dietetics & nutrition, food science, forensic & bioanalytical science, herbal medicinal science, human biology/nutrition, international/ public health nutrition, medical bioscience, medical genetics, obesity & weight management, personal training and fitness consultancy, pharmaceutical science, pharmacology, sports dance therapy, sports psychology & coaching, sport science & PE, sports rehabilitation & therapy, sports therapy

### School of Psychology; www.londonmet.ac.uk/depts/flsdops

psychology, addiction & mental health, psychology of health, counselling psychology, child adolescent & family psychology, business/consumer/criminal/forensic/occupational/organisational psychology, cognitive behaviour therapy; BSc(Hons), DipHE, FdSc, GradDip/Cert, MOst, MOstMed, MSc, Prof Doc

## Faculty of Law, Governance and International Relations; www.londonmet.ac.uk/ depts/hale/lgr

law, law & business management, business/international/European/human rights/ law, international banking & insurance law, trade, transport & maritime law, comparative IP law, European law, human rights law and social justice, international law & politics, governance & international relations/law, international commercial law & business, legal practice, international development, peace & conflict studies, politics, European studies, international relations (globalization/interdisciplinary), international security studies, peace & conflict studies, public service management/administration; BA(Hons), BSc(Hons), FdG, LlB, LlM, MA, PGCE

## London Metropolitan Business School; www.londonmet.ac.uk/lmb

accounting & finance/business management, aviation management, banking & finance, business management & marketing/law, communication, development & leadership, financial markets & derivatives, financial mathematics, business/operations management, corporate finance & investment, international finance /banking & finance, international financial strategy, economics/& finance, international business/ economics & finance, HRM & employment law, international business/business management & business law, international/human resources & employment management, HRM, organisational change & consultancy, business management/studies/administration, corporate social, marketing, network management & security, advertising, marketing communications & PR, digital & experiential marketing, digital media, media & communication/journalism, international marketing communications, fashion marketing/buying & retailing/PR, marketing, PR, marketing & business management/journalism, arts & heritage management, aviation management, events management, international events management & PR, international hospitality/tourism management/hotel & restaurant management, international sustainable tourism, management & development, international trade & transport, international/sports management, logistics & supply chain management, music industry & media digital business, purchase & supply chain management, executive & professional courses; DPS, FdSc, GradConv, HND, MA, MBA, MSc, PGDip, ProfDoc

## THE LONDON SCHOOL OF OSTEOPATHY
## www.lso.ac.uk

osteopathy; MOst

## LONDON SOUTH BANK UNIVERSITY
## www.lsbu.ac.uk

### Faculty of Arts and Human Sciences; www.lsbu.ac.uk/#ahs

#### Arts, Media; www.lsbu.ac.uk/ahs/departments/artsmedia

digital film & video/media arts/photography, game cultures, independent film practice/editing & montage, music & sonic media, photographic culture; BA(Hons), MA, MPhil, PhD

#### Culture, Writing & Performance; www.lsbu.ac.uk/ahs/departments/cwp

arts & festivals management, communications, critical/arts management, creative writing, drama & performance, English studies, cultural management, journalism, independent film practice, media studies, photographic culture, film studies, cultural & media studies, multimedia journalism, creative media industries, media arts/writing, new media, theatre practice; BA(Hons), MA, PhD, MPhil

#### Education; www.lsbu.ac.uk/departments/education

PCGE: early years, graduate teacher training/PGCE with QTS (primary/secondary maths), education, learning and teaching, in HE, education for sustainability, post-compulsory education, secondary mathematics, sustainability equality & diversity; BA(Hons), Cert, FdA, MA, MPhil, PhD, PgDip/Cert, EdDoc, PGCHE

#### Law; www.lsbu.ac.uk/departments/law

business/criminal/medical/family law, common law, crime & litigation, human rights, international human rights and development/criminal law, law, legal studies, criminality; GradDip, LlB(Hons), LLM, CPE

#### Psychology; www.lsbu.ac.uk/departments/psychology

addiction psychology & counselling, investigative forensic psychology, psychology, criminology, clinical psychology, child development; BSc(Hons), GradDip, MSc, PhD

#### Social Sciences; www.lsbu.ac.uk/ahs/departments/socialsciences

criminology with law/psychology, development studies, development & urbanisation, education for sustainability, gender & sexuality, international planning, international politics, refugee studies, social policy, social research methods, sociology; BA(Hons), BSc(Hons), MSc, PhD, PGDip/Cert

#### Urban, Environmental & Leisure Studies; www.lsbu.ac.uk/ahs/departments/uels

built environment studies, housing studies, international tourism & hospitality/travel management, planning policy and practice, town planning, urban planning design, sustainable communities, urban and environmental planning/regeneration and community development, urban planning design/regeneration, tourism, leisure & hospitality management; BA(Hons), FdA, HNC, MA, MSc, PGCert/Dip, MPhil, PhD

### Faculty of Business; www.bus.lsbu.ac.uk

accounting, business administration/management/project management/studies/enterprise, international business by e-learning, finance, corporate governance, international finance/banking/investment/business with finance/accounting, management in civil society, financial management, business information technology/intelligence, computing, computer systems management, high performance/human centred computing, international investment & finance/banking/accounting/intelligent systems/management, IT, internet & database systems, multimedia computing, small business development, strategic information IT, web design/& mobile computing, digital marketing, public administration, HRM/D, HR practice, international business, international health services & hospital management, international human resources/HRM/management/marketing, learning & development in practice, management in civil society, marketing & fundraising, marketing/communications management, Chinese business practice, charity finance/& accounting, public administration, management in civil society/financial management/fundraising & marketing; MA, D/MBA, PGDip/Cert, MSc, BTEC, HND, DMS, CM, BSc(Hons), BA(Hons), MPA, CM

## *Faculty of Engineering, Science & Built Environment: www.lsbu.ac.uk/esbe*

### Dept of Applied Sciences; www.lsbu.ac.uk/esbe/departments/appsci

applied biology, applied science, chemical & process engineering, biochemistry, culinary art, engineering, environmental biology, food & nutrition, food safety & control, food science, forensic science/with criminology, human biology, human nutrition, microbiology, petroleum engineering, sport & exercise science, sport coaching & analysis; BA(Hons), BEng(Hons), BSc(Hons), FdSc, MSc/PgCert/PgDip

### Dept of Engineering & Design; www.lsbu.ac.uk/esbe/departments/engdes

biomedical engineering & instrumentation, computer-aided design/engineering, computer systems & networks, design & manufacturing management, electrical & electronic engineering, engineering product design, enterprise, mechanical engineering/design, mechatronics/engineering, power distribution, product design, sports product design, telecommunications & computer networks engineering, embedded & distributed systems, quality engineering management systems for environmental services; BEng(Hons), BSc(Hons), FdEng, HNC, HND, MRes, MSc, PgDip

### Dept of the Built Environment; www1.lsbu.ac.uk/esbe/departments/builtenv

architecture, architectural technology, built environment, commercial management (quantity surveying), construction/management/project management, planning buildings for health, property development & planning management, property management (building surveying), surveying (building or quantity building surveying, real estate; BA(Hons), FdSc, HNC, PgDip/Cert, MSc

### Dept of Urban Engineering; www1.lsbu.ac.uk/esbe/departments/urbeng

architectural engineering, building services engineering, civil engineering, environmental & architectural acoustics, structural engineering, transport engineering & planning, sustainable energy systems; BEng(Hons), BSc(Hons), FdEng, HNC, HND, MSc, PgDip/Cert

## *Faculty of Health & Social Care: www.lsbu.ac.uk/faculties/hsc*

health & social care (hospital care/maternity support/mental health care/primary care/rehabilitation therapy), health visiting (specialist community practice nursing), nursing (advanced/children's/learning disabilities/mental health/neonatal), midwifery, professional nursing practice (adult), children's adv nursing practice, children's high dependency nursing, radiography (diagnostic/therapeutic/reporting), clinical technology, operating dept practice, occupational therapy, perioperative practice, social work, primary & social care, neuromusculoskeletal management, non medical prescribing, breast imaging, ultrasound, child health studies, acute & psychiatric intensive care, cognitive behaviour therapy, forensic/mental health practice, careers development/guidance, health visiting, mental health/& primary care, occupational health nursing, public health & health promotion, schools nursing, continuous professional development, traditional Chinese medicine (acupuncture), workplace health management; FdSc, BSc, BSc(Hons), DipHE(Hons), MSc, PgDip/Cert, PhD, University AdvDip, ProfDoc, MCMAc

# UNIVERSITY OF EAST LONDON
# www.uel.ac.uk

### School of Arts and Digital Industries; www.uel.ac.uk/ad

acting, animation, computer games design/development, fine art, film & video, graphic design, fashion, independent film & video & new screen media, heritage studies, international fashion management, illustration, interactive media, magazines, multimedia design technology, photography, printed textile design, print design, textiles & fashion, theatre directing, writing imaginative practice; BA(Hons), BSc/BA, FdA, GradCert, MA, MPhil, MSc, PGC, PhD, ProfDoc

### School of Combined Honours; www.uel.ac.uk/combined

range of subjects for which combined honours courses are conducted

### School of Architecture, Computing and Engineering; www.uel.ac.uk/ace

architecture/computing/design, architecture interpretation & theories/sustainability & design, urban design environments, landscape architecture, business information systems, computing networks, computing, computer games/networks/systems engineering/forensics, information technology/security, computer systems engineering, technology management, media & communications, mobile communications, software engineering, civil engineering surveying, construction management, structural engineering, electrical & electronic engineering, product design, environmental adaptability and sustainability, geotechnics & energy management, renewable energy & built environment; BA/BEng(Hons), BA/BSc, BSc(Hons), MPhil, MSc, PhD, ProfDoc

### Royal Docks Business School; www.uel.ac.uk/business

accounting, business management (finance/HR/marketing) investment/risk management, economics, entrepreneurship, finance, financial management, healthcare management, hospitality & international tourist management, HRM, international accounting/HRM/marketing/risk business/finance, Islamic finance, financial & risk/investment, leadership/& international business communication/international business, music industry management, mathematics, project management, retail, brand management, marketing, sports/tourism management, sustainability & energy management; BA(Hons), DBA, HND, LlB, MA, MBA, MPhil, MSc, PGDip, PhD

### Cass School of Education & Communities; www.uel.ac.uk/education

approved mental health practice, children & young people, their families and carers/social work with adults, helping professions, couple psychoanalytic psychotherapy, creative leadership in education, ELT, inter-professional practice (children's workforce development, international social work with community development/refugee studies, learning and teaching in HE, multilingualism, PGCE secondary education (numerous subjects), PGCE (primary education, early years, modern languages, English, mathematics, special educational needs, special schools, inclusion, English as additional language), psychological therapies with children, young people and families, PGCE secondary design & technology (food & textiles), special educational needs, strategic leadership and management, teaching and learning, child care, early years education, enhancement programme, secondary/primary education, post-compulsory training, primary/secondary teaching, professional development, social work, teacher training, teaching assistants, youth & community work; BA(Hons), EdD, FdA, MA, PGCE, PGDip, ProfDoc, UnivCert

### School of Health, Sport and Bioscience; www.uel.ac.uk/hsb

applied biology, adv practice for health professions, biochemistry, bioinformatics/promotion, biomedical science, biotechnology, cellular & molecular pharmacy, clinical science, conservation, fitness & health, forensic science, health promotion/services, human biology, immunology, medical/microbiology/biotechnology/physiology, molecular medical microbiology, paediatrics, professional nursing practice, toxicology, public health, pharmacology, pharmaceutical science, physiotherapy, podiatry, sports & exercise science/rehabilitation, sports coaching/development/psychology/therapy, strength & conditioning; BA(Hons), BSc(Hons), FdSc, MPhil, MSc, PGCert, PhD, ProfDoc

### School of Law & Social Science; www.uel.ac.uk/lss

law, criminology/ & criminal justice, human rights, international development/relations, innovation, NGOs & management, Islamic & Middle East law, native American studies, psychosocial studies, social sciences, sociology, refugee studies, transport sustenance & science, anthropology/& human rights and justice, applied systemic theory, art/systemic psychotherapy, attachment, psychoanalysis and the couple relationship, child and adolescent primary mental health care work, child protection and complex child care, child psychoanalytic psychotherapy, child, adolescent and family mental well-being: multidisciplinary practice, conflict, displacement and human security, consultation and the organisation/psychoanalytic approaches, counselling in educational settings, emotional factors in learning and teaching, fostering and adoption studies, infant mental health, information and communication technologies and development, international development and health, international business/law and criminal justice, international law and financial markets/international relations/world economy, international relations, Islamic & middle eastern studies, law general, leadership and organisational analysis, narrative research, narrative research, NGO and management, psychoanalytic observational studies/ psychotherapy with children, parents and young people, studies, psychodynamic approaches to working with adolescents/people with learning disabilities, psychodynamic psychosocial nursing, psychosocial perspectives on working with people with personality disorders, social enterprise: health & social care, systemic psychotherapy, terrorism studies, therapeutic communication with children, transport, sustainability and society, working with groups, working with people with eating disorders, voluntary sector management; BA(Hons), BSc(Hons), LlB, LlM, MSc, PostGDip, DChPsych, MSystPsych, MPsych, DConsOrg

### School of Psychology; www.uel.ac.uk/psychology

counselling, mentoring, psychology, critical/developmental/forensic/educational/child psychology, psychosocial studies, spiritual, religious & cultural care, applied educational and child psychology, applied / positive psychology, applied psychology/psychosynthesis, business psychology, career/coaching, clinical and community psychology, clinical psychology, coaching/psychology, counselling and psychotherapy, counselling children in schools/psychology, international humanitarian psychosocial consultation, occupational /and organisational psychology, couple and individual psychodynamic counselling and psychotherapy, psychosexual and relationship therapy, psychosynthesis counselling/foundations/studies, transpersonal and integrative supervision; BA(Hons), BSc(Hons), ClinPSyD, FdA, GradDip/Cert, MA, MSc, ProfDoc, DAppEdChPsych, MPsych, UnivCert

## UNIVERSITY OF WEST LONDON
## www.uwl.ac.uk

### Faculty of the Arts; www.uwl.ac.uk/the_university/faculties_and_schools/Faculty_of_the_Arts

**London College of Music; www.uwl.ac.uk/music/London_College_of_Music**

adv music technology, electronic music composition, music technology/management, music (performance & composition), management & artist development, performance/technology, composing concert music or film or TV, music industry management, record production, pop music; performance BA, BMus, BSc, DipHE, FdA, FdMus, MA, MMus, PGCert, PGDip

**School of Art, Design, & Media; www.uwl.ac.uk/art_design_media/School_of_Art_Design_and_Media**

advertising, digital animation/media production, fashion & textiles, graphic design, photography, digital imaging, web design, broadcast journalism, media studies, PR, video production & film studies; BA, FdA, MA, DipHE

### Faculty of Health & Human Studies; www.uwl.ac.uk/the_university/faculties_and_schools/Faculty_of_Health_and_Human_Sciences

**School of Psychology, Social Care & Human Sciences; www.uwl.ac.uk/school_of_psychology_social_work_and_human_sciences/School_of_Psychology_Social_Work_and_Human_Sciences**

substance use & misuse studies, clinical hypnotherapy, communicable diseases, enhancing professional practice, forensic sciences, health psychology, principles of public health, leadership for health & care, psychology, psychology & health/criminology/counselling theory, nutritional nutrients/therapy, principles of healthcare, psychology, nutrients in metabolism & health, social work/care; BSc, CertHE, DipHE, FdSc, MA, MPhil, MSc, PGCert, PGDip, PhD

**School of Nursing, Midwifery & Healthcare; www.uwl.ac.uk/school_of_nursing_midwifery_and_healthcare/School_of_Nursing_Midwifery_and_Healthcare**

advancing practice/community, CPD, community & primary healthcare, matron/midwifery, health & social care, healthcare, enhancing professional practice, learning disability/adult/child/mental health nursing, midwifery/& women's health, nursing & healthcare, operating department practice, health promotion & public health, primary care, strategic workplace planning, working with children & young people; BSc, DipHE, MA, MM, MPhil, PGDip, PhD, FdSc

### Faculty of Professional Studies

**West London Business School; www.uwl.ac.uk/businessschool/Business_School**

accounting & finance, business studies/finance/internship/marketing/administration, contemporary marketing, credit management, English studies, finance & risk management, global capital markets, HRM, marketing, management, managing human resources, information & communication, international business management/marketing hotel management, corporate communication, management studies (health & social care), project management, PR, purchasing & supply, tourism management; DMS, FdA, GradCert, GradDip, HND, MA, MBA, MPhil, MSc, PGDip, PhD

**Ealing Law School; www.uwl.ac.uk/law/Ealing_Law_School**

law, criminology, employment law, intellectual property law, investment & arbitration law, international/business & commercial/banking & finance/investment law, finance law, legal practice; GradDip, LLB, LLM, PhD

**London School of Hospitality & Tourism; www.uwl.ac.uk/hospitality/London_School_of_Hospitality_Tourism**

airline & airport management, events management, food & professional cookery, hospitality/operations management, hospitality management & food studies, fundraising & special events management, gastronomic food management, international culinary arts/hotel management, tourism, travel communication, travel & tourism/management; BA, DipHE, FdA, GradCert, HND, MA, MPhil, PGDip, PhD

**School of Computing & Technology; www.uwl.ac.uk/computing/School_of_Computing_and_Technology**

applied sound engineering, computing/science, computing & information systems, digital service architecture, information systems/for business, computer interaction design, information management, intelligent computer systems, electronic/electrical engineering, information & communications technology, mechanical engineering, mechatronics, microelectronics, network & mobile communications, software engineering, sustainability & built environment, civil & environmental engineering, built environment: construction management/architectural technology; BSc, FdSc, HND, MSc, MPhil, PhD

## UNIVERSITY OF LONDON; BIRKBECK
## www.bbk.ac.uk

### *School of Arts; www.bbk.ac.uk/arts*

English & humanities, contemporary/medieval/ literature & culture/modern literature, creative writing/producing, culture & critical studies, medical humanities, theatre & drama studies, gender, sexuality & culture, media & cultural studies, medieval literature & culture, Renaissance studies, romantic studies, theatre studies & English/humanities, theatre directing, Shakespeare & contemporary performance, Victorian studies

linguistics & language/culture, history & language, kinship & community, Iberian & Latin American cultural/studies, French, Spanish, German, Japanese/linguistics & language, Polish, Portuguese

film & media strategy/management, Japanese & film/media, language & film, film curating, film, TV & screen media, TV history & practice, world cinema, performance dance, arts management/policy, creative industry, Japanese culture studies, /creative industries, journalism, digital media management, design & devlopment

### *School of Business, Economics and Informatics; www.bbk.ac.uk/business*

applied statistics, accounting with business/finance, business, business ethics/innovation, corporate governance/responsibility & sustainability, economics, financial economics/engineering/management, e-business, finance, finance and commodities/accounting, HRM, international business, investment management, marketing, mathematics, econometrics, statistics, economic and social policy, economics and business, mathematics and accounting/economics/management, professional studies, services & retail marketing, statistics, international business & development/EU, public sector management, sports management, adv computing/financial services, computing technology, creative industries, information & web technologies, information science & management, intelligent techniques, information technology, business computing/technology, cloud & data technology, web techniques; BSc(Econ), BSc, CertHE, MPhil, PhD, MSc, MRes

### School of Law; www.bbk.ac.uk/law

law, criminology & criminal justice, constitutional law, theory & practice, law (general), human rights, international economic law/justice & development, law & social justice, criminology & criminal justice, human rights law, international criminal law & social justice, legal practice; LlB, MPhil, PhD, LlM, BSc

### School of Science; www.bbk.ac.uk

science, analytical chemistry (forensic & environmental analysis), analytical bioscience, bioinformatics & systems biology, health & diseases, microbiology, biomedical science, chemistry, chemical & molecular biology, biological science, geology, earth sciences, environmental geology, planetary science & astronomy, psychology, cognition & computation, cognitive neuroscience, & neuropsychology, psychological research methods, functional neuroimaging; MRes, PGDip, BSc, MPhil, PhD, FD

### School of Social Sciences, History and Philosophy; www/bbk.ac.uk

applied linguistics & intercultural communication, linguistics & language (Italian, German, Japanese, Portuguese, Spanish), international leadership, environmental management, community development & public policy, development studies with environment, environmental management/science, geology, social science, business strategy & the economy, children, young people & international development, climate change management, development studies & sociology, anthropology, GIS, voluntary & public sector studies, linguistics studies, language teaching, TESOL, history, archaeology, classical archaeology/civilisations/classics, contemporary history & politics, European history, gender, sexuality & sociology/culture, history in Britain, history of ideas, London, cities & culture, medical science & culture, psychology & history, world history, politics, philosophy & history, social science, psychosocial studies, culture, diaspora, ethnicity, psychoanalytical history & culture, education, power & social change, psychodynamics of human development; BA, BSc, MA, MRes, MPhil, PhD, MPhilSt, CertHE, FDSc

## UNIVERSITY OF LONDON; COURTAULD INSTITUTE OF ART
## www.courtauld.ac.uk

conservation of easel paintings, curating the art museum, history of art, painting (conservation of wall painting), curating the art museum; BA(Hons), GradDip, MA, PGDip, MPhil, PhD

## UNIVERSITY OF LONDON; GOLDSMITHS
## www.goldsmiths.ac.uk

### Dept of Anthropology; www.gold.ac.uk/anthropology

anthropology, anthropology & media/sociology/history, cultural politics, applied anthropology & community development, Latin American studies, development & rights, history, sociology & political science, social/visual anthropology, applied anthropology & community development/community & youth work, development & rights; BA(Hons), MPhil, PhD, MRes

### Dept of Art; www.gold.ac.uk/art

fine art & history of art, art writing, curating; BA(Hons), MFA, MPhil, PhD

### Centre for English Language & Academic Writing; www.gold.ac.uk/eap

humanities & social science, media, communication, design, music, music computing; GradDip, IntCert

### Centre for Cultural Studies; www.gold.ac.uk/cultural-studies

cultural studies/industry, creating social media, interactive media: post-colonial culture & global policy; MA, MPhil, PhD

### Dept of Computing; www.gold.ac.uk/computing

computing, business computing, computer science, computational arts, computer games & entertainment, computational studio arts, creative computing, creative & cultural entrepreneurship, digital journalism/sociology, games programming, information systems, music computing; BMus, BA/BSc(Hons), MFA, MPhil, MSc, PhD, MA

### Dept of Design; www.gold.ac.uk/design

design, design education, design & technology, design – critical practice/ & entertainment, creative & cultural entrepreneurship, fashion, innovation in practice; BA(Hons), BSc(Hons), BEng/MEng, MPhil, MRes, PhD, GradDip/Cert, PGCE,

### Dept of Educational Studies; www.gold.ac.uk/educational-studies

artist teachers & contemporary practice, education, culture & identity, education: culture, language & society/school-based exploration, writer/teacher, education teacher training (PGCE) – primary/secondary (standard/flexible), multilingual & linguistic education, social & cultural strategy; BA(Hons), DPS, MA, MPhil, PhD, PGCE

### English Studies, Comparative Literature & English Language; www.gold.ac.uk/ecl

American literature, applied linguistics, comparative literary studies, creative/& life writing, drama, English, history, media & sociocultural linguistics, comparative literature, multilingualism, linguistics & education, creative writing/media & English, writer/teacher; BA(Hons), MA, MPhil, MRes, PhD

### Dept of History; www.gold.ac.uk/history

history, history & anthropology/history of ideas/politics, English & history; BA(Hons), MA, MPhil, MRes, PhD

### Institute for Creative and Cultural Entrepreneurship; www.gold.ac.uk/ccl

creative cultural entrepreneurship, cultural policy/& tourism, social entrepreneurship, fashion, diplomacy, arts administration & cultural politics; MA, MPhil, PhD

### Institute of Management Studies; www.gold.ac.uk/institute-management-studies

business computing, global leadership, management of innovation, digital entrepreneurship studies, management & entrepreneurship, occupational psychology; MSc, BSc

### Dept of Media and Communications; www.gold.ac.uk/media-communications

advertising & marketing, anthropology & media, media & communications/sociology/English, brands communications & culture, creative & cultural entrepreneurship, digital media/journalism, filmmaking, gender & culture, journalism, promotional media/PR, global media & transnational communications, photography: the image & the electronics age, radio, screen documentary, screen & film studies, script writing, media & communications, political communications; BA(Hons), MA, MPhil, PhD, MRes

### Dept of Music; www.gold.ac.uk/music

arts administration & cultural policy, composition, contemporary music studies, pop music, creative practice, creative & cultural entrepreneurship, ethnomusicology, historical musicology, music, music computing/performance & related studies, studio composition; BMus(Hons), BMus/BSc(Hons), MA, MMus, MPhil, PGCert, PhD, GradDip

### Dept of Politics; www.gold.ac.uk/politics

applied social & political science, art & politics, Chinese, critical Asian studies, economics, politics & public policy, history, international studies, politics, sociology, political science; BA(Hons), DPS, MA, MPhil, MRes, PhD

### Dept of Theatre & Performance; www.gold.ac.uk/theatre-performance

drama, drama and theatre arts/English, applied theatre: drama in educational community and social contexts, arts administration and cultural policy, black British writing, drama and performance, contemporary African theatre & performance, creative and cultural entrepreneurship, musical theatre, performance making, performance & culture, writing for performance; BA(Hons), MA, PGCE

### Dept of Psychology; www.gold.ac.uk/psychology

cognitive (& clinical) neuroscience, music, mind & brain, clinical psychology/& health services, organizational behaviour, psychology, science of psychology, genetics & education; FD, BSc(Hons), MPhil, MSc, PhD

### Dept of Sociology; www.gold.ac.uk/sociology

critical & creative analysis, digital sociology, gender, media & culture, photography & urban cultures, social research, sociology & anthropology/media/politics/political science, sociology, visual sociology, world cities & urban life; BA(Hons), MA, MPhil, PhD

**Dept of Visual Cultures; www.gold.ac.uk/visual-cultures**
aural & visual cultures, contemporary art theory/history, fine art, global arts, history of art, research architecture; BA(Hons), MA, MPhil, PGDip, PhD

## UNIVERSITY OF LONDON; HEYTHROP COLLEGE
## www.heythrop.ac.uk

Abrahamic religions, biblical studies, canon law, Christian spirituality/theology, Christianity & inter-religious relations, contemporary ethics, divinity, pastoral/mission/theology, philosophy, religion & ethics/theology, philosophy in education, psychology of religion, study of religions, theology; BA, Certs, FD, GradDip, MA, MRes, MPhil, PhD

## UNIVERSITY OF LONDON; INSTITUTE IN PARIS
## www.ulip.ac.uk

Paris studies – history & culture; BA, MA, MPhil, PhD

## UNIVERSITY OF LONDON; INSTITUTE OF EDUCATION
## www.ioe.ac.uk

teacher training: primary PGCE, secondary PGCE: numerous secondary subjects, post-compulsory education, adult literacy/numeracy/language, religious education, teaching & ESOL, lifelong learning, leadership, education/studies, professional practice in lifelong learning sector, psychology with teaching, developmental and educational psychology, teaching, education, gender and international development, clinical education, early years education, applied educational leadership and management, curriculum, pedagogy and assessment, advanced educational practice, social pedagogy: working with children and families, lifelong learning: policy, teaching and learning, bilingual learners, child development, education and technology, philosophy of education, music education, special and inclusive education, geography education, bilingual learners, child development, education and technology, higher and professional education, philosophy of education, history of education, educational and social research, adult literacy, education, health promotion and international development, art and design in education, education (citizenship/history/ religious education), economics of education, museums and galleries in education, comparative education, social justice and education, educational neuroscience, teaching and learning in higher and professional education, psychosocial studies and education, primary education (policy and practice), inspection and regulation, joint professional practice: language and communication, literacy learning and literacy difficulties, development education, leadership, education (psychology), educational leadership, media, culture and education, educational planning, economics and international, policy analysis and evaluation, sociology of childhood and children's rights, specific learning difficulties, psychology of education, educational assessment, TESOL, mathematics education, English education, science education, education and international development, policy studies in education, HE management, learning technologies, reading recovery and literacy leadership, effective learning and teaching, English, globalization and language policy, sociology of education; BEd, Certs, DedPsy, EdD, GradDip, MA, MBA, MPhil, MRes, MSc, MTg, PGCE, PhD, MTL, BA/BSc

# UNIVERSITY OF LONDON; KING'S COLLEGE LONDON
# www.kcl.ac.uk

## The School of Arts & Humanities: www.kcl.ac.uk/humanities

adv musical studies, ancient history, biblical studies, Byzantine/modern Greek studies, Christianity & the arts, classics, classical studies/archaeology/art & archaeology, comparative literature, conflict resolution in divided societies, critical methodology, cultural & creative industries, digital asset management/ culture & society/humanities/information & asset management, early modern Eng lit/history, English (1850–present), 18/19th-century studies, European public policy/studies (French/German/Spanish), European politics/history, film studies, French, German, Turkish/modern Greek, French literature & culture, German & comparative literature, global history, Greek tradition, Hispanic studies, liberal arts, medieval/history, history of philosophy, international political economy, language & cognition, life writing, war studies, Jewish studies, late antique & Byzantine studies, linguistics, medical humanities, medieval history, medieval England, sex, gender & culture, Middle East & Mediterranean studies, mathematics/ philosophy & physics, music, political economy of Middle East, philosophy/of medicine/mental disorder/psychology, Portuguese & Brazilian studies, religion in the contemporary world, Spanish & Portuguese, Latin American studies, religion, systematic theology, philosophy & ethics, religion/ philosophy/politics & sociology, theatre & performance studies, Shakespeare studies, theology/& religious studies, war studies, world history & culture; BA(Hons), MA, MMus, MRes, MSc, GradDip, MPhil, PhD

## School of Biomedical Sciences: www.kcl.ac.uk/biohealth

analytical science/toxicology, anatomy, biotechnology, developmental & human biology, aviation medicine, biomedical science/& scientific English, biomedicine & molecular science, biopharmaceuticals, chemistry with biomedicine, drug discovery/ development, forensic science, human & applied physiology, medical physiology, molecular genetics, neuroscience, pain science & society, clinical/pharmacology, pharmacy/practice, pharmaceutical analysis & quality control/technology, pharmacology molecular genetics, space physiology & health, translational medicine; BSc, DHC, MB, MPharm, MRes, MSc, GradDip, PGDip/Cert, MPhil, PhD, MD

## Dental Institute; www.kcl.ac.uk/dentistry

adv interventional dentistry, dentistry, adv general dental practice, aesthetic dentistry, conscious sedation, dental public health, developmental & human biology, endodontics, maxillofacial & craniofacial/ prosthodontal treatment, regenerative dental technology, orthodontics, paediatric dentistry, periodontology, fixed & removable/prosthodontics, sedation & special care dentistry; BDS, MClinDent, MOrth, MScDL, PGDip

## Institute of Psychiatry; www.iop.kcl.ac.uk

addiction studies, adv care in dementia, biostatistics, child & adolescent psychiatry, clinical forensic psychiatry/neuroscience/psychology, cognitive behavioural therapies/for psychosis, early intervention in psychosis, epilepsy, family therapy, forensic mental health, genes, environment & development, global mental health, health psychology, mental health in learning disorder studies, neuroscience, neuroimaging, organizational psychiatry & psychology, psychology, social, genetic & developmental psychiatry, war & psychiatry; BSc, DClinPsy, GradCert, MSc, PGDip, MPhil, PhD, MD

## School of Law; www.kcl.ac.uk/law

construction law & dispute resolution, criminology & criminal justice, English & French/German/American/Hong Kong/Australian/EU law, politics, philosophy & law, medical ethics & law, EU competition/ competition law, European/EU law, global ethics & human values, intellectual property & information law, international business/financial law, medical law, law & transnational legal studies, medical ethics & law, UK/US/EU copyright law; LlB, LLM, MA, MPhil, MSc, PhD

## School of Medicine; www.kcl.ac.uk/schools/medicine

medicine, nutrition, chemistry with biomedicine, adv neuromusculoskeletal physiotherapy, dietetics, physiology, cardiovascular res, immunology, translational cancer medicine, clinical pharmacology, drug development, clinical/medical imaging, medical engineering/physics, radiopharmaceutics, medical/vascular ultrasound, nuclear medicine, pain, science & society, palliative care, primary health care, public health, adv physiotherapy/paediatrics, clinical dermatology, imaging, rheumatology, translational medicine; MBBS, MPH, MSc, DDip/Cert, MD, MPhil, PhD

### Florence Nightingale School of Nursing & Midwifery; www.kcl.ac.uk/nursing

midwifery/ studies, nursing practice, nursing studies (adult nursing, children's nursing, mental health nursing), nutrition & dietetics, advanced practice (cancer nursing/cardiac care/child health/critical care/ dermatology nursing/diabetes care/district nursing/ infection control/leadership/midwifery/neuroscience care/nurse practitioner/community matron/case manager/palliative care/specialist community public health nursing/ health visiting/school nursing/ women's healthcare), clinical nursing, clinical research, education for healthcare professionals, health studies; BSc(Hons), DipHE, DHC, DPhil, MRes, MSc, PGCert/Dip

### School of Natural & Mathematical Sciences; www.kcl.ac.uk/nms

adv computing, biomedical engineering, chemistry with biomedicine, computer science/with management/mathematics/robotics/intelligent systems, adv software engineering, bioinformatics, complex systems modelling, computing & internet systems/ security/IT, law & management, mobile & personal communication, mobile internet research, telecommunications/& internet technology, web intelligence

mathematics: mathematics & philosophy/physics/ computer science/management & finance, financial mathematics

physics: physics & mathematics/philosophy/medical applications/ theoretical physics, robotics & intelligent systems

electronic engineering/engineering with business management, robotics; BEng, BSc, MSc, MPhil, MSci, GradDip, PhD

### School of Social Science and Public Policy; www.kcl.ac.uk/sspp

Management: business management, accounting, accountability & financial management, HRM & organizational analysis, international management/ marketing, public service policy & management, risk analysis

Education & Professional Studies: assessment in education, education studies, assessment, child studies, creative arts in the classroom, education – professional studies/management/policy & society/ arts & cultural setting/English, ELT/& applied linguistics, English language & communication, health promotion/health & society, ICT education, inclusive education & technology, international/ child studies, language & cultural diversity, ministry & leadership, teaching & learning, FE management, PGCE (various subjects), science/mathematics education, science engagement & communication, physics with mathematics, bible & ministry, ethics/mission in modern age, religious/Christian/Jewish education, contemporary ecclesiology/worship, theology, politics & faith-based organisations, youth ministry

[txtPolitical Economy: politics of international economy, international politics/studies/conflict studies, European public policy, public policy & ageing, political economy

War Studies: air power in the modern world, history of warfare, defence studies, international security & strategy/war science, peace & security/relations/studies, terrorism, security & society, war in the modern world, war studies & history/philosophy, science & security, S.Asia & global security, politics of international economics, conflict security & development, geopolitics, territory & security, intelligence & international security, non-proliferation & international security, risk analysis

Geography: geography, creative cities, disasters, adaptation & development, carbon science, society & change, environment & development/politics & globalization, environmental monitoring/modelling/ management, geopolitics, global environmental change, acquatic resource management, social science & health, sustainable cities, water science, tourism, environment & development

Social Science, Health & Medicine: ageing & society, bioethics & society, gerontology, global health & social medicine/justice, health & society/promotion, medicine, science & society, ageing & public policy, public services, research methods; BA, MA, MSc, MRes, GradDip, PGDip/Cert, FD, DThMin, DrPS, MPhil, PhD, EdD

# UNIVERSITY OF LONDON; LONDON SCHOOL OF ECONOMICS & POLITICAL SCIENCE
# www.lse.ac.uk

## Departments at LSE:

**Accounting, Anthropology, Economics, Finance, Geography & Environment, Government, International History, International Relations, Law, Management, Mathematics, Media and Communications, Philosophy, Logic and Scientific Method, Social Policy, Sociology, Statistics**

accounting & finance, anthropology/& law, social anthropology, actuarial science, business management statistics, statistics with finance, economic history/with economics, economics/with mathematical economics, economic history, environment/& development, environmental policy & economics, geography/with economics, government/environment/history, politics & philosophy, international history, history, international relations, language studies, English literature & society, law, management, mathematics & economics, philosophy, logic & scientific method, philosophy & economics, social policy & criminology/economics/sociology/government, social psychology, sociology, European/public and economic policy, international development, public policy and management/social policy, international relations, international political economy, global media and communications, global studies: a European perspective, diplomacy and international strategy, finance, health economics, policy and management, law, management, political economy of Europe, accounting and finance, accounting, organisations and institutions, anthropology and development/management, applicable mathematics, china in a comparative perspective, city design and social science, comparative politics, conflict studies, criminal justice policy, culture and society, development management/studies, diplomacy and international strategy, economics/and management/philosophy, economy, risk and society, empires, colonialism and globalisation, environment and development, environmental economics and climate change/regulation, European and comparative social policy, European political economy, European studies/ideas and identities, finance and economic/private equity, financial mathematics, gender/development and globalisation/ media and culture, policy and inequalities, global history/politics, health, community and development, health economics, policy and management, health policy, planning and financing, health, population and society, history of international relations, human geography and urban studies, human rights, international development and humanitarian emergencies, international employment relations and HRM, international health policy/health economics, international migration and public policy, international management, international relations theory, law and accounting, law, anthropology and society, local economic development, management/and human resources, management, information systems and innovation, management, organisations and governance, management science/decision sciences/ operational research, management and strategy, media and communications/communication governance/development, non-governmental organisations, organisational behaviour, organisational and social psychology, philosophy and public policy, philosophy of science, philosophy of the social sciences, political economy of Europe/late development, political science and political economy, political sociology, political theory, politics and government in the European union, population and development, public management and governance, real estate economics and finance, regional and urban planning studies, religion in the contemporary world, regulation, risk and finance/stochastics, social anthropology/learning and cognition, social and cultural psychology, social policy/and development/non-governmental organisations, social policy (social policy and planning/ European and comparative social policy, social and public communication, social research methods, sociology/contemporary social thought/research, statistics, theory and history of international relations, urbanisation and development; BA(Hons), BSc(Hons), Dips, EMBA, LlM, ELLM, MBA, MPA, MPhil, MRes, MSc, MA, PhD

## UNIVERSITY OF LONDON; LONDON SCHOOL OF JEWISH STUDIES
## www.lsjs.ac.uk

Jewish education, Jewish studies, applied professional studies; BA(Hons), MA

## UNIVERSITY OF LONDON; QUEEN MARY
## www.qmul.ac.uk

*Humanities & Social Sciences*

### School of Business & Management; www.busman.qmul.ac.uk

business & management, accounting & management, international/global business, management & organisational innovation, marketing, international business & politics/financial management/HRM & employment relations, public administration
In addition to the above taught degrees there are numerous compulsory modules, a number of which are required to be taken on MSc courses; BSc, MSc, MPH, MRes, PhD

### School of Economics & Finance; www.econ.qmul.ac.uk

accounting, banking, business finance, economics/& finance/management/geography, finance & econometrics, finance, geography, investment & finance, law, statistics & management, mathematics, statistics & financial economics, mathematical finance, statistics; BSc, MPhil, MSc(Econ), PhD

### School of English and Drama: www.sed.qmul.ac.uk

**Dept of Drama**

drama, drama & English/French/German/Hispanic studies/Russian/film studies, theatre & performance theory

**Dept of English**

English/& drama/film studies/history/modern language/French/German/Hispanic studies/Russian, English literature & linguistics, 18th century literature & romanticism, writing in the modern age, Renaissance & early modern studies; BA(Hons), MA, MRes, PhD

### School of Languages, Linguistics & Film; www.sllf.qmul.ac.uk

honours combinations of French, German, Hispanic studies, Russian, Catalan languages, Portuguese, with English language, business management, film studies, linguistics, politics, history, drama, Anglo-German cultural relations, comparative literature, documentary practice, linguistics, language teaching; BA(Hons), MA, PhD

### Dept of Geography; www.geog.qmul.ac.uk

cities & cultures, community organizing, environmental geography/science, environmental science with business management, geography, integrated management of freshwater environment, globalization & development, London studies, physical/human/environmental geography; BA(Hons), BSc(Econ), BSc(Hons), MA, MSc, PhD

### Dept of History; www.history.qmul.ac.uk

modern & contemporary/medieval/history, history & politics/film studies/English/German language/French, comparative literature, Islam & the West, European Jewish history, medieval history, modern & contemporary British history, history of political thought & intellectual history; BA(Hons), MA, PhD

### School of Law; www.law.qmul.ac.uk

banking & finance law, commercial & corporate law, comparative & international dispute resolution, competition law, computer & communications law, economic regulation, English and European law, environmental law, human rights law, insurance law, intellectual property law, international business/shipping law, law & development/politics, legal theory & history, trade mark law & practice, insurance law, international dispute resolution, medical law, public international law, public law, tax law, media law, senior status; Dips, LlB, LlM, MPhil, MSc, PGDip, PhD

### Dept of Philosophy; www.philosophy.qmul.ac.uk

philosophy; MPhil, PhD

### School of Politics & International Relations; www.politics.qmul.ac.uk

international relations, international/public policy, politics, politics & economics/law/geography/business management/French/German/Russian/Hispanic studies, critical theory & global politics, globalization & development, history of politics, international business & politics, thought & intellectual history, numerous postgraduate modules available; BA(Hons), MA, MPhil, MRes, PhD

## *School of Medicine & Dentistry; www.smd.qmul.ac.uk*

### Barts and The London School of Medicine and Dentistry; www.smd-edu.qmul.ac.uk/medicine/

medicine, surgery, dentistry, dental surgery, biomedical engineering, clinical specialisations, community & public health, aesthetic plastic surgery, burn care, cancer therapeutics, clinical dermatology, clinical drug development, clinical microbiology, critical care, endocrinology & diabetes, forensic medical sciences, gastroenterology, global public health & policy, healthcare research methods, health systems & global policy, inflammation/cellular & vascular aspects, international primary health care, mental health/psychological therapies/transcultural mental health care, molecular pathology & genomics, neuroscience & translational medicine, sport & exercise science, surgical skills & science, trauma science (military & austere); dental clinical science/public health/technology, endodontic practice, experimental oral practice, oral biology/medicine, orthodontics, paediatric dentistry, periodontology, prosthodontics; MBBS, BDS, BSc

### Research Institutions;

**Barts Cancer Institute**
**Bizard Institute of Cell and Molecular Science**
**Institute of Dentistry**
**Institute of Health Science and Education**
**William Harvey Research Institute**
**Wolfson Institute of Preventative Medicine**

BDS, BMedSci, FD, BDental Science, MBBS, MClinDent, MD, MRes, MPhil, MSc, NVQ, PGDip, PhD, MPrth, PG Cert/Dip

## *Department of Science & Engineering*

### School of Biological and Chemical Sciences; www.sbcs.qmul.ac.uk

aquatic biology, biochemistry, biology, biomedical sciences, chemistry, evolutionary biology, marine ecology & environmental management, medical/genetics, pharmaceutical chemistry, psychology, zoology with aquatic biology; BSc(Hons), FD, MPhil, MSci, PhD

### School of Electronic Engineering & Computer Science; www.eecs.qmul.ac.uk

audio systems engineering, computer science/& mathematics/business management, computer vision, computing/& information systems, digital music/signal processing, electrical engineering, electronic engineering with computing/telecommunications, information/systems/management & communication technologies/business management, multi/media & arts technology, software engineering, telecommunications systems, mobile & wireless networks; BEng, BSc(Eng), MEng, MSc, PhD

### School of Engineering and Materials Science; www.sems.qmul.ac.uk

aerospace engineering, biomedical engineering, clinical materials, computer-aided engineering, design & innovation, materials & design, materials science & engineering/research, dental materials, biomaterials, mechanical engineering, medical materials/engineering/electronics & physics, polymer science & technology, sustainable energy systems/engineering/materials; BEng, BSc, MEng, MPhil, MRes, PhD

### School of Mathematical Sciences; www.maths.qmul.ac.uk

mathematics, pure mathematics, statistics, astrophysics, financial economics, finance & accounting, mathematical finance, maths with business management; BSc(Hons), MPhil, MSc, MSci, PGDip/Cert, PhD

### School of Physics & Astronomy; www.phy.qmul.ac.uk

astrophysics, astronomy, physics, theoretical physics, particle physics; BSc(Hons), MSc, MSci, PGDip, PhD

# UNIVERSITY OF LONDON; ROYAL HOLLOWAY
# www.rhul.ac.uk

## *Faculty of Arts; www.rhul.ac.uk/departments/arts*

### Dept for Classics; www.rhul.ac.uk/classics

ancient history & philosophy, classics & philosophy, comparative literature & culture & philosophy, late antique & Byzantine studies, combinations of: classics, English & classical studies/Latin/philosophy, rhetoric, Greek, Latin, Hellenic studies, philosophy, classical studies & drama/Italian/French, music & philosophy, philosophy, politics & international relations, classical art & archaeology, moderrn philosophy; BA(Hons), MPhil, PhD

### Dept of Drama & Theatre; www.rhul.ac.uk/drama

applied & participative theatre, drama, drama & creative writing/philosophy/French/German/Italian/music/classical studies, theatre studies, contemporary performance practices, playwriting; BA(Hons), MPhil, PhD

### Dept of English; www.rhul.ac.uk/english

English, English & philosophy/classics/comparative literature/modern languages/film studies/drama, creative writing, English literature, modern & contemporary literature, medieval studies, poetic practice, Shakespeare, Victorian literature, art, culture; BA, MA

### Dept of Media Arts; www.rhul.ac.uk/media-arts

documentary by practice, international broadcasting, production, media arts, film & TV studies, screenwriting/producing for TV & film; BA(Hons), MA, MPhil, PhD

### Dept of Modern Languages, Literature & Culture; www.rhul.ac.uk/mllc

French, German, Italian, Spanish, Hispanic studies, contemporary literature & culture, film studies, critical theory, film, visual & performing arts, linguistics, comparative literature & culture; BA, BSc, MA, MA by Research

### Dept of Music; www.rhul.ac.uk/Music

music, composition, ethnomusicology, fusion electronics, sonic art, multimedia & film-making, pop music, documenting performance, musicology, performance, music with performance studies, music history; BA(Hons), BMus, MMus, MPhil, PhD

## *Faculty of History & Social Sciences; www.rhul.ac.uk/departments/hss*

### Centre for Criminology & Sociology; www.rhul.ac.uk/criminology & sociology

criminology & sociology/psychology, consumption, culture & marketing; BSc, MA

### Dept of Economics; www.rhul.ac.uk/economics

economics, economics & management/mathematics, financial & business economics, policy economics, finance, economic studies; BSc, MSc, PhD

### Dept of European Studies; www.rhul.ac.uk/EuropeanStudies

European studies (French/Spanish/Italian/German), European research, social science; BA

### Dept of Social Work; www.rhul.ac.uk/socialwork

social work, work with children & families; BA(Hons), MA, MSc

### Dept of History; www.rhul.ac.uk/history

history, public history, late antique & Byzantine studies, crusader studies, medieval studies, modern history & politics, political thought & intellectual history; BA, MA, PhD

### School of Management; www.rhul.ac.uk/management

management with accounting/entrepreneurship/HR/business/information systems, consumption, culture & marketing, marketing, international accounting/business/HRM, leadership & management in health, management, project management, Asia Pacific business & management, sustainability/& management; BSc, MA

### Dept of Politics & International Relations; www.rhul.ac.uk/politicsandir

politics & international relations/theory/philosophy, economics, politics & philosophy, European studies/politics/French/German/Italian/Spanish/contemporary political theory, global politics, democracy, economics, politics & international relations, history governance, new political communication, transnational security studies; BA(Hons), BSc(Hons) MA, MBA, MSc, MPhil, PhD, PGCert, Grad Dip, PGDip

## Faculty of Science; www.rhul.ac.uk/departments/science

### School of Biological Sciences; www.rhul.ac.uk/biological-sciences

biochemistry, biology, ecology & environment, molecular biology, biomedical sciences, medical biochemistry, plant molecular sciences, psychology, zoology; BA(Hons), BSc(Hons), MSc, PhD

### Dept of Computer Science; www.cs.rhul.ac.uk

computer science & artificial intelligence/mathematics/business management, business information systems, computational finance, data science & analytics, machine learning; BSc(Hons), MPhil, MSc, PhD

### Dept of Earth Sciences; www.rhul.ac.uk/earthscience

environmental geology/geoscience, geology, geoscience, petroleum geology/geoscience, environmental geology/diagnosis & management, physical geography & geology, petroleum geoscience (basin evolution/tectonics); BSc, MSC, MSci, PhD

### Dept of Geography; www.rhul.ac.uk/geography

cultural geography, earthscience, geography, geology, human/physical geography, politics & international relations, practising sustainable development, sustainability & management, quarternary science, creative writing, place, environment, writing, geopolitics & security; BA, BSc, MA, MSc, PhD

### Dept of Mathematics; www.ma.rhul.ac.uk

information security, mathematics, mathematics for applications, maths of cryptology & communication, statistics, physics, philosophy, joint degrees; BSc(Hons), MSc, MSci, PhD

### Dept of Physics; www.rhul.ac.uk/physics

physics/with mathematics/philosophy/music, applied physics, astrophysics, low temperature physics, nanotechnology, particle physics, theoretical physics; BSc(Hons), MPhil, MPhys, MSc, PhD

### Dept of Psychology; www.rhul.ac.uk/psychology

applied/social psychology, applied cognitive behavioural theory, psychology with biology/mathematics/music, psychological development & developmental disorders, clinical psychology & mental health, cognitive neuroscience; BSc(Hons), DClinPsych, MSc, PhD

# UNIVERSITY OF LONDON; ROYAL VETERINARY COLLEGE
www.rvc.ac.uk

bioveterinary sciences, comparative pathology, control of infectious diseases in animals, intensive/livestock health & production, veterinary nursing/medicine, wild animal health/biology, veterinary pathology/physiotherapy/education/epidemiology, public health, risk analysis & food safety; BSc(Hons), BVetMed, FdSc, MPhil, PhD, MVMed, MRes, MSc, PGDip/Cert

# UNIVERSITY OF LONDON; SCHOOL OF ORIENTAL AND AFRICAN STUDIES
www.soas.ac.uk

### Faculty of Languages & Cultures; www.soas.ac.uk/languagecultures

African language and culture/literature/studies, ancient Near Eastern languages/studies, afropone, Amharic, black art studies, anthropological research, applied linguistics & language pedagogy, Arabic cultural studies/language teaching/literature, Arabic/& Islamic studies, Asian politics, Bantu, Bengali, Chinese (modern and classical), Chinese/literature/studies, comparative literature (Africa/Asia), contemporary Pakistan, cultural studies, gender studies, Burmese (Myanmar), Hausa, Hebrew & Israeli studies, Hindi, Indonesian, international management & SE Asian studies, Iranian studies, Islamic law/studies/societies, Japanese literature/studies/linguistics, Korean studies, languages & cultures of south Asia, language documentation & description, languages & literatures of south east Asia, linguistics,

Near & Middle Eastern studies, Nepali, Pacific Asian studies, Persian, Sandskrit, Sinology, Somali, south Asian/area studies, Taiwan studies, Thai, theory & practice of translation (Asian & African studies), Turkish studies, Urdu, Vietnamese, Yoruka

**Faculty of Law & Social Sciences; www.soas.ac.uk/lawsocialsciences**

African environment & development, comparative political thought, development economics, development studies (central Africa), economics, international politics, international management (China/Japan & Korea/Middle East & North Africa), law in M East & N Africa, S Asian law, globalisation & development, African politics, development economics, development studies/C Asia, economics (reference Asia/S Asia/Asia Pacific region/M East), finance & development, financial law, international development, labour, social movements & development, ME politics, migration mobility & development, political economy of development, political studies, politics of China, politics of international rights & justice, research, state, society & development, violence, conflict & development

**Faculty of Arts & the Humanities; www.soas.ac.uk/artshumanities**

arts of Asia & Africa, history of art (Asia, Africa, Europe), history of art &/archaeology, study of religions, music, social anthropology/of development/food/media, anthropological research methods/& Nepali, anthropology of travel, tourism & pilgrimage/food, art & archaeology of E Asia, art & archaeology of Islamic M East, film & history, history, music in development, medical anthropology, music & development, religions of Asia & Africa, religious arts of Asia, traditions of yoga & meditation, global creative & cultural industries, historical research methods, migration & diaspora studies, ethnomusicology, performance; BA(Hons), LlB, LlM, MMus, MPhil, MSc, PGDip, PhD

## UNIVERSITY OF LONDON; THE SCHOOL OF PHARMACY
## www.pharmacy.ac.uk

clinical pharmacy, international practice & policy, drug delivery, drug discovery & development/pharmacy management, pharmacognosy, pharmacy; Certs, MPharm, MSc, PGDip, PhD

## UNIVERSITY OF LONDON; UNIVERSITY COLLEGE LONDON (UCL)
## www.ucl.ac.uk

### *UCL School of Life and Medical Science (including UCL Medical School); www.ucl.ac.uk/slms*

**Faculty of Brain Sciences; www.ucl.ac.uk/brain-sciences**

**Faculty of Life Sciences; www.ucl.ac.uk/life-sciences**

**Faculty of Medical Sciences; www.ucl.ac.uk/medical-sciences**

**Faculty of Population Health Sciences; www.ucl.ac.uk/populationhealth-sciences**

**Brain Sciences**

Psychology & language Sciences: linguistics, psychology, speech science, language science, cognitive and decision sciences, cognitive neuroscience, human-compute, neuroscience, language and communication, phonetics, psychoanalytic developmental psychology, developmental neuroscience and psychopathology, research methods in psychology, social cognition, speech and language sciences, speech, language and cognition, theoretical psychoanalytical studies, cognitive, behavioural therapy for children and young people, developmental psychology and clinical, low intensity cognitive behavioural interventions, clinical psychology, educational and child psychology, psychotherapy (child and adolescent psychoanalytic psychotherapy), speech and language therapy

Ophthalmology: biology of vision, clinical ophthalmology, ophthalmology (cataract, rectinal)

Ear: adv/audiology, ENT practice (ontology), audiological surgery, audiovestibular medicine

Neurology: adv neuroimaging, brain & mind science, clinical neurology, clinical neuroscience

Mental Health Sciences: psychiatric research, clinical neuroscience, cognitive neuroscience

**Life Sciences**

biochemistry, biological sciences (genetics, human genetics, environmental biology and zoology), biomedical sciences, biotechnology, human sciences, immunology, molecular biology, natural sciences, neuroscience, pharmacology, physiology, history of medicine, biosciences, biomedical sciences, clinical pharmacy, international practice and policy, drug delivery, pharmacogenetics and stratified medicine, pharmacognosy, pharmacy practice

**Popular Health Sciences**

**Medical Sciences**

anatomy cell and developmental biology, clinical sciences, history of medicine, human genetics/genetics, immunology infection and cell pathology, global health, medical anthropology, medical physics and bioengineering, neuroscience, orthopaedic science, paediatrics and child health, pharmacology, physiology, physiology and pharmacology, philosophy, medicine and society, primary health care, psychology, surgical sciences

**Population Health Sciences**

child health, paediatrics & child health, international health, women's health & communicable disease, prenatal genetics, fetal medicine, reproductive science & women's health, haemoglobinopathology, epidemiology & healthcare, health informatics, dietetics & public health, health & society, social epidemiology, health physiology, sexually transmitted disease, & HIV, cardiovascular science, cancer, cardiorespiratory sciences, general & adolescent paediatrics, genes, development & disease, infection & immunity, neurosciences & mental health, nutritional & surgical sciences, population health sciences; BSc(Hons), DipCDSc, IbSc, MBBS, MClinDent, MD(Res), MPhil, MRes, MSc, MSci, PGCert/Dip, PhD

## *The Bartlett, Faculty of the Built Environment*

### Built Environment: www.barlett.ucl.ac.uk

School of Architecture: architectural/& interdisciplinary studies, architectural design, urban design, architectural history/& theory, professional management & practice in architecture

School of Construction & Project Management: project management for construction, construction economics & management, project enterprise & management, strategic management of projects, infrastructure investment and finance,

Development Planning: building and urban design in development, development administration & planning, environment and sustainable development, social development practice, urban development planning, urban economic development, energy demand studies, economics and policy of energy and the environment, adaptive architecture & computation, advanced architectural studies, environmental design & engineering, facility & environment management, heritage science, light & lighting, sustainable heritage, built environment

School of Planning: urban planning, design & management, urban studies, planning and real estate, inter-disciplinary urban design, dip spatial planning, international planning, international real estate & planning, urban regeneration, sustainable urbanism, planning, design & development, mega infrastructure planning appraisal, housing development, transport and city planning; BSc(Hons), Diplomas, EngD, MA, MArch, MPhil, MSc, PhD, PGDip, MRes

## *Faculty of Engineering Sciences; www.ucl.ac.uk/engineering*

### Civil, Environmental & Geomatic Engineering; www.rege.ucl.ac.uk

civil engineering, earthquake engineering with disaster management, environmental engineering/mapping, environmental systems engineering, GIS, hydrographic surveying, remote sensing, transport studies

### Biochemical Engineering; www.ucl.ac.uk/biochemeng

biochemical engineering, bioprocessing of new medicines

### Chemical Engineering; www.ucl.ac.uk/chemeng

chemical engineering/with biochemical engineering, chemical process engineering

### Computer Science; www.cs.ucl.ac.uk/

computer science, computational statistics & machine learning, computer graphics, vision & imaging, financial systems engineering/computation, human-computer interaction with ergonomics, ICT innovation, information security, machine learning, mathematical computation, networked computer systems, software systems engineering, web science & big data analytics

### Electronic and Electrical Engineering; www.ee.ucl.ac.uk

electronics engineering with communications engineering/computer science/nanotechnology, electrical & electronic engineering, internet engineering, nanotechnology, photonics systems, spacecraft technology/& satellite communications, telecommunications/engineering/with business, wireless & optical communications

### Management Science and Innovation; www.ucl.ac.uk/msi

business economics, corporate strategy, information management for business, innovation management, entrepreneurship: theory & practice, entrepreneurial finance, fraud, ethics & forensic accounting, international business, management, project management, marketing communications, managing information & IT, mergers & valuation, technology entrepreneurship

### Mechanical Engineering; www.ucl.ac.uk/mecheng

engineering with business/ finance, marine engineering, mechanical engineering, naval architecture, power systems engineering, biomaterials & tissue engineering, engineering with innovation & enterprise

### Medical Physics & Bioengineering; www.ucl.ac.uk/medphys

human physiology, medical imaging, physics/& medical physics, medical physics, physics & engineering in medicine; MEng, BSc, Certs, MEng, MPhil, MRes, MSc, PgDip, PhD

## *Faculty of Mathematical and Physical Sciences: www.ucl.ac.uk/maps-faculty*

### Chemistry; www.ucl.ac.uk/chemistry

chemistry, chemical physics, drug discovery, chemical research, energy & the environment, medical chemistry, molecular measurement in medicine

### Earth Sciences; www.ucl.ac.uk/es

earth science, environmental geoscience, geology, geophysical hazards, geophysics, geosciences, natural hazards for insurers, natural sciences, risk & disaster reduction

### Mathematics; www.ucl.ac.uk/mathematics

mathematics with mathematical physics/economics/ modern languages/management studies/physics/statistical science, mathematical modelling, financial mathematics

### Physics and Astronomy; www.phys.ucl.ac.uk

astronomy, astrophysics, physics, theoretical physics, high energy physics, planetary science, ultra precision techniques & applications, managing nanotechnology

### Science and Technology Studies; www.ucl.ac.uk/sts

arts & science, history, sociology of science & technology, natural sciences, philosophy & social studies of science, science, science & society, science, technology, medicine & society

### Space and Climate Physics; www.mssl.ucl.ac.uk

astrophysics, climate extremes, cryogenics, space plasma physics, plasma science, solar & stellar physics, space science & engineering, space plasma physics, systems engineering management

### Statistical Science; www.ucl.ac.uk/stats

economics, finance, statistics, statistical science, statistics/& management for business, medical statistics; BSc, BSc(Econ), EngD, MRes, MSc, MSci, PhD

## *Faculty of Arts & Humanities; www.ucl.ac.uk/ah*

English Language & Literature: English linguistics, issues in modern culture, Shakespeare in history, old & middle English literature, film studies

European Social & Political Studies, Dutch, French, German, Italian, Russian, Spanish, Scandinavian studies, Spanish & Latin American studies, East European language & culture, Hebrew & Jewish studies, anthropology, economics, geography, planning, political science, philosophy, international relations, history, law

Greek & Latin: classics: languages & literature, ancient world studies, reception of classical world

Hebrew & Jewish studies: Jewish history, language & culture, holocaust studies, modern Israeli studies, history (central & E Europe)

Information Studies: library & information studies, electronic communication/& publishing, archive & information studies/records management, digital humanities publishing, programming, information systems/science, web technologies, database systems

Philosophy: philosophy of mind & language, politics & modern philosophy, metaphysics & epistemology, history of philosophy, political philosophy, ethics, Aristotle, early Wittgenstein, epistemology, moral philosophy etc

European Languages, Culture & Society: French, Dutch, German, Spanish & Latin American studies, comparative literature, translation studies, modern languages, language culture & history

**Slade School of Art**

painting, fine art, sculpture, media, history & theory of art, critical studies; BA(Hons), BFA, MA, MPhil, MRes, PhD, MFA

## *Faculty of Law; www.ucl.ac.uk/laws*

law, law & adv studies/another legal system (Australia, Singapore), French/German/Hispanic law, competition/comparative/corporate law, criminal justice, family & social welfare, dispute resolution, environmental law & policy, family law, human rights/intellectual property law, international banking & finance/commercial law, international law, jurisprudence & legal theory, legal history, litigation & dispute resolution, maritime law, public law, law with another legal subject, law & economics, EU law, LlB and Baccalaureus Legum, LlBHons, LlM, MPhil, PhD

## *Faculty of Historical and Social Sciences; www.ucl.ac.uk/shs*

### Anthropology; www.ucl.ac.uk/anthropology

anthropology, digital/social & cultural anthropology, culture, materials & design, human evolution & behaviour, human science, medical anthropology, materials & visual culture, anthropology & modern European studies; BA(Hons), BSc(Hons), MA, MPhil, MRes, MSc, PhD

### Archaeology; www.ucl.ac.uk/archaeology

archaeology & anthropology, archaeology of eastern Mediterranean/& Middle East, artefact studies, ancient history & Egyptology, classical archaeology & classical civilization, comparative art & archaeology, conservation for archaeology & museums, culture, materials & design, culture & heritage of Asia, cultural heritage studies, Egyptian archaeology, environmental archaeology, forensic archaeological science, GIS, managing archaeological sites, museum studies, palaeoanthropology & palaeolithic archaeology, principles of conservation, public archaeology, skeletal & dental bioarchaeology, technology & analysis of archaeological materials; BA(Hons), BSc(Hons), MA, MPhil, MSc, PhD

### Economics; www.ucl.ac.uk/economics

economics, econometrics, economics & business with East European studies, economics & geography/statistics/philosophy/mathematics, microeconomics, macroeconomics, statistics & economics & finance/languages, economic policy; BSc(Hons), MSc, PhD

### Geography; www.geog.ucl.ac.uk

geography, aquatic science, climate change, environmental mapping/modelling/geography, environment, science & society, ecology, geography/& economics, geography (international), geospatial analysis, global migration, globalization, GIS, natural resources/water management, population/political/physical/human geography, quaternary science, remote sensing, urban studies; BA(Hons), BSc(Hons), MSc, PhD

### History; www.ucl.ac.uk/history

history, ancient history, Dutch & the golden age, ancient history & Egyptology, late antique & Byzantine studies, European history, history of political thought & intellectual history, medieval & Renaissance studies, transnational studies, China, health & humanity; BA(Hons), MA, MPhil, PhD

### History of Art; www.ucl.ac.uk/art-history

history of art/with material studies, contemporary politics of the image: Germany, human & non human in medieval art, cannibalism & the early modern image, vision, tourism imperialism, photographic cultures, seriality & polarism; BA(Hons), MA, MPhil, PhD

### Political Science; www.ucl.ac.uk/spp

political science & international relations, European social & political studies, human rights, security studies, democracy & comparative politics, European public policy, global government & ethics, international public policy, legal & political theory; MA, MPhil, MSc, PhD

### School of Slavonic and Eastern European Studies; www.ssees.ucl.ac.uk

central SE/E European studies, comparative business economics, comparative economics & politics, Russian studies, politics/security & integration, history, identity, culture and power, Russian & East European literature & culture; BA(Hons), MA, MPhil, MRes, PhD

# UNIVERSITY OF LOUGHBOROUGH
## www.lboro.ac.uk

*Faculty of Engineering; www.lboro.ac.uk/eng*

### Aeronautical and Automotive Engineering; www.lboro.ac.uk/departments/tt/

advanced methods/aeronautical engineering, automotive engineering/systems engineering

### Chemical Engineering; www.lboro.ac.uk/departments/cg

advanced/chemical engineering/IT & management, advanced process engineering, chemical engineering/management/IT, science & engineering

### Civil and Building Engineering; www.lboro.ac.uk/departments/cv

air transport management, architectural engineering & design management, building services engineering, civil engineering, commercial management & quantity surveying, construction engineering management/project management/construction business management, construction management, low energy building, transport & business management, building surveying, low carbon building design, transport, building, infrastructure in emergencies, services engineering, water & waste engineering/environmental management

### Electronic, Electrical & Systems Engineering; www.lboro.ac.uk/departments/el

digital communication systems, security & forensics, digital/mobile communication, electronic & electrical engineering, electronics & computer systems engineering/software engineering, networked communications, renewable energy systems technology, signal processing in communication systems, systems engineering

### Mechanical and Manufacturing; www.lboro.ac.uk/departments/mm

adv engineering, adv manufacturing engineering & management, engineering design & manufacture, innovative manufacturing engineering, mechanical engineering, mechatronics, product design engineering, sports technology, sustainable engineering; BEng, BSc(Hons), MDes, MRes, MSc, PhD, Cert, Dip

*Faculty of Science; www.lboro.ac.uk/sci*

### Faculty of Chemistry; www.lboro.ac.uk/departments/cm

analytical & pharmaceutical science, analytical chemistry/& environmental science, chemistry/& analytical science/sport science, environmental studies, pharmaceutical science & medicinal chemistry, medicinal & pharmaceutical chemistry; BSc, MSc, PhD

### Dept of Computer Science; www.lboro.ac.uk/departments/co

computer science/& mathematics, AI, IT management for business, computing & management, international computing for the internet, internet computing & network security, IT, networks, visual systems & technology; BSc(Hons), MSc, PhD, PGDip/Cert

### Dept of Information Science; www.lboro.ac.uk/departments/is

information management & computing/web development/business studies, business technology, information & knowledge management, library management, publishing with English, information & business technology; BSc(Hons), MPhil, PhD

### Dept of Materials; www.lboro.ac.uk/departments/materials

automotive materials, design with engineering materials, materials engineering/science & technology, polymer science & technology; BEng/MEng, BSc(Hons), Diploma in Industrial Studies, MSc, PGDip/Cert, PhD

### School of Mathematical Sciences; www.lboro.ac.uk/departments/ma

financial mathematics, industrial mathematical modelling, mathematical finance, mathematics, financial mathematics, mathematics & accounting & financial management/sports science/computer science/economics/management/mathematics education/statistics; BSc(Hons), MSc, PhD

### Dept of Physics; www.lboro.ac.uk/departments/ph

astrophysics & cosmology, engineering physics, nanoscience, physics, physics & maths/management/sports science/cosmology/IT/computing, psychophysics, quantum, string & phase transition, quantum information & computing, science of the internet, surface physics, experimental/theoretical condensed matter physics; BSc(Hons), MSc, PhD

## *Faculty of Social Sciences and Humanities; www.lboro.ac.uk/ssh*

### School of the Arts; www.lboro.ac.uk/departments/sota

3D design/new practice, fine art, graphic communication, illustration, textile innovation & design, 2D/3D visualisation, art & design; studio practice, arts & the public sphere, studio ceramics, method design & practice; BA(Hons), MA, MSc, MPhil, PhD

### School of Business & Economics; www.lboro.ac.uk/departments/sbe

Business: accounting & financial management, banking, finance & accounting, business analysis & management, finance & management, international business/marketing/management, management sciences, marketing, management, HRM, ailing marketing & management

Economics: economics, business economics & finance/accounting, international economics, banking & finance/financial markets, money

Executive Education: management & leadership, automotive management, occupational health & safety management, security management, healthcare management; BSc, MA, MSc, MRes, MPhil, PhD, Cert, Dip, MBA

### Loughborough Design School; www.lboro/departments/ds

design/ergonomics, ergonomics (human factors in design/in health & community care), product/industrial design & technology, design for innovation & sustainability, human factors in transport/for inclusive design, international design; BA, MA, MSc, MDes, PGCE with QTS

### Dept of English & Drama; www.lboro.ac.uk/departments/ea

creative writing, drama, English, history, English & sports studies/history, American studies, performance & multi-media, sports science; BA(Hons), MA, PhD

### Dept of Politics, International Relations & European Studies; www.lboro.ac.uk/departments/eu

history & geography/English, international relations, politics, res methods (European & international studies), international finance & PR; BSc(Hons), MPhil, MSc, PhD

### Dept of Geography; www.lboro.ac.uk/departments/gy

environmental monitoring for management, geography, geography & management/economic, sports management & science, globalization & society/sport science/history, human geography research, international financial & political relations, space & sport; BSc, MPhil, MSc, PhD

### School of Sport, Exercise and Health Sciences; www.lboro.ac.uk/departments/ssehs

human biology, physical activity & public health, physical education & QTS, psychology, PE & QTS, sociology of sport, sport biomechanics, sport coaching, sports science & management, sport and exercise nutrition/psychology/science, exercise science/physiology, psychology, sport management/science; BSc(Hons), MPhil, MSc, PhD

### Dept of Social Sciences; www.lboro.ac.uk/departments/ss

communications and media studies, conversation analysis, discursive psychology, criminology & social policy, digital media & culture, global media & cultural industries, media & cultural analysis, social psychology, sociology; BSc(Hons), MPhil, MSc, PhD

## *Teacher Education Unit; www.lboro.ac.uk/departments/teu*

design & technology, PE, science, physics with mathematics, initial teacher training; MSc, PGCE, QTS

# UNIVERSITY OF MANCHESTER
## www.manchester.ac.uk

*Faculty of Engineering and Physical Sciences: www.eps.manchester.ac.uk*

### School of Chemical Engineering and Analytical Science; www.ceas.manchester.ac.uk

biotechnology, bio-catalysis, systems biology, analytical and separation science, chemical engineering /& business management, instrumentation and measurement science, chemical process design, process design for energy and the environment, product formulation, colloids, crystals and interfaces, theory and modelling of fluids, polymers, proteins and foams, chemical engineering/with chemistry/environmental technology/management/design, environmental & sustainable technologies, refinery design & operation, petroleum engineering; BEng, MEng, MSc, PhD

### School of Chemistry; www.chemistry.manchester.ac.uk

chemistry/& analytical chemistry, forensic & analytical/medicinal chemistry/industrial experience, polymer & materials science & engineering; BSc(Hons), EngD, MChem, MEnt, MPhil, MSc, PhD

### School of Computer Science; www.cs.manchester.ac.uk

adv web technologies, AI, computer science/security, computer science with/business & management/ mathematics, computer systems engineering, computing for business applications, data & knowledge management, digital biology, engineering, internet computing, multicore computing, semantic technology, software engineering; BSc(Hons), MEng, MEnt, MPhil, MSc, PhD

### School of Earth, Atmospheric & Environmental Sciences; www.seaes.manchester.ac.uk

earth sciences, applications in/environmental sciences/policy & management, geochemistry, geography, geology, planetary science, environmental & resource geology, petroleum engineering, geoscience/ engineering, pollution & environmental control; BSc(Hons), MEarthSci, MEng, MSc, PhD

### School of Electrical and Electronic Engineering; www.eee.manchester.ac.uk

communication engineering, advanced control & systems engineering, digital image & signal processing, electrical /& electronic engineering/industrial experience, electrical energy conversion systems, electrical power systems engineering, mechatronic engineering, renewable & clean technology; BEng(Hons), Dip, BSc(Hons), EngD, MEng(Hons), MPhil, MSc, PhD

### School of Materials; www.materials.manchester.ac.uk

advanced/engineering materials/composites, biomaterials/science & tissue engineering, corrosion control engineering, design management for fashion retailing, fashion & textile retailing, international fashion retailing, materials & surface design, materials science & engineering, marketing & management of fashion textiles, polymer material science & engineering, textile design & design management/technology; BSc, MEng, MPhil, PhD

### School of Mathematics; www.maths.manchester.ac.uk

actuarial science, applied maths, computational science, mathematical finance, mathematics, statistics, pure mathematics & logic, mathematics jt degrees; BSc, MMath, MPhil, MSc, PhD

### School of Mechanical, Aerospace and Civil Engineering; www.mace.manchester.ac.uk

adv manufacturing technology & systems management, aerospace engineering/with management, civil engineering/enterprise, maintenance engineering & asset management, management of projects, mechanical engineering/design management, nuclear engineering, structural engineering, thermal power & fluid engineering, renewable energy & clean technology; BEng, EngD, MEng, MEnt, MPhil, MSc, PhD

### School of Physics & Astronomy; www.physics.manchester.ac.uk

physics, physics & astrophysics/mathematics/theoretical physics/philosophy, nuclear science & technology, radio imaging & sensing; BSc, EngD, MMath & Phys, MPhys, MSc, PhD

## *Faculty of Humanities; www.humanities.manchester.ac.uk*

### School of Arts, Languages and Cultures; www.arts.manchester.ac.uk

Archaeology; archaeology and anthropology, art history/and visual studies, history of art

Classics and Ancient History; ancient history, classical studies, classics, Latin and English literature/Italian/linguistics/Spanish/French

Art History & Visual Studies; art gallery & museum studies, art history, arts management policy & practice

Drama; Drama/& English literature/screen studies/music, applied theatre, arts management, policy & practice, screen studies, theatre & performance

East Asian Studies; combinations of Chinese, Japanese, linguistics, screen studies, Chinese studies, English language, French, German, Italian, Japanese studies, modern language and business & management (Chinese)/business & management (Japanese), Portuguese, Russian, Spanish, conference interpreting, intercultural communication, languages & cultures, translation & interpreting studies

English, American Studies and Creative Writing; American studies (history/literature & culture), English/literature & American studies, creative writing, history and American studies, arts management, policy & practice, contemporary literature & culture, gender, sexuality & culture, literature & culture (1200–1700), medieval studies, post 1900 literatures, theories & cultures, postcolonial literatures & cultures

French Studies; English language and French, English literature and French, European studies and French, French and Chinese/German/Italian/Japanese/linguistics/Portuguese/Russian/screen studies/Spanish, French Studies, History and French, history of art and French, modern language and business and management (French), conference interpreting, intercultural communication, languages & linguistics, languages & cultures, translation & interpreting

German Studies; English language and German, English literature and German, European studies and German, combinations of German with French, Chinese, Italian, Japanese, linguistics, Portuguese, Russian, screen studies, Spanish, German studies, history and German, history of art and German, business and management & German, conference interpreting, intercultural communication, languages & cultures, languages & linguistics, translation & interpreting

History and American Studies; sociology, modern history with economics/politics, history, history of science, technology & medicine, medieval studies

Humanitarian Conflict Response Institute; humanitarian & conflict response, international disaster management, peace building

Italian Studies; English literature/European studies/history of art and Italian, combinations with Italian or English literature/French/German/History/Chinese/linguistics/Portuguese/Russian/Spanish, Italian studies, business and management & Italian, intercultural communication, languages & cultures, languages & linguistics, translation & interpreting

Linguistics and English Language; linguistics in combination with one of Chinese/English literature/French/German/Italian, Linguistics, and a Middle Eastern language (Arabic, Hebrew, Persian or Turkish), Japanese/Portuguese/Russian/screen studies/social anthropology/sociology/ Spanish, English language, intercultural communication, languages & linguistics, linguistics

English Language; English language and a Middle Eastern language (Arabic, Hebrew, Persian or Turkish)/ Chinese/French/ German/Italian/Japanese/Portuguese/Russian/screen studies/Spanish

Middle Eastern Studies; Middle Eastern language and French, German, Italian, Spanish or Russian with Middle Eastern Languages: Arabic and Hebrew, Any two Middle Eastern languages from Arabic, Persian, Turkish and Hebrew, conference interpreting, languages & cultures, translation & interpreting

Arabic Studies; English language and (Arabic or Hebrew), Hebrew and Israel studies, linguistics and Arabic or Hebrew, Middle Eastern Studies and Arabic/Hebrew/Persian/Turkish/screen studies, modern Middle Eastern history and Arabic/Hebrew/Persian/Turkish, Business and Management & Arabic

Music; music, music and drama, arts management, policy & practice, composition, electroacoustic music composition, musicology

Religions and Theology; comparative religion and social anthropology, study of religion & theology, theological studies in philosophy and ethics, biblical studies, Jewish studies, medieval studies, religion & political life, south Asian studies

Russian and East European studies; English language and Russian, English literature/European studies and Russian, Russian in combination with French, German, history, history of art, Italian, or linguistics, Middle Eastern language and Russian, business and management & Russian, Russian & Chinese/Japanese/Portuguese/screen studies/Spanish, Russian

studies, intercultural communication, languages & cultures, languages & linguistics, translation & interpreting
Spanish, Portuguese and Latin American Studies; English language and Portuguese/Spanish, English literature & Portuguese/Spanish, European studies and Portuguese/Spanish, intercultural communication, languages & cultures, languages & linguistics, translation & interpreting, Latin American & Caribbean studies
Translation & Intercultural Studies: French, Portuguese, Spanish, German, History, history of art, Italian, Latin American studies and screen studies, linguistics, business and management, Chinese, Russian, conference interpreting, intercultural communication, translation & interpreting, history; BA(Hons), MA, MMus, PhD

## School of Education; www.education.manchester.ac.uk

counselling, digital technology, communication & education, education (international), educational leadership & school improvement, educational technology & TESOL, English language & education, language, critical learning, disability studies, profound & complex learning disabilities, management & leisure, PGCE primary/secondary (business education, design technology, English, mathematics, modern languages, science), psychology of education, intercultural communication, teaching & learning; BA(Hons), DCons, DEd, EdD, MA, MEd, MPhil, MSc, PGCE, PGCert/Dip, PhD, UGCert/Dip

## School of Environment and Development; www.sed.manchester.ac.uk

economics & management of rural environment, environmental impact assessment and management, environmental monitoring/management, modelling and reconstruction, international development: environment and development/economics and management of rural development, development economics and policy, development finance, environmental governance/impact assessment & management, geography with international studies geography/geology, geography with planning, globalisation and development, industry, trade and development, competition, modelling & reconstruction regulation and development, international development: public policy and management, poverty, politics and welfare in international development, development studies, international development: politics and governance/ poverty, conflict and reconstruction/social policy and social development, poverty and development, architecture and urbanism, global urban development and planning, planning, planning and environmental management, urban regeneration and development, management and human resources in international development, HRD/M(international development), HRM management and development, international development/development management, management and implementation of development projects, organisational change and development, information systems and information science, GIS, ICT for development, management and information systems: change and development/change and development, town & country studies; BSc, MA, MPlan, MSc, MTCP, PGDip, PhD, MGeog

## School of Law; www.law.manchester.ac.uk

law, criminology, law & politics, international business & commercial law/intellectual property law/ international financial law/ international trade transactions, law and development, corporate governance, public international & European law, health care ethics and law, intellectual property law, law and development, criminology, crime, law and society, criminology and socio-legal studies, health care ethics and law, health care ethics; BA, LlB, LlM, MA, MPhil, MRes, PGDip, PhD

## Manchester Business School; www.mbs.manchester.ac.uk

accounting, IT management for business, international business, finance and economics/management, international management with American business studies, management, management (accounting and finance/human resources/innovation, sustainability and entrepreneurship/international business economics/international studies/marketing, management with compliance/trusts and estate worldwide business and management education, accounting and finance, business analytics: operational research and risk analysis, Chinese business and management, corporate communications and reputation management, finance/and business economics, global business analysis, healthcare management, HRM and industrial relations/comparative industrial relations (international), information systems: business IT/e-business technology/organisations and management, innovation management and entrepreneurship, international business and management, management, managerial psychology, marketing, operations, project and supply chain management, organisational psychology, quantitative finance: financial engineering, quantitative finance: risk management, healthcare governance, international commercial and contract management, enterprise, business administration; BA, BSc, MBA, MBus, MDA, MEnt, MPA, MRes, MSc, PhD, DBA, PGCert

**School of Social Sciences; www.socialsciences.manchester.ac.uk**

Accounting and Finance; economics /and finance, Business and Management, business studies, business studies and economics/politics/sociology, economics and finance

Criminology; economics/philosophy/politics/social anthropology/sociology & criminology

Development Studies; development studies & economics/politics/sociology, business studies, economics & business studies, development studies/philosophy/criminology/finance/politics, sociology, politics, philosophy and economics

Government, Politics and International Relations; politics & development studies/economics/criminology/social anthropology/international relations/sociology

Philosophy; philosophy/ & criminology/politics/social anthropology/sociology, politics & business studies/development studies/economics/philosophy/criminology/social anthropology, international relations/sociology, health care, philosophy

Social Anthropology; social anthropology & politics/criminology/philosophy/sociology, economics/ & philosophy/criminology/finance /politics/sociology, politics, philosophy, economics, anthropological research, social anthropology (cities and migration/Latin American studies/visual anthropology

Economics; development economics and policy, econometrics, economics (economics of health/environmental economics, financial economics

Politics; business studies and politics, development studies and politics, economics and politics, philosophy and politics, politics & criminology/social anthropology/international relations, sociology, politics, philosophy and economics, human rights – law/political science

International Development; politics and governance, international politics, international political, political science – democracy and elections/ govern economy/international relations/theoretical political economy/finance/business & employment/political economy of dev/society, space & environment and public policy/political theory, politics

Social Statistics; social change, social research methods and statistics

Sociology; business studies/development studies/economics/politics/social anthropology/criminology/philosophy/social research methods & statistics, BAEcon, BSc, MA, MRes, MSc, PGDip, PhD

## *Faculty of Life Sciences: www.lf.manchester.ac.uk*

anatomical sciences, biochemistry, biology with science & society, bioinformatics & systems biology, biological sciences, biology, biomechanics, biomedical sciences, biotechnology/& enterprise, cell biology, cancer research & molecular biomedicine, cognitive neuroscience and psychology, developmental biology, genetics, history of science, technology and medicine, immunology and immunogenetics, integrative biology, life sciences, medical biochemistry, microbiology, molecular biology/parasitology & vector biology, neuroscience, optometry, pharmacology, physiology, plant sciences, zoology; BSc, MNeuroSci, MRes, MSc, PhD

## *Faculty of Medical & Human Sciences; www.mhs.manchester.ac.uk*

**School of Dentistry; www.dentistry.manchester.ac.uk**

dental implantology, dental public health, dentistry, endodontics, fixed & removable prosthodontics, oral & maxillofacial surgery, oral health sciences, orthodontics, periodontology, restorative & aesthetic dentistry; BDS, BSc, MDen, MDPH, MSc, MSc(Clin), PGDip/Cert, PhD

**School of Medicine; www.medicine.manchester.ac.uk**

medicine, surgery, pathology, audiology, clinical biochemistry, clinical and health psychology, clinical research, clinical rheumatology, cognitive brain imaging, community pharmacy public health services, deaf education, dementia care, advanced practice interventions for mental health, digital biology, forensic mental health, genetic counselling, health care ethics and law, health and social care, investigative ophthalmology and vision sciences. medical education, medical imaging/microbiology/mycology/virology, modelling and simulation in pharmacokinetics and pharmacodynamics, occupational hygiene, occupational medicine, oral and maxillofacial surgery, pharmaceutical industrial advanced training, primary mental health care, psychiatry, psychosocial interventions for psychosis, advanced practice interventions for mental health, public health, social work; ChB, MB, MD/ChM, MPH, MPhil, MRes, MSc, PGCert, PGDip, PhD, BSc(Hons), APIMH

### School of Nursing and Midwifery & Social Work; www.nursing.manchester.ac.uk

advanced nursing/midwifery studies, clinical research, health & social care, midwifery, adult/child/mental health nursing, psychosocial interventions for psychosis, dementia care, primary health care, social work; BMidwif, BNurs, MA, MClinRes, MPhil, MRes, MSc, PGCert, PGD, PGDip, PhD

### School of Pharmacy & Pharmaceutical Sciences; www.pharmacy.manchester.ac.uk

clinical & health services pharmacy, community pharmaceutical public health service, pharmaceutical industrial advanced training, pharmacy, modelling & simulation in pharmacokinetics/dynamics; MPharm, MPhil, MSc, PGCert/Dip, PhD

### School of Psychological Sciences; www.psych-ci.manchester.ac.uk

audiology, clinical & health psychology, cognitive brain imaging, cognitive neuroscience & psychology, deaf education, psychology, adv audiology studies; BSc, MPhil, MRes, MSc, PGDip, PhD, ClinPsyD

# MANCHESTER METROPOLITAN UNIVERSITY
## www.mmu.ac.uk

## *Manchester School of Art; www.artdes.mmu.ac.uk*

acting, architecture/& urbanism/digital fabrication/heritage, contemporary art history, film & video/curating, interactive art/design, creative practice/multimedia, design (animation/ceramics/furniture/glass/jewellery), embroidery, fashion (knitwear/menswear/womenswear), film & media studies, filmmaking, fine art, illustration, interior design, graphic art & design, interior/3D design, landscape architecture/design, media arts, photography, product design, textiles in practice; BA(Hons), BArch, BL and Arch, MA, MEnterprise, MPhil, PGDip/Cert, PhD

## *Faculty of Health, Psychology & Social Care; www.hpsc.mmu.ac.uk*

### Health Professions; Nursing; Social Work & Social Change

acupuncture, adult nursing, community health/psychology, contemporary health practice, counselling, CPD, criminology, critical psychology, disability studies, emergency medicine, forensic psychology, health & social care, psychoanalytical studies, practice development, psychology, physiotherapy, social work/adv practice/ leadership, social care, speech pathology, musculoskeletal/neurological physiotherapy, public health/school nursing, health visiting; BA(Hons), BSc(Hons), BA/BSc, MA, FdA, DipHE, PGCert/Dip, PhD, MPhil

## *Faculty of Humanities, Law & Social Science; www2.hlss.mmu.ac.uk*

applied criminology/& sociology, applied/linguistics, sociology, digital media, communications, contemporary European/film & culture/literature & history, culture, critical theory, film, the Gothic, multimedia journalism, English studies/contemporary literature & film/critical theory, English & American literature, creative writing, business/(French, German, Spanish, Italian), medieval/modern/political/social/local & American history, European urban culture/philosophy, library & information management, informatics, information management/& communications, linguistics, philosophy, politics, public services, global change, social history, sociology, web development, TESOL, TEFL; BA(Hons), BSc(Hons), PGDip/Cert, MA, MPhil, PhD, LlB, LlM, MSc

## *Faculty of Science & Engineering; www.sci-eng.ac.uk*

### School of Healthcare Science; www.shs.mmu.ac.uk

biomedical science, clinical physiology, dental technology, healthcare science, human biology, physical activity & health, physiology; BSc(Hons), MSc, PGCert/Dip

### School of Computing, Mathematics & Digital Technology; www.scmdt.mmu.ac.uk

adv/computing, computing forensics & security, computer games technology, computer science, games design & development, information systems, management production technology, media technology, multimedia & web computing, software engineering, mathematics, financial mathematics; FDSc, BSc(Hons), MSc PGDip/Cert, PhD

### School of Engineering; www.soe.mmu.ac.uk

automotive engineering, applied physics, automation & control, computer & network technology, electrical & electronic engineering, design engineering, engineering, engineering & technology/management, electronic systems design, computer & network technology, industrial communications & automation, mechanical engineering, product/design & technology, computer networks; BSc(Hons), BEng(Hons), MSc, PGDip/Cert, MPhil, PhD

### School of Science & the Environment; www.ssty.mmu.ac.uk

#### Biology & Conservation Ecology

animal behaviour, biology, biological recording, conservation biology, ecology & conservation, environmental management & business/sustainable development, forensic & analytical science, wildlife biology, ornithology, applied/GIS, GI technology, microbiology & molecular biology, countryside/ environmental management, sustainable aviation, zoo studies/conservation biology; BSc(Hons), MSc, PGDip/Cert, MPhil, PhD

#### Chemistry & Environmental Science

applied chemistry, chemistry, chemical & pharmaceutical science, environmental science, forensic/ medicinal & biochemical/pharmaceutical chemistry; MChem, BSc(Hons)

#### Geography & Environmental Management

geography, environmental management & sustainability, human/physical geography, GIS studies; BSc(Hons), PGCert/Dip, MSc, MPHil, PhD

## *Manchester Metropolitan University Business School; www.business.mmu.ac.uk*

accounting, advertising management & brand marketing, finance, creative management, financial planning & wealth management, PR, business/administration/management, business management/ enterprise, digital media/business management, business finance/HRM/economics/management, economics & financial management, financial planning & wealth management, IT, HRM, marketing, business economics, financial services, international business management/marketing/creative advertising/HRM, sports marketing/management, internet retailing, leadership/ in health & social care, logistics & supply chain management, marketing management/communications, PR /& digital communication studies, professional accounting, project management, retail marketing management, strategic financial management, sustainable performance management; BA(Hons), BSc(Hons), MA, MSc, MBA, DBA, PhD, FD

## *Institute of Education; www.ioe.mmu.ac.uk*

childhood studies, early childhood/years studies, education studies, art-maker teacher, initial teacher training (CPD: supporting teaching & learning; education), PGCE: primary education with QTS/ secondary education (numerous subjects), language education, leadership & management, primary early years education, (QTS), professional studies (early years education/careers education and guidance/ education/special educational needs), school administration/business management, specific learning difficulties, teaching, youth & community work; BA(Hons), BA/BSc, Certs, EdD, FD, MA, MPhil, MSc, PGDip/Cert, PhD

## *Hollings Faculty; www.hollings.mmu.ac.uk*

### Department of Clothing Design & Technology

fashion materials & technology, clothing product design, fashion buying & merchandising, fashion design/sportswear/technology (womenswear/sportswear), int fashion marketing/practice/promotion, fashion design & technology, strategic fashion buying; BA(Hons)

### Department of Food & Tourism Management

events/ tourism management, environmental health, food management/safety/innovation, hospitality & licensed retail management, international food management/events management/tourism management/ hospitality management, hospitality with culinary arts, hospitality events/business management/nutrition & health, hospitality/business management, nutrition science, occupational health, safety & environment; BA(Hons), BSc(Hons), FdA, FdSc, HND, MA, MPhil, PhD, BTech, HND

## *MMU Cheshire; www.cheshire.mmu.ac.uk*

### Dept of Business & Management Studies; www.cheshire.mmu.ac.uk/bms

business, business management (financial management/HRM/ legal studies/marketing), HRM, marketing/management, strategic leadership & change; BA/BSc, BA(Hons), FD, HNC, HND, MBA, MSc, MPhil, PhD

### Dept of Contemporary Arts; www.cheshire.mmu.ac.uk/dcu

contemporary arts, contemporary theatre & performance, creative music production, creative writing, dance, drama, music, popular music; BA(Hons), MA, MPhil, PhD

### Dept of Exercise & Sports Science; www.cheshire.mmu.ac.uk/exspsci

coaching and sport development, coaching studies, exercise & sport/biomechanics/coaching studies/physiology/psychology/sport development/sport injuries, PE & sports pedagogy, sport/development/science, sport & exercise science, psychology of sport and exercise; BA, BSc, FD, MA, MSc

# MIDDLESEX UNIVERSITY
# www.mdx.ac.uk

### School of Arts and Design; www.mdx.ac.uk/aboutus/Schools/art-and-design

**Visual Arts**

animation, 3D animation, illustration, photography, fine art, graphic design

**Fashion & Interiors**

fashion design, fashion communication & styling, fashion textiles, interior architecture, interior design, fashion; BA(Hons), MA, FdA, MSc

### Middlesex University Business School; www.mdx.ac.uk/aboutus/Schools/business-school

Economics and International Development; Accounting and Finance; International Management and Innovation; Leadership, Work and Organisation

banking & finance, business accounting/economics, financial services, business management/finance/marketing/human resources/innovation/project management/supply chain management, international business/business administration/business management/HRM, business & trade, investment & finance, financial management, Islamic finance, innovation management & enterprise, HR practice, marketing, e-marketing & social media, marketing communications/management; BA(Hons), BSc(Hons), MA, MSc

### School of Health and Education; www.mdx.ac.uk/aboutus/Schools/health-and-education

early teaching studies, education, inclusive education, PGCE (early years, primary education, secondary education – numerous subjects), midwifery, nursing (adult children, mental health), health care supervision, health promotion, leadership and management in care services, children & families mental health work, leading & developing public & community services, promoting mental health in young people; CertHE, DipHE, BSc, MSc, PGDip, PGCE

### School of Law; www.mdx.ac.uk/aboutus/Schools/law

criminology, criminology (social justice/youth justice/policing/psychology), sociology (criminology), law/general, employment law, human rights & business, international business, law, legal research; BA(Hons), Grad Dip, LlM, PGDip/Cert

### School of Media and Performing Arts; www.mdx.ac.uk/aboutus/Schools/performing-arts

media, performing arts, advertising and PR, creative writing/technology, dance, English literature and language, film/& TV technology, journalism/& media, music, media & cultural studies, performing arts, publishing, TV production, theatre arts (design & technology/performance/solo performance), theatre directing, education (dance), music and theatre arts, digital media, media arts, culture and communication; BA(Hons), MA, MSc

### School of Science and Technology; www.mdx.ac.uk/aboutus/Schools/science-and-technology

Computer & Communications Engineering; Computer Science, Design Engineering & Mathematics; Natural Sciences
biomedical science (haematology & transfusion science/medical microbiology), biological science, clinical biochemistry, cellular pathology, business information systems/technology, computer & network security, computer communications & networks, creative technology, computer systems engineering, electronic security & digital forensics, engineering & computing mobile systems & telecommunication, design engineering/& electronics, /embedded systems, mechatronics, environmental policy/culture, environmental health, sustainable environmental management/development, natural sciences, complementary health (herbal medicine, acupuncture, traditional Chinese medicine), applied public health, environmental health, occupational safety & health management, risk management, building information modelling management, design engineering manufacturing management, engineering management, mobile telecommunications, project management, telecommunications engineering; BSc(Hons), BEng, MEng, MA, MSc

## UNIVERSITY OF NEWCASTLE UPON TYNE
## www.ncl.ac.uk

### *Faculty of Humanities and Social Sciences; www.ncl.ac.uk/hass*

### School of Architectural Planning and Landscape; www.ncl.ac.uk/apl

architecture, architecture & practice/management/urban planning, architectural design research/theory & criticism, digital architecture, future landscape, geography & planning, architectural planning/landscape, planning & environmental research, planning in developing countries/studies/practice, planning for sustainable & climate change, spatial planning, sustainable building & environment, town planning, urban design; BA, BArch, Cert, Dip, MA, MPhil, MSc, PGCert, PhD, MPlan

### School of Arts and Cultures; www.ncl.ac.uk/sacs

**Music; www.ncl.ac.uk/sacs/music/**

folk & traditional music, music, music & education, popular & contemporary music, composition, performance, musicology, ethnomusicology; BA, BMus, Diploma, MA, MLitt, MMus, MPhil, PhD

**Fine Art; www.ncl.ac.uk/sacs/fineart/**

fine art, history of art; BA(Hons), MFA, MPhil, PhD

**Digital Media & Cultural Studies; www.ncl.ac.uk/sacs/digitalmedia/**

digital media/theoretical foundations/techniques, media, communication & culture, media journalism/PR, international media journalism, digital film production; Dip, BA(Hons), MA, MRes, PhD

**Museum, Gallery and Heritage Studies; www.ncl.ac.uk/sacs/icchs/**

art museum & gallery studies, art as enterprise, heritage studies, management, museum studies, practice; MA, MPhil, MPrac, PGCert, PGDip, PhD

### Business School; www.ncl.ac.uk/nubs

accounting, advanced business management, arts, business & creativity, banking, business accounting, business management, e-business (information systems/emarketing), economics/& business management, economics/accounting, business & marketing, economics & politics, finance, e-marketing, financial & business economics, financial regulation, international/finance & law with cross culture, communication & international management, HRM, innovation, creativity & entrepreneurship, international business management/economics & finance/financial analysis/HR/marketing, Islamic finance, law, management, marketing, operations management & logistics/supply chain management, strategic planning & investment, quantitative finance & management, transport & business management; BA, BSc, DBA, MA, MBA, MSc, PhD

### School of Education, Communication and Language Sciences; www.ncl.ac.uk/ecls

applied linguistics & TESOL, cross-cultural communication & applied linguistics/education/international management/marketing/international relations, coaching & mentoring, education, evidence-based practice, educational research, innovative pedagogy & curriculum, education & communication/applied linguistics, cross cultural communication & integration, international development & education, pedagogy & education, practitioner enquiry (leadership & management), evidence-based practice in common disorders, PGCE primary/secondary (numerous subjects), educational psychology, education, speech & language science, language pathology; BA(Hons), BSc(Hons), DedPsych, EdD, MA, MEd, MSc, PGCE, PhD, QTS

### School of English Literature, Language, Linguistics; www.ncl.ac.uk/elll

English language/literature, English lit: 1500–1900, linguistics, creative writing, film theory, language practice acquisition, modern & contemporary studies; BA(Hons), MA, MLitt, MPhil, PGCert, PhD

### Geography, Politics and Sociology; www.ncl.ac.uk/gps

applied policy research, geography (human, physical), geography & planning, local & regional development, European Union studies, international political economy, international politics (global justice & ethics/critical geopolitics/globalization, politics/& economics/sociology/history, poverty, development), sociology, social research, world politics & popular culture; BA(Hons), BSc(Hons), MA, MSc, PhD

### Global Urban Research Unit; www.ncl.ac.uk/guru

cities and international development, power, place & materiality, planning & environmental dynamics, cities, security & vulnerability; MPhil, PhD

### Institute of Health and Society; www.ncl.ac.uk/ihs/

public health & health services research, social sciences, social sciences & health research; MSc, PGDip/Cert

### School of History, Classics & Archaeology Studies; www.ncl.ac.uk/historical

ancient history, archaeology, British history, Byzantine & Roman archaeology, classical studies, classics, early medieval & Byzantine archaeology, east Asian history, ethnohistory, late/European pre history, Greek & Roman/Byzantine archaeology, history, politics/& history, history of medicine, history of the Americas, Latin American studies, Roman frontier studies; BA(Hons), MA, MLitt, MPhil, PhD

### Newcastle Law School; www.ncl.ac.uk/nuls

environmental regulation & sustainable development, criminology, European legal studies, international legal studies, international business law, law (complete range of legal areas taught at undergrad level); LlB, LlM, MPhil, PhD

### Centre for Learning and Teaching; www.ncl.ac.uk/cflat

PGCE primary & secondary education, educational leadership and management, education, education research, education & communication, graduate skills enhancement, information, communication and entertainment technology, inclusive education, international development & education, practitioner enquiry, pedagogy & learning, educational psychology; EdD, MA, MEd, PGCE

### Newcastle Centre for the Literary arts/ www.ncl.ac.uk/ncla

creative writing; MA, PhD, PGCert

### School of Modern Languages; www.ncl.ac.uk/sml

Chinese, French, German, Japanese, Spanish, Portuguese & Latin American studies, Catalan, Dutch, Quecha, cultural studies, linguistics, professional translation for European languages, Latin American interdisciplinary studies, linguistics & language acquisition, modern languages & business studies/ linguistics, film theory & practice, Spanish, translating and interpreting – Chinese strand; BA(Hons), MA, MLitt, PhD

#### Policy, Ethics and Life Sciences Research Centre; www.ncl.ac.uk/peals

reproduction & genetic medicine, families, kinship & childhood, embodiment & identity; PhD

### Centre for Research in Linguistics and Language Science; www.ncl.ac.uk/linguistics

applied lingustics & TESOL, clinical linguistics research, cross-cultural communication, education (TESOL), English language & literature, evidence-based practice with communication disorders, European or Asian linguistics, language acquisition/ pathology, linguistics, speech & language science; MA, MEd, MSc, PhD

### Centre for Urban and Regional Development Studies; www.ncl.ac.uk/curds

local/and regional development; MA, PhD

## Faculty of Medical Sciences: www.ncl.ac.uk/aboutpeoplestudies academic/biosciences

### School of Biomedical Science; www.ncl.ac.uk/biomedicine

biochemistry, biomedical genetics/science, medical microbiology, biotechnology, medical science, pharmacology, psychological science, clinical education/psychology, sociology; BSc, MB, MSci, BA, MD, PhD

### Biomedicine

medicine, surgery, infection prevention & control, public health & health services, medical & molecular bioscience, minimal access surgery, oncology & palliative care, therapeutics, social services & health, clinical research, clinical education, clinical psychology/transplantation, cognitive behavioural therapy, high/low intensity psychological therapies, medical sciences, clinical sciences (physiological sciences – cardiac, vascular, respiratory and sleep science, gastrointestinal physiology and urodynamic science), clinical sciences (medical physics with specialisms in: radiotherapy physics, radiation safety, imaging with ionising radiation, imaging with non-ionising radiation, oncology and palliative care, cancer studies, psychology (foundations in clinical and health psychology), public health and health services research, social science and health research, clinical/ & health psychology, neuroscience, ageing and health, animal behaviour, biosciences, biotechnology and business enterprise, cancer, cardiovascular science in health and disease, diabetes, epidemiology, evolution and human behaviour, immunobiology, medical molecular biosciences, medical genetics, medical sciences, mitochondrial biology and medicine, molecular microbiology, nanomedicine, neuromuscular diseases, neuroscience, stem cells and regenerative medicine, systems biology, toxicology, translational medicine and therapeutics, transplantation; BSc(Hons), DClinPsychol, MB, MClinEd, MClinRes, MD, MRes, MSc, MSci, PGCert/Dip, PhD, MClinRes, MBBS

### Dentistry; www.ncl.ac.uk/dental

clinical dental implants, conscious sedation in dentistry, dental surgery, endodontics, orthodontics, restorative dentistry, dental hygiene & therapy; BDS, DDS, MSc, PGDip, PhD

## Faculty of Science, Agriculture & Engineering: www.ncl.ac.uk/ aboutpeoplestudies/academic/sage

### School of Agriculture, Food and Rural Development; www.ncl.ac.uk/afrd

adv food marketing, agri-business management, agricultural & environmental science, agriculture (agronomy, animal production/science, behaviour & welfare, farm business management), biodiversity, conservation & ecosystems management, countryside management, organic farming & food production systems, environmental resource assessment/science, food & human nutrition, food & rural development, food marketing & nutrition, medicinal plants & functional foods, rural social science/studies; BSc(Hons), MPhil, MSc, PhD

### School of Biology; www.ncl.ac.uk/biology

biology, cellular & molecular biology, conservation & ecotourism, ecological & environmental biology, ecological consultancy, industrial & commercial biotechnology, biology & psychology, zoology; BSc(Hons), MSc, MRes, PhD

### School of Chemical Engineering and Advanced Materials; www.ncl.ac.uk/ceam

applied process control, bioprocessing engineering, identical product, chemical engineering, chemical & processing engineering, clean technology, industrial quality technology, materials and process engineering, materials, design & engineering, process automation/control, sustainable chemical engineering; BEng(Hons), MEng(Hons), MSc, PGDip

### School of Chemistry; www.ncl.ac.uk/ chemistry

chemistry, drug chemistry, medicinal & synthetic product, chemistry, chemical nanoscience, structural chemistry & spectroscopy; BSc(Hons), MChem, MPhil, MSc, PhD

### Civil Engineering and Geosciences; www.ncl.ac.uk/ceg

civil engineering, environmental engineering/consultancy, geochemistry, geotechnical engineering, GIS, petroleum geochemistry/geoscience, engineering geology, environmental & petroleum intelligent transport systems & intelligent mobility, transport engineering & operations, structural engineering, surveying & mapping science, physical geography, applied hydrology, flood risk management, transport planning, hydroinformatics & water management, hydrology & climate change, water environment; BEng, BSc(Hons), MEng, MPhil, MSc, PhD

**Computing Science; www.cs.ncl.ac.uk/**
computer game engineering, cloud computing, computer security and resilience, computer science – bioinformatics, computational systems biology, adv/ computing science, mobile & distributed systems, games engineering, biocomputing, security & resilience, human-computer interaction, software engineering, e-business & information systems, neuroinformatics, synthetic biology; BSc(Hons), MPhil, MSc, MComp, PhD

**Electrical, Electronic and Computer Engineering; www.ncl.ac.uk/eece**
adv sensor technology, automation and control, communications & signal processing, digital electronics, electrical & electronics engineering, electronics BEng, EngD, MEng, MPhil, PhD

*Newcastle Institute for Research on Sustainability; www.ncl.ac.uk/*
research projects; MPhil, MRes, PhD

*Digital Institute; www.ncl.ac.uk/iri*
research projects; PhD

*Newcastle Centre for Railway Research; www.ncl.ac.uk/newrail*
rail freight & logistics; MSc, PhD

**School of Marine Science and Technology; www.ncl.ac.uk/marine**
aquaculture enterprise & technology, engineering & science in marine environments, international marine environmental consultancy, marine & offshore power systems/technology, marine biology, marine engineering/structures & integrity/transport & management/technology/oceanography, marine zoology, marine electrical power technology, marine/naval architecture, oceanography, offshore & environmental technology, offshore engineering, pipeline engineering, transport & management, ring, renewable energy enterprise & management, small craft technology/design, tropical coastal management; BEng, BSc(Hons), MEng, MRes, MSc

**Mathematics and Statistics; www.ncl.ac.uk/maths**
applied/financial mathematics/with management/ biology, mathematics/with statistics, mathematical sciences, pure mathematics, statistics; BSc(Hons), MMath, MMathStat, MPhil, PhD

**School of Mechanical & Systems Engineering; www.ncl.ac.uk/mech**
bioengineering, biomedical engineering, manufacturing engineering, mechanical engineering/design, mechatronics, mechanical engineering/with microsystems, microsystems engineering, low carbon transport engineering, rail freight & logistics; BEng, MEng, MSc

**Centre for Rural Economy;**
www.ncl.ac.uk/cre
food & rural development; MPhil, MSc, PhD, MRes

**Sir Joseph Swan Institute for Energy Research; www.ncl.ac.uk/energy**
bioenergy, renewable energy, novel geoenergy, energy conversion, storage & distribution, social impact; MRes, MSc, PhD

## UNIVERSITY OF NORTHAMPTON
## www.northampton.ac.uk

*School of Science & Technology: www.northampton.ac.uk/science-technology*

**Division of Computing;**
www.northampton.ac.uk/about-us/academic-schools/school-of-science-and-technology/subject-areas/computing
computing, computing (computer networks engineering/computer systems engineering/graphics and visualisation/internet technology and security/mobile computing/software engineering, computing (internet technology and security/computer networks engineering/software engineering/immersive technologies/ environmental informatics; BA/BSc, BSc(Hons), HND, MSc, PhD

**Division of Engineering;**
www.northampton.ac.uk/about-us/academic-schools/school-of-science-and-technology/subject-areas/engineering

electrical and electronic engineering, lift/& escalator engineering/technology, mechanical/production engineering, non-destructive testing; BSc(Hons), BTEC, FdSc, HNC, HND, MSc, ProfCert

**Environmental & Geographical Sciences;**
www.northampton.ac.uk/about-us/academic-schools/school-of-science-and-technology/subject-areas/environmental-and-geographical-sciences
biology, biological conservation, wildlife conservation, environmental management/science, geography; BA/BSc, BSc(Hons), FdSc, HND, MBA, MSc, UnivCerts

**Leather Technologies;**
www.northampton.ac.uk/about-us/academic-schools/school-of-science-and-technology/subject-areas/leather-technology
leather technology (international environmental management/marketing), environment, leather technology (leather science/environment/marketing & business); BSc(Hons), BTEC NC, Cert/Dip, MSc, PhD/MPhil

**Wastes Management;**
www.northampton.ac.uk/about-us/academic-schools/school-of-science-and-technology/subject-areas/wastes-management
wastes management, environmental science, waste management pollution technology; BSc(Hons), MSc, FdSc

## *The School of The Arts:*
www.northampton.ac.uk/about-us/academic-schools/school-of-the-arts

**Division of Design; www2.northampton.ac.uk/arts/home/Design**
architectural technology, graphic communication, illustration, interactive digital media, interior design, product design, design (textiles/footwear/graphic communication/photographic communication/product & spatial innovation); BA(Hons), BSc(Hons), MA, HND

**Division of Fine Art; www2.northampton.ac.uk/arts/home/Fine Art**
drawing, fine art, painting, photographic practice; BA(Hons), FDA, MA

**Division of Media, English and Culture; www2.northampton.ac.uk/arts/home/Media-English-Culture**
creative writing, English, film & TV studies, journalism, media production, digital film making, screen studies, modern English studies; BA(Hons), MA

**Division of Performance Studies; www2.northampton.ac.uk/arts/home/performance**
acting, dance, drama, music production/practice, popular music, theatre practice, performing arts; BA(Hons), HND, MA, PhD

**Division of Fashion; www2.northampton.ac.uk/arts/home/Division-of-Fashion**
fashion, footware & accessories, printed textile fashion, surface design & printed textiles; BA(Hons), MA

## *School of Education:*
www.northampton.ac.uk/about-us/academic-schools/school-of-education
early years education, early childhood studies, education (primary), early years (primary/early years/secondary/PGCE), education studies, counselling children & young people, developmental & educational psychology, graduate teacher programme (GTP), initial teacher training, learning & teaching, special education needs & inclusion, post-compulsory education & training, primary mathematics; QTS, GTI, BA(Hons), GTP, PGCE, BSc(Hons), BA/BSc, FD, CertHE, FD, PhD

## *School of Health;*
www.northampton.ac.uk/about-us/academic-schools/school-of-health
dental nursing, health studies, applied cancer studies, children, young people, families & care, sociology & community development, health & social care, child & adolescent mental health, health studies, human bioscience, leadership in health & social care, mental health & learning disabilities, midwifery, non-medical prescribing, nursing (adult/children's/learning disabilities/mental health), occupational therapy, palliative & supportive care, paramedic science, podiatry, physical activity & health, sport studies/therapy, sport & recreational activity; BSc(Hons), MPhil, PGCert, PhD, FD

## *Northampton Business School;*

www.northampton.ac.uk/about-us/academic-schools/northampton-business-school
accounting, advertising, applied management, banking & financial planning, business/& management, business computing systems/entrepreneurship/studies, construction management, corporate governance tendering, international accounting/banking & finance/business/business communications/development/logistics & trade financing, IT service management, leadership & management, management (financial analysis/HR/international logistics/international/IT services/marketing/tourism), marketing management, sports marketing/enterprise, travel & tourism management, web design; BA(Hons), BA/BscHons, CMS, DBA, DMS, FdA, HND, MA, MBA, MSc, PGDip (marketing), MBL, ProfDip

## *School of Social Sciences:*

www.northampton.ac.uk/about-us/academic-schools/school-of-social-sciences

### History;

www.northampton.ac.uk/about-us/academic-schools/school-of-social-sciences/subject-areas/history
history, social & cultural history

### Law;

www.northampton.ac.uk/about-us/academic-schools/school-of-social-sciences/subject-areas/law
international business law/criminal law & security, law, appl criminal justice, offender management, police & criminal justice

### Psychology;

www.northampton.ac.uk/about-us/academic-schools/school-of-social-sciences/subject-areas/psychology
child & adolescent health, development & educational/sport & exercise psychology, counselling, psychology, transpersonal psychology & consciousness

### Sociology;

www.northampton.ac.uk/about-us/academic-schools/school-of-social-sciences/subject-areas/sociology
international relations, sociology, police & criminal justice service, probation & policing, urban affairs

### Politics;

www.northampton.ac.uk/about-us/academic-schools/school-of-social-sciences/subject-areas/politics
media studies, philosophy, politics, media, philosophy, politics, international relations, politics, international relations

### Criminology;

www.northampton.ac.uk/about-us/academic-schools/school-of-social-sciences/subject-areas/criminology
criminology

### Human Geography;

www.northampton.ac.uk/about-us/academic-schools/school-of-social-sciences/subject-areas/human-geography
geography (human/physical)

### Police and criminal justice;

www.northampton.ac.uk/about-us/academic-schools/school-of-social-sciences/subject-areas/police-and-criminal-justice
police & criminal justice studies, offender management

### Urban Affairs;

http:/ www.northampton.ac.uk/about-us/academic-schools/school-of-social-sciences/subject-areas/urban-affairs
sustainable communities
FdA, BA(Hons), BSc(Hons), BA/BSc, MA, LlB, LlM, PhD

### Youth and Community Work

youth and community work
MA

# UNIVERSITY OF NORTHUMBRIA AT NEWCASTLE
## www.northumbria.ac.uk

## *Faculty of Business & Law*

### Newcastle Business School: www.northumbria.ac.uk/sdacademic/bs

accounting, business administration/communication/development, business creation/management/studies, business leadership & corporate management, business with financial management/HRM/international management/logistics & supply chain management/materials management/tourism management, business with arts management/financial management/entrepreneurship/hospitality management/HRM/international management/legal management/logistics & supply chain management, music management/public administration, business & law (MBA), HRM & Dev, global financial management/banking, global/logistics & supply chain management, hospitality & tourism management, investment management, international business management with French/Spanish, international business administration/hospitality & tourism management/HRM/management/banking & finance/business, investment management, leadership & corporate management/performance coaching/development, marketing management/studies, public administration, tourism & hospitality management, strategic marketing, travel & tourism management; BA, DBA, MA, MBA, MSc, PhD

### Northumbria School of Law: northumbria.ac.uk/sd/academic/law

advanced legal practice, law (undergraduate, traditional/innovative/specialist/flexible), bar practice, business/commercial/employment law, business with legal management, employment law in practice, information rights law and practice, international commercial/trade law, law with business/international business/environment/property management, legal practice, medical law, mental health law, policy & practice, solicitors; GradCert, LlM, LlB, LPC, PGCert, MLaw, MSc, MBA

### School of Life Sciences: www.northumbria.ac.uk/sd/academic/lifesciences

#### Biology, Food & Nutrition Science

applied biology, applied sciences, biology with forensic biology, biotechnology, food science & nutrition, human nutrition, nutrition science, microbiology

#### Chemical & Forensic Science

applied sciences, biomedical sciences, human biosciences, forensic science, drug design with pharmacology, science (chemistry)

#### Biomedical Sciences; www.northumbria.ac.uk/sd/academic/lifesciences/ad/biomed/bmsug

applied science, biomedical science, chemistry, human biology, medical science

#### Psychology

psychology with criminology/sport science, psychology, health psychology, occupational psychology, organisational psychology, psychology of health & wellbeing, psychology of sport & exercise behaviour

#### Sport & Exercise Science

applied science with coaching/exercise science, psychology & sport science, sport exercise & nutrition, clinical exercise psychology, psychology of sport & exercise behaviour, strength & conditioning

#### Sport Development

sport, sport coaching, sport development/management, athlete lifestyle, international sport management; BA(Hons), BSc(Hons), MSc, ProfDoc

## *Faculty of Arts, Design & Social Sciences: www.northumbria.ac.uk/sd/academic/sass*

### Dept of Arts; www.northumbria.ac.uk/sd/academic/sass/about/arts

arts, arts & media management, art & design, music management & promotion, conservation of fine art, cultural/environment/heritage management, dance, drama & applied theatre/scriptwriting, performance, events & conference management, film & TV studies, fine art/& education, music management, museum & heritage management, contemporary photographic practice, preventive conservation; MA, MSc, MERes, BA(Hons), FD

### Dept of Humanities; www.northumbria.ac.uk/sd/academic/sass/about/humanities

American studies, applied linguistics, TESOL, creative writing, English literature/& place, gender studies, history/ & politics, journalism & English literature, history (America/British/European/early modern), linguistics, English language/literature; BA(Hons), MA, PGCert, MRes, PhD

### Dept of Media; www.northumbria.ac.uk/sd/academic/sass/about/media

advertising & marketing, mass communication/management/PR & business, media, media & journalism, media production, media, culture & society, journalism/& English literature, advertising; BA(Hons), MA

### Dept of Social Sciences; www.northumbria.ac.uk/sd/academic/sass/about/socscience

criminology & sociology/crime & criminal justice/psychology, history & English literature/politics, international development, public administration/services, social sciences, politics, sociology; BA(Hons), BSc, MSc, MPA, MRes, MA, PhD

### Northumbria Design;

3D design, design for industry, design/management, fashion management & entrepreneurship/communication/marketing/graphic design, interactive media design, interior design, motion graphics & animation, multidisciplinary design & innovation; BA(Hons), BSc(Hons), MA, MSc, MRes, MPA, PhD, PGCert/Dip

## *Faculty of Engineering & Environment: www.northumbria.ac.uk/sd/academic/ee*

Built & Natural Environment; Business Information Systems; Computing; Engineering; Mathematics & Statistics; Physics

### Built & Natural Environment

architectural technology/engineering/studies, architecture, building design management/project management/services engineering, building surveying, built environment, quantity surveying, construction management, civil engineering, project management/for construction, environmental management/health, geography/& environment, disaster management & development, housing policy/with professional practice, interior architecture, housing policy & management, international/real estate management, occupational safety & health, planning & real estate/development/quantity surveying, project management, surveying (minerals), sustainable development in the built environment; BA(Hons)

### Business Information Systems

business information management/systems; BSc

### Computing

computer animation & VFX, computer games programming, computer & network technology/IT, ethical hacking for computer security, IT management, web design & development/computing, digital & computer forensics; BSc, BEng, MEng

### Engineering

electrical & electronic engineering, electronic design engineering, mobile communication engineering, mechanical design/engineering, microelectronic & communications engineering, pipeline integrity management, product design technology, professional engineering, renewable sustainable energy technologies; BSc, BEng, MEng

### Mathematics & Statistics

mathematics/with business management; BSc(Hons)

### Physics

physics, astrophysics; BSc(Hons), BA(Hons), FdSc, MA, MSc, PGDip/Cert, PhD, ProfDip

## *Faculty of Health & Life Sciences*

### School of Health, Community & Education Studies: www.northumbria.ac.uk/sd/academic/shes

Health: emergency care practice, midwifery studies, nursing studies/registered nurse/child/mental health/adult/learning disabilities, leadership & management in integrated children/services, occupational therapy, operating dept practice, physiotherapy; AdvDipHE, BSc, MSc, PGDip

Education: academic practice, autism, early primary education, early years education, PGCE early years & primary/secondary, education studies/leadership, professional practice, graduate teacher training, post-compulsory education & training, literacy/HE/curriculum development/teaching & learning, adult learners with learning difficulties/disablement, teaching assistants, lifelong learning/English literacy/(CPD)/mathematics/numeracy/maths; BA(Hons), MSc, MA, MTL, Cert/DipHE, PGDipCert

Social Work: social work/with children, young people & their families/in mental health services; BSc(Hons), PGDip/Cert, ProfDoc

### School of Life Sciences: www.northumbria.ac.uk/sd/academic/lifesciences

#### Biology, Food & Nutrition Science

applied biology, applied sciences, biology with forensic biology, biotechnology, food science &

nutrition, human nutrition, nutrition science, microbiology; BSc(Hons), MSc

**Chemical & Forensic Science**

applied sciences, biomedical sciences, human biosciences, forensic science, drug design with pharmacology, science (chemistry); BSc(Hons), MC

**Biomedical Sciences; www.northumbria.ac.uk/sd/academic/lifesciences/ad/biomed/bmsug**

applied science, biomedical science, chemistry, human biology, medical science; BSc(Hons)

**Psychology**

psychology with criminology/sport science, psychology, health psychology, occupational psychology, organisational psychology, psychology of health & wellbeing, psychology of sport & exercise behaviour; BSc(Hons), MSc, MRes

**Sport & Exercise Science**

applied science with coaching/exercise science, psychology & sport science, sport exercise & nutrition, clinical exercise psychology, psychology of sport & exercise behaviour, strength & conditioning; BSc(Hons), MSc, MRes

**Sport Development**

sport, sport coaching, sport development/management, athlete lifestyle, international sport; BA(Hons), BSc(Hons), MSc

## UNIVERSITY OF NOTTINGHAM
## www.nottingham.ac.uk

### *Faculty of Arts; www.nottingham.ac.uk/arts*

#### School of American and Canadian Studies; www.nottingham.ac.uk/american

American & Canadian literature/history & culture, American studies & European studies, American studies with English/history/Latin American studies, American studies with visual culture; BA(Hons), MA, MRes, PhD

#### Dept of Archaeology; www.nottingham.ac.uk/archaeology/index.aspx

archaeological science, archaeology/& ancient history/classical civilisation, history, Viking studies, natural science; BA(Hons), BSc(Hons), MA, MPhil

#### Art History; www.nottingham.ac.uk/art-history

art history & classical civilisation/English studies/archaeology/history, visual culture; BA(Hons), MA

#### Dept of Classics; www.nottingham.ac.uk/classics

classical civilisation, ancient history/archaeology, classical literature, classics, Greek (ancient), Latin, ancient drama & its reception, visual culture of classical antiquity, history; BA(Hons), MPhil/PhD

#### Dept of Culture, Film & Media; www.nottingham.ac.uk/cfm

cultural studies, cultural industries & entrepreneurship, international media & communications studies, critical theory & politics/cultural studies, contemporary Middle East studies & critical theory, modern languages, film & TV studies, numerous jt degrees; BA(Hons), MA, MPhil

#### School of English Studies; www.nottingham.ac.uk/english

English, English language & literature, applied linguistics, communication & entrepreneurship, creative & professional practice in arts & education, English studies/language teaching, creative writing, literary linguistics, the 20th century & contemporary literature, Viking & Anglo Saxon studies, English literature, the long 19th century; BA(Hons), MA, MPhil, MSc, PGDip, PhD

#### Dept of French & Francophone Studies; www.nottingham.ac.uk/french

French studies, French & Canadian studies, classical civilization, critical theory & cultural studies, modern European studies, modern language & critical theory, medieval studies, francophone & post-colonial studies, French culture & society, early modern French studies, 20th/21st-century French thought, numerous jt degrees; BA(Hons), MA, MPhil, PhD

#### Dept of German Studies; www.nottingham.ac.uk/german

German, classical civilization, German cultural studies, beginner's German, E European civilization, modern & contemporary German studies, law & German law, modern language studies, modern languages & critical theory, numerous jt degrees; BA(Hons), MA, MPhil, PhD

### School of History; www.nottingham.ac.uk/history

history, ancient history, archaeology, British history, church history, gender history, women's studies & global gender history, environmental/international history, contemporary Chinese studies, art history, politics, local & regional history, medieval studies, modern history, Viking studies, warrior societies; BA(Hons), MA, MPhil, PhD

### School of Humanities; www.nottingham.ac.uk/humanities

archaeology, art history, classics, music, culture, languages & area studies, philosophy/& theology, theology & religious studies, systemic & philosophical theology, church history; BA(Hons), BSc(Hons), MA, MSci, MSc, MPhil, PhD

### School of Culture, Languages & Area Studies; www.nottingham.ac.uk/clas

American & Canadian studies, culture, film & media, comparative literature, combined studies with languages, Chinese (English) translation & interpreting, French & Francophone studies, German studies, Russian & Slavonic studies, Spanish Portuguese & Latin American & Canadian studies, translation studies & interpreting; BA(Hons), MA, MPhil, PhD

### Music; www.nottingham.ac.uk/music

music, early music, music on stage & screen, music theory & analysis, musicology, history & culture; BA(Hons), MPhil, PhD

### Dept of Philosophy; www.nottingham.ac.uk/philosophy

philosophy, theology, philosophy & literature, systematic & philosophical theology, metaphysics, mind & knowledge, ethics, philosophy of language, aesthetics, numerous jt degrees; BA(Hons), MA, MPhil, PhD

### Russian & Slavonic Studies; www.nottingham.ac.uk/slavonic

Russian studies, international media communications, Serbian & Croatian studies, Russian and East European civilisations, Serbo-Croatian, Slovene; BA(Hons), MA, MPhil

### Spanish, Portuguese and Latin American Studies; www.nottingham.ac.uk/splas

Hispanic studies, Portuguese/Spanish (beginners), American/Hispanic & Latin American studies, Portuguese & Lusophone studies, modern language studies/& critical theory; international media & communication studies; BA(Hons), MA, MPhil, PhD

## *Faculty of Science; www.nottingham.ac.uk/science*

### School of Biology; www.nottingham.ac.uk/biology

biology, biochemistry & genetics, zoology, human/genetics, numerous MRes subjects; BSc(Hons), MSc, MRes, MSci, Phd

### School of Biosciences; www.nottingham.ac.uk/biosciences

#### Plant and Crop Sciences; www.nottingham.ac.uk/biosciences/divisions/plantcrop/index.aspx

agriculture & biotechnology, applied biology, crop improvement/science, technology & entrepreneurship, environmental biology & genetics, genomic & proteomic science, integrative systems biology, plant genetic manipulation, plant science

#### Animal Sciences; www.nottingham.ac.uk/biosciences/divisions/animal/index.aspx

animal science, preveterinary science, numerous MRes subjects

#### Food Sciences; www.nottingham.ac.uk/biosciences/divisions/food/index.aspx

applied biomolecular technology, biopharmacological, food & biotechnical industries, brewing science, food production management, food microbiology, food science, industrial biochemistry, microbiology, nutrition & food science, sustainable energy/bioenergy

#### Nutritional Sciences; www.nottingham.ac.uk/biosciences/divisions/nutritional/index.aspx

advanced dietetic practice, dietetics, food science, nutrition, nutritional biochemistry; BSc(Hons), Cert, Grad Dip, MRes, MSc, MNutrition, MPhil, PhD

### School of Chemistry; www.nottingham.ac.uk/chemistry

biochemistry, medical/ & biological chemistry, chemistry, nanoscience, chemistry/& entrepreneurship, molecular physics, medicinal chemistry; BSc(Hons), MChem, MPhil, MSc, MSci, PhD

### School of Computer Science; www.nottingham.ac.uk/computerscience

artificial intelligence, adv/computer science, computer science & entrepreneurship/IT/mathematics/economics/management/artificial intelligence, human-computer interaction, management/of information technology, scientific computation, software engineering; BSc(Hons), MPhil, MSc

### School of Mathematical Sciences; www.maths.nottingham.ac.uk/

financial mathematics, gravity, particles & fields, mathematics, mathematical physics, numerical techniques for finance, pure mathematics, statistics, scientific computation/with industrial mathematics/ mathematical medicine & biology, statistics with applied probability, natural sciences; BSc(Hons), MSc, PhD

### School of Pharmacy; www.nottingham.ac.uk/pharmacy

medicinal & biological chemistry, pharmacy, drug discovery & pharmacological science; MPharm, MRes, MSc, MSci, PhD

### School of Physics & Astronomy; www.nottingham.ac.uk/physics

astronomy, mathematical physics, medical physics, nanoscience, physics, physics & philosophy, theoretical astrophysics/physics, chemistry & molecular physics, condensed matter theory, particle theory; BSc(Hons), MSc, MSci, PhD, MRes, MPhil

### School of Psychology; www.nottingham.ac.uk/psychology

cognitive neuroscience, brain imaging, neuroimaging, psychology/& philosophy; BSc(Hons), MSc, PhD, DAppPsych, DEdPsych

## *Faculty of Engineering; www.nottingham.ac.uk/engineering*

### Dept of Architecture & Built Environment; www.nottingham.ac.uk/abe

architectural environment engineering, architecture, architecture & environmental design, design, energy conversion & management, environmental design, renewable energy & architecture, sustainable built environment/energy & entrepreneurship, sustainable tall buildings/building technology, technology, theory & design, urban design; BA(Hons), BArch (Hons), BEng (Hons), Dip Arch, MEng, MPhil, PhD

### Dept of Chemical and Environmental Engineering; www.nottingham.ac.uk/scheme

chemical engineering/with environmental engineering, environmental & resource engineering; BEng (Hons), MEng(Hons), MPhil, MRes, MSc, PhD

### Dept of Electrical & Electronic Engineering; www.nottingham.ac.uk/eee

biophotonics, bioengineering, imaging & sensing, computational engineering: electromagnetics electrical/& electronic engineering, electrical technology for sustainable & renewable energy systems, electrical engineering & renewable energy systems, electronic & communications engineering, computer engineering, electrical technology for sustainable & renewable energy systems, sustainable & renewable energy systems, sustainable transportation & electrical power systems, electromagnetics design, electronic communications & computer engineering, photonic & optical engineering, power electronics & drive, machines & drives, sustainable energy engineering; BEng, MEng, MPhil, MRes, MSc, PGDip, PhD

### Dept of Civil Engineering; www.nottingham.ac.uk/civil

civil engineering, civil engineering: engineering surveying/environmental fluid mechanics/management/& environmental engineering, engineering surveying & GIS/geodesy, environmental management & earth observation, GNNS technology, pavement engineering, infrastructure, structural engineering, transportation, positioning & navigation technology, risk & reliability methods; BEng(Hons), MEng(Hons), MPhil, MSc, PhD

### Dept of Mechanical, Materials and Manufacturing Engineering; www.nottingham.ac.uk/schoolm3

advanced materials/manufacture, aerospace technology, applied ergonomics, biomedical materials science, bioengineering; biomaterials & biomechanics/imaging & sensing, computational fluid dynamics, computational engineering: finite element analysis, design engineering, materials failure and analysis, human factors, manufacturing engineering & management, mechanical engineering, product design & manufacture; BEng, MEng, MSc, PGCert, PhD

## *Faculty of Medicine & Health Science; www.nottingham.ac.uk/mhs/index.aspx*

### School of Biology; www.nottingham.ac.uk/biology

biochemical genetics, biology, human genetics, zoology, numerous MRes topics; BSc, MSc, MSci, PhD, MRes

### School of Biomedical Sciences; www.nottingham.ac.uk/biomedsci

biochemistry, biological chemistry, genetics, pharmacy, pharmacology, physiology, medicine, molecular medicine, neuroscience, integrated physiology in health & disease, sport & exercise science; BSc(Hons), MPhil, MRes, MSc, PhD, BMBS, BMedSci

### School for Clinical Sciences; www.nottingham.ac.uk/scs

assisted reproduction/stem cell technology, sports & exercise medicine, translational neuroimaging; DM, MSc, PhD

### School of Community Health Sciences; www.nottingham.ac.uk/chs

applied epidemiology, applied psychology, applied/work & organization/rehabilitation/work & occupational/management/occupational health/criminological/health psychology, medicine, mental health studies, occupational health & safety leadership, primary care, psychiatry, rehabilitation & ageing, workplace health & wellbeing, public health, psychological research methods; MBBS, BMedSci, MMedSci, MPH, MSc, PGDip/Cert, PhD

### School of Graduate Entry Medicine & Health; www.nottingham.ac.uk/gem

health care science, medical physiology & therapeutics; BSc, MRes, MPhil, PHD, DM

### School of Molecular Medical Sciences; www.nottingham.ac.uk/mol

clinical microbiology, molecular medicine, microbiology/& immunology, immunology & allergy, cancer immunology & biotechnology, micro biology & immunology, molecular genetics & diagnostics, oncology; MSc, PhD

### School of Nursing, Midwifery & Physiotherapy; www.nottingham.ac.uk/nursing

nursing science, healthcare studies/practice, adult/critical care, advanced clinical practice/skills, advanced nursing, clinical leadership for innovative practice, cognitive behaviour therapy, nursing (adult/child/mental health), health and social care/practice teacher, health communication, health care sciences, midwifery, physiotherapy/manual therapy/neurohabilitation, practice teacher in health BMid(Hons), BSc(Hons), DHSci, MA, MNursSci, MPhil, MSc, PGDip/Cert, PhD

### School of Veterinary Medicine & Science; www.nottingham.ac.uk/vet

veterinary medicine & surgery/science, veterinary, biomedical, statistical science, veterinary science/business & management/education; BVMBVS, BVMedSci, MPhil, MRes, PhD, DVM, DVS

### Institute of Work, Health & Organisations; www.nottingham.ac.uk/who

applied psychology, management studies, clinical psychology, work & organisational psychology, occupational health & safety leadership, clinical psychology, psychology & health, forensic/criminological/rehabilitation psychology, workplace health & wellbeing; MSc, MPhil, PhD, DocClinPsych, DocForPsych

## *Faculty of Social Sciences, Law & Education; www.nottingham.ac.uk/social-sciences/index.aspx*

### School of Contemporary Chinese Studies; www.nottingham.ac.uk/chinese

Chinese/English translation & interpreting, accounting & finance for contemporary Chinese, business & economy of contemporary China, corporate finance/banking & financial markets/management in contemporary China, international relations & contemporary Chinese studies; BA, MSc, MSci, PhD

### Economics; www.nottingham.ac.uk/economics

applied economics, behavioural economics, economic development & policy analysis, economics, economics with modern languages/philosophy/mathematics/politics, economics & international economics/Chinese studies, international/development/financial economics, econometrics; BA(Hons), BSc(Hons), MPhil, PGDip, PhD

### School of Education; www.nottingham.ac.uk/education

counselling/children & young people, creative professional practice in arts & education, education, initial teacher training, school direct/school central ITT, (PGCE) – secondary (English, geography, history, humanistic counselling, mathematics, modern languages, science), PGCE (primary), mentoring & coaching, educational leadership & management, special needs, international HE, trauma studies, TESOL, learning technology & education, special needs, TESOL, creative & professional writing, fine art, humanities, teaching Chinese; BA(Hons), MA, MPhil, MRes, PGCE, PGCert/Dip, PhD, SCITT, EdD

### School of Geography; www.nottingham.ac.uk/geography

geography, environmental management/history, GIS, human geography/with Chinese, physical geography, landscape & culture, contaminated land management, economy, space, society; BA(Hons), PhD

**School of Law; www.nottingham.ac.uk/law**
law, French/German/Spanish/Euro/Chinese/Canadian/New Zealand/South East Asian/Australian/American law, environmental law, human rights law, international law/commercial law/criminal justice and armed conflict, criminal law, European law, international law, international law/and development, law & environmental science, maritime law, public international law, public procurement law, security & terrorism, senior status, sociolegal & criminal research; BA(Hons), LlB, LlM, MA, MSc, PhD

**Nottingham University Business School; www.nottingham.ac.uk/business**
banking & finance, corporate social responsibility/strategy and governance, entrepreneurship & communication/computer science/cultural studies/sustainable energy, finance, accounting & management, finance & investment, industrial economics/engineering & operations management, international business/management, global supply chain management, logistics & supply chain management, management studies, management studies with Chinese studies/French/German/Spanish, manufacturing systems, marketing, operations management & manufacturing systems, risk management, supply chain & operations management, sustainable environment/communications/entrepreneurship; BA(Hons), ExecMBA, MA, MBA, MSc

**Politics & International Relations; www.nottingham.ac.uk/politics**
diplomacy, international relations & global issues, international security & terrorism, politics/& economics/contemporary history/American studies/German/French, social and global justice, war & contemporary conflict, European politics; BA(Hons), MA, MPhil, MRes, PhD

**School of Sociology and Social Policy; www.nottingham.ac.uk/sociology**
global citizenship, identities & human rights, science & technology public administration/policy, social & cultural studies, international/social policy, social work, sociology, trauma studies; BA(Hons), MA, MPA, MPhil, MSWS, PhD, PGCert

## NOTTINGHAM TRENT UNIVERSITY
## www.ntu.ac.uk

**School of Animal, Rural and Environmental Sciences; www.ntu.ac.uk/ares**
animal biology/studies, biodiversity conservation, environmental design & management/conservation science, equestrian practice & sports science, equine health & welfare/sports science, geography, endangered species recovery & conservation, wildlife conservation, zoo biology; BSc(Hons), MSc/MRes/PGCert/PGDip, FdSc

**School of Architecture, Design and Built Environment; www.ntu.ac.uk/adbe**
adv property design engineering, architecture, architectural technology & design, built environment studies, commercial management, construction, interior architecture & design, international real estate investment & finance, civil engineering, furniture & product design, building/quantity surveying, planning & development, real estate, construction management, planning, urban design & sustainable development, product design, innovation management, project management, property finance & investment, innovation & management, structural engineering/with management/materials, smart design; BSc(Hons), MA, MSc, MArch, PGDip/Cert, PhD

**School of Art & Design: www.ntu.ac.uk/art**
branding & identity design, costume design & making, curation by registered provision, contemporary craft practice, creative pattern design, decorative arts, design for film & TV/events/publication, fashion accessory design/knitwear design and knitted textiles/management/design/communication & promotion/marketing and branding/marketing communications/textile design/business, film practice, fine art, furniture, graphic design, international fashion business, multimedia, photography, puppetry and digital animation, textile design and innovation, theatre design; BA(Hons), GradDip, MA, MPhil, PhD

**School of Arts & Humanities: www.ntu.ac.uk/hum**
English, broadcasting/magazine/newspaper/media journalism, broadcasting, creative writing, global studies, European studies, history, games & play, Holocaust & genocide studies, museum & heritage

management, environmental change, English language/literature research, international development, linguistics, media, philosophy, French, Spanish, Latin American studies, TESOL; BA(Hons), MA, PGDip/Cert, MPhil, PhD

### Nottingham Business School: www.ntu.ac.uk/nbs

business management, management and leadership, business, management, business management and accounting and finance/economics/entrepreneurship/business management and human resources/marketing, economics/finance and banking, business economics, business finance/accounting and finance, marketing/management, international business/with French/Spanish, international business administration, management and entrepreneurial ebusiness, management and human resource/entrepreneurship/marketing, international business investment strategy, marketing, marketing/advertising and communications/management, economics and finance, international finance, strategic accounting and finance, international business, HRM, global management and leadership; BA(Hons), DBA, MBA, MSc

### School of Education; www.ntu.ac.uk/edu

business & educational development, education, education studies, early years & educational development/& psychology & education, special & inclusive education & educational development, educational support, HE, ICT & education, physical science education, primary education, psychology & education/educational development, sport & leisure, teaching adult literacy, numerous PGCE secondary courses, TESOL, teacher training; BA(Hons), MA, PGCE, PGCert, ProfCert, ProfDoc

### Nottingham Law School:

www.ntu.ac.uk/nls

law, corporate/commercial law, European law, international criminal justice, employment law, health law, human rights, insolvency law, international intellectual property law, competition law, corporate law, international/trade law, law & criminality/psychology, sports law, public international law, legal practice; GDL, GradDip, LlB, LlM, LPC, PhD

### School of Science & Technology; www.ntu.ac.uk/sat

biological sciences, biomedical science, biochemistry, microbiology, pharmacology, chemistry/pharmaceutical and medicinal chemistry, computer science, computer science/games technology, software engineering, computer systems engineering/networks/forensic and security, computing, digital media technology, information systems; information and communications technology

mathematics, financial mathematics, computer science/sport science and mathematics

physics/ with nuclear technology, forensic applications, astrophysics

chemistry, advanced materials engineering, analytical chemistry, pharmaceutical analysis, pharmaceutical and medicinal science

applied biosciences, bioinformatics, biotechnology, environmental management, molecular cell biology, pharmacology, neuroscience, biomedical science

sport science & management/coaching, sport & exercise science, exercise, health & nutrition, computer science, computing systems, computer games systems, internet and security, internet and enterprise computing, multimedia engineering, multimedia games engineering, engineering, cybernetics and communications), engineering (electronics), engineering management, computer science, electronic systems, games and play

forensics, forensic science/technology

sport science, sport and leisure management, international performance analysis of sport, campaigning, performance nutrition/analysis, biomechanics and kinesiology, sport and exercise

physics, medical and materials imaging

FdSc, MChem, MRes, MSc, MSci, PhD

### School of Social Sciences;

www.ntu.ac.uk/soc

applied child psychology, adv professional practice, careers/guidance, child care practice, counselling/psychotherapy, criminology, children's services, counselling & psychotherapy, forensic mental health/health & wellbeing psychology, health & social care, health & safety risk management, international relations, psychology with criminology/sociology, psychological research methods, politics, public health, safety & environment, social work, sociology, youth justice/work; BA(Hons), MA, MRes, MSc, PGDip/Cert, PhD, ProfDoc

# *Degrees validated by Nottingham Trent University offered at:*

## SOUTHAMPTON SOLENT UNIVERSITY
www.solent.ac.uk

**Art & Design; www.solent.ac.uk/courses/course-areas/art-design.aspx**

Advertising Communications; creative advertising
Animation; animation, computer-generated imagery, special effects
Fashion; fashion, fashion buying and merchandising/graphics/management with marketing/photography/promotion and communication/with PR, make-up and hair design, fashion merchandise management/fashion styling
Graphic Design; graphic design
Interactive Design; computer & video games
Interior Design; interior design/decoration
Media & Fashion Styling; fashion styling/make-up for media, make-up & hair design
Media Production, Media Technology, Media Writing, Media Studies; media production, special effects, media, communication & culture, pop music performance, live & studio sound, music studio technology, song writing, English & advertising/film/magazine, film & TV studies (film, sports broadcasting), multimedia journalism, journalism/media/PR, media writing, music festival industries, song writing, screenwriting, creative writing, industry & practice, writing fashion & culture, media
Photography; photography
Visual Arts; fine art, illustration, visual arts
BA(Hons), BSc(Hons), HNC, FdA, LLB(Hons), BEng

**Business & Law; www.solent.ac.uk/courses/course-areas/business-law.aspx**

Accountancy; accountancy and finance
Business; business (professional development), business and finance/management/marketing, business management/studies, international business management, business economics, business (customer service/management/organisational improvement), mentoring skills, social enterprise governance and leadership
Education; blended learning
Events Management; events management
Human Resources/Personnel; HRM, personnel and development
Law; Legal Practical Course, law (LPC)
Management; leadership and management development, management/and finance/international business
Marketing; marketing/with advertising management, marketing management, marketing fundamentals
Sport; monitoring and evaluation for sport and development; BA(Hons), MA, PgDip/Cert, LPC, LlB

**Computing; www.solent.ac.uk/courses/course-areas/computing.aspx**

Business IT; business information technology/for business/management
Computer Networking; computer networks and web design, computer systems and networks, network security management
Computing (including internet); computer games development, computing, software engineering, software engineering management
Web Design; web design and development; BSc(Hons), MSc

**Engineering & Construction; www.solent.ac.uk/courses/course-areas/engineering-construction.aspx**

Architecture; architectural technology
Civil Engineering; civil engineering
Construction; construction management
Electrical/Electronic Engineering; electronic engineering
Mechanical Engineering; mechanical design, mechanical engineering
Surveying; quantity surveying
BA(Hons), BSc(Hons), HNC, BEng,

**Entertainment Technology; www.solent.ac.uk/courses/course-areas/entertainment-technology.aspx**

Acoustics; competence in building acoustics measurement, competence in environmental noise measurement, acoustics and noise control
Film & TV Studies; film & sport broadcasting
Media Technology; audio technology, live & studio sound, media technology, music studio/technology
Music & Music Technology; sound technology, sound for film, TV & games
Outside Broadcasting; outside broadcasting (production/operations), music festivals, pop music performance, song writing; BA(Hons), MA

### Maritime; www.solent.ac.uk/courses/course-areas/maritime.aspx

Geography; geography with environmental studies/marine studies
Maritime Industry; marine engineering & management, marine operations management/engineering/operations, maritime business, ship and port management, international maritime studies – ship & shipping management/shipping and logistics, shipping operations/engineering
Yacht and Boat Design; yacht and powercraft design, yacht production and surveying, watersports technology; BEng, BSc(Hons), HNC

### Media; www.solent.ac.uk/courses/course-areas/media.aspx]Advertising/Communications;

Advertising/& PR, promotional media, PR/ & communication
Fashion; fashion writing
Film and TV Studies; film/& TV/studies, film, sports broadcasting
Graphic Design; graphic design
Journalism; journalism, magazine journalism & feature writing, multimedia/photo/sport journalism, writing fashion & culture, PR & sports journalism
Journalism and Media Writing; publishing, multimedia journalism
English & Writing; English, English & development/film/magazine journalism/media/PR
Media Production; media culture/& production media, communication and culture, popular media production, special effects
Media Studies; media, popular music
Media Writing; English, English & advertising film, magazine journalism, English & media/PR/screenwriting, media writing, creative writing, writing fashion and culture, multimedia communications
Music and Music Technology; digital music, music promotion, popular music journalism/performance, music festival industries, song writing, sound engineering, sound for film & TV
Performing Arts; comedy – writing and performance, performance
Public Relations; PR, advertising, communications
Television Production; TV & video production/post-production/studio production television
Visual Arts; illustration, fine art, visual art; BA(Hons), MA

### Social Sciences; www.solent.ac.uk/courses/course-areas/social-sciences.aspx

Business; communications in crisis management
Criminology; criminal investigation with psychology, criminology/& psychology/criminal justice, politics, applied social science
Housing; managing change in the workplace
Psychology; psychology (counselling/criminal behaviour/education/health psychology)
Social Work; adult social care, social work/with adults; BA(Hons), BSc(Hons), MA

### Sport and Tourism; www.solent.ac.uk/courses/course-areas/sport-tourism.aspx

Health and Fitness; fitness/management & personal training, health, exercise & physical activityLeisure Management; introduction to special event logistics/staging Coaching; sport coaching/& development-Marketing; promoting & marketing sports activities, marketing/with advertisingOutdoor & Water Sports; extreme sports managementSport; football studies/& business, sports studies & business, sport coaching & development, sports studies, applied sport science, sports coaching, sport & development Tourism; cruise industry management, international/tourism management; BA(Hons), BSc(Hons), MA

## THE OPEN UNIVERSITY
## www.open.ac.uk

### Arts and Humanities Studies; www3.open.ac.uk/study/undergraduate/arts-and-humanities/index.htm

art history, classical studies, English language & literature, history, humanities, literature, music, politics, philosophy, religious studies; BA(Hons), MA, PGDip

### Business and Management; www3.open.ac.uk/study/undergraduate/business_and_management/index.htm

accounting, business management/administration/studies, computing & IT, finance, financial services/strategy, leadership and management, retail management, clinical leadership, HRM; BA/BSc, Diplomas, DipHE, FD, MA, MSc, PGDip, MBA

**Childhood and Youth; www3.open.ac.uk/study/undergraduate/childhood-and-youth/index.htm**
childhood practice, childhood & youth studies, early years, primary teaching & learning, youth work, working with young people, youth justice studies; BA(Hons), Diplomas, DipHE, Certificates

**Computing and ICT; www3.open.ac.uk/study/undergraduate/computing-and-ICT/index.htm**
advanced networking, communication & information technology, computing & IT/practice, information systems, management of software, software development, web technology; BSc(Hons), Certs, Diplomas, DipHE, FD, MSc, PGDip

**Education; www3.open.ac.uk/study/undergraduate/education/index.htm**
childhood practice, childhood & youth studies, early years, education, mathematics & its learning, online & distance education, primary teaching & learning, QTS, professional studies in education, working together for children, working with young people, youth work; BA/BSc, Certs, DipHE, FD, MA, PGCE

**Engineering, Technology & Design; www3.open.ac.uk/study/undergraduate/engineering_and-technology-and-design/index.htm**
adv networking, computing and IT/practice, design & innovation, engineering, information systems, materials fabrication & engineering, systems thinking in practice, technology management; BEng, FD, MBA, MEng, MSc, PGDip, DipHE

**Environment, Development and International Studies; www3.open.ac.uk/study/undergraduate/environment-development-and-international-studies/index.htm**
conflict/environment & development, development management, environmental science/studies, environmental, international studies, environment management & technology, global development, human rights & development; BSc(Hons), MSc, PGDip/Cert

**Health and Social Care; www3.open.ac.uk/study/undergraduate/health-and-social-care/index.htm**
adult nursing, advancing professional practice/healthcare practice, childhood & youth studies, counselling, health studies/science, health & social care, healthcare practice, managing care, mental health nursing, nursing practice, paramedical science, promoting public health, social working with young people, sport & fitness/& coaching, social work, youth justice, youth work; BA(Hons), BA/BSc, CertHE, DipHE, FD

**Languages; www3.open.ac.uk/study/undergraduate/languagesstudies/index.htm**
French, German, Spanish, applied linguistics, language studies, Spanish, English language & literature, humanities, education; BA(Hons), Dip/CertHE

**Law; www3.open.ac.uk/study/undergraduate/law/index.htm**
law, agreements, ownership & trusts, legal system, criminal justice, business, development, human rights & corporate responsibility, international law, company law, employment law, English law; Certs, Dips, LlB(Hons), PGDip

**Mathematics and Statistics; www3.open.ac.uk/study/undergraduate/mathematics_and_statistics/index.htm**
computing & IT/economics & mathematical sciences, statistics, mathematics, mathematics & physics, education, mathematics & its learning; BA/BSc, BSc(Hons), MMath, MSc, UGCert

**Psychology & Counselling; www3.open.ac.uk/study/undergraduate/psychology-and-counselling/index.htm**
counselling, psychology, philosophy psychological studies, combined social studies, behaviour & psychological studies, psychological studies & criminology; BA/BSc, MSc, PGDip, UGDip

**Science; www3.open.ac.uk/study/undergraduate/science/index.htm**
astronomy, biology, chemistry, geography, planetary science/studies, earth science, environmental studies/science, health sciences, mathematics & physics, medicinal chemistry, medical physics, natural sciences, paramedic sciences, physics, professional science, science & society; BSc(Hons), DipHE, FD, MSc

**Social Sciences; www3.open.ac.uk/study/undergraduate/social_sciences/index.htm**
counselling, economics, environmental studies, criminology/& social policy, criminology & psychology, philosophy & social sciences, combined social sciences, financial services, politics, philosophy, economics; BA(Hons), BA/BSc, FD, MA, PGDip

# UNIVERSITY OF OXFORD
## www.ox.ac.uk

*Division of Humanities: www.ox.ac.uk/divisions/humanities*

### Rothermere American Institute; www.rai.ox.ac.uk/
American studies/history/politics/literature; MSt

### Faculty of Classics; www.classics.ox.ac.uk
ancient & modern history, classics, classics & modern languages/English/oriental studies, classical archaeology & ancient history, classical philology & linguistics, Greek and Latin languages & literature/history, late antique & Byzantine studies, philosophy; BA(Hons), MPhil, MSt

### Ruskin School of Drawing and Fine Art; www.ruskin-sc.ox.ac.uk
art history & theory, contemporary art, drawing, fine art, theoretical & practice-led research, history of art & visual culture; BFA, MLitt, DPhil

### Faculty of English, Language & Literature; www.english.ox.ac.uk
English language and literature (650–1550; 1550–1700; 1600–1830; 1800–1914; 1900–present day), English & modern languages/classics/history, literature in English, English & American studies, history & English, medieval studies, history & English, Shakespeare, women's studies: film aesthetics, studio world literatures in English; BA(Hons), DPhil, MLitt, MPhil, MSt

### History of Art Department; www.hoa.ox.ac.uk
history of art, authenticity & replication in art and visual culture, image & theory, media & modernity in mass culture 1880–2000, portraiture as genre, medieval art: Gothic; artistic originality & transmission of style & mass culture, 1880–2000, theories of vision, women, art & culture in early modern Europe; BA(Hons), DPhil, MLitt, MSt

### Faculty of History; www.history.ox.ac.uk
ancient & modern history, economic & social history, English local history, international global & imperial history, general history, modern s. Asian studies, Gothic, history of science, medicine, technology, media & modernity: art & mass culture, late antique & Byzantine studies, medieval history/studies, modern British & European history, US history, women, art & culture in early modern Europe; BA(Hons), DPhil, MPhil, MSc, MSt, MLetters

### Faculty of Linguistics, Philology and Phonetics; www.ling-phil.ox.ac.uk
comparative philology & comparative philosophy, historical philology, history & structure of language, Indo-European languages, linguistics theory, philology & phonetics, modern languages & linguistics, Romance linguistics; BA, MPhil, PhD, MSt

### Faculty of Medieval & Modern Languages; www.mod-langs.ox.ac.uk
Celtic, comparative literature or medieval literature, cultural studies, Czech, Catalan, Galician, French, German, linguistics, literature, modern Greek, Italian, medieval literature, language history, linguistics/medieval & modern languages, European enlightenment/cultural studies, European & mid European languages, film, Polish, Portuguese, Russian, Spanish, Slavonic languages, Yiddish; BA(Hons), DPhil, MPhil, MSt

### Faculty of Music; www.music.ox.ac.uk
chamber music, choral studies/conducting performance, composition & analysis, dance music, musicology, ethnomusicology, historical musicology, jazz, musical history/theory, the motet in the 14/15th centuries, orchestration, music analysis & criticism, performance & interpretation, psychology of music, theory & analysis, source studies, technology of composition, s. Western music theory; BMus, DPhil, MA(Hons), MPhil, MSt, MLitt

### Faculty of Oriental Studies; www.orinst.ox.ac.uk
Arabic, Persian, Turkish, Sanskrit, Buddhist studies, Chinese studies, classic & oriental studies, eastern Christianity, Egyptology & ancient Near East, European & Middle East languages, Asia & Near Asian studies, Hebrew & Jewish studies, Islamic world, Japanese studies, Korean studies, theology & oriental studies; BA(Hons), DPhil, MPhil, MSt

### Faculty of Philosophy; www.philosophy.ox.ac.uk
philosophy & modern language/theology/physics/mathematics, aesthetics, Aquinas, Aristotle, ethics, formal logic, history of philosophy Descartes to Kant, knowledge & reality, logic & language, medieval

philosophy, philosophy of science/psychology/social science/behavioural science/religion, language & logic, Plato, post-Kantian philosophy, PPP Russell, Wittgenstein; BA(Hons), BPhil, MPhil, PhD

### Faculty of Theology; www.theology.ox.ac.uk

applied theology, theology/& pastoral studies/religious studies, oriental studies, pastoral studies, the Old Testament/New Testament studies, biblical interpretation, ecclesiastical history, cannon law, Christian ethics/doctrine/spirituality & theology, confession studies, philosophy & theology, philosophical theology, eastern Christian studies, interfaith dialogue, Judaism & Christianity in Graeco-Roman world, sociology of religion, study of religion; BA(Hons), BTh, MTh, MSt, MLitt, MPhil, DPhil, PGDip/Cert

## *Division of Mathematical, Physical and Life Sciences: www.ox.ac.uk/divisions/mpls*

### Dept of Chemistry; www.chemistry.ox.ac.uk

chemical biology, inorganic chemistry, mathematical techniques, medical chemistry, molecular biochemistry/& chemical biology, organic chemistry/reactions/synthesis, organometallic chemistry, physical & theoretical chemistry, quantum mechanics, reaction mechanisms, solid state chemistry, spectroscopy, theoretical chemistry, thermodynamics; DPhil, MChem, MSc

### Dept of Computer Science; www.cs.ox.ac.uk

computer science, mathematics, modelling & scientific computing, mathematics & foundations of computer science/philosophy/mathematics, software engineering, software & systems security; BA(Hons), MSc, DPhil

### Dept of Engineering Science; www.eng.ox.ac.uk

automotive engineering, biomedical engineering, chemical engineering, computer engineering, process engineering, civil & offshore engineering, electrical engineering, electronic & information engineering, structures, materials & dynamics, engineering science, engineering, economics & management, information/control & vision engineering, materials engineering, mechanical/civil/structural engineering, structural & mechanical engineering; DPhil, MEng, MSc

### Life Science Interface; Doctoral Training Centre; www.lsi.ox.ac.uk

biological systems, organic chemistry, molecular genetics & cell biology, mathematical biology, medical imaging & signals, bioinformatics, evolution & genetics, statistical data systems; DPhil

### Division of Materials; www.materials.ox.ac.uk

materials science, materials structures & mechanical properties of metals, electrical/mechanical properties, nanoelectronics, materials economics, non-metallic materials, composites, polymers, packaging/superconducting/semiconducting materials, etc; DPhil, MEng, MSc, MS, MEm

### Mathematical Institute; www.maths.ox.ac.uk

algebra, analysis, applied maths, mathematics & foundations of computer science, mathematics & scientific computing, mathematical finance, mathematical modelling & scientific computing, statistics, geometry, pure maths; BA(Hons), DPhil, MCF, MFoCS, MS, MSc, MMath

### Dept of Physics; www.physics.ox.ac.uk

physics, atmospheric oceanic & planetary physics, astrophysics, condensed matter physics, cosmology, sub-atomic physics, particle physics, physics, atomic & laser/theoretical physics; BA(Hons), DPhil, MPhys, MPhysPhil

### Dept of Plant Science; www.lps.plants.ox.ac.uk/plants

biochemistry & systems biology, cell biology/physiology, cell & development biology, comparative developmental genetics, ecology, evolution & systematics, plant science; BA(Hons), DPhil, MRes, MSc

### Dept of Statistics; www.stats.ox.ac.uk

applied statistics, mathematics & statistics; BA(Hons), DPhil, MMath, MSc, PGDip

### Dept of Zoology; www.zoo.ox.ac.uk

animal behaviour/welfare, ageing biology, biological science, disease, ecology, evolution, food science, molecular biology & bioinformatics, indigenous biology, ornithology, integrative bioscience, wildlife conservation; BA(Hons), DPhil, MRes, MSc

## Division of Medical Sciences; www.ox.ac.uk/divisions/medical_science

### Medical Sciences; www.medschool.ox.ac.uk

pre-clinical/post-clinical medicine, global health, immunology, biomedical science, biochemistry, experimental psychology, medicine, clinical embryology, endovascular neurosurgery (interventional neuroradiology), integrated immunology, global health science, neuroscience, radiation biology, athletic performance, psychological research, pharmacology, diagnostic imaging, neuroradiology, musculoskeletal sciences, medicinal chemistry for cancer, health care, therapeutics; MB, BCh, MSc, DPhil, PhD

### Dept of Biochemistry; www.bioch.ox.ac.uk

biochemistry (molecular & cellular), biomedicine, chromosome & developmental biology, genetics & molecular biology, immunity & translational medicine, infection, integrated systems, medical sciences, neuroscience, structural biology, systems approach to biomedical science; DPhil, MBiochem, MSc, PhD

### Dept of Cardiovascular Medicine; www.cardiov.ox.ac.uk

cardiovascular science; DPhil

### Nuffield Dept of Clinical Laboratory Sciences; www.ndcls.ox.ac.uk

blood research, inherited disease; DPhil, MSc

### Dept of Clinical Neurology; www.clneuro.ox.ac.uk

clinical immunology, cardiovascular disease, structural biology, genetics, developmental biology, cancer, endocrinology, functional neurosurgery & experimental neurology, remedial repair, neurodegeneration, neurology, neurogenetic immunology/pathology, epidemiology, integrated immunology, multiple sclerosis; DPhil, MSc

### Nuffield Dept of Clinical Medicine; www.ndm.ox.ac.uk

cancer biology, clinical immunology, bioinformation & statistics/computational biology, immunity & infectious diseases, musculoskeletal medicine, physiology, cellular & molecular biology, clinical trials & epidemiology, endricinology & metabolic medicine, genetics & genomics, physiology, cellular & molecular biology, medical statistics, professional science & structural biology, tropical & global med; PhD, MSc

### Dept of Pharmacology; www.pharm.ox.ac.uk

clinical pharmacology, experimental therapeutics, practical drug therapy, medical chemistry for cancer; MSc, DPhil

### Dept of Experimental Psychology; www.psy.ox.ac.uk

clinical/experimental psychology, psychology, philosophy & linguistics, neuroscience, psychological research; BA(Hons), DPhil, MSc

### Dept of Oncology; www.oncology.ox.ac.uk

oncology, radiation biology, experimental therapeutics, clinical pharmacy, medical oncology, radiation oncology & biology, radiobiology; DPhil, MRes, MSc

### Wellcome Trust Centre for Human Genetics; www.well.ox.ac.uk

biology, immunity, cardiovascular medicine, neuroscience, structural biology, genetic medicine; PhD

### Wetherall Institute of Molecular Medicine; www.imw.ox.ac.uk

clinical genetics, computational biology, stem cell biology, HIV immunity, global health, paediatrics, haematopietic stem cell biology, human immunology, neuroscience, molecular immunology/oncology/parasitology/haematology; DPhil

### Nuffield Dept of Obstetrics & Gynaecology; www.obs-gyn.ox.ac.uk

clinical embryology, human reproduction, obstetrics, gynaecology, antenatal care, sexual & reproductive health; MSc, DPhil

### Nuffield Laboratory of Ophthalmology; www.eye.ox.ac.uk

retinal genetics, artificial vision, bodyclocks, clinical trials, ocular biology, vision & disease, gene therapy, genetic/ocular biology, photoreceptors, ophthalmology, neuroscience, sleep; DPhil, MSc

### Nuffield Department of Clinical Neuroscience; www.clneuro.ox.ac.uk

cerebrovascular disease, anaesthesia, functional neurosurgery, muliple sclerosis, pain, simulation, neurodegeneration/genetics/muscular/immunology/muscular pathology;

### Nuffield Department of Orthopaedics, Rheumatology and Musculoskeletal Sciences; www.ndorms.ox.ac.uk

orthopaedics, rheumatology, musculoskeletal sciences; MSc, DPhil

### Dept of Paediatrics; www.paediatrics.ox.ac.uk

paediatric infection & immunity & translational medicine, gastroenterological & nutrition/neurology/vaccine/endocrine & diabetes, childhood care; PhD, MSc

### Dept of Physiology, Anatomy and Genetics; www.dpag.ox.ac.uk

ion channels, transporters & signalling, metabolism & endrinoconology, functional genomics, neuroscience, cardiac science, development and reproduction; MPhil, MSc, DPhil

### Dept of Psychiatry; www.psychiatry.ox.ac.uk

child & adolescent psychiatry, clinical neuroscience, eating disorders, evidence-based mental health, experimental psychopathology, behaviour & cognitive neuroscience, forensic psychiatry, global child development & mental health, molecular neuropathology, mood disorders, neurobiology of ageing, neuroimaging, psychopharmacology, schizophrenia & psychosis, self harm & suicide, social psychiatry; DPhil, MRCPsych

### Division of Primary Care Health Science; www.dphpc.ox.ac.uk

cancer, monitoring & diagnosis, tobacco addiction, health therapeutics, infectious disease, health services & policy, global health science, health economics/services; DPhil, MSc

### Nuffield Dept of Surgical Science; www.surgery.ox.ac.uk

endovascular neurosurgery, diagnostic imaging, integrated immunology, surgical science & practice; DPhil, MCh, MSc

## *Division of Social Sciences; www.socsci.ox.ac.uk*

### School of Anthropology and Museum Ethnography; www.anthro.ox.ac.uk

anthropology & mind, human science, social/& cultural anthropology, medical anthropology, cognitive & evolutionary anthropology, visual, material & museum anthropology, migration studies, refugee & forced migration studies, material anthropology & museum ethnography; BA, BSc, DPhil, MPhil

### Pitt Rivers Museum; www.prm.ox.ac.uk

material anthropology, museum ethnography, sound & music; DPhil, MPhil, MSc

### School of Archaeology; www.arch.ox.ac.uk

archaeology & anthropology, bioarchaeology, Eurasian prehistory, classical archaeology & ancient history, materials & material cultures, palaeolithic, archaeological science; BA(Hons), DPhil, MLitt, MSc, MSt

### SAID Business School; www.sbs.ox.ac.uk

accounting, economics & management, major project management, law/& finance, financial strategy/economics, general management, global business, law management science, marketing, innovation/change/organizational behaviour/leadership, materials/economics & management, major programme management, general management, public policy, strategy & innovation; BA, Dip, Exec MBA, MSc

### Dept of Economics; www.economics.ox.ac.uk

economics/financial development, engineering/materials/economics & management, history & economics, econometrics, financial economics, microeconomics, macroeconomics, philosophy, politics & economics, quantitative economics, comparative demographic studies, economics of developing countries, international economics, public economics; BA(Hons), DPhil, MEng, MSc

### Dept of Education; www.education.ox.ac.uk

applied linguistics & second language acquisition, child development and education, comparative & international education, education, e-learning, educational research methodology, learning and teaching/in HE/technology, PGCE (numerous secondary subjects), teaching English in university setting; DPhil, MSc, PGCE, PGDip

### School of Geography & the Environment; www.geog.ox.ac.uk

African societies, biodiversity, biogeography, conservation, climate systems & policy, climate change, landscape dynamics, biogeography, conservation & management, dryland environment, earth systems processes/dynamics, earth science, environmental change & management, environmental geography, European integration, forensic geography, geographical techniques/controversies, geographical technology, geography & finance, nature, quaternary period, society & environmental policy, transport, water science, policy & management; BA(Hons), DPhil, MSc

### School of Interdisciplinary Area Studies; www.area-studies.ox.ac.uk

African studies, modern Japanese studies, contemporary Chinese studies, Russian & east European studies, public policy in Latin America, contemporary India; MSc, MPhil, DPhil

### Dept of International Development; www.qeh.ox.ac.uk

development studies, economics for development, international development, refugee & forced migration studies, global governance, diplomacy; Cert/Dip, DPhil, MPhil, MSc

### Oxford Internet Institute; www.oii.ox.ac.uk

social science of the internet, information, communication & the social sciences; DPhil, MSc

### Faculty of Law; www.law.ox.ac.uk

common/comparative/company/competition/corporate/labour law, constitutional & administration/criminal law, criminology & criminal justice, philosophy of/criminology, environmental law, EU/family/human rights law, intellectual property law, international human rights law, judicial process, law & finance, law of obligation, legal history/studies, media law, property & trusts, Roman law, socio-legal studies; BA(Hons), BCL, Dip, DPhil, MJur, MLitt, MPhil, MSc, MSt, PGDip

### Oxford Martin School; www.oxfordmartin.ox.ac.uk

research in health & medicine, energy & environment, technology & society, ethics & governance

### Oxford-Man Institute of Quantitative Finance; www.oxford-man.ox.ac.uk

research in quantitative finance, alternative investment etc

### Dept of Politics & International Relations; www.politics.ox.ac.uk

history and politics, international relations, philosophy, political theory, philosophy, politics and economics, politics (comparative government/European politics and society/political theory), PPE; BA(Hons), DPhil, MLitt, MPhil, MSc

### Dept of Social Policy & Intervention; www.spi.ox.ac.uk

comparative social policy, educational policy, evidence-based social intervention, family policy, ageing, poverty, inequality, health & social policy, housing & homelessness, social policy & the environment, labour markets/policy; BA, MPhil, MSc

### Dept of Sociology; www.sociology.ox.ac.uk

political sociology, human sciences, history & politics, philosophy, politics & economics, quantitative methods in politics and sociology, sociological theory, introduction to/sociology, sociology of industrial societies; BA(Hons), DPhil, MPhil, MSc

## OXFORD BROOKES UNIVERSITY
## www.brookes.ac.uk

## *Faculty of Business; www.brookes.ac.uk/about/faculties/business*

### Business School; www.business.brookes.ac.uk

accounting & finance, business & economics/marketing management, economics, finance & international business/politics & international relations, international business/management, business management, applied accounting, international management/& international relations, international transport & logistics, HRM, business, management & communications, business & enterprise, e-business, international business/economics/trade & logistics, marketing; BA(Hons), BSc(Hons), Certs, DCM, DBA, Dips, FdA, MA, MBA, MRes, MSc, PhD

### Oxford International Centre for Publishing; www.publishing.brookes.ac.uk

publishing, book history, print culture, digital publishing, international publishing, publishing & law; BA(Hons), European Master's in Publishing, MA

### Oxford School of Hospitality; www.hospitality.brookes.ac.uk

international hospitality management/& tourism management, international tourism & hotel marketing, food, wine & culture; BSc(Hons), MSc

## *Faculty of Human & Life Sciences; www.hls.brookes.ac.uk*

### Dept of Biological & Medical Sciences; www.bms.brookes.ac.uk

animal behaviour & welfare/biology & conservation, biological sciences, biology, biomedical science, biotechnology/with business, conservation ecology, environmental management/science, human biology, infection, prevention & control, biosciences, medical science/statistics, equine science/& management/thoroughbred management, life sciences; BA(Hons)/BSc(Hons), MSc, PGDip, PhD, BMedSci

### Dept of Clinical Health Care; www.chc.brookes.ac.uk

adult/children's nursing, adv practice, cancer studies, children's nursing, emergency care, health and social care, nursing studies, leadership in clinical practice, non-medical prescribing, palliative care, paramedic emergency care; BScHons, FdSC, MA, MSc

### Dept of Psychology; www.psychology.brookes.ac.uk

psychology, developmental psychology; BSc(Hons), BA(Hons), MPhil, PhD, MSc, PGDip/Cert

### Dept of Social Work & Public Health; www.swph.brookes.ac.uk

management in/health & social care/studies, health promotion, social work, children, young people & family wellbeing, community children's nursing/in the home, district nursing, higher professional education, infection prevention & control, medical education, midwifery, public health, specialist community public health nursing; BSc(Hons), BA(Hons), PGDip/Cert, Cert HE, MA, MSc

### Dept of Sport & Health Science; www.shs.brookes.ac.uk

management in health & social care, physiology, higher professional education, sport & exercise science, sports coaching & PE, sports science, applied human nutrition, applied sports & exercise nutrition, contemporary occupational therapy, rehabilitation; BSc(Hons), MSc, PGDip/Cert, MOst, MSc, PhD

## *Faculty of Humanities & Social Sciences; www.brookes.ac.uk/about faculties/hss*

### School of Education; www.education.brookes.ac.uk

early/childhood studies, early years specialisation, early years, e-pedagogy, education/studies, adv educational practice, CPD, gifted & talented education, artist teacher studies, educational studies, education & lifelong learning, English language & communications, education (leadership & management/TESOL), mentoring new teachers, working with literacy difficulties, PGCE primary/secondary/post-compulsory education, learning & teaching, primary teacher education, special educational needs support for learning; BA(Hons), BSc(Hons), CertEd, FdA, MA, MPhil, PGCE, PGDip, PhD

### Dept of English & Modern Languages: www.english-language.brookes.ac.uk

English, creative writing, drama, European business, culture & language, French, Spanish, Japanese studies; BA(Hons), MA

### Dept of History, Philosophy & Religion; www.history.brookes.ac.uk

history, history of medicine, history of art, philosophy, religion & theology, communication, media & culture, ministry; BA(Hons), MA, FdA

### School of Law; www.law.brookes.ac.uk

law, international/economic/human rights/trade & commercial law, international law & international relations, public international law, legal practice; BA/BSc, LlB, PGDip, GradDip, LlM

### Dept of Social Sciences;

www.social-sciences.brookes.ac.uk

anthropology, geography, international relations /& politics, primate conservation, international studies (international relations/global political economy/environment/security), international management & international relations/law, sociology, policing; BA/BSc, MA, MSc, GradDip, FdA

## *Faculty of Technology, Design & Environment; www.brookes.ac.uk/tde*

### School of Architecture;

http:/architecture.brookes.ac.uk

architecture, interior architecture, built environment, development & emergency practice, humanitarian action & conflict, shelter after disaster, regeneration & development, applied design in architecture; BA(Hons), MArch, MArchD, PhD

### School of Arts; http:/arts.brookes.ac.uk

fine art, composition & sonic art, contemporary arts/& music, creative arts & practice, music, fine art: drawing for fine art practice, archaeological illustration, illustration narrative & sequential, contemporary arts/& music, social sculpture, music & popular culture, music on stage and on screen, contemporary practice in composition, music in 19th-century culture, film studies, publishing/media/& language, book history & popular culture, digital international publishing; BA(Hons), BA/BSc, MA, MPhil, PhD

**Dept of Planning;**
http:/planning.brookes.ac.uk
built environment, environmental/impact assessment & management, spatial planning, historic conservation, city & regional planning, planning/& property development, tourism environment & development, urban design/planning development & transitional regions & regional regeneration; BA(Hons), MPlan, MSc, PhD, MPhil, PGCip/Cert

**Dept of Real Estate & Construction;**
http:/rec.brookes.ac.uk
construction management/project management, quantity surveying & commercial management, real estate/management, spatial planning, project management in the built environment; BSc(Hons), MSc, PhD

**Dept of Computing & Communication Technologies;**
http:/cct.brookes.ac.uk
broadband networks, computer science, ebusiness computing, information technology management for business, mobile computing, media technology, computer vision, computer games & animation, ebusiness, network computing, software engineering, multimedia production, sound technology & digital music, mobile & high-speed telecommunications, wireless communication systems, digital media production; BSc(Hons), MSc, PhD

**Dept of Mechanical Engineering & Mathematical Science;**
http:/mems.brookes.ac.uk
mathematics, mathematical sciences, statistics, mechanical engineering, motorsport engineering, automotive engineering, computer aided mechanical engineering, adv engineering design, racing engine design, medical statistics; BSc(Hons), BA(Hons), BEng, MEng, MSc, MRes, MPhil, PhD

## UNIVERSITY OF PLYMOUTH
## www.plymouth.ac.uk

### *Faculty of Arts; www.plymouth.ac.uk/faculties/arts*

**School of Architecture, Design and Environment; www1.plymouth.ac.uk/schools/ade/**
architecture, architectural technology & the environment, architectural conservation, 3D design, design/service practice/spatial practice, sustainable futures, design thinking, building surveying & the environment, sustainable construction/cost management/project management, construction management & the environment; BA(Hons), MA, MRes, MArch, MSc

**School of Art & Media; www.plymouth.ac.uk/schools/artmedia**
creativity & enterprise, creative practice, digital art & technology, media & animation, graphic communication with typography, film & video, fine art, media arts, contemporary art/film practice, photography/& the book, publishing, TV arts; BA(Hons), MA, MArch, GradDip, MRes, PhD, MSc, BSc

**School of Humanities & Performing Arts; www.plymouth.ac.uk/schools/hpa**
art history, computer music, dance, literature, English & creative writing/history/French/Spanish/culture, fine art & art history, history with international relations/politics, music, performance practice, theatre & performance, the speaking dance; BA(Hons), MA, PGDip/Cert, MRes, PhD

### *Faculty of Health, Education & Society; www.plymouth.ac.uk/faculties/health*

**School of Social Science & Social Work; www.plymouth.ac.uk/schools/sssw**
health & social care studies, mental health, social work, sociology, cognitive behavioural therapy, social & market/education research, social research & evaluation, sociology; BA(Hons), BSc(Hons), MA, MSc, PGDip

**School of Nursing & Midwifery; www.plymouth.ac.uk/schools/nm**
midwifery, adult/child health/mental health nursing, adv practice in education for health professionals, healthcare/service improvement, genetic healthcare; BSc(Hons), MSc, PGDip

### School of Health Professions; www.plymouth.ac.uk/schools/hp

dietetics, mental health, neurological rehabilitation, adv/occupational therapy, adv professional practice (dietetic/neurological rehabilitation/occupational therapy/paediatric dietetics/physiotherapy), operating dept practice, optometry, paramedic practitioner (community emergency/studies), physiotherapy, podiatry, women's health, work & wellbeing; BSc(Hons), DipHE, MSc, PGCert, PGDip

### School of Education; www.plymouth.ac.uk/schools/education

primary – art & design, digital literacy, early childhood studies, English, humanities, mathematics, music, PE, science, special education: early childhood studies (IMP) education, learning for sustainability, teaching & learning, PGCE: primary/early years, secondary (large range of secondary subjects), special educational needs coordination; BEd, Cert Ed, MA, MSc, Masters in Teaching & Learning, PGCE, Dip, PGCert, ProfDoc

## *Plymouth Business School; www.plymouth.ac.uk/faculties/pbs*

### Plymouth Law School; www.plymouth.ac.uk/schools/law

criminology & criminal justice studies, law, law with business studies/politics/psychology/sociology, legal practice, police/law & criminal justice studies; BA(Hons), BSc(Hons), LlB, LlM, MSc, PGDip

### School of Management; www.plymouth.ac.uk/schools/man

accounting, business admin/economics/management/studies, finance, business & management, marketing, economics/with international relations/law/politics, financial economics, global security & development, HRM, international relations with French/law/politics/psychology, international supply chain shipping management, international business/economics/finance/logistics/management/trade & operations management/supply chain management/shipping, maritime business & logistics/management/law, marketing management, shipping & logistics, supply chain management, technology strategy, public administration/management, public service/policies; BA(Hons), BSc(Hons), MA, MBA, DBA, MSc, PGCert/Dip, DMS, DPA

### School of Tourism & Hospitality; www.plymouth.ac.uk/schools/th

business & tourism, cruise management, event management, international/hospitality management, hospitality tourism & events management, international tourism & marketing, tourism & hospitality management; BSc(Hons), BA(Hons), MSc, PGDip

## *Faculty of Science & Technology; www.plymouth.ac.uk/faculties/scitech*

### School of Biomedical & Biological Sciences; www.plymouth.ac.uk/schools/bio

animal behaviour/welfare, applied bioscience (aquaculture/plant sciences), biomedical/biological science/diversity, healthcare science, nutrition, exercise & health, health & fitness, healthcare (life sciences), human biosciences, environmental biology, life science, physiological sciences, sustainable aquaculture systems/horticulture & food production, zoo conservation; BSc(Hons), PGDip, MSc

### School of Computing & Mathematics; www.plymouth.ac.uk/schools/compmath

applied statistics/with management science, computing, civil engineering, computer networking/systems & networking/engineering, computing & games development, electrical & electronic engineering, mathematics/with statistics/education/finance, multimedia computing, robotics, signal processing, web applications dev; BSc, MSc, MRes

### School of Geography, Earth & Environmental Sciences; www.plymouth.ac.uk/schools/sogees

chemistry, applied/geology, environmental science/consultancy, extended science, holistic science, geography/& international relations/ocean science, physical geography, planning, sustainable environmental management; BA(Hons), BSc(Hons), MGeol, MSc, MRes, PGCert

### School of Marine Science & Engineering; www.plymouth.ac.uk/schools/mse

applied marine science, civil/coastal engineering, marine & composites technology, marine biology & coastal ecology/oceanography, marine technology, marine renewable energy, mechanical design & manufacture, mechanical engineering/with composites, ocean exploration/science, coastal engineering, hydrography, marine sport science/technology, navigation & marine science, ocean exploration science; BSc(Hons), MEng, MRes, MSc, BEng, FdSc, PGDip

**School of Psychology;**
**www.plymouth.ac.uk/schools/psychology**
psychological studies, adv/psychology/with law, human biology/sociology, criminology & criminal justice studies, psychology research methods; BSc(Hons), MSc, PGDip

*Plymouth University Peninsular School of Medicine and Dentistry;*
*www.plymouth.ac.uk/peninsular*
medicine, surgery, dentistry, dental studies, oral & dental health, cancer, clinical science/education, infection & immunisation, remote treatment, environmental & human health, gastroenterology, obesity & diabetes, cardiovascular risk & ageing, neuroscience, health services, professional studies, public health, simulation & palliative studies/primary care/restorative dentistry/leadership/trauma; MBBS, BDS, MD, MS, MPhil, PhD

## *Degrees validated by the University of Plymouth offered at:*

---

## SOUTH DEVON COLLEGE
www.southdevon.ac.uk

animal science, biosciences, business, computing, creative digital media, teaching in the lifelong learning sector, law, early years care & education, education, electrical & electronics engineering, engineering technology, exercise science & fitness, events & conference management, healthcare practice, illustrative arts, modern music production, outdoor education, performance practice & events management, 3D design, sustainable construction & building, tourism & hospitality management, uniformed public services, yacht operations; BSc(Hons), FD, HNC, HND, PGCE

---

## TRURO & PENWITH COLLEGE
www.trurocollege.ac.uk

action photography, applied media, archaeology, bioscience, children & young people's workforce, commercial fashion/music, community & cultural studies, computer techniques, contemporary world jazz, community studies, complementary body therapies, counselling, dance, digital visualization, early childhood education, education/and training, education in lifelong learning sector, English studies, environmental & public health/nutrition, exercise, health & fitness, hairdressing & salon management, history & heritage, information, advice & guidance, interior design, law, libraries, museums & archives, management & business resources, media advertising, post-compulsory education & training, music performance, outdoor education, photography & digital imaging, public services, salon & spa management, silversmithing & jewellery, sound engineering, sports coaching & therapy/rehabilitation, web technology; BA(Hons), BSc, FdA, FdSc, HNC, HND, PCET, PGCE, UnivCert/Dip

## UNIVERSITY OF PORTSMOUTH
## www.port.ac.uk

### *Portsmouth Business School; www.port.ac.uk/departments/faculties/portsmouthbusinessschool*

**Accounting & Finance, Economics, Human Resource & Marketing Management, Law, Strategy & Business Systems**

accountancy and financial management, accounting and business/finance, business/and HRM/management, business economics/enterprise development/information technology, business with business communication, digital marketing, economics/and management/law, economics, finance and banking, European business, finance and management business communication, hospitality management/tourism, HRM with psychology, international business, law, law with business/business communication/criminology/European studies/international relations, leadership/business and management, marketing/with business communication/psychology, business and management, business economics, finance and banking, coaching and development, corporate governance and law, digital marketing, economics for business, finance, financial decision analysis, forensic accounting, HRD/M, innovation management and entrepreneurship, international business and English, international HRM, law, leadership and management, leadership in health and wellbeing, marketing, master of business administration/executive, project management/and leadership, risk management, sales management, strategic quality management, sustainable environmental management, training management and consultancy; BA(Hons), BSc(Hons), MSc, BSc(Econ)(Hons), PGDip/Cert, MPhil, PHD, LlB, LlM, MBA

### *Faculty of Creative and Cultural Industries; www.port.ac.uk/departments/faculties/facultyofcreativeartsandindustries*

**Portsmouth School of Architecture; www.port.ac.uk/departments/academic/architecture/**

architecture, interior design, professional practice, sustainable architecture, urban design, historic building conservation; BA(Hons), MA, MArch, MSc

**School of Art, Design and Media; www.port.ac.uk/departments/academic/adm**

design for digital media, art, contemporary fine art, fashion & textile design, fine art, graphic design, illustration, photography; BA(Hons), MA

**School of Creative Arts, Film and Media; www.port.ac.uk/departments/academic/scafm**

creative & media writing, drama/& performance, English/& creative writing/film studies, entertainment technology, film & TV studies, media studies/& entertainment technology; BA(Hons), MA

**School of Creative Technologies; www.port.ac.uk/departments/academic/ct**

animation, computational sound, computer animation/games enterprise/technology, computing & digital sound, creative professional practice, digital media, entertainment technology, film studies & creative writing, TV & film production/broadcasting, video & games technology; BA(Hons), BSc(Hons), FdSc, MSc

### *Faculty of Humanities and Social Sciences; www.port.ac.uk/departments/faculties/facultyofhumanities*

**Institute of Criminal Justice Studies; www.port.ac.uk/departments/academic/icjs**

counter fraud & counter corruption studies, crime & criminology, investigation & evidence, police studies, risk & security management, crime science, investigation & intelligence, criminology & community safety/criminal justice/criminal psychology/crime cultures, security management, policing, international criminal justice, policing, policy & leadership, security management, law & criminology, sociology & criminology, forensic computing/accounting, forensic IT; BSc(Hons), FdA, LlB, MScDCrim Studs, DCrimJ

**School of Education and Continuing Studies; www.port.ac.uk/departments/academic/iecs**

childhood & youth studies/with psychology, early childhood studies/with psychology, early years care & education, education administration, education &

training studies/management, PGCE in numerous subject courses/post-compulsory education, investigation & evidence, learning support, learning & teaching/in HE; BA(Hons), CertEd, FdA, MA, MSc, PGCE, PGCert, EYPS

### School of Languages & Area Studies; www.port.ac.uk/departments/academic/slas

American studies & history, applied languages, combined modern languages, communication & English studies, English language & international relations, EU studies, European studies, French/German studies, international trade & business, international development studies/& languages, international relations/& trade/business communication, international trade, logistics & busness communications, languages & European studies/law, linguistics & business English, logistics, Spanish & Latin American studies, applied linguistics & TESOL; BA(Hons), MA

### School of Social, Historical and Literary Studies; www.port.ac.uk/departments/academic/sshls

English & history/media studies/languages & literature, English literature/psychology, European law & policy/studies, government, history/& politics, history of war, culture & society, international relations & history/politics/European studies, journalism/with English literature/language/media studies, media studies, politics, psychology, sociology/& criminology/psychology/literature, culture & identity, public administration; BA(Hons), BSc(Hons), FdA, MPA, MSc

## *Faculty of Science; www.port.ac.uk/departments/faculties/facultyofscience*

### School of Biological Sciences; www.port.ac.uk/departments/academic/biology

applied aquatic biology, biology, biochemistry, marine biology; BSc(Hons), MSc, MPhil, PhD, MRes

### School of Earth and Environmental Sciences; www.port.ac.uk/departments/academic/isees

engineering geology & geotechnics/contamination, crisis & disaster management, environmental science, geological hazards, geological & environmental hazards, geology, marine environmental science, palaeobiology; BSc(Hons), MEng(Hons), MSc

### Department of Geography; www.port.ac.uk/departments/academic/geography

environmental geography, coastal & marine resources management, geography & GIS, human geography, physical geography; BA(Hons), BSc(Hons), MSc

### The Dental Academy; www.port.ac.uk/departments/academic/dentalacademy

dental hygiene/therapy, science & dental therapy; BSc (Hons), CertHE, FdSc

### School of Health Sciences and Social Work; www.port.ac.uk/departments/academic/shssw

acute clinical healthcare, human physiology/comunication, speech, language & communication science, operating dept practice, paramedic science, social work, radiography (diagnostic/therapy), langauge & communication science; DipHE, FdSc, GradDip, BSc(Hons), MSc

### Pharmacy & Biomedical sciences; www.port.ac.uk/departments/academic/pharmacy/

applied/biomedical science, healthcare sciences, pharmacy/practice, pharmacology, biomedicine; FdSc, BSc(Hons), MSc

### Psychology; www.port.ac.uk/departments/academic/psychology/

psychology, forensic/psychology, applied psychology of intellectual disabilities, child forensic studies; BSc(Hons), MSc, PGCert, MPhil, PhD

### Sport & Exercise Science; www.port.ac.uk/departments/academic/sportscience/

sport & exercise science/psychology, exercise & fitness practice, sports development/business management/performance, clinical exercise science; BSc(Hons), MSc

## *Faculty of Technology; www.port.ac.uk/departments/faculties/facultyoftechnology*

### Civil Engineering & Surveying; www.port.ac.uk/departments/academic/sces

civil engineering, construction engineering management, property development, civil engineering with environmental/geotechnical/structural engineering, construction project management, quantity surveying; BSc(Hons), BEng(Hons), MEng, MSc

### Computing; www.port.ac.uk/departments/academic/comp

business information systems, computer science, computing & information systems/digital image/information security, forensic computing, computing & information technology, information systems/technology, software engineering, web technologies, forensic/IT; BSc(Hons), MSc

### Mathematics; www.port.ac.uk/departments/academic/maths

mathematics, mathematics for finance & management/with statistics, logistics & transportation/supply chain management, supportability management; BSc(Hons), MSc, PgCert/Dip, MPhil, PhD

### Engineering; www.port.ac.uk/departments/academic/eng

communication systems/engineering, computer-aided product design, computer engineering/networks, computer network planning & management, electronic engineering, electronic systems engineering, engineering & technology, mechanical & manufacturing engineering, mechanical engineering, petroleum engineering, product design & modern materials/innovation, adv manufacturing technology, technology management, adv manufacturing technology, communication network planning & management, computer network administration & management, digital systems engineering, electronic engineering, mechanical engineering, technology management; BSc(Hons), BEng(Hons), MEng, MSc

### Learning at Work; www.port.ac.uk/departments/academic/learning atwork

occupational health & safety management; PGCert, MSc

## QUEEN MARGARET UNIVERSITY COLLEGE
## www.qmuc.ac.uk

### School of Arts, Social Sciences & Management; www.qmuc/assam

### School of Health Sciences; www.qmuc/hs

**Undergraduate Courses**

Biological Sciences; applied pharmacology, human biology, nutrition

Health Professions; diagnostic radiography, dietetics, hearing aid audiology, nursing, occupational therapy, physiotherapy, podiatry, radiography, occupational therapy, physiotherapy – conversion courses – speech and language therapy/therapeutic radiography

Hospitality and Tourism; international hospitality and tourism management

Business Management; business management

Performing Arts; acting for stage and screen, costume design and construction, drama and performance

Psychology and Sociology; psychology, psychology and sociology

Public Relations, Marketing and Events; events management, PR & marketing/media

Theatre, Film and Media; film and media, media, theatre and film studies

**Postgraduate Courses**

Business and Management; public services governance, international management and leadership/with hospitality; MBA/hospitality

Creativity and Culture; arts, festival and cultural management, creative enterprise

Dietetics and Nutrition; dietetics, public health nutrition

Education; collaborative working: education and therapy, professional and higher education

International Health; applied social development, conflict, social development and health, global health systems, human resources for global health, international health, sexual and reproductive health, social development and health, social justice, development and health

Nursing; cognitive behavioural therapy, nursing, community health nursing, palliative care, public health practice

Occupational Therapy and Arts Therapies; music therapy (nordoff-robbins), occupational therapy, transactional analysis counselling psychotherapy, dance movement psychotherapy, art psychotherapy (international)

Physiotherapy; physiotherapy

Podiatry and Diabetes; diabetes, podiatric medicine, podiatry, theory of podiatric surgery

Public Relations; public affairs, PR

Professional Doctorate; professional doctorate – health and social sciences

Radiography; diagnostic radiography, mammography, radiotherapy, radiotherapy and oncology, clinical research
Social Justice; environmental justice, gender and social justice, social justice

Speech and Hearing Sciences; audiology, rehabilitative audiology, speech and language therapy (pre-registration);BA(Hons), BSc(Hons), MA, MBA, PgDipCert, MSc, PhD

## UNIVERSITY OF READING
## www.reading.ac.uk

### *Faculty of Arts & Humanities; www.reading.ac.uk/fah*

#### School of Arts & Communication Design; www.reading.ac.uk/sacd

Art: art, fine art, history of art, art & philosophy/history of artfilm & theatre/psychology, history of art & ancient history/classics/English/architecture
Film, Theatre and Television: film & theatre & TV/English literature/art/film/German/Italian/history of art, theatre/film studies, theatre & history of art/German/Italian, English literature, TV studies
Typography & Graphic Communication: graphic communication, book/information/typeface design, typography & graphic communication;
BA(Hons), MA, MA(Res), MFA, MPhil, PhD

#### School of Humanities; www.reading.ac.uk/humanities

Classics: ancient history & history/history of art, the city of Rome, classical & medieval studies, classical studies & English/English literature/history of art, the classical tradition, classics, museum studies, ancient maritime trade & navigation, archaeology, architectural history, classical studies
History: history, modern history, history & economics/English/European literature & culture/international relations/modern European languages/medieval studies
Philosophy: philosophy, philosophy & classical studies/English literature/French/German/Italian/politics/international relations, ethics & political theory, politics, philosophy & economics;
BA(Hons), MA, MPhil, PhD

#### School of Literature & Languages; www.reading.ac.uk/literature-and-languages

**Dept of Modern Languages & European Studies; www.reading.ac.uk/modern-languages-and-european-studies/mles-home.aspx**

French
French, French & history of art/economics/English language/English literature/German/international relations/Italian/management/politics/history/philosophy, international management and business administration with French, Franco-British history, French studies
German
German, German and history of art, economics/English language/English literature/French/ international relations/Italian/management/politics/history/philosophy, international management and business administration with German, German studies
Italian
Italian, Italian & economics/English language/English literature/German/ international relations/Italian/management/politics/history/philosophy, international management and business administration with Italian, modern Italian history, Italian studies
European studies/European literature and culture, European studies, European studies with a major European language, European cultures and history; BA(Hons), MA, MA(Res), PhD

**Dept of English Language & Applied Linguistics; www.reading.ac.uk/english-langauge-and-applied-linguistics/elel/home.aspx**

English language/literature, applied linguistics, English language teaching; BA(Hons), MA, MA(Res), PhD

**Dept of English Literature; www.reading.ac.uk/english-literature**

English literature, classical studies and English literature, English and European literature and culture, English and film & theatre/philosophy, English literature with French/French studies/German studies/history/history of art & architecture, Italian studies/international relations, English and politics/English literature and international relations, English, modern and contemporary writing, children's literature, early modern literature and drama, nineteenth-century literature; BA(Hons), MA, MA(Res), PhD

## Faculty of Social Sciences; www.reading.ac.uk/internal/fss

### Institute of Education; www.reading.ac.uk/education

children's development & learning, early years, education (art/English/music/mathematics specialism), theatre arts, education & deaf studies, PGCE (secondary, primary, graduate teacher programme, subject knowledge enhancement), mathematics specialist teaching, professional development, EYPS; BA(Hons), FdA, PGCE, PhD, EdD

### School of Law; www.reading.ac.uk/law

law, law & economics, advanced legal studies, European Union law & citizenship/governance, legal studies in Europe, international law & world order/commercial law/corporate finance/financial regulation/banking law, law & society, oil & gas; DPhil, LlB, LLM, MARes, MRes, MScPhD

### School of Politics & International Relations; www.reading.ac.uk/spirs

international relations & politics/economics/English literature/history/philosophy/modern European language, politics & economics/English literature/history/philosophy/modern European language, philosophy & politics, public policy, international relations diplomacy, international law & world order/international security/strategy, war, peace & international relations, military history & strategic studies; BA(Hons), MA, MPhil, MRes, PhD

### The School of Economics; www.reading.ac.uk/economics

banking and finance/business & management in emerging economies, business economics, economics, econometrics, economic development in emerging markets, economics of climate change, economics of international business & finance, financial & economic development, international business & economic development, public policy, international banking & financial services; BA(Hons), BSc(Hons), MSc, PhD

### Henley Business School; www.henley.ac.uk

accounting, finance, informatics, management, real estate & planning, planning, coaching, business & management; MBA, DBA, Masters, PhD

## Faculty of Life Sciences; www.reading.ac.uk/internal/lifesci

### School of Agriculture, Policy & Development; www.reading.ac.uk/apd

agriculture, agricultural business management/development economics, agricultural economics, agriculture & development, applied development studies, animal science, climate change & development, communications for innovation & development, consumer behaviour & marketing, development finance/policy, environment & development, environmental & countryside management, food marketing/& business economics, food economics & marketing, food security & development, research agricultural & food economics, social development & sustainable livelihoods; BA(Hons), BSc(Hons), MPhil, PhD

### School of Biological Sciences; www.reading.ac.uk/biologicalsciences

ecology & wildlife conservation, biochemistry, biological sciences, biomedical sciences, ecology & wildlife conservation, microbiology, plant diversity, species identification & survey skills, wildlife management & conservation, zoology; BSc(Hons), MPhil, MSc, PhD

### School of Chemistry; www.reading.ac.uk/chemistry

chemistry, chemistry with analytics/education, research groups; bioanalysis and analytical methods, nanostructured polymers and biopolymers, atmospheric chemistry and environmental research, photoredox processes and structure of functional materials, interfacial chemistry; BSc(Hons), MSc, MChem, PhD

### School of Chemistry, Food & Pharmacy; www.reading.ac.uk/fcfp

chemistry, food science/technology, forensic analysis, medical chemistry, nutrition & food science, pharmacy, quality assurance; BSc(Hons), MPharm, MSc, PhD, MChem

### School of Psychology & Clinical Language Sciences; www.reading.ac.uk/pcls

psychology, childhood and ageing, psychology & biology/philosophy/art/neuroscience, psychology – mental & psychological health/practice, clinical science, speech & language therapy, cognitive neuroscience, development & psychopathology; BSc(Hons), MSc, PhD

## *Faculty of Science; www.reading.ac.uk/internal/facsci*

### School of Systems Engineering; www.reading.ac.uk/sse

artificial intelligence, adv computer science/ and informatics, cybernetics, digital signal processing & communications, electronic engineering, IT, robotics, software engineering, systems engineering; BEng, BSc(Hons), FdSc, MEng, MPhil, MRes, MSc, PhD

### School of Construction Management and Engineering; www.reading.ac.uk/CME

building/quantity surveying, construction management, construction in emerging economies, design & management of sustainable built environment, built environment & surveying, project management, intelligent buildings, renewable energy, technology & sustainability; BSc(Hons), MPhil, MSc, PGDip, PhD

### School of Mathematical & Physical Sciences; www.smps.reading.ac.uk/

meteorology, computational mathematics, biometry, data assimilation & inverse methods in geography, financial economics mathematics, mathematics and financial & investment banking/economics/meteorology/psychology/statistics, applicable numerical mathematics, statistics/applied statistics; BSc(Hons), MMath, MPhil, MSc, PhD

### School of Human & Environmental Science; www.reading.ac.uk/shes

archaeology/with ancient history/classical studies/history/museum studies, environmental science, medieval archaeology, geoarchaeology, geography/physical/human, economics, environmental management/science, soils & environmental pollution; BSc(Hons), MSc, MA, MPhil, PhD

# ROBERT GORDON UNIVERSITY
www.rgu.ac.uk

## *Faculty of Health and Social Care*

### School of Applied Social Studies: www.rgu.ac.uk/social

applied social sciences, corporate responsibility & energy, social care/work, sociology; BA(Hons), GradCert, MSW, MSc, PGDip, PhD

### School of Health Sciences; www.rgu.ac.uk/health

Health Professions; Health & Exercise Professions; Laboratory, Biomedical & Sport Sciences

applied biomedical science, adv nursing/district nursing, bioscience, biomedicine, biochemistry, clinical biomechanics/pharmacological practice, health practice/promotion & public health, forensic & analytical science, clinical practice, diagnostic radiography, mental health nursing, nutrition, occupational therapy, pharmacy, physiotherapy, applied sport & exercise science, sports nutrition & dietetics, sport biomedicine, laboratory, biochemical & sport sciences, instrumental analytical science (proteomics & metabolomics/drug analysis & toxicology/sport biomedicine/oilfield chemicals), public health; BSc(Hons), CertHE, MPhil, MSc, PhD, MN, BN, MPhysiotherapy

### School of Nursing & Midwifery; www.rgu.ac.uk/nursing

acute/adult/children's/mental health/community nursing occupational health, adv clinical practice, children & young people, community health, midwifery; BN, DipHE, MPhil, MSc, PhD, MN, MRes, MNurs

### School of Pharmacy & Life Sciences; www.rgu.ac.uk/pharmacy-life

applied/biomedical science, adv pharmacy practice, bioscience, nutrition, dietetics, pharmacy, prescribing science, clinical pharmacy, forensic & analytical science, instrumental analytical science; MPharm, MSc, PGDip, PhD, DocProfPract

## *Aberdeen Business School; www.rgu.ac.uk/abs*

Accounting & Finance: accounting, finance, strategic accounting, financial management, oil & gas accounting

Management: int/business/management, business administration, management with HRM, marketing, management studies, project management, energy management, health, safety & risk management, international business/tourism management, oil & gas management, project management, PR, public administration, purchasing & supply chain management, quality management, events/fashion management, international hospitality & tourism

management, management & marketing, corporate communication & public affairs, international marketing management
Law: law, law & management, online law, construction law & arbitration, employment law, international commercial law/trade, oil & gas law, legal practice; BA/BA(Hons), DBA, DInfSc, LlB, LlM, MBA, MPA, MPhil, MSc, PGDip/Cert, PhD

## *Faculty of Design & Technology*

### School of Computing, Science & Digital Media; www.rgu.ac.uk/computing

business information systems, computer science, computer graphics & animation, computer network management & development, computer information systems technology, computing for internet & multimedia, information & network security, computing engineering with network management, digital media: design, production & development, computing information engineering, computing software with network management, information engineering/software technology, IT for oil & gas industry, multimedia development; BSc(Hons), MSc, PGCert/Dip

### School of Engineering; www.rgu.ac.uk/eng

electrical/electronic/mechanical/offshore engineering, oil & gas/drilling & well/petroleum production engineering, computer network management & design; BSc, BSc(Hons), MPhil, MSc, PhD

### Gray's School of Art, Design & Craft; www.rgu.ac.uk/grays

communication design, commercial photography/design, contemporary art practice, design for digital media, fashion & textile design, fine art, painting, 3D design; BA/BA(Hons), BDes/BDes(Hons), MDes, MRes, PGDip/MAa

### The Scott Sunderland School of Architecture and Built Environment; www.rgu.ac.uk/sss

architecture studies, architecture, architectural technology, construction/project management, design management, property development, quantity/surveying; GradDip, MArch, MSc, PhD, BSc(Hons)

## ROEHAMPTON UNIVERSITY
## www.roehampton.ac.uk

### Dept of Dance; www.roehampton.ac.uk/dance

ballet studies, dance anthropology/choreography/studies, SE Asia dance studies, choreography/& performance, community dancing, global dancing/identities & institutions; BA, MA, PGDip/Cert, MRes

### Dept of Drama, Theatre & Performance; www.roehampton.ac.uk/drama-theatre-and-performance

drama, drama studies, theatre & performance studies, performance & creative research; BA(Hons), MPhil, MRes, MA, PhD

### Dept of English & Creative Writing; www.roehampton.ac.uk/English-and-creative-writing

creative/& professional writing, modern literature & culture, English literature, children's literature; BA, MA, MPhil, PhD

### Dept of Humanities; www.roehampton.ac.uk/humanities

classical civilization, classics, history, philosophy, Christian ministry, historical research, studies in contemporary Catholicism, theology & religious studies, religion & gender, ministerial theology; BA, MTh, PGDip, MPhil, PhD

### Department of Education; www.roehampton.ac.uk/education

applied music studies/(education), applied psychology in education, art, craft and design education, education, education leadership & management, early childhood studies, English education, PGCE (primary education/secondary education), social research methods, special & inclusive education needs & inclusion, sports coaching, supporting learning & teaching; BA(Hons), BA/BSc, EdD, FdA, Froebel Cert and Grad Cert, MA, MPhil, PGCE Primary/Secondary, PhD

### Dept of Life Sciences: www.roehampton.ac.uk/life-sciences

anthropology, biological anthropology, social anthropology, biological sciences, biomedical sciences, biomechanics, health sciences, nutrition & health, ecology, clinical neuroscience/nutrition, life sciences, nutrition & health, obesity: risks & prevention, primate biology, behaviour & conservation, stress &

health, sport psychology, sport & exercise physiology/science/psychology, zoology; BA, BSc, MSC, MPhil, PGDip, PhD

### Dept of Media, Culture & Language; www.roehampton.ac.uk/media-culture-and-language

accessibility & film-making, applied linguistics & TESOL, audiovisual translation, English language & linguistics, EFL, journalism, film/& TV/screen cultures, language testing & assessment, mass communication, media & culture studies, modern languages/ translation, photography, Spanish, French, TESOL, translation and interpreting, media, culture & identity; BSc, BA, MA, MRes, MPhil, PGDip, PhD

### Dept of Psychology; www.roehampton.ac.uk/psychology

applied music psychology, art/psychotherapy, art & play therapy, drama therapy, counselling, counselling psychology/psychotherapy, forensic psychology, integrative counselling, psychology & communication, psychotherapy, play/music/drama/dance movement therapy, attachment studies, applied psychological research; BSc, PsychD, MA, MPhil, PhD

### Dept of Social Sciences; www.roehampton.ac.uk/social-sciences

criminology, human rights & society/international relations/policy & practice, sociology; BA/BSc, MA, PGDip/Cert, PhD

### Roehampton Business School; www.roehampton/business

business management & accounting/economics/ entrepreneurship/retail marketing/HRM/digital media, international business/management, marketing, international management with finance/HRM/ information systems/marketing, HRM, marketing & multimedia, web & creative technologies, finance, project mnagement; MBA, PGDip/Cert, BA/BSc, BSc(Hons), MSc, MPhil, PhD

## THE ROYAL ACADEMY OF DANCE
## www.rad.org.uk

ballet education, dance education, professional dancers' teaching diploma; BA, PGCert

## ROYAL ACADEMY OF DRAMATIC ART
## www.rada.org

acting, technical theatre & stage management, theatre lab/directing, text & performance; BA, MA, PGDip, FD

## ROYAL AGRICULTURAL UNIVERSITY
## www.rau.ac.uk

agriculture (livestock production, crop production, farm mechanisation, farm business, countryside management, agricultural science & sustainable soil management), animal science & management, adv farm management, agricultural & farm management, business management, equine business & management, equine science, food production & supply management, environmental conservation & heritage management, international & agricultural business management, international food & agribusiness, international rural development, real estate land management, property agency & management, rural/environmental estate management, rural/land management, sustainable agriculture & food security; FdSc, BSc(Hons), BSc(Hons) Top-up, GradDip, MSc, MA, MBA

## ROYAL BALLET SCHOOL
## www.royalballetschool.co.uk

classical ballet training, performing dancing/arts, professional dance; BTEC, NatDip

## ROYAL COLLEGE OF ART
## www.rca.ac.uk

### School of Architecture; www.rca.ac.uk/Default.aspx?ContentID=160131

architecture, interior design

### School of Communication; www.rca.ac.uk/Default.aspx?ContentID=160132

animation, information experience design, visual communication

### School of Design; www.rca.ac.uk/Default.aspx?ContentID=501976

design interactions/products, global innovation design engineering, service design, vehicle design

### School of Fine Art; www.rca.ac.uk/Default.aspx?ContentID=160134

painting, photography, printmaking, sculpture

### School of Humanities; www.rca.ac.uk/Default.aspx?ContentID=160135

critical writing in art & design, curating contemporary art, critical and historical studies, history of design

### School of Material; www.rca.ac.uk/Default.aspx?ContentID=160133

ceramics & glass, fashion menswear/womenswear, goldsmithing, metalwork & jewellery, silversmithing, textiles;MA, MPhil, PGCert, PhD

## ROYAL COLLEGE OF MUSIC
## www.rcm.ac.uk

advanced vocal performance, composition, composition for screen, conducting, contemporary culture, ensemble production, opera, performance, historical/orchestral performance, music/in context, performance studies, physics & musical performance, vocal studies; DipRCM, BMus, BSc, PGDip, MMus, DMus, GradDip, MPerf, MSc, ArtDip

## THE ROYAL COLLEGE OF ORGANISTS
## www.rco.org.uk

teaching, choral directing; CertRCO, ARCO, FRCO, LTRCO, DipCHD

## ROYAL CONSERVATOIRE OF SCOTLAND
## www.rcs.ac.uk

### School of Music

keyboard, education, vocal studies, opera, piano for dance, strings, woodwind, brass, repetiteurship, timpani & percussion, Scottish music, composition, conducting, jazz; BA(Hons), BMus(Hons), MA, MMus, MOpera, MPhil, PGDip, PhD

**School of Drama & Dance**

acting, classical & contemporary text, contemporary performance practice, digital film & TV, modern ballet, technical & production arts & design, musical theatre/directing/performance, modern ballet;BA(-Hons), BMus(Hons), MA, MMus, MOpera, MPhil, PGDip, PhD

## ROYAL NORTHERN COLLEGE OF MUSIC
## www.rncm.ac.uk

composition, conducting & repetiteurship studies, chamber music, keyboard studies, strings, vocal studies, wind, brass & percussion, music, musicology, music psychology, orchestral studies, popular music practice/performance, solo performance, specialist instrument techniques; BA(Hons), MusB, MMus, MPhil, PhD, BA(Hons)

## UNIVERSITY OF ST ANDREWS
## www.st-andrews.ac.uk

### *Faculty of Arts*

**School of Art History;**

www-ah.st-andrews.ac.uk

art history (with numerous joint degrees), history of photography, archaeology, modern languages (French & German) & ancient history, museum & gallery studies: GradCert, GradDip, MA, MLitt, MPhil, PhD

**School of Classics; www.st-andrews.ac.uk/classics**

ancient history, classics, classical studies, Greek, Latin; MA, MLitt, MPhil, PGDip, PhD

**School of Economics & Finance;**

www.st-andrews.ac.uk/economics

analytical finance, finance, applied economics, economics, international strategy & economics, financial economics, money, banking & finance, microeconomics, macroeconomics, sustainable development; BSc, MA, MSc, MPhil, PhD, MA/BSc

**School of English; www.st-andrews.ac.uk/english**

creative writing, English, medieval English, 18th century, Romantic 18th century studies, Scottish/Irish/American literature; GradDip, MA, MLitt, MPhil, PhD

**School of History; www.st-andrews.ac.uk/history**

Arabic, book history, central & Eastern European studies, environmental history, history, Iranian studies, medieval history/& archaeology, Middle East studies/history, early/modern history, reformation studies, Scottish historical studies/history; GradDip, MA, DLitt, MPhil, PhD

**School of International Relations;**

www.st-andrews.ac.uk/intrel

international relations (numerous jt hons degrees), international security studies, international political theory, Middle East & Central Asian security studies, peace & conflict, terrorism studies; MA, MLitt, MPhil, MRes, PhD

**School of Management;**

www.st-andrews.ac.uk/management

sociology of finance, international marketing, HRM, scenario thinking, non-governmental organisations, corporate social responsibility, accounting and reporting, consuming culture, social history of advertising, entrepreneurship and small business development, change complexity and innovation, international business/banking, strategies for global business management, social theory and work organisations, sustainable development and management, creative industries, management of change, corporate finance and control, finance & management, management & information technology, marketing, management studies; BSc, DipRes, MA, MLitt, MSc, MRes, PhD

**School of Modern Languages;**

www.st-andrews.ac.uk/modlangs

Arabic, comparative literature, cultural identity studies, French/German/Italian studies, language/& linguistics, modern Hispanic literature & film, Russian, Central & Eastern European studies, Persian,

Spanish, Spanish & Latin American studies, medieval studies, language & linguistics; DLang, MA, MLitt, MPhil, PGDip, PhD

### School of Philosophical, Anthropological & Film Studies; www.st-andrews.ac.uk/philosophy

Philosophy: analytical/classical/philosophy, logic & philosophy of science, philosophers of Scottish enlightenment, Kant, metaphysics, political philosophy, advanced logic, philosophy of perception, contemporary metaphysics, origins & history of analytical philosophy

Social Anthropology: African studies, social anthropology & Pacific studies, Amerindian studies, anthropology, art & perception, numerous jt degrees

Film Studies: film studies, film culture/techniques & aesthetics, theory of entertainment film theory & history, world cinema

Music: opera, advanced performance, Scottish/bagpipe/electronic music;

BSc, MA, MLitt, MPhil, MRes, PhD, PGDip

## *Faculty of Divinity*

### School of Divinity; www.st-andrews.ac.uk/divinity

bible & the contemporary world, biblical studies, divinity, Hebrew, New Testament, Old Testament, theological studies/interpretation of scripture, biblical language & literature, scripture & theology, systematic & historical theology, theology, imagination & the arts; BD, MA, MLitt, MPhil, MTheol, PGDip, PhD

## *Faculty of Medicine*

### Bute Medical School; www.medicine.st-andrews.ac.uk

health psychology, medicine, surgery, community health, molecular medicine; BSc, MD, MPhil, MSc, PhD, MRes

## *Faculty of Science*

### School of Biology; www.biology.st-andrews.ac.uk

behavioural biology, biochemistry, biology, biology & geology/psychology, cell biology, cell structure & function, comparative physiology, ecology & conservation/evolutionary biology, biology/& geography/geology/psychology, marine biology, molecular biology, neuroscience, psychology with biology, zoology, marine mammal science, ecosystem-based management of marine systems, behavioural & neural sciences, sustainable aquaculture; BSc, MPhil, MRes, PhD, PG Dip/MSc

### School of Chemistry; www.st-andrews.ac.uk/chemistry

biomolecular/chemical sciences, biological chemistry, chemical science, inorganic/physical/organic chemistry, materials chemistry, medicinal chemistry; BSc, MChem, MSci, PGDip, PhD, PG Dip/MSc

### School of Computer Science; www.cs.st-andrews.ac.uk

advanced/computer science, AI, human-computer interaction, internet computer science, information technology, computing/management & IT, networks & distributed systems, software engineering; BSc, MPhil, MSc, PhD, MSci(Hons)

### School of Geography & Geosciences; www.st-andrews.ac.uk/gg

environmental earth science, evolutionary biology, chemistry & geology, environmental biology & geology, geography, geoscience, geology, general sciences, earth sciences, managing environmental change; BSc, MA, MLitt, MPhil, MRes, MSc, PGCert, PGDip, PhD, MGeol

### School of Mathematics & Statistics; www.maths.mcs.st-andrews.ac.uk

applied mathematics/statistics, mathematics, pure mathematics, statistics; BSc, GradDip, MA, MLitt, MMath, MPhil, MSc, PhD

### School of Physics & Astronomy; www.st-andrews.ac.uk/physics

astrophysics, physics, theoretical physics, photonics & optoelectronic devices, physics & mathematics/computer science/logic & philosophy of science; BSc, EngDoc, MPhys, MSc, PhD, MSci

### School of Psychology & Neuroscience; www.psy.st-andrews.ac.uk

behavioural & neural sciences, evolutionary & comparative psychology, learning disabilities, neuroscience, perception, psychology, health psychology, adult support, protection & safeguarding; BSc, MA, MPhil, MRes, MSc, PhD

# UNIVERSITY OF SALFORD
**www.salford.ac.uk**

## *College of Arts & Social Sciences: www.famss.salford.ac.uk*

### School of Arts & Media; www.salford.ac.uk/arts-media

3D design, animation, computer and video games, English, film studies, graphic design, journalism (broadcast/multimedia/news), journalism and English, media technology, music (interactive music and studio production/popular music and recording/popular musicology), performance (comedy practices/contemporary practice/dance theatre/drama and theatre/media performance), photography, TV and radio, visual arts, art and design: communication design/contemporary fine art/creative education/creative technology/design management/museum and heritage interpretation/product innovation, children's digital media production, digital performance, digital production for TV and film: post production, fashion innovation: communication/design/digital/entrepreneurship, fiction film production, film screenwriting, international and online journalism, journalism, ludic interfaces, media, music, performance, social media, television documentary production, TV and radio scriptwriting, wildlife documentary production; BA(Hons), BSc(Hons), PGDip, MA, PGDip/Cert, PhD, MRes

### School of Humanities, Languages & Social Sciences; www.salford.ac.uk/humanities

contemporary history & politics, contemporary military & international history, criminology/& sociology, drama, creative writing, English, English language/& linguistics/English literature, international relations & politics, law with criminology, modern language studies (Arabic/French/Spanish/French and EFL/Italian), politics, psychology & criminology, sociology, intelligence & security services, translation & interpreting (combinations of Arabic/EFL/Chinese/French/German/Italian), international relations & globalisation, literary culture & production, terrorism & security, TESOL & applied linguistics, translating for foreign management & business; BA(Hons), MA, PGDip/Cert

## *College of Business & Law; www.salford.ac.uk/cbl*

### Salford Business School; www.salford.ac.uk/business-school

accounting and finance, business and economics/financial management/management/tourism management, business information technology, business management with sport, HRM, international business, international events management, marketing, business and management studies/with law/financial management/HRM/international business management/marketing management/quantitative business management, hospitality and tourism management, hospitality management, leisure and tourism management, sport and leisure management, tourism management, financial services management, global management, HRM/D, information systems management, international banking and finance/business/corporate finance/events management, Islamic banking and finance, management, procurement, logistics and supply chain management, project management, the Salford MBA;

BA(Hons), BSc(Hons), CertHE, DipHE, FD, GradCert/dip, MA, MBA, MPhil, ProfDip, ProfPGDip, PhD

### Salford Law School; www.salford.ac.uk/law

construction law & practice, environmental/health case law, international business law & regulation, international social justice, law/& criminality/finance/Spanish; LlB, LlM, MA, MSc, PGCert/Dip

## *College of Health & Social Care; www.fhsc.salford.ac.uk*

### School of Health Sciences; www.salford.ac.uk/health-sciences

sports science (strength & conditioning), diagnostic radiography, exercise, physical activity & health, occupational therapy, physiotherapy, podiatry, prosthetics & orthotics, psychology & counselling/criminology, psychology, sport rehabilitation, adv medical imaging (radiology/ultrasound), adv occupational therapy, advancing physiotherapy, applied psychology (therapies), dental implantology, lower limb health, disease & rehabilitation, upper limb orthopaedics, media psychology, nuclear medicine imaging, psycho-oncology, public health, sports injury rehabilitation, strength & conditioning, surgical practice, trauma orthopaedics; BSc(Hons), MSc, PgDip/PgCert, MPhil, PhD

### School of Nursing, Midwifery & Social Work; www.salford.ac.uk/nmsw

midwifery, nursing/RN children & young people's/ adult/mental health, counselling & psychotherapy, integrated practice in learning disability nursing/& social work, social policy, adv practice (health & social care/neonatal), cognitive behavioural psychotherapy/therapy, child & adolescent mental health, counselling & psychotherapy, international hospital & health care management, leadership & management for health care practice, nursing, (education, research, practice, international), midwifery, health & social care, health care, counselling, adult care, child care, therapeutic interventions, enhancing professional health care practice; BSc(Hons), MA, ProfDoc, MSc, PgDip/PgCert

## *College of Science & Technology; www.fsee.salford.ac.uk*

### School of the Built Environment; www.sobe.salford.ac.uk

architectural design & technology, BIM & integrated design, building/quantity surveying, construction project management, construction law & practice/ management, project management in construction, real estate development/management, real estae & property management; BSc(Hons), DBEnv, DConst-Mangt, DRealEst, MSc, MPhil, PGDip/Cert, PhD, ProfDoc

### School of Computing, Science & Engineering; www.cse.salford.ac.uk

audio acoustics, adv computer science, aeronautical engineering, aircraft engineering/technology with pilot studies, animation with virtual environments, civil/& architectural engineering, computer networks/science, data telecommunications & networks, databases and web-based systems, digital media & audio production, environmental acoustics, gas engineering & management, industrial & commercial combustion engineering, information security, internet, mathematics, mechanical engineering, multimedia & internet technology, petroleum & gas engineering, physics with acoustics, pure & applied/ physics, robotics & embedded systems, software engineering, structural engineering, transport engineering & planning, video, audio & social technologies; BEng, BSc(Hons), HND, MEng, MEnt(Tech), MPhys, MSc, PGDip, PG(Tech)

### School of Environmental & Life Sciences; www.els.salford.ac.uk

applied microbiology, biology, human biology & infectious diseases, wildlife & practical conservation, wildlife conservation with zoo biology, zoology

Biomedicine: biochemistry, biomedical science, pharmaceutical science

Environment: environmental studies/health/management, geography

Bioscience: analytical bioscience & drug design, biotechnology, molecular parasitology & vector biology

Geography: GIS, geography

Environmental Studies: environmental assessment & management, environmental/& public health, occupational safety & health, safety, health & environment

Housing & Regeneration: housing, regeneration & sustainability

Wildlife: wildlife documentary production; BSc(Hons), BA(Hons), MSc, MA, FD

## *Degrees validated by University of Salford offered at:*

---

## RIVERSIDE COLLEGE, HALTON
www.riversidecollege.ac.uk

business & management, childcare, counselling, health and social care, sport, teaching in the lifelong learning sector; Dip, FD, FdSc, PGDip, BA(Hons), BSc(Hons)

# UNIVERSITY OF SHEFFIELD
# www.sheffield.ac.uk

## *Faculty of Arts & Humanities; www.sheffield.ac.uk/faculty/arts-and-humanities*

### Dept of Archaeology; www.sheffield.ac.uk/archaeology

archaeology, archaeology, religion, theology & the bible, archaeological materials, archaeology & history/Slavonic studies/Hispanic studies/French/German, Aegean archaeology, archaeology of the classical Mediterranean, classical & ancient world, classical & historical archaeology, environmental archaeology & palaeoeconomy, prehistorical archaeology, experimental archaeology, geoarchaeology, human osteology and funerary archaeology, landscape archaeology, material culture studies, palaeoanthropology, cultural heritage management, medieval archaeology, environmental archaeology & palaeoeconomy, osteoarchaeology, cultural heritage management; BA(Hons), BSc(Hons), MA, MPhil, MSc, PhD, MSt

### Dept of Biblical Studies; www.sheffield.ac.uk/biblicalstudies

archaeology, religion, theology & the bible & ancient cultures, religion, theology & the Bible/& linguistics, religion, conflict & the media, biblical literature and English, French/German/philosophy & religion, theology and music, theological studies, social scientific biblical studies; BA(Hons), MA, PGDip/Cert

### Dept of French; www.sheffield.ac.uk/french

French studies, French & archaeology/business management/economics/English/German/Hispanic studies/history/journalism/linguistics/music/philosophy/politics/religion/Russian, modern languages, French & Dutch, Czech, Japanese & Luxembourgish; BA(Hons), MA, MPhil, PhD

### School of English Literature, Language and Linguistics; www.sheffield.ac.uk/english

19th-century studies, applied linguistics with TESOL, creative writing, cultures of the British Isles, English language studies, English literature, English language & linguistics, language acquisition, language & literature, English & theatre studies, English studies, theatre & performance studies; BA(Hons), MA, MPhil, PhD

### Dept of Germanic Studies; www.sheffield.ac.uk/german

German studies, German & archaeology/business management/economics/English/French/Hispanic studies/history/journalism/linguistics/music/philosophy/politics/religion/Russian, modern languages, comparative Germanic linguistics, linguistics of Dutch, Dutch literature, modern German political culture, post-war German politics, 19th/20th century German literary writing; BA(Hons), MPhil, PhD

### Dept of Hispanic Studies; www.sheffield.ac.uk/hispanic

Hispanic studies & archaeology/business management/economics/English/French/history/journalism/linguistics/music/philosophy/politics/religion/Russian, applied Hispanic studies, Catalan studies, Portuguese studies, Latin American studies, modern language studies; BA(Hons), MA, MPhil, PhD

### Dept of History; www.sheffield.ac.uk/history

history, 18th/19th-century studies, American history, early/modern history, historical research, international/medieval history, numerous jt degrees; BA(Hons), MA, MPhil, PhD

### School of Languages & Cultures; www.sheffield.ac.uk/slc

Catalan, Czech, Dutch, French, German, Hispanic studies, European gender studies, cultural narratives, intercultural communication, modern languages, multilingual information management, Polish, Russian, Russian and Slavonic studies, Spanish, Luxembourgish, screen translation, translation studies; BA(Hons), MA, MPhil, PhD

### Department of Music; www.sheffield.ac.uk/music

ethnomusicology, music, music management/performance, music psychology in education, psychology of music/for musicians, sonic arts, world music, numerous jt degrees; BA(Hons), BMus(Hons), DPhil, MA, MMus, PhD

### Dept of Philosophy; www.sheffield.ac.uk/philosophy

philosophy, metaphysics, epistemology, logic, philosophy of language & the mind, ethics, politics &

value, political theory, cognitive studies, numerous joint degrees; BA(Hons), MA, MPhil, PhD, PGDip

### Russian & Slavonic Studies; www.sheffield.ac.uk/russian

Russian studies, Polish studies, Czech, translation studies, screen translation, intercultural communication, multilingual information management, modern language studies, gender studies in Europe, numerous jt degree courses; BA(Hons), MA, MPhil, PhD

## *Faculty of Engineering; www.sheffield.ac.uk/faculties/engineering*

### Dept of Aerospace Engineering; www.sheffield.ac.uk/aerospace

aerospace materials/engineering, aerospace engineering with private pilot instruction, aerostructures & aerodynamics, adv manufacturing technologies, avionics, control systems, mechatronics & robotics; BEng, MEng, MPhil, MSc, PhD, PGDip, MSc(Res)

### Dept of Automatic Control & Systems Engineering; www.sheffield.ac.uk/acse

control systems, gas turbine control, computer systems engineering, electronic/mechanical systems engineering, mechatronic & robotic engineering, systems & control engineering; BEng, MEng, MPhil, MSc, PhD

### Dept of Bioengineering; www.sheffield.ac.uk/bioengineering

bioengineering, biomedical engineering, biomaterials science with tissue engineering, biomaterials & regenerative medicine, dental matetials science, biological systems bioprocessing, medical devices & systems; BEng, MEng

### Dept of Chemical & Biological Engineering; www.sheffield.ac.uk/cbe

biological and bioprocessing engineering, chemical engineering, chemical engineering with energy/chemistry/biotechnology/nuclear technology, chemical & process engineering, environmental & energy engineering, fuel technology, process safety & loss prevention; BEng, MEng, MPhil, MSc, MSc(Eng), PhD

### Dept of Civil & Structural Engineering; www.sheffield.ac.uk/civil

architectural engineering design, civil/structural engineering, civil structures, blast protection design, contaminant hydrogeology, earthquake & civil engineering dynamics, environmental management of urban land & water, steel construction, structural/& concrete engineering, structural engineering & architecture, urban water engineering & management; BEng, MEng, MPhil, MSc, PGDip/Cert, PhD

### Dept of Computer Science; www.sheffield.ac.uk/dcs

advanced computer science, advanced software engineering, computer science with speech & language processing, enterprise computing, IT for business, software engineering, AI, data communications, information systems, information technology management for business, software systems & internet technology; BEng, BSc, MComp, MEng, MPhil, MSc, MSc(Eng), PhD

### Dept of Electronic & Electrical Engineering; www.sheffield.ac.uk/eee

avionic systems, computer vision engineering, data communications, digital electronics, semiconductor photonics & electronics, electrical/communications/electronic engineering, microelectronics, wireless communcations systems; BEng, MEng, MPhil, MSc, PhD

### Dept of Materials Science & Engineering; www.sheffield.ac.uk/materials

aerospace materials, adv metallurgy, materials science & engineering, biomaterials/& regenerative medicine, metallurgy, ceramic science & engineering, polymers & polymer composites, adv solid state chemistry, nuclear environmental science/technology/engineering, nanomaterials for nanoengineering, bionanotechnology; BEng, EngD, MEng, MPhil, MSc, MRes, PhD, MMet

### Dept of Mechanical Engineering; www.sheffield.ac.uk/mecheng

advanced mechanical engineering, advanced manufacturing technology, aerodynamics & aerostructures, automotive engineering, mechatronics & robotics, mechanical engineering with Spanish/French/Italian/German/industrial management, nuclear technology; BEng, MEng, MPhil, MSc, MSc(Res), PhD

## *Faculty of Medicine, Dentistry & Health; www.sheffield.ac.uk/faculties/medicine-dentistry-health*

### The Medical School; www.sheffield.ac.uk/medicine

cancer, human metabolism/nutrition, infection & immunity, medicine, medical education, molecular/& genetic medicine, musculoskeletal science, nephrology, neuroscience, orthoptics, surgery, vision & strabismus, pharmacokinetics/dynamics; BMedSci, MBChB, MD, PhD, PGCert/Dip

**Dept of Cardiovascular Science; www.sheffield.ac.uk/cardiovascularscience**
cell biology, coronary artery disease, haemostasis, medical physics, molecular medicine – cardiovascular pathway, human nutrition, molecular medicine & genetics, non-mammalian models, pulmonary vascular, platelets, inflammatory signals, reproductive & developmental medicine, translational neuroscience, vascular biology; MPhil, PhD, DM

**School of Clinical Dentistry; www.sheffield.ac.uk/dentalschool**
clinical dentistry, dental hygiene and therapy, dental implantology, dental materials science, dental public health, dental surgery, dentistry, endodontics, oral pathology, oral health, orthodontics, paediatric dentistry, periodontics, prosthodontics, social science & oral health; BDS, ClinDent, Diploma, MSc, MClinD, MDPH, MMedSci, MPhil, PhD

**Health & Related Research; www.sheffield.ac.uk/scharr**
adv emergency care, clinical research, health services, public health (management & leadership), economics/health economics & decision modelling, European public health, health informatics, international health & technical assessment, pricing & reimbursement, psychotherapy studies, social science & health, statistics appl to medicine; MSc, PGDip/Cert, MPH, MEuro PubHealth

**Dept of Human Communication Sciences; www.sheffield.ac.uk/hcs**
speech & cleft palate studies, child communication studies, clinical/human communication sciences, language & communication impairment in children, speech/difficulties/science; AdvCert, BMedSci(Hons), BSc(Hons), MMedSci, MPhil, MSc, PGCert/Dip, PhD

**Dept of Human Metabolism; www.sheffield.ac.uk/humanmetabolism**
molecular medicine, translational neuroscience, human nutrition, vision & strabismus; B/MMedSci, MSc, MRCPsych, PGCert, PhD, MD

**Dept of Infection & Immunity; www.sheffield.ac.uk/infectionandimmunity**
molecular medicine, translational neuroscience; BMedSci, MSc, MRCPsych

**Dept of Neuroscience; www.sheffield.ac.uk/neuroscience**
translational neuroscience; BMedSci, MSc, MRCPsych

**Dept of Oncology; www.sheffield.ac.uk/oncology**
clinical oncology, cancer studies, supportive care, surgical oncology, urology, inflammation & tumour targeting, translational medicine; MSc, MSD, PhD

**School of Nursing & Midwifery; www.sheffield.ac.uk/snm**
acute care, cancer care, adult nursing studies, advanced practice, health & social care studies/human sciences, high dependency & critical care, infection control, long term conditions, maternity care, midwifery, neonatal intensive care, nursing studies, occupational health nursing, palliative care, public health, primary/critical/cancer/neonatal intensive care; BMedSci, MMedSci, MMid, MPhil, PGCert, PhD

## *The Faculty of Science; www.sheffield.ac.uk/faculties/science*

**Dept of Animal & Plant Sciences; www.sheffield.ac.uk/aps**
animal behaviour, biology, conservation & biodiversity, ecology, plant sciences, evolution & behaviour, plant-environment interaction/science, ecology & conservation biology/environment, plant & microbial biology, molecular science, plant science, plant-environment interchange, population & community ecology, zoology; MBiolSci, PhD, MPhil, MEnv Sci

**Dept of Biomedical Science; www.sheffield.ac.uk/bms**
biomedical science/with biomaterials & tissue engineering, molecular & cellular basis of human disease, developmental & cell biology, integrated ecology, molecular biology, pathobiology, physiology & pharmacology, medical science, stem cell & regenerative medicine; BSc(Hons), MSc, PhD

**Dept of Chemistry; www.sheffield.ac.uk/chemistry**
chemistry, polymers for advanced technologies, science communication, biological chemistry, chemical physics; BSc, MChem, MPhil, MPhys, PhD

**Dept of Molecular Biology & Biotechnology; www.sheffield.ac.uk/mbb**
biochemistry, biology, genetics, human & molecular biosciences, medical genetics/microbiology/

biochemistry, microbiology, molecular/cell biology/ biology, mechanistic biology, microbrewing; BSc(Hons), MBiolSci, PhD

### Dept of Physics & Astronomy; www.sheffield.ac.uk/physics

astronomy, astrophysics, medical physics, nanoscale science and technology, nanoelectronics & nanomechanics, physics, physics & philosophy/computer science, theoretical physics; BS(Hons), MPhys, MSc, PhD

### Dept of Psychology; www.sheffield.ac.uk/psychology

cognitive studies/neuroscience, cognitive & computational neuroscience, human neuroimaging, science communication, psychology, psychological research studies; BA(Hons), BSc(Hons), DClinPsych, MA, MPhil, MSc, PhD

### School of Mathematics & Statistics; www.sheffield.ac.uk/maths

mathematics, statistics, financial maths, statistics with medical applications; BSc, MSc, PhD, MMath, MComp

## *Faculty of Social Science; www.sheffield.ac.uk/faculty/social-science*

### School of Architecture; www.sheffield.ac.uk/architecture

architecture, architectural design, architecture regeneration, designing learning environments, structural engineering & architecture, digital design & international built environment, sustainable architectural studies, urban design; BA(Hons), MArch, MPhil, MSc, PhD, MEng

### School of East Asian Studies; www.sheffield.ac.uk/seas

Chinese studies, East Asian studies, Japanese studies, Korean studies, teaching Chinese as a foreign language; BA(Hons), MA, PhD

### Dept of Economics; www.sheffield.ac.uk/economics

development economics & policy, accounting & financial management & economics, business finance, economics, economics & mathematics/politics/philosophy/finance/business management, financial economics, health economics, international finance and economics, money, banking & finance; Adv Cert, BA(Hons), BSc(Hons), MSc, PhD

### Sheffield School of Law; www.sheffield.ac.uk/law

biotechnological law and ethics, commercial law, law (European & international), law with French/German/Spanish/criminology, social policy & criminology, European health law & policy, French/German/Spanish, law, international law, international criminology, international commercial law & practice, global policy & law, European law, politics & governance, legal practice; LlB, LlM, MAPhil, PhD, GradDip

### Sheffield Management School; www.sheffield.ac.uk/management

accounting & financial management/& economics/informatics/mathematics, HRM, information systems management, business management & economics/informatics/sociology/social policy/various foreign language studies/mathematics, entrepreneurship, enterprise computing, global marketing management, information systems management, international business management/management & marketing, leadership, management, logistics & supply chain management, management (creative & cultural industries/international business), marketing management practice, occupational/work psychology; MSc, MPhil, PhD, Sheffield MBA, ExecMBA

### Dept of Politics; www.sheffield.ac.uk/politics

politics, European law/& global affairs/governance & politics, contemporary global security, international politics/relations/history/political economy/security studies, sociology, global politics and law, security/justice, globalisation & development, governance & public policy, politics/ & history/sociology/economics/philosophy/French/German/Russian, European global affairs, international studies/politics & security studies, philosophy, political theory; BA, MA, MPhil, PhD

### Dept of Sociological Studies; www.sheffield.ac.uk/socstudies

business management & social policy/sociology, social policy & criminology, global & international/social policy, social policy/work, sociology & English language/history/politics/criminology, professional practice with children & families; BA(Hons), MA, MPhil, PhD

### Dept of Town & Regional Planning; www.sheffield.ac.uk/trp

architecture/ & town & regional planning, commercial property, geography & planning, international development & planning, planning/& development, town & regional planning, urban studies/design & planning, TR; BA(Hons), MA, MPlan, PhD

### The School of Education; www.sheffield.ac.uk/education

education, culture & childhood, education, education: early childhood education/working with communities, globalising education, policy & practice, PGCE (English, geography, history, mathematics, modern languages & science), school direct, initial teacher education, psychology & education, languages, education & research, educational research; EdD, MA, MEd, MPhil, PhD, PCHE

### Dept of Geography; www.sheffield.ac.uk/geography

arid land studies, environmental science/change & international development, geoarchaeology, geography & planning, human geography, international development, polar & alpine change, social & cultural geography, environmental analysis of terrestrial systems, physical geography, social & spatial inequalities; BA(Hons), BSc(Hons), MEnvSci, PhD

### School of Information; www.sheffield.ac.uk/is

accounting & financial management & informatics, business management & information, electronic & digital library management, health informatics, information management, information systems/management, librarianship, multilingual information management; MA, MChem, MSc, MSc(Res), PhD/MPhil

### Dept of Journalism Studies; www.sheffield.ac.uk/journalism

global/magazine/web journalism, journalism studies, international political communication, broadcast & web journalism, print/science journalism; BA, MPhil, PhD

### Dept of Landscape; www.sheffield.ac.uk/landscape

landscape architecture, landscape management, architecture & landscape, landscape studies, landscape research; BA(Hons), BSc(Hons), MA, PGDip, PhD, MLA, BA/BSc

## SHEFFIELD HALLAM UNIVERSITY
## www.shu.ac.uk

### *Faculty of Arts, Computing, Engineering & Science; www.shu.ac.uk/art/faculties.aces*

### Art & Design; www.shu.ac.uk/prospectus/subject/art-design/

creative art practice, fashion design, fine art, graphic design, industrial practice/design, interior design, packaging design, product design: jewellery & fashion/furniture, product design; BA(Hons), MA, MArt, MDes

### Media, PR & Journalism; www.shu.ac.uk/prospectus/subject/media-pr-journalism/

international broadcast journalism, PR, film & media production, media, sports journalism, international documentary production, cultural policy & management, marketing communication & advertising, photography, PR & media, games development; BA(Hons), MA, MPhil, PhD, PGCert/Dip

### Computing; www.shu.ac.uk/prospectus/subject/computing/

animation for special effects/computer games, applied computing, big data analysis, business information systems, business & ICT, computing, computer & network engineering/information security, computer science, computer security with forensics, computer & network engineering, database professionals, digital media production, electronics/management & IT, enterprise systems professional, forensic & security technologies, games & interactive technology, games/software design/development, interactive media with animation, IT professional (databases), IT with business studies/& management (data bases), informatics, information systems/security/with SAP, internet media with animation, internet & management, mobile computing applications, multimedia technology, networking technology & management/design/management, software engineering, web & cloud computing, web systems design; BEng, BSc(Hons), FDSc, GradDip, HND, MComp, MSc, MPhil, PhD

### Engineering; www.shu.ac.uk/prospectus/subject/engineering/

advanced engineering/management, aeronautical/aerospace/electronic engineering, advanced design/aeronautical materials engineering/engineering metals, automation & control engineering, automotive engineering, automotive design/manufacturing engineering/technology, computer & network engineering, electrical & electronic engineering, energy engineering, food engineering, forensic engineering, intelligent robotics, industrial management, integrated engineering, materials engineering, mechanical engineering, mobile computing applications, product design, railway engineering, sports technology/engineering, telecommunication engineering; BSc(Hons), BEng, FdSc, MBA, MSc, PhD

### Mathematics; www.shu.ac.uk/mathematics

specialist teaching, education with QTS, mathematics education, mathematics, PGCE secondary mathematics, subject knowledge/mathematics; BSc(Hons), MSc, PhD, PGCE

### Media Arts; www.shu.ac.uk/prospectus/subject/media-arts/

animation/& special effects, digital media production, fashion & media, media, interactive media, games design/software development, international documentary production, fine art, journalism, games & interactive media technology, photography, PR & media; BA(Hons), MA, MComp, MArt, MSc

## *Faculty of Development & Society; www.shu.ac.uk/faculties/ds*

### Architecture & Planning; www.shu.ac.uk/prosectus/subject/architecture-and-planning

architecture & environmental development, architectural technology, architecture, technical architecture, PGCE art & technology; BSc(Hons), MSc, PGDip/Cert, PGCE

### Built Environment; www.shu.ac.uk/prospectus/subject/construction-building-surveying/

architectural technology, architecture, construction & community management, environmental design, building surveying/studies, built environment, construction/management & real estate, planning & property development, project management, quantity surveying, real estate; BSc(Hons), HNC, HND, MPhil, MSc, PGDip/Cert, PhD

### Criminology & Community Justice; www.shu.ac.uk/prospectus/subject/law/

criminology & psychology/sociology/politics, law & criminology, forensic criminology/science/law, international commercial law, English & French law; BEng, BSc(Hons), FdSc, MA/PgDip/PgCert, MSc

### Education; www.shu.ac.uk/prospectus/subject/education-studies/

Asperger's syndrome, autism spectrum, children & playwork, early/childhood studies, early years/education with QTS/teaching, design & technology, education, educational studies with psychology & counselling, English & educational studies, languages & TESOL, learning & teaching in HE/in primary education with QTS, mentoring & coaching in educational leadership/early years mathematics with education, PE & school sport, post-16 education & training, technologically enhanced learning, analysis & change, teaching & learning in the primary sector/with QTS/early years, special needs coordination, education studies, learning & skills, primary ed with QTS, design & technology/science with education & QTS, PGCE (early years education, learning & skills, mathematics education, primary, secondary – broad range of taught subjects – secondary citizenship), post-16 education & training, youth work; BA(Hons), CertE, EdD, FdA, MA, MPhil, MSc, PGCert/Dip, PhD, PGCE

### Environment; www.shu.ac.uk/prospectus/subject/environment/

environmental management/conservation/science; BSc(Hons), MPlan, MSc/PGDip/PGCert

### English; www.shu.ac.uk/prospectus/subject/english/

creative writing, writing, English & history, English/language/literature, TESOL, English language teaching; BA(Hons), MA, PgDip, MPhil, PhD

### History; www.shu.ac.uk/prospectus/subject/history/

history, English & history, criminology, politics, local & global history, imperialism & culture; BA(Hons), MA, PGDip, MPhil, PhD

### Stage & Screen; www.shu.ac.uk/prospectus/subject/stage-screen/

animation & visual effects, film studies, film and media/production, international documentary production, performance & professional practice/for stage & screen, film & screenwriting; BA(Hons), FdA, MA, MA/PGDip/PGCert

### Geography; www.shu.ac.uk/prospectus/subject/geography/

geography/with planning, GIS, human geography; BA(Hons), BSc(Hons), MSc, PGDip/Cert

### Forensics; www.shu.ac.uk/forensics

analytical chemistry, biochemical laboratory sciences, biomedical sciences, biology, biotechnology, chemistry, human biology, molecular & cell biology, analytical criminology/engineering/psychology, intelligence & forensics management, forensic & security technologies, forensic science, pharmaceutical analysis, pharmacology & biotechnology; BSc(Hons), FdSc, MSc

### Law; www.shu.ac.uk/prospectus/subject/law/

antisocial behavioural law & strategy, business law, criminality & international commercial law, English & French law, forensic & security techniques, forensic engineering, forensic accounting/criminology/psychology/science, law, law and criminology, mâîtrise en droit Frañcais; LlB, LLM, MSc, PGCert/Dip

### Planning, Regeneration & Housing; www.shu.ac.uk/planning/

geography & planning, GIS, human geography, transport/planning and management, urban and regional/environmental planning/building, urban regeneration; BA(Hons), BSc(Hons), MPlanning and Transport, MSc/PGDip, DipHE

### Psychology; www.shu.ac.uk/psychology

psychology, applied cognitive neuroscience, cognitive analytic therapy, criminology & psychology, developmental/forensic/industrial/organizational psychology, education with psychology & counselling, health psychology, psychology & sociology, sexual & relationship psychotherapy, sport & exercise psychology; BSc(Hons), MRes/PGDip/PGCert, MSc

### Sociology & Politics; www.shu.ac.uk/prospectus/subject/sociology-politics/

applied social science, business, cultural studies, criminology, sociology, education, health & society, history, human geography, international relations, politics, psychology/& sociology, public health, social sciences, social work, planning and policy, youth & community work, working with children, young people & families; BA(Hons), GradDip, MA, MPhil/PhD, MRes/PgDip/PgCert

## *Faculty of Health & Wellbeing; www.shu.ac.uk/faculties/hwb*

### Sport and Active Lifestyles; www.shu.ac.uk/prospectus/subject/sport-active-lifestyles/

PE & youth sport, sport performance/coaching, sport, culture & community/society, sport & coaching, sport journalism/technology/engineering, physical activity, health & exercise science, secondary physical education, sports journalism, sport & exercise science, international/sport business management, physical education & youth sport, sport technology; BA(Hons), BSc(Hons), MA, MSc, PgDip/Cert, PRofDoc

### Biosciences & Chemistry; www.shu.ac.uk/bio/

analytical chemistry, biology, biomedical laboratory science, biosciences, biotechnology, chemistry, forensic science, human biology, molecular & cell biology, pharmaceutical analysis, pharmacology and biotechnology, secondary science; BSc(Hons), MSc/PGDip/PGCert, ProfDocBiomedSci

### Diagnostic Radiography; www.shu.ac.uk/prospectus/subject/diagnostic-radiography/

advanced diagnostic imaging practice, applying radiography, breast imaging & diagnosis, diagnostic radiography, medical imaging, medical ultrasound, radiological studies, health & social care; DocProf Studies (Health and Social Care), BA(Hons), BSc(Hons), MSc/PGDip/PGCert

### Management and Leadership; www.shu.ac.uk/faculties/hwb/cpod/

clinical audit/management, health & social care, medical leadership/management/services management; BA(Hons), DipHE, MSc, PhD, MBA

### Nursing & Midwifery; www.shu.ac.uk/faculties/lwb/departments/nursing-midwifery

clinical education, applied nursing (learning disabilities) and generic social work, specialist community public health nursing/health visiting, health and social care leadership, learning disabilities & generic social work, maternal health care, midwifery, adult nursing studies, child or mental health nursing, supportive and palliative care, primary care nursing/district nursing, professional practice (nursing/midwifery), health visiting and school nursing, primary care radiological studies, social work;

AdvDip, AdvProfDev, BA(Hons), BSc(Hons), DocProfStud, FD, MSc/PGDip/PGCert

### Medical & Dental; www.shu.ac.uk/faculties/hwb/medical/

cardiovascular medicine, clinical education; MSc, PGCert/Dip

### Occupational Therapy; www.shu.ac.uk/occupational

applying/occupational therapy, clinical audit, paediatric practice, vocational rehabilitation, health and social care leadership; BSc(Hons), DocProf, MSc/PGDip/PGCert

### Operating Department Practice; www.shu.ac.uk/odp/

operating dept practice, health & social care leadership; BA(Hons), BSc(Hons), DipHE, DocProfStud, MSc/PGDip/Cert

### Paramedic Studies; www.shu.ac.uk/paramedic/

paramedic practice, health and social care leadership; DipHE, MSc, PGDip/Cert, ProfDoc

### Physiotherapy; www.shu.ac.uk/physio/

advancing/applying physiotherapy, physiotherapy (practice based), sport injury, adv professional practice (paediatrics), radiological studies, health and social care leadership; BA(Hons), BSc(Hons), MSc, PGCert, PGDip, ProfDoc

### Radiotherapy and Oncology; www.shu.ac.uk/radiotherapy/

radiotherapy planning, radiotherapy & oncology in practice, supportive and palliative care, health and social care leadership, radiological studies, professional studies; BA(Hons), BSc(Hons), DipHE, MSc/PGDip/PGCert, ProfDoc

### Social Work; www.shu.ac.uk/socialwork/

applied nursing & generic social work (learning disability), social work, specialist mental health practice/practitioner, working with children, young people & families, youth & community work studies, youth work, health and social care leadership; BA(Hons), GradDip, MScPgDip, MSW, PGCert, Doc SocWork

## *Sheffield Business School; www.shu.ac.uk/sbs/*

### Accounting, Banking & Finance; www.shu.ac.uk/prospectus/subject/accounting-banking-finance/

accounting & finance, business & finance, international banking/finance & economics/banking management/finance & marketing, business accounting/economics/financial management, forensic accounting, risk management; BA(Hons), MA, MSc, PGDip/Cert

### Business & Management; www.shu.ac.uk/prospectus/subject/business-management/

business and management/marketing/HRM, business admin/economics/studies, charity research management, city region leadership, coaching & mentoring, cooperative & social enterprise management, finance, financial management, food marketing management, global supply chain management, HRM/D, HR leadership, international business/studies/with languages, IT with business studies, global marketing/business/strategic marketing, HRM/HR development, leadership & management, logistics & supply chain management, organisational development & consultancy, industrial management, international business & management/HRM/marketing/business studies, languages with business, marketing, total quality management & organisational excellence, sports business management, strategic operations management, tourism; BSc(Hons), DBA, FD, GradDip, HNC, HND, MBA, MPhil, MSc, PGCert, PGDip, PhD

### Facilities Management; www.shu.ac.uk/prospectus/course/875/

food management, events management, tourism, hospitality & facilities management; BA(Hons), BSc(Hons), Cert, FD, MA, MPhil, MSc, PGCert, PGDip, PhD

### Languages; www.shu.ac.uk/prospectus/subject/languages/

business & English, English language teaching, languages with TESOL/international business/tourism, international business studies & languages (French/German/Spanish), teaching English for academic purposes; GradDip/Cert, MPhil, PGCert, PhD

**Tourism, Hospitality & Events Management; www.shu.ac.uk/prospectus/subject/tourism-hospitality-events/**
events management with arts & entertainment, international events and conference management, international hospitality/& tourism management/hotel management, international events management/with tourism, tourism management, hospitality business management with conference & events; BSc(Hons), FdSc, HND, MA, MPhil, MSc, PGCert, PGDip, PhD

## UNIVERSITY OF SOUTH WALES: www.southwales.ac.uk

### *Faculty of Business & Society; http:/fbs.glam.ac.uk*

**Newport Business School**
accounting and finance, insurance, finance (financial planning), accounting/ and finance, forensic accounting, international accounting, business and accounting/finance, finance, finance and investment, forensic audit and accounting, Islamic banking and finance, management and development of international financial systems, business management, marketing, HRM, logistics and supply chain management, event management, business studies, business and accounting/finance/HRM/marketing/supply chain management, international business, business administration (MBA), international business and enterprise, leadership and management, engineering management, management, international logistics and supply chain management, retailing, marketing and management, advertising, PR and media communications, marketing, international fashion marketing, PR, strategic procurement, sports management, sports development/psychology; BA(Hons), BSc(Hons), BEng, FdSc, DBA, MBA, MSc, MScSta, MPhil, PhD, FD

### *Faculty of Humanities & Social Sciences; http:/fbs.glam.ac.uk/schools/humanities*

Art; art and design, art practice, arts practice (art, health and wellbeing)
Criminology; criminology and criminal justice/law/psychology/sociology
English; creative and professional writing, English, English literature, English and history/professional Welsh/TESOL, culture writing, literature, English by research
History; history, English and history, history with American studies/education/professional Welsh, history by research, social & cultural history
Welsh; professional Welsh with education/English/history/TESOL/law
Public Services; public services, health and public service management, public service management, community regeneration
Sociology; sociology, sociology with criminology/education/psychology;
FD, BA(Hons), BSc(Hons), MA, LlB, MPhil, PhD

**Accounting & Finance Courses**
insurance, finance (financial planning), accounting & finance, forensic accounting, international accounting, finance, business & accounting/finance, finance & investment, forensic audit & accounting, Islamic banking & finance, management & development of international financial systems; FD, BSc(Hons), MSc

**Law Courses**
paralegal studies, legal practice, law, law & criminology/professional Welsh, international/commercial law; BSc(Hons), LlB, MLaw, LlM, FD

**Psychology & Early Years**
psychology, applied psychology, developmental psychology, sports psychology, psychology with criminology/sociology/education, behavioural analysis & therapy, clinical & abnormal psychology, health psychology, play & therapeutic play, play therapy, psychology by research, behavioural analysis supervised practice;
Early Years; early years development & education, childhood studies, childhood & youth;
PgC, BSc(Hons), MSc

### *Faculty of Advanced Technology; http:/courses.glam.ac.uk/faculties/4-fat*

aeronautical engineering, aeronautical systems engineering with avionics, automotive engineering, civil engineering, computer systems engineering, electrical and electronic engineering, electronic and communication engineering, mechanical engineering, aircraft maintenance engineering, civil engineering, computer forensics, computer games development, computer science, computer security, computing, computing mathematics, financial mathematics, information communication technology, information technology/management for business, lighting design and technology, live event technology, mathematical sciences, mathematics, mathematics and accounting/education, mechanical engineering, project management (surveying), quantity surveying and commercial management, renewable energy systems, software engineering, sound, lighting and live event technology, computer forensics and security, aircraft maintenance systems, asset management and development, building information modelling and sustainability, civil and structural engineering, civil engineering and environmental management, computer systems engineering, computer systems security, computing and information systems, construction project management, electronic mobile communications, electronic product design, electronics and information technology, embedded systems design, energy systems engineering, environmental management, geographical information systems, mobile and satellite communications, mobile computing, professional engineering, safety, health and environmental management, sustainable business risk management, sustainable power technology, total quality; BSc(Hons), BEng, MSc, FD

## *Cardiff School of Creative & Design Industries; http:/glam.ac.uk/faculties/2-cci*

animation, computer animation, computer games enterprise, creative industries, fashion, fashion promotion, film and video, film studies, game art, graphic communication, interior design, journalism, media production, media, culture and journalism, performance and media, photography, photojournalism, popular music, radio, scriptwriting, TV and film set design, visual effects and motion graphics, fashion marketing and retail design, contemporary music performance, creative industries (popular music technology), media technology, music technology, sound technology, music industry entrepreneurship, research in media, culture and communication, drama, film producing, graphic communication, journalism/international; BA(Hons), BSc(Hons), BDes(Hons), BMus(Hons), MSc, MA

## *Faculty of Health, Sport & Science; http:/heasas.glam.ac.uk/subj*

**Health & Social Care**

community health studies (community children's nursing, professional practice, endocrinology, diabetes, specialist community public health nursing (occupational/health nursing/health visiting), community mental health practice, professional practice (violence reduction), nursing (adult/learning disabilities/child/mental health), care of the older person, professional practice, community health studies (children's community nursing/community learning disabilities nursing/district nursing/practice nursing), acute and critical care, palliative care, health and social care worker education, health care nursing support worker education, diagnostic clinical ultrasound (abdomen and small parts/clinical echocardiography/gynaecology/musculoskeletal/obstetrics and related gynaecology) vascular ultrasound, clinical practice for nurses and midwives, community health studies (community children's nursing/district nursing/learning disabilities nursing/practice nursing), professional practice (vulnerable person), human physiological science, disaster healthcare, education for health and social care professionals, specialist community public health nursing (health visiting), advanced clinical practitioner, clinical endodontics, professional practice (social care management/learning disability/research/health care studies/nursing/mental health), specialist community public health nursing (school health nursing), occupational health (technician/nursing), public health

Chiropractic; chiropractic

Counselling & Phsychotherapy; systemic counselling, psychotherapy

Social Work & Health & Social Care; social work, post qual social work, health & social care

Midwifery; midwifery, professional practice

Pharmacology & Prescribing; independent prescribing, advanced clinical practice

Nutrition; nutition, physical activity & community health

**Sport & Coaching**

sport and exercise science, sport management/development/psychology/science and rugby/studies, rugby/football coaching and performance, community football coaching and development, sports coaching and performance, sports/football/rugby coaching and performance, sport, health and exercise science, youth sports coaching, performance coaching

**Science**

Astronomy; observational astronomy

Chemistry & Pharmaceutical Science; chemistry, pharmaceutical science, forensic health/science

Natural History; natural history

Biology; biology, human biology, international wildlife, medical science

Geography; physical/human geography, sustainable energy science, disaster management & environmental hazards, renewable energy & resource management, conservation & GIS, environmental conservation management
Environment & Sustainability; renewable energy & resource management, conservation & GIS, environmental resource management, disaster management for environment, sustainable energy science
Forensic & Police Science: forensic science/chemistry, police science studies, security risk & investigation, community & partnership, international policing; BSc(Hons), BA(Hons), FD, MSc, PhD

## UNIVERSITY OF SOUTHAMPTON
## www.soton.ac.uk

### *Faculty of Business and Law; www.southampton.ac.uk/faculties/faculty_business_law.html*

#### School of Law; www.soton.ac.uk/law

commercial & corporate law, European & comparative property law, European law/legal studies, finance & law, general law, insurance law, IT & commerce/telecommunications law, international law/business law/legal studies, maritime law, socio-legal studies; LlB, LlM, MPhil, PhD

#### Southampton Management School; www.southampton.ac.uk/management

accounting/& financial management, business & administration, business analytics & management studies, corporate risk & security management, digital marketing, entrepreneurship, finance, HRM/strategies, international banking/marketing, international financial markets, financial studies/markets/marketing, global enterprise & entrepreneurship, knowledge & information systems management, management science & accounting, marketing analytics, management/& finance, risk management, organisational development & facilitation, strategy & innovation; BSc(Hons), MSc, PhD, MBA, DBA

#### Winchester School of Art; www.soton.ac.uk/wsa

advertising design, communication/fashion/textiles design, design/fashion management, fashion & textile design, graphic/communications design, fashion design (knitwear for fashion/textiles/woven textiles), fashion marketing, graphic arts/design, illustration, luxury brand management, photography, motion graphics, fine art, fashion promotion & marketing, photography, motion graphics, printmaking, textile design; BA(Hons), MA, MPhil, PhD

### *Faculty of Engineering & the Environment; www.southampton.ac.uk/engineering*

**Acoustical Engineering**

acoustical engineering, acoustics & music, engineering; BEng, MEng, BSc(Hons)

**Aerospace Engineering**

aeronautics & astronautics, aeronautics & astronautics/advanced materials/aerodynamics/airvehicle systems design/engineering management/spacecraft engineering/structural design, aerospace engineering engineering, space systems engineering; BHEng, MEng

**Audiology**

environmental science, healthcare science (audiology); BSc(Hons), MSc, DClinPract

**Civil & Environmental Engineering**

civil engineering/& architecture, environmental engineering; BEng, MEng

**Environmental Sciences**

environmental sciences; BSc, BSc(Hons), MEnvSci(Hons)

**Mechanical Engineering**

mechanical engineering, mechanical engineering/advanced materials/aerospace/automotive/bioengineering/engineering management/mechatronics/naval engineering/sustainable energy systems; BEng, MEng

**Ship Science**

engineering, ship science, ship science/advanced materials/engineering management/naval architecture/naval engineering/yacht & small craft; BEng, MEng

**Taught Masters (MSc) Degrees**

Taught Research Degrees (MSc)
Audiology; audiology
Engineering; engineering, engineering and the environment, advanced tribology, aerodynamics and computation, bioengineering (advanced mechanical

engineering science), civil engineering, coastal and marine engineering and management, computational engineering design (advanced mechanical engineering science), energy and sustainability (energy, environment and buildings/energy and sustainability/energy resources and climate change), engineering in the coastal environment, engineering materials, marine technology/classification and survey/marine technology/defence/general/marine technology/marine engineering/marine technology/naval architecture/marine technology/offshore engineering/small craft design, maritime engineering science/advanced materials/maritime engineering science/marine engineering/maritime computational fluid dynamics/naval architecture/ship science/yacht and small craft, mechatronics, race car aerodynamics, sound and vibration studies, space systems engineering, sustainable energy technologies, transportation planning & engineering, unmanned vehicle systems design/air-vehicle/marine

Environmental Management; biodiversity & conservation, environmental monitoring & assessment, environmental pollution control, integrated environmental water resources;

MSc, MPhil, PhD, EngD

## *Faculty of Health Sciences; www.soton.ac.uk/healthsciences*

clinical practice/specialist practice, clinical practice (adv nursing practice/children & young people/critical care/district nursing/children's community nursing/midwifery/neonatal care), community nursing, healthcare science (cardiovascular & respiratory & sleep science), healthcare management, policy & resources, nursing (adult, children, mental health), midwifery, occupational therapy, physiotherapy, podiatry, health & social care, public health practice, mental health practitioner, health & rehabilitation, clinical leadership in cancer, palliative & end of life care, clinical research, health science (health & rehabilitation), leadership & management health & social care, mental health studies, public health practice, specialist community public health nursing; BSc(Hons), MSc, PGDip, MPhil, PhD, MRes, DocClinPract

## *Faculty of Humanities; www.soton.ac.uk/about/faculties/faculty_humanities*

### Archaeology; www.southampton.ac.uk/archaeology/

archaeology & history/geography, archaeological computing (spatial technologies/virtual pasts), Rome & provinces, ceramic & Lithic/maritime/social archaeology, osteoarchaeology, maritime conservation, archaeological survey & landscape, palaeolithic archaeology & human origins, social archaeology

### English; www.southampton.ac.uk/english/

English, English & jt degrees, English literary studies, language & linguistics, 18th-century studies, 20th/21st century literature, medieval & Renaissance culture, creative writing

### Film; www.southampton.ac.uk/film/

film studies/ film & cultural management, film (jt degrees)

### History; www.southampton.ac.uk/history/

history, modern history, jt hons incl archaeology, English, foreign language, philosophy, Jewish history & culture studies, 18th century studies, medieval & Renaissance studies

### Modern Languages; www.southampton.ac.uk/ml/

modern languages – contemporary Europe/English language studies/French/German/linguistics studies/Spanish, Portuguese and Latin American studies

### Music; www.southampton.ac.uk/music/

acoustics & music, performance, composition, music therapy, musicology, 18th century studies, medieval & Renaissance studies, jt degrees

### Philosophy; www.southampton.ac.uk/philosophy/

philosophy: jt hons degrees incl sociology, politics, mathematics, foreign language, aesthetics

BA(Hons), MA, MRes, MPhil, PhD, CetHE, MMus

## *Faculty of Medicine; www.southampton.ac.uk/faculties/faculty_medicine.html*

### Medicine; www.southampton.ac.uk/medicine

allergy, biomedical sciences/cell biology & immunology of cancer, immunology & infection, medicine, surgery, stem cell science, medicine, public health/nutrition; BM, MSc, BMedSci, PGDip/Cert, PhD, DM

## *Faculty of Natural and Environmental Sciences; www.soton.ac.uk/about/faculties/faculty_natural_environmental-sciences*

### Biological Sciences; www.soton.ac.uk/biosc

biochemistry, biology, biomedical sciences, biological sciences & chemistry, cellular & molecular sciences, molecular biosciences, natural sciences, ocean & earth sciences, neurosciences, pharmacology, wildlife conservation, zoology, ecology & the environment; BSc(Hons), Cert/DipHE, MPhil, PhD, B/BNatSci

### Chemistry; www.soton.ac.uk/chemistry

chemistry/with biological sciences/ocean & earth sciences/mathematics/medicinal science, electrochemistry, computational systems chemistry, instrumental analytical chemistry, molecular diagnostics & therapeutics, magnetic resonance, molecular assembly, function & structure; BSc(Hons), B/MNatSci, MPhil, PhD

### National Oceanography Centre, Southampton; www.noc.soton.ac.uk

marine biology, oceanography, geology, geophysics; BSc, MSc, MSci

### School of Ocean and Earth Science; www.soton.ac.uk/soes

geology, geophysics, geophysical sciences, oceanography, earth & climate science, engineering in the coastal environment, physical geography, marine science/biology/policy & law, marine resource management/geology & geography, engineering in the coastal environment, marine environment & resources, ocean science/chemistry, ocean, earth & climate science, vertebrate palaeontology; BSc(Hons), MSci, BNatSci, MRes, MPhil, PhD

## *Faculty of Physical and Applied Sciences; www.soton.ac.uk/about/faculties/faculty_physical-applied_sciences*

### Electronics and Computer Science; www.ecs.soton.ac.uk

bionanotechnology, computer science/& software engineering, AI, distributed networks, engineering & sustainability with electrical power engineering, information technology in organisations, microelectromechanical systems, microelectronics systems design/mechanical systems, nanoelectronics & nanotechnology, open data technology, software engineering, systems-on-a-chip, systems & signal processing, web science/technology, image & multimedia systems, mobile & secure systems, software/electrical/electronic/electromechanical engineering, optical communication, power systems, wireless communications; BEng, MEng, MSc, MComp, PhD

### Optoelectronics Research Centre; www.orc.soton.ac.uk

photonics, photonic technologies; MSc, PhD

### Physics & Astronomy; www.phy.soton.ac.uk

astronomy, adv quantum mechanics, coherent light/matter, particle physics, physics/ with astronomy/nanotechnology/space science/photonics/mathematics; BSc(Hons), European Masters, MPhy, PhD

## *Faculty of Social and Human Sciences; www.soton.ac.uk/about/faculties/facultysocial_human-sciences*

### School of Education; www.southampton.ac.uk/education

education, education & training (primary), educational studies with psychology/training, education (management & leadership/practice & innovation/specific learning difficulties (dyslexia)/mathematics & science), PGCE (primary, numerous secondary subjects/learning & skills), school direct, PCET; BSc(Hons), BA(Hons), MSc, MA(Ed), CertEd, MPhil, PhD, EdD

### Geography & Environment; www.soton.ac.uk/geography

geography, geology, physical geography, oceanography, applied GIS & remote sensing/earth observation, city & regional development, geo-information science & earth sciences; BSc(Hons), BA(Hons), MA, MSc, MPhil, PhD

### School of Mathematics; www.soton.ac.uk/maths

actuarial science, mathematical studies, mathematics with actuarial science/astronomy/biology/computer science/economics/finance/management science/music/OR/physics/statistics, OR/& finance, mathematics, statistics with applications in medicine; BSc(Hons), MMath, MSc, PGDip, PhD

### School of Psychology; www.southampton.ac.uk/psychology

psychology/& education, foundations of clinical psychology, psychology, research methods, BTC (mental health problems/long term health problems/cognitive therapy for anxiety & depression); BSc(Hons), MSc, MPhil, PhD, PGDip

**School of Social Sciences; www.southampton.ac.uk/socsci**
accounting and economics, applied social sciences, applied social sciences (anthropology/criminology and psychological studies/criminology), criminology, economics, economics and actuarial science/finance/ management sciences/philosophy, international relations, modern history and politics, mathematics, operational research, statistics and economics, philosophy and politics/sociology, politics, politics and economics/French/German/international relations/ Spanish (or Portuguese) and Latin American studies, population and geography, social policy and criminology, sociology, sociology and criminology, social ageing/gerontology, economics, politics & international relations, social statistics & demography, sociology & social policy; BSc(Hons), BA(Hons), MEcon, MSc, MPhil, PGDip, PhD

**Southampton Statistical Sciences Research Institute; www.southampton.ac.uk/s3ri**
official statistics, social statistics and demography; PhD

## STAFFORDSHIRE UNIVERSITY
## www.staffs.ac.uk

### *Faculty of Business, Education & Law; www.staffs.ac.uk/academic _depts/fbel*

**Staffordshire University Business School; www.staffs.ac.uk/business**
Accounting & Finance: accounting & business/ finance, business administration, finance
Business, Management & Enterprise: business management, business management & enterprise, business start-up, international business management, business administration (finance/HRM/international), economics for business analysis, economics of globalisation & European integration, business marketing management
Economics: economics for business analysis, economics of international trade & European integration, business & economics education
Human Resource Management: HRM, strategic HRM, personnel practice, professional development
Marketing: marketing management, international marketing, business & marketing management
Tourism & Events: tourism management, events management
Professional Courses
BA, BSc, HNC, HND, MA, MBA, MPhil, MSc, PGCert/Dip, PhD, PGCE

**School of Education: www.staffs.ac.uk/ depts._education**
education, early childhood studies, post-compulsory education, teaching assistants, cognitive difficulties/ education in the lifelong learning sector, PGCE (primary, secondary education/various subjects, for QTS), education (learning & assessment/negotiated/ educational leadership), teaching in the lifelong learning sector; BA(Hons), MA, MPhil, PhD, EdD, FD, PGCert

**School of Law; www.staffs.ac.uk/ academic_depts/law**
law, business law, criminology, family law, healthcare & ethics, international sports law, international trade & commerce, legal practice; LlB, LlM, MPhil, PhD, GradDip

### *Faculty of Arts & Creative Technologies; www.staffs.ac.uk/academic_depts/fact*

**School of Art & Design; www.staffs.ac.uk/ academic _ depts/artanddesign**
art, design, 3D design, ceramics/contemporary jewellery & fashion accessories/design crafts, advertising & brand management, animation, cartoon & comic arts, design for outdoor living, entrepreneurship, fine art, photography, graphic design, heritage interior design, illustration, interior design, photojournalism, product design, retail design, stop motion animation & puppet-making, surface pattern design, textile surfaces, transport design, visual effects & concept design

**School of Film, Sound and Vision: www.staffs.ac.uk/academic _ depts/fsv**
advertising & commercial film production, arts & creative technologies, CGI & digital effects, computer games design & programming, 3D games modelling, digital film & post production techniques/3D animation techniques, digital feature film production, drama, performance & theatre arts, experimental film production, film, games concept design/design & technology, TV & radio studies, film production/

practice & theory/& visual art/techniques, media (film) production, music technology, radio production, screenwriting & film studies, theatre studies & technical stage production

### School of Journalism, Humanities & Social Sciences: www.staffs.ac.uk/academic_depts/hss

journalism, broadcast journalism, music journalism and broadcasting, sports journalism, sports PR and journalism, creative writing, crime, deviance and society, crime, deviance and society and sociology, English literature, English and creative writing, modern history, modern and international history, sociology, arts and creative technologies by negotiated study, community and participatory arts, community practice, continental philosophy, crime, terrorism and global security, global society and media communication, international history, international policy and diplomacy, international relations, regeneration, social and cultural theory, sociology, sports broadcast journalism, transnational organised crime, youth and community work
BA, FdA, MA, MFA, MPhil, MSc, PhD

## *Faculty of Computing, Engineering & Science; www.staffs.ac.uk/academic_depts/fecs*

### School of Computing; www.staffs.ac.uk/academic_depts/computing;

applied computing, information technology studies, applied/business computing science for business, computer games programming, mobile computer systems, computer systems e-learning, digital forensics, cybersecurity, computer networks & security, computer science, cloud computing, web development/design/programming

### School of Engineering; www.staffs.ac.uk/academic_depts/engineering

automotive engineering, motorsport engineering, motorsport technology, aeronautics technology, electronic engineering, electrical engineering, telecommunications engineering, mathematics & statistics, PGCE in mathematics, mechanical engineering, mechatronics, product design engineering, mechanical/manufacturing technology, advanced technology, professional education

### School of Sciences; www.staffs.ac.uk/acamemic_depts/sciences

animal biology & conservation, biology/& microbiology, biomedical science, forensic biology, human biology, nautical management & conservation, ecology & conservation, urban ecology & conservation, molecular biology, healthcare science management, forensic/investigative science, policing & criminal investigation, crime scene investigation, fire investigation, firearm examination, questioned documents, human/physical geography, environment & sustainability, geography & mountain leadership, governance & sustainable development
BA, BEng, BSc, FdSc, HND, MEng, MSc, MPhil, MRes, PGCE, PGCert, PGDip, PhD

## *Faculty of Health Sciences; www.staffs.ac.uk/academic_depts/health*

### School of Nursing & Midwifery; www.staffs.ac.uk/academic_depts/nursingandmidwifery

adv/clinical practice, adv forensic practice, adult/children's/mental health nursing, healthcare practice, health visiting/specialist community public health nursing, integrated care practice, midwifery, public health nursing, school nursing, specialist community nursing in the home

### School of Psychology, Sport & Exercise; www.staffs.ac.uk/academic-depts/pse

psychology, forensic psychology, sport development & coaching, PE & youth coaching, psychology & child development/counselling/criminology, applied sport & exercise psychology/science, sport studies/therapy, clinical biomechanics/& diabetes/orthotic therapy/pain management in the lower limb, clinical podiatric biomechanics, clinical psychology, cognitive behavioural therapy, counselling, footwear in diagnosis & therapy, health psychology, basic counselling skills, musculoskeletal diagnosis, psychotherapy

### School of Social Work, Allied & Public Health; www.staffs.ac.uk/academic-depts/swaph

health & social care, health studies, hypnosis & stress management, operating department practice, osteopathy, paramedic science, peri-operative care, social welfare law, policy & advice practice, social work, ageing, mental health & dementia, health management & policy, medical education, physical activity & public health; BSc, MA, MPhil, MSc, PGCert, PGDip, PhD

# UNIVERSITY OF STIRLING
# www.external.stir.ac.uk

## School of Applied Social Science; www.stir.ac.uk/socialscience

applied social research, sociology & social policy, criminology, housing studies, applied studies (child welfare & protection/management & leadership in social services), adult services, criminological research/social work, dementia studies/training/& gerontology, social work studies, drug & alcohol studies, dementia studies, child welfare & protection, criminology, crime & justice, social policy, sociology, social enterprise; BA, GradCert, MSc, PGCert, PGDip, PhD

## School of Arts & Humanities; www.stir.ac.uk/schools/arts-and-humanities

### Dept of English Studies; www.english.stir.ac.uk

English studies, creative writing, English language & linguistics, the Gothic imagination, modern Scottish writing, post-colonial studies, international publishing management, publishing studies, Renaissance studies; BA, MLitt, MPhil, MRes, MSc, PhD

### Dept of Film, Media & Journalism; www.fmj.stir.ac.uk

film & media studies, journalism studies, digital media, media management, publishing & law, media & culture, strategic PR; BA, MLitt, MPhil, MSc, PGDip, PhD

### History & Politics; www.historyandpolitics.stir.ac.uk

history, politics, environmental history, medieval history, Scottish history, the American revolution, colonial America, eighteenth-century British history, the French revolution, European history, African history, urban history, the history of medicine, religious history, international conflict & cooperation; BA(Hons), MSc, MRes, MA, DPhil, PhD

### School of Languages, Culture and Regions; www.slcr.stir.ac.uk

hermeneutics, humanities, French/Spanish & Latin American studies, translation studies, TESOL, film studies, religion & global cinema & culture, global cinema & culture; BA, MLitt, MRes, PhD

### Dept of Philosophy; www.philosophy.stir.ac.uk

philosophy, philosophy of logic & language, legal, moral & social philosophy, epistemology & philosophy of mind, history of early analytical philosophy; BA, MLitt, MPhil, PhD

### Stirling Law School; www.law.stir.ac.uk

law, international commercial law/energy law & policy, financial law & finance, environmental policy & governance, digital media, publishing & law, corporate social responsibility, business/commercial law, law; BA, LLB, LLM, MSc, MLitt, PhD

## School of Education; www.ioe.stir.ac.uk

education (primary/secondary), tertiary education (TQFE/TQAE), English language teaching, EFL, educational leadership, applied linguistics, computer-assisted language learning, international policing, professional learning & leadership, enquiry, teaching qualifications in adult education/FE, TESOL with translational studies/applied linguistics, tertiary education, educational research; BA, BSc, EdD, MEd, MPhil, MRes, MSc, PGCert/Dip, PhD, UnivCert

## School of Natural Sciences; www.stir/schools/natural-sciences

### Institute of Aquaculture; www.aqua.stir.ac.uk

aquaculture & the environment/development/business management/biotechnology, aquacultural business management/biotechnology/veterinary studies/pathobiology, marine biology, sustainable aquaculture; BSc, MPhil, MSc, PGCert, PGDip, PhD

### School of Biological & Environmental Sciences; www.sbes.stir.ac.uk

animal/cell/conservation biology, biology/ & professional education/psychology, cell biology, conservation biology & management, conservation & sustainability, ecology, energy & the environment, environmental geography/history/management/professional education/science/outdoor education, sports & exercise science; BSc, MPhil, MRes, MSc, PGCert, PGDip, PhD

**Dept of Computing Science & Mathematics; www.cs.stir.ac.uk**
advanced/computing, business computing, computing science, computing for financial markets/business, IT, mathematics/& its applications, information technology, software engineering; BSc, MSc, PhD, MBA

**Dept of Psychology; www.psychology.stir.ac.uk**
psychology, health psychology, psychological research methods, autism/child development/evolution & behaviour/measuring perception/psychology of faces, evolutionary psychology, psychology applied to health, psychological therapy in primary care; BA, BSc, MSc, PGDip, PhD

*School of Nursing & Midwifery & Health; www.nm.stir.ac.uk*
advanced/professional practice/care practice, health & wellbeing of the older person, non-medical prescribing, health profession & paramedical practice, studies/research, midwifery, nursing (adult, mental health), supporting self-care; BM, BN, BSc, DAHP, DM, DN, MPhil, MRes, MSc, PGDip, PhD, DipHE

**School of Sport; www.sports.stir.ac.uk**
health & exercise sciences, performance coaching, psychology of sport, sport & exercise science, sport coaching/management/nutrition, sports studies; BA, BSc, MPhil, MSc, PGDip, PhD

*Stirling Management School; www.stir.ac.uk/management*
accountancy, finance, international accounting & finance, investment analysis, computing for financial markets, business & management, business administration, business studies, HRM, international business, marketing, management science & socio-economic development, retailing, retail marketing/management, public service management, social marketing, behavioural change, money, banking & finance, economics, environmental economics, energy management; BA, BSc, MBA, MSc, PhD, BAcc, MPhil, PGDip, MBA, MRes

**Institute for People-Centred Healthcare Management**
PhD

**Institute for Retail Studies**
retail studies; PhD

**Institute for Social Marketing**
PhD

**Institute for Socio-Management**
PhD

## STOCKPORT COLLEGE
## www.stockport.ac.uk

access to HE, art & design, media, building/services/construction, business & IT technology/management, child development & wellbeing, early childhood studies, photography, enterprise computing, illustration, graphic art & design, health & social care, engineering, forensic science, graphic communication, social work/counselling; BA, FdA, FDSc

## UNIVERSITY OF STRATHCLYDE
## www.strath.ac.uk

*Strathclyde Business School; www.strath.ac.uk/business*
Undergraduate Courses:
accounting, business/administration/enterprise, business technology, economics, finance, hospitality & tourism studies, HRM, management/science, marketing, business law
Postgraduate Courses:
applied economics, business analysis & consulting, business & management, European financial management, finance, HRM, hospitality & tourism leadership, international accounting & finance/banking/hospitality & tourism management/management/HRM/marketing, investment & finance, marketing, equality in pay & reward, leadership studies, management, management of IT, operational

research, qualitative finance, supply chain management; BA, MSc, MBA, DBA, MPhil, PhD, MRes, PGCert/Dip, MBM

## *Faculty of Engineering; www.strath.ac.uk/engineering*

### Dept of Architecture; www.strath.ac.uk/architecture

architecture, adv architectural design/studies, sustainable engineering, urban design; BSc, MArch, MRes, MSc, PGCert, PGDip

### Bioengineering Unit; www.strath.ac.uk/bioeng

medical devices, biomedical engineering, medical technology, prosthetics & orthotics, rehabilitation studies; EngD, MPhil, MRes, MSc, PGCert, PGDip, PhD

### Dept of Chemical & Process Engineering; www.strath.ac.uk/chemeng

adv chemical & processing engineering, chemical engineering, chemical processing, chemical/process & technology management; BEng, MEng, MSc, PGCert, PGDip

### Dept of Civil & Environmental Engineering; www.strath.ac.uk/civeng

civil & environmental engineering, civil engineering, environmental engineering/health, entrepreneurship, hydrogeology, sustainability & environmental studies; BEng, BSc, MEng, MPhil, MRes, MSc, PhD

### Dept of Design, Manufacture & Engineering Management; www.strath.ac.uk/dmen

adv engineering technology & systems, computer-aided engineering design, digital creativity, global innovation management, lean six sigma for process, mechatronics & automation, operations management in engineering, product design engineering/design & innovation, production engineering design, production engineering & management, sports engineering, supply chain & ops management, management, sustainable engineering/product development; BEng, BSc, MEng, MSc, PGCert, PGDip

### Dept of Electronic & Electrical Engineering; www.strath.ac.uk/eee

communications/technology & policy, computer & electronic systems, electrical energy systems, electrical & electronic engineering with/business studies/international studies, electrical & mechanical engineering, electrical power engineering with business, electronic & digital systems, signals processing engineering, wind engineering systems; BEng, MEng, MSc, PGCert, PGDip

### Dept of Mechanical & Aerospace Engineering; www.strath.ac.uk/mecheng

adv mechanical engineering, aero-mechanical/enviro-mechanical/mechanical engineering, mechanical engineering with aeronautics/financial management, materials engineering, power plant engineering/technologies, sustainable renewable energy systems & the environment; BEng, MEng, MPhil, PGCert, PGDip, PhD

### Dept of Naval Architectural & Marine Engineering; www.strath.ac.uk/na-me

marine engineering/technology, naval architecture with marine engineering/ocean engineering/small craft engineering, subsea engineering, offshore renewable energy/floating systems, technical ship management, ship & offshore structures/technology; BEng, MEng, MPhil, MSc, PGCert, PGDip, PhD

### Biomedical Engineering; www.strath.ac.uk/biomedeng

prosthetics & orthotics, rehabilitation studies, medical devices/technology, biomedical engineering; BSc, MRes, MSc, PGCert, PGDip, EngD, PhD

## *Faculty of Humanities & Social Sciences; www.strath.ac.uk/humanities*

### School of Applied Social Sciences; www.strath.ac.uk/humanities/school-of-appliedsocialsciences

adv professional studies, social work/management, residential child/community care, mental health officer social work, sociology, social research, refugee & migration studies; BA(Hons), Cert, MPhil, PhD, MSc, MRes, MLitt

### School of Education; www.strath.ac.uk/humanities/schoolofeducation

autism, adv professional studies, adult guidance, childhood practice, early childhood studies, education, applied educational research, educational support, management & leadership in education, philosophy with children, school leadership & management, PGCE (primary, secondary education), supporting bilingual learners/teacher learning; BA, BSc, EdD, BEd, MSc, PGCE, PGCert, MEd, MPhil, PGDE, PGDip, PhD

**School of Government & Public Policy; www.strath.ac.uk/humanities/schoolofgovernmentandpublicpolicy**
European/international public policy, political research, politics, public policy; BA, MSc, PhD

**School of Humanities; www.strath.ac.uk/humanities/schoolofhumanities**
creative writing, English, history, French, Spanish, Italian, politics, journalism, psychology, sociology, law, literary/digital/investigative journalism, hospitality & tourism, literary culture & philosophy, music, Renaissance studies; MA, MLitt, MPhil, MRes, PGDip/Cert, PhD

**School of Law; www.strath.ac.uk/humanities/lawschool**
law, advocacy, construction law, criminal justice & penal change, human rights law, international economic law, international law & sustainable development, internet law & policy, mediation & conflict resolution; BA, LLB, LLM, PGCert, PGDip, MSc, MPhil, PhD

**School of Psychological Science & Health; www.strath.ac.uk/humanities/schoolofpsychologicalsciencehealth**
psychology, sport & physical activity, speech & language pathology, educational psychology, counselling skills, research methods; BA, BSc, MRes, DEdPsy, PGCert/Dip, MCounselling

*Faculty of Science; www.strath.ac.uk/science*

**Dept of Pure & Applied Chemistry; www.chem.strath.ac.uk**
chemistry, applied chemistry & chemical engineering, forensic & analytical chemistry, chemistry with drug discovery, chemistry with teaching, forensic science; BSc, MChem, MSc, PGDip, PhD

**Dept of Computer & Information Sciences; www.strath.ac.uk/cis**
business information systems, computer & electronic systems, adv/computer science/with law, information & library studies, information management; BEng, BSc, MEng, MPhil, MRes, MSc, PGCert, PGDip

**Dept of Mathematics & Statistics; www.mathstat.strath.ac.uk**
mathematics, mathematics & computer science/statistics/accountancy/economics/finance/management, research topics; BSc, MSc, PhD

**Dept of Physics; www.strath.ac.uk/physics**
physics, nanoscience, optical technologies, high power frequency science & engineering, photonics & device fabrication, quantum information & coherence, physics with teaching; BSc, MPhys, MSc, PhD

**Strathclyde Institute of Pharmacy & Biomedical Sciences; www.strath.ac.uk/sipbs**
biomedical sciences, biochemistry, biotechnology, quality & good manufacturing practice, analysis of medicines, clinical pharmacy, pharmacy, pharmaceutical analysis, drug delivery sustainability/discovery, neuroscience; BSc, MPharm, MPhil, MSc, PGCert, PGDip, PhD

## UNIVERSITY CAMPUS SUFFOLK
## www.ucs.ac.uk

**School of Arts & Humanities; www.ucs.ac.uk/SchoolsAndNetwork/SchoolOfArtsAndHumanities**
arts practice, design context & practice, computer games design, dance, English, history, fashion, film, fine art, graphic/design/illustration, interior architecture & design, photography, journalism; BA, FdA, MA, PGCert, PGDip

**School of Science, Technology & Health; www.ucs.ac.uk/SchoolsAndNetwork/UCSSchools/SchoolofScienceTechnologyandHealth**

**Division of Health**
advanced healthcare practice (advanced nurse practitioner; allied health professionals), health & well-being, diagnostic radiography, radiotherapy & oncology, health sciences (diagnostic imaging), health administration, health & social care practice, operating department practice, health sciences

(mammography), non-medical prescribing, specialist community public health nursing, acute healthcare practice

**Division of Science and Technology**

bioscience, nutrition & human health, sport & exercise science, regenerative medicine, science of healthy ageing;

FdSc, MA, PGCert, PGDip, Cert/DipHE, BSc(Hons), MSc

### School of Nursing & Midwifery; http:/ www.ucs.ac.uk/SchoolsAndNetwork/ UCSSchools/ SchoolofNursingandMidwifery/ SchoolofNursingandMidwifery.aspx

adult/children's/mental health nursing, health care practice, midwifery, care practitioner, continuing care, clinical practice, education for health & social care professionals, leadership & service innovation; BSc(Hons), FdA, MA

### School of Applied Social Sciences: www.ucs.ac.uk/SchoolsAndNetwork/ UCSSchools/ SchoolofAppliedSocialSciences

**Children, Young People and Education**

children, young people & policy, children's care, learning & development, criminology/& youth studies, early childhood studies, early learning, SCITT, childhood & youth studies, learning & teaching

**Psychology, Social Policy and Social Work**

criminology & youth studies, psychology & criminology/sociology/youth studies, sociology & youth studies, social care practice, social work;

BA(Hons), BSc(Hons), FdAPG Cert, PG Dip, MA

### School of Business, Leadership & Enterprise; www.ucs.ac.uk/ SchoolsAndNetwork/UCSSchools/ SchoolofBusiness, LeadershipandEnterprise/Courses

accounting & business, business management with finance/HRM/marketing/law/entrepreneurship, business administration/management & HRM/marketing, business & management studies, community leadership & social innovation, event management, HR strategy, HRM, leisure/tourism management, management for the heritage sector, maritime tourism, marketing management, network & communication technologies, sustainable business; BA, FdA, FdSc, MHRStrat, MBA, PGDip

## UNIVERSITY OF SUNDERLAND
## www.sunderland.ac.uk

## *Faculty of Applied Sciences; www.sunderland.ac.uk/faculties/apsc*

### Dept of Computing, Engineering & Technology; www.sunderland.ac.uk/ faculties/apsc/ourdepartments/cet

applied business computing/engineering, automotive/electronic & electrical/manufacturing/engineering, business computing, computer systems engineering, computing, computer forensics/science, electronics & electrical engineering, engineering management, games software engineering, health information management, information communications technology, IT management, maritime engineering, mechanical engineering, management & assessment/health & safety, network systems/computing, project management, telecommunications engineering; BA, BEng, BSc, FdSc, MSc

### Dept of Pharmacy, Health & Well-being; www.sunderland.ac.uk/faculties/apsc/ ourdepartments/phw

biomedical sciences, biopharmaceutical science, clinical skills, community & public health, clinical pharmacy, cognitive behavioural therapy, drug & alcohol studies, drug discovery & development, environmental health & safety, environmental health & social care, healthcare science/physiological sciences/life sciences, medicine management, proteomics & metabolomics, public health, nursing, pharmacological science, pharmacy, pharmaceutics, biopharmaceutical formulation, psychological science; BA, BSc, FdA, MPharm, MSc, PGCE, Univ Dip, PGDip, Adv Dip

### Dept of Psychology; www.sunderland.ac.uk/faculties/apsc/ ourfaculty/ourdepartments/psychology

counselling, psychology; BA, FdA, MA, MSc

**Dept of Sport & Exercise Sciences; www.sunderland.ac.uk/faculties/apsc/ourdepartments/sport/**
sport & exercise development/sciences, sport studies, sports coaching/journalism, exercise health & fitness; BA, BSc, FdA, MSc

## *Faculty of Arts, Design & Media; www.sunderland.ac.uk/faculties/adm/*

**Dept of Arts & Design; www.sunderland.ac.uk/faculties/adm/ourfaculty/ourdepartments/departmentofartsdesign**
applied music practice, community music, curating, design studies/multimedia & graphics, fashion production/promotion, jazz, pop & commercial music, performing arts, advertising/animation & design, dance, drama, music, design, fine art, glass & ceramics, photography; BA, BSc, FdA, MA

**Dept of Media; www.sunderland.ac.uk/faculties/adm/ourfaculty/ourdepartments/departmentofmedia**
graphic communication, illustration & design, applied art, art & design, calligraphy & design, curating, creative practice, digital film production, fine art, photography, media, culture & communication, video & data imagery, media & cultural studies/communication, film; BA, BSc, FdA, MA

## *Faculty of Business & Law; www.sunderland.ac.uk/faculties/bl*

**Sunderland Business School; www.sunderland.ac.uk/faculties/bl/departments/business/**
accounting & finance, accountancy & management, applied management, banking & finance, business & finance/financial management, business management/administration, business & management/enterprise management/HRM/marketing, financial management, health & safety management, international tourism & hospitality management, HRM, innovation & enterprise, events/travel management, international management, leadership & management, marketing/management, sports management, supply chain management; BA(Hons), FD, CertHE, MBM, MBA, MA, MSc, PgDip

**Dept of Law; www.sunderland.ac.uk/faculties/bl/departments/law/**
law, criminology, business law, legal practice, criminal law & procedure, human rights; LlB, LlM, LPC, BA(Hons)

**Dept of Tourism, Hospitality & Events; www.sunderland.ac.uk/faculties/bl/departments/tourism/**
international hospitality & tourism management, tourism management, events management, travel & tourism, tourism (jt degrees); BA(Hons), BA/BSc, FD, BSc(Hons)

## *Faculty of Education & Society*

**Dept of Education; www.sunderland.ac.uk/faculties/es/ourfaculty/ourdepartments/departmentofeducation**
secondary education, curriculum studies, English education, education & care, GTP, history, mathematics education, advanced pedagogy, post compulsory education & training, professional learning & teaching, training & work-based learning, knowledge based enhancement – science/chemistry/physics/mathematics, advanced professional practice, science with chemistry education, PGCE (primary/secondary/business/geography/design & technology), teaching & learning with ICT, TESOL, international education, children's literature, social work, special needs & inclusive education, teaching & learning with ICT, TESOL; BA, BSc, MA, PGCE, FD, Dip, MSc

**Dept of Culture; www.sunderland.ac.uk/faculties/es/ourfaculty/ourdepartments/departmentofculture**
English & creative writing, English education/language & literature, TESOL, history, politics, religious studies, French, German, Spanish, EFL, world literatures; BA, BSc, MA, PGCE

**Dept of Social Sciences; www.sunderland.ac.uk/faculties/es/ourfaculty/ourdepartments/departmentofsocialsciences**
career guidance, childhood studies, community & youth studies, children, young people & families, criminology, early years professional status, education & care/curriculum studies, health & social care, interprofessional practice education, social work, sociology, understanding community development, working with young people; BA, FdA, MA, BA(Hons), BEng(Hons), BSc(Hons), EdEng, FdSc, LLM, MBA, MSc, PGCE, PGCert

## Degrees validated by University of Sunderland offered at:

### CITY OF SUNDERLAND COLLEGE
www.citysun.ac.uk

applied arts/music, art and design, business & management, counselling, early years, education & care, health & social care, network security technology, practice dance, drama, biomedical science, exercise health & fitness, health & safety management, leadership & management, sports coaching, travel & tourism; FdA, FdSc

## UNIVERSITY OF SURREY
**www.surrey.ac.uk**

### Faculty of Arts & Human Sciences; www.surrey.ac.uk/fahs/

**School of Arts; www.surrey.ac.uk/schoolofarts**

acting, contemporary theatre making, dance/& culture, dance, film & theatre, digital media, film studies, creative writing, theatre studies, music, creative music technology, music & sound recording, professional acting, musical theatre, practice of voice & singing, professional production skills; BA(Hons), MA, BMus, MMus, MPhil, PGDip, PhD

**School of English & Languages; www.surrey.ac.uk/englishandlanguages**

French/German/Spanish & translation, French/German/Spanish/ for international communication, business management & French/German/Spanish, English literature/with creative writing, audiovisual translation, business translation & interpreting, liberal arts & science, monolingual subtitling & audio description, public service interpreting, translation/studies/with intercultural communication, business interpreting in Chinese & English, communications & international marketing, intercultural communication with international business, translation with French/German/Spanish, English literature/& English for international communication, public service interpreting, creative writing; BA(Hons), BSc(Hons), MA, PhD

**School of Politics; www.surrey.ac.uk/politics**

politics, international politics/with English for international communication, international politics with French/German/Spanish, politics & sociology/economics, politics with policy studies, international relations, European & international politics, European politics, law & policy; BA(Hons), BSc(Hons), MSc, MPhil, PhD

**School of Psychology; www.surrey.ac.uk/psychology**

psychology, environmental/forensic/health/social psychology, occupational & organisational psychology, research methods, supervision & consultation: psychotherapeutic organisational approaches, psychological intervention, liberal arts & science; BSc(Hons), MSc, PsychD, PhD

**School of Sociology; www.surrey.ac.uk/sociology**

sociology, criminology, criminal justice & social research, media, culture and society, law with social work, social research methods, media studies; BA(Hons), BSc(Hons, MA, MSc, PsychD, PGDip, LlB

**Dept of Economics; www.econ.surrey.ac.uk**

finance, economics, energy economics & policy, business economics & finance, business/international economics, finance & development; BSc, MSc, PhD

**Dept of Music & Sound Recording; www.surrey.ac.uk/music-sound**

creative music technology, music, music & sound recording, musicology, musical theatre, the practice of music & singing; BMus, BSc, BA(Hons), MMus, MPhil, MRes, PGDip, PhD

### Faculty of Engineering & Physical Sciences; www.surrey.ac.uk/feps

**Dept of Computing; www.surrey.ac.uk/computing**

computer science/& engineering, computing & information technology, computational intelligence & computational science, information systems, internet computing, security technologies & applications; BSc, MSc, PhD

### Dept of Electronic Engineering; www.ee.surrey.ac.uk

advanced systems (communications/nanotechnology/space science, communications networks & software, satellite communications engineering, electronic engineering/with computer systems, medical imaging, microwave engineering & wireless subsystems, mobile & satellite communication, mobile communication systems, multimedia technology & systems, nanotechnology & nanoelectronic devices, signal processing & machine intelligence, satellite communications systems, space technology & planetary exploration; BEng, MEng, MPhil, MSc, PhD

### Dept of Mathematics; www.maths.surrey.ac.uk

mathematics, financial mathematics, statistics, mathematics/with physics, integrated professional training; BSc, MMath, MSc, PhD

### Dept of Physics; www.surrey.ac.uk/physics

astronomy, radiation detection & instrumentation, medical imaging, Euromaster, medical physics, physics, nuclear astrophysics, satellite technology, radiation & environmental protection; BSc, MSc, MPhys

### Division of Chemistry; www.surrey.ac.uk/chemistry

chemistry/with forensic investigation, medicinal chemistry, drug discovery; BSc, MSc, MChem, MRes, PhD

### Division of Civil, Chemical & Environmental Engineering; www.surrey.ac.uk/cce

**Dept of Civil & Environmental Engineering**

civil engineering, bridge engineering, structural engineering, water & environmental engineering

**Dept of Chemical & Process Engineering**

chemical engineering, chemical & petroleum engineering, chemical & biosystems engineering, petroleum refining, information & processing, environmental systems engineering, renewable energy, process systems engineering

BEng, MEng, MSc, PGCert, PGDip, Phd

### Division of Mechanical, Medical & Aerospace Engineering; www.surrey.ac.uk/mma

advanced materials, aerospace/mechanical engineering, biomedical/medical engineering; BEng, MEng, MSc, PGCert, PGDip, PhD, MPhil

## *School of Health & Social Care; www.surrey.ac.uk/healthandsocialcare*

Department of Biochemistry & Physiology; Department of Microbial & Cellular Sciences; Department of Nutrition & Metabolism; School of Health & Social Care

biochemistry, biomedical science, food science, microbiology, midwifery, nursing studies, nutrition and dietetics, operating department practice, paramedic practice, veterinary biosciences, veterinary medicine, advanced gynaecological endoscopy, applied toxicology, clinical pharmacology, clinical practice, education for professional practice, genetic toxicology and environmental mutagenesis, health and clinical sciences, human nutrition, medical microbiology, nutritional medicine, pharmaceutical medicine, primary and community care, professional practice, public health practice, systems biology, toxicology, veterinary microbiology

BSc(Hons), MSc, DipHE, PGCert/Dip, PhD, DClinPract

## *Faculty of Business, Economics & Law; www.surrey.ac.uk/fbel*

### Surrey Business School; www.surrey.ac.uk/sbs

accounting & finance, banking & finance, business/& retail management, business analytics/administration, corporate environment management, entrepreneurship, finance, HRM, international business management, international financial/marketing/management, operations & logistics management, international retail management, marketing management; BSc, DBA, MBA, MSc, PhD

### School of Law; www.surrey.ac.uk/law

law, health/European/international/international commercial law, law & international studies/criminology; LLB, LLM, MA, PhD

### School of Hospitality & Tourism Management; www.surrey.ac.uk/shtm

food management, international hospitality/& tourism management, international event/hotel management, tourism development/management/marketing, sustainable tourism; BSc(Hons), MSc, PhD, MBA

## *Department of Health Care Management and Policy; www.surrey.ac.uk/hcmp*

health care management; MSc, PhD

## Degrees validated by the University of Surrey offered at:

### FARNBOROUGH COLLEGE OF TECHNOLOGY
www.farn-ct.ac.uk

accounting, aeronautical engineering, business management/& computing, complementary therapies, computing with gaming/networking/software engineering, education (early childhood studies/early years practice/learning support), early years (children & education), electrical/electronic engineering, English literature & criminology/sociology/contemporary education, film production & screenwriting, graphic design, animation & interactive media, hospitality management, mechanical engineering, mechatronics, modern history & contemporary education/criminology/English literature, media/music production, multimedia, photography, psychology & marketing/criminology, public service (uniformed), salon & spa management, sports science/human performance/performance & personal training, theatre, dance & film; BA(Hons), BSc(Hons), FdA, FdSc, FdEng, PGEd

### NESCOT (NORTH EAST SURREY COLLEGE OF TECHNOLOGY)
www.nescot.ac.uk

acoustics, environment & noise control, biomedical science, business management, psychodynamic counselling, health & social care, computing, early years, music technology, orthopaedic medicine, osteopathy, photography, photo-imaging, perfusion science, sports therapy, teacher training, teaching & learning in lifelong learning sector, travel & tourism management; BA(Hons), BSc(Hons), DipHE, FdA, FdSc, HNC, HND, MSc, PGDip, Masters, MOst

### ST MARY'S COLLEGE
www.smuc.ac.uk

applied physics, business law, creative and professional writing, drama, drama and applied/physical theatre/theatre arts, education and social science, English, screen media, geography, history, Irish studies, law, management studies, media arts, nutrition, philosophy, physical and sport education, primary education/with QTS, psychology, sociology, sport rehabilitation, sport science, sports coaching science, strength and conditioning, theology and religious studies, tourism/management, applied linguistics & ELT, Gothic: culture, subculture, counterculture, Irish studies, physical theatre, sports journalism, theatre directing, psychology and counselling, charity management, international business practice, international tourism development, managing for sustainability, applied sport and exercise physiology, applied sports nutrition, applied sport psychology, nutrition and physical activity for public health, sport rehabilitation, strength and conditioning, healthcare chaplaincy, pastoral ministry, youth ministry, bioethics and medical law, theology, Catholic school leadership – principles and practice, religion, politics and conflict resolution; BA, BSc, FdA, LlB, LLM, MA, MPhil, MSc, PGCE, PGCert, PGDip, PhD

## UNIVERSITY OF SUSSEX
**www.sussex.ac.uk**

### *Brighton & Sussex Medical School; www.bsms.sussex.ac.uk*

anaesthesia & perioperative medicine, cardiology, clinical education, commissioning & leadership, dementia studies, epidemiology, education in clinical setting, evidence-based practice, geriatric medicine, global health, health & social care, diabetes, leadership & management in health care, medical education, medical toxicology, medicine, nephrology, psychiatry, psychopharmacology, public health, surgery, trauma & orthopaedics; MA, MSc, MRes, MD, MPhil, PGCert, PGDip, PhD

## *School of Business, Management & Economics; www.sussex.ac.uk/aboutus/schoolsdepartments/bmec*

### Dept of Business & Management; www.sussex.ac.uk/Units/spru/bams

accounting & finance, banking & finance, business & management studies, business administration, financial risk management, international banking & finance/business, international accounting & corporate governance, business & HRM, global supply chain & logistics management, international management/marketing, law with business, management & entrepreneurship/finance, managing innovation & projects, marketing & management; BA, BSc, MSc, PGDip, LlB, MPhil, DPhil

### Dept of Economics; www.sussex.ac.uk/economics

economics, economics & international development/international relations/management studies/politics, finance & business, mathematics with economics, PPE, international economics, international finance; BA, BSc, GradDip, MSc, MPhil, MMath, DPhil

### Dept of Science & Technology Policy Research (SPRU); www.sussex.ac.uk/spru

science & technology policy, energy policy for sustainability, innovation & sustainability for international development, technology & innovation management; DPhil, MPhil, MSc

## *School of Education & Social Work; www.sussex.ac.uk/aboutus/schoolsdepartments/esw*

### Dept of Education; www.sussex.ac.uk/education

childhood & youth: theory & practice, education, education studies, working with children & young people, initial teacher education, PGCE: primary, 11–18/7–14 maths/moderrn foreign languages/secondary (numerous subjects)/international, school direct, secondary course leader; BA, MA, PGCE, PGCert/ Dip, EdD, MPhil, DPhil, MSc, QTS

### Dept of Social Work & Social Care; www.sussex.ac.uk/socialwork

childhood & youth studies, leadership & management in integrated children's services/& supervison in children's services, supervision of children's services, effective practice in children's services, practice education, social work, social research methods; BA, DPhil, MA, MPhil, MSc, PGCert

## *School of Engineering & Informatics www.sussex.ac.uk/ei*

Engineering & Design: advanced mechanical engineering, automotive/mechanical engineering, electrical/electronic/computer engineering, digital communications & business management, product design, satellite communications & space systems, sustainable engineering technology
Informatics: computer science, adv/computing & AI, computing for business & management, computing with digital media, evolutionary & adaptive systems, games & multimedia environments, human-computer interaction, IT with business & management, intelligent systems, management of IT
BA, BSc, BEng, MEng, DPhil, MA, MComp, MPhil, MSc, PGCert

## *School of English; www.sussex.ac.uk/aboutus/schoolsdepartments/english*

English language/literature/studies, American studies, drama & English/studies, drama, media & performance, drama studies, early modern literature & culture, English (jt degrees), English language & literature, English literature, English literature & culture 1700–1900, literature, film & visual culture, literature, modern & contemporary culture & thought, sexual dissidence in literature & culture, creative & critical writing, critical theory, literature & philosophy, applied linguistics; BA, DPhil, MA, MPhil

## *School of Global Studies; www.sussex.ac.uk/aboutus/schoolsdepartments/global*

### Dept of Anthropology; www.sussex.ac.uk/anthropology

anthropology, anthropology & cultural studies/history/modern languages, anthropology & international development/geography/international relations, anthropology of development/social transformation; BA, DPhil, MA, MSc

### Dept of Geography; www.sussex.ac.uk/geography

geography, geography & international relations/development/anthropology/modern languages, applied geomorphology, climate change & policy/

development, migration studies; BA, BSc, DPhil, MA, MPhil, MSc

**International Development; www.sussex.ac.uk/development**
international development, international development & anthropology/economics/geography/French/German/Spanish, anthropology & international development, environmental development & policy, gender & development, globalization, social development, human rights; BA, MA, MPhil, DPhil

**Dept of International Relations; www.sussex.ac.uk/ir**
conflict, security & development, geopolitics & grand strategy, global political economy, international relations & anthropology/contemporary European studies/law/modern languages/politics/sociology/economics/geography/development, international security; BA, LlB, DPhil, MA

## *School of History, Art History & Philosophy; www.sussex.ac.uk/aboutus/schoolsdepartments/hahp*

**Dept of American Studies; www.sussex.ac.uk/americanstudies**
American studies, American studies with history/English/film studies/politics/law/psychology/art history; BA, MA, MPhil, DPhil, LlB

**Dept of Art History; www.sussex.ac.uk/arthistory**
art history & museum curating/with philosophy/cultural studies/film studies, English; BA, MA, MPhil, DPhil

**Dept of History; www.sussex.ac.uk/history**
contemporary history, history/& American studies/English/philosophy/sociology/anthropology/film studies, intellectual history/politics, modern European history; BA, MPhil, DPhil, MA

**Dept of Philosophy; www.sussex.ac.uk/philosophy**
philosophy, philosophy & cognitive science, philosophy & English/history/political science, PPE, social & political thought; BA, MA, MPhil, DPhil

## *School of Law, Politics & Sociology; www.sussex.ac.uk/aboutus/schoolsdepartments/lps*

**Dept of Politics; www.sussex.ac.uk/politics**
contemporary European studies, corruption & governance, European politics, politics & international relations/languages/history/law/sociology/philosophy/American studies/economics, PPE; BA, DPhil, MPhil

**Sussex Law School; www.sussex.ac.uk/law**
law, criminal law & criminal justice, international criminal law/trade law/commercial law, law & business/American studies/international relations; CPE, DPhil, GradDip, LLB, LLM, MPhil, MSc

**Dept of Sociology; www.sussex.ac.uk/sociology**
sociology/with cultural studies/politics/psychology/media studies/international relations/philosophy/politics/history/international development, gender studies, social sciences; BA, DPhil, MA, MPhil, MSc

## *School of Mathematical & Physical Sciences; www.sussex.ac.uk/aboutus/schoolsdepartments/mps*

**Dept of Mathematics; www.sussex.ac.uk/maths**
mathematics, corporate & financial risk management, financial mathematics, mathematics with computer science/economics/physics, scientific computation; BSc, DPhil, MMath, MPhil, MSc, PGDip

**Dept of Physics & Astronomy; www.sussex.ac.uk/physics**
astronomy, astrophysics, cosmology, physics, astrophysics, theoretical/particle/neutrino physics, quantum optics; BSc, DPhil, MPhil, MPhys

## *School of Life Sciences; www.sussex.ac.uk/aboutus/schoolsdepartments/lifesci*

**Biochemistry & Molecular Biology; www.sussex.ac.uk/lifesci/biochemistry/**
biochemistry, biomedical science, genetic manipulation & molecular cell biology, molecular biology. biosciences

**Evolution, Behaviour & Environment; www.sussex.ac.uk/lifesci/ebe/**
biology, ecology & environment, biosciences

**Genome Danger & Stability; www.sussex.ac.uk/gdsc/**
various research topics

**Neuroscience; www.sussex.ac.uk/lifesci/neuroscience/**
neuroscience, medical neurosciences, neuroscience with cognition science/psychology, biosciences; BSc, DPhil, MPhil, MChem, MSc

## *School of Media, Film & Music; www.sussex.ac.uk/aboutus/schoolsdepartments/mfm*

### Dept of Media & Film; www.sussex.ac.uk/mediaandfilm/

English & film studies, film studies & American studies/art history/drama studies/English/history/French/Spanish/Italian, creative media practice, digital documentary/media, film studies, gender & media/cultural studies, media practice/studies, global film culture, international/journalism, journalism & documentary production, media & communication/cultural studies, media practice for international development, media studies & English, sociology & cultural studies/media studies

### Dept of Music; www.sussex.ac.uk/music/

music, music technology, music & sonic media; BA, BSc, DPhil, MA, MPhil, PhD, PGDip

## *School of Psychology; www.sussex.ac.uk/aboutus/schoolsdepartments/psychology*

psychology, psychology with American studies/cognitive science/neuroscience/sociolology, applied/social psychology, experimental psychology, clinical psychology & mental health, health psychology, cognitive/ neuroscience, psychological methods/therapy; BSc, MRes, MSc, PGDip

# SWANSEA UNIVERSITY
# www.swansea.ac.uk

## *College of Arts & Humanities; www.swansea.ac.uk/artand humanities*

classics and classical civilisation, Egyptology, English language and literature, TEFL, language and communication, Welsh, European languages, ancient, medieval, early modern and modern history, medieval studies, media studies including public and media relations and film studies, politics and international relations, philosophy, politics and economics or philosophy, politics and law, political communication (politics and media), translation studies and war and society, ancient history and classical culture, ancient narrative literature, classics, comparative journalism, creative writing, development and human rights, digital media, early modern history, English language studies, English literature, journalism and media within globalization, translation with language technology, literary translation, gender and culture, history, international communication and development, international relations, international security and development, literary translation, medieval studies, modern history, politics, media practice and PR, public policy, Chinese-English translation and language teaching, translation and interpreting, translation with language technology, Welsh writing in English, war and society; BA, MA, MPhil, MSc, MScEcon, PhD

## *College of Business & Economics & the Law; www.swansea.ac.uk/business*

### Swansea University Business School; www.swansea.ac.uk/business

accounting & finance, business management, business management (accounting/business/information systems/finance), business management and economics/ law, international business management, marketing, finance, international banking and finance, management, management (entrepreneurship/marketing/HRM/finance/international management/international); BA, BSc, MBA, MPhil, MSc, MScEcon, PhD

### School of Law; www.swansea.ac.uk/law

law, law & American studies/criminology/economics/French/German/law & history/Italian/politics/Spanish/Welsh, law with business, international maritime/trade/commercial and maritime law, intellectual property & commercial practice, legal practice, higher rights of audience, continuing professional development; Ll, LlM, GDL

### Dept of Economics; www.swansea.ac.uk/economics

economics, business economics/& accountancy/finance/computing/international business economics, financial economics/& accountancy, economics with international banking, PPE; BSc(Hons), BA(Hons), LlB, MSc, PhD

### Dept of Criminology; www.swansea.ac.uk/criminology

criminology/& criminal justice, criminology & social policy/law, applied criminal justice & criminology; BSc(Hons), LlB, MA

## *College of Engineering; www.swansea.ac.uk/engineering*

aerospace engineering, civil engineering, electronic and electrical engineering, electronics with computing science, electronic engineering with nanotechnology, telecommunications engineering, sports materials, mechanical engineering, medical engineering, electronic engineering with nanotechnology, sports materials, sports science/and engineering; computational engineering, computer modelling in engineering mechanics, /engineering, computational engineering, environmental management, materials engineering, steel technology, steel process & product development, nanoscience to nanotechnology; BEng, EngD, MEng, MPhil, MRes, MSc

## *College of Human & Health Sciences; www.swansea.ac.uk/Human & HealthSciences*

adult/child/mental health nursing, health and social care, healthcare science (audiology/cardiac physiology/nuclear medicine/radiotherapy physics/respiratory and sleep sciences), medical sciences and humanities, midwifery, osteopathy, paramedic science, psychology, social work, social policy, criminology/economics/politics/social history & social policy, ageing studies, childhood studies, developmental and therapeutic play, education for health professions, advanced practice in health care/infection control, approved mental health professional, chronic conditions management, community and primary health care practice, health care law & ethics, infection prevention and control, public health & health promotion/partnerships in care, social work, health care management, abnormal and clinical psychology, cognitive neuroscience, research methods in psychology, social research methods

BA, BSc, BMid, BN, DipHE, HND, LLB, MA, MPhil, MSc, MScEcon, PGCert/Dip, PhD, DipHE, MOst, BScEcon

## *College of Medicine; www.swansea.ac.uk/medicine*

medical genetics, medical biochemistry, trauma surgery, biochemistry general medicine, liquid chromatography & mass spectrometry, health service research, basic biomedical & physiological science, bioinformatics, cell biology of cancer & reproduction, diabetes, immunity & allergy, medical physics & clinical engineering, microbiology & infection, neuroscience & molecular psychiatry, nanomedicine & medical devices; BSc, MBBCh, MD, MPhil, MSc, PhD

## *College of Science; www.swansea.ac.uk/science*

### Dept of Biosciences; www.swansea.ac.uk/biosci

biology, biological science & genetics, maritime biology, zoology, environmental biology, conservation & resource management, aquatic ecology & conservation, sustainable aquaculture & fisheries

### Dept of Computer Science; www.swansea.ac.uk/compsci

computer science, computing/& communications, computer science & pure mathematics/physics/geoinformatics, adv computer science, software technology, human–computer interaction, visual computing, safety & secure systems

### Dept of Geography; www.swansea.ac.uk/geography

geography, human geography, physical earth geography, geography & geoinformatics/European studies, environmental dynamics & climate change, geographical information & climate change, global migration

### Dept of Physics; www.swansea.ac.uk/physics

physics, theoretical physics, physics & nanotechnology, particle physics & cosmology, modelling, uncertainty & data

### Dept of Mathematics; www.swansea.ac.uk/maths

mathematics, pure/applied mathematics, mathematics for finance, mathematics & physics/geoinformatics/computing for finance, modelling, uncertainty & data; BSc, MEng, MMath, MPhil, MPhys, MRes, MSc, PhD

# UNIVERSITY OF TEESSIDE
## www.tees.ac.uk

### School of Arts & Media; www.tees.ac.uk/schools/sam

Art: digital arts & design, interior architecture, fine art

Design: design for creative industries, graphic design, interior architecture/design, product design, future design

English: English studies, creative writing

History: history, cultural history, European history, local & regional history

Media & Journalism: media production, journalism/ & news practice, media studies, multimedia journalism/PR, TV & film production, mass communication

Performing Arts: contemporary music creation, music technology, dance, performance & events, professional dance practice, performing arts, performance for live & recorded media

BA(Hons), BSc(Hons), FdA, MA, MPhil, MSc, PhD

### School of Computing; www.tees.ac.uk/schools/scm

computer animation, /games, computer animation & visual effects, computer character animation, computing, computer games AI/production, computer games/art/design/programming, games & animation, independent games development, creative digital media, concept art form, computer science, computing networking/mathematics, information & communication technology, creative digital media, web & multimedia, web design, computer & digital forensics, computing security & information, IT project management, mobile application development, software engineering, user experience; BA, BSc, DProf, FdSc, MA, MPhil, MProf, MSc, PGDip, PhD,

### School of Health & Social Care; www.tees.ac.uk/schools/soh

adult/social care, dental hygiene and dental therapy, dental nurse practice, diagnostic radiography, midwifery, nursing studies (adult/child/learning disabilities/mental health), occupational therapy, operating department practice, physiotherapy, social work, nursing in the home/district nursing, professional health studies, professional nursing studies, specialist community public health nursing (health visiting/occupational health/school nursing), environmental health, food and nutrition

advanced clinical practice (cardiac care/management of long-term health conditions/manipulative therapy/neurological rehabilitation), advancing practice, applied behaviour analysis, autism practice, clinical psychology, clinical research, cognitive behaviour therapy, diagnostic radiography, evidence-based medicine/anaesthesia, evidence-based practice, forensic radiography, health and social care, health and social care sciences (end of life care/generic pathway/public health), innovation and transformational change, leadership in health and social care, manipulative therapy, medical ultrasound, midwifery studies, neurological rehabilitation, nursing (advanced cardiac care/advanced nurse practitioner/advanced surgical care practitioner/ specialist field, occupational therapy studies, orthopaedics, physiotherapy studies, public health, rehabilitation (occupational therapy/physiotherapy), service improvement, social work, surgical care practitioner (cardiothoracic surgery/general surgery/obstetric and gynaecology surgery/orthopaedic surgery), the management of long-term health conditions, transformational leadership in health and social care; BA, BSc, Cert/DipHE, FdSc, HND, MA, MPhil, MSc, PGCert/Dip, MRes, DClinPsy, Doc Health & Social Care

### Science & Engineering; www.tees.ac.uk/schools/sse

adv manufacturing systems, aeronautical/aerospace engineering, automotive engineering, chemistry, biological sciences, biotechnology, chemical/civil engineering, computer & digital forensics, control & electronics, crime & investigation, crime scene science, disaster management, electrical & electronic engineering, electronics & communications, energy & environmental engineering, engineering/management, environmental science/health, fire scene investigation, food, nutrition & health science, food science & engineering, forensic biology/science/psychology, instrumentation & control engineering, mechanical engineering, petroleum technology, policing & investigation, project management, renewable energy engineering; BEng, BSc, FdEng, HNC, HND, MPhil, MRes, MSc, PGDip, PhD

### School of Social Sciences & Law; www.tees.ac.uk/schools/ss

business/medical law, childhood & youth studies, crime & investigation, criminal investigation/law, criminology with sociology/law/psychology/youth studies/investigation, contemporary drug use, early childhood studies, education/professional studies, exercise therapy, legal/& forensic psychology, global development & social research, health psychology, international/criminal law, investigative skills, law, movement science & multimodal rehabilitation, outdoor education/leadership, police studies, policing & investigation, professional policing, promoting inclusive practice in education, social sciences/research, sociology, sport & exercise (exercise science/sport science/coaching science/personal training), sports therapy/development, fitness instruction & sports massage, adv sports therapy & rehabilitation science, strength & conditioning psychology/development/therapy & rehabilitation), teaching in lifelong learning, youth & community studies/criminology/psychology, youth work; BA, BSc, DProf, FdA, FdSc, FdSocSc, GradCert, HNC, CertEd, HND, LLB, LLM, MA, MPhil, MProf, MSc, PhD

### Teesside Business School; www.tees.ac.uk/schools/tubs/

accounting & finance, applied accounting & business finance, business administration/finance/management, business with law, coaching for transformational change, economic crime management, financial investigation & financial crime, fraud management, hospitality management, HRM, international management, management, leadership & management, marketing/& advertising/management, project management, tourism & aviation, tourism management, travel & tourism/management; BA, BSc, DBA, FdA, FdSc, MA, MBA, MSc, PGDip

## TRINITY COLLEGE LONDON
## www.trinitycollege.co.uk

dance, drama & speech, music, performing arts, English language, teaching English; PGDip, SfL, TESOL

## UNIVERSITY OF ULSTER
## www.ulster.ac.uk

### *Faculty of Art, Design & the Built Environment; www.adbe.ulster.ac.uk*

#### School of Architecture & Design; www.adbe.ulster.ac.uk/schools/archi_design

3D design (interior, product & furniture design), architectural studies/technology & management, architecture, interior design; BA(Hons), BDes, BSc(Hons), CertHE, MArch, MLA, MSc

#### School of Art & Design; www.adbe.ulster.ac.uk/schools/art_design

art & design, contemporary applied arts, design for animation, multidisciplinary design, textile art, design & fashion, fine & applied arts, fine art, photography; BA, BDes, BSc, MA, MDes, MFA, PGDip

#### School of the Built Environment; www.adbe.ulster.ac.uk/schools/built_environment

building engineering & materials, building services & energy engineering, built environment building surveying, civil engineering, construction engineering & project management, construction business & project management, energy & building services engineering, environmental health, fire safety engineering, housing management/studies, hydrogen safety engineering, infrastructure engineering, property investment, appraisal & development, planning & property development, property development, appraisal quantity surveying & commercial management, renewable engineering & energy management, transportation, transport management; BEng, BSc, MEng, MPhil, MSc, PGCert, PGDip, PhD

### *Faculty of Arts; www.arts.ulster.ac.uk*

applied languages and translation (French/German/Spanish), arts, Celtic studies, Chinese, creative technologies, cultural heritage and museum studies,

dance, dance with drama/Irish/music, design for creative practice, documentary practice, drama, drama with advertising/computing/dance/Irish/marketing/music/ psychology, English, English: jt degrees in number of subjects, film studies, film studies: jt degrees in number of subjects, French, French: jt degrees in number of subjects, German, German: jt degrees in number of subjects, history, history; jt degrees in number of subjects, humanities, interactive media arts, Irish, Irish; jt degrees in number of subjects, Irish history, Irish history & politics/society, Irish language/and literature, Irish literature in English, journalism, journalism; jt degrees in number of subjects, media management and policy, media studies, media studies and production, media studies; jt degrees in number of subjects, modern Irish, modern languages – French/German/Spanish, museum practice and management, music, music with dance/drama/Irish/psychology, photo imaging minor, professional translation, Spanish, Spanish; jt degrees in number of subjects;
BA(Hons), MA, MPhil, PGDip, PhD, MRes, BMus, MMus, MDes, CertHE

## *Faculty of Computing & Engineering; www.compeng.ulster.ac.uk*

### School of Computing & Information Engineering; www.compeng.ulster.ac.uk/cie

computing, computing artificial intelligence/digital games development/internet systems, telecommunications & internet systems, computing with accountancy/business, education/geography/psychology; BSc, MSc, PGDip, PhD

### School of Computing & Intelligent systems; www.scis.ulster.ac.uk

creative computing (games/design), information & communications technologies, computer science (intelligent systems/mobile computing/software systems development), computer games development, computer engineering, multimedia computer games/modelling, computing with accounting/HRM/management studies/marketing, computing & creative technologies/intelligent systems/financial services; BEng, BSc, MSc, PGDip, PhD

### School of Computing & Mathematics; www.infj.ulst.ac.uk/cm/

computing & information systems, computational finance, computer security, computing science/& mathematics, computing/web technologies/healthcare informatics, computing systems, creative computing, information & communication technologies, interactive multimedia design, computing science (artificial intelligence/healthcare/technologies/network technologies), software engineering; BSc, MSc, PGCert, PGDip, PhD

### School of Engineering; www.seng.ulster.ac.uk/eme

biomedical engineering, clean technology, electronic engineering, engineering management, mechanical engineering, mechatronics engineering, sports technology, technology/design, adv composites & polymers, manufacturing management, nanotechnology; BSc, BEng, MEng, MSc, PGDip, PhD

## *Faculty of Life & Health Sciences; www.science.ulster.ac.uk*

### School of Biomedical Sciences; www.biomed.science.ulster.ac.uk

applied biosciences, biology, biomedical science, biotechnology, cataract & refractory studies, clinical visual sciences, dietetics, food regulatory affairs, food & forensic studies, human nutrition, optometry, pathology, pharmaceutical sciences, pharmacy/management, stem cell biology, systems biology, veterinary; public health; BSc, DMedSc, GradCert, MPharm, MSc, PGCert, PGDip

### School of Environmental Sciences; www.science.ulster.ac.uk/envsci

coastal zone management, coastal & marine tourism, environmental management/science/studies/toxicology & pollution monitoring, GIS, geography, marine science/spatial planning; AB, BSc, DEnvSci, MPhil, MRes, MSc, PGCert, PGDip, PhD

### School of Health Sciences; www.science.ulster.ac.uk/health

advanced practice, clinical physiology research/cardiology/respiratory, health science, occupational therapy, physiotherapy, podiatry, radiography (diagnostic/therapeutic), speech & language therapy; BSc, MClinRes, MSc

### School of Nursing; www.science.ulster.ac.uk/nursing

community & public health nursing, dementia studies, health promotion & population health, health & social care/wellbeing, independent & supplementary prescribing, learning disabilities, midwifery, nursing practice/adult/public health, palliative care, primary care & general practice, specialist midwifery/nursing practice; BSc, CertHE, MSc, PGCert, PGDip, MPhil, PhD

### School of Psychology; www.science.ulster.ac.uk/psychology

applied behaviour analysis, applied psychology (mental health), careers guidance, health psychology, psychology; BSc, MSc, PGDip

### Ulster Sports Academy; www.ulster.ac.uk/science

physical activity & population health, sport & exercise sciences, applied sport & exercise psychology, sports management/coaching/studies/technology/development, sports & exercise nutrition; BSc, FdSc, MPhil, MSc, DPhil, PGDip, PhD

## *Faculty of Social Sciences; www.socsci.ulster.ac.uk*

### School of Communication; www.socsci.ulster.ac.uk/comms

advertising & marketing, PR, counselling/& therapeutic communication, communication with advertising/counselling/PR, political lobbying & public affairs, language & linguistics with advertising/communications/counselling/PR, linguistics/in advertising; BSc, MPhil, MSc, PGCert, PGDip, PhD

### School of Economics; www.socsci.ulster.ac.uk/ecompolitics

applied/business economics, economics, economics with accountancy/marketing/politics; BSc, MSc, PGDip

### School of Education; www.socsci.ulster.ac.uk/education

PGCE (post-primary, primary, in numerous school subjects, FE), Certificate in Teaching, contemporary society, educational leadership & management, education with numerous jt degree subjects, ICT, inclusive & special education, international development, teaching & learning, library & information management; TESOL, MEd, PGCE, PGCert, PGDip, BA(Hons), BSc(Hons)

### School of Law; www.socsci.ulster.ac.uk/law

law, law & criminology/politics, human rights law & transitional justice, clinical legal education; LLB, LLM

### School of Criminology, Politics & Social Policy; www.socsci.ulster.ac.uk/policy

criminology/& criminal justice, health & social care policy, politics, public administration, social policy, international studies, procurement executive development, politics with criminology/economics sociology/law/international studies; BSc, MPA, PGCert, PGDip

### School of Sociology & Applied Social Studies; www.socsci.ulster.ac.uk/sociology

community development/youth work, restorative practices, profession development/in social work, sociology/with international politics/social work/criminology/HRM/law/politics; BSc, MSc, PGCert, PGDip

### Graduate School of Professional Legal Education; www.socsci.ulster.ac.uk/gsple

legal practice; PGDip

## *Ulster Business School; www.business.ulster.ac.uk*

accounting & law/advertising/HRM/managerial finance/marketing, advertising, advertising and HRM, advertising with accounting/computing/drama/Irish psychology, business administration, business, business management, business studies/with specialisms, business with specialisms, consumer studies, creative advertising technologies, culinary arts management, finance and investment analysis, HRM, HRM & marketing, international hospitality management, international travel and tourism management, international travel and tourism studies with languages, leisure and events management, management and leadership development, management practice, marketing, social enterprise, advanced accounting, applied management, business administration master, business development and innovation, business improvement, business studies, cultural management, event management, executive leadership, financial services, innovation management in the public service, international business, international hotel and tourism management, international tourism development, management & corporate governance, marketing, sport management; BSc, BSc(Hons), MBS, CertHE, AdvDip, MBA, MSc, PGDip

## UNIVERSITY OF WALES: GLYNDWR UNIVERSITY
## www.glyndwr.ac.uk

### *Institute forArts, Science & Technology; www.glyndwr.ac.uk/en/ UniversityInstitutes/ ArtsScience&Technology*

### Creative Industries, Media & Performance; www.glyndwr.ac.uk/en/ UniversityInstitutes/ ArtsScienceandTechnology/Cre

Applied Art; design: applied arts, art practice, design practice
Design Communication & Digital Art; design: animation, visual effects and game art/film and photography/graphic design and multimedia/illustration, graphic novels and children's publishing, creative media, communications & digital art
Fine Art; fine art
Creative Media Technology; music technology, sound technology, television production and technology
Broadcasting & Journalism; broadcasting, journalism and media communications
Creative Writing; creative writing and history/ English
English; English, English and creative writing/history
History; history, creative writing/English and history
Information Management; library and information practice/management
BEng(Hons), FdEng, MSc, PhD, MPhil, MRes

### Engineering and Applied Physics; www.glyndwr.ac.uk/en/ UniversityInstitutes/ ArtsScienceandTechnology/eng

Electrical and Electronic Engineering; electrical and electronic engineering, digital and radio frequency communication systems, advanced electronic techniques, electrical and electronic systems, renewable energy systems and sustainability/distributed generation
Aeronautical Engineering; aeronautical and mechanical engineering/manufacture, aircraft maintenance, aircraft electronics & control, composites
Performance Car Technology; performance car technology, motorsport design and management, renewable energy and sustainable technologies
Industrial Engineering; industrial engineering
Mechanical Engineering; mechanical engineering, manufacture, manufacturing engineering
Digital and Radio Frequency Communication Systems; advanced electronic techniques, electrical and electronic systems, renewable energy systems and sustainability/distributed generation
BSc(Hons), MSc, MRes, FdEng, BEng, MEng, MPhil, PhD

### Computing; www.glyndwr.ac.uk/en/ UniversityInstitutes/ ArtsScienceandTechnology/Cor

applied computing, computer game development, computer network management and security, creative media computing, app design, IT management for business, information technology support, business management and IT, applied computing, creative media computing, library and information practice; computer networking, computer science, creative audio technology, computing, high performance computing, creative media technology; BSc(Hons), FdSc, MSc, MRes, PhD, MPhil

### Biology & the Environment; www.glyndwr.ac.uk/en/ UniversityInstitutes/ ArtsScienceandTechnology/Biol

Built environment: architectural design technology, building studies (construction/maintenance management), facilities management, housing studies, housing & sustainable communities, supported housing, rural business
Animal Studies & Equine Science: animal studies, equestrian psychology, equine science & welfare
Wildlife & Plant Biology
Science & Environment: formulation science, photovoltaics, polymer & biopolymer science
BSc(Hons), FdSc, MPhil, PhD

### Chemistry; www.glyndwr.ac.uk/en/ UniversityInstitutes/ ArtsScienceandTechnology/Chemistry/

forensic science, polymer & biopolymer science; BSc(Hons), MSc

### Management & Business; www.glyndwr.ac.uk/en/ UniversityInstitutes/ ArtsScienceandTechnology

accounting and finance, business management/and IT, entrepreneurship, app design, business marketing, business and events management, professional education and training, IT management for business, business management/with accounting/marketing, rural business, HRM, executive/MBA, international business, IT management, marketing, management BA(Hons), FdA, PhD, MPhil, MA, MBA, MSc, ProfDoc

## *Institute for Health, Medical Science & Society; www.glyndwr.ac.uk/en/UniversityInstitutes/HealthMedicalScienceandSociety*

**Applied Social Services**

criminology & criminal justice, therapeutic childcare, health & social care, youth & community work/studies, social work, counselling with children & young people, counselling work

**Education**

post-compulsory education and training, professional education and training, compulsory education sector, learning support: learning and teaching/SEN, education, education (psychology and counselling/additional learning needs/special educational needs), dyslexia, e-learning: theory and practice, professional development in HE, professional development (education), teaching of psychology, professional education, youth and community studies, youth studies

**Health, Psychology & Social Care**

counselling; person-centred and experiential counselling and psychotherapy, health care studies, health and social care, health and care studies, nursing post-registration

Community Practice; community specialist practice (community children's nursing/district nursing/general practice nursing), health studies, healthcare leadership and management, specialist community public health nursing (health visiting/school nursing), clinical/community practice

Occupational Health and Safety; environmental health management (environmental and public health/occupational health, safety and environmental management

Occupational Therapy; occupational therapy

Health and Medical Science; nursing and healthcare studies, advanced clinical practice, leadership in health and social care, professional education, counselling studies with children and young people

**Childhood & Family Studies**

childhood studies, education & childhood studies, early childhood care & education, childhood studies/babies & young children/play/early childhood education

**Psychology**

psychology, psychology of religion, teaching of psychology

BA(Hons), BSc(Hons), FdSc, MSc, MPhil & Childhood Studies

## Science & Environment

polymer science & technology; MRes, MPhil, PhD

## Society & Community

Counselling: counselling studies, person-centred & experiential counselling & psychotherapy

Criminal Justice: criminology & criminal justice

Social Care: social work, therapeutic childcare, counselling & psychotherapy, counselling studies/with children & young people

Social Science: public & social policy

Youth & Community: youth & community work/studies; Cer/DiptHE, BA(Hons), FdA, MPhil, PhD, MA, ProfDoc

## Social Sciences

social science; MRes, MPhil, PhD

## Sport & Exercise Sciences; www.glyndwr.ac.uk/en/UniversityInstitutes/HealthMedicalSciencesandSociety/SportandExerciseSciences

sport & exercise sciences, sports coaching; BSc(Hons), MRes, MPhil, PhD

## UNIVERSITY OF WALES: SWANSEA METROPOLITAN UNIVERSITY
## www.smu.ac.uk

### *Faculty of Applied Design & Engineering; www.smu.ac.uk/index.php/potential-students/faculty-of-applied-design-and-engineering*

#### School of Applied Computing; www.smu.ac.uk/index.php/potential-students/faculty-of-applied-design-and-engineering/school-of-applied-computing

applied computing, business information technology, computer games development, computer networks/systems & electronics, computer network technology, computing & information systems, e-commerce, electronic engineering, software engineering, web development; BEng, BSc, HND, MSc

#### School of Automotive Engineering; www.smu.ac.uk/index.php/potential-students/faculty-of-applied-design-and-engineering/school of automotive engineering

automotive engineering, motorcycle engineering, motorsport engineering & design/technology; BEng, BSc, HND

#### School of Built & Natural Environment; www.smu.ac.uk/index.php/potential-students/faculty-of-applied-design-and-engineering/school-of-natural-environment

building studies, civil engineering & environmental management, facilities management, project & construction management, quantity surveying, environmental conservation/management; BSc, MSc

#### School of Digital Media; www.smu.ac.uk/index.php/potential-students/faculty-of-applied-design-and-engineering/school-of-digital-media

3D/computer animation, creative computer games design, creative sound production, creative digital media, computer animation, digital media development, multimedia, music technology, visual effects; BA, BSc, HND, MA, MSc

#### School of Industrial Design; www.smu.ac.uk/index.php/potential-students/faculty-of-applied-design-and-engineering/school-of-industrial-design

automotive design, industrial design, product design/& innovation, transportation design; BA, BSc, MA, MSc

#### School of Logistics & Manufacturing Engineering; www.smu.ac.uk/index.php/potential-students/faculty-of-applied-design-and-engineering/school-of-logistics-and-manufacturing

logistics, lean & agile manufacturing, mechanical & manufacturing engineering, food logistics, motorsport management, non-destructive testing & evaluation, logistics & supply chain management; BSc, BEng, MA, MSc

#### Welsh School of Architectural Glass; www.smu.ac.uk/index.php/faculty-of-applied-design-and-engineering/welsh-school-of-architectural-glass

architectural glass, stained glass; BA, MA

### *Faculty of Art & Design; www.smu.ac.uk/index.php/potential-students/faculty-of-art-and-design*

#### School of Visual Communication; www.smu.ac.uk/index.php/potential-students/faculty-of-art-and-design/vis

graphic/design for advertising, advertising & brand design, general illustration; BA(Hons)

#### School of Fine Arts; www.smu.ac.uk/index.php/potential-students/faculty-of-art-and-design/school-of-fine-arts

Fine art: combined media/painting & drawing/3D & sculpture

Photography: photography in the arts, photojournalism, documentary video, video arts, fashion & visual culture, digital film & TV production, new media production

Surface Pattern (textiles): surface pattern design (contemporary arts practice/textiles for fashion/for interiors)

Visual Communication: graphic design, advertising & brand design, general illustration

Postgraduate: fine art/photography/visual communication/textiles – contemporary dialogue
BA, FdA, MA

### Faculty of Humanities; www.smu.ac.uk/faculty-of-humanities

#### Swansea School of Education; www.smu.ac.uk/index.php/faculty-of-humanities/swansea-school-of-education

educational studies, post-compulsory education & training, professional development (education & training/teaching & learning/education), language & learning, introduction to teaching, mentoring & coaching, thinking studies, research in maths education, PGCE primary/secondary (in numerous subjects), secondary education, primary education (Welsh medium), post-compulsory education & training; BA, MA, FD, MRes, MA, GradDip, MEd, CertHE, MPhil, PhD

### Faculty of Business & Management; www.smu.ac.uk/faculty-of-business-and-management

#### Swansea Business School; www.smu.ac.uk/index.php/faculty-of-humanities/swansea-business-schools

accounting, business & finance, business, HRM, HR development, financial services, financial management/learning & development, management & leadership, marketing management, international business, international tourism, events management, leisure management, tourism management, international travel & tourism management, sports management; BA, FdA, GradDip, HND, MA, MA(Ed), MRes, PGCE, MBA, MSc

#### School of Public Service Leadership; www.smu.ac.uk/index.php/faculty-of-humanities/school-of-public-service-leadership

health & social care, public services; BA, MPhil, PhD

## UNIVERSITY OF WALES: TRINITY SAINT DAVID
## www.trinitysaintdavid.ac.uk

### Faculty of Humanities; www.trinitysaintdavid.ac.uk/en/facultyofhumanities/

#### School of Archaeology, History & Anthropology; www.trinitysaintdavid.ac.uk/en/archaeologyhistoryandanthropology/

Archaeology; archaeology professional practice, ancient civilisations, ancient history & art, archaeology (environmental), archaeology & classical civilisations/history/medieval studies
History; medieval studies, modern historical studies, ancient & medieval history
Anthropology; archaeology & anthropology/ancient history, religious studies & anthropology
Postgrad; cultural astronomy & astrology, local history, landscape management & environmental archaeology, heritage studies
BA(Hons), MA, PhD

#### School of Cultural studies; www.trinitysaintdavid.ac.uk/en/schoolofculturalstudies

Chinese studies, Chinese civilisation (jt degrees), creative writing, creative & script writing, English & creative writing/TEFL, medieval & early modern literature, modern literature, applied/philosophy, European philosophy
BA(Hons), MA

#### School of Classics; www.trinitysaintdavid.ac.uk/en/schoolofclassics/

ancient history/civilizations/religions, ancient history & archaeology, classical studies, ancient & medieval history, classics, Greek, Latin; BA, MA, MPhil, PhD, PGCert/Dip

#### Dept of Theology & Religious Studies & Islamic Studies; www.trinitysaintdavid.ac.uk/en/schooloftheologyreligiousstudiesand islamicstudies/

biblical interpretation, Christian theology, church history, Islamic studies, philosophy, religious history/studies, with education, study of religions, religion & society, jt hons in numerous subjects, theology; BA, DMin, DPT, LTh, MA, MMin, MTh, CertHE

### *Faculty of Arts & Social Studies; www.trinitysaintdavid.ac.uk/en/facultyofartsandsocialstudies/*

**School of Business; www.trinitysaintdavid.ac.uk/en/schoolofbusiness/**

business information technology/management, computing, internet computing, internet/computing, management & information technology, prof practice, social/entrepreneurship, HRM, information security/management, leadership, marketing, professional practice, professional arts management, heritage tourism management, technology enhanced learning; BA, MBA, MA, MSc, MPhil, PhD, PGCert/Dip

**School of Creative Arts; www.trinitysaintdavid.ac.uk/en/creativearts**

applied art, art & design, 3D designer maker-craft product, ceramics & jewellery, design, digital illustration, fashion: apparel design & construction, fine art, graphic communication, textiles art, design, craft, film & visual culture, new media production, fine art: contemporary practice, painting, drawing & printmaking, sculpture, photography; BA(Hons), MA, FD, MPhil, PhD

**School of Sport, Health & Outdoor Education; www.trinitysaintdavid.ac.uk/en/schoolofsporthealthandoutdooreducation/**

health, nutrition & lifestyle, PE with QTS, health & exercise/sport studies, outdoor education; BA, BSc, MA, MPhil

**School of Performing Arts; www.trinitysaintdavid.ac.uk/en/schooloftheatreandperformance/**

acting, theatre design & production, drama & education – context & practices, theatre & society; BA, MA

### *Faculty of Education & Training; www.trinitysaintdavid.ac.uk/en/facultyofeducationandtraining*

**School of Early Childhood; www.trinitysaintdavid.ac.uk/en/schoolofearlychildhood/**

early childhood, nursery management, Welsh & bilingual practice in early years, foundation phase; MA, BA, CertHE, PGDip

**School of Initial Teacher Training & Education; www.trinitysaintdavid.ac.uk/en/schoolofinitialteachereducationandtraining/**

primary education with QTS, professional development, education; MA, BA, GradDip/Cert

**School of Welsh & Bilingual Studies; www.trinitysaintdavid.ac.uk/en/schoolofwelshandbilingualstudies/**

Celtic studies, bilingualism & multilingualism; BA, MA, MPhil, PhD

**Welsh International Academy of Voice; www.trinitysaintdavid.ac.uk/en/schoolofwelshandbilingualstudies/**

advanced vocal studies; MA

**School of Social Justice & Inclusion; www.trinitysaintdavid.ac.uk/en/schoolofsocialjusticeandinclusion**

primary education studies, applied psychology, social media, youth & community work, inclusive studies, youth & community work, special educational needs, adolescence studies; BA(Hons), MA, FD, GradCert

## UNIVERSITY OF WARWICK
## www.warwick.ac.uk

### *Faculty of Arts; www2.warwick.ac.uk/fac/arts*

**Dept of Classics & Ancient History; www2.warwick.ac.uk/fac/arts/classics**

ancient history & classical archaeology, ancient visual & material culture, visual & material culture in ancient Rome, classical civilization/with philosophy, classics, English & Latin literature, Italian & classics, Italian literature; BA, MA, MPhil, PhD

**Dept of English & Comparative Literary Studies; www2.warwick.ac.uk/fac/arts/english**
English literature, creative writing, English & theatre studies, pan-romanticisms, philosophy, film & literature, world literatures, writing, English & French/German/Latin/Italian, translation studies; BA, MA, MPhil, PhD

**Dept of Film & TV Studies; www2.warwick.ac.uk/fac/arts/film**
film & literature/TV studies, research in film & TV, history & film; BA, MA, MPhil, PhD

**Dept of French Studies; www2.warwick.ac.uk/fac/arts/french**
English & French, French studies with history of art/German/Italian studies/film studies/ stage & theatre German/history/international studies/Italian/politics/film/sociology, film, French culture & thought, French & francophone studies, translation, writing & cultural difficulties, theatre studies; BA, MA, MPhil, PGDip, PhD

**Dept of German Studies; www2.warwick.ac.uk/fac/arts/german**
German cultural studies, German studies, German with business studies/French/international studies/Italian/Spanish/history, pan-romanticism, translation, writing & cultural differences; BA, MA, MPhil, PGDip, PhD

**Dept of History; www2.warwick.ac.uk/fac/arts/history**
history, 18th-century studies, comparative American history, global history, history & politics/sociology/Italian/French/German/culture, history, history of race in America, literature & culture of the Americas, historical studies, modern European, modern history, medieval world, histography, history of medicine, religious/cultural & social history, 1500–1700; BA, MA, MPhil, PhD

**Dept of History of Art; www2.warwick.ac.uk/fac/arts/arthistory**
history of art, art history with Italian, history of art/& French, Venice, British art; BA, MA, MPhil, PGDip, PhD

**Dept of Italian; www2.warwick.ac.uk/fac/arts/italian**
comparative Italian/& European studies, Italian studies & French/German/Classics/theatre studies/international studies/history of art/European literature, translation, writing & cultural differences; BA, MA, MPhil, PGDip, PhD

**School of Comparative American Studies; www2.warwick.ac.uk/fac/arts/cas**
comparative American studies, literature, film & politics of the USA, history, literature & culture of the Americas; BA, MA, PhD

**School of Theatre, Performance & Cultural Policy Studies; www2.warwick.ac.uk/fac/arts/Theatre_s**
theatre consultancy, international cultural policy & management/performance research, creative & media enterprise, global media & communication, theatre & performance studies; BA, MA, MPhil, PhD

## *Faculty of Medicine; www2.warwick.ac.uk/fac/med*

**Warwick Medical School**
medicine & surgery, advanced clinical practice for health care, child health, diabetes, diabetes (paediatrics), digital healthcare, dentistry, endodontics, healthcare systems improvement, health sciences, health sciences (musculoskeletal care/plastic surgery/retinal screening – diabetes), health services management, implant dentistry/with supervised oral surgery clinical training, interdisciplinary biomedical research, medical education/leadership, orthodontics/with supervised dental clinical training, philosophy & ethics of mental health, pre-hospital critical care, public health, research methods in health sciences, restorative dentistry with supervised dental clinical training, trauma and orthopaedic surgery, biomedical cell biology, health science, mental health & well-being, metabolic & vascular health, microbiology; MBChB, MD, MMedSci, MPhil, MSc, MA, MS, PhD, PGCert, MPH

## *Faculty of Science; www2.warwick.ac.uk/fac/sci*

**Dept of Life Sciences; www2.warwick.ac.uk/fac/sci/lifesci**
biochemistry, biomedical science, biological sciences, biotechnology, bioprocessing & business management, cell biology, food science, environmental resources, environmental bioscience in changing climate, food security, integrative bioscience/with business & virology, medical microbiology, molecular genetics, sustainable crop production; BSc, MD, MPhil, MSc, PhD

### Dept of Chemistry; www2.warwick.ac.uk/fac/sci/chemistry

analytical science, biomedical chemistry, chemical biology, chemistry/with management, molecular/physical chemistry, chemical physics, materials chemistry, medicinal chemistry, synthetics, polymer chemistry, chemistry with scientific writing; BSc, MChem, MSc, PhD

### Dept of Computer Science; www2.warwick.ac.uk/fac/sci/dcs

computer & management sciences/business studies, cognitive systems, computer science/& applications, computing systems, discrete mathematics; BSc, MEng, MPhil, MSc, PhD

### School of Engineering; www2.warwick.ac.uk/fac/sci/eng

automotive engineering, biomedical engineering, civil engineering, computer & information engineering, electronic engineering/systems, electronic systems with communications/sensor technology, engineering with business studies/management, engineering systems, energy & power electronic systems, engineering/& business, engineering business management, general engineering, fluid dynamics, manufacturing & mechanical engineering/systems, mechanical systems, robotics, sustainability, systems engineering, tunnelling & underground space; BEng, BSc, EngD, MPhil, MSc, PhD

### Dept of Mathematics/Warwick Mathematics Institute; www2.warwick.ac.uk/fac/sci/maths

financial/interdisciplinary mathematics, mathematics, mathematics & business studies/economics/philosophy; BSc, MMath, MSc, PhD

### Dept of Physics; www2.warwick.ac.uk/fac/sci/physics

mathematics & physics, physics/& business studies, Master project options; BSc, MPhys, MSc, PhD, MMathPhys

### Dept of Psychology; www2.warwick.ac.uk/fac/sci/psych

philosophy with psychology, behavioural & economic science, clinical applications of psychology, psychology, psychological research; BSc, MPhil, MSc, PhD

### Dept of Statistics; www2.warwick.ac.uk/fac/sci/statistics

statistics & mathematics/economics, operational research; MMathStat, MPhil, MSc, PgDip, PhD

## *Faculty of Social Studies; www2.warwick.ac.uk/fac/soc*

### Centre for Applied Linguistics; www2.warwick.ac.uk/fac/soc/al

English language teaching/for young learners/specific purposes/ICT & multimedia/testing & assessment methods, intercultural communication/for business & the professions; BEd, BA(Hons), EdD, MA, MPhil, PGCert, PGDip, PhD

### Dept of Economics; www2.warwick.ac.uk/fac/soc/economics

economics, economics & industrial organisation/politics & international studies, finance & economics, mathematics, international financial economics, economics, behavioural & economic science, PPE; BA, BSc, BSc/Ec, MEcMSc, PGDip, PhD

### Dept of Philosophy; www2.warwick.ac.uk/fac/soc/philosophy

continental philosophy, philosophy, philosophy & literature/maths/psychology/classical civilisation, philosophy of mind, philosophy, politics & economics; BA, BSc, MA, MPhil, PGDip, PhD

### Dept of Politics & International Studies; www2.warwick.ac.uk/fac/soc/pais

politics & international studies/French/ German/sociology, globalization & development, economic policy, 7 international studies, international politics & East Asia/Europe, international relations/security/political economy, politics, political theory, public policy/& comparative politics; BA, MA, MPhil, PhD

### Dept of Sociology; www2.warwick.ac.uk/fac/soc/sociology

sociology, social policy, gender studies, cultural studies, sociology/& law/politics/French, social policy, research methods; BA, MA, MPhil, PGDip, PhD

### School of Health & Social Studies; www2.warwick.ac.uk/fac/soc/shss

applied social studies, health studies, health & social studies, specialist social work; MA, MPhil, PGDip, PhD

### Warwick Business School; www2.wbs.warwick.ac.uk/fac/soc/

accounting & finance, business (behavioural science/finance & accounting/marketing/analytics & consulting), finance & IT/economics/behavioural science, financial mathematics, global economics, industrial relations & managing human resources, information systems, management & innovation & management, information & technology, international business/

employment relations/management, management & organizational analysis, management science & operational research, marketing & strategy, applied/ management; BA, BSc, MA, MBA, MPA, MPhil, MSc, PGDip, PhD

### Warwick Institute of Education; www2.warwick.ac.uk/fac/soc/wie

accreditation of prior learning, adv teaching of Shakespeare, childhood, education & society, drama & theatre education, educational assessment/leadership/innovation studies/management mathematics education, religion & education, PGCE: early years, schools direct, primary/secondary/qualified teacher programme; BA, EdD, FdA, MA, MPhil, MSc, PGCE, PhD

### Warwick School of Law; www2.warwick.ac.uk/fac/soc/law

law, advanced legal studies, European law, international corporate governance & financial regulation, international economic/ development law & human rights, law & business/sociology/humanities; BA, LLB, LLM, MPhil, PhD, PGCert, PGDip

## UNIVERSITY OF WEST OF SCOTLAND
## www.uws.ac.uk

### School of Business & Creative Industries; www.uws.ac.uk/schools/school-of-creative-and-cultural-industries/

### Business School; www.uws.ac.uk/schools/business-school

accounting, business, business administration, international finance & accounting/hospitality management/ HRM/management/marketing, financial management/marketing/HRM/marketing management, event management/& tourism, HRM, management & new technology, marketing, law, logistics & supply chain management, retail management, tourism management; BA, BSc, MSc, MBA, EMBA, PGDip/ Cert

### School of Creative and Cultural Industries; www.uws.ac.uk/schools/school-of-creative-and-cultural-industries

broadcast journalism/production, commercial music/ sound production, contemporary art practice/screen acting, creative media/industry practice, digital art, film-making & screen writing, journalism, musical theatre, music, innovation & entrepreneurship, photography, songwriting & performance, sports journalism, research methods for business, cultural & social research; BA, BA(Hons), BAcc, ExecMBA, MA, MSc, PGDip, PhD

### School of Science; www.uws.ac.uk/schools-of-science

adv/applied biomedical science, biotechnology, applied bioscience & zoology, biomedical science, chemistry, environmental health, forensic science, occupational safety & health, exercise & health science, sport & exercise science, sports coaching/ development, biotechnology, drug design & discovery, personal fitness & practice, project management, psychological science, waste & clean technologies; BSc/BSc(Hons), CertHE, GradDip/Cert, MSc, PhD

### School of Engineering; www.uws.ac.uk/schools/school-of-engineering

civil/chemical/mechanical/aircraft/motorsport design engineering, computer-aided design, product design & development, engineering management, physics/ nuclear technology, product design & development, mechatronics, sensor design; BEng(Hons), PGDip/ Cert, MSc

### School of Health, Nursing & Midwifery; www.uws.ac.uk/schools/school-of health-nursing-and-midwifery

adv clinical/paediatric/neonatal practice, acute & critical care, cancer care, child protection, cognitive behaviour therapy, health studies, non-medical prescribing, midwifery, adult/mental health/public health/nursing, maternal & child health, health care, occupational health, orthopaedic care, integrated public services, non-medical prescribing, cancer & palliative care, sexual & reproductive health, veterinary nursing, vulnerability, working with older people; BSc(Hons), MSc, PGCert/Dip, DipHE

### School of Social Sciences; www.uws.ac.uk/schools/school-of-social-sciences

alcohol & drug studies, careers guidance & development, criminal justice, politics, psychology, race equality, social policy, social sciences, social studies, social work, sociology; BA, BA(Hons), MSc, Grad Cert, PGDip/Cert, Cert HE

**School of Computing; www.uws.ac.uk/schools/school-of-computing**
advanced computer systems development, business technology, computer animation with digital art, computer games development/technology/networking, computing, enterprise software systems, information technology, web authoring/technology, mobile web design, multimedia technology, music technology, web & mobile design; BA(Hons), BSc, BSc(Hons), MSc, PGDip/Cert, CertHE

**School of Education; www.uws.ac.uk/schools/school-of-education**
artist teacher, chartered teacher, childhood practice/studies, community learning & participation, education, coaching therapy, enhanced education practice, leadership for learning, leadership & learning in HE, inclusive education, mental health & education, primary/secondary education; BA, BEd MEd, PGCert/Dip

## THE UNIVERSITY OF WESTMINSTER
## www.wmin.ac.uk

*School of Architecture & the Built Environment; www.westminster.ac.uk/schools/architecture*
architectural technology, architecture, architecture & digital media, cultural identity & globalisation, interior design, international architecture, building engineering/surveying, business & property, construction project/property/management, facilities & property management, international planning & sustainable development, logistics & supply chain management, property & planning/construction, quantity surveying/& commercial management, real estate development, tourism & planning, air/transport planning & management, tourist & events management, events & conference management, tourism management, tourism with healthcare, travel & tourism, urban & regional planning/design, urban design; BA, BSc, MA, MPhil, MSc, PGCert, PGDip, PhD, MArch

*School of Electronics & Computer Science; www.westminster.ac.uk/schools/computing*
business & information systems, business intelligence & analytics, computer games development/science, computer network/systems engineering, computer network security, computer forensics, database systems, microelectronic systems design, mobile wireless & broadband communications, multimedia, multimedia computing & animation, networks & communications, multimedia communications, electronic engineering, embedded systems, multimedia, mobile & web computing, software engineering; BEng, BSc, MEng, MPhil, MSc, PhD

*School of Law; www.westminster.ac.uk/schools/law*
law/with French law, commercial/corporate finance law, conflict & dispute prevention & resolution, entertainment law, EU law, European legal studies, international & commercial dispute resolution, international commercial/banking /law, legal practice, solicitors exemption; GradDip, LLB, LLM, LPC

*School of Life Sciences; www.westminster.ac.uk/schools/science*
applied/microbiology & biotechnology, biochemistry, biochemical engineering, biological sciences (cancer biology/forensic biology/molecular biosystems) biomedical sciences, biotechnology, cellular pathology, Chinese medicine/acupuncture, clinical chemistry, complementary therapies, drug discovery & development, environmental biotechnology, forensic biology, human & medical science, nutritional therapy, integrated governance of healthcare community, international/public health nutrition, herbal medicine, haematology, human nutrition (nutrition & exercise science)/microbiology, sport & exercise nutrition, medical biotechnology/microbiology/molecular biology, genetics, nutrition/& medical science, nutritional therapy, nutrition & exercise science, physiology & pharmacology & physiology; BSc, FdSc, MA, MPhil, MSc, PGCert, PhD

*School of Media, Arts & Design; www.westminster.ac.uk/schools/media*
animation, applied sound for interactive media, audio production, clinical photography, commercial music performance, communication/policy, contemporary media practice, design for communication,

diversity, fashion/buying/business management, management/design/merchandise management, film & TV directing/production/theory, culture & industry, global media, graphic communication design, illustration & visual communication, international media, journalism (international/broadcasting/online/print), media development/management/business, mixed media, media & development, fine art, film & TV, music business management, clinical photography, photographic arts/studies, photography & digital imaging technology, photojournalism, medical journalism, PR/& development, radio production, social media, TV production, theory, culture & industry; BA, BMus, BSc, FdA, GradDip, MA, PGDip

### School of Social Sciences, Humanities & Languages; www.westminster.ac.uk/schools/humanities

creative writing/writing the city, cultural & entertainment studies, criminal justice, English literature & creative writing/French/German/Spanish/linguistics, cultural & critical studies, English language & Arabic/Chinese/creative writing/French/German/Spanish/linguistics, development studies & international relations, various jt degree combinations of (English language, English literature and Arabic/Chinese/French/Spanish/ creative writing/sociology), history & politics/sociology, international liaison & culture, international relations & Arabic/Chinese/French/German/Spanish/politics/democratic politics/security, TESOL & creative writing, visual culture, bilingual translation, conference interpreting, museums, galleries & contemporary culture, specialist & technical translation, linguistics & Arabic/Chinese/English language, translation studies (Chinese/Arabic/French German), interpreting, politics, contemporary political theory, applied cognitive neuroscience/rehabilitation, business/health psychology, applied market & social research, sociology & criminology, criminal justice, sociology, social policy/sociology/& criminology, visual culture; BA, MA, MPhil, PhD

### Westminster Business School; www.westminster.ac.uk/schools/business

Accounting, Finance & Economics; accounting with international business economics, business management(accounting/economics/finance & financial services), finance with management, finance & accounting, finance, banking & insurance, global finance, international economic policy & analysis, investment & risk financeBusiness & Management; business – international, business management (accounting/economics/entrepreneurship/finance & financial services/HRM/international business/law), operation & supply chain management, international business (with Arabic/Chinese/French/German/Spanish), international marketing, marketing communication/management, business communication for digital economy, international business & management, international development management/HRM, management, business management (MBA), project management, health & social careHuman Management Resource; HRM, international HRMMarketing: business management – marketing, international marketing, marketing communication/managementBA, MA, MBA, MPhil, MSc, PGCert, PhD

## THE UNIVERSITY OF WINCHESTER
## www.winchester.ac.uk

### Faculty of Arts; www.winchester.ac.uk/aboutus/universitystructure

American studies/literature, creative arts (creative writing/critical writing/performing arts), dance practice & production, cultural & arts management, English language studies/literature in context, English & American literature, digital media design/development, film & cinema techniques, film studies/production, journalism, media production/studies, cultural studies, choreography & dance, devised performance, global radio production, performing arts (contemporary performance), drama, media & production/studies, popular/devised performance, modern liberal arts, street arts, theatre & media as development, theatre production (stage & arts management), vocal & choral studies, writing for children; BA, FdA, MA, PGCert/Dip, PhD

## Faculty of Humanities and Social Sciences; www.winchester.ac.uk/aboutus/universitystructure/hss

### Dept of Archaeology; www.winchester.ac.uk/academicdepartments/archaeology/Pages/Archaeology.aspx

archaeology, archaeological practice, ancient, classical & medieval studies, cultural heritage & resource management, regional & local history & archaeology

### Dept of Applied Social Studies; www.winchester.ac.uk/academicdepartments/applied-social-studies

criminology, fashion: media & marketing, forensic science, sociology

### Dept of Theology and Religious Studies; www.winchester.ac.uk/academicdepartments/theology/Pages/TheologyandReligiousStudies.aspx

history, civilisations & belief, religious studies, theology & religious studies, death, religion & culture, orthodox studies, religion, ethics & society

### Dept of History; www.winchester.ac.uk/academicdepartments/history/Pages/history.aspx

history, regional and local history &/or archaeology, historical studies, history & the medieval world/modern world, global history & politics, ancient, classical & medieval studies

### Dept of Psychology; www.winchester.ac.uk/academicdepartments/psychology/Pages/Welcome.aspx

psychological science/disorders, psychology & child development/cognition, psychology, psychological research methods

BA, BSc, MA, MPhil, MRes, MSc, PGCert, PGDip, PhD

## Faculty of Education, Health & Social Care; www.winchester.ac.uk/aboutus/universitystructure/Educationhealthsocialcare

childhood studies, childhood, youth & community studies, early years professional studies, education, educational studies, modern liberal arts, early childhood/years, health, community & social care studies, humanistic counselling, interprofessional studies (children, health, social work, & community), modern liberal arts, primary practice, youth & community studies, teacher education; PGCE secondary/(RE)/primary ed with QTS, health & social care practice/wellbeing, medical education, nursing studies, social care studies, social work; BA, FdA, BEd, MA(Ed), MRes, MPhil, PGCE, PhD, Dip

## Faculty of Business Law & Sport; www.winchester.ac.uk/startinghere/Registrationinformation/Newstudentinformation2013/Facultyofbusinesslawandsport/Pages/FacultyofBusiness,LawandSport.aspx20sport/pages/facultyofbusinesslawandsport.aspx

### Winchester Business School;

www.winchester.ac.uk/academic-departments/winchester-business-school

accounting & finance, business management, enterprise & innovation, business administration/management, events management, fashion media & marketing, HRM, management, managing contemporary issues with environment & development, marketing, sustainable business; BA, FdA, MBA, MSc, PGCert, PGDip, FD

### Dept of Law; www.winchester.ac.uk/academicdepartments/Law/Pages/LawDepartment.aspx

law, public/European/criminal/contract & restitution/equity law, property/medical/ecclesiastical law, media law & ethics; BA/LLB, LLB, GradDip

### Dept of Sports Studies; www.winchester.ac.uk/academicdepartments/SportsStudies/Pages/Sportsstudies.aspx

sports coaching & development/management/science/studies, sport & society, applied sport & exercise science; BA, BSc, FdA

## UNIVERSITY OF WOLVERHAMPTON
## www.wlv.ac.uk

### School of Applied Sciences; www.wlv.ac.uk/default.aspx?page=6878

medical science, animal behaviour and wildlife conservation, applied biological sciences, applied microbiology, biochemistry, biomedical science, biotechnology, environmental health, forensic science/ and criminology, genetics and molecular biology, healthcare science (physiological sciences/biomedical sciences), human biology, pharmaceutical science, pharmacology, psychology, psychology (counselling psychology/criminal behaviour), pharmacy, biomedical science (cellular pathology/clinical biochemistry/ haematology/medical microbiology), climate change management, cognitive behaviour therapy, computational bioinformatics, environmental management/ pollution control/technology, fire scene investigation, forensic genetics and human identification, forensic mark comparison, medical biotechnology, molecular biology with bioinformatics, occupational psychology, oil and gas management, pharmaceutical science (drug discovery and design/pharmaceutical analysis/ pharmaceutical manufacturing/pharmaceutical quality assurance/pharmacological sciences), waste and resource management, applied child psychology, prescribing studies, counselling psychology; BSc, DBMS, FdSc, PGCert, BMdSci, PractDoc, MPharm, MSc, PGDip

### School of Art & Design; www.wlv.ac.uk/ default.aspx?page=6963

animation, applied arts, art & design, computer games design, commercial video production, design & applied arts, digital & visual communication, fashion & textiles, fine art, graphic design, illustration, interior design, photography, product design, video & film production, visual communication; BA, FdA, HND, MA

### School for Educational Futures; www.wlv.ac.uk/default.aspx?page=6965

adult numeracy/literacy, childhood, family & community studies, conductive education, CPD, early years/services/learning, education (generic/learning in a digital age/leadership in education/learning & teaching), primary ed, education studies/social policy/sociology/special needs & inclusive education/ deaf studies, learning assistants, TESOL, post-compulsory education, PGCE (numerous secondary subjects/early/primary education/adult education/ numeracy/literacy), schools direct, ESOL, learning assistants, preparing to teach, special needs & inclusion studies, subject specialists in English (ESOL/literacy/mathematics/numeracy), social policy, sociology, special needs & inclusive study, support of children in primary years; BA, EdD, FdA, MA, PGCert, PGDip, PhD

### School of Technology; www.wlv.ac.uk/ default.aspx?page=24367

advanced technology management, architecture, architectural studies/design technology, CAD for construction, interior architecture & property development, automotive systems engineering, building services engineering, building surveying/studies, civil engineering/management/& environmental engineering, computer science/games development/ software development/security, computer systems engineering, computer networks/security, computing, software development, games design, commercial management & quantity surveying, computer-aided design & construction, construction, construction law/management/project management, design technology, electronics & communications engineering, engineering design management, business information systems, information technology/management, interior mathematics, mechanical engineering, mechatronics, polymer engineering, project & progress management, rapid production design & development, strategic IT management, sustainable design & manufacture; BDes, BEng, BSc, FdSc, FDEng, MEng, MSc, PGCert

### School of Health & Wellbeing; www.wlv.ac.uk/default.aspx?page=6067

Community Health: specialist community public heath nursing (district/general practice/health/school)

Midwifery; midwifery

Nursing; palliative and end of life care, health and social care practice (lymphoedema care/orthopaedic care/acute care/cardiac care/stroke care/renal care), emergency practitioner, nursing studies (acute care/ cancer care/cardiac care/diabetes care/emergency care/critical care/neonatal intensive care/orthopaedic care/renal care/stroke care/palliative and end of life care), nursing studies (learning disabilities/mental health and psychological interventions/offender health), adult/children's/learning disability/mental health nursing

Health and Wellbeing; health and wellbeing, public health, commissioning for health and social care, emergency planning resilience and response, lymphoedema care, palliative and end of life care, primary health care/practice, mental health, health and social care, health, social care and allied professionals, emergency planning resilience and response, management of passenger transport emergency incidents, mental health/practice, specialist community nursing, specialist social work studies, therapeutic practitioner

Psychology; psychology, psychology (counselling/criminal behaviour), occupational/applied child/counselling psychology

Social Care; social care and health studies/sociology/and social policy

Social Work; social work

BA, BSc, BNurs, Cert/DipHE, DipHE, FdA, GradDip, MA, MPH, MSc, PGCert, PGDip, Doc Health & Wellbeing

### School of Law, Social Sciences & Communications

conflict studies, contemporary media, creative & professional writing/& English, deaf studies, education studies, English/language/& linguistics, film studies, history, HRM, inclusion & deaf studies, interpreting, language & information processing, linguistics, media & communication/cultural studies, philosophy, policing, politics, popular culture, public sector, religious studies, social policy, sociology, TESOL, transmedia screenwriting, war studies, world & sign language, law, law & accounting/business/HRM/social policy, international corporate and financial law, international commercial and financial law (oil and gas), legal practice; BA, FdA, LLB, LLM, MA

### School of Sport, Performing Arts & Leisure; www.wlv.ac.uk/default.aspx?page=6970

creative music production, dance/& drama/science, drama & performance/creative professional writing/English/film studies, event & venue management, international hospitality management, music/theatre/& popular music/technology, music performance/& pop, physical activity, exercise & health, physical education, sound production, sport & exercise science, sport coaching/studies, tourism management; BA, BSc, FdA, FdSc, MA, MSc

### University of Wolverhampton Business School; www.wlv.ac.uk/default.aspx?page=6971

accounting & finance, business administration, international/business management, business & finance/HRM/marketing management/accounting, coaching & mentoring, employability & enterprise, HRM, HRD & organisational change, innovation & entrepreneurship, management studies, marketing & enterprise management/HRM, marketing management, healthcare leadership, medical education, leadership, HRD/M; BA, FdA, HND, MA, MBA, PGDip/Cert, MSc

## UNIVERSITY COLLEGE WORCESTER
## www.worc.ac.uk

### Institute of Education; www.worc.ac.uk/departments/institute-of-education

early childhood/years, education (early years), education studies, education & Christian discipleship, integrated working with children & families, educational management & leadership, integrated children's service, church school leadership, leading learning & training, learning support, teaching & learning in HE, English/PGCE (primary, secondary, graduate teacher), leading early years practice, primary intial teacher, professional practice, mentoring & coaching for leadership, mentoring in early childhood, religious education, special & inclusive education, technology & learning; BA, CertHE, FdA, MA, MSc, PGCE, PGCert, PGDip

### Institute of Health & Society; www.worc.ac.uk/departments/institute-of health-and society

district nurse practitioner, healthcare visitor, hospital medical prescription, public health & wellbeing, community health, midwifery, nursing, psychology, social care, social work; BSc, DipHE, FdA, FdSc, GradDip, MA, MSc, PGCert, PGDip

### Institute of Humanities & Creative Arts; www.worc.ac.uk/departments/institute-of-humanities-and-creative-arts

animation, art & design, creative & professional writing, creative digital media, dance, drama/& performance, digital film production, English language/literary studies/literature, film making/studies, fine art practice, graphic design & multimedia, illustration, history, journalism, media & cultural studies, performance (costume & make-up), politics & people power, screenwriting, sociology, urban & electronic music; BA, HND, MA, MSc

**Institute of Science & the Environment; www.worc.ac.uk/departments/institute-of-science-and-the-environment**
animal biology, arboriculture, archaeology & heritage studies/landscape studies, airborne infectious agents & allergies, biochemical biology, archaeological landscapes, conservation ecology, ecology, environmental management/science, human/physical/geography, forensic & applied biology, human nutrition/biology, medical communication, sustainable horticulture, plant science, sustainable developmental advocacy; BSc, FdSc, HNC, HND, MSc, PGCert, PGDip

**Institute of Sport & Exercise Science; www.worc.ac.uk/departments/652.html**
applied sport science, cricket coaching & management, football business management & coaching, outdoor adventure leadership & management/education, PE/& outdoor education, sport & exercise psychology/science, sports coaching/management/performance & coaching/therapy/studies, sports business management & events management, sport development & coaching; BSc, HND, MSc

**Worcester Business School; www.worc.ac.uk/departments/655.html**
accountancy, accounting, advertising, business administration/entrepreneurship, business IT/management, business finance & accounts, computer game design & development, computing, economics, entrepreneurship, executive leadership & management (health & social care), finance, financial management, hospitality, retail, tourism & travel, HRM, HR & management, innovation, international business/management, IT for education, leadership, management/studies, management & human resources, marketing/advertising & PR/management, web design/development, many joint degrees with combinations of the above subjects; BA, BSc, DMS, GradCert, MBA, MSc

## UNIVERSITY OF YORK
## www.york.ac.uk

**Dept of Archaeology; www.york.ac.uk/depts/arch**
archaeology, archaeology of buildings, archaeological information systems, bioarchaeology, field/medieval archaeology, conservation studies, cultural heritage management, digital heritage, early prehistory, heritage studies, historical archaeology, mesolithic studies, zooarchaeology; BA, BSc, MA, MPhil, MSc, PhD

**Dept of Biology; www.york.ac.uk/depts/biol**
biology, biochemistry, bioscience technology, biotechnology & microbiology, computational biology, ecology & environmental management, post-genomic biology, genetics, molecular cell biology; BSc, MPhil, MRes, MSc, PhD

**Dept of Chemistry; www.york.ac.uk/depts/chemistry**
chemistry, chemistry with biological & medicinal biological & medical chemistry, chemistry/management & industry/resources & the environment, computational biology, green chemistry & sustainable industrial technology; BSc, MChem, MPhil, MSc, PhD

**Dept of Computer Science; www.cs.york.ac.uk/depts**
computer science/with AI/embedded systems/software engineering/philosophy/mathematics, automaton, robotics engineering, computing, cyber security, human-centred interactive technologies, information technology, safety critical systems engineering, social media & interactive technology, systems security; BEng, BSc, MEng, MMath, MPhil, MSc, PGCert, PGDip

**Dept of Economics & Related Studies; www.york.ac.uk/depts/econ**
economics, economics & finance, economics & econometrics/economic history/social history, economic history/sociology/philosophy/politics, environmental economics & management, development economics & emerging markets, health/public/economics, economic & social policy analysis, politics, philosophy & economics; BA, BSc, MSc, PGCert, PGDip, PhD

## Dept of Education; www.york.ac.uk/depts/educ

applied linguistics for English/language teaching, English in education, psychology in education, educational studies, language & literature in education, teaching English (young learners/TESOL), PGCE (English, history, maths, foreign languages, sciences, teaching & learning), global & international citizenship, science education & learning, sociology & education; BA, MA, MPhil, PhD

## Dept of Electronics; www.york.ac.uk/depts/elec

avionics, automaton & robotic engineering, communications engineering, computer engineering, digital systems engineering & signal processing, digital media systems, electronic engineering, electronics & communication, engineering management, internet & wireless technology, music technology/systems, electrical engineering with nanotechnology/business management, computer engineering; BEng, MEng, MSc, MPhil, PhD

## Dept of English & Related Literature; www.york.ac.uk/depts/engl

English, English & history/history of art/linguistics/philosophy/politics, culture & thought after 1945, cultures of empire, resistance & postcoloniality, eighteenth century studies, English literary studies, film & literature, medieval literatures, modern & contemporary literature & culture, nineteenth-century literature & culture, Renaissance literature, 1500–1700, romantic & sentimental literature 1770–1830; BA, MA, MPhil, PhD

## Dept of Environment; www.york.ac.uk/depts/eeem

environmental economics & environmental management, environmental geography/science, environmental science & management, ecology & environmental management, environment, economics & ecology, corporate social responsibility & environmental management, marine environmental development; BSc, MPhil, MSc, PGDip, PhD

## Dept of Health Sciences; www.york.ac.uk/depts/healthsciences

applied health research, haematopathology, health sciences, health & social care, public health, midwifery practice, nursing studies (adult/child/learning disability/mental health); BA, BSc, DipHE, MPhil, MSc, PGCert, PGDip, PhD, MPH, FD

## Dept of History; www.york.ac.uk/depts/hist

history, history with politics/history of art/philosophy/economics/French/English, contemporary history & international politics, 18th century studies, medieval history, railway studies & transport history, Renaissance/& early/modern history, public history, women's studies; BA, GradCert, MA, MPhil, PhD

## Dept of History of Art; www.york.ac.uk/depts/histart

history of art, stained glass conservation & heritage management; BA, MA, MPhil, PhD

## Hull York Medical School; www.hyms.ac.uk

undergraduate qualifying medical courses, human science, medical education, public health; MBBS, MSc, PGCert, MD, PhD, MPhil

## Dept of Language & Linguistic Science; www.york.ac.uk/depts/lang

linguistics, phonetics & phonology, psycholinguistics, sociolinguistics, combinations of French/German/Spanish/English, linguistics & French/German/Spanish, philosophy & French/German, syntax & semantics, phonological development, forensic speech science; BA, MA, MPhil, MSc, PhD

## York Law School; www.york.ac.uk/depts/law

law, international corporate & commercial law, international human rights & practice; LLB, LLM, MPhil, PhD

## Dept of Mathematics; www.york.ac.uk/depts/maths

mathematics, mathematics with computer science/economics/physics/statistics/finance/linguistics/philosophy, financial engineering, statistics & computational finance, mathematical finance; BA, BSc, MMath, MPhil, MRes, MSc, PGCert, PGDip, PhD

## Dept of Music; www.york.ac.uk/depts/music

music, community music, music technology, composition, performance; BA, MA, MPhil, PhD

## Dept of Philosophy; www.york.ac.uk/depts/phil

philosophy, history of philosophy, philosophy with computing/economics/physics/English/German/mathematics/linguistics, PPE; BA, BSc, GradDip, MA, MPhil, PGCert, PGDip, PhD

**Criminology; www.york.ac.uk/criminology**
criminology, sociology with criminology, applied social science & crime, criminal justice; BA

**Dept of Physics; www.york.ac.uk/depts/physics**
physics, physics with astrophysics, theoretical physics, fusion energy; BA, BSc, MMath, MPhil, MPhys, MSc, PhD, GradDip

**Dept of Politics; www.york.ac.uk/depts/poli**
politics with international relations/English/history/economics/philosophy/contemporary history & international politics, political research, conflict, governance & development, international political economy/relations, political philosophy, public administration & public policy/international development, PPE, postwar recovery, public policy; BA, MA, PGDip, PhD

**Dept of Psychology; www.york.ac.uk/depts/psych**
developmental/cognitive neuroscience, applied/forensic psychology, development disorders & clinical psychology, psychology; BSc, MPhil, MRes, MSc, PhD

**Dept of Social Policy & Social Work; www.york.ac.uk/depts/spsw**
applied social science (children & young people/crime & criminal justice), applied social science & social policy, international development, public administration, public policy & management, social policy, social work, sociology & political science, comparative & international social policy; BA, MA, MPhil, MRes, PGCert, PhD, MPA

**Dept of Sociology; www.york.ac.uk/depts/soci**
sociology/with criminology/crime/economics/education/philosophy/politics/social psychology/political science, social research, social media & management/interactive technology; BA, MA, MPhil, MSc, PhD

**School of Social & Political Sciences; www.york.ac.uk/sps**
social & political sciences, comparative cultural class analysis, environmental policy, science & technology, social media & communications, urban social science & criminology, women's studies; BA(Hons), MA, MRes, PhD

**Dept of Theatre, Film & Television; www.york.ac.uk/depts/tft**
cinema, contemporary cinema & TV, digital film & TV production, TV & society, post-production with visual effects/sound design, theatre, film & TV production, theatre writing, directing & performance; BA, MA, MPhil, MSc, PhD

**York Management School; www.york.ac.uk/depts/management**
accounting, business finance & management, business management, global markets, international business & strategic management, financial management, management with business finance, management studies, HRM; BA, BSc, MA, MPhil, MRes, MSc, PhD

## YORKSHIRE COAST COLLEGE
## www.yorkshirecoastcollege.ac.uk

**Higher education; www.yorkshirecoastcollege.ac.uk/highereducation/index.php**
historical & performance costume for stage & screen, fine art, teacher education; BA, FdA, GradCert

# Part 5

# Qualifications Awarded by Professional and Trade Associations

# THE FUNCTIONS OF PROFESSIONAL ASSOCIATIONS

## Qualifications

Some associations qualify individuals to act in a certain professional capacity. They also try to safeguard high standards of professional conduct. Few associations have complete control over the profession with which they are concerned. Some professions are regulated by the law, and their associations act as the central registration authority. Entry to others is directly controlled by associations that alone award the requisite qualifications. If a profession is required to be registered by the law and is controlled by the representative council, a practitioner found guilty by his or her council of misconduct may be suspended from practice or completely debarred by the removal of his or her name from the register of qualified practitioners. In other professions the consequence of misdemeanour may not be so serious, because the profession does not exercise the same degree of control.

The professions registered by statute, and therefore subject to restrictions on entry and loss of either privileges or the right to practise on erasure, are listed in Table 5.1. Certain other professions are closed.

**Table 5.1** Professions registered by statute

| Profession | Statutory committee controlling professional conduct |
|---|---|
| Architects | Architects Registration Board |
| Dentists | General Dental Council |
| Doctors | General Medical Council |
| Professions supplementary to medicine: arts therapists, biomedical scientists, chiropodists/podiatrists, clinical scientists, dieticians, hearing aid dispensers, occupational therapists, operating department practitioners, orthoptists, paramedics, physiotherapists, practitioner psychologists, prosthetists/orthotists, radiographers, speech and language therapists and social workers | Health and Care Professions Council (HCPC) |
| Nurses and midwives | Nursing and Midwifery Council |
| Opticians | General Optical Council |
| Osteopaths | General Osteopathic Council |
| Patent agents | Chartered Institute of Patent Attorneys |
| Pharmacists | General Pharmaceutical Council |
| Teachers | The Teaching Agency |

## Study

Some associations give their members an opportunity to keep abreast of a particular discipline or to undertake further study in it. Such associations are especially numerous in medicine, science and applied science. Many qualifying associations also provide an information and study service for their members. Some of the more famous learned societies confer added status upon distinguished practitioners by electing them to membership or honorary membership.

## Protection of Members' Interests

Some associations exist mainly to look after the interests of individual practitioners and the group. A small number are directly concerned with negotiations over salary and working conditions.

# MEMBERSHIP OF PROFESSIONAL ASSOCIATIONS

## Qualifying associations

The principal function of qualifying associations is to examine and qualify people who wish to become practitioners in the field with which they are concerned. As already indicated, some regulate professional conduct and many offer opportunities for further study. Membership is divided into grades, usually classified as corporate and non-corporate. Non-corporate members are those not yet admitted to full membership, mainly students; they are divided from corporate membership by barriers of age and levels of responsibility and experience. The principal requirement for admission to membership is the knowledge and ability to pass the association's exams; candidates may be exempted from the association's exams if they have acceptable alternative qualifications.

## Non-corporate or affiliated members

Non-corporate members are those who are as yet unqualified or only partly qualified. They are accorded limited rights and privileges, but may not vote at meetings of the corporate body. Most associations have a student membership grade. Students are those who are preparing for the exams that qualify them for admission to corporate membership. Some associations have licentiate and graduate membership grades, which are senior to the student grade. Graduates are those who have passed the qualifying exams but lack other requirements, such as age and experience, for admission to corporate membership.

## Corporate or full members

Corporate members are the fully qualified constituent members of incorporated associations. They are accorded full rights and privileges and may vote at meetings of the corporate body. Corporate membership is often divided into two grades: a senior grade of members or fellows and a general grade of associate members or associates.

## Honorary members

Some associations have a special class of honorary members or fellows for distinguished members or individuals who have made an outstanding contribution to the profession in question.

## Examinations and requirements

Professionals normally become corporate members by exam or exemption, with or without additional requirements. Many final professional exams are of degree standard, and a number of professional qualifications are accepted by employers as evidence of competence at operational level. Ongoing professional development is encouraged by most associations to ensure members' skills and knowledge are up to date and relevant.

The transition from the general grade of membership to the senior can be automatic in some associations (for instance, on reaching a prescribed age), but in others the higher grade is reached only after the submission of evidence of research or progress in the profession.

Qualifying exams are usually conducted in two or more stages. The first stage leads to an Intermediate or Part I qualification, the second leads to a Final or Part II or Part III qualification, which is about the standard of a degree.

## Gaining professional qualifications

Prospective students can study by any of the following means:

- correspondence courses (distance learning and/or online support);

- personal attendance at the schools maintained by some associations (eg the Architectural Association School of Architecture);
- further and higher education institutions.

# ACCOUNTANCY

## *Membership of Professional Institutions and Associations*

### ASSOCIATION OF ACCOUNTING TECHNICIANS

140 Aldersgate Street
London EC1A 4HY
Tel: 0845 863 0802
Fax: 020 7397 3009
E-mail: aat@aat.org.uk
Website: www.aat.org.uk

AAT is the UK's leading qualification and membership body for accounting professionals. We have over 125, 000 members including students, people working in accountancy and self-employed business owners, in more than 90 countries worldwide. Established in 1980 to ensure consistent training and regulation for accounting staff, our qualifications provide a progression route to CIMA, CIPFA, ICAS, ICAEW and ACCA.

*MEMBERSHIP*
Student member
Affiliate member
Full member (MAAT)
Fellow member (FMAAT)

*QUALIFICATION/EXAMINATIONS*
AAT Accounting Qualification
AAT Access Level 1 in accounting
AAT Level 2 Certificate in Bookkeeping

*DESIGNATORY LETTERS*
MAAT and FMAAT

### ASSOCIATION OF CHARITY INDEPENDENT EXAMINERS

The Gatehouse
White Cross
South Road
Lancaster
Lancashire LA1 4XQ
Tel: 01524 34892
Fax: 01524 34892
E-mail: info@acie.org.uk
Website: www.acie.org.uk

ACIE provides support, training, conferences, resources and qualifications for independent examiners of charity accounts throughout the UK (*subscriptions apply*). Further information at the website: www.acie.org.uk

Registered charity in E&W 1139609 & SC039066. Registered company limited by guarantee 7461134; registered in England at 4-6 Grimshaw St, Burnley BB11 2AZ.

*MEMBERSHIP*
Affiliate
Full Member (with category of Associate or Fellow)

*QUALIFICATION/EXAMINATIONS*
Associate (limited re: size and type of charity by 1 of 5 authorisation bands – see website for details): ACIE
Fellow (all UK charities eligible for IE): FCIE

*DESIGNATORY LETTERS*
ACIE, FCIE

## CHARTERED INSTITUTE OF INTERNAL AUDITORS

13 Abbeville Mews
88 Clapham Park Road
London SW4 7BX
Tel: 020 7498 0101
Fax: 020 7978 2492
E-mail: membership@iia.org.uk
Website: www.iia.org.uk

The Chartered Institute of Internal Auditors (IIA) is the only professional body in the UK and Ireland focused exclusively on internal auditing and we are passionate about supporting, promoting and training the professionals who work in it. Every year we help internal auditors at every stage of their career with training, qualifications and technical resources.

*MEMBERSHIP*
Student Member
Affiliate Member
Voting Member (PIIA, CMIIA)
Head of Internal Audit Service Member
Fellow (FIIA, CFIIA)

*QUALIFICATION/EXAMINATIONS*
IIA Certificate in Internal Audit and Business Risk (IA Cert)
IIA Diploma (PIIA)
IIA Advanced Diploma (CMIIA)
IT Auditing Certificate

*DESIGNATORY LETTERS*
IA Cert, PIIA, CMIIA, FIIA, CFIIA

## CIMA – THE CHARTERED INSTITUTE OF MANAGEMENT ACCOUNTANTS

26 Chapter Street
London SW1P 4NP
Tel: 020 8849 2251
E-mail: cima.contact@cimaglobal.com
Website: www.cimaglobal.com

CIMA is the employers' choice when recruiting financially qualified business leaders.

The Chartered Institute of Management Accountants, founded in 1919, is the world's leading and largest professional body of Management Accountants, with 183, 000 members and students operating at the heart of business in 168 countries. CIMA works closely with employers and sponsors leading-edge research, constantly updating its qualification, professional experience requirements and continuing professional development to ensure it remains the most relevant international accountancy qualification for business.

*MEMBERSHIP*
Member
Associate (ACMA)
Fellow (FCMA)

*QUALIFICATION/EXAMINATIONS*
Certificate in Business Accounting
CIMA Professional
Certificate in Islamic Finance
Diploma in Islamic Finance

*DESIGNATORY LETTERS*
ACMA, FCMA

## ICAEW (THE INSTITUTE OF CHARTERED ACCOUNTANTS IN ENGLAND AND WALES)

Metropolitan House
321 Avebury Boulevard
Milton Keynes MK9 2FZ
Tel: 01908 248 250
E-mail: careers@icaew.com
Website: icaew.com/careers

ICAEW is a world leading professional membership organisation that promotes, develops and supports over 140, 000 chartered accountants worldwide. We provide qualifications and professional development, share our knowledge, insight and technical expertise, and protect the quality and integrity of the accountancy and finance profession.

*MEMBERSHIP*
ACA (Associate of the Institute of Chartered Accountants in England and Wales) FCA (Fellow Chartered Accountant)

*QUALIFICATION/EXAMINATIONS*
The ICAEW chartered accountancy qualification, the ACA, is one of the most advanced learning and professional development programmes available. It has integrated components which give an in-depth understanding across accountancy, finance and business. Combined they help build the technical knowledge, professional skills and practical experience needed to become an ICAEW Chartered Accountant. There is more than one way to start the ACA, find out more at icaew.com/careers
The ICAEW Certificate in Finance, Accounting and Business (ICAEW CFAB) provides fundamental knowledge and skills in finance, accounting and business. ICAEW CFAB consists of the same six exam modules as the first level of the ACA qualification. It can be studied as a stand-alone qualification or as an entry route to the ACA. There are no entry requirements and it is achievable in as little as 12 months through online learning, self-study or classroom tuition. Find out more at icaew.com/cfab

*DESIGNATORY LETTERS*
ACA, FCA

## ICAS (INSTITUTE OF CHARTERED ACCOUNTANTS OF SCOTLAND)

CA House
21 Haymarket Yards
Edinburgh EH12 5BH
Tel: 0131 347 0100
E-mail: caeducation@icas.org.uk
Website: icas.org.uk

ICAS is a professional body for around 19, 000 world class business professionals who work in the UK and in more than 100 countries around the world. Our members have all achieved the internationally recognised and respected CA qualification. We are an educator, examiner, regulator, and thought leader. ICAS is the first professional body for accountants and was created by Royal Charter in 1854.

*MEMBERSHIP*
To qualify as a CA, trainees must enter and complete a training contract with an ICAS authorised employer for a prescribed period, normally three years. They must achieve relevant work experience requirements and key competencies, study for and pass three stages of examinations and complete a course and assignment in Business Ethics. For further information please see the ICAS website.

*QUALIFICATION/EXAMINATIONS*
The CA qualification syllabus contains ten subjects leading to three stages of exams.
Test of Competence (TC) contains five subjects: Financial Accounting, Principles of Auditing and Reporting, Finance, Business Management, Business Law.

Test of Professional Skills (TPS): Taxation, Advanced Finance, Financial Reporting, Assurance and Business Systems.
Test of Professional Expertise (TPE) contains a multidisciplinary case study designed to apply theoretical knowledge and practical skills to a real-life situation.

In addition to including ethics within the three levels, Business Ethics forms a standalone subject and assessment.

*DESIGNATORY LETTERS*
CA

## INSTITUTE OF FINANCIAL ACCOUNTANTS

Burford House
44 London Road
Sevenoaks
Kent TN13 1AS
Tel: 01732 458080
Fax: 01732 455848
E-mail: mail@ifa.org.uk
Website: www.ifa.org.uk

The IFA was established in 1916 and is the oldest body of non-Chartered Accountants in the world. We represent members and students in more than 80 countries, providing qualifications for those wishing to work in financial management and accountancy, and CPD for qualified Financial Accountants, particularly in SMEs.

*MEMBERSHIP*
Financial Accounting Executive
Associate (AFA)
Fellow (FFA)

*QUALIFICATION/EXAMINATIONS*
IFE Level 4 Award for SME Tax Advisers (QCF)
IFA Level 4 Award for SME Financial Accounting (International Standards) (QCF)
IFA Level 4 Diploma for SME Financial Accountants (QCF)
IFA Level 5 Diploma for SME Financial Managers (QCF)
IFA Level 5 Diploma for SME Finance and Business Managers (QCF)
The Diploma in IFRS for Accounting Professionals and the Diploma in IFRS for Business

*DESIGNATORY LETTERS*
QCF

## INTERNATIONAL ASSOCIATION OF BOOK-KEEPERS

Suite 5
20 Churchill Square
Kings Hill
West Malling
Kent ME19 4YU
Tel: 0844 3303527
Fax: 0844 3303514
E-mail: mail@iab.org.uk
Website: www.iab.org.uk

The IAB specializes in providing high-quality, accredited and regulated financial and business qualifications. We continue to be the leading international membership body for professional book-keepers. Established in 1973, we now have many thousands of students and members worldwide.

*MEMBERSHIP*
Associate (AIAB)
Member (MIAB)
Fellow (FIAB)

*QUALIFICATION/EXAMINATIONS*
Award in Bookkeeping (Level 1)
Award in Manual Bookkeeping (Level 1)
Award in Computerized Bookkeeping (Level 1)
Certificate in Bookkeeping (Level 2)
Award in Manual Bookkeeping (Level 2)
Award in Computerized Bookkeeping (Level 2)
Certificate in Bookkeeping (Level 1)
Certificate in Bookkeeping (Level 3)
Diploma in Bookkeeping (Level 3)
Certificate in Manual Bookkeeping (Level 3)
Award in Computerized Bookkeeping (Level 3)
Diploma in Accounting to International Standards (Level 4)
Certificate in Payroll (Level 1)
Certificate in Payroll (Level 2)
Award in Computerized Payroll (Level 2)
Diploma in Payroll (Level 2)
Diploma in Payroll (Level 3)
Award in Computerized Payroll (Level 1)
Award in Computerized Payroll for Business (Level 1)
Certificate in Computerized Payroll for Business (Level 2)
Certificate in Computerized Payroll for Business (Level 3)
Award in Computerized Payroll (Level 3)
Award in Computerized Accounting for Business (Level 1)
Certificate in Computerized Accounting for Business (Level 2)
Certificate in Computerized Accounting for Business (Level 3)
Diploma in Accounting and Advanced Bookkeeping (Level 3)
Diploma in Small Business Financial Management (Level 3)
Diploma in Cost and Management Accounting (Level 3)
Diploma in Financial Information for Managers (Level 4)
Diploma in Personal and Business Tax (Level 4)

*DESIGNATORY LETTERS*
NCF, QCF

## THE ASSOCIATION OF CHARTERED CERTIFIED ACCOUNTANTS

London WC2A 3EE
Tel: 020 7059 5000
Fax: 020 7059 5050
E-mail: info@accaglobal.com
Website: www.accaglobal.com

ACCA is the largest and fastest-growing international accountancy body, with over 424, 000 students and 147, 000 members in 170 countries. The ACCA Qualification is an established route to professional status, and we offer continued support to our members throughout their careers.

*MEMBERSHIP*
Associate (ACCA)
Fellow (FCCA)

*QUALIFICATION/EXAMINATIONS*
Foundations in Accountancy
Certificate in International Finance Reporting
Certificate in International Finance Reporting Standard for SMEs
Diploma in International Finance Reporting
The ACCA Qualification
MBA (awarded by Oxford Brookes University; accredited by the Association of MBAs)

*DESIGNATORY LETTERS*
ACCA, FCCA

## THE ASSOCIATION OF CORPORATE TREASURERS

51 Moorgate
London EC2R 6BH
Tel: 020 7847 2540
Fax: 020 7374 8744
E-mail: enquiries@treasurers.co.uk
Website: www.treasurers.org

The ACT is the international body for professionals working in treasury, risk and corporate finance. We are the leading examining body for international treasury, providing the widest scope of benchmark qualifications and continuing development through training, conferences and publications – including *The Treasurer* magazine.

*MEMBERSHIP*
Student Member
Faculty Member
Associate Member (AMCT)
Member (MCT)
Fellow (FCT)
Corporate Representative
International Affiliate

*QUALIFICATION/EXAMINATIONS*
Advanced Diploma in Treasury Risk and Corporate Finance (MCT)
Diploma in Treasury (AMCT)
Certificate in Financial Fundamentals (CertFin)
Certificate in International Treasury Management (CertITM)
Certificate in Corporate Finance and Funding (CertCFF)
Certificate in Financial Maths and Modelling (CertFMM)
Certificate in International Cash Management (CertICM)
Certificate in Risk Management (CertRM)

*DESIGNATORY LETTERS*
AMCT, MCT, FCT

## THE ASSOCIATION OF INTERNATIONAL ACCOUNTANTS

Staithes 3
The Watermark
Metro Riverside
Newcastle upon Tyne
Tyne & Wear NE11 9SN
Tel: 0191 493 0277
Fax: 0191 493 0278
E-mail: aia@aiaworldwide.com
Website: www.aiaworldwide.com

AIA was founded in 1928 as a global accountancy body and has recognition as a Recognised Qualifying Body for statutory auditors, supervisory status for its members in the Money Laundering Regulations 2007 and an Awarding Body in the UK. AIA is a Prescribed Body in the ROI and is recognised in over 30 countries worldwide.

*MEMBERSHIP*
Student Member
Graduate Member
Affiliate Member (AMIA)
Academic Member
Associate (AAIA)
Fellow (FAIA)
Honorary Member
Retired Member

*QUALIFICATION/EXAMINATIONS*
Professional Accountancy Qualification
Statutory Audit Qualification
Audit Diploma
Corporate Finance Diploma
IFRS Diploma
Management Accounting & Costing Diploma

*DESIGNATORY LETTERS*
AMIA, AAIA, FAIA

## THE CHARTERED INSTITUTE OF PUBLIC FINANCE AND ACCOUNTANCY

3 Robert Street
London WC2N 6RL
Tel: 020 7543 5600
Fax: 020 7543 5700
E-mail: students@cipfa.org.uk
Website: www.cipfa.org.uk

The CIPFA is the professional body for people in public finance. Our 14, 000 members work throughout the public services and as the only UK professional accountancy body to specialize in public services, CIPFA's qualifications are the foundation for a career in public finance.

*MEMBERSHIP*
Affiliate
Associate
Full Member

*QUALIFICATION/EXAMINATIONS*
CIPFA Professional Qualification
Certificate in Charity Finance and Accountancy
Certificate in International Public Sector Financial Reporting
Certificate in International Public Sector Accounting Standards
Certificate in Financial Reporting for Academies

## THE INSTITUTE OF CERTIFIED BOOKKEEPERS

London Underwriting Centre
3 Minster Court
Mincing Lane
City of London EC3R 7DD
Tel: 0845 060 2345
Fax: 01635 298960
E-mail: info@bookkeepers.org.uk
Website: www.bookkeepers.org.uk

The ICB is the largest bookkeeping institute in the world. Our aims are to promote bookkeeping as a profession, to improve training in the principles of bookkeeping, and to establish qualifications and the award of grades of membership that recognize academic attainment, work experience and professional competence, and thereby enable qualified bookkeepers to gain recognition as an integral part of the financial world.

*MEMBERSHIP*
Registered Student
Affiliate
Associate Member (AICB)
Member (MICB)
Fellow (FICB)

*QUALIFICATION/EXAMINATIONS*
Level 1: Certificate in Basic Bookkeeping
Level 2: (Intermediate): Certificate in Computerized Bookkeeping
Level 2: (Intermediate): Certificate in Manual Bookkeeping
Level 3: (Advanced): Diploma in Computerized Bookkeeping
Level 3: (Advanced): Diploma in Manual Bookkeeping
Level 3: (Advanced): Diploma in Payroll Management
Level 3: (Advanced): Diploma in Self-Assessment Tax Returns
Level 4: (Advanced): Diploma in Financial Management (Drafting Financial Statements, Management

Accounting, Personal Taxation and Business Taxation)

*DESIGNATORY LETTERS*
AICB, MICB, FICB

# ACOUSTICS

## *Membership of Professional Institutions and Associations*

### INSTITUTE OF ACOUSTICS

St Peter's House
45–49 Victoria Street
St Albans
Hertfordshire AL1 3WZ
Tel: 01727 848195
Fax: 01727 850553
E-mail: ioa@ioa.org.uk
Website: www.ioa.org.uk

The IOA is the UK's professional body for those working in acoustics, noise and vibration, and has more than 3, 000 members in research, educational, environmental, government and industrial organizations. It offers professionally recognized courses and is licensed by the Engineering Research Council to offer registration at Chartered and Incorporated Engineer levels.

*MEMBERSHIP*
Student
Affiliate
Technician Member (TechIOA)
Associate Member (AMIOA)
Member (MIOA)
Fellow (FIOA)
Honorary Fellow (HonFIOA)
Incorporated Engineer (IEng)
Chartered Engineer (CEng)
Sponsor

*QUALIFICATION/EXAMINATIONS*
Certificate of Competence in Environmental Noise Measurement
Certificate of Competence in Workplace Noise Risk Assessment
Certificate Course in the Management of Occupational Exposure to Hand–Arm Vibration
Certificate Course in Building Acoustics Measurements
Diploma in Acoustics and Noise Control

*DESIGNATORY LETTERS*
TechIOA, AMIOA, MIOA, FIOA, HonFIOA, IEng, CEng

# ADVERTISING AND PUBLIC RELATIONS

## *Membership of Professional Institutions and Associations*

### CHARTERED INSTITUTE OF PUBLIC RELATIONS

52–53 Russell Square
London WC1B 4HP
Tel: 020 7631 6900
Fax: 020 7631 6944
E-mail: info@cipr.co.uk
Website: www.cipr.co.uk

The CIPR, founded in 1948, is the professional body for PR practitioners and has more than 9, 000 members, to whom it offers information, advice, support and training. Our aim is to raise standards within the profession through the promotion of best practice and our members abide by our strict code of professional conduct.

*MEMBERSHIP*
Student
Affiliate
Associate (ACIPR)
Member (MCIPR)
Fellow (FCIPR)
Global Affiliate

*QUALIFICATION/EXAMINATIONS*
Foundation Award in Public Relations
Advanced Certificate
Diploma

*DESIGNATORY LETTERS*
ACIPR, MCIPR, FCIPR

### INSTITUTE OF PRACTITIONERS IN ADVERTISING

44 Belgrave Square
London SW1X 8QS
Tel: 020 7235 7020
Fax: 020 7245 9904
E-mail: web@ipa.co.uk
Website: www.ipa.co.uk

The IPA is the UK's leading professional body for advertising, media and marketing communications agencies. We promote the services of our member agencies, which have access to a range of services and benefits, including a Legal Department, Information Centre and training courses provided by our Professional Development Department.

*MEMBERSHIP*
Personal Member (MIPA)
Fellow/Honorary Fellow (FIPA)
Member Agency

*QUALIFICATION/EXAMINATIONS*
Foundation Certificate
Advanced Certificate
LegRgs Certificate
Commercial Certificate
Search Certificate
Excellence Diploma
Eff Test

*DESIGNATORY LETTERS*
MIPA, FIPA

## INSTITUTE OF PROMOTIONAL MARKETING

70 Margaret Street
London W1W 8SS
Tel: 020 7291 7730
E-mail: enquiries@theipm.org.uk
Website: www.theipm.org.uk

The Institute of Promotional Marketing represents promoters, agencies and service partners engaged in promotional marketing in the UK by protecting, promoting and progressing effective sales promotion across all media channels through its education, legal advice, awards, and other products and services.

*MEMBERSHIP*
Corporate Member

*QUALIFICATION/EXAMINATIONS*
Certificate in Experiential Marketing
Diploma in Motivation
Certificate in Promotional Marketing
Diploma in Promotional Marketing

*DESIGNATORY LETTERS*
MISP

## LONDON SCHOOL OF PUBLIC RELATIONS

118A Kensington Church Street
London W8 4BH
Tel: 020 7221 3399
Fax: 020 7243 1730
E-mail: info@lspr-education.com
Website: www.lspr-education.com

Established in 1992, the London School of Public Relations (LSPR) provides up-to-date training courses for those wishing to enter public relations as a career or for those already in PR or an information/communications job who require up-to-date practical training awarded with a professional development qualification.

LSPR provides the following courses:

**DIPLOMA:**

- PR & Reputation Management

**ADVANCED CERTIFICATES:**

- Branding and Brand Management
- Corporate Social Responsibility
- Issues and Crisis Management
- Leadership and Personal Branding

**CERTIFICATES:**

- Writing for Business
- Feature Writing
- Social Media

Our Diploma, *PR & Reputation Management*, is awarded to delegates upon successful completion of a 10-day full-time intensive course or an 8-week part-time evening course (twice weekly, 6.30pm-8.30pm).

The Advanced Certificate courses run for 5 days, Monday-Friday. The Certificated courses are offered as day and evening courses.

LSPR also runs training programmes in Leadership, CSR, Reputation Management, Stakeholder Analysis, Crisis and Issues Management, Branding, Corporate Identity, Media Relations and Feature and Press Release Writing. Courses are also offered in-house for clients.

LSPR training programmes are approved and recognised by the Institute of Training and Occupational Learning (ITOL). LSPR operates globally with franchises, in association with international PR bodies and agencies.

*MEMBERSHIP*
Institute of Training and Occupational Learning

*QUALIFICATION/EXAMINATIONS*

- Diploma: Examination, Assessment and a Final project
- Advanced Certificates: Critical Thinking Exercises
- Certificates: Projects and exercises

# AGRICULTURE AND HORTICULTURE

## *Membership of Professional Institutions and Associations*

## INSTITUTE OF HORTICULTURE

Capel Manor College
Bullsmoor Lane
Enfield
Middlesex EN1 4RQ
Tel: 01992 707025
E-mail: ioh@horticulture.org.uk
Website: www.horticulture.org.uk

The IoH represents all those professionally engaged in horticulture in the UK and the Republic of Ireland. Our main aim is to promote the profession and its importance in food and ornamental plant production, improving the environment, providing employment and as the leisure pursuit of gardening. We are also developing CPD and mentoring schemes for our members and liaise with government and other bodies on matters of interest or concern.

*MEMBERSHIP*
Student Member, Affiliate, e-Affiliate, Associate (AI Hort), Member (MI Hort), Fellow (FI Hort), Group Membership

*DESIGNATORY LETTERS*
AI Hort, MI Hort, FI Hort

## ROYAL HORTICULTURAL SOCIETY

RHS Qualifications
RHS Garden Wisley
Woking
Surrey GU23 6QB
Tel: 0845 260 9000
E-mail: qualifications@rhs.org.uk
Website: www.rhs.org.uk

RHS Qualifications is a recognized awarding body offering a range of qualifications in horticultural knowledge and skills. Part-time courses leading to RHS qualifications are offered by approved centres throughout the UK and Ireland, and by distance-learning providers. The RHS School of Horticulture provides courses in practical horticultural skills.

*QUALIFICATION/EXAMINATIONS*
RHS Level 1 Award in Practical Horticulture
RHS Level 2 Certificate in the Principles of Plant Growth, Propagation and Development
RHS Level 2 Certificate in the Principles of Garden Planning, Establishment and Maintenance
RHS Level 2 Certificate in the Principles of Horticulture
RHS Level 2 Certificate in Practical Horticulture
RHS Level 2 Diploma in the Principles and Practices of Horticulture
RHS Level 3 Certificate in the Principles of Plant Growth, Health and Applied Propagation
RHS Level 3 Certificate in the Principles of Garden Planning, Construction and Planting
RHS Level 3 Certificate in Practical Horticulture
RHS Level 3 Diploma in the Principles and Practices of Horticulture
Master of Horticulture (RHS)
Wisley Diploma in Practical Horticulture
Certificate in Practical Horticulture
Specialist Option Certificates in:
Ornamental Horticulture
Fruit Cultivation
Rock and Alpine Gardening
Orchid Culture and Glasshouse Technique

Estate Management with Arboriculture

Plant Centre Management Skills

## THE ROYAL BOTANIC GARDEN EDINBURGH

20A Inverleith Row
Edinburgh EH3 5LR
Tel: 0131 552 7171
Fax: 01312 482901
E-mail: education@rbge.org.uk
Website: www.rbge.org.uk

The RBGE was founded in the 17th century as a physic garden, growing medicinal plants. Now it extends over four gardens boasting a rich living collection of plants, and is a world-renowned centre for plant science and education.

*QUALIFICATION/EXAMINATIONS*
Certificate in Botanic Illustration
Certificate in Herbology
Certificate in the Principles of Horticulture (RHS Level 2)
Certificate in Practical Field Botany
Certificate in Practical Horticulture
Diploma in Botanical Illustration
Diploma in Garden Design
Diploma in Garden History
Diploma in Herbology
HND/BSc in Horticulture with Plantsmanship
MSc in The Biodiversity and Taxonomy of Plants

# AMBULANCE SERVICE

## *Membership of Professional Institutions and Associations*

## AMBULANCE SERVICE INSTITUTE

Suite 183
Maddison House
226 High Street
Croydon CR9 1DF
E-mail: enquiries@asi-international.com
Website: www.asi-international.com

The ASI is a non-union, non-political, independent institute whose membership is dedicated to raising the standards and quality of ambulance provision and thereby improving the professionalism and quality of care available to patients. Membership is open to non-NHS personnel as well as to employees of NHS Ambulance Services.

*MEMBERSHIP*
Student
Member (MASI)
Licentiate (LASI)
Associate (AASI)
Graduate (GASI)
Fellow (FASI)

*QUALIFICATION/EXAMINATIONS*
The Institute offers professional examinations and qualifications in the areas of Pre-Hospital Care, Control and Communications, and Management, for those who desire a career in the ambulance service.

*DESIGNATORY LETTERS*
MASI, LASI, AASI, GASI, FASI

# ARBITRATION

## *Membership of Professional Institutions and Associations*

### THE CHARTERED INSTITUTE OF ARBITRATORS

12 Bloomsbury Square
London WC1A 2LP
Tel: 020 7421 7444
Fax: 020 7404 4023
E-mail: info@ciarb.org
Website: www.ciarb.org

The CIArb is a not-for-profit, UK-registered charity with 12, 000 members worldwide that exists to promote and facilitate the settlement of private disputes by arbitration and alternative dispute resolution. We provide training for arbitrators, mediators and adjudicators and act as an international centre for practitioners, policy-makers, academics and those in business concerned with the cost-effective and early settlement of disputes.

*MEMBERSHIP*
Associate (ACIArb)
Member (MCIArb)
Fellow (FCIArb)

*QUALIFICATION/EXAMINATIONS*
Introductory Certificate
Advanced Certificate
Diploma

*DESIGNATORY LETTERS*
ACIArb, MCIArb, FCIArb

# ARCHAEOLOGY

## *Membership of Professional Institutions and Associations*

### INSTITUTE FOR ARCHAEOLOGISTS

Miller Building
University of Reading
Whiteknights
Reading
Berkshire RG6 6AB
Tel: 0118 378 6446
Fax: 0118 378 6448
E-mail: admin@archaeologists.net
Website: www.archaeologists.net

The IfA is a professional organization for all archaeologists and others involved in protecting and understanding the historic environment, with more than 3000 members. We advance the practice of archaeology and allied disciplines by promoting professional standards and ethics for conserving, managing, understanding and enjoying our heritage.

*MEMBERSHIP*
Student
Affiliate
Practitioner (PIfA)
Associate (AIfA)
Member (MIfA)
Registered Organization

# ARCHITECTURE

## *Membership of Professional Institutions and Associations*

### ARCHITECTS REGISTRATION BOARD

8 Weymouth Street
London W1W 5BU
Tel: 020 7580 5861
Fax: 020 7436 5269
E-mail: info@arb.org.uk
Website: www.arb.org.uk

The ARB is the regulatory body for architects in the UK. Only individuals registered with the Board can use the title 'architect'. Applicants must have passed the recognized exams at a school of architecture in the UK (or have an equivalent non-UK professional qualification) and have at least 2 years' practical experience working under the supervision of an architect.

### CHARTERED INSTITUTE OF ARCHITECTURAL TECHNOLOGISTS (CIAT)

397 City Road
London EC1V 1NH
Tel: 020 7278 2206
Fax: 020 7837 3194
E-mail: info@ciat.org.uk
Website: www.ciat.org.uk

CIAT represents professionals working and studying in the field of Architectural Technology. We are internationally recognised as the qualifying body for Chartered Architectural Technologists (MCIAT) and Architectural Technicians (TCIAT).

*MEMBERSHIP*
Student member
Profile candidate
Associate (ACIAT)
Architectural Technician (TCIAT)
Chartered Architectural Technologist (MCIAT)
Honorary Member (HonMCIAT)

*DESIGNATORY LETTERS*
ACIAT, TCIAT, MCIAT

### ROYAL INSTITUTE OF BRITISH ARCHITECTS

66 Portland Place
London W1B 1AD
Tel: 020 7580 5533
Fax: 020 7255 1541
E-mail: info@riba.org
Website: www.architecture.com

The Royal Institute of British Architects is the UK body for architecture and the architectural profession. We provide support for our 40, 500 members worldwide in the form of training, technical services, publications and events, and set standards for the education of architects, both in the UK and overseas. We also work with government to improve the design quality of public buildings, new homes and new communities.

*MEMBERSHIP*
Student Member

Affiliate Member
Associate Member
Chartered Member
Chartered Practice

# ART AND DESIGN

## *Membership of Professional Institutions and Associations*

### BRITISH ASSOCIATION OF ART THERAPISTS

Claremont
24–27 White Lion Street
London N1 9PD
Tel: 020 7686 4216
E-mail: info@baat.org
Website: www.baat.org

The BAAT is the professional organization for art therapists in the UK and has its own Code of Ethics of Professional Practice. We maintain a comprehensive directory of qualified art therapists and work to promote art therapy in the UK through 20 regional groups. We also have a European section and an international section.

*MEMBERSHIP*
Trainee Member
Associate Member
Full Member
Honorary Member
Fellow
Corporate Member

*QUALIFICATION/EXAMINATIONS*
The BAAT organizes a programme of CPD courses for Art Therapists. For details see the website.

### BRITISH ASSOCIATION OF PAINTINGS CONSERVATOR-RESTORERS

PO Box 258
Norwich NR13 4WY
Tel: 01603 516237
Fax: 01603 510985
E-mail: office@bapcr.org.uk
Website: www.bapcr.org.uk

The BAPCR (founded in 1943 as the Association of British Picture Restorers) is the professional association for conservator-restorers of paintings and has more than 400 members worldwide. Our aims are to advance the profession by providing means for CPD to our members and thereby a service to the public.

*MEMBERSHIP*
Associate (Student)
Associate
Fellow

## D&AD (BRITISH DESIGN & ART DIRECTION)

Britannia House
68-80 Hanbury Street
London E1 5JL
Tel: 020 7840 1111
Fax: 020 7840 0840
E-mail: info@dandad.co.uk
Website: www.dandad.org

Founded in 1962, D&AD is a professional association and educational charity with a membership of more than 2, 000, working on behalf of the design and advertising communities. Our mission is to set creative standards, educate and inspire the next creative generation, and promote the importance of good design and advertising to business as a whole.

*MEMBERSHIP*
Awarded
Professional
Education Network

## SOCIETY OF DESIGNER CRAFTSMEN (SDC)

24 Rivington Street
London EC2A 3DU
Tel: 07531 798983
E-mail: info@societyofdesignercraftsmen.org.uk
Website: www.societyofdesignercraftsmen.org.uk

The Society, which was founded in 1887 as the Arts and Crafts Exhibition Society, is the largest and oldest multi-craft society in the UK. Our aim is to emphasize designer-making where innovation, originality and quality are important; we provide promotional services and exhibiting opportunities to members.

*MEMBERSHIP*
Associate
Licentiate (LSDC)
Member (MSDC)
Fellow (FSDC)

*DESIGNATORY LETTERS*
LSDC, MSDC, FSDC

## THE CHARTERED SOCIETY OF DESIGNERS

1 Cedar Court
Royal Oak Yard
Bermondsey Street
London SE1 3GA
Tel: 020 7357 8088
Fax: 020 7407 9878
E-mail: info@csd.org.uk
Website: www.csd.org.uk

The CSD, which was founded in 1930, is the professional body for designers and has more than 3, 000 members. We promote sound principles of design in all areas in which design considerations apply, further design practice and encourage the study of design techniques for the benefit of the community.

*MEMBERSHIP*
Student Member

Associate (Assoc. CSD)
Member (MCSD)
Fellow (FCSD)

*DESIGNATORY LETTERS*
MCSD, FCSD

## THE INDEX OF PROFESSIONAL MASTER DESIGNERS

Kensington House
33 Imperial Square
Cheltenham Spa
Gloucestershire GL50 1QZ
Tel: 08701 161823
Fax: 08702 626146
E-mail: masterdesigners@kensington-house.com

The Index was formed to provide a register of designers practising in all areas of design. Our objectives are to enable designers to achieve recognition and attain qualifications and also to accredit schools and training organizations offering suitable courses.

*MEMBERSHIP*
Student
Professional Designer (IPMD (DIP))
Master Designer (IPMD (MAS))

*QUALIFICATION/EXAMINATIONS*
Certificate of Excellence – Interior Design Students

*DESIGNATORY LETTERS*
IPMD (DIP), IPMD (MAS)

# ASTRONOMY AND SPACE SCIENCE

## *Membership of Professional Institutions and Associations*

## THE BRITISH INTERPLANETARY SOCIETY

27/29 South Lambeth Road
London SW8 1SZ
Tel: 020 7735 3160
Fax: 020 7587 5118
E-mail: info@bis-space.com
Website: www.bis-space.com

The BIS was formed in 1933 and has been at the forefront of actively promoting new ideas on space exploration at technical, educational and popular levels for 80 years. We serve the interests of those professionally involved with space, promote fundamental space research, technology and applications, encourage technical and scientific space studies, and undertake educational activities on space topics.

*MEMBERSHIP*
Member
Fellow (FBIS)

*DESIGNATORY LETTERS*
FBIS

# AVIATION

## Membership of Professional Institutions and Associations

### THE GUILD OF AIR PILOTS AND AIR NAVIGATORS

Cobham House
9 Warwick Court
London WC1R 5DJ
Tel: 020 7404 4032
Fax: 020 7404 4035
E-mail: gapan@gapan.org
Website: www.gapan.org

The Guild, an active Livery Company of the City of London, represents pilot and navigator interests within all areas of aviation. Most of our members are, or have been, professional licence holders, or hold a private licence. Our aims include promoting the highest standards of air safety, liaising with all authorities connected with licensing, training and legislation, providing advice and facilitating exchange of information.

*MEMBERSHIP*
Associate
Freeman
Upper Freeman

*QUALIFICATION/EXAMINATIONS*
Master Air Pilot Certificate
Master Air Navigator Certificate
Master Rearcrew Certificate

### THE GUILD OF AIR TRAFFIC CONTROL OFFICERS

4 St Mary's Road
Bingham
Nottingham
Nottinghamshire NG13 8DW
Tel: 01949 876405
Fax: 01949 876405
E-mail: caf@gatco.org
Website: www.gatco.org

Founded in 1954, GATCO is an independent professional organization that exists to promote honourable practice and the highest standards in all aspects of aviation. It is dedicated to the safety of all who seek their livelihood or pleasure in the air.

*MEMBERSHIP*
Student Member
Associate Non-Operational Member
Associate Operational Member
Full Member
Corporate Member

*QUALIFICATION/EXAMINATIONS*
Qualifying criteria apply to all membership categories. Further information should be sought from GATCO Ltd, Central Administrative Facility (CAF).

# AWARDS

## Membership of Professional Institutions and Associations

### CONSORTIUM OF PROFESSIONAL AWARDING BODIES (COPAB)

40 Archdale Road
East Dulwich
London SE22 9HJ
Tel: 0845 643 6832
Fax: 0845 643 6834
E-mail: secretary@copab.net; profblankson@ssm.org.uk
Website: www.copab.net

Consortium of Professional Awarding Bodies (COPAB) was incorporated in 2012. It strives to become the best and the biggest global professional awarding body representing educational, vocational, technical, scientific and professional awarding bodies worldwide. It also aims to foster the ideals and objectives of professional, career membership and registering bodies on a global scale.

*MEMBERSHIP*
There is only one membership grade: Member Consortium of Professional Awarding Bodies.

*QUALIFICATION/EXAMINATIONS*
To join COPAB, you must be a professional awarding body operating in the United Kingdom and/or internationally.

*BENEFITS (AMONG OTHERS)*
- To promote information on professional bodies by discussions and lectures
- To encourage the study of various professional bodies
- To join other professional bodies for convocations
- To cooperate with other members;
- To promote reciprocal agreements, where necessary
- To receive COPAB's wall shield
- To receive COPAB's Journal
- To use COPAB's logo on letterheads and advertising materials

*DESIGNATORY LETTERS*
MCOPAB

# BANKING

## Membership of Professional Institutions and Associations

### IFS SCHOOL OF FINANCE

8th Floor
Peninsular House
36 Monument Street
London EC3R 8LJ
Tel: 0207 4447111
Fax: 0207 4447115
E-mail: customerservices@ifslearning.ac.uk
Website: www.ifslearning.ac.uk

The ifs School of Finance is a world-class provider of financial learning, and has more than 50, 000 students in over 90 countries. Having built a reputation for excellence in learning, all the qualifications it provides combine innovation and quality, and draw from over 130 years of educational experience.

*MEMBERSHIP*
Member

Student Member
Associate
Fellow
Chartered Associate
Chartered Fellow

*QUALIFICATION/EXAMINATIONS*
The ifs offers a wide range of qualifications for those employed or aspiring to a career in the financial services industry, and for consumers. For details see www.ifslearning.ac.uk

## THE CHARTERED INSTITUTE OF BANKERS IN SCOTLAND

Drumsheugh House
38B Drumsheugh Gardens
Edinburgh EH3 7SW
Tel: 0131 473 7777
Fax: 0131 473 7788
E-mail: info@charteredbanker.com
Website: www.charteredbanker.com

The Chartered Institute of Bankers in Scotland provides world-class professional qualifications for both the UK and international markets. Our vision for the financial services industry is one of professionalism. We are the only organisation in the world entitled to award the designation 'Chartered Banker' to its members.

*MEMBERSHIP*
Student
Affiliate
Associate (ACIBS)
Member (MCIBS)
Fellow (FCIBS)

*QUALIFICATION/EXAMINATIONS*
Certificate
Diploma
Advanced Diploma
Chartered Banker

*DESIGNATORY LETTERS*
ACIBS, MCIBS, FCIBS

# BEAUTY THERAPY AND BEAUTY CULTURE

## *Membership of Professional Institutions and Associations*

## BRITISH ASSOCIATION OF BEAUTY THERAPY AND COSMETOLOGY LTD

BABTAC Limited
Ambrose House, Meteor Court
Barnett Way
Barnwood
Gloucester GL4 3GG
Tel: 0845 250 7277
Fax: 01452 611599
E-mail: info@babtac.com
Website: www.babtac.com

BABTAC was formed in 1977 and is a non-profit-making organization for beauticians and therapists in the UK. Members work to a rigorous code of ethics and good practice, both in terms of the treatments and therapies they offer and the way they conduct their relationships with their clients. CIBTAC, an international, educational awarding body that works closely with BABTAC, offers over 30 internationally recognized diplomas in beauty and complementary therapies to accredited colleges and students in the UK and abroad.

*MEMBERSHIP*
Student Member
Associate Member
Full Therapist member
Full Hairdresser member
Salon and Spa member
International member

*QUALIFICATION/EXAMINATIONS*
BABTAC offers a programme of short courses. For details see the BABTAC website. For CIBTAC diplomas see www.cibtac.com/courses_home.htm

## BRITISH INSTITUTE AND ASSOCIATION OF ELECTROLYSIS LTD

40 Parkfield Road
Ickenham
Middlesex UB10 BLW
Tel: 08445 441373
E-mail: sec@electrolysis.co.uk
Website: www.electrolysis.co.uk

The BIAE is a non-profit-making organisation that demands a high standard of skill and ethical conduct from its members, who are spread throughout the UK and overseas. Candidate Electrolysists must complete the rigorous assessments, both theoretical and practical, of the BIAE Examining Board before being accepted onto the Register.

*MEMBERSHIP*
Member

*QUALIFICATION/EXAMINATIONS*
Certificate in Remedial Electrolysis (CRE)

## FEDERATION OF HOLISTIC THERAPISTS

18 Shakespeare Business Centre
Hathaway Close
Eastleigh
Hampshire SO50 4SR
Tel: 023 8062 4350
Fax: 023 8062 4396
E-mail: info@fht.org.uk
Website: www.fht.org.uk

The FHT is the leading and largest professional beauty, sports and complementary therapist association in the UK, which has been representing the interests of holistic therapists since 1962. The FHT leads the industry by offering its members a Code of Conduct and Professional Practice, public liability insurance, access to regulation, a robust CPD programme with auditing, class-leading journal, local therapist network, and comprehensive business and public affairs updates.

*MEMBERSHIP*
Student
Affiliate
Associate
Member
Fellow
International

*QUALIFICATION/EXAMINATIONS*
Please see the FHT's website.

*DESIGNATORY LETTERS*
MFHT, FFHT, AFHT, AfFHT

## ITEC

2nd Floor, Chiswick Gate
598–608 Chiswick High Road
London W4 5RT
Tel: 020 8994 4141
Fax: 020 8994 7880
E-mail: info@itecworld.co.uk
Website: www.itecworld.co.uk

ITEC is an international examination board offering a variety of qualifications in the beauty therapy, complementary therapy and sports therapy sectors worldwide. We also offer teacher training courses in: Skincare; Make-up; Manicure and Pedicure; Waxing; Holistic Massage; Aromatherapy; Reflexology; Body Treatments; and other areas as required.

*QUALIFICATION/EXAMINATIONS*
Please see the ITEC website.

# BIOLOGICAL SCIENCES

## *Membership of Professional Institutions and Associations*

## INSTITUTE OF BIOMEDICAL SCIENCE

12 Coldbath Square
London EC1R 5HL
Tel: 020 7713 0214
Fax: 020 7837 9658
E-mail: mail@ibms.org
Website: www.ibms.org

The IBMS is the professional body for biomedical scientists in the UK. We aim to promote and develop the role of biomedical science within healthcare to deliver the best possible service for patient care and safety.

*MEMBERSHIP*
Associate
Licentiate (LIBMS)
Member (MIBMS)
Fellow (FIBMS)
Company member

*QUALIFICATION/EXAMINATIONS*
Certificate of Competence (also required for registration with the Health and Care Professions Council (HCPC))
Specialist Diploma in:
Cellular Pathology, Clinical Biochemistry, Clinical Immunology, Cytopathology, Haematology & Transfusion Science, Histocompatibility & Immunogenetics (developed in conjunction with BSHI), Medical Microbiology, Transfusion Science, Virology.
Diploma of Specialist Practice
Higher Specialist Diploma in:
Cellular Pathology, Clinical Chemistry, Cytopathology, Haematology, Immunology, Histocompatibility & Immunogenetics (developed in conjunction with BSHI), Medical Microbiology, Transfusion Science, Virology.
Diploma of Higher Specialist Practice
Complementary qualifications/examinations related to areas of scientific expertise (available to Members and/or Fellows)
Certificates and Diplomas of Expert Practice
Advanced Specialist Diplomas

*DESIGNATORY LETTERS*
LIBMS, MIBMS, FIBMS

## SOCIETY OF BIOLOGY

Charles Darwin House
12 Roger Street
London WC1N 2JU
Tel: 020 7685 2550
E-mail: info@societyofbiology.org
Website: www.societyofbiology.org

The Society of Biology aims to be a single unified voice for biology: advising government and influencing policy; advancing education and professional development; supporting members; and engaging and encouraging public interest in the life sciences.

*MEMBERSHIP*
Associate Member (AMSB)
Member (MSB)
Fellow (FSB)
Chartered Biologist (CBiol)
Affiliate
Sudent
BioNet

*DESIGNATORY LETTERS*
AMSB, MSB, FSB, CBiol

# BREWING

## *Membership of Professional Institutions and Associations*

## INSTITUTE OF BREWING & DISTILLING

33 Clarges Street
Mayfair
London W1J 7EE
Tel: 020 7499 8144
Fax: 020 7499 1156
E-mail: enquiries@ibd.org.uk
Website: www.ibd.org.uk

The IBD is a members' organization dedicated to the education and training needs of brewers and distillers and those in related industries. We do this by offering a range of internationally recognized qualifications and the training to support them, through either direct instruction or distance learning.

*MEMBERSHIP*
Member
Honorary Member
Senior Member
Fellow (FIBD)
Honorary Fellow
Corporate Member
Student Member
Member in Retirement
Certificate Member

*QUALIFICATION/EXAMINATIONS*
Certificate in the Fundamentals of Brewing and Packaging of Beer (FBPB) (City & Guilds Level 2)
Certificate in the Fundamentals of Distilling (FD) (City & Guilds Level 2)
General Certificate in Brewing (GCB) (City & Guilds Level 3)
General Certificate in Distilling (GCD) (City & Guilds Level 3)
General Certificate in Packaging (GCP) (City & Guilds Level 3)
Diploma in Packaging (Dipl.Pack) (City & Guilds Level 4)
General Certificate in Spirits Packaging
General Certificate in Malting
Diploma in Brewing (Dipl.Brew) (City & Guilds Level 4)

Diploma in Distilling (Dipl.Distil) (City & Guilds Level 4)
Master Brewer (MBrew)

*DESIGNATORY LETTERS*
Dipl.Brew, Dipl.Distil, Dipl.Pack, MBrew, FIBD, Hon FIBD

# BUILDING

## *Membership of Professional Institutions and Associations*

### INSTITUTE OF ASPHALT TECHNOLOGY

PO Box 17399
Edinburgh EH12 1FR
Tel: 01506 238397
E-mail: info@instituteofasphalt.org
Website: www.instofasphalt.org

The IAT is the UK's professional body for persons working in asphalt technology and those interested in aspects of the manufacture, placing, technology and uses of materials containing asphalt or bitumen. A fully audited CPD system for members has been available since 1994 and is now also offered in computerized format for ease of data entry and auditing, via members' own PCs.

*MEMBERSHIP*
Student (SIAT)
Technician (TIAT)
Affiliate (AIAT)
Member (MIAT)
Fellow (FIAT)
Associate Member (AMIAT)
Honorary Fellow (Hon FIAT)

*DESIGNATORY LETTERS*
Tech IAT, AIAT, MIAT, FIAT

### THE CHARTERED INSTITUTE OF BUILDING

Englemere
Kings Ride
Ascot
Berkshire SL5 7TB
Tel: 01344 630700
Fax: 01344 630777
E-mail: reception@ciob.org.uk
Website: www.ciob.org

The CIOB is the international voice of the construction industry. CIOB members are largely Construction Managers engaged in managing the development, conservation and improvement of the built environment, with a common commitment to achieving and maintaining the highest possible standards.

*MEMBERSHIP*
Student Member
Associate (ACIOB)
Incorporated (ICIOB)
Member (MCIOB)
Fellow (FCIOB)
Chartered Environmentalist (CENV)
Student in Employment
Educationalist
Concessionary

*QUALIFICATION/EXAMINATIONS*
The CIOB has routes to membership to suit a range of professionals from those with degrees or vocational qualifications to those with experience but no formal qualifications. All our members have a strong

commitment to improve and develop themselves in a challenging and exciting career.

Chartered Member status is recognized internationally as the mark of a skilled professional in the construction industry. CIOB members are from a wide range of professions in the construction industry.

To find out more about our membership qualifications and joining the CIOB just visit our website www.ciob.org

The CIOB Awarding Body offers a suite of qualifications to enable site operatives to progress into management roles.

Level 3 Diploma in Site Supervisory Studies
Level 4 Certificate in Site Management
Level 4 Diploma in Site Management

The CIOB qualifications develop the skills and confidence to manage and coordinate all types of construction projects. The site management qualifications are nationally recognized and allow the learner to progress to higher education and National Vocational Qualifications (NVQs).

For more information on the Site Management Qualifications visit the website at www.ciob.org.uk/education/courseinfo/sitemanagement

*DESIGNATORY LETTERS*

ACIOB, ICIOB, MCIOB, FCIOB, CENV

## THE INSTITUTE OF CARPENTERS

32 High Street
Wendover
Buckinghamshire HP22 6EA
Tel: 0844 879 7696
Fax: 01296 620981
E-mail: info@instituteofcarpenters.com
Website: www.instituteofcarpenters.com

The IOC was founded in 1890 to oversee training for carpenters and joiners and maintain high professional standards at a time when many feared that traditional skills were being lost. Today, while remaining committed to our original aims, we embrace many other wood craftsmen, such as shopfitters, furniture and cabinetmakers, boat builders (woodworking skills), structural post & beam carpenters (heavy structural timber framers), wheelwrights, wood carvers and wood turners, and offer professional status to those holding recognized qualifications.

*MEMBERSHIP*

Student
Mature Student
Affiliate
Licentiate (LIOC)
Member (MIOC)
Fellow (FIOC)
College Member
Corporate Member
Corporate Associate

*QUALIFICATION/EXAMINATIONS*

Foundation Examination
Intermediate Examination
Advanced Craft Examination
Fellowship Examination
Setting-Out Course

*DESIGNATORY LETTERS*

LIOC, MIOC, FIOC

## THE INSTITUTE OF CLERKS OF WORKS AND CONSTRUCTION INSPECTORATE OF GREAT BRITAIN INC

28 Commerce Road
Lynch Wood
Peterborough PE2 6LR
Tel: 01733 405160
Fax: 01733 405161
E-mail: info@icwci.org
Website: www.icwci.org

---

The ICWCI is the professional body that supports quality construction through inspection. As a membership organization, we provide a support network of meeting centres, technical advice, publications and events to help keep our members up to date with the ever-changing construction industry.

*MEMBERSHIP*
Student
Licentiate (LICWCI)
Member (MICWCI)
Fellow (FICWCI)
Life Member
Honorary Member

*DESIGNATORY LETTERS*
LICWCI, MICWCI, FICWCI

# BUSINESS STUDIES

## *Membership of Professional Institutions and Associations*

## ASSOCIATION OF BUSINESS RECOVERY PROFESSIONALS (R3)

8th Floor
120 Aldersgate Street
London EC1A 4JQ
Tel: 020 7566 4200
Fax: 020 7566 4224
E-mail: association@r3.org.uk
Website: www.r3.org.uk

---

The Association of Business Recovery Professionals (known by its brand name 'R3') is the leading professional association for insolvency, business recovery and turnaround specialists in the UK. A not-for-profit organization, it promotes best practice for professionals working with financially troubled individuals and businesses, and provides a forum for debate on key issues facing the profession.

*MEMBERSHIP*
New Professional (Student) Member
New Professional (Networking) Member
Associate Member (AABRP)
Full Member (MABRP)
Fellow (FABRP)

*QUALIFICATION/EXAMINATIONS*
R3 provides comprehensive Continuing Professional Education in the field of Insolvency and Restructuring. For details of courses see R3's website.

*DESIGNATORY LETTERS*
AABRP, MABRP, FABRP

## INSTITUTE OF ASSESSORS AND INTERNAL VERIFIERS

PO Box 1138
Warrington WA4 9GS
Tel: 01925 485 786
E-mail: office@iavltd.co.uk
Website: www.iavltd.co.uk

The IAV is the professional organization representing assessors and internal verifiers in the UK in vocational training and assessment.

*MEMBERSHIP*
Affiliate Member
Associate Member
Licentiate Member

## THE ACADEMY OF EXECUTIVES & ADMINISTRATORS

Head Office
Warwick Corner
42 Warwick Road
Kenilworth
Warwickshire CV8 1HE
Tel: 01926 259342
E-mail: info@academyofexecutivesandadministrators.org.uk
Website: www.academyofexecutivesandadministrators.org.uk

The Academy of Executives & Administrators was founded in 2002 to give professional status and recognition to the knowledge and skills of executives and administrators. We encourage excellence and flexibility in the changing environment of executive and administrative roles, and support lifelong learning to help members fulfil their career ambitions.

*MEMBERSHIP*
Student Member (StudAEA)
Associate Member (AMAEA)
Member (MAEA)
Fellow (FAEA)
Companion (CAEA)

*QUALIFICATION/EXAMINATIONS*
Certified Business Economist
Certified Financial Manager
Certified Assistant Accountant
Certified Assistant Corporate Accountant
Certified Trainer
Certified Administration Practitioner
Certified Executive Practitioner

## THE ACADEMY OF MULTI-SKILLS

Head Office
219 Bow Road
London
Middlesex E3 2SJ
Tel: (0)709 201 2910
E-mail: The MSAcademy@yahoo.co.uk
Website: www.academyofmultiskills.co.uk

The Academy of Multi-Skills was founded in 1995 to give professional recognition to multi-skilled personnel, skilled trades, crafts and professions. The Academy encourages a positive and energetic attitude to the challenges of careers that require diversity, creativity and intellect, and recognizes the valuable contribution that these skills provide to society.

*MEMBERSHIP*
Technician (TAMS)
Associate (AAMS)
Fellow (FAMS)
Doctoral Fellow (DFAMS)

*QUALIFICATION/EXAMINATIONS*
Members may choose to enhance their qualifications via our diploma, HND, post-graduate and doctoral diploma courses.

We have arrangements with other prestigious organisations which our members may choose to join to obtain further qualifications.
Discounts are available to our members from organisations ranging from books to overseas conferences.

*DESIGNATORY LETTERS*
TAMS, AAMS, FAMS, DFAMS

## THE FACULTY OF SECRETARIES AND ADMINISTRATORS (1930) WITH THE ASSOCIATION OF CORPORATE SECRETARIES

Brightstowe
Catteshall Lane
Godalming
Surrey GU7 1LL
Tel: 01483 427323
E-mail: facultyofsecretaries@gmail.com
Website: www.facultyofsecretaries.co.uk

The Faculty and Association is a professional body for company and corporate secretaries whose prime qualified designation is that of Certified Public or Corporate Secretary.

*MEMBERSHIP*
Membership Fellows (FFCS)
Associates (AFCS)
Member (MACS)
Ordinary Member
Student Member
Licentiate (AFCS)
Corporate

*QUALIFICATION/EXAMINATIONS*
Part 1 The Generic Business Assessment to ONC/D Level
Part 2 Professional Papers in Company Secretarial Practice, Company Law and Management, Secretarial and Administrative Practice, Commercial Law
Part 3 Professional Meetings Law and Procedure, Company Taxation, Accountancy and Finance, Company Law

*DESIGNATORY LETTERS*
FFCS, AFCS, MACS

## THE INSTITUTE OF CHARTERED SECRETARIES AND ADMINISTRATORS

16 Park Crescent
London W1B 1AH
Tel: 020 7580 4741
Fax: 020 7323 1132
E-mail: studentsupport@icsaglobal.com
Website: www.icsaglobal.com

The Institute of Chartered Secretaries and Administrators is the international qualifying and membership body for the Chartered Secretary profession. With a global community of 37, 000 members we provide Chartered Membership, training and a professional qualifying scheme to set you on the path to a diverse, challenging and rewarding career.

*MEMBERSHIP*
Affiliate
Graduate (GradICSA)

Associate (ACIS)
Fellow (FCIS)

*QUALIFICATION/EXAMINATIONS*
Chartered Secretaries Qualifying Scheme (CSQS)
Certificate in Offshore Finance and Administration
Diploma in Offshore Finance and Administration
Certificate in Company Secretarial Practice and Share Registration Practice
Certificate in Irish Company Secretarial Practice and Share Registration Practice
Certificate in Employee Share Plans
Postgraduate Certificate in Charity Management
ICSA Certificate in Further Education Governance

*DESIGNATORY LETTERS*
GradICSA, ACIS, FCIS

# CATERING AND INSTITUTIONAL MANAGEMENT

## *Membership of Professional Institutions and Associations*

### BII

Wessex House
80 Park Street
Camberley
Surrey GU15 3PT
Tel: 01276 684449
E-mail: info@bii.org
Website: www.bii.org

Founded in 1981, BII is the professional body for the licensed retail sector with a remit to raise standards throughout the industry. BIIAB, the wholly owned awarding body of BII, does this through offering qualifications specifically tailored to, and designed in conjunction with, the industry.

*MEMBERSHIP*
There is a wide range of membership grades available, from those who have just started their careers in licensed retailing to those who have been in the industry for many years. The grade of membership awarded depends on both experience and qualifications and is determined by a points system. Member of the Hotel Catering and Management Association, HCIMA.

*QUALIFICATION/EXAMINATIONS*
Qualifications for licensing
Award for Designated Premises Supervisors (Level 2)
Award for Licensing Practitioners (Alcohol) (Level 2)
Award for Personal License Holders (Level 2)
Award for Upskilling Door Supervisors (Level 2)
Award for Upskilling Door Supervisors (Scotland)
Award in Door Supervision (Level 2)
Award in Door Supervision (Scotland)
Award in Door Supervision (Northern Ireland)
Award in CCTV Operations (Public Space Surveillance) (Scotland)
Award in Crime Scene Preservation (Level 2)
Award in Drug Awareness for Licensed Hospitality Staff (Level 2)
Award in Fire Safety (Level 2)
Scottish Certificate for Licensees (Drugs Awareness)
Award in Isle of Man Licensing Law
Award in Jersey Licensing Law
Qualifications for new licensed retail managers
Award in Licensed Retailing (Level 2)
Award in Beer and Cellar Quality (Cask and Keg) (Level 2)
Award in Beer and Cellar Quality (Keg) (Level 2)
Scottish Certificate in Licensed Retailing

Qualifications for staff development
Award in Kitchen Management (Level 3)
Award in Introduction to Employment in the Hospitality Industry (Level 1)
Professional Barperson's Qualification
Award in Conflict Management for Licensed Premises Staff (Level 2)
Award in Customer Service Excellence (Licensed Hospitality)
Award in Food Safety in Catering (Level 2)
Award in Health and Safety in the Workplace (Level 2)

Isle of Man Security Staff Qualification

Qualifications for management development

Award in Licensed Hospitality Operations (Level 2)
Certificate in Licensed Hospitality Operations (Level 2)
Certificate in Licensed Hospitality Skills (Level 2)
Award in Hospitality Business Management (Level 3)
Certificate in Hospitality Business Management (Level 3)
Certificate in Multiple Licensed Premises Management (Level 4)

Qualifications for personal and social responsibility

Award in Alcohol Awareness (Level 1)
Award in Assessment of Licensed Premises (Social Responsibility) (Level 2)
Award in Assessment of Licensed Premises (Social Responsibility) (Scotland)

## GUILD OF INTERNATIONAL PROFESSIONAL TOASTMASTERS

Life President: Ivor Spencer
22 Great Mead
Denmead
Waterlooville
Hampshire PO7 6HH
Tel: 07802 250477
E-mail: info@guildoftoastmasters.co.uk
Website: www.guildoftoastmasters.co.uk

The Guild of Professional Toastmasters was established over 30 years ago to improve standards in the profession and support its members. A 5-day course is offered to prospective members, who may apply for membership upon successful completion of the course. Applications are considered by the Fellows of the Guild.

*MEMBERSHIP*
Fellow (FGIntPT)

*DESIGNATORY LETTERS*
FGIntPT

## INSTITUTE OF HOSPITALITY

Trinity Court
34 West Street
Sutton
Surrey SM1 1SH
Tel: 020 8661 4900
Fax: 020 8661 4901
E-mail: accreditation@instituteofhospitality.org
Website: www.instituteofhospitality.org

The Institute of Hospitality is the professional body for managers and aspiring managers in the hospitality, leisure and tourism industries. We are an accredited awarding body in the UK and have more than 10, 000 members worldwide, whose professional and career development we promote to ensure the highest standards.

*MEMBERSHIP*
Student Member
Affiliate
Associate (AIH)
Member (MIH)
Fellow (FIH)

*DESIGNATORY LETTERS*
AIH, MIH, FIH

# CHEMISTRY

## *Membership of Professional Institutions and Associations*

### SOCIETY OF COSMETIC SCIENTISTS

Suite 5
Langham House West
Mill Street
Luton
Bedfordshire LU1 2NA
Tel: 01582 726661
Fax: 01582 405217
E-mail: gem.bektas@btconnect.com
Website: www.scs.org.uk

---

The main object of the Society, which was formed in 1948, is to advance the science of cosmetics. We endeavour to do this by attracting highly qualified scientists with both academic and industrial experience in cosmetics or a related science to our membership of around 900 members, and by means of our publications, educational programmes and scientific meetings.

*MEMBERSHIP*
Student
Affiliate
Associate Member
Member – B Grade
Member – A Grade
Honorary Member

*QUALIFICATION/EXAMINATIONS*
Certificate of Higher Education in Cosmetic Science

### THE OIL AND COLOUR CHEMISTS' ASSOCIATION

The Oval
14 West Walk
Leicester LE1 7NA
Tel: 0116 257 5488
Fax: 0116 257 5499
E-mail: admin@occa.org.uk
Website: www.occa.org.uk

---

OCCA, founded in 1918, is a learned society comprising individual qualified persons employed in, or associated with, the worldwide surface coatings industries. Most of our members work in a technical capacity, but there are senior personnel from throughout the surface coating industries. The word 'oil' in our title refers to vegetable oils, which once formed a major part of surface coatings' formulations.

*MEMBERSHIP*
Student Member
Ordinary Member
Honorary Member
Licentiate (LTSC)
Associate (ATSC)
Fellow (FTSC)
Chartered Scientist (CSci)

*DESIGNATORY LETTERS*
LTSC, ATSC, FTSC, CSci

## THE ROYAL SOCIETY OF CHEMISTRY

Thomas Graham House
Science Park
Milton Road
Cambridge CB4 0WF
Tel: 01223 420066
Fax: 01223 423623
E-mail: membership@rsc.org
Website: www.rsc.org

The RSC is the UK professional body for chemical scientists and an international learned society for advancing the chemical sciences. With over 46, 000 members worldwide and an internationally acclaimed publishing business, our activities span education and training, conferences, science policy and the promotion of the chemical sciences to the public.

*MEMBERSHIP*
Affiliate
Associate Member (AMRSC)
Member (MRSC)
Fellow (FRSC)

*QUALIFICATION/EXAMINATIONS*
NVQ Analytical Chemistry (Level 5)
Registered Scientist and Registered Science Technician
MSc in Chemical Technology and Management
Mastership in Chemical Analysis (MChemA)
Chartered Chemist (CChem)
Chartered Scientist (CSci)

*DESIGNATORY LETTERS*
AMRSC, MRSC, FRSC, CChem

# CHIROPODY

## *Membership of Professional Institutions and Associations*

## BRITISH CHIROPODY AND PODIATRY ASSOCIATION

The New Hall
149 Bath Road
Maidenhead
Berkshire SL6 4LA
Tel: 01628 632440
Fax: 01628 674483
E-mail: membership@bcha-uk.org
Website: www.bcha-uk.org

The BChA, formed in 1959, is the largest professional organization in the UK representing the interests of independent private chiropodists / podiatrists. Since 2005 we have added foothealth practitioners to include our 7, 000 members, most of whom work mainly in private practice. Those who are registered with the Health Professions Council may work in the NHS or in education.

*MEMBERSHIP*
Member (MSSCh & MBChA) – Podiatrists
Fellow (FSSCh) – Podiatrist
Associate members are foothealth practitioners trained by The SMAE Institute.

*QUALIFICATION/EXAMINATIONS*
Diploma in Podiatric Medicine (DipPodMed)
Foothealth practitioners carry the qualification – MAFHP

*DESIGNATORY LETTERS*
MSSCh, MBChA, FSSCh and MAFHP

## THE INSTITUTE OF CHIROPODISTS AND PODIATRISTS

150 Lord Street
Southport
Merseyside PR9 0TL
Tel: 01704 546141
Fax: 01704 500477
E-mail: secretary@iocp.org.uk
Website: www.iocp.org.uk

---

The IOCP represents all levels of the profession and our CPD is open to both members and non-members, as by elevating professional standards we aim to improve public safety. We have branches throughout the UK and the Republic of Ireland, and members overseas, and hold lectures, seminars and workshops to enable members to keep up to date.

*MEMBERSHIP*
Full Member
Student
Associate

## THE SOCIETY OF CHIROPODISTS AND PODIATRISTS

1 Fellmongers Path
Tower Bridge Road
London SE1 3LY
Tel: 020 7234 8620
E-mail: enq@scpod.org
Website: www.scpod.org

---

The SCP is the professional body and trade union for registered podiatrists. Membership is restricted to those qualified for registration and the Society represents around 10, 000 NHS podiatrists, private practitioners and students. We monitor standards of undergraduate education and provide opportunities for CPD for our members.

*MEMBERSHIP*
Member (MChS)
Associate

*DESIGNATORY LETTERS*
MChS

# CHIROPRACTIC

## *Membership of Professional Institutions and Associations*

## MCTIMONEY CHIROPRACTIC ASSOCIATION

Crowmarsh Gifford
Wallingford
Oxfordshire OX10 8DJ
Tel: 01491 829211
Fax: 01491 829492
E-mail: admin@mctimoney-chiropractic.org
Website: www.mctimoneychiropractic.org

---

The McTimoney Chiropractic Association is the professional association for McTimoney chiropractors, who in the UK are registered with the General Chiropractic Council.

*MEMBERSHIP*
Provisional Member
Full Member
Fellow

*DESIGNATORY LETTERS*
MMCA

## SCOTTISH CHIROPRACTIC ASSOCIATION

1 Chisholm Avenue
Bishopton
Renfrewshire PA7 5JH
Tel: 0141 404 0260
E-mail: admin@sca-chiropractic.org
Website: www.sca-chiropractic.org

---

The SCA was formed in 1979 and now has more than 60 members practising in Scotland and over 120 associated members elsewhere in the UK and abroad. Our aims are to enhance the chiropractic profession in the UK, maintain high standards of professional practice, and provide advice and support to our members.

*MEMBERSHIP*
Member

## UNITED CHIROPRACTIC ASSOCIATION

1st Floor
45 North Hill
Plymouth
Devon PL4 8EZ
Tel: 01752 658785
Fax: 01752 658786
E-mail: admin@united-chiropractic.org
Website: www.united-chiropractic.org

---

The UCA is a UK-based organization for qualified, professional, principal-based chiropractors, associates and students. Full membership is open to qualified, GCC-registered chiropractors from any recognized school of chiropractic.

*MEMBERSHIP*
Student
Associate
Affiliate
1st Year Graduate
2nd Year Graduate
Full Member
Overseas Member

# THE CHURCHES

## Membership of Professional Institutions and Associations

### BAPTIST UNION OF SCOTLAND

48 Speirs Wharf
Glasgow G4 9TH
Tel: 0141 423 6169
Fax: 0141 424 1422
E-mail: admin@scottishbaptist.org.uk
Website: www.scottishbaptist.org.uk

The Baptist Union of Scotland was formed in 1869, when 51 churches with a total congregation of about 3, 500 united. Today, with 168 churches and about 11, 450 members, the Union strives for simplicity in organizational structure and promotes increasing contact between the local churches and the National Team, who function under the overall direction of the General Director.

*QUALIFICATION/EXAMINATIONS*
BD or BA in Theology
Graduate Diploma in Applied Theology through Work Based Learning
Graduate Diploma in Pastoral Studies
(awarded by the Scottish Baptist College, Paisley, and validated by the University of Paisley)

### BRISTOL BAPTIST COLLEGE

The Promenade
Clifton Down
Clifton
Bristol BS8 3NJ
Tel: 0117 946 7050
Fax: 0117 946 7787
E-mail: reception@bristol-baptist.ac.uk
Website: www.bristol-baptist.ac.uk

The central aim of the College is to train men and women for ministry in the Church and in the world. We do this by enabling critical reflection upon the Bible and Christian theological tradition and on the contexts from which we come and within which we are placed.

*QUALIFICATION/EXAMINATIONS*
Certificate in Theological Studies
Diploma in Theological Studies
BA in Theological Studies
MA in Christian Theology
(all validated by the University of Bristol)

## METHODIST CHURCH IN IRELAND

1 Fountainville Avenue
Belfast BT9 6AN
Tel: 028 9032 4554
Fax: 028 9023 9467
E-mail: secretary@irishmethodist.org
Website: www.irishmethodist.org

*MEMBERSHIP*
Candidates for training must normally have the standard of general education for university entrance. They must be accredited Local Preachers of the Methodist Church, and are examined by written papers in Biblical Studies and Theology and by oral aptitude and personality tests. After admission to training, candidates normally spend 3 years at Edgehill Theological College, Belfast, studying for a diploma or degree of Queen's University, Belfast, in New Testament Greek, Hebrew, the English Bible, Theology, Church History, Pastoral Psychology, or Homiletics. This is followed by 3 years as a probationer Minister working under a superintendent Minister. During probation the candidate continues study within a tutorial system and is examined by continuous assessment.

## THE CHURCH OF ENGLAND

Ministry Division of The Archbishops' Council
Church House
Great Smith Street
London SW1P 3AZ
Tel: 020 7898 1000
E-mail: david.way@churchofengland.org (ordination training) susan.hart@churchofengland.org (Reader training)
Website: www.churchofengland.org/clergy-office-holders/ministry.aspx
www.archbishopofcanterbury.org/1027

The Church of England's Ministry Division oversees training for ordination and issues certificates for successful completion for Reader ministry. Enquiries about entry into training should be directed to the candidate's own diocese. In addition, The Archbishop's Examination in Theology offers means of study at three postgraduate levels.

*QUALIFICATION/EXAMINATIONS*
Archbishop's Examination:
PG Diploma of Student of Theology
Master of Philosophy
Doctor of Philosophy

## THE CHURCH OF SCOTLAND

Church of Scotland Offices
121 George Street
Edinburgh EH2 4YN
Tel: 0131 225 5722
Website: www.churchofscotland.org.uk

The Ministries Council runs an enquiry process to help those who sense a call to any of the ministries within the Church of Scotland to consider it in a supportive environment. Attendance at one of our enquirers' conferences, which are held twice each year, is the first stage of the enquiry process. For more information see: www.churchofscotland.org.uk/serve/ministries_in_the_church/training_for_ministries

## THE METHODIST CHURCH

Formation in Ministry Office (Initial Development of Ministries)
25 Marylebone Road
London NW1 5JR
Tel: 020 7486 5502
E-mail: helpdesk@methodistchurch.org.uk
Website: www.methodist.org.uk

Candidates for Diaconal or Presbyteral Ministry in the Methodist Church must have been members of the Methodist Church at least 2 years and are expected to offer at least 10 years of ministerial service. The first stage of preparation is Foundation Training, which requires 1 year (FT) or 2 years (PT) to complete, during which a person may apply to become a candidate for ordained ministry. The process of selection takes 6 months. To enter into training for Presbyteral Ministry, a candidate must be a trained Local Preacher, which involves taking the Methodist Local Preachers' Training Course, Faith & Worship. Deacons become members of the Methodist Diaconal and are not required to be preachers. Accepted candidates for either order receive 1 or 2 years of further theological training, which in most cases leads to a degree or diploma in Theology or Ministry. Upon completion of training, a candidate serves as a Methodist Minister for 2 years on probation before ordination. For Presbyters, the appointment may be to an itinerant appointment (stipendiary) or to a local appointment (usually non-stipendiary) or as licensed to minister in secular employment. Deacons are always itinerant.

## THE MORAVIAN CHURCH IN GREAT BRITAIN AND IRELAND

Moravian Church House
5–7 Muswell Hill
London N10 3TJ
Tel: 020 8883 3409
Fax: 020 8365 3371
E-mail: office@moravian.org.uk
Website: www.moravian.org.uk

Candidates for Moravian Church Service must be members of the Moravian Church and would normally have completed the Lay Training Course and have the support of their local church committee. They should make an initial application to the Provincial Board of the Moravian Church. Their qualifications are examined by the Church Service Advisory Board, which reports on them to the Provincial Board, with whom the final decision rests. Normally the standard of education required for the work of the Ministry is a university Divinity degree or Certificate together with a thorough acquaintance with the history, principles and methods of the Moravian Church. Candidates receive guidance for the Ministry during a period of supervised service under the direction of experienced Ministers. A class of non-stipendiary Ministers has been established for those who wish to serve on a non-maintained basis. Training varies according to candidates' needs. In all cases applications should be made to the address given above.

## THE PRESBYTERIAN CHURCH IN IRELAND

The Director of Ministerial Studies
Union Theological College
108 Botanic Avenue
Belfast BT7 1JT
Tel: 02890 205088
Fax: 02890 205099

Qualifications required: Under 30 – a non-theological degree; over 30 but under 40 (as reckoned on 1 October following application) – either a non-theological degree or 2 years, non-graduating Arts or 4 modules of PT BD study or 6 modules of PT study in Humanities acceptable to the Board of Studies; over 40 – not normally accepted, except in exceptional circumstances, where candidate is already possessed of good educational background and/or professional experience.

## THE PRESBYTERIAN CHURCH OF WALES

Tabernacle Chapel
81 Merthyr Road
Whitchurch
Cardiff CF14 1DD
Tel: 02920 627465
Fax: 02920 616188
E-mail: swyddfa.office@ebcpcw.org.uk
Website: www.ebcpcw.org.uk

The Presbyterian Church of Wales (PCW) is a Protestant non-conformist denomination. Ordination is dependent on successful application through the local church and Presbytery to the Candidates and Training Department.

*MEMBERSHIP*
Ministers are ordained to the full-time, part-time or non-stipendiary ministry.

*QUALIFICATION/EXAMINATIONS*
Pastoral Studies course

## THE ROMAN CATHOLIC CHURCH

Candidates for the priesthood in the RC Church attend a residential seminary course of at least 6 years. Among subjects studied are Philosophy, Psychology, Dogmatic and Moral Theology, Scripture, Church History, Canon Law, Liturgy, Catechetics, Communications and Pastoral Theology. Each college/seminary has its own arrangements for the university education of its students. Those who do not attend university take a final internal exam.

## THE SALVATION ARMY

UK Headquarters
101 Newington Causeway
London SE1 6BN
Tel: 020 7367 4500
E-mail: info@salvationarmy.org.uk
Website: www.salvationarmy.org.uk

Salvation Army officers engaged in FT service are ordained ministers of religion, and are commissioned following a 2-year period of residential training at the William Booth College, Denmark Hill, London SE5 8BQ. This course – an HE Diploma in Salvation Army Officer Training – may now be undertaken by distance learning, or a mixture of residential and distance learning. Officers may be appointed to corps (church) work, to social services centres (for which additional professional qualifications are required) or to administrative posts.

## THE SCOTTISH EPISCOPAL CHURCH

Theological Institute of the Scottish Episcopal Church
Forbes House
21 Grosvenor Crescent
Edinburgh EH12 5EE
Tel: 0131 225 6357
Fax: 0131 346 7247
E-mail: tisec@scotland.anglican.org
Website: www.scotland.anglican.org

Candidates are trained for lay and ordained, stipendiary and non-stipendiary ministries in the Scottish Episcopal Church, Methodist Church and the United Reformed Church.

The curriculum is delivered centrally through residential sessions and regionally through diocesan groups. The Diploma in Theology for Ministry course run by the Institute is validated by York St John's University. Some students undertake further studies through universities, leading to degree qualifications.

## THE SCOTTISH UNITED REFORMED AND CONGREGATIONAL COLLEGE

113 West Regent Street
Glasgow G2 2RU
Tel: 0141 248 5382
E-mail: Scottishcollege@urcscotland.org.uk
Website: www.scotland.urc.org.uk

The College is recognized as a resource centre for learning by the General Assembly of the United Reformed Church and is one of the institutions charged with responsibility for initial ministerial education.

*QUALIFICATION/EXAMINATIONS*

The College awards only its own certificate, which is part of the process of accreditation of ordinands as ministers of the United Reformed Church. Students, however, are normally concurrently matriculated for a degree, normally in Theology or Religious Studies, at a university.

## THE UNITARIAN AND FREE CHRISTIAN CHURCHES

Essex Hall
London WC2R 3HY
Tel: 020 7240 2384
Fax: 020 7240 3089
E-mail: info@unitarian.org.uk
Website: www.unitarian.org.uk

Candidates accepted for training for the ministry in the Unitarian and Free Christian Churches take courses of training either at Manchester Academy & Harris College, Oxford (2 to 4 years' study for an Oxford degree in Theology/or Theology & Philosophy or an Oxford Certificate in Theology/Religious Studies), or at the Unitarian College (Luther King House, Brighton Grove, Rusholme, Manchester; an individually designed contextual theology course of the Partnership for Theological Education which may lead to a degree or other academic qualification validated by Chester or Manchester University). Alternative arrangements can be made for candidates wishing to study through the Welsh language. Placement work and Unitarian studies are also integral to ministerial preparation. Training normally takes 2 or more years.

## THE UNITED REFORMED CHURCH

Church House
86 Tavistock Place
London WC1H 9RT
Tel: 020 7916 2020
Fax: 020 7916 2021
E-mail: urc@urc.org.uk
Website: www.urc.org.uk

Candidates for the Ministry of Word and Sacraments must have been a member of the URC for at least 2 years, and go through a candidating process to decide whether they should be sponsored for training. Most then take a 3- or 4-year course of academic study alongside a minimum of 800 hours of pastoral placements, through 1 of 3 Resource Centres for Learning. The minimum required outcome is a Diploma for Higher Education, in Theology. Candidates for stipendiary service normally train full-time; candidates for non-stipendiary service normally train part-time. **Church-related Community Workers** help to lead and strengthen the local church's mission through community development in an area where specialist help is required to meet unusual needs. Candidates must be members of the URC and show capabilities for leadership. They are required to obtain at least a Diploma in Theology and a Diploma in Community Work before being commissioned.

**Lay Preacher's Certificate:** Training for Learning & Serving is the qualifying course for this. The course takes 3 years. Work is done in local groups and there are 3 residential weekend courses each year. Candidates are also expected to undertake some practical work in churches.

## THE WESLEYAN REFORM UNION

Wesleyan Reform Church House
123 Queen Street
Sheffield S1 2DU
Tel: 0114 272 1938
E-mail: gen.sec@thewru.co.uk
Website: www.thewru.com

The Wesleyan Reform Union has no training college of its own and encourages candidates for its Ministry to enter a Bible College for 2 or 3 years. All candidates are, however, under the personal supervision of a Union Tutor, who directs a Biblical Studies & Training Department offering fairly extensive courses. Candidates attend Headquarters once a year for an oral exam in Theology conducted by the Tutor in the presence of the Union Examination Committee; they also take written exams.

## UNITED FREE CHURCH OF SCOTLAND

11 Newton Place
Glasgow G3 7PR
Tel: 01413 323435
Fax: 01413 331973
E-mail: office@ufcos.org.uk
Website: www.ufcos.org.uk

The United Free Church of Scotland is a small presbyterian denomination which came into being in 1929. Those seeking to become candidates for the ministry should normally have been members of the denomination for at least a year. They will require to undertake a degree course in theology.

## THE CHURCH IN WALES

St Michael's College
Llandaff
Cardiff CF5 2YJ
Tel: 029 205 63379
Fax: 029 208 38008
Website: www.stmichaels.ac.uk

The Church in Wales expects candidates for ordination to satisfy the requirements of recognized theological courses. University graduates usually spend at least 2 years at a theological college, and if they are non-theological graduates, they are encouraged to study for a university degree or diploma in Theology. Non-graduate candidates must have at least 5 passes at GCSE and normally study for a university diploma in Theology or a degree in Theology if they have obtained the necessary grades at A level. These requirements may be modified in the case of older candidates.

# CINEMA, FILM AND TELEVISION

## *Membership of Professional Institutions and Associations*

### BRITISH KINEMATOGRAPH SOUND AND TELEVISION SOCIETY (BKSTS)

Pinewood Studios
Pinewood Road
Iver Heath
Buckinghamshire SL0 0NH
Tel: 01753 656656
E-mail: info@bksts.com
Website: www.bksts.com

The BKSTS was founded in 1931 to serve the growing film industry and today arranges meetings, presentations, seminars, international exhibitions and conferences, as well as organizing an extensive programme of training courses, lectures, workshops and special events. We ensure that our members remain up to date with the latest techniques through master classes and our print and electronic publications.

*MEMBERSHIP*
Student Member
Intermediate Member
Associate Member
Full Member (MBKS)
Retired Member
Fellow (FBKS)

*DESIGNATORY LETTERS*
MBKS, FBKS

### THE LONDON FILM SCHOOL

24 Shelton Street
Covent Garden
London WC2H 9UB
Tel: 020 7836 9642
Fax: 020 7497 3718
E-mail: info@lfs.org.uk
Website: www.lfs.org.uk

The LFS is one of the foremost independent film schools in Europe and is recognized by Skillset as a Centre of Excellence. It is a registered charity and a non-profit-making company, limited by guarantee. Since 1956 we have trained thousands of directors, cinematographers, editors and other film professionals from around the world.

*QUALIFICATION/EXAMINATIONS*
MA in Filmmaking (validated by London Metropolitan University)
MA in Screenwriting (validated by London Metropolitan University)
MA International Film Business
PhD Film by Practice

### THE NATIONAL FILM AND TELEVISION SCHOOL

Beaconsfield Studios
Station Road
Beaconsfield
Buckinghamshire HP9 1LG
Tel: 01494 671234
Fax: 01494 674042
E-mail: info@nfts.co.uk
Website: www.nfts.co.uk

A Skillset Screen & Media Academy, the UK's leading film and television school offers full-time MA and Diploma courses in all the key film and television disciplines, from Animation to VFX. Purpose-built studios include two film stages, a large television studio, and post-production facilities rivalling those of many professional companies.

*QUALIFICATION/EXAMINATIONS*
Diploma (in 1 of 3 disciplines)
MA in Film and Television (specializing in 1 of 13 disciplines)

# CLEANING, LAUNDRY AND DRY CLEANING

## *Membership of Professional Institutions and Associations*

### BRITISH INSTITUTE OF CLEANING SCIENCE

9 Premier Court
Boarden Close
Moulton Park
Northampton NN3 6LF
Tel: 01604 678710
Fax: 01604 645988
E-mail: info@bics.org.uk
Website: www.bics.org.uk

The BICSc is the largest independent professional and educational body within the cleaning industry. Our aim is to raise the status and standards of the cleaning industry through training and education. We offer our 5, 000 members a range of assessment schemes and training courses, together with a telephone and e-mail helpline.

*MEMBERSHIP*
Student
Competent
Technical
Member with Diploma
Fellow

*QUALIFICATION/EXAMINATIONS*
Cleaning Professional Skills Suite (CPSS)
Qualifications and Credit Framework

## THE GUILD OF CLEANERS AND LAUNDERERS

56 Maple Drive
Larkhall
South Lanarkshire ML9 2AR
Tel: 01698 322669
E-mail: enquiries@gcl.org.uk
Website: www.gcl.org.uk

The Guild, formed in 1949, is a technical and professional society whose aim is to further knowledge and skill in all branches of the industry. We keep our members up to date through lectures, seminars and written reports, exchange information of mutual benefit with other organizations in the industry, and voice our opinion in relevant forums.

*MEMBERSHIP*
Young Guilder
Member
Associate (AGCL)
Advanced Member (AdGCL)
Licentiate (LGCL)
Fellow (FGCL)
Guild Plus Member

*DESIGNATORY LETTERS*
AGCL, AdGCL, LGCL, FGCL

# COLOUR TECHNOLOGY

## *Membership of Professional Institutions and Associations*

## PAINTING AND DECORATING ASSOCIATION

32 Coton Road
Nuneaton
Warwickshire CV11 5TW
Tel: 024 7635 3776
Fax: 024 7635 4513
E-mail: info@paintingdecoratingassociation.co.uk
Website: www.paintingdecoratingassociation.co.uk

The PDA is a registered trade and employers' organization, catering exclusively for the needs of professional painting and decorating trade employers. The Association conducts no examinations, but all membership applications are scrutinized at branch level to ensure that only bona fide firms that agree to abide by our code of conduct are admitted.

*MEMBERSHIP*
Full Member
Associate

## THE SOCIETY OF DYERS AND COLOURISTS

Perkin House
82 Grattan Road
Bradford BD1 2LU
Tel: 01274 725138
Fax: 01274 392888
E-mail: members@sdc.org.uk
Website: www.sdc.org.uk

An educational charity, professional body and chartered society, serving globally all aspects of the coloration industries including the textile supply chain through the knowledgeable and enthusiastic involvement of its professional members and industry partners.

Recognized as the authority for colour science and technology, delivering high-quality international qualifications and training programmes.

*MEMBERSHIP*
Individual Voting Member
Individual Non-voting Member
Individual Student Member
Educational Institute Member
Corporate (Company) Member

*QUALIFICATION/EXAMINATIONS*
Diploma of Fellowship (FSDC)
Diploma of Associateship (ASDC)
Diploma of Licentiateship (LSDC)
Chartered Colourist (CCol

*DESIGNATORY LETTERS*
FSDC, ASDC, LSDC, CCol.

# COMMUNICATIONS AND MEDIA

***Membership of Professional Institutions and Associations***

## THE PICTURE RESEARCH ASSOCIATION

c/o 10 Marrick House
Mortimer Crescent
London NW6 5NY
Tel: 0771403017
E-mail: chair@picture-research.org.uk
Website: www.picture-research.org.uk

The PRA, founded in 1977, is a professional organization for picture researchers, picture editors and anyone specifically involved in the research, management and supply of visual material to the media industry. Our aims are to provide information and give support to our members, and to promote their interests and specific skills to potential employers.

*MEMBERSHIP*
Introductory Member
Full Member
Sponsors

*QUALIFICATION/EXAMINATIONS*
To qualify as a member of the Association your need a minimum of 2 years experience as a qualified picture researcher/picture editor, eg you were involved in the online search of images, working to a specific brief or project. You would have supplied both digital or analogue files for reproduction. You would also be required to have knowledge and experience of fee negotiations, clearances, copyright and licensing of photographic images from a selection of photographic sources and collections.
Sponsors: A full or part time employee of a picture library, picture agency or image archive who are directly involved in the supply of images to the media in general.

# COMPUTING AND INFORMATION TECHNOLOGY

## *Membership of Professional Institutions and Associations*

### ASSOCIATION OF COMPUTER PROFESSIONALS

ACP
Chilverbridge House
Arlington
East Sussex BN26 6SB
Tel: 01323 871874
Fax: 01323 871875
E-mail: admin@acpexamboard.com
Website: www.acpexamboard.com

---

The ACP is an independent professional examining body, founded in 1984 to set and maintain standards of education that reflect the constantly changing requirements of the computer industry, both in the UK and overseas. We do so through the provision of course syllabuses and examinations to our carefully vetted training centres around the world.

*MEMBERSHIP*
Student
Practitioner
Graduate (GradACP)
Licentiate (LACP)
Associate (AACP)
Member (MACP)
Fellow (FACP)

*QUALIFICATION/EXAMINATIONS*
Please see the ACP's website for details of certificates and diplomas.

*DESIGNATORY LETTERS*
GradACP, LACP, AACP, MACP, FACP

### BRITISH COMPUTER SOCIETY

1st Floor, Block D
North Star House
North Star Avenue
Swindon
Wiltshire SN2 1FA
Tel: 01793 417417
Fax: 01793 417444
E-mail: customerservices@hq.bcs.org.uk
Website: www.bcs.org.uk

---

The BCS is the professional membership and accreditation body for IT and has more than 70, 000 members, including practitioners, businesses, academics and students, in the UK and internationally. Our aim is to promote the academic study and professional practice of computing and to show the public that IT is about far more than simply using a PC.

*MEMBERSHIP*
Student
Affiliate
Associate Member (AMBCS)
Professional Fellow (FBCS)
Honorary Fellow
Distinguished Fellow
Incorporated Engineer (IEng)
Chartered Engineer (CEng)
Chartered IT Professional (MBCS CITP)
Chartered Fellow (FBCS CITP)
Chartered Scientist (CSci)
Education Affiliate (institutional member)

*QUALIFICATION/EXAMINATIONS*
Certificate in IT
Certificate in IT for Insurance Professionals (developed jointly with The Chartered Insurance Institute)
Diploma in IT
Professional GradDip in IT

See the BCS website for details of other qualifications.

## INSTITUTE FOR THE MANAGEMENT OF INFORMATION SYSTEMS

Suite A (Part) 2nd Floor
3 White Oak Square
London Road
Swanley
Kent BR8 7AG
Tel: 0845 850 0006
Fax: 0845 850 0007
E-mail: imis@bcs.org
Website: www.imis.org.uk

IMIS is one of the leading professional associations in the IT sector. A registered charity, it plays a prominent role in fostering greater understanding of IS management, in working to enhance the status of those engaged in the profession, and in promoting higher standards through better education and training worldwide.

*MEMBERSHIP*
Student Member
Practitioner Member
Licentiate Member (LIMIS)
Associate Member (AIMIS)
Full Member (MIMIS)
Fellow (FIMIS)

*QUALIFICATION/EXAMINATIONS*
Foundation
Diploma
Higher Diploma

*DESIGNATORY LETTERS*
LIMIS, AIMIS, MIMIS, FIMIS

## INSTITUTION OF ANALYSTS AND PROGRAMMERS

Boundary House
Boston Road
London W7 2QE
Tel: 020 8434 3685
E-mail: admin@iap.org.uk
Website: www.iap.org.uk

The IAP is a professional organization for people who work in the development, installation and testing of business systems and computer software. Our aim is to promote high standards of competence and conduct among our members, to encourage them to develop their skills and progress their career, and to facilitate the advancement and spreading of knowledge within the profession.

*MEMBERSHIP*
Licentiate
Graduate (GradIAP)
Associate Member (AIAP)
Member (MIAP)
Fellow (FIAP)

*DESIGNATORY LETTERS*
GradIAP, AIAP, MIAP, FIAP

# COUNSELLING

## *Membership of Professional Institutions and Associations*

### COUNSELLING LTD

Registered Office
5 Pear Tree Walk
Wakefield
West Yorkshire WF2 0HW
E-mail: E-mail via the website
Website: www.counselling.ltd.uk

Counselling, a registered charity founded in 1998, is a membership organization for counsellors and psychotherapists in the UK that has established a network of about 2, 700 affiliated CCC-registered counsellors, many of whom are able to provide occasional free or discounted face-to-face counselling with clients on low incomes.

*MEMBERSHIP*
Affiliate

### COUNSELLORS AND PSYCHOTHERAPISTS IN PRIMARY CARE

PO Box 3379
Littlehampton BN16 9HL
Tel: 01243 870701
E-mail: cpc@cpc-online.co.uk
Website: www.cpc-online.co.uk

CPC is a professional membership association for individual practitioners, whose names are entered in a Register of Members. The aims of the Association are to represent counsellors and psychotherapists working in an NHS setting and to lead the way in establishing national standards and guidelines for further development of professional and effective counselling throughout the NHS.

*MEMBERSHIP*
Student
Subscriber
Intermediate Member
Registered Member
Supervisor
Organizational Member

*QUALIFICATION/EXAMINATIONS*
PGDip in Supervision for the Primary Care Setting

### CSCT COUNSELLING TRAINING

13 Coleshill Street
Sutton Coldfield
West Midlands B72 1SD
Tel: 0121 321 1396
Fax: 0121 355 5581
E-mail: info@counsellingtraining.com
Website: www.counsellingtraining.com

CSCT has been producing counselling training courses for over 25 years, during which time we have trained over 50, 000 students. Our courses are offered PT via a network of colleges and private providers throughout the UK. Our training materials are written to the specifications of the appropriate awarding body and we provide 24-hour e-mail and telephone support from Client Services and the Academic Team.

*QUALIFICATION/EXAMINATIONS*
Please see the CSCT's website.

# CREDIT MANAGEMENT

## *Membership of Professional Institutions and Associations*

### INSTITUTE OF CREDIT MANAGEMENT

The Water Mill
Station Road
South Luffenham
Oakham
Leicestershire LE15 8NB
Tel: 01780 722900
Fax: 01780 721333
E-mail: info@icm.org.uk
Website: www.icm.org.uk

The ICM is the largest professional credit management organization in Europe and the only one accredited by Ofqual as an awarding body. We represent the credit profession across trade, consumer and export credit, as well as in related activities such as collections, credit reporting, credit insurance and insolvency, promote excellence in credit management and raise awareness of its vital role in business and the community.

*MEMBERSHIP*
Affiliate
Associate Member (AICM)
Graduate Member (MICM(Grad))
Member (MICM)
Fellow (FICM)
Corporate Member

*QUALIFICATION/EXAMINATIONS*
Certificate in Credit Management
Diploma in Credit Management
Level 5 Diploma in Credit Management
Certificate in Debt Collection
Diploma in Debt Collection
Certificate in Money and Debt Advice
Diploma in Money and Debt Advice
Certificate in High Court Enforcement (Level 4)
Diploma in High Court Enforcement (Level 4)
Diploma in High Court Enforcement (Level 5)

*DESIGNATORY LETTERS*
AICM, MICM (Grad), MICM, FIFA

# DANCING

## Membership of Professional Institutions and Associations

### BRITISH BALLET ORGANIZATION

Woolborough House
39 Lonsdale Road
Barnes
London SW13 9JP
Tel: 020 8748 1241
Fax: 020 8748 1301
E-mail: info@bbo.org.uk
Website: www.bbo.org.uk

The BBO, founded in 1930, is an awarding body offering teacher training and examinations in classical ballet, tap, modern dance and jazz. We have schools throughout the UK and in several other countries.

*MEMBERSHIP*
Student Member
Senior Student Member
Affiliated Member
Student Teacher Member
Teacher Member

*QUALIFICATION/EXAMINATIONS*
Please see the BBO website for details.

### IMPERIAL SOCIETY OF TEACHERS OF DANCING

Imperial House
22/26 Paul Street
London EC2A 4QE
Tel: +44 (0)20 7377 1577
Fax: +44 (0)20 7247 8829
E-mail: via website
Website: www.istd.org

The ISTD is a registered educational charity and examinations board. We aim to promote knowledge of dance, to maintain and improve teaching standards, and to qualify (by examination) teachers of dancing. Our dance techniques cover more than 12 different genres and are taught by more than 7, 500 members by our members worldwide.

*MEMBERSHIP*
A range of 9 categories from Student to Life Membership.

*QUALIFICATION/EXAMINATIONS*
Please see our website www.istd.org or www.dance-teachers.org

*DESIGNATORY LETTERS*
ISTD

### INTERNATIONAL DANCE TEACHERS' ASSOCIATION LIMITED

International House
76 Bennett Road
Brighton BN2 5JL
Tel: 01273 685652
Fax: 01273 674388
E-mail: via website
Website: www.idta.co.uk

The IDTA is one of the world's largest dance examination boards, with more than 7, 000 members in 55 countries. Our aims are to promote knowledge and foster the art of dance in all its forms, to maintain and improve dancing standards, and to offer a comprehensive range of professional qualifications in all dance genres.

*MEMBERSHIP*
Associate (AIDTA)
Licentiate (LIDTA)
Fellow (FIDTA)

*DESIGNATORY LETTERS*
AIDTA, LIDTA, FIDTA

### THE BENESH INSTITUTE

36 Battersea Square
London SW11 3RA
Tel: 020 7326 8031
Fax: 020 7924 3129
E-mail: beneshinstitute@rad.org.uk
Website: www.benesh.org

The Benesh Institute is the international centre for Benesh Movement Notation (BMN) founded in 1962 to promote, develop and offer education in BMN. We also function as an examining body and professional centre, and are responsible for coordinating technical developments. Since 1997 The Benesh Institute has been incorporated within the Royal Academy of Dance.

*QUALIFICATION/EXAMINATIONS*
Certificate in Benesh Movement Notation (CBMN) (validated by the Royal Academy of Dance)
Diploma for Professional Benesh Movement Notators (DPBMN) (validated by the Royal Academy of Dance)
Associate of the Institute of Choreology (AI Chor)

# DENTISTRY

## *Membership of Professional Institutions and Associations*

### GENERAL DENTAL COUNCIL

37 Wimpole Street
London W1G 8DQ
Tel: 0845 222 4141
E-mail: information@gdc-uk.org
Website: www.gdc-uk.org

The GDC regulates dental professionals in the UK. All dentists, clinical dental technicians, dental hygienists, dental nurses, dental technicians, dental therapists and orthodontic therapists must be registered with the GDC in order to work in the UK.

## THE BRITISH DENTAL ASSOCIATION

64 Wimpole Street
London W1G 8YS
Tel: 020 7935 0875
Fax: 020 7487 5232
E-mail: enquiries@bda.org
Website: www.bda.org

The BDA, which was founded in 1880, is the professional association and trade union for dentists in the UK. Our aims are to advance the science, arts and ethics of dentistry, improve the UK's oral health, and promote the interests of our members. Membership, which is voluntary, stands at around 23, 000, mostly in general practice.

*MEMBERSHIP*
Essential
Extra
Expert

## BRITISH SOCIETY OF DENTAL HYGIENE AND THERAPY

3 Kestrel Court
Waterwells Business Park
Gloucester GL2 2AT
Tel: 01452 886365
Fax: 01452 886468
E-mail: enquiries@bsdht.org.uk
Website: www.bsdht.org.uk

The BSDHT is the only nationally recognized body that represents dental hygienists, dental hygienist-therapists and students of dental hygiene. We have a membership of more than 3, 500 in the UK and beyond, and look after their interests through liaising with the Department of Health, General Dental Council, British Dental Association and other organizations.

*MEMBERSHIP*
Member

## BRITISH ASSOCIATION OF DENTAL NURSES

PO Box 4, Room 200
Hillhouse International Business Centre
Thornton-Cleveleys
Lancashire FY5 4QD
Tel: 01253 338360
E-mail: admin@badn.org.uk
Website: www.badn.org.uk

The BADN represents dental nurses, whether qualified or unqualified, working in general practice, hospital, the community, the armed forces, industry, practice management or reception, and has representation on the National Examining Board, the Dental Nurses Standards and Training Advisory Board and its Registration Committee, the Joint Consultative Committee, and other bodies.

*MEMBERSHIP*
Associate Member
Full Member

## BRITISH ASSOCIATION OF CLINICAL DENTAL TECHNOLOGY

44-46 Wollaton Road
Beeston
Nottingham N69 2NR
Tel: 0115 957 5370
Fax: 0115 925 4800
E-mail: info@bacdt.org.uk
Website: www.bacdt.org.uk

The CDTA provides political and educational representation for its members, who are registered with the General Dental Council and trained in designing, creating, constructing, repairing and rebasing removable appliances to ensure optimal fit, maximum comfort and general wellbeing of patients. We are committed to team dentistry and ensure that our members work to the highest professional standards.

*MEMBERSHIP*
Full Membership
In training Membership
Practice Membership
Multi Practice Membership

## DENTAL TECHNOLOGISTS ASSOCIATION

3 Kestral Court
Waterwells Drive
Waterwells Business Park
Gloucester GL2 2AT
Tel: 01452 886366
E-mail: via website
Website: www.dta-uk.org/

The DTA is an organization that supports the development of the dental technology profession by encouraging and promoting education, including CPD, and for the exchange of views between dental technicians. We advise, develop and support dental technicians and maintain links with the government, other dental organizations, service providers and the public.

*MEMBERSHIP*
Member

# DIETETICS

## *Membership of Professional Institutions and Associations*

### THE BRITISH DIETETIC ASSOCIATION

5th Floor
Charles House
148–49 Great Charles Street Queensway
Birmingham B3 3HT
Tel: 0121 200 8080
Fax: 0121 200 8081
E-mail: info@bda.uk.com
Website: www.bda.uk.com

The BDA, established in 1936, is the UK's leading professional association and trade union for dietitians. Our aims are to advance the science and practice of dietetics and associated subjects, to promote education and training in the science and practice of dietetics and associated subjects, and to regulate relations between our 6, 700+ members and their employers.

*MEMBERSHIP*
Full Member
Associate Member
Affiliate Member
Alliance Member
Student Member
International Member

# DISTRIBUTION

## *Membership of Professional Institutions and Associations*

### THE CHARTERED INSTITUTE OF LOGISTICS AND TRANSPORT (UK)

Earlstrees Court
Earlstrees Road
Corby
Northamptonshire NN17 4AX
Tel: 01536 740104
Fax: 01536 740103
E-mail: membership@ciltuk.org.uk
Website: www.ciltuk.org.uk

The Chartered Institute of Logistics and Transport in the UK – CILT(UK) – is the independent professional body for transport, logistics, supply chain management and has more than 18, 000 members in the industry. Our aim is to facilitate the development of personal and professional excellence.

*MEMBERSHIP*
Learner Affiliate
Student Affiliate
Affiliate
Member (MILT)
Chartered Member (CMILT)
Chartered Fellow (FCILT)
Corporate Member

*QUALIFICATION/EXAMINATIONS*
Regulated Qualifications (cover eight professional sectors in Supply Chain, Transport Planning, Rail, Active Travel and Travel Planning, Bus & Coach, Ports Maritime and Waterways, Freight Forwarding and Aviation)
Award (Level 1)
Award (Level 2)
Award (Level 3)
Certificate (Level 2)

Certificate (Level 3)
Diploma (Level 2)
Professional Diploma (Level 5)
Advanced Diploma (Level 6)

Accredited Qualifications
Humanitarian Logistics (3 programmes)
Supply Chain Practitioner Award (Foundation, Professional and Master programmes)

Partnerships
Certified European Logistician (Junior, Senior, Master programmes)
MSc in International Transport and Logistics or International Logistics and Supply Chain Management

*DESIGNATORY LETTERS*
MILT, CMILT, FCILT

# DIVING

## *Membership of Professional Institutions and Associations*

### DIVING CERTIFICATES

Health & Safety Executive, Diving Operations Strategy Team
Redwing House, Hedgerows Business Park
Colchester Road, Springfield
Chelmsford
Essex CM2 5PB
Tel: 01245 706256
Fax: 01245 706222
E-mail: advice@hse.gsi.gov.uk
Website: www.hse.gov.uk/diving

The Health and Safety Executive (HSE) issues diver competence certificates to divers who have been assessed as competent by an HSE-recognized diver-training organization (a list of which can be obtained from the HSE) for the following competencies: SCUBA, Surface Supplied, Surface Supplied (top-up) and Closed Bell.

# DRAMATIC AND PERFORMING ARTS

## *Membership of Professional Institutions and Associations*

### DRAMA UK

Woburn House
20 Tavistock Square
London WC1H 9HB
Tel: 020 3393 6141
E-mail: info@dramauk.co.uk
Website: www.dramauk.co.uk

Drama UK was formed in 2012 following the merger of the National Council for Drama Training and the Conference of Drama Schools.

We act as an advocate for quality drama training; offer advice to students of all ages; and award a quality mark to the very best drama training available.

## EQUITY

Guild House
Upper St Martins Lane
London WC2H 9EG
Tel: 020 7379 6000
E-mail: info@equity.org.uk
Website: www.equity.org.uk

Equity is the UK trade union representing professional performers and other creative workers from across the entertainment, creative and cultural industries. The main function of Equity is to negotiate minimum terms and conditions of employment for its members and to represent its members' interests to the government and other bodies.

*MEMBERSHIP*
Student Member
Graduate Member
Full Member

## THE BRITISH (THEATRICAL) ARTS

12 Deveron Way
Rise Park
Romford
Essex RM1 4UL
Tel: 01708 756263
E-mail: sally.chennelle1@ntlworld.com
Website: www.britisharts.org

The British Arts is a non-profit-making organization dedicated to maintaining and where necessary raising the standard of the teaching of Performing Arts subjects. We work to encourage a strong technical foundation combined with an understanding of professional theatrical presentation and conduct exams in Dramatic Art, Classical & Stage Ballet, Mime, Tap, Musical Theatre and Modern Dance.

*MEMBERSHIP*
Student Member
Companion
Associate (Teaching and Non-teaching)
Member (Teaching and Non-teaching)
Advanced Teacher Member
Fellow

*QUALIFICATION/EXAMINATIONS*
Please see the British Arts website.

# DRIVING INSTRUCTORS

## Membership of Professional Institutions and Associations

### REGISTER OF APPROVED DRIVING INSTRUCTORS

The Axis Building
112 Upper Parliament Street
Nottingham NG1 6LP
Tel: 0300 200 1122
E-mail: ADIReg@dsa.gsi.gov.uk

The Register of Approved Driving Instructors (ADI) and the licensing scheme for trainee instructors (PDI) are administered under the provisions of the Road Traffic Act 1988 by the Department for Transport (DfT). It is an offence for anyone to give professional instruction (that is instruction paid for by or in respect of the pupil) in driving a motor car unless: (a) his or her name is on the Register of Approved Driving Instructors; or (b) he or she holds a 'trainee's licence to give instruction' issued by the Registrar.

QUALIFICATION/EXAMINATIONS

Please see the Business Link website (www.businesslink.gov.uk) for details of the qualifying examinations.

# EMBALMING

## Membership of Professional Institutions and Associations

### INTERNATIONAL EXAMINATIONS BOARD OF EMBALMERS

146 Alexandra Road
Great Wakering
Essex SS3 0GW
Tel: 01702 218907
E-mail: admin@iebe.co.uk

The Board examines candidates who wish to become qualified members of the British Institute of Embalmers (qv), which is not itself an examining body but can provide information packs (also available from the above address) that contain lists of approved schools and accredited tutors.

### THE BRITISH INSTITUTE OF EMBALMERS

Anubis House
21c Station Road
Knowle
Solihull
West Midlands B93 0HL
Tel: 01564 778991
Fax: 01564 770812
E-mail: enquiry@bioe.co.uk
Website: www.bioe.co.uk

The BIE, founded in 1927, is an organization for professional embalmers. Its objectives include supporting and protecting the status, character and interests of embalmers, promoting the efficient tuition of persons seeking to become embalmers, and encouraging the study and practice of improved methods of embalming.

*MEMBERSHIP*
Member (MBIE)
Fellow (FBIE)

*DESIGNATORY LETTERS*
MBIE, FBIE

# EMPLOYMENT AND CAREERS SERVICES

## *Membership of Professional Institutions and Associations*

### RECRUITMENT AND EMPLOYMENT CONFEDERATION

Dorset House
First Floor
27-45 Stamford Street
London SE1 9NT
Tel: 020 7009 2100
E-mail: info@rec.uk.com
Website: www.rec.uk.com

The REC is the representative body for the UK's £27 billion private recruitment and staffing industry, with a membership of more than 8, 000 Corporate Members comprising agencies and businesses from all sectors, and 6, 000 members of the Institute of Recruitment Professionals (IRP) made up of recruitment consultants and other industry professionals.

*MEMBERSHIP*
Affiliate (AIRP)
Member (MIRP)
Fellow (FIRP)

*QUALIFICATION/EXAMINATIONS*
Certificate in Recruitment Practice (QCF)
Diploma in Recruitment Practice (QCF)
Diploma in Recruitment Management (QCF)

*DESIGNATORY LETTERS*
AIRP, MIRP, FIRP

### THE INSTITUTE OF CAREER GUIDANCE

Ground Floor
Copthall House
1 New Road
Stourbridge
West Midlands DY8 1PH
Tel: 01384 376464
Fax: 01384 440830
E-mail: hq@icg-uk.org
Website: www.icg-uk.org

The ICG is the largest UK-wide professional association for career guidance practitioners. Our aim is to promote access to high-quality career guidance and development services, delivered by professionally qualified staff working within an appropriate ethical framework, and to underpin this our members adhere to a strict code of ethics.

*MEMBERSHIP*
Student Member
Full Member

Affiliate Member

*QUALIFICATION/EXAMINATIONS*
Qualification in Career Guidance (QCG)
Certificate in Professional Practice (CPP)
Certificate in Career Guidance Theory (CCGT)

# ENGINEERING, AERONAUTICAL

## *Membership of Professional Institutions and Associations*

### ROYAL AERONAUTICAL SOCIETY

4 Hamilton Place
Hyde Park Corner
London W1J 7BQ
Tel: 020 7670 4300
Fax: 020 7670 4309
E-mail: raes@aerosociety.com
Website: www.aerosociety.com

The RAeS, founded in 1866 to further the science of aeronautics, is a multidisciplinary professional institution dedicated to the global aerospace community. We work on our members' behalf to promote the highest professional standards in all aerospace disciplines, to provide specialist information and act as a central forum for the exchange of ideas, and to play a leading role in influencing opinion on aviation matters.

*MEMBERSHIP*
Student Affiliate
Affiliate
Associate (ARAeS)
Associate Member (AMRAeS)
Member (MRAeS)
Companion (CRAeS)
Fellow (FRAeS)
Apprentice

# ENGINEERING, AGRICULTURAL

## *Membership of Professional Institutions and Associations*

### BRITISH AGRICULTURAL AND GARDEN MACHINERY ASSOCIATION

Middleton House
2 Main Road
Middleton Cheney
Oxfordshire OX17 2TN
Tel: 01295 713344
Fax: 01295 711665
E-mail: info@bagma.com
Website: www.bagma.com

BAGMA is the trade association representing agricultural and garden machinery dealers in the UK. We have some 850 dealer members and 75 affiliated suppliers and allied industry companies. We offer a range of training and assessment courses through our online learning package and at approved Training and Assessment Centres.

*QUALIFICATION/EXAMINATIONS*
Please see the BAGMA website.

## THE INSTITUTION OF AGRICULTURAL ENGINEERS

The Bullock Building
University Way
Cranfield
Bedford
Bedfordshire MK43 0GH
Tel: 01234 750876
Fax: 01234 751319
E-mail: secretary@iagre.org
Website: www.iagre.org

The IAgrE is the professional body for engineers, scientists, technologists and managers in agricultural and allied land-based industries, including forestry, food engineering and technology, amenity, renewable energy, horticulture and the environment. The IAgrE also administers the Landbased Engineering Technician Accreditation schemes (LTA) for the industry.

*MEMBERSHIP*
Student
Associate (AIAgrE)
Associate Member (AMIAgrE)
Member (MIAgrE)
Fellow (FIAgrE)
Honorary Fellow

*QUALIFICATION/EXAMINATIONS*
Chartered Engineer (CEng), Chartered Environmentalist (CEnv), Incorporated Engineer (IEng), Engineering Technician (EngTech)

*DESIGNATORY LETTERS*
AIAgrE, AMIAgrE, MIAgrE, FIAgrE

# ENGINEERING, AUTOMOBILE

***Membership of Professional Institutions and Associations***

## INSTITUTE OF AUTOMOTIVE ENGINEER ASSESSORS

The Firs
High Street
Whitchurch
Buckinghamshire HP22 4JU
Tel: 01296 642895
Fax: 01296 640044
E-mail: sally@theiaea.org
Website: www.iaea-online.org

The IAEA, a Professional Affiliate of the Engineering Council, was founded in 1932 and now represents more than 1, 500 automotive engineer assessors responsible for activities such as vehicle damage assessment, accident reconstruction, investigation of mechanical failures, electrical failures and vehicle fires, providing expert witness testimony, repair assessment, car fleet surveys, and conciliation and arbitration.

*MEMBERSHIP*
Student
Associate
Member (MInstAEA)
Fellow (FInstAEA)
Honorary Fellow (HFInstAEA)

*QUALIFICATION/EXAMINATIONS*
Basic Principles of Maths & Physics Application to Accident Reconstruction
Motor Vehicle Legislation as related to Insurance Principles
Principles and Practice of Vehicle Damage Assessment
Motor Insurance

*DESIGNATORY LETTERS*
IMInstAEA, MInstAEA, FInstAEA

## THE INSTITUTE OF THE MOTOR INDUSTRY

Fanshaws
Brickendon
Hertford SG13 8PQ
Tel: 01992 511521
Fax: 01992 511548
E-mail: comms@theimi.org.uk
Website: www.motor.org.uk and www.automotivetechnician.org.uk

The IMI is the professional association for individuals working in the motor industry and exists to help individuals and employers improve professional standards and performance by qualifying, recognizing and developing people. We are the Sector Skills Council for the automotive retail industry, a Licensed Member of the Engineering Council and the governing body for Automotive Technician Accreditation (ATA) – the UK's first national voluntary assessment system for vehicle technicians.

*MEMBERSHIP*

Affiliate (AffIMI)
Licentiate (LIMI)
Associate (AMIMI)
Member (MIMI)
Fellow (FIMI)

For technicians only, there are two special IMI awards recognizing technical qualifications and experience:

AAE (Advanced Automotive Engineer)
CAE (Certificated Automotive Engineer)

*DESIGNATORY LETTERS*

AffIMI, LIMI, AMIMI, MIMI, FIMI, AAE, CAE

# ENGINEERING, BUILDING SERVICES

## *Membership of Professional Institutions and Associations*

## THE CHARTERED INSTITUTION OF BUILDING SERVICES ENGINEERS

222 Balham High Road
London SW12 9BS
Tel: 020 8675 5211
Fax: 020 8675 5449
Website: www.cibse.org

CIBSE is the professional body for people involved in the design, construction, operation and maintenance of the engineering elements of a building other than its structure and enables it to operate efficiently by saving energy and contributing to a low carbon built environment. This includes heating, ventilation, air conditioning, electrical services, lighting etc.

*MEMBERSHIP*

Student Affiliate
Affiliate
Graduate
Companion
Licentiate (LCIBSE)
Associate (ACIBSE)
Member (MCIBSE)
Fellow (FCIBSE)

CIBSE is a licensed institution of the Engineering Council. This means that, as well as joining CIBSE, you will be Registered as a Chartered Engineer (CEng), Incorporated Engineer (IEng) or Engineering Technician (EngTech) when you have reached the appropriate level of qualification and professional skill.

*QUALIFICATION/EXAMINATIONS*

Please see the CIBSE website for more information www.cibse.org

*DESIGNATORY LETTERS*

LCIBSE, ACIBSE, MCIBSE, FCIBSE

# ENGINEERING, CHEMICAL

## *Membership of Professional Institutions and Associations*

### THE INSTITUTION OF CHEMICAL ENGINEERS

Davis Building
Railway Terrace
Rugby
Warwickshire CV21 3HQ
Tel: 01788 578214
Fax: 01788 560833
E-mail: customerservices@icheme.org
Website: www.icheme.org

The IChemE, founded in 1922, is an international professional membership organization for chemical, biochemical and process engineers, and we have some 30, 000 members in more than 113 countries. We promote competence and a commitment to sustainable development, advance the discipline for the benefit of society, and support the professional development of our members.

*MEMBERSHIP*
Student
Affiliate
Associate Member (AMIChemE)
Member (MIChemE)
Fellow {FIChemE)
Chartered Chemical Engineer (CEng MIChemE)
Chartered Engineer (CEng)
Chartered Scientist (CSci)
Chartered Environmentalist (CEnv)
Associate Fellow

*DESIGNATORY LETTERS*
AMIChemE, MIChemE, FIChemE, CEng MIChemE, CEng, CSci, CEnv

# ENGINEERING, CIVIL

## *Membership of Professional Institutions and Associations*

### INSTITUTION OF CIVIL ENGINEERS

1 Great George Street
Westminster
London SW1P 3AA
Tel: 020 7222 7722
E-mail: membership@ice.org.uk
Website: www.ice.org.uk

The ICE is a UK-based international organization with 80, 000 members that strives to promote and progress civil engineering around the world. Our purpose is to qualify professionals engaged in civil engineering, exchange knowledge and best practice, and support our members, and in the UK we liaise with government and publish reports on civil engineering issues.

*MEMBERSHIP*
Student
Graduate
Affiliate
Technician Member
Associate Member (AMICE)
Member (MICE)
Companion
Fellow (FICE)

# ENGINEERING, ELECTRICAL, ELECTRONIC AND MANUFACTURING

## *Membership of Professional Institutions and Associations*

### INSTITUTION OF LIGHTING PROFESSIONALS

Regent House
Regent Place
Rugby
Warwickshire CV21 2PN
Tel: 01788 576492
E-mail: info@theilp.org.uk
Website: www.theilp.org.uk

The ILP is a professional lighting association with about 2, 000 members, including lighting designers, consultants and engineers. We are dedicated to excellence in lighting and to raising awareness about the important contribution of lighting in road safety, crime prevention and the environment. We support members by providing technical advice and encourage their CPD through our monthly journal and by holding a wide range of conferences, regional meetings, seminars and courses.

*MEMBERSHIP*
Student
Affiliate
Associate Member (AMILP)
Member (MILP)
Fellow (FILP)
Corporate Member
Engineering Technician (EngTech)
Incorporated Engineer (IEng)
Chartered Engineer (CEng)

*QUALIFICATION/EXAMINATIONS*
Exterior Lighting Diploma
LET Diploma in Lighting

*DESIGNATORY LETTERS*
AMILP, MILP, FILP, EngTech, IEng, CEng

### THE INSTITUTION OF ENGINEERING AND TECHNOLOGY

Michael Faraday House
Stevenage
Hertfordshire SG1 2AY
Tel: 01438 313311
Fax: 01438 765526
E-mail: postmaster@theiet.org
Website: www.theiet.org

The IET is a world leading professional organisation sharing and advancing knowledge to promote science, engineering and technology across the world. It is the professional home for life for engineers and technicians, and a trusted source of essential engineering intelligence. The IET has more than 150, 000 members in 127 countries.

*MEMBERSHIP*
Student
Associate
Member (MIET)
Fellow (FIET)
Honorary Fellow
ICT Technician (ICTTech)
Engineering Technician (EngTech)
Incorporated Engineer (IEng)
Chartered Engineer (CEng)

*DESIGNATORY LETTERS*
FIET, ICTTech, EngTech, IEng, CEng, MIET

# ENGINEERING, ENERGY

## *Membership of Professional Institutions and Associations*

### ENERGY INSTITUTE

61 New Cavendish Street
London W1G 7AR
Tel: 020 7467 7100
Fax: 020 7255 1472
E-mail: info@energyinst.org
Website: www.energyinst.org

The EI is the chartered professional membership body for the energy industry, providing learning and networking opportunities, professional recognition and energy knowledge resources for individuals and companies worldwide. We offer professional qualifications including Chartered, Incorporated and Engineering Technician status for engineers, as well as Chartered Scientist, Chartered Energy Manager and Chartered Environmentalist.

*MEMBERSHIP*

Student Member
Affiliate
Graduate Member (GradEI)
Member (MEI)
Fellow (FEI)
Engineering Technician (EngTech)
Incorporated Engineer (IEng)
Chartered Engineer (CEng)
Chartered Scientist (CSci)
Chartered Environmentalist (CEnv)
Chartered Energy Manager (exclusive EI title)
Chartered Energy Engineer (exclusive EI title)
Chartered Petroleum Engineer (exclusive EI title)

*DESIGNATORY LETTERS*

GradEI, MEI, FEI, EngTech, IEng, CEng

# ENGINEERING, ENVIRONMENTAL

## *Membership of Professional Institutions and Associations*

### INSTITUTE OF ENVIRONMENTAL MANAGEMENT AND ASSESSMENT

Saracen House
Lincoln LN6 7AS
Tel: 01522 540069
Fax: 01522 540090
E-mail: info@iema.net
Website: www.iema.net

The IEMA is a not-for-profit membership organization that provides recognition and support to environmental professionals and promotes sustainable development through improved environmental practice and performance. We have about 15, 000 individual and corporate members in 87 countries, in the public, private and non-governmental sectors.

*MEMBERSHIP*

Student Member
Affiliate Member
Graduate Member
Associate (AIEMA)
Full Member (MIEMA)
Fellow (FIEMA)
Chartered Environmentalist (CEnv)
Corporate Member

*QUALIFICATION/EXAMINATIONS*

Foundation Certificate in Environmental Management
Associate Certificate in Environmental Management
Diploma

*DESIGNATORY LETTERS*

AIEMA, MIEMA, FIEMA, CEnv

## THE CHARTERED INSTITUTION OF WATER AND ENVIRONMENTAL MANAGEMENT

15 John Street
London WC1N 2EB
Tel: 020 7831 3110
Fax: 020 7405 4967
E-mail: via website
Website: www.ciwem.org

---

Founded in 1895, CIWEM is an independent professional body and registered charity with 12, 000 members that advances the science and practice of water and environmental management for a clean, green and sustainable world by promoting environmental excellence and professional development and training, supplying independent advice and evidence-based opinion, and providing a forum for debate through conferences, technical meetings and its publications.

*MEMBERSHIP*
Student

Associate ACIWEM
Graduate
Member MCIWEM C.WEM
Fellow FCIWEM C.WEM
Environmental Partner
Chartered Engineer (CEng)
Chartered Environmentalist (CEnv)
Chartered Scientist (CSci)

*QUALIFICATION/EXAMINATIONS*
Online training courses in partnership with Staffordshire University, accredited university courses at 12 leading institutions, CPD modules and Rural Environmental Management Programme

*DESIGNATORY LETTERS*
CEng, CEnv, CSi, C.WEM

## THE SOCIETY OF ENVIRONMENTAL ENGINEERS

The Manor House
High Street
Buntingford
Hertfordshire SG9 9AB
Tel: 01763 271209
Fax: 01763 273255
E-mail: office@environmental.org.uk
Website: www.environmental.org.uk

---

The SEE, founded in 1959, is a professional society that promotes awareness of the discipline of environmental engineering (the measurement, modelling, control and simulation of all types of environment). We provide members with information, training and representation within this field and encourage communication and good practice in quality, reliability, and cost-effective product development and manufacture.

*MEMBERSHIP*
Student
Member
Corporate Member
Engineering Technician (EngTech)
Incorporated Engineer (IEng)
Chartered Engineer (CEng)

*DESIGNATORY LETTERS*
EngTech, IEng, CEng

# ENGINEERING, FIRE

## *Membership of Professional Institutions and Associations*

### ASSOCIATION OF PRINCIPAL FIRE OFFICERS

9-11 Pebble Close
Amington
Tamworth
Staffordshire B77 4RD
Tel: 01827 302300
Fax: 01827 302399
E-mail: enquiries@apfo.org.uk
Website: www.apfo.org.uk

The APFO is the staff association of the most senior Fire Officers in the UK. Our objectives are: to represent and promote the interests of members in conditions of service and legal and employment matters; to negotiate and promote the settlement of disputes involving members; to provide assistance to members and their dependants in exceptional circumstances; and to provide support to members in matters concerning employment or a work-related injury.

*MEMBERSHIP*
Associate Member
Lifetime Past Member

### CHIEF FIRE OFFICERS' ASSOCIATION

9–11 Pebble Close
Amington
Tamworth
Staffordshire B77 4RD
Tel: 01827 302300
Fax: 01827 302399
Website: www.cfoa.org.uk

The CFOA is a professional membership association of the most senior fire officers in the UK. We provide independent advice to the government, local authorities and others. Our aim is to reduce loss of life, personal injury and damage to property by improving the quality of fire fighting, rescue, fire protection and fire prevention in the UK.

*MEMBERSHIP*
Member

## THE INSTITUTION OF FIRE ENGINEERS

IFE House
64-66 Cygnet Court
Timothy's Bridge Road
Stratford-upon-Avon CV37 9NW
Tel: 01789 261 463
Fax: 01789 296 426
E-mail: info@ife.org.uk
Website: www.ife.org.uk

The IFE, founded in 1918, is a non-profit-making professional body for fire professionals and has more than 12, 000 members worldwide. Our aim is to encourage and improve the science and practice of fire extinction, fire prevention and fire engineering, to enhance technical networks, and to give advice and support to our members for the benefit of the community at large.

*MEMBERSHIP*
Student
Affiliate Member
Technician (TIFireE)
Graduate (GIFireE)
Associate (AIFireE)
Member (MIFireE)
Fellow (FIFireE)
Engineering Technician (EngTech)
Incorporated Engineer (IEng)
Chartered Engineer (CEng)
Affiliate Organization

*QUALIFICATION/EXAMINATIONS*
IFE Certificate in Fire Science, Operations and Safety (Level 2)
IFE Certificate in Fire Science, Operations, Fire Safety and Management (Level 3)
IFE Diploma in Fire Science and Fire Safety (Level 3)

*DESIGNATORY LETTERS*
TIFireE, GIFireE, AIFireE, MIFireE, FIFireE, EngTech, IEng, CEng

# ENGINEERING, GAS

## *Membership of Professional Institutions and Associations*

## THE INSTITUTION OF GAS ENGINEERS AND MANAGERS

IGEM House
High Street
Kegworth
Derbyshire DE74 2DA
Tel: 0844 375 4436
Fax: 01509 678198
E-mail: general@igem.org.uk
Website: www.igem.org.uk

IGEM is licensed by EC(UK) and serves a wide range of professionals in the UK and international gas industry through membership and technical standards, having a diverse membership ranging from university students to qualified professionals. Anyone working or interested in the gas industry can form positive connections to enhance their career through IGEM.

*MEMBERSHIP*
Student Member
Associate (AIGEM)
Associate Member (AMIGEM)
Graduate Member (GradIGEM)
Member Manager (MIGEM)
Technician Member (Eng Tech (MIGEM))
Incorporated Member (I Eng (MIGEM))

Chartered Member (C Eng (MIGEM))
Fellow (C Eng (FIGEM))

*DESIGNATORY LETTERS*
MIGEM, Eng Tech (MIGEM), I Eng (MIGEM), C Eng (MIGEM), C Eng (FIGEM)

# ENGINEERING, GENERAL

## *Membership of Professional Institutions and Associations*

### ASSOCIATION OF COST ENGINEERS

Lea House
Sandbach
Cheshire CW11 1XL
Tel: 01270 764798
Fax: 01270 766180
E-mail: enquiries@acoste.org.uk
Website: www.acoste.org.uk

The ACostE represents the professional interests of those with responsibility for the prediction, planning and control of resources for engineering, manufacturing and construction. As a Professional Affiliate of The Engineering Council, we can propose suitably qualified members for the award of the titles of Chartered Engineer (CEng) and Incorporated Engineer (IEng).

*MEMBERSHIP*
Student
Associate (AA Cost E)
Companion (Companion A Cost E)
Graduate (Grad A Cost E)
Member (MA Cost E)
Fellow (FA Cost E)
Honorary Fellow (Hon FA Cost E)
Certified Cost Engineer (CCE)
Engineering Technician (EngTech)
Incorporated Engineer (IEng)
Chartered Engineer (CEng)

*DESIGNATORY LETTERS*
AA Cost E, Companion A Cost E, Grad A Cost E, MA Cost E, FA Cost E, CCE, EngTech, IEng, CEng

### INSTITUTE OF MEASUREMENT AND CONTROL

87 Gower Street
London WC1E 6AF
Tel: 020 7387 4949
Fax: 020 7388 8431
E-mail: membership@instmc.org.uk
Website: www.instmc.org.uk

The IMC is a multidisciplinary body that brings together thinkers and practitioners from the many disciplines that have a common interest in measurement and control. Our object is to promote for the public benefit, by all available means, the general advancement of the science and practice of measurement and control technology and its application.

*MEMBERSHIP*
Student Member
Affiliate Member
Associate Member
Member (MemInstMC)
Fellow (FInstMC)
Honorary Fellow (HonFInstMC)

## SEMTA – THE SECTOR SKILLS COUNCIL FOR SCIENCE, ENGINEERING AND MANUFACTURING TECHNOLOGIES

14 Upton Road
Watford
Hertfordshire WD18 0JT
Tel: 0845 643 9001
E-mail: via website
Website: www.semta.org.uk

Semta is part of the Skills for Business network of 25 employer-led Sector Skills Councils in the UK and works with employers in the aerospace, automotive, electrical, electronics, marine, mechanical, metals and science & bioscience sectors to ascertain their current and future skills needs and provide short- and long-term solutions to meet those needs.

## THE ENGINEERING COUNCIL

2nd Floor
246 High Holborn
London WC1V 7EX
Tel: 020 3206 0500
Fax: 020 3206 0501
Website: www.engc.org.uk

The Engineering Council holds the national registers of Engineering Technicians (EngTech), Incorporated Engineers (IEng), Chartered Engineers (CEng) and Information and Communications Technology Technicians (ICTTech). We set and maintain internationally recognised standards of competence and ethics, ensuring that employers, government and society can have confidence in registrants' skills and commitment.

*DESIGNATORY LETTERS*
EngTech, IEng, CEng, ICTTech

## WOMEN'S ENGINEERING SOCIETY

Michael Faraday House
Six Hills Way
Stevenage
Herts SG1 2AY
Tel: 01438 765506
E-mail: info@wes.org.uk
Website: www.wes.org.uk

The WES, founded in 1919, is a professional, not-for-profit network of women engineers, scientists and technologists, who offer inspiration, support and professional development. Working in partnership, we campaign to encourage women to participate and achieve as engineers, scientists and as leaders.

*MEMBERSHIP*
Student Member
Associate
Full Member (MWES)
Fellow
Company Member

*DESIGNATORY LETTERS*
WES

# ENGINEERING, MARINE

## Membership of Professional Institutions and Associations

## THE INSTITUTE OF MARINE ENGINEERING, SCIENCE AND TECHNOLOGY

33 Aldgate High Street
London EC3N 1EN
Tel: +44 (0)20 7382 2600
Fax: +44 (0)20 7382 2670
E-mail: via website
Website: www.imarest.org

---

The IMarEST, established in 1889, is the leading international membership body and learned society for marine professionals and has more than 15, 000 members worldwide. We have a strong international presence, with a network of 50 international branches, affiliations with major marine societies around the world, representation on the key marine technical committees and non-governmental status at the International Maritime Organization.

*MEMBERSHIP*

**Membership Categories**

IMarEST membership is open to everyone with an interest in the marine world across scientific, engineering and technological disciplines and applications.

Categories of membership are available to those who are seeking professional recognition, those who are currently studying or just starting out in their careers, or those who simply have a general interest in the IMarEST and its activities. There are no academic requirements for Non-corporate Membership of the IMarEST. However, professionals seeking Corporate Membership will require certain academic qualifications according to the type of membership being sought.

**Corporate Membership Categories**

Fellow (FIMarEST)

Fellows are those who qualify for the category of Member and have demonstrated to the satisfaction of Council a level of knowledge and understanding, competence and commitment involving superior responsibility for the conceptual design, management or the execution of important work in a marine related profession, and have given a commitment to abide by the Institute's Code of Professional Conduct.

Member (MIMarEST)

Members are those who qualify for the category of Associate Member and have demonstrated to the satisfaction of Council that they have achieved a position of professional standing having normally been professionally engaged in the marine sector for a period of 5 years that includes significant responsibility and have given a commitment to abide by the Institute's Code of Professional Conduct.

Associate Member (AMIMarEST)

Associate Members are those demonstrating to the satisfaction of Council that they have achieved a position as a technician, or are professionally engaged in Initial Professional Development or occupy an occupational role in the marine sector, and have given a commitment to abide by the Institute's Code of Professional Conduct.

**Non-corporate Membership Categories**

Affiliate

Affiliates may either be those with an interest in, or who may contribute to, the activities of the Institute; or persons who, in the opinion of Council, can contribute to, or wish to have access to, the technical services of the Institute, being resident in a recognized overseas territory and also members of a professional society with which the Institute has a reciprocal arrangement.

Student (SIMarEST)

Student members are those enrolled on a programme of further or higher education accredited or recognized by the IMarEST.

**Professional Registration**

In addition to membership, the IMarEST is licensed to provide a range of registers covering the fields of engineering, science and technology. In addition, the IMarEST's Royal Charter empowers the Institute to offer registers designed to meet the specific needs of the marine profession. Corporate members can become registered (chartered) as follows:

**Engineers**

Chartered Engineer (CEng)

Chartered Marine Engineer (CMarEng)

Incorporated Engineer (IEng)
Incorporated Marine Engineer (IMarEng)
Engineering Technician (EngTech)
Marine Engineering Technician (MarEngTech)
**Scientists**
Chartered Scientist (CSci)
Chartered Marine Scientist (CMarSci)
Registered Marine Scientist (RMarSci)
Marine Technician (MarTech)
**Technologists**
Chartered Marine Technologist (CMarTech)
Registered Marine Technologist (RMarTech)
Marine Technician (MarTech)

*DESIGNATORY LETTERS*
SIMarEST, AMIMarEST, MIMarEST, FIMarEST

# ENGINEERING, MECHANICAL

## *Membership of Professional Institutions and Associations*

### INSTITUTION OF MECHANICAL ENGINEERS

1 Birdcage Walk
Westminster
London SW1H 9JJ
Tel: 020 7222 7899
E-mail: enquiries@imeche.org
Website: www.imeche.org

The IMechE is a professional engineering body with about 80, 000 members. Our aims are to promote sustainable energy and engineering sustainable supply, economic growth while mitigating and adapting to climate change and the depletion of natural resources, and safe, efficient transport systems to ensure less congestion and emissions, and to inspire, prepare and support tomorrow's engineers so we can respond to society's changes.

*MEMBERSHIP*
Affiliate
Associate Member (AMIMechE)
Member (MIMechE)
Fellow (FIMechE)
Engineering Technician (EngTech)
Incorporated Engineer (IEng)
Chartered Engineer (CEng)

*DESIGNATORY LETTERS*
AMIMechE, MIMechE, FIMechE, EngTech, IEng, CEng

# ENGINEERING, MINING

## *Membership of Professional Institutions and Associations*

### INSTITUTE OF EXPLOSIVES ENGINEERS

Suite 3,
7-8 Mill Street
Stafford ST16 2AJ
Tel: 01785 240154
Fax: 01785 240154
E-mail: secretariat@iexpe.org
Website: www.iexpe.org

The Insitute of Explosives Engineers promotes the occupational competency, education and professional standing of those who work with explosives and provides consultative facilities for organizations and government departments within the explosives field.

*MEMBERSHIP*
Student
Associate (AIExpE)
Member (MIExpE)
Fellow (FIExpE)
Company
Company Affiliate

*QUALIFICATION/EXAMINATIONS*
CEng, IEng, Eng Tech

*DESIGNATORY LETTERS*
AIExpE, MIExpE, FIExpE

## THE INSTITUTE OF MATERIALS, MINERALS AND MINING (IOM$^3$)

1 Carlton House Terrace
London SW1Y 5DB
Tel: 020 7451 7300
Fax: 020 7839 1702
E-mail: via website
Website: www.iom3.org

IOM$^3$ is a major UK engineering institution whose activities encompass the whole materials cycle, from exploration and extraction, through characterization, processing, forming, finishing and application, to product recycling and land reuse. We promote and develop all aspects of materials science and engineering, geology, mining and associated technologies, mineral and petroleum engineering and extraction metallurgy, as a leading authority in the worldwide materials and mining community.

*MEMBERSHIP*
Student
Graduate
Affiliate
Member (MIMMM)
Fellow (FIMMM)
Associate (AIMMM)
Technician (Eng Tech)

*DESIGNATORY LETTERS*
MIMMM, FIMMM, AIMMM, Eng Tech

## THE INSTITUTE OF QUARRYING

McPherson House
8a Regan Way
Chetwynd Business Park
Chilwell
Nottingham NG9 6RZ
Tel: 0115 945 3880
Fax: 0115 948 4035
E-mail: mail@quarrying.org
Website: www.quarrying.org

The Institute of Quarrying, which dates from 1917, is the international professional body for quarrying, construction materials and related extractive and processing industries, and has 6, 000 members in some 50 countries. Our aim is to improve all aspects of operational performance through education and training at supervisory and management level.

*MEMBERSHIP*
Student
Associate
Member (MIQ)
Fellow (FIQ)

*QUALIFICATION/EXAMINATIONS*
Professional Examination

*DESIGNATORY LETTERS*
MIQ, FIQ

# ENGINEERING, NUCLEAR

## *Membership of Professional Institutions and Associations*

### THE NUCLEAR INSTITUTE

CK International House
1-6 Yarmouth Place
London WJ1 7BU
Tel: 020 3475 4701
Fax: 020 3475 4708
E-mail: admin@nuclearinst.com
Website: www.nuclearinst.com

The NI (a Nominated Body of the Engineering Council) is a registered charity established to support the nuclear sector. We organize lectures, seminars and events at a regional and national level, and can award EngTech, IEng and CEng to suitably qualified individuals.

*MEMBERSHIP*
Student Member
Learned Member
Graduate Member
Technician Member (TNucI)
Associate Member (AMNucI)
Member (MNucI)
Fellow (FNucI)
Honorary Fellow

*DESIGNATORY LETTERS*
TNucI, AMNucI, MNucI, FNucI

# ENGINEERING, PRODUCTION

## *Membership of Professional Institutions and Associations*

### THE INSTITUTE OF OPERATIONS MANAGEMENT

CILT(UK)
Earlstrees Court
Earlstrees Road
Corby
Northamptonshire NN17 4AX
Tel: 01536 740105
E-mail: info@iomnet.org.uk
Website: www.iomnet.org.uk

The Institute of Operations Management (IOM) is the UK professional body for operations management in manufacturing, service industries and the public sector. Our aim is to equip operations professionals with the skills and resources they need to maximize individual potential and organizational process.

*MEMBERSHIP*
Learner Affiliate
Student Affiliate
Associate Member (MIOM)
Fellow (FIOM)
Corporate Membership
APICS Membership

*QUALIFICATION/EXAMINATIONS*
Regulated Qualifications
Certificate in Operations Management COM (Level 3)
Diploma in Operations Management DOM (Level 5)
Award in Supply Chain and Inventory Management (Level 5)
Partnerships

APICS Certified in Production and Inventory Management (CPIM) APICS Certified Supply Chain Professional (CSCP)

*DESIGNATORY LETTERS*
MIOM, FIOM

# ENGINEERING, REFRACTORIES

## *Membership of Professional Institutions and Associations*

### INSTITUTE OF REFRACTORIES ENGINEERING

575 Trentham Road
Burton
Stoke on Trent
Staffs ST3 3BN
Tel: 01782 310 234
Fax: 01782 310 234
E-mail: secretary@ireng.org
Website: www.ireng.org

The IRE is a non-profit-making organization dedicated to fostering the science, technology and skills of refractories engineering and to serving the needs of refractories engineers worldwide. Our members have a background in R&D, design, engineering, manufacturing and installation contracting in the iron & steel, cement, non-ferrous, glass, chemical/petrochemical incineration, power generation, ceramics/bricks and similar industries.

*MEMBERSHIP*
Student
Associate Member (AMI Ref Eng)
Member (MI Ref Eng)
Fellow (FI Ref Eng)

*DESIGNATORY LETTERS*
AMI Ref Eng, MI Ref Eng, FI Ref Eng

# ENGINEERING, REFRIGERATION

## *Membership of Professional Institutions and Associations*

### THE INSTITUTE OF REFRIGERATION

Kelvin House
76 Mill Lane
Carshalton
Surrey SM5 2JR
Tel: 020 8647 7033
E-mail: ior@ior.org.uk
Website: www.ior.org.uk

The IOR is the professional body for the refrigeration and air conditioning industries. We promote the technical advancement and perfection of refrigeration, and the minimization of its effects on the environment, encourage the extension of refrigeration, air conditioning and heat pump services for the benefit of the community, and provide advice, CPD and support to our members.

*MEMBERSHIP*
Student
Technician Affiliate
Associate Member (AMInstR)
Member (MInstR)
Service Engineering Section
Air Conditioning and Heat Pump Institute of the IOR

*QUALIFICATION/EXAMINATIONS*
REAL Zero CPD, REAL Skills Europe CPD

*DESIGNATORY LETTERS*
AMInstR, TMInstR

# ENGINEERING, ROAD, RAIL AND TRANSPORT

## *Membership of Professional Institutions and Associations*

## INSTITUTE OF HIGHWAY ENGINEERS

De Morgan House
58 Russell Square
London WC1B 4HS
Tel: 020 7436 7487
Fax: 020 7436 7488
E-mail: cherrie.ouerghi@theihe.org
Website: www.theihe.org

The IHE is the professional body for highway and traffic professionals. We are run by engineers for engineers and technicians, and work to keep the standards of the profession high, to safeguard the interests of our members, and to ensure that their contribution is recognised.

*MEMBERSHIP*
Student Member
Graduate Member
Associate Member (AMIHE)
Member (MIHE)
Fellow (FIHE)
Engineering Technician (EngTech)
Incorporated Engineer (IEng)
Chartered Engineer (CEng)

*QUALIFICATION/EXAMINATIONS*
Prof Cert in Traffic Sign Design
Prof Cert in Traffic Signal Control
Prof Cert in Transport Development Management

*DESIGNATORY LETTERS*
AMIHE, MIHE, FIHE, EngTech, IEng, CEng

## INSTITUTION OF RAILWAY SIGNAL ENGINEERS

4th Floor
1 Birdcage Walk
Westminster
London SW1H 9JJ
Tel: 020 7808 1180
Fax: 020 7808 1196
E-mail: hq@irse.org
Website: www.irse.org

The Institution of Railway Signal Engineers, known more usually as the IRSE, is an international organization, active throughout the world. It is the professional institution for all those engaged or interested in railway signalling and telecommunications and allied disciplines. Membership is open to anyone engaged or interested in the management, planning, design, installation, telecommunications or associated equipment.

*MEMBERSHIP*
Student
Associate
Accredited Technician
Associate Member
Member
Fellow
Companion

*QUALIFICATION/EXAMINATIONS*
Professional Examination

*DESIGNATORY LETTERS*
AMIRSE, MIRSE, FIRSE, CompIRSE

## SOCIETY OF OPERATIONS ENGINEERS

22 Greencoat Place
London SW1P 1PR
Tel: 020 7630 1111
Fax: 020 7630 6677
E-mail: soe@soe.org.uk
Website: www.soe.org.uk

SOE is a professional membership organisation representing more than 16, 000 individuals and companies in the engineering industry. It was formed in 2000 by the merger of the Institute of Road Transport Engineers (IRTE) and the Institution of Plant Engineers (IPlantE). The Society's third Professional Sector, the Bureau of Engineer Surveyors (BES), joined in 2004.

*MEMBERSHIP*
Associate Member (AMSOE)
Member (MSOE)
Fellow (FSOE)
Engineering Technician (EngTech)
Incorporated Engineer (IEng)
Chartered Engineer (CEng)

## THE CHARTERED INSTITUTION OF HIGHWAYS AND TRANSPORTATION

119 Britannia Walk
London N1 7JE
Tel: 020 7336 1555
Fax: 020 7336 1556
E-mail: info@ciht.org.uk
Website: www.ciht.org.uk

The CIHT is a learned society and membership organization concerned with the planning, design, construction, maintenance and operation of land-based transport systems and infrastructure. CIHT provides professional development and networking opportunities to members, with routes to qualifications, cutting-edge technical conferences and exciting social events.

*MEMBERSHIP*
Student
Associate Member (AMCIHT)
Member (MCIHT)
Fellow (FCIHT)

*QUALIFICATION/EXAMINATIONS*
Transport Planning Professional (TPP) status (awarded jointly with the Transport Planning Society (TPS))

*DESIGNATORY LETTERS*
AMCIHT, MCIHT, FCIHT

# ENGINEERING, SHEET METAL

## Membership of Professional Institutions and Associations

### INSTITUTE OF SHEET METAL ENGINEERING

102 Richmond Drive
Perton
Wolverhampton
West Midlands WV6 7UQ
Tel: 07891 499146
E-mail: ismesec@googlemail.com
Website: www.isme.org.uk

The ISME is a learned body with individual membership open to those employed in the sheet metal and associated industries and corporate membership open to relevant companies. Our aims are to promote the science of working and using sheet metal by providing opportunities for the exchange of ideas and information, and to encourage the professional development of our members.

*MEMBERSHIP*
Student Member
Member (MISME)
Fellow (FISME)
Corporate Member

*DESIGNATORY LETTERS*
MISME, FISME

# ENGINEERING, STRUCTURAL

## Membership of Professional Institutions and Associations

### THE INSTITUTION OF STRUCTURAL ENGINEERS

11 Upper Belgrave Street
London SW1X 8BH
Tel: 020 7235 4535
Fax: 020 7235 4294
E-mail: membership@istructe.org
Website: www.istructe.org

The Institution of Structural Engineers, founded in 1908, is the world's largest membership organization dedicated to the art and science of structural engineering. Our aims include: maintaining professional standards for structural engineering; ensuring continued technical excellence; advancing safety, creativity and innovation; and promoting a sustainable approach to both the structural engineering profession and the built environment.

*MEMBERSHIP*
Student
Graduate
Technician (TIStructE)
Associate Member (AMIStructE)
Chartered Member (MIStructE)
Fellow (FIStructE)

*DESIGNATORY LETTERS*
TIStructE, AMIStructE, MIStructE, FIStructE

# ENGINEERING, WATER

## *Membership of Professional Institutions and Associations*

### INSTITUTE OF WATER

4 Carlton Court
Team Valley
Gateshead
Tyne and Wear NE11 0AZ
Tel: 0191 422 0088
Fax: 0191 422 0087
E-mail: info@instituteofwater.org.uk
Website: www.instituteofwater.org.uk

---

The IW is the only institute concerned with the UK water industry. Our aim is to promote high standards of integrity, conduct and ethics, and to provide our members with an opportunity for CPD and growth through sharing knowledge, experience and networking opportunities.

*MEMBERSHIP*
Student Member
Associate Member
Full Member
Fellow
Honorary Member
Engineering Technician (EngTech)
Incorporated Engineer (IEng)
Chartered Engineer (CEng)
Chartered Environmentalist (CEnv)
Company Member

*DESIGNATORY LETTERS*
EngTech, IEng, CEng, CEnv

# ENGINEERING DESIGN

## *Membership of Professional Institutions and Associations*

### THE INSTITUTION OF ENGINEERING DESIGNERS

Courtleigh
Westbury Leigh
Westbury
Wiltshire BA13 3TA
Tel: 01373 822801
Fax: 01373 858085
E-mail: via website
Website: www.ied.org.uk

---

Established in 1945, the IED represents 4, 000 members worldwide working in engineering design, product design and CAD. Benefits include a bimonthly journal, access to an extensive library, legal advice helpline, local branch activities, and guidance and support to registration with the EC(UK) for suitably qualified members.

*MEMBERSHIP*
IED membership has two divisions: Engineering Design, and Product Design and Technology.
Each division has a range of membership grades: Student Member (StudIED), Graduate/Diplomate Member (GradIED/DipIED), Competent Draughting Associate (CDAIED), Associate (AIED), Member (MIED), Fellow (FIED), Affiliate

*QUALIFICATION/EXAMINATIONS*
Registration with EC(UK) for suitably qualified members

*DESIGNATORY LETTERS*
AIED, MIED, FIED

# ENVIRONMENTAL SCIENCES

## *Membership of Professional Institutions and Associations*

### CHARTERED INSTITUTE OF ECOLOGY AND ENVIRONMENTAL MANAGEMENT

43 Southgate Street
Winchester
Hampshire SO23 9EH
Tel: 01962 868626
E-mail: enquiries@cieem.net
Website: www.cieem.net

Founded in 1991 to advance the science, technology and practice of ecology, environmental management and sustainable development to further conservation and the enhancement of biodiversity through education, training, study and research. CIEEM now has more than 4, 700 members drawn from local authorities, government agencies, industry, environmental consultancy, teaching/research and NGOs.

*MEMBERSHIP*
Student Member
Affiliate Member
Graduate Member (Grad CIEEM)
Associate Member (ACIEEM)
Full Member (MCIEEM)
Fellow (FCIEEM)

*DESIGNATORY LETTERS*
Grad CIEEM, ACIEEM, MCIEEM, FCIEEM

# EXPORT

## *Membership of Professional Institutions and Associations*

### THE INSTITUTE OF EXPORT

Export House
Minerva Business Park
Lynch Wood
Peterborough PE2 6FT
Tel: 01733 404400
E-mail: via website
Website: www.export.org.uk

Established since 1935 offering training and professional qualifications to those working within international trade. We are the only professional institute in the UK offering qualifications ranging from the new 14–19 Diploma up to a level 5 Diploma as well as standard and bespoke training courses for individuals and companies.

*MEMBERSHIP*
Affiliate
Student
Associate
Member MIEx (Grad)
Member MIEx
Fellow
Business

*QUALIFICATION/EXAMINATIONS*
Diploma in International Trade (DIT)
Certified International Trade Advisor (CIT)
Advanced Certificate in International Trade (ACIT)
Young International Trader (YIT)
Certificate in International Trade (CIT)
Foundation Degree (FdA)

# FISHERIES MANAGEMENT

## *Membership of Professional Institutions and Associations*

### INSTITUTE OF FISHERIES MANAGEMENT

PO Box 679
Hull
East Yorkshire HU5 9AX
Tel: 0845 388 7012
E-mail: info@ifm.org.uk
Website: www.ifm.org.uk

The Institute of Fisheries Management is an international organization of persons sharing a common interest in the modern and sustainable management of recreational and commercial fisheries. It is a non-profit-making body and is a constituent body of the Society for the Environment.

*MEMBERSHIP*
Subscriber
Student Member
Associate Member (AMIFM)
Registered Member (MIFM)
Fellow (FIFM)
Honorary Fellow (Hon FIFM)
Corporate Member
Honorary Member (Hon MIFM)

*QUALIFICATION/EXAMINATIONS*
Certificate
Diploma (accredited by The Open University)

*DESIGNATORY LETTERS*
AMIFM, MIFM, FIFM, Hon FIFM, Hon MIFM

# FLORISTRY

## *Membership of Professional Institutions and Associations*

### BRITISH FLORIST ASSOCIATION

PO Box 674
Wigan
Lancashire WN1 9LL
Tel: 0844 800 7299
E-mail: via website
Website: www.britishfloristassociation.org

The BFA, founded in 1951, is an awarding body that promotes the highest standards in professional floristry. We are responsible for preparing and setting the highest floristry qualifications and for designing programmes for the training of SOF judges and examiners. We provide help, advice and information to our more than 1, 000 members, who include business owners, florists, training providers, and students.

*MEMBERSHIP*
Florist Individual
Student
Corporate
Associate
College Member
Honorary Member

# FOOD SCIENCE AND NUTRITION

## *Membership of Professional Institutions and Associations*

### INSTITUTE OF FOOD SCIENCE AND TECHNOLOGY

5 Cambridge Court
210 Shepherd's Bush Road
London W6 7NJ
Tel: 020 7603 6316
E-mail: info@ifst.org
Website: www.ifst.org

---

IFST is the leading independent qualifying body for food professionals in Europe and the only professional body in the UK concerned with all aspects of food science and technology. As a registered charity we are independent of government, industry, lobby or special interest groups.

*MEMBERSHIP*
Associate
Member (MIFST)
Fellow (FIFST)
Chartered Scientist (CSci)
Registered Scientist (RSci)
Registered Science Technician (RSciTech)
Professional Food Sensory Group

*DESIGNATORY LETTERS*
MIFST, FIFST, CSci, RSci, RSciTech

# FORESTRY AND ARBORICULTURE

## *Membership of Professional Institutions and Associations*

### INSTITUTE OF CHARTERED FORESTERS

59 George Street
Edinburgh EH2 2JG
Tel: 0131 240 1425
Fax: 0131 240 1424
E-mail: icf@charteredforesters.org
Website: www.charteredforesters.org

---

The ICF is the Royal Chartered body for foresters and arboriculturists in the UK. We have over 1, 000 members, to whom we offer advice, guidance and support. We also strive to foster a greater public understanding and awareness of the profession, as the environment and its management become more relevant to everyone.

*MEMBERSHIP*
Student Member
Supporter
Associate Member
Professional Member (MICFor)
Fellow (FICFor)

*QUALIFICATION/EXAMINATIONS*
Professional Membership Entry (PME) exam

*DESIGNATORY LETTERS*
MICFor, FICFor

## THE ARBORICULTURAL ASSOCIATION

The Malthouse
Stroud Green
Standish
Stonehouse
Gloucestershire GL10 3DL
Tel: 01242 522152
Fax: 01242 577766
E-mail: admin@trees.org.uk
Website: www.trees.org.uk

---

The Arboricultural Association, founded in 1964, is the leading body in the UK for the amenity tree care professional in either civic or commercial employment at craft, technical, supervisory, managerial or consultancy level. There are currently over 2, 000 members of The Arboricultural Association in a variety of membership classes.

*MEMBERSHIP*
Student Member
Ordinary Member
Associate Member
Technician Member
Professional Member
Fellow
Fellow Retired
Corporate Member

*QUALIFICATION/EXAMINATIONS*
Arboricultural Association Approved Contractor
Arboricultural Association Registered Consultant

*DESIGNATORY LETTERS*
TechArborA; MArborA; FArborA

## THE ROYAL FORESTRY SOCIETY

The Hay Barns
Home Farm Drive
Upton Estate
Banbury OX15 6HU
Tel: 01295 678588
Fax: 01295 670798
E-mail: rfshq@rfs.org.uk
Website: www.rfs.org.uk

---

The RFS was founded in 1882 and now has over 3, 600 members. We are dedicated to promoting the wise management of trees and woodlands, and to increasing people's understanding of forestry. We publish a popular magazine, the *Quarterly Journal of Forestry,* arrange outdoor meetings, organize woodland study tours in the UK and overseas, run exams in arboriculture and manage model woodlands.

*MEMBERSHIP*
Member
Corporate Member
Full-time Student

# FOUNDRY TECHNOLOGY AND PATTERN MAKING

## *Membership of Professional Institutions and Associations*

### THE INSTITUTE OF CAST METALS ENGINEERS

National Metalforming Centre
47 Birmingham Road
West Bromwich
West Midlands B70 6PY
Tel: 01216 016979
Fax: 01216 016981
E-mail: info@icme.org.uk
Website: www.icme.org.uk

The ICME is the professional body for those in the castings and associated industry. It was formed in 1904, granted its first Royal Charter in 1921, a Third Supplemental Charter in 1994 and changed its name in 2001. The granting of the Third Supplemental Charter aligned its membership requirements with those of the EC(UK).

*MEMBERSHIP*
Student
Member (MICME)
Professional Member (Prof MICME)
Fellow (FICME)
Engineering Technician (EngTech)
Incorporated Engineer (IEng)
Chartered Engineer (CEng)
European Engineer (EurIng)

*DESIGNATORY LETTERS*
MICME, Prof MICME, FICME, EngTech, IEng, CEng, EurIng

# FREIGHT FORWARDING

## *Membership of Professional Institutions and Associations*

### BRITISH INTERNATIONAL FREIGHT ASSOCIATION (BIFA)

Redfern House
Browells Lane
Feltham
Middlesex TW13 7EP
Tel: 020 8844 2266
Fax: 020 8890 5546
E-mail: bifa@bifa.org
Website: www.bifa.org/content/home

BIFA is the principal trade association providing representation, training and support to British companies engaged in the international movement of freight to and from the UK by air, rail, road and sea. It is a not-for-profit organisation. Members are encouraged to contribute to the running of the Association.

*MEMBERSHIP*
Associate Member
Trade Member

# FUNDRAISING

## Membership of Professional Institutions and Associations

### INSTITUTE OF FUNDRAISING

Park Place
12 Lawn Lane
London SW8 1UD
Tel: 020 7840 1000
Fax: 020 7840 1001
E-mail: enquiries@institute-of-fundraising.org.uk
Website: www.institute-of-fundraising.org.uk

The Institute of Fundraising is the professional body for fundraisers in the UK, representing over 5000 individual fundraisers and 340 organisations. We offer professional support, act as a voice for fundraisers and promote best practice. We offer professional qualifications and training, and the annual IoF National Convention is the largest fundraising conference of its type in Europe.

*MEMBERSHIP*
Associate
Full Member (MInstF)
Fully Certificated Member MInstF(Cert)
Diploma Qualified Member MInstF(Dip)
Organisational Member

*QUALIFICATION/EXAMINATIONS*
Introductory Certificate in Fundraising
Certificate in Fundraising
Diploma in Fundraising
Advanced Diploma in Fundraising (in development)
Certificate in Direct Marketing

*DESIGNATORY LETTERS*
MInstF, MInstF(Cert), MInstF(Dip), FInstF, FInstF(-Cert), FInstF(Dip)

# FUNERAL DIRECTING, BURIAL AND CREMATION ADMINISTRATION

## Membership of Professional Institutions and Associations

### NATIONAL ASSOCIATION OF FUNERAL DIRECTORS

618 Warwick Road
Solihull
West Midlands B91 1AA
Tel: 0845 230 1343
Fax: 0121 711 1351
E-mail: info@nafd.org.uk
Website: www.nafd.org.uk

The NAFD, founded in 1905, is an independent trade association whose members include more than 3, 200 funeral homes throughout the UK, suppliers to the profession, and overseas funeral directing businesses. We provide support to our members and offer informed opinion to government.

*MEMBERSHIP*
Funeral Director (Category A) Member
Supplier (Category B) Member
Overseas Member

*QUALIFICATION/EXAMINATIONS*
Diploma in Funeral Arranging and Administration (Dip.FAA)
Diploma in Funeral Directing (Dip.FD)

## NATIONAL ASSOCIATION OF MEMORIAL MASONS

1 Castle Mews
Rugby
Warwickshire CV21 2AL
Tel: 01788 542264
Fax: 01788 542276
E-mail: enquiries@namm.org.uk
Website: www.namm.org.uk

The NAMM was formed in 1907 to promote excellence and craftsmanship within the memorial masonry trade. Our services to members include training, business advice, technical advice, promotion, a legal helpline, a conciliation and arbitration service, trade exhibitions and a conference. We protect members' interests through representation to the British Standards Institution (BSI) and the Burial & Cemeteries Advisory Group (BCAG).

*MEMBERSHIP*
Individual Associate Member
Affiliate Member
Full Retail and Wholesale Members
Company Associate Member
Corporate Associate Member
Overseas Member
Overseas Affiliate Member

## THE INSTITUTE OF BURIAL AND CREMATION AUTHORITIES

41 Salisbury Road
Carshalton
Surrey SM5 3HA
Tel: 020 8669 4521
Fax: 020 8669 4521
E-mail: fbcasec@btconnect.com
Website: www.fbca.org.uk

*MEMBERSHIP*
Student
Registered Licentiate (LInstBCA)
Associate Member (AInstBCA)
Member (MInstBCA)
Fellow (FInstBCA)

*QUALIFICATION/EXAMINATIONS*
Diploma
Final Diploma

*DESIGNATORY LETTERS*
LInstBCA, AInstBCA, MInstBCA, FInstBCA

# FURNISHING AND FURNITURE

## *Membership of Professional Institutions and Associations*

## FLOORING INDUSTRY TRAINING ASSOCIATION

4c St Marys Place
The Lace Market
Nottingham NG1 1PH
Tel: 0115 9506836
E-mail: info@fita.co.uk
Website: www.fita.co.uk

---

FITA was set up and is fully supported by the CFA and the NICF to provide training for the floor-covering industry. We have a fully equipped training centre at Loughborough, where the majority of our courses are run. We also offer tailor-made courses to suit individual specifications and requirements.

*QUALIFICATION/EXAMINATIONS*

FITA Training Courses

The Flooring Industry Flooring Association was set up by, and is fully supported by the CFA and NICF to provide training.

FITA has a fully equipped training centre at Loughborough in Leicestershire where the majority of our standard courses are run. FITA also offers tailor-made courses to suit your specifications and requirements, quotations on request.

FITA instructors have all passed assessments and knowledge exams and are supported on courses by technicians with specialist knowledge from the trade.

FITA also enjoys the support of a considerable number of suppliers who freely donate materials, accessories and tools.

Fully trained staff are an asset to any company. The outlay for training courses far outweighs the initial cost.

Please be sure to book early to reserve your place on a course. Go to our Course Dates page for details of our latest courses and the training centres where they are being held.

Training courses considered suitable for Domestic Installers

Carpet Fitting – Basic
Carpet Fitting – Intermediate
Domestic Sheet Vinyl Fitting
Profitable Measuring and Quoting
Subfloor Preparation – Domestic

Training courses considered suitable for Commercial Installers

Commercial Vinyl Fitting – Advanced
Commercial Vinyl Fitting – Basic
Commercial Vinyl Fitting – Intermediate
Cost Effective Estimating and Planning
Linoleum Installation – Intermediate
Subfloor Preparation – Commercial

Training courses considered suitable for Domestic & Commercial Installers

Carpet Fitting – Advanced
Laminate and Wood Fitting – Basic
Linoleum Installation – Basic
Moisture – Preventing floor failures
Resilient / Luxury Vinyl Tile Fitting – Advanced
Resilient / Luxury Vinyl Tile Fitting – Basic
Wood Fitting – Advanced
Wood Fitting – Intermediate
Wood Sanding and Finishing

Assessments designed for FITA QA Accreditation

QA Card Adhered Carpet Assessment
QA Card Carpet Tile Assessment
QA Card Floating Timber Assessment
QA Card Resilient Sheet Assessment
QA Card Subfloor Preparation Assessment
QA Card Vinyl Tile Assessment

### NATIONAL INSTITUTE OF CARPET AND FLOORLAYERS

4c St Marys Place
The Lace Market
Nottingham NG1 1PH
Tel: 0115 9583077
Fax: 0115 9412238
E-mail: info@nicfltd.org.uk
Website: www.nicfltd.org.uk

The NICF furthers the interests of its members by promoting excellence in the field of carpet and floorlaying and providing a range of benefits, products and services.

*MEMBERSHIP*
Master Fitter Member
Fitter Member
Trainee Fitter Member
Retailer Member
Associate Member
Patron Member

*QUALIFICATION/EXAMINATIONS*
Fitter qualification assessment
Master Fitter qualification assessment

# GEMMOLOGY AND JEWELLERY

## *Membership of Professional Institutions and Associations*

### THE GEMMOLOGICAL ASSOCIATION OF GREAT BRITAIN

21 Ely Place
London EC1N 6TD
Tel: 020 7404 3334
Fax: 020 7404 8843
E-mail: information@gem-a.com
Website: www.gem-a.com

The Gemmological Association of Great Britain (Gem-A), a UK-registered charity, is the world's longest established provider of gem and jewellery education, our first diploma having been awarded in 1913. We are committed to promoting the study of gemmology and to providing CPD to our members – an international community of gem professionals and enthusiasts.

*MEMBERSHIP*
Member
Fellow (FGA)
Diamond Member (DGA)
Corporate Member

*QUALIFICATION/EXAMINATIONS*
Foundation Certificate in Gemmology
Diploma in Gemmology
Diamond Diploma

*DESIGNATORY LETTERS*
FGA, DGA

## THE NATIONAL ASSOCIATION OF GOLDSMITHS

78A Luke Street
London EC2A 4XG
Tel: 020 7613 4445
E-mail: nag@jewellers-online.org
Website: www.jewellers-online.org

The NAG, established in 1894, serves and supports the jewellery industry of Great Britain and Ireland. We promote high professional standards among our members, who must adhere to a code of professional practice. In return, we offer them advice, support and CPD in the form of distance learning courses, seminars and tutorials.

*MEMBERSHIP*
Alumni Member
Allied Member
Affiliate Member
Ordinary Member

*QUALIFICATION/EXAMINATIONS*
Professional Jewellers' Diploma (JET 1 Certificate)
Professional Jewellers' Diploma (JET 2 Diploma)
Professional Jewellers' Management Diploma (JETPlus)
Professional Jewellers' Business Development Diploma (JETPro)
Certificate of Appraisal Theory (CAT)

# GENEALOGY

## *Membership of Professional Institutions and Associations*

## SOCIETY OF GENEALOGISTS

14 Charterhouse Buildings
Goswell Road
London EC1M 7BA
Tel: 020 7251 8799
Fax: 020 7250 1800
E-mail: info@sog.org.uk
Website: www.sog.org.uk

The Society (founded 1911) is the National Family History Centre. A registered educational charity, it was founded to encourage and foster the study, science and knowledge of genealogy. This it does chiefly through its library, publications and extensive education programme of courses and events. It currently does not hold exams.

*MEMBERSHIP*
Member
Fellow (FSG)
Honorary Fellow (FSG Hon)

*DESIGNATORY LETTERS*
FSG, FSG Hon

## THE HERALDRY SOCIETY

53 Hitchin Street
Baldock
Herts SG7 6AQ
Tel: 01869 246188
E-mail: memsec@theheraldrysociety.com
Website: www.theheraldrysociety.com

The Heraldry Society is a registered charity that aims to encourage interest in heraldry through publications, lectures, visits and related activities. Members receive *The Heraldry Gazette*, which contains heraldic news and comments, and Society information quarterly. We maintain contact with heraldic societies in many parts of the UK and abroad.

*MEMBERSHIP*
Associate Member
Ordinary Member
Fellow (FHS)
Honorary Fellow (Hon FHS)

*QUALIFICATION/EXAMINATIONS*
Elementary Certificate
Intermediate Certificate
Advanced Certificate
Diploma (DipHS)

*DESIGNATORY LETTERS*
FHS, Hon FHS

## THE INSTITUTE OF HERALDIC AND GENEALOGICAL STUDIES

79–82 Northgate
Canterbury
Kent CT1 1BA
Tel: 01227 768664
Fax: 01227 765617
E-mail: via website
Website: www.ihgs.ac.uk

The IHGS, founded in 1961, is an independent educational charitable trust that offers a wide range of courses on family history, heraldry and related historical subjects, and has an extensive library, archive and research facilities. We also publish a monthly e-mail newsletter and a quarterly journal, *Family History*.

*MEMBERSHIP*
Associate Member
Graduate Member

*QUALIFICATION/EXAMINATIONS*
Correspondence Course in Genealogy
Higher Certificate in Genealogy
Diploma in Genealogy

*DESIGNATORY LETTERS*
LHG, FHG

# GEOGRAPHY

## *Membership of Professional Institutions and Associations*

### ROYAL GEOGRAPHICAL SOCIETY (WITH THE INSTITUTE OF BRITISH GEOGRAPHERS)

1 Kensington Gore
London SW7 2AR
Tel: 020 7591 3000
Fax: 020 7591 3001
E-mail: via website
Website: www.rgs.org

The RGS-IBG is the learned society and professional body for geography. We aim to foster an understanding and informed enjoyment of our world: developing, supporting and promoting geographical research, expeditions and fieldwork, education, public engagement, and providing geography input to policy.

*MEMBERSHIP*
Young Geographer
Member
Postgraduate Fellow
Fellow
Chartered Geographer (CGeog)
Corporate Member

*DESIGNATORY LETTERS*
FRGS, CGeog

# GEOLOGY

## *Membership of Professional Institutions and Associations*

### THE GEOLOGICAL SOCIETY

Burlington House
Piccadilly
London W1J 0BG
Tel: 020 7434 9944
Fax: 020 7439 8975
E-mail: enquiries@geolsoc.org.uk
Website: www.geolsoc.org.uk

The Geological Society, founded in 1807, is the UK's national organization for professional Earth scientists. The normal grade of membership is Fellow. Students may become Candidate Fellows. Members of the public not eligible for any other status may join as Friends.

*MEMBERSHIP*
Friend
Candidate Fellow
Fellow
Chartered Geologist

*DESIGNATORY LETTERS*
FGS, CGeol

# GLASS TECHNOLOGY

## *Membership of Professional Institutions and Associations*

### BRITISH SOCIETY OF SCIENTIFIC GLASSBLOWERS

Unit W1, MK2 Business Centre
Barton Road
Bletchley
Milton Keynes
Buckinghamshire MK2 3HU
Tel: 01908 821191
Fax: 01908 821195
E-mail: bssg@biochemglass.co.uk
Website: www.bssg.co.uk

The Society was founded in 1960 for the benefit of those engaged in Scientific Glassblowing and its associated professions, and to uphold and further the status of Scientific Glassblowers. We welcome written submissions to our quarterly journal, which is circulated to members.

*MEMBERSHIP*
Associate
Student Member
Fellow
Full Member
Master
Honorary Member
Retired Member
Overseas Member

### SOCIETY OF GLASS TECHNOLOGY

9 Churchill Way
Chapeltown
Sheffield
South Yorkshire S35 2PY
Tel: 0114 2634455
Fax: 0871 8754085
E-mail: info@sgt.org
Website: www.sgt.org

The objects of the Society of Glass Technology are to encourage and advance the study of the history, art, science, design, manufacture, after treatment, distribution and end use of glass of any and every kind.

*MEMBERSHIP*
Personal Member
Fellow (FSGT)
Fellow Emeritus
Honorary Fellow (HonFSGT)
Corporate Member

*QUALIFICATION/EXAMINATIONS*
Peer review by the Board of Fellows

*DESIGNATORY LETTERS*
FSGT, HonFSGT

# HAIRDRESSING

## *Membership of Professional Institutions and Associations*

### HABIA

Oxford House
Sixth Avenue
Sky Business Park, Robin Hood Airport
Doncaster
South Yorkshire DN9 3GG
Tel: 0845 6 123555
Fax: 01302 774949
E-mail: info@habia.org
Website: www.habia.org

Habia is the government-appointed standards-setting body for hair, beauty, nails, spa therapy, barbering and African-type hair, and creates the standards that form the basis of all qualifications, including NVQs, SVQs, apprenticeships, diplomas and foundation degrees, as well as industry codes of practice.

*MEMBERSHIP*

Habia offers a membership programme for training providers (Habia Members) and a wider, free membership for industry professionals and educators.

### THE GUILD OF HAIRDRESSERS

Archway House
Barnsley S71 1AQ
Tel: 01226 786555
Fax: 01226 208300

The Guild of Hairdressers dates back to 1340, when it was part of the Guild of Barbers and Surgeons. Then in the late 16th century, when the surgeons split off, it became the Guild of Hairdressers, Wigmakers and Perfumers. Today it still exists for the benefit of its members, who adhere to a code of ethics and to whom it provides help and advice.

# HEALTH AND HEALTH SERVICES

## *Membership of Professional Institutions and Associations*

### BRITISH OCCUPATIONAL HYGIENE SOCIETY – FACULTY OF OCCUPATIONAL HYGIENE

5/6 Melbourne Business Court
Millennium Way
Pride Park
Derby DE24 8LZ
Tel: 01332 298101
Fax: 01332 298099
E-mail: admin@bohs.org
Website: www.bohs.org

BOHS is a Chartered professional membership organisation and learned society, promoting public and professional awareness, good practice and high standards of occupational hygiene, to help reduce work-related ill-health. The Faculty is our professional arm and examining board, and administers examinations and awards qualifications in occupational hygiene and allied subjects.

*MEMBERSHIP*
Individual
Student
Affiliate (corporate)
Retired
Associate (AFOH)
Licentiate (LFOH)
Chartered Member (CMFOH)
Specialist Member (MFOH(S))
Chartered Fellow (CFFOH)

*QUALIFICATION/EXAMINATIONS*
A range of UK and international qualifications in occupational hygiene and related subjects, which include stand-alone modules covering general principles and practical applications at the technician level, through to BOHS's own professional level Certificate and Diploma qualifications.
The Occupational Hygiene Modules are aimed at those who want to gain a qualification in a particular topic of occupational hygiene to demonstrate technical expertise in that area or, grouped together, to gain exemption from the Faculty's professional level Certificate Core examination.
The International Occupational Hygiene Modules are based on the Occupational Hygiene Modules, without specific reference to UK or other legislation.
The Proficiency Modules cover both theory and practical training in a specific subject, and are aimed at those needing to demonstrate a level of proficiency to carry out the area of work covered by the Module.
Our professional qualifications are as follows: The Certificate of Competence in an individual subject is for candidates wanting to establish their competence in a specific field, and follows on from successful completion of one of the Occupational Hygiene Modules. This is an oral examination, supported by submission of a written report. The Certificate of Operational Competence in Occupational Hygiene is the qualification required to join the Faculty of Occupational Hygiene as a Licentiate, and demonstrates knowledge and competence in the broad principles and practice of occupational hygiene. This is a two-part written and oral examination. The Diploma of Professional Competence in Occupational Hygiene is the highest professional occupational hygiene qualification. Candidates must already hold the Certificate of Operational Competence, and be able to demonstrate 5 years' experience in the field of occupational hygiene. Award of the Diploma qualifies the holder to become a Member of the Faculty, and demonstrates knowledge of, and competence in, assessment of health hazards and the extent of risk in various workplace circumstances, and an ability to advise on suitable control procedures. This is also a two-part, written and oral, examination. Practising members who hold the Diploma are awarded the title of Chartered Occupational Hygienist.
For further information see
www.bohs.org/education/examinations/

*DESIGNATORY LETTERS*
AFOH, LFOH, CMFOH, CFFOH, MFOH(S)

## CHARTERED INSTITUTE OF ENVIRONMENTAL HEALTH

Chadwick Court
15 Hatfields
London SE1 8DJ
Tel: 020 7928 6006
Fax: 020 7827 5862
E-mail: via website
Website: www.cieh.org

The CIEH is a professional, awarding and campaigning body at the forefront of environmental and public health and safety.

*MEMBERSHIP*
Student member
Associate
Accredited Associate
Graduate Member
Voting Member
Fellow
Chartered Environmental Health Practitioner

*QUALIFICATION/EXAMINATIONS*
The CIEH offers a range of Ofqual-regulated qualifications at four levels in health and safety, food safety, environmental protection and train the trainer.

## ERGONOMICS SOCIETY

Elms Court
Elms Grove
Loughborough
Leicestershire LE11 1RG
Tel: 01509 234904
Fax: 01509 235666
E-mail: iehf@ergonomics.org.uk
Website: www.ergonomics.org.uk

The Ergonomics Society, founded in 1949, is a UK-based professional society for ergonomists worldwide. We encourage and maintain high standards of professional practice through education, accreditation and development, promote the interests of our members across government, academia, business and industry, and raise awareness of ergonomics in general.

*MEMBERSHIP*
Student Member
Associate Member
Graduate Member
Registered Member (MErgS)
Fellow (FErgS)
Technical Member
Retired Member

## INSTITUTE OF HEALTH PROMOTION AND EDUCATION

c/o Helen Draper
School of Dentistry, University of Manchester
Coupland 3, Oxford Road
Manchester M13 9PL
Tel: 01612 756610
E-mail: honsec@ihpe.org.uk
Website: www.ihpe.org.uk

The IHPE was established 50 years ago to bring together professionals with a common interest in health education and promotion to share their experience, ideas and information. Our members come from a diverse range of backgrounds, including nursing, midwifery, health visiting, medicine, dentistry, public health, stress management, psychology and teaching.

*MEMBERSHIP*
Student Member
Associate Member (AIHPE)
Full Member (MIHPE)
Fellow (FIHPE)
Corporate Member

*DESIGNATORY LETTERS*
MIHPE, AIHPE, FIHPE

## INSTITUTE OF HEALTH RECORDS AND INFORMATION MANAGEMENT

Marshall House
Heanor Gate Road
Heanor
Derbyshire DE75 7RG
Tel: 01773 713927
Fax: 01773 713927
E-mail: ihrim@zen.co.uk
Website: www.ihrim.co.uk

IHRIM was founded in 1948, primarily as an educational body, to provide qualifications as well as career and professional assistance to members. We encourage professionalism and high standards among our members who work in the fields of health records, information management, clinical coding and information governance.

*MEMBERSHIP*
Student
Affiliate
Licentiate
Certificated Member (CHRIM)
Accredited Clinical Coder (ACC)
Associate (AHRIM)
Fellow (FHRIM)
Corporate Affiliate

*QUALIFICATION/EXAMINATIONS*
Certificate of Technical Competence
Foundation exam
Certificate exam
Diploma exam
National Clinical Coding Qualification

*DESIGNATORY LETTERS*
CHRIM, ACC, AHRIM, FHRIM

## INSTITUTE OF HEALTHCARE ENGINEERING AND ESTATE MANAGEMENT

2 Abingdon House
Cumberland Business Centre
Northumberland Road
Portsmouth PO5 1DS
Tel: 023 92 823186
Fax: 023 92 815927
E-mail: office@iheem.org.uk
Website: www.iheem.org.uk

IHEEM is the learned society and professional body for those working in the Healthcare Estates sector. Our members are architects, builders, engineers, estate managers, surveyors, medical engineers and other related professionals. We provide benefits to members to keep them up to date with developing technology and changing regulations.

*MEMBERSHIP*
Graduate (GIHEEM)
Associate Member (AMIHEEM)
Member (MIHEEM)
Fellow (FIHEEM)

*DESIGNATORY LETTERS*
GIHEEM, AMIHEEM, MIHEEM, FIHEEM

## INSTITUTE OF HEALTHCARE MANAGEMENT

John Snow House
59 Mansell Street
London E1 8AN
Tel: 020 7265 7321
Fax: 020 7265 7301
E-mail: education@ihm.org.uk
Website: www.ihm.org.uk

The IHM is the professional organization for managers throughout healthcare, including the NHS, independent providers, healthcare consultants and the armed forces. Our focus is on improving patient/user care by publishing standards of management practice, promoting the IHM Code (which covers behavioural and ethical aspects of management practice) and establishing a CPD framework for our members.

*MEMBERSHIP*
Associate Member
Full Member (MIHM)

*QUALIFICATION/EXAMINATIONS*
Certificate in Health Management Studies (CertHMS)
Certificate in Health Services Management (CertHSM)
Certificate in Managing Health Services (CertMHS)
Certificate in Managing Health & Social Care (CertMHSC)
Diploma in Health Services Management (DipHSM)

*DESIGNATORY LETTERS*
MIHM, FIHM, CIHM

## THE ROYAL SOCIETY FOR PUBLIC HEALTH

John Snow House
59 Mansell Street
London E1 8AN
Tel: 020 7265 7300
Fax: 020 7265 7301
E-mail: via website
Website: www.rsph.org.uk

The RSPH was formed in October 2008 by the merger of the Royal Society for the Promotion of Health (RSPH/RSH) and the Royal Institute of Public Health (RIPH). We offer a wide range of vocationally related qualifications in the fields of food safety and nutrition, hygiene, health and safety, pest control, health promotion and the built environment.

*MEMBERSHIP*
Associate (ARSPH)
Licentiate (LRSPH)
Member (MRSPH)
Fellow (FRSPH)
Student

*QUALIFICATION/EXAMINATIONS*
Please see the RSPH's website.

*DESIGNATORY LETTERS*
ARSPH, LRSPH, MRSPH, FRSPH

# HORSES AND HORSE RIDING

***Membership of Professional Institutions and Associations***

## THE BRITISH HORSE SOCIETY

Contact: Equestrian Qualifications GB Limited
c/o The British Horse Society
Abbey Park
Kenilworth
Warwickshire CV8 2XZ
Tel: 02476 840500
Fax: 02476 840501
E-mail: enquiry@bhs.org.uk
Website: www.bhs.org.uk

The British Horse Society offers vocational and work-based examinations for grooms, stable managers, riding instructors and coaches. Founded in 1947, the BHS exams system is world renowned as credible and rigorous, producing competent, practical people who follow safe practices. We also offer competency certificates for the recreational rider.

*MEMBERSHIP*
Individual Member
Trade Member
Corporate Member

*QUALIFICATION/EXAMINATIONS*
Equestrian Qualifications GB Limited awards examinations and qualifications for grooms, stable managers, riding instructors and coaches on behalf of The British Horse Society and British Equestrian Federation. Please see the EQL website, www.equestrian-qualifications.org.uk, for details.

# HOUSING

## *Membership of Professional Institutions and Associations*

### THE CHARTERED INSTITUTE OF HOUSING

Octavia House
Westwood Way
Coventry CV4 8JP
Tel: 024 7685 1700
E-mail: customer.services@cih.org
Website: www.cih.org

The CIH is the professional body for people involved in housing and communities. We are a registered charity and not-for-profit organization. We have a diverse and growing membership of over 22, 000 people – both in the public and private sectors – living and working in over 20 countries on five continents across the world.

*MEMBERSHIP*

From January 2012 two new grades of membership have been introduced and replaced the previous six grades of membership.

CIH Member (formerly Student, Affiliate, Practitioner, Associate)

CIH Chartered Member (formerly Corporate and Fellow).

Visit www.cih.org to find out more about CIH membership.

*QUALIFICATION/EXAMINATIONS*

Certificate Courses

The CIH offers a range of certificated courses at Levels 2, 3 and 4 delivered at various centres across the UK. They are also available by distance learning. We also offer a suite of certificated courses in repairs and maintenance, also at Levels 2, 3 and 4, developed in partnership with the Chartered Institute of Building (CIOB).

Professional Qualifications

The CIH Professional Qualification can be achieved at either undergraduate or postgraduate level, FT or PT.

Please see the CIH's website for details.

*DESIGNATORY LETTERS*

CIH Members: CIH Member or CIHM, CIH Chartered Members: CIH Chartered Member or CIHCM (existing Fellows can continue to use FCIH and Honorary Members can use (Hon).

# INDEXING

## *Membership of Professional Institutions and Associations*

### SOCIETY OF INDEXERS

Woodbourn Business Centre
10 Jessell Street
Sheffield S9 3HY
Tel: 01142 449561
E-mail: admin@indexers.org.uk
Website: www.indexers.org.uk

The Society of Indexers is the professional body for indexing in the UK and Ireland, and exists to promote indexing, the quality of indexes and the profession of indexing. We offer information to publishers and other organizations on commissioning indexes and our online directory 'Indexers Available' provides an up-to-date guide to indexers currently working in a wide range of fields.

*MEMBERSHIP*
Student Member
Member
Professional Member (MSocInd)
Advanced Professional Member (MSocInd(Adv))
Fellow (FSocInd)
Corporate Member

*QUALIFICATION/EXAMINATIONS*
Training in Indexing course
Advanced Test
Fellowship index submission

*DESIGNATORY LETTERS*
MSocInd, MSocInd(Adv), FSocInd

# INDUSTRIAL SAFETY

## *Membership of Professional Institutions and Associations*

### BRITISH SAFETY COUNCIL

70 Chancellors Road
London W6 9RS
Tel: 020 8741 1231
Fax: 0844 583 4731
E-mail: info@britsafe.org
Website: www.britsafe.org

The BSC is one of the world's leading health and safety organizations. Our mission is to keep people healthy and safe at work. Our range of charitable initiatives, such as free health and safety qualifications for school children, is supported by a broad mix of commercial activities centred on membership, training, auditing and qualifications.

*MEMBERSHIP*
UK Member
International Member

*QUALIFICATION/EXAMINATIONS*
Award in COSHH Risk Assessment (Level 2)
Award in DSE Risk Assessment (Level 2)
Award in Fire Risk Assessment (Level 2)
Award in Manual Handling Risk Assessment (Level 2)
Award in Risk Assessment (Level 2)
Award in Supervising Staff Safely (Level 2)
Certificate in Occupational Health and Safety (Level 3)
Diploma in Occupational Health and Safety (Level 6)
International Certificate in Occupational Health and Safety
International Diploma in Occupational Health and Safety
Entry Level Award in Workplace Hazard Awareness
Award in Health and Safety at Work (Level 1)
Certificate in Fire Safety and Risk Management
National Certificate in Construction Health and Safety

## HEALTH & SAFETY EXECUTIVE APPROVED MINING QUALIFICATIONS

Mining Qualifications, The Health & Safety Executive
2nd Floor, Foundry House
3 Millsands, Riverside Exchange
Sheffield
South Yorkshire S3 8NH
Tel: 0114 291 2394
Fax: 0114 291 2399
E-mail: sarah.johnson@hse.gsi.gov.uk
Website: www.hse.gov.uk/mining

The HSE issues First and Second Class Certificates of Qualification as required under the Management and Administration of Safety and Health at Mines Regulations (MASHAM) 1993 for the appointment of a manager and undermanager respectively, in mines of coal, shale and fireclay in the UK. It also issues certificates to Mining Mechanical and Mining Electrical Engineers, Mechanics and Electricians Class I and Class II, Mines Surveyor, and Mines Deputy. For details see: www.hse.gov.uk/mining

## INTERNATIONAL INSTITUTE OF RISK AND SAFETY MANAGEMENT

Suite 7a
77 Fulham Palace Road
London W6 8JA
Tel: 020 8741 9100
Fax: 020 8741 1349
E-mail: info@iirsm.org
Website: www.iirsm.org

The IIRSM is a professional body for health & safety practitioners and specialists in associated professions. Our aim is to advance professional standards in accident prevention and occupational health throughout the world. We have more than 8, 100 members, in the UK and over 70 other countries, to whom we provide support and offer advice via a technical helpline.

*MEMBERSHIP*
Student
Affiliate
Associate (AIIRSM)
Member (MIIRSM)
Specialist Member (SIIRSM)
Fellow (FIIRSM)
Specialist Fellow (SFIIRSM)

*DESIGNATORY LETTERS*
AIIRSM, MIIRSM, SIIRSM, FIIRSM, SFIIRSM

## NEBOSH (THE NATIONAL EXAMINATION BOARD IN OCCUPATIONAL SAFETY AND HEALTH)

Dominus Way
Meridian Business Park
Leicester LE19 1QW
Tel: (+44) 116 263 4700
Fax: (+44) 116 282 4000
E-mail: info@nebosh.org.uk
Website: www.nebosh.org.uk

NEBOSH offers globally recognized qualifications designed to meet the health, safety, environmental and risk management needs of all places of work. Courses leading to NEBOSH qualifications attract over 35, 000 candidates annually in over 100 countries around the world.

*MEMBERSHIP*

NEBOSH's National General Certificate, National Certificate in Fire Safety and Risk Management, National Certificate in Construction Health and Safety, and the International General Certificate are all accepted as meeting the academic requirements to apply for Technical Membership (Tech IOSH) of the Institution of Occupational Safety and Health (IOSH).

In partnership with the Association for Project Safety (APS) the NEBOSH National and International Certificates in Construction Health and Safety meet the headline entrance criteria requirements for Construction Safety Associate membership (AaPS).

In addition holders of either the NEBOSH National or International Diploma in Occupational Health and Safety and either the NEBOSH National or International Certificate in Construction Health and Safety meet the headline qualification entrance criteria requirements for Registered Construction Safety Practitioner (RMaPS).

NEBOSH environmental management qualifications are now being accepted by CIWEM (The Chartered Institution of Water and Environmental Management) as meeting its membership requirements.

The NEBOSH Certificate in Environmental Management will be accepted for its new Technician Membership grade entitling the use of post-nominal designation (TechCIWEM).

The NEBOSH National Diploma in Environmental Management fulfils the qualification requirements for non-chartered Member of CIWEM (MCIWEM). Progression on to chartered membership is a further opportunity.

NEBOSH's National Diploma and International Diploma are accepted as meeting the requirements to apply for Graduate Membership (Grad IOSH) of the Institution of Occupational Safety and Health (IOSH).

A NEBOSH Diploma provides a sound basis for progression to MSc level: a number of UK universities offer MSc programmes that accept the National Diploma as a full or partial entry requirement.

NEBOSH will be offering a Master's Degree from September 2013, in partnership with the University of Hull.

The new Masters of Research (MRes) Degree is open to holders of a NEBOSH Diploma who wish to further their career in Health and Safety and/or Environment. It will be delivered by distance learning through research directly relevant to the candidate's own work.

*QUALIFICATION/EXAMINATIONS*

NEBOSH Health and Safety at Work Qualification
NEBOSH Health, Safety and Environment in the Process Industries Qualification
NEBOSH National Certificate in Construction Health and Safety
NEBOSH Certificate in Environmental Management
NEBOSH National Certificate in Fire Safety and Risk Management
NEBOSH National General Certificate in Occupational Health and Safety
NEBOSH International General Certificate in Occupational Health and Safety
NEBOSH International Technical Certificate in Oil and Gas Operational Safety
NEBOSH National Certificate in the Management of Health and Well-being at Work
NEBOSH International Certificate in Construction Health and Safety
NEBOSH International Certificate in Fire Safety and Risk Management

NEBOSH National Diploma in Environmental Management
NEBOSH National Diploma in Occupational Health and Safety
NEBOSH International Diploma in Occupational Health and Safety
MRes in Occupational Health and Safety Management (in partnership with the University of Hull)

### THE INSTITUTION OF OCCUPATIONAL SAFETY AND HEALTH

The Grange
Highfield Drive
Wigston
Leicestershire LE18 1NN
Tel: 0116 257 3100
Fax: 0116 257 3101
E-mail: membership@iosh.co.uk
Website: www.iosh.co.uk

---

IOSH is the world's largest organization for health and safety professionals, with more than 36, 000 members worldwide, including 13, 000 Chartered Safety and Health Practitioners. The Institution was founded in 1945 and is an independent, not-for-profit organization that sets professional standards, supports and develops members, and provides authoritative advice and guidance on health and safety issues.

*MEMBERSHIP*
Affiliate Member
Associate Member
Technician Member (Tech IOSH)
Graduate Member (Grad IOSH)
Chartered Member (CMIOSH)
Chartered Fellow (CFIOSH)

*DESIGNATORY LETTERS*
Tech IOSH, Grad IOSH, CMIOSH, CFIOSH

# INSURANCE AND ACTUARIAL WORK

## *Membership of Professional Institutions and Associations*

### ASSOCIATION OF AVERAGE ADJUSTERS

1 St Katherine's Way
London E1W 1UN
Tel: 020 748 1250
E-mail: aaa@rtiForensics.com
Website: www.average-adjusters.com

---

The AAA was founded in 1869 to promote correct principles in the adjustment of marine insurance claims and general average, uniformity of practice among average adjusters and the maintenance of good professional conduct. It ensures the independence and impartiality of its members by imposing a strict code of conduct and has close links with other international associations and insurance markets.

*MEMBERSHIP*
Subscriber
Associate
Fellow

*QUALIFICATION/EXAMINATIONS*
The Association's examination consists of 6 modules. Passes in Modules 1 & 2 are required for Associateship, passes in Modules 3–6 for Fellowship. For details see the Association's website.

## THE CHARTERED INSTITUTE OF LOSS ADJUSTERS

51–55 Gresham Street
London EC2V 7HQ
Tel: 020 7216 7580
E-mail: info@cila.co.uk
Website: www.cila.co.uk

The CILA, which was founded in 1941, is the professional body representing the claims specialists who investigate, negotiate and agree the conclusion of insurance and other claims on behalf of insurers and policyholders. We safeguard the interests of our members and maintain the high standards of the profession by requiring them to abide by our code of professional conduct.

*MEMBERSHIP*
Student Member
Ordinary Member
Certificate Member (Cert CILA)
Associate (ACILA)
Fellow (FCILA)
Honorary Member

*QUALIFICATION/EXAMINATIONS*
ACILA examination

*DESIGNATORY LETTERS*
Cert CILA, Dip CILA, ACILA, FCILA

## THE CHARTERED INSURANCE INSTITUTE

42–48 High Road
South Woodford
London E18 2JP
Tel: 020 8989 8464
Fax: 020 8530 3052
E-mail: customer.serv@cii.co.uk
Website: www.cii.co.uk

The CII is the premier professional body for those working in the insurance and financial services industry. We are dedicated to promoting higher standards of competence and integrity through the provision of relevant qualifications for employees at all levels across all sectors of the industry.

*MEMBERSHIP*
Ordinary Member
Qualified Member
Associate Member (ACII)
Fellow (FCII)

*QUALIFICATION/EXAMINATIONS*
Award in Financial Planning
Certificate in Equity Release
Certificate in Financial Planning
Certificate in Insurance
Certificate in Life and Pensions
Certificate in Mortgage Advice
Diploma in Financial Planning
Diploma in Insurance
Advanced Diploma in Financial Planning
Advanced Diploma in Insurance
Award for the Foundation Insurance Test
Award in General Insurance
Award in London Market Insurance
Award in Customer Service Insurance
Award in Financial Administration
Award in Bancassurance
Award in Investment Planning
Certificate in Contract Wording
Certificate in Insurance and Financial Services
Certificate in London Market Insurance Specialisation
Certificate in Discretionary Investment Management
Certificate in Paraplanning
Certificate in Securities Advice and Dealing
Certificate in Investment Operations
Diploma in Regulated Financial Planning
Msc in Insurance and Risk Management
Msc in Wealth Management

*DESIGNATORY LETTERS*
ACII, FCII

## THE FACULTY AND INSTITUTE OF ACTUARIES

Faculty of Actuaries
Maclaurin House
18 Dublin Street
Edinburgh EH1 3PP
Tel: 0131 240 1313
E-mail: faculty@actuaries.org.uk
Website: www.actuaries.org.uk

Institute of Actuaries
Staple Inn Hall
High Holborn
London WC1V 7QJ
Tel: 020 7632 2111
E-mail: institute@actuaries.org.uk

Napier House
4 Worcester Street
Oxford OX1 2AW
Tel: 01865 268211
E-mail: institute@actuaries.org.uk

---

Actuaries are experts in assessing the financial impact of tomorrow's uncertain events. They enable financial decisions to be made with more confidence by analysing the past, modelling the future, assessing the risks involved, and communicating what the results mean in financial terms.

*MEMBERSHIP*
Student Member
Affiliate Member
Associate (AFA or AIA)
Fellow (FFA or FIA)
Honorary Fellow

*QUALIFICATION/EXAMINATIONS*
Certificate in Financial Mathematics

*DESIGNATORY LETTERS*
AFA, AIA, FFA, FIA

# JOURNALISM

## *Membership of Professional Institutions and Associations*

## NATIONAL COUNCIL FOR THE TRAINING OF JOURNALISTS

NCTJ Training Ltd
The New Granary
Newport
Saffron Walden
Essex CB11 3PL
Tel: 01799 544014
Fax: 01799 544015
E-mail: info@nctj.com
Website: www.nctj.com

---

The NCTJ provides a range of journalism training products and services in the UK, including: accredited courses; qualifications and examinations; awards; careers information; distance learning; short courses and CPD; information and research;

publications and events. We play an influential role in all areas of journalism education and training.

*QUALIFICATION/EXAMINATIONS*
Advanced Level Apprenticeship in Journalism
Diploma in Journalism
Diploma in Press Photography and Photojournalism
National Certificate Examination (NCE) for Press Photographers and Photo-Journalists
National Certificate Examination (NCE) for Sub-editors
National Certificate Examination (NCE) for Sports Reporters
National Qualification in Journalism (NQJ) for Reporters

## THE CHARTERED INSTITUTE OF JOURNALISTS

2 Dock Offices
Surrey Quays Road
London SE16 2XU
Tel: 020 7252 1187
Fax: 020 7232 2302
E-mail: memberservices@cioj.co.uk
Website: www.cioj.co.uk

The CIoJ, which dates back to 1884, is a professional body and trade union for journalists. We expect our members to uphold high standards in the way they work and to adhere to a strict code of conduct, and in return we champion journalistic freedom, protect their interests in the workplace and campaign for better working conditions.

*MEMBERSHIP*
Student Member
Affiliate Member
Trainee Member
Full Member
International Member

*DESIGNATORY LETTERS*
MCIJ – Member, FCIJ – Fellow

# LAND AND PROPERTY

## *Membership of Professional Institutions and Associations*

## RICS (ROYAL INSTITUTION OF CHARTERED SURVEYORS)

Parliament Square
London SW1P 3AD
Tel: 024 7686 8555
Fax: 020 7334 3811
E-mail: contactrics@rics.org
Website: www.rics.org/careers

RICS, an independent, not-for-profit organization, has around 100, 000 qualified members and more than 50, 000 students and trainees in some 140 countries, and provides the world's leading professional qualification in land, property, construction and associated environmental issues. We accredit over 600 courses at leading universities worldwide and provide impartial, authoritative advice on key issues for business, society and governments.

*MEMBERSHIP*
Student
Associate (AssocRICS)
Member (MRICS)
Fellow (FRICS)

*DESIGNATORY LETTERS*
AssocRICS, MRICS, FRICS

## THE COLLEGE OF ESTATE MANAGEMENT

Whiteknights
Reading
Berkshire RG6 6AW
Tel: 0118 921 4696
Fax: 0118 921 4620
E-mail: enquiries@cem.ac.uk
Website: www.cem.ac.uk

The College of Estate Management is the leading provider of supported distance learning for real estate and construction professionals. We have been playing a key role in the property world for over 90 years. At any one time we have over 4, 000 students based all over the world.

*QUALIFICATION/EXAMINATIONS*
BCSC Diploma in Shopping Centre Management
BSc(Hons) Building Surveying
BSc(Hons) Construction Management
BSc(Hons) Estate Management
BSc(Hons) Property Management
BSc(Hons) Quantity Surveying
Postgraduate Diploma/MSc Conservation of the Historic Environment
Postgraduate Diploma/MSc Surveying
MBA Real Estate and Construction Management
Postgraduate Diploma/MSc Facilities Management
Postgraduate Diploma/MSc Property Investment
RICS Professional Membership Graduate Route – Adaptation 1

## THE INSTITUTE OF REVENUES, RATING AND VALUATION

Northumberland House
5th Floor
303–306 High Holborn
London WC1V 7JZ
Tel: 020 7831 3505
Fax: 020 7831 2048
E-mail: education@irrv.org.uk
Website: www.irrv.org.uk

The Institute offers professional and technical qualifications for all those whose professional work is concerned with local authority revenues and benefits, valuation for rating, property taxation and the appeals procedure. Our qualifications are widely recognized throughout the profession.

*MEMBERSHIP*
Student Member
Affiliate Member
Graduate Member
Technician Member (Tech IRRV)
Corporate Member (IRRV)
Diploma Member (Dip IRRV)
Honours Member (IRRV Hons)
Honorary Member
Fellow (FIRRV)

*QUALIFICATION/EXAMINATIONS*
Level 3 Certificate in Local Taxation and Benefits OR Business Rates
Level 3 Local Taxation & Benefits (QCF) / SCQF
Professional Diploma in Local Taxation and Benefits
Honours

*DESIGNATORY LETTERS*
Tech IRRV, IRRV, IRRV (Dip), IRRV (Hons), FIRRV

## THE NATIONAL FEDERATION OF PROPERTY PROFESSIONALS AWARDING BODY

Arbon House
6 Tournament Court
Edgehill Drive
Warwick CV34 6LG
Tel: 0845 250 6008
Fax: 01926 417789
E-mail: quals@nfopp.co.uk
Website: www.nfopp-awardingbody.co.uk

The NFOPP Awarding Body is committed to raising standards within agency through the provision of accredited, nationally recognized qualifications. We are recognized by the Qualifications and Examinations Regulator (Ofqual) and have to follow strict guidelines and maintain quality standards in the provision of all our qualifications.

*MEMBERSHIP*
For membership details of the following organizations please refer to the relevant website:
APIP: www.apip.co.uk
ARLA: www.arla.co.uk
ICBA: www.icba.uk.com
NAEA: www.naea.co.uk
NAVA: www.nava.org.uk

*QUALIFICATION/EXAMINATIONS*
NFoPP Level 3 Technical Award in Commercial Property Agency (QCF)
NFoPP Level 3 Technical Award in Real Property Auctioneering (QCF)
NFoPP Level 3 Technical Award in Residential Letting and Property Management (QCF)
NFoPP Level 3 Technical Award in Sale of Residential Property (QCF)
NFoPP Level 3 Technical Award in Chattels Auctioneering (QCF)
NFoPP Level 4 Certificate in Residential Letting & Property Management
NFoPP Level 4 Certificate in Sale of Residential Property
NFoPP Level 4 Certificate in Commercial Property Agency

## THE PROPERTY CONSULTANTS SOCIETY

Basement Office
Surrey Court
1 Surrey Street
Arundel
West Sussex BN18 9DT
Tel: 01903 883787
E-mail: info@propertyconsultantssociety.org
Website: www.propertyconsultantssociety.org

The Property Consultants Society is a non-profit-making organization that offers advice to qualified surveyors, architects, valuers, auctioneers, land and estate agents, master builders, construction engineers, accountants and members of the legal profession to help them to undertake their property consultancy in a competent, legitimate and publicly acceptable way.

*MEMBERSHIP*
Student (SPCS)
Licentiate (LPCS)
Associate (APCS)
Fellow (FPCS)
Honorary Member

*DESIGNATORY LETTERS*
SPCS, LPCS, APCS, FPCS

# LANDSCAPE ARCHITECTURE

## *Membership of Professional Institutions and Associations*

### LANDSCAPE INSTITUTE

Charles Darwin House
12 Roger Street
London WC1N 2JU
Tel: 020 7685 2640
E-mail: membership@landscapeinstitute.org
Website: www.landscapeinstitute.org

The LI is an educational charity and chartered body responsible for protecting, conserving and enhancing the natural and built environment for the benefit of the public. We champion well-designed and well-managed urban and rural landscape. Our 6, 000 members include chartered landscape architects, academics and scientists working for local authorities, government agencies and in private practice, and students.

*MEMBERSHIP*
Student Member
Affiliate Member
Licentiate Member
Chartered Member (CMLI)
Fellow (FLI)
Academic

*QUALIFICATION/EXAMINATIONS*
Pathway to Chartership oral examination conferring chartered professional status (CMLI)

*DESIGNATORY LETTERS*
CMLI, FLI

# LANGUAGES, LINGUISTICS AND TRANSLATION

## *Membership of Professional Institutions and Associations*

### INSTITUTE OF TRANSLATION & INTERPRETING

Milton Keynes Business Centre
Foxhunter Drive
Linford Wood
Milton Keynes MK14 6GD
Tel: 01908 325250
Fax: 01908 325259
E-mail: info@iti.org.uk
Website: www.iti.org.uk

The Institute of Translation & Interpreting is one of the primary sources of information on these services to government, industry, the media and the general public. We promote the highest standards, providing guidance to those entering the profession and advice to those who offer language services and to their customers.

*MEMBERSHIP*
Associate (AITI)
Student
Qualified Member (MITI)
Corporate Member
Fellow

*QUALIFICATION/EXAMINATIONS*
Applicants for qualified membership must take an exam (translators) or attend an interview (interpreters).

## THE CHARTERED INSTITUTE OF LINGUISTS

Saxon House
48 Southwark Street
London SE1 1UN
Tel: 020 7940 3100
Fax: 020 7940 3101
E-mail: info@iol.org.uk
Website: www.iol.org.uk

The Chartered Institute of Linguistics, founded in 1910, is a respected language assessment and accredited awarding body, with about 6, 500 members. Our aims include promoting the learning and use of modern languages, improving the status of all professional linguistics, and ensuring the maintenance of high professional standards through adherence to our code of conduct.

*MEMBERSHIP*
Registered Student
Associate Member (ACIL)
Member (MCIL)
Fellow (FCIL)
Chartered Linguist (CL)

*QUALIFICATION/EXAMINATIONS*
Certificate in Bilingual Skills (CBS)
Diploma in Public Service Interpreting (DPSI)
International Diploma in Bilingual Translation (IDBT)
Diploma in Translation (DipTrans)

*DESIGNATORY LETTERS*
ACIL, MCIL, FCIL, CL

## THE GREEK INSTITUTE

34 Bush Hill Road
London N21 2DS
Tel: 020 8360 7968
Fax: 020 8360 7968
E-mail: info@greekinstitute.co.uk
Website: www.greekinstitute.co.uk

The Greek Institute, which was founded in 1969, is a non-profit-making cultural organization that promotes Modern Greek studies and culture through lectures, publications, literary competitions, Greek cultural evenings and the award of Certificates and a Diploma which are recognized by many UK universities as equivalent to GCSE and GCE A level Modern Greek.

*MEMBERSHIP*
Member
Associate (AGI)
Fellow (FGI)

*QUALIFICATION/EXAMINATIONS*
Certificate in Greek Conversation – Basic Stage: Levels 1 and 2
Certificate in Greek Conversation – Intermediate Stage: Levels 3 and 4
Certificate in Greek Conversation – Higher Stage: Levels 5 and 6
Preliminary Certificate
Intermediate Certificate
Advanced Certificate
Diploma in Greek Translation (DipGrTrans)

*DESIGNATORY LETTERS*
AGI, FGI

# LAW

## ENGLAND AND WALES

### MAGISTRATES

The President of the Courts of England and Wales, The Lord Chief Justice, is head of the Judiciary. He is responsible for the welfare, training and deployment of magistrates, for approving the names of the candidates recommended for appointment and for disciplinary action, short of removal. He also has responsibility for the protection of judicial independence and for working to ensure that the magistracy reflects the diversity of society as a whole.

There are six key qualities that a magistrate must possess: good character, understanding and communication, social awareness, maturity and sound temperament, sound judgement, commitment and reliability.

Before sitting in court, magistrates must undertake some basic training, which includes structured observations in court. This covers practice and procedure in court, structured decision making, sentencing, etc. New magistrates are assigned a mentor for their first two years. Consolidation training takes place at the end of the first year; this is designed to help magistrates plan for their ongoing development and prepare for their first appraisal which takes place about 12 to 18 months after appointment. Magistrates only sit in adult courts when first appointed. Having got that experience they may apply to sit in youth courts and family courts and have to undertake more training before they can sit.

### JUDGES

All judicial office holders are Her Majesty's Judges and as such all appointments are made by the Queen or her Ministers. Since 2006 all candidates for judicial appointment in England and Wales have been selected by the independent Judicial Appointments Commission (JAC), which passes its recommendations to the Lord Chancellor for approval. The key statutory responsibilities of the JAC are to select candidates solely on merit; to select only people of good character; to have regard to the need to encourage diversity in the range of people available for selection for appointments.

Once the JAC's selections have been received, the actual appointments are made in slightly different ways depending on the type of post. The Lord Chancellor himself appoints Deputy District Judges and most members of tribunals. He also appoints the 30, 000 unpaid magistrates (who are selected by local Advisory Committees, not by the JAC). The Queen appoints High Court and Circuit Judges, Masters, Registrars and District Judges, District Judges (Magistrates' Courts) and Recorders on the advice of the Lord Chancellor. Lord Chief Justices and Heads of Division are appointed by a special panel convened by the JAC. All Court of Appeal judges are senior judges with lengthy judicial experience and they are appointed by The Queen on the recommendation of a selection panel convened by the JAC. Scotland and Northern Ireland have their own separate court systems, with their own arrangements for appointing members of the judiciary.

The Supreme Court has jurisdiction over the whole of the UK, so its Justices are not selected by the JAC, which is an England and Wales body. Rather, a special committee is set up, which is made up of the three judicial appointments bodies from around the UK (England and Wales, Scotland and Northern Ireland), who recommend a name to Ministers. The Queen appoints the Justices on the basis of advice from the Prime Minister.

Appointments to salaried or fee-paid judicial posts are made from among judges or practising lawyers. In general the requirement for appointment is that the candidate must have been a practising barrister or solicitor for at least 10 years (for appointment to the Circuit Bench or above) or for five years (appointments to the District Bench and to most tribunal posts). Certain posts are also open to legal executives, patent agents and trademark agents of the required seniority. Candidates for appointment as Justices of the Supreme Court must have held high judicial office for two years or must have been practising barristers or solicitors of the senior courts for at least 15 years.

#### *OFFICERS OF THE COURT*

Officers of the Court include judicial and administrative staff; the former include Masters and Registrars, the latter secretaries and clerks to the judges and the staff who administer the court service. Details are given in *The English Legal System*, 14th edition, 2013–14 (Routledge). Qualifications for the judicial offices vary somewhat, but most appointments are limited to established barristers and solicitors.

## THE LEGAL PROFESSION

The legal profession consists of two branches. Each performs distinct duties, although there is a degree of overlap in some aspects of their work.

*Solicitors* undertake all ordinary legal business for their clients (with whom they are in direct contact). They may also appear on behalf of a client in the magistrates' and county courts and tribunals, and with specialist training are able to represent them in the higher courts (Crown Court, High Court and Court of Appeal).

*Barristers* (known collectively as the 'Bar' and collectively and individually as 'Counsel') advise on legal problems submitted by solicitors and conduct cases in court when instructed by a solicitor; only barristers or qualified solicitor advocates may represent clients in the higher courts.

## LEGAL EXECUTIVES

Both graduates and non-graduates can work in a legal office with the option of qualifying as a solicitor through further vocational training.

## CORONERS

Coroners must be barristers, solicitors or legally qualified medical practitioners of not less than five years' standing. They are appointed by local authorities. There are approximately 110 coroners' jurisdictions in England and Wales. Coroners are independent judicial officers. When not engaged in coronal duties, coroners (apart from 'whole-time' coroners) continue in their legal or medical practices. On 22 May 2012 the first Chief Coroner of England and Wales was announced. He will oversee the implementation of the Coroner and Justice Act 2009. Further information from the Coroners' Society of England and Wales, website: www.coronersociety.org.uk

## BARRISTERS

### Qualification as a barrister at the Bar of England and Wales

There are three stages that must be completed to qualify as a barrister. The academic stage consists of an undergraduate degree in law or in any other subject with a minimum of a 2:2. For those with an undergraduate degree in a subject other than law a one-year conversion course (CPE/GDL) must be completed.

Before commencing the vocational stage candidates must join one of the four Inns and then undertake the Bar Professional Training Course (BPTC), which is either one year full time or two years part time. The main skills taught on the BPTC are: case work skills, legal research, general written skills including opinion-writing (that is, giving written advice), interpersonal skills including conference skills (interviewing clients), resolution of disputes out of court (ReDOC) and advocacy (court or tribunal appearances). The main areas of legal knowledge taught on the BPTC are: civil litigation and remedies, criminal litigation and sentencing, evidence, professional ethics, and two optional subjects selected from a choice of at least six.

Three examinations are set by a Central Examinations Board comprised of experienced legal practitioners and academics appointed by the Bar Standards Board (BSB). The examinations are Civil Litigation, Criminal Litigation and Ethics. Applicants will also have to take the Bar Course Aptitude Test. It aims to test critical thinking and reasoning, but does not test legal knowledge. Practise tests are available on the BSB website. The Aptitude Test will ensure that those undertaking the BPTC have the required skills to succeed.

Once the BPCT has been successfully completed candidates are 'Called to the Bar' by their Inn. The Pupillage Stage consists of one year spent in an authorized pupillage training organization. Pupillage is divided into two parts: the non-practising six months (also known as 'the first six') and the practising six months (also known as 'the second six').

To find out more about all three stages of qualification as a barrister visit www.barcouncil.org.uk

## SOLICITORS

### Qualification as a solicitor in England and Wales

To practise as a solicitor in England and Wales a person must have been admitted as a solicitor, his or her name having been entered on the Roll of Solicitors, and must hold a practising certificate issued by The Solicitors Regulation Authority (SRA) (Solicitors Regulation Authority, The Cube, 199 Wharfside Street, Birmingham B1 1RN; Tel: 0870 606 2555).

The SRA is the independent regulatory body of the Law Society of England and Wales. People will be admitted as solicitors only if they have passed the appropriate academic and vocational course and have completed a training contract and Professional Skills course, or have transferred from another jurisdiction or the Bar. The SRA controls the training of solicitors. Most solicitors become members of the Law Society, but membership is not compulsory. Intending solicitors other than Fellows of the Institute of Legal Executives and Justices' Clerk's Assistants, and qualified lawyers from other jurisdictions, are required to serve a period of training with a practising solicitor after they have completed the legal practice course.

All new entrants to the profession are required to complete a Criminal Records Bureau standard disclosure prior to admission. Candidates wishing to start training must enrol as a student with the SRA and satisfy it that they have successfully completed the academic stage of training and there are no issues that may call their character and suitability into question.

It is not necessary for the first degree to be in law as about 20 per cent of solicitors qualify via the non-law graduate route. The key stages of this are:

- degree in any subject;
- Common Professional Examination/Graduate Diploma in Law;
- Legal Practice course;
- practice-based training incorporating the Professional Skills course;
- admission to the roll of solicitors.

*THE COMMON PROFESSIONAL EXAMINATION (CPE) OR GRADUATE DIPLOMA IN LAW (GDL)*

The seven taught modules are the foundation subjects prescribed by the Joint Academic Stage Board on behalf of the Law Society and General Council of the Bar: Criminal Law, Contract Law, The Law of Tort, Equity and Trusts, Public Law, European Law and Land Law. For an up-to-date list of course providers for the CPE, see the SRA website: www.sra.org.uk/students/courses/trainingprovidersearch.page

*THE LEGAL PRACTICE COURSE*

Stage 1 covers core practice areas: Litigation, Property Law and Practice (PLP), Business Law and Practice (BLP); Course Skills: Research, Writing, Drafting, Interviewing and Advising, and Advocacy – these skills form an integral part of the compulsory and elective subjects; Solicitors Accounts and Professional Conduct and Regulation; Taxation, and Wills and Administration of Estates. Stage 2 covers three vocational electives: from a range of corporate client or private client topics (the range of elective available can differ from institution to institution). An up-to-date list of course providers for the LPC is available from the SRA website: www.sra.org.uk/students/courses/trainingprovidersearch.page

*TRAINING CONTRACT*

The training contract to be served by all intending solicitors, other than Fellows of the Institute of Legal Executives and Justices' Clerk's Assistants, is two years full time or a maximum of four years part time. The training contract can also be a part-time-study training contract that normally lasts between three and four years. During this period the trainee works and is studying the last two years of a part-time qualifying law degree, the part-time Common Professional Examination course and/or the part-time Legal Practice course.

The law graduate who holds a qualifying law degree must complete the Legal Practice course at a recognized institution, and then serve under the training contract for two years. The non-law graduate must first pass the Common Professional Exam (CPE) or the Postgraduate Diploma in Law, having attended either a one-year full-time or two-year part-time preparatory course. He or she may then serve under the training contract for two years after completion of a Legal Practice course. A Professional Skills course must be attended and successfully completed during the training contract.

Fellows of the Institute of Chartered Legal Executives may obtain partial or full exemptions from the CPE and Justices' Clerk's Assistants courses by virtue of similar subjects passed in their Fellowship exams or the Diploma in Magisterial Law. After passing or being exempted from the CPE, the Fellow/Justices' Clerk's Assistant may be exempt from serving under a training contract following successful completion of an LPC. A Professional Skills course must be taken prior to application for admission.

*THE PROFESSIONAL SKILLS COURSE*

The aim of the Professional Skills course is to build on the foundations laid in the LPC so as to develop a trainee's professional skills. Providers of the course, trainees and their employers are encouraged to regard the course as the first stage of a trainee's lifetime professional development.

Built upon the LPC, the course provides training in three subject areas: financial and business skills; advocacy and communication skills; client care and professional standards. Elective topics will also be chosen, which fall within one or more of these three core areas. All trainees have to complete all sections of the course satisfactorily before being admitted. The course consists of face-to-face instruction on the core subjects, for a minimum of 18 hours each for financial and business skills and advocacy and communication skills, and a minimum of 12 hours for client care and professional standards. The elective topics require a minimum total of 24 hours, of which a minimum of 12 hours must be face to face. The instruction must be completed during the training contract. The PSC is offered by accredited external course providers.

### QUALIFIED LAWYERS FROM OTHER JURISDICTIONS

UK and EU lawyers together with lawyers from certain foreign jurisdictions can apply for admission under the Qualified Lawyers Transfer Scheme Regulations 2011. They need to obtain a QLTS Certificate of Eligibility.

Under the European Communities Directive No 2005/36/EC, lawyers from EU jurisdictions may apply for admission if they can prove they have met the requirements of the Directive and implementing legislation. Any lawyer applying for admission under the Directive may be required to pass one or more QLTS Assessments. All international applicants must satisfy the requirements and pass all of the QLTS Assessments. The Assessments are in three parts. Part 1 is a multiple-choice test; Part 2 is a practical examination that will test interviewing and advocacy skills; Part 3 is a technical legal skills test that will test the skills of legal research, drafting and writing. The Solicitors Regulation Authority has appointed Kaplan QLTS as the sole assessment organization for the first three years of the operation of the assessments (www.kaplanqlts.com).

EEA, Northern Irish and Scottish lawyers, and barristers qualified in England and Wales will be individually assessed against the Day One Outcomes. All transferees are required to prove their character and suitability to be a solicitor by taking the SRA Suitability Test. Candidates who have passed the LPC can get exemption from the Part 1 (MCT) assessment.

Prospective candidates wanting more information on QLTS can consult the website www.sra.org.uk/solicitors/qlts/key-features.page for guidance, or contact the SRA on 0870 606 2555.

## SCOTLAND

The Court of Session, High Court of Justiciary, Sheriff Courts and Justice of the Peace Courts are administered by the Scottish Court service, an Executive Agency of the Scottish Government. For further information on Scottish Courts go to www.scotcourts.gov.uk

### The Legal Profession

The profession consists of solicitors and advocates.

#### Qualification as a Solicitor in Scotland

Solicitors in Scotland have their names inserted in a Roll of Solicitors and are granted annual Certificates entitling them to practise by The Law Society of Scotland (26 Drumsheugh Gardens, Edinburgh EH3 7YR; Tel: 0131 226 7411; Fax: 0131 225 2934; e-mail: lawscot@lawscot.org.uk; website: www.lawscot.org.uk). A Certificate is granted to candidates who have passed approved exams, completed a term of practical training and been admitted as solicitors. (The Law Society can provide copies of its Careers Information leaflet on request.)

*THE QUALIFYING EXAMINATIONS*

The standard route to qualification is the LLB (the Ordinary degree is a three-year course, the Honours is four years) followed by the Diploma in Professional Legal Practice (Professional Education and Training Stage 1: PEAT 1) and then the traineeship, the period of paid in-office training working towards the standard of the qualified solicitor (Professional Education and Training Stage 2: PEAT 2). Outcomes in 'professionalism, professional ethics and standards', 'professional communication' and 'business, commercial, financial and practice awareness' apply across both PEAT 1 and 2, linking them and providing real clarity across the two stages.

All trainees are required to undertake trainee Continuing Professional Development (CPD). All solicitors are required to undertake CPD for a minimum of 20 hours each year. To support solicitors in their CPD activities, the Society provides basic templates, which can be completed online, to assist with identifying training needs, recording CPD undertaken and evaluating the outcome of the training. A wide range of activities are acceptable as CPD, including structured and formalized one-to-one training, coaching and online training.

An alternate route to qualifying as a solicitor in Scotland is by a combination of the Law Society's own examinations and three years' pre-Diploma training. To be eligible to sit the Law Society's examinations, non-law graduates must find full-time employment as a pre-Diploma trainee with a qualified solicitor practising in Scotland. A pre-Diploma training contract lasts for three years. During the period of the training contract, a pre-Diploma trainee will study for the Law Society's examinations. European Law must be passed prior to admission as a solicitor, but can be obtained during post-Diploma training. The two routes to qualification (degree and Law Society exams) merge at this point as all intending solicitors are required to complete the Diploma in Professional Legal Practice. Upon successful completion of the Diploma the graduate will enter into a two-year post-Diploma training contract with a qualified solicitor practising in Scotland.

**Qualification as an advocate in Scotland**

Barristers in Scotland are called Advocates. Scottish Advocates are not only members of the Faculty of Advocates but also members of the College of Justice and officers of the Court. The procedure for the admission of 'Intrants' is subject in part to the control of the Court and in part to the control of the Faculty; the Court is responsible for most of the formal procedures and the Faculty for the exams and periods of professional training. To become an Intrant, applicants must produce evidence that they hold one of the following standard of degree: a degree with Honours, Second Class (Division 2) or above, in Scottish Law at a Scottish university, or a degree in Scottish Law at a Scottish university together with a degree with Honours, Second Class (Division 2) or above, in another subject at a UK university or an ordinary degree with distinction in Scottish Law at a Scottish university. A Diploma in Legal Practice from a Scottish University is also required, although in exceptional cases this requirement may be waived.

Once this evidence is provided and the relevant references obtained, a notice is posted outside Parliament House for a period of 21 days declaring the candidate's intention to present a Petition. At the end of this period the Petition is presented to the Court. After the Petition has been remitted by the Court to the Faculty and signed off by the Clerk of Faculty and Dean of Faculty the candidate is considered to have matriculated as an Intrant.

An Intrant must also comply with the professional training required by the Faculty, which consists of a period of 21 months' training in a solicitors' office (in some cases 12 months). Subject-for-subject exemptions are granted to Intrants who have passed exams at this standard in the course of a curriculum for a law degree at a Scottish university. Every Intrant must pass or be exempted from exams in nine compulsory subjects and two optional subjects. The compulsory subjects include Roman Law of Property and Obligations, Jurisprudence, Constitutional and Administrative Law, Scottish Criminal Law, Scottish Private Law, Commercial Law and Business Institutions, Evidence, International Private Law and European Law and Institutions. In addition, and prior to the commencement of pupillage (also known as 'devilling') every Intrant must sit the Faculty's entrant examination in Evidence, Practice and Procedure. If successfully passed, the Intrant can then commence his or her pupillage.

During the first five or six weeks of pupillage pupils undertake the Foundation course. After about three months of work with their 'devil master', the pupils will participate in the February Skills course, comprising a series of performance workshops involving the use of documents in evidence, the conduct of a procedure roll discussion, workshops on judicial review, section 275 applications and working with expert evidence. Shortly before admission, the pupils attend the May Preparation for Practice course, covering workshops on vulnerable witnesses, longer motions, reclaiming motions, negotiation and mediation, as well as carrying out civil and criminal appeals before a serving judge.

Intrants who have passed all the necessary exams and undergone the necessary professional training as well as successfully completing their pupillage may apply to be admitted to membership of the Faculty and are admitted at a public meeting of the Faculty. Once admitted, Intrants are introduced to the Court by the Dean of Faculty, make a Declaration of Allegiance to the Sovereign in open Court and are then admitted by the Court to the public office of Advocate. For further information on becoming an advocate contact Dean's Secretariat, Faculty of Advocates, Parliament House, Edinburgh EH1 1RF; Tel: 0131 260 5795; e-mail: admissions@advocates.org.uk; website: www.advocates.org.uk

## NORTHERN IRELAND

As in England and Wales, the superior courts are the Court of Appeal, the High Court and the Crown Court. The latter is an exclusively criminal court. The Court of Appeal hears appeals in civil cases from the High Court and in criminal cases from the Crown Court, and cases stated on a point of law from, inter alia, the County Court and the Magistrates' Courts. Appeals lie from the Court of Appeal to the House of Lords.

*Inferior Courts*: as in England and Wales, the county courts are principally civil courts, but in Northern Ireland they also hear appeals from conviction in the Magistrates' Courts for summary offences.

*Magistrates' Courts*: these deal principally with minor criminal offences (summary offences) and are presided over by Resident Magistrates (stipendiaries). Resident Magistrates are appointed by the Crown on the advice of the Lord Chancellor.

*Coroners*: coroners in Northern Ireland must be barristers or solicitors who have practised for not less than five years. They are appointed by the Lord Chancellor.

### The legal profession

The legal profession in Northern Ireland consists of barristers and solicitors belonging to professional bodies organized on similar lines to those in England and Wales.

#### Qualification as a barrister in Northern Ireland

To qualify to practise as a barrister in Northern Ireland a candidate must be admitted to the degree of Barrister-at-Law by the Honourable Society of the Inn of Court of Northern Ireland (enquiries to Under Treasurer, Bar Council Office, The Bar Library, 91 Chichester Street, Belfast BT1 3JQ; e-mail: contact@barlibrary.com; website: www.barlibrary.com). A candidate must have a recognized law degree of 2.1 honours standard or higher, or equivalent (the list of recognized law degrees can be found at www.qub.ac.uk/schools/InstituteofProfessionalLegalStudies/FileStore/).

To be called to the Bar of Northern Ireland the candidate needs to have obtained his or her Certificate of Professional Legal Studies or otherwise be qualified, to have completed and signed a Memorial and Undertaking, and to have submitted two certificates of good character.

#### Qualification as a solicitor in Northern Ireland

The solicitors' professional body in Northern Ireland is the Law Society of Northern Ireland (Law Society House, 96 Victoria Street, Belfast BT1 3GN; Tel: 028 9023 1614; website: www.lawsoc-ni.org). It has overall responsibility for education and admission to the profession.

Admission to training is generally dependent upon possession of a recognized law degree from a university. Details of the recognized law degrees are available on the website of the Institute of Professional Legal Studies (www.qub.ac.uk/schools/InstituteofProfessionalLegalStudies/Admissions/RecognisedLawDegrees/). Details are also available on the Graduate School website (see 'Information Booklet for Applicants', www.socsci.ulster.ac.uk/gsple/info_-booklet.pdf). Law graduates must attend a two-year vocational apprenticeship course at the Institute of Professional Legal Studies, The Queen's University of Belfast, or the Graduate School of Professional Legal Education at the University of Ulster's Magee Campus. On completion of the two-year apprenticeship newly qualified solicitors receive restricted practising certificates, which means that although they are fully qualified they cannot practise on their own account or in partnership for at least two more years.

Non-law graduates must satisfy the Society that they possess an acceptable degree in a discipline other than law and have attained a satisfactory level of knowledge of the following subjects: Constitutional Law, Law of Tort, Law of Contract, Criminal Law, Equity, European Law, Land Law, Law of Evidence; that they have been offered a place in the Institute; and that they have obtained a Master (a solicitor with whom the applicant proposes to serve his or her apprenticeship). It is also possible to be accepted as a student of the Law Society if the applicant is 29 years or older and can demonstrate the required experience, knowledge or relevant qualifications (see the Law Society of Northern Ireland, website: www.lawsoc-ni.org/joining-the-legal-profession).

## Membership of Professional Institutions and Associations

### COUNCIL FOR LICENSED CONVEYANCERS

16 Glebe Road
Chelmsford
Essex CM1 1QG
Tel: 01245 349599
Fax: 01245 341300
E-mail: clc@clc-uk.org
Website: www.clc-uk.org

---

The CLC was established under the provisions of the Administration of Justice Act 1985 as the Regulatory Body for Licensed Conveyancers. Our purpose is to set entry standards and regulate the profession of Licensed Conveyancers effectively. CLC regulates Probate services provided by its licensed practitioners. CLC is an authorised regulator for ABS.

*MEMBERSHIP*
Student
Licensed Conveyancer
Probate Practitioner
ABS

*QUALIFICATION/EXAMINATIONS*
Foundation
Finals
Practical Training

### THE LAW SOCIETY OF SCOTLAND

26 Drumsheugh Gardens
Edinburgh EH3 7YR
Tel: 0131 226 7411
Fax: 0131 225 2934
E-mail: lawscot@lawscot.org.uk
Website: www.lawscot.org.uk

---

The Law Society of Scotland is the membership organization of Scottish solicitors. We promote the interests of the profession and of the public in relation to the profession. Our services include providing initial career advice, overseeing legal education in Scotland, handling admissions to the profession, monitoring trainees, providing post-qualifying legal education, and administering courses and examinations for the Society of Law Accountants in Scotland.

*MEMBERSHIP*
All practising solicitors in Scotland must be members of the Society and must hold a current Practising Certificate which is issued by the Society.

*QUALIFICATION/EXAMINATIONS*
Please see the Law Society of Scotland's website.

## CHARTERED INSTITUTE OF LEGAL EXECUTIVES

Kempston Manor
Kempston
Bedford MK42 7AB
Tel: 01234 841000
E-mail: membership@cilex.org.uk
Website: www.cilex.org.uk

ILEX, founded in 1892, is a professional body representing around 22, 000 practising and trainee legal executives (qualified lawyers who specialize in a particular area of law). Our objectives are to provide for the education, training and development of our Fellows, to advance and protect their interests, and to promote cooperation among everyone engaged in legal work.

*MEMBERSHIP*
Student Member
Affiliate Member
Associate Member (ACILEx)
Graduate Member (GCILEx)
Chartered Legal Executive Lawyer (FCILEx)

*QUALIFICATION/EXAMINATIONS*
Level 2 Award/Certificate/Diploma in Legal Studies
Level 2 Certificate/Diploma for Legal Secretaries
Level 3 Certificate/Diploma for Legal Secretaries
Level 3 Certificate in Law and Legal Practice
Level 3 Professional Diploma in Law and Practice
Level 3 Certificate in Law and Practice
Level 3 Professional Diploma in Law and Practice
Level 6 Certificate in Law
Level 6 Professional Higher Diploma in Law and Practice
Graduate Fast Track Diploma (Level 6)

*DESIGNATORY LETTERS*
ACILEx, GCILEx, FCILEx

## THE ACADEMY OF EXPERTS

3 Gray's Inn Square
Gray's Inn
London WC1R 5AH
Tel: 020 7430 0333
E-mail: admin@academy-experts.org
Website: www.academy-experts.org

The Academy of Experts is a multidisciplinary body established in 1987 to establish and promote high objective standards for those acting as expert witnesses. We act as an accrediting and professional body, offering training, technical guidance and representation. In addition we promote cost-efficient dispute resolution, maintaining a register of qualified dispute resolvers.

*MEMBERSHIP*
Associate Member
Associate Member (AMAE)
Full Member (MAE)
Fellow (FAE)
Practising Corporate Member
Dispute Resolver Member

*QUALIFICATION/EXAMINATIONS*
There are examinations for upgrade.

*DESIGNATORY LETTERS*
AMAE, MAE, FAE, QDR

## THE INSTITUTE OF LEGAL FINANCE AND MANAGEMENT (ILFM)

2nd Floor
Marlowe House
109 Station Road
Sidcup
Kent DA15 7ET
Tel: 020 8302 2867
Fax: 020 8302 7481
E-mail: exec.sec@ilca.org.uk
Website: www.ilca.org.uk

The ILCA, which was founded in 1978, is a non-profit-making professional body dedicated to the education and support of specialist financial and administrative personnel working within the legal community. We encourage the development of our members' skills through educational courses, training workshops, seminars, conferences and our bimonthly magazine, *Legal Abacus*.

*MEMBERSHIP*
Ordinary Member
Diploma Member (ILFM (Dip))
Associate Member (AILFM)
Fellow Member (FILFM)
Affiliated Professional Member

*QUALIFICATION/EXAMINATIONS*
Diploma
Associateship examination

*DESIGNATORY LETTERS*
ILCA (Dip), AILCA, FILCA

# LEISURE AND RECREATION MANAGEMENT

***Membership of Professional Institutions and Associations***

## CHARTERED INSTITUTE FOR THE MANAGEMENT OF SPORT AND PHYSICAL ACTIVITY (CIMSPA)

Sportpark Loughborough University
3 Oakwood Drive
Loughborough
Leicestershire LE11 3QF
Tel: 01509 226474
Fax: 01509 226475
E-mail: info@cimspa.co.uk
Website: www.ispal.org.uk

ISPAL is the membership body for sport, parks and leisure industry professionals. We promote high standards and provide CPD as well as a wide range of training courses to our members in-house and at venues across the UK. We also work hard to influence government policy on behalf of our members.

*MEMBERSHIP*
Student Member
Affiliate Member
Associate Member
Member
Fellow
Companion
Chartered Member
Chartered Fellow
Retired Member

*QUALIFICATION/EXAMINATIONS*
National Pool Plant Operators Certificate
National Pool Plant Foundation Certificate

National Spa Pool Operators Certificate
Supervisory Management Certificate
Fitness Management Certificate
Health and Safety Management Certificate
Higher Professional Diploma in Sport and Recreation Management
Online Continuing Professional Development (CPD) (Entrance and Supervisory Level)
Online Continuing Professional Development (CPD) (Management Level)
Certificate in Leisure Operations (QCF) (1st4sport Level 2)
NVQ Award in Mechanical Ride Operation (QCF) (1st4sport Level 2)
NVQ Certificate in Active Leisure, Learning and Well-being Operational Services (QCF) (1st4sport Level 2)
Certificate in Leisure Management (QCF) (1st4sport Level 3)
NVQ Diploma in Leisure Management (QCF) (1st4sport Level 3)
NVQ Diploma in Sports Development (QCF) (1st4sport Level 3)
Award in Introductory Work in the Outdoors (QCF) (1st4sport Level 2)
NVQ Diploma in Outdoor Programmes (QCF) (1st4sport Level 3)
Award in Coordinating Sports Volunteers (QCF) (1st4sport Level 3)
Certificate in Managing Sports Volunteers (QCF) (1st4sport Level 3)

*DESIGNATORY LETTERS*
NPPO, RoPPPS, CPD, QCF

## INSTITUTE OF GROUNDSMANSHIP

28 Stratford Office Village
Walker Avenue
Wolverton Mill East
Milton Keynes MK12 5TW
Tel: 01908 312511
Fax: 01908 311140
E-mail: iog@iog.org
Website: www.iog.org

The Institute of Groundsmanship is the only membership organization supporting the whole of the grounds care industry. Serving the industry for 75 years, we provide a range of quality products, services and events including education, training and membership services, exhibitions, local information days, an annual conference and awards programme.

*MEMBERSHIP*
Student Member
Associate Member
E-Member
Individual Member
Corporate Member

*QUALIFICATION/EXAMINATIONS*
For details see: www.iog.org/training-training-courses.asp

# LIBRARIANSHIP AND INFORMATION WORK

## *Membership of Professional Institutions and Associations*

### CHARTERED INSTITUTE OF LIBRARY AND INFORMATION PROFESSIONALS

7 Ridgmount Street
London WC1E 7AE
Tel: 020 7255 0500
Fax: 020 7255 0501
E-mail: info@cilip.org.uk
Website: www.cilip.org.uk

CILIP is the professional body representing those working within libraries and the information profession in the UK.

*MEMBERSHIP*
Certified Affiliate (ACLIP)
Chartered Member (MCLIP)
Chartered Fellow (FCLIP)
Revalidated Chartered Member or Fellow
Student Membership

*QUALIFICATION/EXAMINATIONS*
Application for membership qualifications is through the submission of a portfolio of evidence meeting published criteria. Please contact the Institute for further information.

*DESIGNATORY LETTERS*
ACLIP, MCLIP, FCLIP

# MANAGEMENT

## *Membership of Professional Institutions and Associations*

### ASSOCIATION FOR PROJECT MANAGEMENT

Ibis House
Regent Park
Summerleys Road
Princes Risborough
Buckinghamshire HP27 9LE
Tel: 0845 458 1944
E-mail: via website
Website: www.apm.org.uk

The association is a registered charity with over 19, 500 individual and 500 corporate members making it the largest professional body of its kind in Europe. APM's mission statement is 'to develop and promote the professional disciplines of project and programme management for the public benefit'.

*MEMBERSHIP*
Student Member
Associate Member
Full Member (MAPM)
Fellow (FAPM)
Corporate Member
Honorary member/ Fellow (HonFAPM)

*QUALIFICATION/EXAMINATIONS*
Introductory Certificate in Project Management (IC)
APMP
APMP for PRINCE2 Practitioners
Practitioner Qualification (PQ)
Risk level 1
Risk level 2
Pan sector standard:
Registered Project Professional (RPP)

Higher Apprenticeship:
Higher Apprenticeship in Project Management

*DESIGNATORY LETTERS*
MAPM, FAPM, HonFAPM, RPP

## ASSOCIATION OF CERTIFIED COMMERCIAL DIPLOMATS (ACCD)

Commercial Diplomats Regulation Authority
ACCD Global Headquarters
Central Administration Office
PO Box 50561, Canary Wharf,
London E16 3WY
Tel: +44(0)8445 864249
Fax: +44(0)8445 864252
E-mail: enquiries@commercialdiplomats.eu or enquiries@chartereddiplomats.org.uk
Website: www.commercialdiplomats.org.uk

Association of Certified Commercial Diplomats is the first independent regulation authority, and global professional awarding body for commercial diplomats. The umbrella of ACCD covers ambassadors, representatives of government, trade commissioners, advisors and negotiators, arbitrators, negotiators of IIAs, policy-makers & government officials involved in trade, commercial and or investment issues, commercial counsellors, IIA experts, academia, private sector & NGO representatives, officials in government ministries, parastatals, corporations, academic, public and private institutions worldwide. Its principal objectives are to provide accreditation and regulation, and to advance the interests of its members as qualified, certified and competent commercial diplomats. As the global voice, ACCD has overall responsibility, including the setting of policy and guidelines, as well as the qualification and accreditation procedures for the commercial diplomatic profession. ACCD is non-partisan, not-for-profit, independent of government, and uniquely the professional regulatory body for commercial diplomats, and institutions of higher learning providing advanced postgraduate, doctoral, and postdoctoral programmes on commercial diplomacy.

*MEMBERSHIP*
AFFILIATED PROFESSIONAL MEMBERSHIP:
Affiliated Professional Associate
Associate
REGULATED FULL MEMBERSHIP:
Member
Fellow

*QUALIFICATION/EXAMINATIONS*
ACCD REGULATED QUALIFICATIONS/EXAMINATIONS/ACCREDITATIONS
Advanced Certificate of Competency
ACCD REGULATED ACADEMIC QUALIFICATIONS
Master of Commercial Diplomacy
Doctor of Commercial Diplomacy
ACCD REGULATED ACCREDITATIONS:
Qualified Policy Advocate (QA)
Qualified Certified Diplomat (QCD)
Chartered Diplomat (C. Dipl)

*DESIGNATORY LETTERS*
ACDipl, MCD, MCDipl, DCD, DCDipl, FCDipl, QA, QCD, C. Dipl

## AUA

AUA National Office
University of Manchester
Sackville Street Building
Manchester M60 1QD
Tel: 0161 275 2063
Fax: 0161 275 2036
E-mail: aua@aua.ac.uk
Website: www.aua.ac.uk

As a member-led organization with over 3, 500 members, AUA promotes best practice in higher education management and exists to advance and promote professional recognition and development of those who work in higher and further education by encouraging and fostering sound methods of leadership, management and administration, through a range of professional development initiatives.

AUA members are individually and collectively committed to:

- the continuous development of their own and others' professional knowledge, skills and practices;
- actively championing equality of educational and professional opportunity;
- the advancement of higher education through the robust application of professional knowledge, skills and practices;
- the highest standards of fair, ethical and transparent professional behaviours.

AUA is at the forefront of professional development in higher education and has developed a sector-wide framework to support the development of professional services colleagues. Through continuing professional development, individuals, teams and institutions can foster skills and behaviours associated with the profession. AUA also holds the largest professional development annual conference in the UK higher education calendar.

*MEMBERSHIP*
Member (MAUA)
Accredited Member (AAUA)
Fellow (FAUA)
Honorary Member (FAUA)
Student Member (MAUA)

*QUALIFICATION/EXAMINATIONS*
Postgraduate Certificate in Professional Practice (PG Cert)
This programme is validated by The Open University and credits from the course can be used on a number of MA courses.

BIFM
ADVANCING OUR PROFESSION

## BRITISH INSTITUTE OF FACILITIES MANAGEMENT

Number One Building
The Causeway
Bishop's Stortford
Hertfordshire CM23 2ER
Tel: 01279 712651
Fax: 01279 712669
E-mail: qualifications@bifm.org.uk
Website: www.bifm.org.uk

The BIFM is the professional body for facilities management (FM) in the UK. Founded in 1993, the Institute provides information, education, training and networking services for over 13, 000 members – both individual professionals and organizations. The BIFM's mission is to advance the profession – to consolidate FM as a vital management discipline.

*MEMBERSHIP*
Affiliate
Associate (ABIFM)
Member (MBIFM)
Certified Member (CBIFM)
Fellow (FBIFM)
Corporate Member

*QUALIFICATION/EXAMINATIONS*
BIFM Level 2 Certificate in Facilities Services
BIFM Level 2 Certificate in Facilities Services Principles
BIFM Level 3 Award in Facilities Management
BIFM Level 3 Certificate in Facilities Management
BIFM Level 3 Certificate in Facilities Management Practice
BIFM Level 3 Diploma in Facilities Management
BIFM Level 4 Award in Facilities Management
BIFM Level 4 Certificate in Facilities Management
BIFM Level 4 Diploma in Facilities Management
BIFM Level 5 Award in Facilities Management
BIFM Level 5 Certificate in Facilities Management
BIFM Level 5 Diploma in Facilities Management
BIFM Level 6 Award in Facilities Management
BIFM Level 6 Certificate in Facilities Management
BIFM Level 6 Diploma in Facilities Management
BIFM Level 7 Certificate in Facilities Management
BIFM Level 7 Diploma in Facilities Management

*DESIGNATORY LETTERS*
ABIFM, MBIFM, CBIFM, FBIFM

## BUSINESS MANAGEMENT ASSOCIATION

1 High Oak House
Collett Road
Ware
Hertfordshire SG12 7LY
Tel: 0871 231 1689
E-mail: enquiries@businessmanagement.org.uk
Website: www.businessmanagement.org.uk

The Business Management Association is a professional body for business owners and managers. We promote the aims and interests of the small business sector internationally, provide information and advice to our members, encourage networking between members, and seek to provide members with advanced knowledge, skill and qualifications in several aspects of management.

*MEMBERSHIP*
Affiliate (AffBMA)
Associate (ABMA)
Member (MBMA)
Fellow (FBMA)
Companion (CBMA)
Certified Manager (CertMgr)
Certified Master of Management (CMMgt)
Certified Master of Business Administration (CMBA)
Certified Doctor of Business Administration (CDBA)

*QUALIFICATION/EXAMINATIONS*
Entrepreneurs Award (EA)
Diploma In Business Management (DipBMA)

*DESIGNATORY LETTERS*
AffBMA, ABMA, MBMA, FBMA, CBMA, CertMgr, CMMgt, CMBA, CDBA, MCBMA, FCBMA

## DIPLOMATIC ACADEMY OF EUROPE AND THE ATLANTIC

A Global Force for Regional Prosperity
ACCD Global Headquarters
PO Box 50561, Canary Wharf
Greater London E16 3WY
Tel: 08445 857027
Fax: 08445 857077
E-mail: enquiries@eatcd.org
Website: www.eatcd.org

---

Diplomatic Academy of Europe is an authoritative knowledge-based professional diplomatic institution whose activities include advanced research and development, provision of postgraduate and post-qualification education, and contribution to responsible commercial diplomatic practice. A key independent extraterritorial diplomatic organization established for the advancement and development of greater knowledge and skills in commercial diplomacy. The Academy offers complete portfolio of specialized mandatory post-graduate programme on commercial diplomatic practice.

*MEMBERSHIP*
Fellow of the Diplomatic Academy (FDAe)

*QUALIFICATION/EXAMINATIONS*
EXAMINATIONS:
Master of Commercial Diplomacy
Doctor of Commercial Diplomacy
Fellowship of the Diplomatic Academy
Qualified Certified Diplomat (QCD)
PostQualification Fellowship

*DESIGNATORY LETTERS*
MCD, DCD, FDAe

## FACULTY OF PROFESSIONAL BUSINESS AND TECHNICAL MANAGEMENT

Head Office
Warwick Corner
42 Warwick Road
Kenilworth
Warwickshire CV8 1HE
Tel: 01926 259342
E-mail: info@pbtm.org.uk
Website: www.pbtm.org.uk

---

FPBTM was founded in 1983 to forge the link between business and technology. We give professional recognition to the knowledge and skills of managers in business and technology, supporting lifelong learning to help members fulfil their career ambitions and develop their potential.

*MEMBERSHIP*
Student Member (SFPBTM)
Technician Member (TMFPBTM)
Associate Member (AMFPBTM)
Member (MFPBTM)
Fellow (FFPBTM)
Companion (CFPBTM)

## INSTITUTE OF ADMINISTRATIVE MANAGEMENT

6 Graphite Square
Vauxhall Walk
London SE11 5EE
Tel: 020 7091 2600
E-mail: info@instam.org
Website: www.instam.org

The IAM is the leading professional body and UK government-recognized awarding body for those involved in the administration and management of business. We offer a range of qualifications, from an introduction to the subject up to a full BA Hons degree.

*MEMBERSHIP*
Technician (TInstAM)
Associate (AInstAM)
Member (MInstAM)
Fellow (FInstAM)
IAM Student
Non-IAM Student
Graduate
Tutor
Companion

*QUALIFICATION/EXAMINATIONS*
Level 2 Certificate in Principles of Business & Administration (QCF)
Level 2 NVQ Certificate in Business & Administration (QCF)
Level 3 Certificate in Principles of Business & Administration (QCF)
Level 3 NVQ Certificate in Business & Administration (QCF)
Level 3 Certificate in Administration Management (NQF)
Level 4 Certificate in Business & Administration Management (QCF)
Level 4 Diploma in Business & Administration (QCF)
Level 4 Diploma in Business & Administrative Management (QCF)
Level 4 NVQ Diploma in Business & Administration (QCF)
Level 4 Award in Administration for Executive Facilities (QCF)
Level 4 Award in Managing Business Facilities (QCF)
Level 4 Certificate in Business Events Management (QCF)
Level 5 Certificate in Business & Administration Management (QCF)
Level 5 Certificate in Governance, Leadership & Motivation Management (QCF)
Level 5 Diploma in Business & Administrative Management (QCF)
Level 5 Diploma in Leadership & Management (QCF)
Level 5 Award in Organisational Facilities Management (QCF)
Level 5 Certificate in Managing Change (QCF)
Level 6 Diploma in Business & Administrative Management (QCF)
Level 6 Diploma in Business Management (QCF)
Level 6 Extended Diploma in Business & Administrative Management (QCF)
Level 6 Certificate in Strategic Management (QCF)
Level 6 Certificate in Advanced Finance for Decision-Makers (QCF)
Level 6 Certificate in Leadership Skills (QCF)
Level 6 Certificate in Managing Risk in Business (QCF)

*DESIGNATORY LETTERS*
AInstAM, MInstAM, FInstAM

## INSTITUTE OF CONSULTING

4th Floor
2 Savoy Court
Strand
London WC2R 0EZ
Tel: 020 7497 0580
Fax: 020 7497 0463
E-mail: welcome@ibconsulting.org.uk
Website: www.iconsulting.org.uk

The Institute of Consulting was formed in 2007 by the merger of the Institute of Business Advisers and the Institute of Management Consultancy, and we are the professional body for business consultants and advisers. Our aim is to raise the standards of professional practice in support of better business performance.

*MEMBERSHIP*
Student
Affiliate
Associate (AIBC)
Member (MIBC)
Fellow (FIBC)
Certified Business Advisor (CBA)
Certified Management Consultant (CMC)
Practice Member (corporate membership)

*QUALIFICATION/EXAMINATIONS*
Award in Professional Consulting (Level 5) (QCF)
Certificate in Professional Consulting (Level 5) (QCF)
Diploma in Professional Consulting (Level 5) (QCF)
Award in Business Support (Level 5) (QCF)
Certificate in Business Support (Level 5) (QCF)
Diploma in Business Support (Level 5) (QCF)
Award in Professional Consulting (Level 7) (QCF)
Certificate in Professional Consulting (Level 7) (QCF)
Diploma in Professional Consulting (Level 7) (QCF)
Certified Management Consultant Award (CMC)
Certified Business Advisor Award (CBA)

*DESIGNATORY LETTERS*
AIBC, MIBC, FIBC

## INSTITUTE OF DIRECTORS

116 Pall Mall
London SW1Y 5ED
Tel: 020 7766 2601
E-mail: professionaldev@iod.com
Website: www.iod.com/development

The IoD represents professional leaders, with individual members ranging from entrepreneurs of start-up companies to CEOs of multinational organizations. The Institute's principal objectives are to advance the interests of its members as company directors, and to provide them with business facilities and a variety of services.

*MEMBERSHIP*
Student
Associate Member
Member (MIoD)
Fellow (FIoD)
Chartered Director (C Dir)

*QUALIFICATION/EXAMINATIONS*
Certificate in Company Direction (CertIoD)
Diploma in Company Direction (DipIoD)
Chartered Director (C Dir)

*DESIGNATORY LETTERS*
MIoD, FIoD, C Dir

## INSTITUTE OF LEADERSHIP & MANAGEMENT

Stowe House
Netherstowe
Lichfield
Staffordshire WS13 6TJ
Tel: 01543 266867
Fax: 01543 266893
E-mail: customer@i-l-m.com
Website: www.i-l-m.com

---

The ILM supports, develops and informs leaders and managers at every stage of their career. With our broad range of industry-leading qualifications, membership services and learning resources, the ILM provides flexible development solutions that can be blended to meet the specific needs of employers and learners.

*MEMBERSHIP*
Studying Member
Professional Member

*QUALIFICATION/EXAMINATIONS*
Management
Principles of Team Leading including Foundation Award in Management Practice (Level 2)
Award, Certificate in Effective Team Member Skills (Level 2)
Award, Certificate in Leadership and Team Skills (Level 2)
NVQ Certificate in Team Leading (Level 2)
Certificate in Team Leading (Level 2)
NVQ Certificate in Management (Level 3)
Certificate in Effective Management (Level 3)
Certificate in Principles of Leadership and Management (Level 3)
Award, Certificate and Diploma in Leadership and Management (Level 4)
Diploma in Principles of Leadership and Management (Level 5)
NVQ Diploma in Management (Level 5)
Award in Management (Level 6)
NVQ Diploma in Management (Level 7)
Diploma in Strategic Leadership and Executive Management (Level 7)
Award, Certificate and Diploma in Executive Management (Level 7)
Leadership
Certificate in Leadership (Level 3)
Award in Leadership (Level 4)
Award, Certificate and Diploma in Strategic Leadership (Level 7)
Leadership and management
Award, Certificate and Diploma in Leadership and Management (Level 3)
Award, Certificate and Diploma in Leadership and Management (Level 5)
Coaching and mentoring
Certificate in Coaching and Mentoring (Level 3)
Certificate and Diploma in Coaching and Mentoring (Level 5)
Certificate and Diploma in Coaching Supervision (Level 7)
Certificate and Diploma in Executive Coaching and Leadership Mentoring (Level 7)
Specialist management qualifications
Environmental Management
Facilities Management
Equality and Diversity
Managing Volunteers
Sales Management
Waste Management
Business and Enterprise
Certificate in Enterprise (Level 2)
Award and Certificate in Enterprise and Entrepreneurship (Level 3)
Award in Management (Level 5)
Certificate and Diploma in Social Enterprise Support (Level 5)

**Specialist Management Qualifications**
Operational management
Service improvement
Waste management
Equality and diversity
Volunteer management
Management consultancy
Staff and organisational development
Quality improvement

**Scottish Vocational Qualifications (SVQs)**
SVQ 2 in Team Leading (Scottish Level 5)
SVQ 3 in Management (Scottish Level 7)
SVQ 4 in Management (Scottish Level 9)
SVQ 5 in Management (Scottish Level 11)

## INSTITUTE OF MANAGEMENT SERVICES

Brooke House
Lichfield
Staffordshire WS13 6AA
Tel: 01543 266909
Fax: 01543 257848
E-mail: via website
Website: www.ims-productivity.com

The IMS is the primary body in the UK concerned with the promotion, practice and development of methods and techniques for the improvement of productivity and quality. We act as the qualifying body for the management services profession in the UK, focusing developments in practice and knowledge and acting as a forum for information exchange.

*MEMBERSHIP*
Affiliate
Associate (AMS)
Member (MMS)
Fellow (FMS)

*QUALIFICATION/EXAMINATIONS*
Management Services Certificate
Management Services Diploma

*DESIGNATORY LETTERS*
AMS, MMS, FMS

## INSTITUTE OF VALUE MANAGEMENT

PO Box 101
Ledbury
Herefordshire HR8 9JW
Tel: 01531 63144
E-mail: secretary@ivm.org.uk
Website: www.ivm.org.uk

The Institute aims to establish Value Management as a process for achieving value in every sector of the economy and to provide support in the innovative use of value management techniques.

*MEMBERSHIP*
Corporate Membership: Open to any company or organization practising or promoting value techniques. Each corporate member may nominate up to 10 members of their organization as representatives to the Institute. A member nominated by a corporate body can hold executive office and has full voting rights.
Ordinary Membership: Open to any professional person who has an interest in and can demonstrate an involvement in practising value techniques.
Student Membership: Open to students who have an interest in value management and who are registered FT students possessing a valid student card.
Fellow: Awarded to a member as a special honour for outstanding contribution to the field of value management.

*QUALIFICATION/EXAMINATIONS*
Certificate and Training: The Institute has worked closely with the Commission of the European Communities to establish a European Training System and Certification Procedure.
Roll of Practitioners: The Institute maintains an authorized list of value practitioners who are members of the Institute.
It launched its European Training and Certification System in 1998. This European Commission funded initiative offers, through the IVM's Certification Board, certification in the following categories: Certificated Value Analyst (CVA); Professional in Value Management (PVM); Certificated Value Manager (CVM); Trainer in Value Management (TVM). The Certification Board also approves basic and advanced courses in value management that have been designed by trainers in value management. The Institute provides a list of trainers.

## INTERNATIONAL PROFESSIONAL MANAGERS ASSOCIATION

5 Starnes Court
Union Street
Maidstone
Kent ME14 1EB
Tel: 01622 672867
Fax: 01622 755149
E-mail: admin@ipma.co.uk
Website: www.ipma.co.uk

The IPMA is an international examining, licensing and regulatory professional body, which, through its qualifying examinations, enables practising managers to participate in and be part of the process of improving managerial performance and effectiveness in all areas of business, industry and public administration.

*MEMBERSHIP*
Student member
Graduate Member (GRD PMA)
Licentiate Member (LMPMA)
Certified Associate (AMPMA)
Certified Member (MPMA)
Certified Fellow (FPMA)

*QUALIFICATION/EXAMINATIONS*
Certified International Professional Manager (CIPM) examinations

*DESIGNATORY LETTERS*
GRD PMA, LMPMA, AMPMA, MPMA, FPMA, CIPM

## THE ASSOCIATION OF BUSINESS EXECUTIVES

5th Floor, CI Tower
St Georges Square
New Malden
Surrey KT3 4TE
Tel: 020 8329 2930
Fax: 020 8329 2945
E-mail: info@abeuk.com
Website: www.abeuk.com

ABE is a professional membership body and examination board. We develop business and management qualifications at Levels 4, 5, 6 & 7 on the QCF framework. ABE's range of OFQUAL accredited qualifications provide progression routes to degree and Master's programmes worldwide.

*MEMBERSHIP*
Affiliate Member
Student Member
Associate Member (AMABE)
Member (MABE)
Fellow (FABE)

*QUALIFICATION/EXAMINATIONS*
Diploma Levels 4, 5 and 6 in:
Business Management
Management of Information Systems (Pathway)
Financial Management (Pathway)
Human Resource Management
Marketing Management
Travel, Tourism and Hospitality Management
Diploma in Business Development (Level 7)
Diploma in Business Start-Up and Entrepreneurship (Level 4)

*DESIGNATORY LETTERS*
AMABE, MABE, FABE

## THE CAMBRIDGE ACADEMY OF MANAGEMENT

Royal Arsenal Gatehouse
Beresford Square
Woolwich
London SE18 6AR
Tel: 0844 284 7190
E-mail: admin@camuk.org
Website: www.camuk.org.uk

The Cambridge Academy of Management (CAM) is a professional, autonomous, not-for-profit institution established to foster the concept of UK management education made available to all internationally. CAM is built on the foundation of promoting state-of-the-art knowledge and expertise in all facets of management education, training and development for the global educational arena.

*MEMBERSHIP*
Associate Category (ACAM)
Member Category (MCAM)
Fellowship Category (FCAM)

*QUALIFICATION/EXAMINATIONS*
All programmes offered by Cambridge Academy of Management are accredited by Quality Assurance Commission UK. Programmes offered:
CAM International Foundation Diploma
CAM International Certificate in Restaurant & Catering Management
CAM International Diploma in Business Management
CAM International Diploma in Business (Restaurant & Catering Management)
CAM International Diploma in Business (Tourism Management)
CAM International Advanced Diploma in Business Management
CAM International Advanced Diploma in Business (Restaurant & Catering Management)
CAM International Advanced Diploma in Business (Tourism Management)
CAM International Postgraduate Diploma in Hospitality Management
CAM International Postgraduate Diploma in Business
CAM International Postgraduate Diploma in Business with Specialization in: Marketing, Finance, Human Resource

## THE CHARTERED MANAGEMENT INSTITUTE

Membership Department
Management House
Cottingham Road
Corby
Northants NN17 1TT
Tel: 01536 204222
Fax: 01536 201651
E-mail: enquiries@managers.org.uk
Website: www.managers.org.uk

The CMI is the only chartered professional body dedicated to managers and leaders, and to the organizations they work in. As founders of the National Occupational Standards for Management and Leadership excellence, we set the standards that others follow. As a membership organization we give our members the tools they need to make a genuine impact on business in the UK.

*MEMBERSHIP*
Associate (ACMI)
Member (MCMI)
Fellow (FCMI)
Affiliate Chartered Member (CMgr/MCMI)
Chartered Fellow (Mgr/FCMI)

*DESIGNATORY LETTERS*
ACMI, MCMI, FCMI, CMgr

## THE INSTITUTE OF COMMERCIAL MANAGEMENT

ICM House
Castleman Way
Ringwood
Hampshire BH24 3BA
Tel: 01202 490555
Fax: 01202 490666
E-mail: info@icm.ac.uk
Website: www.icm.ac.uk

The Institute is the leading professional body for Commercial and Business Development Managers. It is regulated by Ofqual, the Regulator of UK Qualifications. ICM provides examining and assessment services for those undertaking business and management studies and offers in excess of 200 programmes. It is authorized to offer awards from HNDs to doctorates and works with public and private sector education and training providers in more than 100 countries.

*MEMBERSHIP*
Student Membership

*QUALIFICATION/EXAMINATIONS*
ICM Awards cover the following areas: Accounting & Finance; Business Studies; Commercial Management; Hospitality Management; Human Resource Development; Journalism; Legal Studies; Management Studies; Maritime Management; Marketing Management; Sales Management; Travel & Tourism.

## THE INSTITUTE OF MANAGEMENT SPECIALISTS

Head Office
Warwick Corner
42 Warwick Road
Kenilworth
Warwickshire CV8 1HE
Tel: 01926 259342
E-mail: info@instituteofmanagementspecialists.org.uk
Website: www.instituteofmanagementspecialists.org.uk

The Institute of Management Specialists was founded in 1971 to give professional recognition to the knowledge and skills of managers and specialists. The Institute encourages management excellence and specialist expertise, and supports lifelong learning to help members fulfil their career ambitions.

Specialised Manager Awards are available in a range of specialised areas and IMS offers a CPD (Continuous Professional Development) programme leading to Certified Specialist Manager status.

*MEMBERSHIP*
Student Member (StudIMS)
Associate Member (AMIMS)
Member (MIMS)
Fellow (FIMS)
Companion (CompIMS)

*QUALIFICATION/EXAMINATIONS*
Diploma of Management
Executive Diploma in Business Leadership and Management

## THE SOCIETY OF BUSINESS PRACTITIONERS

PO Box 11
Sandbach
Cheshire CW11 3GE
Tel: 01270 526339
Fax: 01270 526339
E-mail: info@mamsasbp.org.uk
Website: www.mamsasbp.org.uk

SBP is an International Examination Board founded in 1956 by experienced educationalists and executives to fulfill a need to set standards in business practice achieved by examinations/assessments. Inexperienced and mature students should be able to follow careers in further education and/or be proficient in employment and receive the benefits of membership.

*MEMBERSHIP*
Student (StuSBP)
Member (MSBP)
Certified Professional Manager (CPMSBP)
Honorary Fellow
Professional Memberships *(Senior Professional Qualifications)*
Associateship (ASBP)
Licentiateship (LSBP)
Graduateship (GSBP)
Fellowship (FSBP)
These are certified competency-based Membership Awards open to persons occupied in business practice who are considered suitable by the Membership Committee.
CPD programmes are also offered for the Asia region.

*QUALIFICATION/EXAMINATIONS*
Diploma in Business Administration
Advanced Diploma in Business Administration
PGDip in Business Administration
PGDip in International Marketing
Diploma in Computer Studies
Advanced Diploma in Computer Studies
GradDip in IT & E-Commerce
GradDip in Entrepreneurship
Advanced Diploma in Accounting
Diploma & Advanced Diploma in Marketing Management (Joint Award with the Managing & Marketing Sales Association)

*DESIGNATORY LETTERS*
StuSBP, MSBP, CPMSBP, ASBP, LSBP, GSBP, FSBP

# MANUFACTURING

## *Membership of Professional Institutions and Associations*

## THE INSTITUTE OF MANUFACTURING

Head Office
Warwick Corner
42 Warwick Road
Kenilworth
Warwickshire CV8 1HE
Tel: 01926 259342
E-mail: info@instituteofmanufacturing.org.uk
Website: www.instituteofmanufacturing.org.uk

The Institute of Manufacturing was founded in 1978 to give professional recognition to the knowledge and skills of people in all aspects of manufacturing. The Institute supports lifelong learning to help members fulfil their career ambitions and develop their potential.

*MEMBERSHIP*
Student Member (StudIManf)

Associate Member (AMIManf)
Member (MIManf)
Fellow (FIManf)
Companion (CompIManf)

*QUALIFICATION/EXAMINATIONS*
Associate Diploma in Manufacturing
Executive Diploma in Manufacturing
Certified Manufacturing Practitioner

# MARKETING AND SALES

## *Membership of Professional Institutions and Associations*

### LONDON CENTRE OF MARKETING

Buckingham House West
Stanmore
London HA7 4EB
Tel: 020 8385 7766
Fax: 020 8385 7755
E-mail: info@lcmuk.com
Website: www.lcmuk.com

The London Centre of Marketing is an Ofqual accredited, non-political, Awarding Organisation based in London, which exists with the sole aim of providing internationally recognised professional qualifications in marketing and marketing management.

*MEMBERSHIP*
We offer 3 types of memberships:
1. Associate (ALCM)
2. Member (MLCM)
3. Fellow (FLCM)

*QUALIFICATION/EXAMINATIONS*
Diploma, Higher Diploma, Professional Diploma, Graduate Diploma and Postgraduate Dipolma in:
Business Management & Marketing
Human Resource Development & Marketing
Sales & Marketing Management
Travel & Tourism Marketing
Public Relations & Marketing
Entrepreneurship & Marketing

*DESIGNATORY LETTERS*
ALCM/MLCM/FLCM

### MANAGING AND MARKETING SALES ASSOCIATION EXAMINATION BOARD

PO Box 11
Sandbach
Cheshire CW11 3GE
Tel: 01270 526339
Fax: 01270 526339
E-mail: info@mamsasbp.org.uk
Website: www.mamsasbp.org.uk

MAMSA is an international Examination Board offering qualifications in Sales, Marketing and Management and its senior specialist Diploma in Marketing Strategy Diploma. The importance of 'Customer Service' is emphasized throughout all the programmes.

*MEMBERSHIP*
Graduate (GradMAMSA)
Graduate Affliliate (GradAfMAMSA)
Professional (MMAMSA)
Fellow (FMAMSA)

*QUALIFICATION/EXAMINATIONS*
Standard Diploma in Salesmanship
Certificate in Sales Marketing
Higher Diploma in Marketing
Advanced Diploma in Sales Management
Certificate in Marketing Strategy
Diploma in Marketing Strategy & Management (Hypothesis/Thesis)
Diploma in Sales and Marketing Practices (Joint Award with the Society of Business Practitioners)
A CPD programme is also offered.

*DESIGNATORY LETTERS*
GradMAMSA, GradAfMAMSA, MMAMSA, FMAMSA

## MRS (THE MARKET RESEARCH SOCIETY)

The Old Trading House
15 Northburgh Street
London EC1V 0JR
Tel: 020 7490 4911
Fax: 020 7490 0608
E-mail: profdevelopment@mrs.org.uk
Website: www.mrs.org.uk

With members in more than 60 countries, MRS is the world's leading research association. For all those who need, use, generate or interpret the evidence essential to making good decisions for commercial and public policy. We offer various qualifications and membership grades, and are an awarding body for vocationally related qualifications in market and social research.

*MEMBERSHIP*
Student Member
Affiliate Member
Associate Member (AMRS)
Full Member (MMRS)
Fellow (FMRS)
Honorary Member (Hon. MMRS)
Honorary Fellow (Hon. FMRS)

*QUALIFICATION/EXAMINATIONS*
MRS Certificate in Market and Social Reseach
MRS Certificate in Interviewing Skills
MRS Advanced Certificate in Market and Social Research Practice
MRS Diploma in Market and Social Research Practice

*DESIGNATORY LETTERS*
AMRS, MMRS, FMRS, Hon. MMRS, Hon. FMRS

## THE CHARTERED INSTITUTE OF MARKETING

Moor Hall
Maidenhead
Berkshire SL6 9QH
Tel: 01628 427120
Fax: 01628 427158
E-mail: qualifications@cim.co.uk
Website: www.cim.co.uk/learningzone

The Chartered Institute of Marketing is the leading international professional marketing body, with 47, 000 members worldwide. We aim to improve the skills of marketing practitioners, enabling them to deliver exceptional results for their organization. Qualifications from Introductory to Chartered postgraduate level are offered to anyone wanting to develop their career in marketing.

*MEMBERSHIP*
Affiliate (Studying/Professional)
Associate (ACIM)
Member (MCIM)

Fellow (FCIM)
Chartered Marketer

*QUALIFICATION/EXAMINATIONS*
Professional Certificate in Marketing
Professional Diploma in Marketing
Chartered Postgraduate Diploma in Marketing
Diploma in Marketing Communications
Diploma in Digital Marketing
Professional Diploma in Marketing for Business Services and Solutions
Diploma in Digital Marketing (Mobile)
Diploma in Digital Marketing (Metrics and Analytics)
Diploma in Digital Marketing (Media and Branding)
Certificate in Professional Sales Practice
Advanced Certificate in Professional Sales Management Practice
Advanced Certificate in Account Management Practice
Intensive Diploma on Strategic Sales Practice

*DESIGNATORY LETTERS*
ACIM, MCIM, FCIM

## THE INSTITUTE OF DIRECT MARKETING

1 Park Road
Teddington
Middlesex TW11 0AR
Tel: 020 8164 0277
E-mail: enquiries@theidm.com
Website: www.theidm.com

---

The IDM is Europe's leading professional development body for direct, data and digital marketing. Founded in 1987, we are an educational trust and registered charity. We advocate lifelong learning and maintain an up-to-date education portfolio designed to meet the needs of marketing practitioners throughout their career.

*MEMBERSHIP*
Affiliate Member
Associate Member
Member
Fellow
Corporate Member

*QUALIFICATION/EXAMINATIONS*
MSc in Digital Marketing
MSc Marketing Management
IDM Award in Search Marketing
IDM Award in Social Media
IDM Award in Email Marketing
IDM Award in Digital Copywriting
IDM Award in Data Management
IDM Award in Direct and Digital Marketing
IDM Certificate in Digital Marketing
IDM Certificate in Direct and Digital Marketing
IDM Diploma in Digital Marketing
IDM Diploma in Digital Marketing with B2B
IDM Diploma in Direct and Digital Marketing
IDM Diploma in Direct and Digital Marketing with B2B

## THE INSTITUTE OF SALES AND MARKETING MANAGEMENT

Harrier Court
Woodside Road
Lower Woodside
Bedfordshire LU1 4DQ
Tel: 01582 840001
Fax: 01582 849142
E-mail: education@ismm.co.uk
Website: www.ismm.co.uk

The ISMM offers professional qualifications in sales and marketing. The qualifications are accredited by the Qualification and Curriculum Authority, the body set up by the government to regulate qualifications. The programmes are available through ISMM-accredited centres.

*MEMBERSHIP*
Student
Associate (AInstSMM)
Member
Fellow

*QUALIFICATION/EXAMINATIONS*
Level 1 Award in Selling Lawfully and Ethically
Level 1 Award in Understanding the Sales Cycle
Level 1 Award in Understanding Marketing
Level 1 Award in Communication Skills in Sales
Level 1 Award in Sales and Marketing
Level 2 Award in Understanding Laws and Ethics of Selling
Level 2 Award in Understanding Marketing
Level 2 Award in Understanding Buyer Behaviour
Level 2 Award in Sales Targets
Level 2 Award in Selling to Customers
Level 2 Award in Understanding Selling to Customers
Level 2 Award in Telesales
Level 2 Certificate in Sales and Marketing
Level 3 Award in Preparing and Delivering a Sales Presentation
Level 3 Award in Handling Objections, Negotiating and Closing Deals
Level 3 Award in Understanding Influences on Buyer Behaviour
Level 3 Award in Understanding customer segmentation and profiling
Level 3 Award in Understanding sales and marketing in organisations
Level 3 Award in Using market information for sales
Level 3 Award in Time and territory management for sales people
Level 3 Award in Planning for professional development
Level 3 Award in Prospecting for new business
Level 3 Award in Sales pipeline management
Level 3 Certificate in Sales and Marketing
Level 3 Diploma in Sales and Marketing
Level 4 Award in Managing responsible selling
Level 4 Award in Understanding segmentation, targeting and positioning
Level 4 Award in Managing a sales team
Level 4 Award in Operational sales planning
Level 4 Award in Sales negotiations
Level 4 Award in Analysing the marketing environment
Level 4 Award in Finance for sales managers
Level 4 Award in Writing and delivering a sales proposal
Level 4 Certificate in Sales and Marketing Management
Level 4 Diploma in Sales and Marketing Management
Level 5 Award in Understanding and developing customer accounts
Level 5 Award in Understanding the integrated functions of sales and marketing
Level 5 Award in Sales forecasts and target setting
Level 5 Award in Leading a team
Level 5 Award in Motivation and compensation for sales teams
Level 5 Award in Coaching and mentoring
Level 5 Award in Designing, planning and managing sales territories
Level 5 Award in Analysing the financial potential and performance of customer accounts
Level 5 Award in Relationship management for account managers
Level 5 Award in Bid and tender management for account managers
Level 5 Award in Developing a product portfolio

Level 5 Certificate in Sales and Account Management
Level 5 Diploma in Sales and Account Management
Level 6 Award in Leading a culture for responsible selling
Level 6 Award in Leadership and management in sales
Level 6 Award in Planning and implementing sales and marketing strategy
Level 6 Award in Salesforce organisation
Level 6 Award in Sales forecasting and budgeting
Level 6 Award in Developing strategic relationships with major customers
Level 6 Award in Managing sales-related change
Level 6 Award in Developing and using customer insight
Level 6 Certificate in Strategic Sales Management
Level 6 Diploma in Strategic Sales Management

*DESIGNATORY LETTERS*
AInstSMM, MInstSMM, FInstSMM

## THE SOCIETY OF SALES & MARKETING

40 Archdale Road
East Dulwich
London SE22 9HJ
Tel: 0208 693 0555
Fax: 0203 693 0555
E-mail: info@ssm.org.uk
Website: www.ssm.org.uk

The Society is the only professional examining body that awards Certificates and Diplomas in all the four areas of selling, namely selling and sales management, marketing, retail management, and international trade and services. The Society celebrated its Silver Jubilee in style in 2005 at Imperial College London.

*MEMBERSHIP*
Graduate (GSSM)
Associate (ASSM)
Fellow (FSSM)

*QUALIFICATION/EXAMINATIONS*
Candidates for the Certificate, Advanced Certificate or Diploma choose any one of the following: (A) Selling & Sales Management, (B) Marketing, (C) Retail Management and (D) International Trade & Services
(A) Selling & Sales Management subjects:
Certificate: (1) Business Communication, (2) Book-keeping & Accounts, (3) Selling & Sales Management, (4) Fundamentals of Marketing
Advanced Certificate: (5) Marketing Research Management, (6) Consumer Behaviour, (7) Principles of Selling, (8) Consumer Law
Diploma: (9) Management Information Systems, (10) Consumerism, Ethics & Social Responsibility, (11) Marketing Planning & Control, (12) Marketing Communication
(B) Marketing subjects:
Certificate: (1) Business Communication, (2) Book-keeping & Accounts, (3) Selling & Sales Management, (4) Fundamentals of Marketing
Advanced Certificate: (5) Marketing Research Management, (6) Consumer Behaviour, (7) Principles of Selling, (8) Consumer Law
Diploma: (9) Management Information Systems, (10) Consumerism, Ethics & Social Responsibility, (11) Marketing Planning & Control, (12) Marketing Communication
(C) Retail Management subjects:
Certificate: (1) Business Communication, (2) Book-keeping & Accounts, (3) Selling & Sales Management, (4) Retail Management
Advanced Certificate: (5) Marketing Research Management, (6) Consumer Behaviour, (7) Principles of Selling, (8) Consumer Law
Diploma: (9) Management Information Systems, (10) Consumerism, Ethics & Social Responsibility, (11) Fundamentals of Marketing, (12) Marketing Communication
(D) International Trade & Services:
Certificate: (1) Business Communication, (2) Book-keeping & Accounts, (3) International Trade & Services, (4) Fundamentals of Marketing
Advanced Certificate: (5) Marketing Research Management, (6) Import & Export Management, (7) Finance for Export, (8) Consumer Law
Diploma: (9) Management Information Systems, (10) Consumerism, Ethics & Social Responsibility, (11)

Marketing Planning & Control, (12) Marketing Communication

*DESIGNATORY LETTERS*
GSSM, ASSM, FSSM

# MARTIAL ARTS

## *Membership of Professional Institutions and Associations*

### INSTITUTE OF MARTIAL ARTS AND SCIENCES

1 Henrietta Street
Bolton
Lancashire BL3 4HL
Tel: 07792 214993
E-mail: admin@instituteofmartialartsandsciences.com
Website: www.instituteofmartialartsandsciences.com

The IMAS is a professional institute for martial artists. It is dedicated to education and research in the martial arts and offers memberships, accredited training, education and qualifications from the basic up to post graduate level, publishes a quarterly, peer reviewed journal, and an annual yearbook containing its research articles.

*MEMBERSHIP*
Affiliate, Associate (AIMAS)
Member (MIMAS)
Fellow (FIMAS)

*QUALIFICATION/EXAMINATIONS*
Further education/professional development courses available at certificate and diploma level, including accredited instructor training. Higher Educatioal opportunities include: Graduate of the Institute of Martial Arts and Sciences (Grad. IMAS). Masters by Research (MRes) Doctoral studies (PhD) available through associated universities.

*DESIGNATORY LETTERS*
Grad.IMAS, MRes, PhD

# MASSAGE AND ALLIED THERAPIES

## *Membership of Professional Institutions and Associations*

### BRITISH MEDICAL ACUPUNCTURE SOCIETY

BMAS House
3 Winnington Court
Winnington Street
Northwich
Cheshire CW8 1AQ
Tel: 01606 786782
Fax: 01606 786783
E-mail: admin@medical-acupuncture.co.uk
Website: www.medical-acupuncture.co.uk

The BMAS was formed in 1980 as an association of medical practitioners interested in acupuncture and we now have a membership of more than 2, 500 registered doctors and allied health professionals who practise acupuncture alongside more conventional techniques. We believe that acupuncture has an important role to play in healthcare and promote its use as a therapy following orthodox medical diagnosis by suitably trained practitioners. We run training programmes in the UK for doctors, dentists and other healthcare professionals.

*MEMBERSHIP*
Member
Accredited Member
Dental/Veterinary Member
Retired Member
Affiliated
Overseas Member

*QUALIFICATION/EXAMINATIONS*
Certificate of Basic Competence (CoBC)
Diploma of Medical Acupuncture (DipMedAc)
University of Hertfordshire MSc in Western Medical Acupuncture

## LCSP REGISTER OF REMEDIAL MASSEURS AND MANIPULATIVE THERAPISTS

38A High Street
Lowestoft
Suffolk NR32 1HY
Tel: 01502 563344
Fax: 01502 582220
E-mail: admin@lcsp.uk.com
Website: www.lcsp.uk.com

The Register accepts practitioners who currently work in Massage, Sports / Remedial Massage or Manipulative Therapy. Applicants must have completed a course of education at an establishment whose training meets or exceeds the National Occupational Standards. The Register offers heavily discounted comprehensive medical malpractice insurance, business support, regular communications and CPD.

*MEMBERSHIP*
Student Member
Associate Member (LCSP (Assoc))
Full Member (LCSP (Phys))
Affiliate
Fellow (FLCSP)
Honorary Member

*DESIGNATORY LETTERS*
LCSP (Assoc), LCSP (Phys), FLCSP

## NORTHERN INSTITUTE OF MASSAGE LTD

14–16 St Mary's Place
Bury
Greater Manchester BL9 0DZ
Tel: 0161 797 1800
E-mail: information@nim.co.uk
Website: www.nim.co.uk

The NIM was founded in 1924 and offers professional training in Remedial Massage, Advanced Remedial Massage, and Manipulative Therapy. We also offer a number of CPD seminars and short courses to supplement our main training programme. Research is carried out mostly by therapists on patients from their own clinics or by students completing university courses.

*QUALIFICATION/EXAMINATIONS*
Advanced Remedial Massage Diploma
Manipulative Therapy Diploma

## SOCIETY OF HOMEOPATHS

11 Brookfield Duncan Close
Moulton Park
Northampton NN3 6WL
Tel: 01604 817890
Fax: 01604 648848
E-mail: info@homeopathy-soh.org
Website: www.homeopathy-soh.org

The Society of Homeopaths was established in 1978 and is now the largest organization registering professional homeopaths in Europe. Our vision is 'homeopathy for all' and we aim to achieve this both by supporting our members and by raising the profile of homeopathy in general.

*MEMBERSHIP*
Subscriber
Student Member
Student Clinical Member
Registered Member (RSHom)

*DESIGNATORY LETTERS*
RSHom

# MATHEMATICS

## *Membership of Professional Institutions and Associations*

## EDINBURGH MATHEMATICAL SOCIETY

School of Mathematics, Edinburgh University
James Clerk Maxwell Building
Mayfield Road
Edinburgh EH9 3JZ
Tel: 01316 505060
Fax: 01316 506553
E-mail: queries@maths.ed.ac.uk
Website: www.maths.ed.ac.uk

The EMS, founded in 1883, is the principal mathematical society for the academic community in Scotland as well as mathematicians in industry and commerce. We organize meetings, publish a journal and support mathematical activities through various funds.

*MEMBERSHIP*
Ordinary Member
Reciprocal Member
Honorary Member

## THE INSTITUTE OF MATHEMATICS AND ITS APPLICATIONS

Catherine Richards House
16 Nelson Street
Southend-on-Sea
Essex SS1 1EF
Tel: 01702 354020
Fax: 01702 354111
E-mail: post@ima.org.uk
Website: www.ima.org.uk

The IMA, founded in 1964, is the UK's learned society for mathematics and its applications. We promote mathematical research, education and careers, and the use of mathematics in business, industry and commerce. In 1990 the Institute was incorporated by Royal Charter and subsequently granted the right to award the status of Chartered Mathematician, Chartered Scientist and Chartered Mathematics Teacher.

*MEMBERSHIP*
Student
Affiliate
Associate Member (AMIMA)
Member (MIMA)
Fellow (FIMA)
Chartered Mathematician (CMath)
Chartered Mathematics Teacher (CMathTeach)
Chartered Scientist (CSci)

*DESIGNATORY LETTERS*
AMIMA, MIMA, FIMA, CMath, CMathTeach, CSci

## THE MATHEMATICAL ASSOCIATION

259 London Road
Leicester LE2 3BE
Tel: 01162 210013
Fax: 01162 122835
E-mail: office@m-a.org.uk
Website: www.m-a.org.uk

The MA dates from 1871 and supports and improves the teaching and learning of mathematics and its applications, and provides opportunities for communication and collaboration between teachers and students of mathematics. We publish a number of books, journals and magazines, hold an annual conference and regional meetings, and organize CPD events for our members. We also confer with government re the curriculum and assessment.

*MEMBERSHIP*
Student Member
Personal Member
Institutional Member

# MEDICAL HERBALISM

## Membership of Professional Institutions and Associations

### THE NATIONAL INSTITUTE OF MEDICAL HERBALISTS

Clover House
James Court
South Street
Exeter
Devon EX1 1EE
Tel: 01392 426022
Fax: 01392 498963
E-mail: info@nimh.org.uk
Website: www.nimh.org.uk

The NIMH is the UK's leading professional organization of qualified medical herbal practitioners. We maintain high standards of practice and patient care, and work to promote the benefits of western herbal medicine. We provide codes of conduct, ethics and practice, and represent the profession, patients and the public through participation in external processes.

*MEMBERSHIP*

Member (MNIMH) Membership is open to graduates holding a BSc(Hons) degree in Herbal Medicine from: Middlesex University, Lincoln College or University of Westminster. There is also a student affiliate membership scheme for those who are undergraduates of any of the above schools.

*QUALIFICATION/EXAMINATIONS*

The NIMH has historically managed its own accreditation process, with universities currently offering a BSc(Hons) degree in Herbal Medicine at Middlesex University, Lincoln College, University of Westminster.

From 2011 accreditation of the above courses transferred to The European Herbal and Traditional Medicine Practitioners Association (EHTPA), as an umbrella body of Professional Herbal Medicine Associations, although graduates will continue to be eligible to apply for NIMH membership.

*DESIGNATORY LETTERS*

MNIMH, FNIMH

# MEDICAL SECRETARIES

## Membership of Professional Institutions and Associations

### ASSOCIATION OF MEDICAL SECRETARIES, PRACTICE MANAGERS, ADMINISTRATORS AND RECEPTIONISTS

Tavistock House North
Tavistock Square
London WC1H 9LN
Tel: 020 7387 6005
Fax: 020 7388 2648
E-mail: info@amspar.co.uk
Website: www.amspar.com

AMSPAR is a professional membership and educational organization. We work with City & Guilds to provide non-clinical qualifications for health administration within the UK qualification frameworks. We aim to promote quality and coherence in the delivery of qualifications, and encourage and support standards of excellence in the pursuit of continuous professional development and lifelong learning.

*MEMBERSHIP*
Associate Member (AAMS)
Member (MAMS)
Fellow (FAMS)

*QUALIFICATION/EXAMINATIONS*
The Level 5 Diploma in Primary Care & Health Management
The Level 5 Certificate in Primary Care & Health Management
The Level 3 Diploma for Medical Secretaries
The Level 3 Certificate in Medical Administration
The Level 3 Certificate in Medical Terminology
The Level 3 Award in Legal Aspects of Medical Administration
The Level 3 Award in Medical Principles for the Administrator
The Level 3 Award in Medical Word Processing
The Level 3 Award in Production of Medical Documents from Recorded Speech
The Level 2 Diploma in Medical Administration
The Level 2 Certificate in Medical Administration
The Level 2 Award in Medical Terminology
The Level 2 Award in Working in the NHS
The Level 2 Award in Medical Word Processing
The Level 2 Award in Production of Medical Documents from Recorded Speech

*DESIGNATORY LETTERS*
AAMS, MAMS, FAMS

# MEDICINE

A student who wishes to qualify as a doctor in the UK must first obtain a primary qualification. Medical students in the UK typically study for five years to receive their medical degrees (or four years for a graduate entry programme). After graduation, a trainee doctor will enter the two-year Foundation Programme. The trainee is provisionally registered with a licence to practise with the General Medical Council (GMC) while completing the first year and full registration is awarded upon completion of year one.

The GMC is charged with the responsibility under the Medical Act 1983 of keeping a register of all duly qualified medical practitioners. General Medical Council, Regent's Place, 350 Euston Road, London NW1 3JN; Tel: 0161 923 6602; e-mail: gmc@gmc-uk.org; website: www.gmc-uk.org For information on how to apply to join the register, see www.gmc-uk.org/doctors/registration_applications/join_the_register.asp

## PRIMARY QUALIFICATIONS

A qualifying examination for the purposes of Part II of the Medical Act is an examination held for the granting of one or more primary medical qualifications (PMQs) by any one of the bodies or combinations of bodies in the United Kingdom that are included in a list maintained by the GMC and published on the GMC's website (www.gmc-uk.org/education/undergraduate/awarding_bodies.asp).
Subject to the provisions of the Act any person whose fitness to practise is not impaired and who a) holds one or more primary United Kingdom qualifications and has satisfactorily completed an acceptable programme for provisionally registered doctors; or b) being a national of any relevant European State, holds one or more primary European qualifications, is entitled to be registered as a fully registered medical practitioner.

## LICENSING AND REVALIDATION

A qualifying examination for the purposes of Part II of the Medical Act is an examination held for the granting of one or more primary medical qualifications (PMQs) by any one of the bodies or combinations of bodies in the United Kingdom that are included in a list maintained by the GMC and published on the GMC's website (www.gmc-uk.org/education/undergraduate/awarding_bodies.asp).
Subject to the provisions of the Act any person whose fitness to practise is not impaired and who a) holds one or more primary United Kingdom qualifications and has satisfactorily completed an acceptable

programme for provisionally registered doctors; or b) being a national of any relevant European State, holds one or more primary European qualifications, is entitled to be registered as a fully registered medical practitioner.

▯ Revalidation is a new way of regulating licensed doctors that will give extra confidence to patients that their doctors are up to date and fit to practise. Licensed doctors will have to revalidate, usually every five years, by having regular appraisals based on the GMC's core guidance for doctors, *Good Medical Practice*. It is planned that revalidation will be introduced across the UK in early December 2012 and the majority of licensed doctors will be revalidated for the first time by the end of March 2016.

## Membership of Professional Institutions and Associations

### COLLEGE OF OPERATING DEPARTMENT PRACTITIONERS

130 Euston Road
London NW1 2AY
Tel: 0870 121 5414
E-mail: office@codp.org
Website: www.codp.org.uk

The CODP is the professional body for Operating Department Practitioners. It is a membership, not-for-profit organization that sets standards of education for the pre-registration aspect of the profession and promotes the enhancement of knowledge and skills, in the context of the multidisciplinary team, through regional, national and international networks.

*MEMBERSHIP*
Student Member
Association Member
Full College Member

### ROYAL COLLEGE OF GENERAL PRACTITIONERS

30 Euston Square
London NW1 2FB
Tel: 020 3188 7400
Fax: 020 3188 7401
E-mail: info@rcgp.org.uk
Website: www.rcgp.org.uk

The aims of the College are to encourage, foster and maintain the highest possible standards in general medical practice. Full entry to the College is by exam undertaken whilst in training for General Practice, or assessment as a qualified GP.

*MEMBERSHIP*
Associate in Training
Associate
Member (MRCGP)
Fellow (FRCGP)
International

Undergraduate medical students and Foundation programme students may register with the College's Student Forum, which exposes the students to life in general practice.

*QUALIFICATION/EXAMINATIONS*
Assessment for Membership of the RCGP (MRCGP)

*DESIGNATORY LETTERS*
MRCGP, FRCGP

## ROYAL COLLEGE OF OBSTETRICIANS AND GYNAECOLOGISTS

27 Sussex Place
London NW1 4RG
Tel: 020 7772 6200
E-mail: library@rcog.org.uk
Website: www.rcog.org.uk

The RCOG encourages the study and advancement of the science and practice of obstetrics and gynaecology. We do this through postgraduate medical education and training development, and the publication of clinical guidelines and reports on aspects of the specialty and service provision. The RCOG International Office works with other international organizations to help lower maternal morbidity and mortality in under-resourced countries.

*MEMBERSHIP*
Affiliate
Associate
Diplomate
Trainee – pre-membership
Member without Examination (MRCOG)
Member (MRCOG)
Fellow (FRCOG)
Fellow *honoris causa*
Fellow *ad eumdem* (FRCOG)
Honorary Fellow (FRCOG)

*QUALIFICATION/EXAMINATIONS*
MRCOG (Membership Exam)
FRCOG (Diploma)

*DESIGNATORY LETTERS*
MRCOG, FRCOG

## ROYAL SOCIETY OF MEDICINE

1 Wimpole Street
London W1G 0AE
Tel: 020 7290 2900
Fax: 020 7290 2989
E-mail: membership@rsm.ac.uk
Website: www.rsm.ac.uk

The RSM, founded in 1805, is a medical charity that promotes the exchange of information and ideas in medical science. We provide a broad range of educational activities and opportunities for doctors, dentists, veterinary surgeons, students of these disciplines and allied healthcare professionals, organize conferences, and publish books and journals through our publishing division, RSM Press.

*MEMBERSHIP*
Student
Associate
Fellow
Corporate

## THE FEDERATION OF ROYAL COLLEGES OF PHYSICIANS OF THE UNITED KINGDOM

MRCP(UK)
11 St Andrews Place
Regent's Park
London NW1 4LE
Tel: +44 (0)20 3075 1515
E-mail: part1@mrcpuk.org
Website: www.mrcpuk.org

The Federation is a partnership between the Royal College of Physicians of Edinburgh, the Royal College of Physicians and Surgeons of Glasgow and the Royal College of Physicians of London. Working together, the colleges develop and deliver membership and specialty examinations that are recognized around the world as quality benchmarks.

*MEMBERSHIP*
Membership of the Royal Colleges of Physicians (MRCP(UK)): Once candidates have successfully completed their final Part of the examination they must then submit and complete the Form of Faith and a testimonial for election to membership. The testimonial must be completed by a Fellow or Member of the Royal Colleges of Physicians of the United Kingdom. The latter should have worked with the candidate within the previous 3 years and must be a holder of MRCP(UK) for at least 8 years.

*QUALIFICATION/EXAMINATIONS*
The Federation is responsible for a portfolio of examinations: MRCP(UK) Diploma (Membership of the Royal Colleges of Physicians of the United Kingdom): Candidates for the MRCP(UK) Diploma may enter through the Royal College of Physicians of Edinburgh, the Royal College of Physicians and Surgeons of Glasgow, the Royal College of Physicians of London, or through the online application system. There are three components to the MRCP(UK) Diploma. The part 1 examination has a two-paper format. Each paper is 3 hours in duration and contains 100 multiple choice questions in one from five (best of five) format, where a candidate chooses the best answer from five possible answers. The part 2 written examination has a three-paper format. All papers in the MRCP(UK) part 2 written examination are 3 hours in duration and contain up to 100 multiple choice questions. The questions will usually have a clinical scenario, may include the results of investigations and may be illustrated. The Part 2 clinical examination (PACES) consists of five clinical stations, each assessed by two independent examiners. Candidates will start at any one of the five stations, and then move round the carousel of stations at 20-minute intervals until they have completed the cycle. There is a 5-minute period between each station. Candidates may apply to sit the MRCP(UK) part 1 examination provided they graduated at least 12 months in advance of the examinations date (and have had at least 12 months' experience in medical employment). Candidates who have passed the part 1 examination can proceed to complete the remaining components. The MRCP(UK) Examination provides valid, reliable evidence of attainment in knowledge, clinical skills and behaviour, and is a mandatory component of assessment for Core Medical Training (CMT). The Specialty Certificate Examinations (SCEs): The Federation of Royal Colleges of Physicians of the UK, in association with the Specialist Societies, has developed a programme to deliver Specialty Certificate Examinations within the new specialist training structure. The aim of these national assessments is to ensure that trainees have sufficient knowledge of their specialty to practise safely and competently as consultants. The Specialty Certificate Examination is delivered in computer-based format (referred to as CBT) at a Pearson VUE test centre. Each paper is based on the MRCP(UK) written paper format and contains 100 multiple choice questions in 'best of five' format. A Specialty Certificate Examination is now a compulsory component of assessment for Certificate of Completion of Training (CCT) for all UK trainees whose specialist training began in or after August 2007 and is in one of the following specialties: Dermatology; Endocrinology and Diabetes; Gastroenterology, Geriatric Medicine; Infectious Diseases; Medical Oncology; Nephrology; Neurology; Palliative Medicine; Respiratory Medicine and Rheumatology.

## THE INSTITUTE OF CLINICAL RESEARCH

10 Cedar Court
Grove Park
White Waltham Road
Maidenhead
Tel: 0845 521 0056
E-mail: info@icr-global.org
Website: www.icr-global.org

The ICR was founded in 1978 and is now the largest professional clinical research body in Europe and India. Our aim is to promote knowledge and understanding by engaging with the healthcare community and the general public, to support and facilitate communication between our members, and to provide opportunities for learning and development to enhance professional competence.

*MEMBERSHIP*
Affiliate
Registered Member (RICR)
Professional Member (MICR)
Fellow (FICR)
Honorary Fellow (Hon FICR)

*QUALIFICATION/EXAMINATIONS*
Please see the ICR's website.

*DESIGNATORY LETTERS*
RICR, MICR, FICR, HonFICR

## THE ROYAL COLLEGE OF ANAESTHETISTS

Churchill House
35 Red Lion Square
London WC1R 4SG
Tel: 020 7092 1500
Fax: 020 7092 1730
E-mail: info@rcoa.ac.uk
Website: www.rcoa.ac.uk

The RCA, which dates from 1948, is the professional body responsible for the specialty of anaesthesia throughout the UK. Our principal responsibility is to ensure the quality of patient care through the maintenance of standards in anaesthesia, pain management and intensive care. We set and run examinations, and provide CPD for all practising anaesthetists.

*MEMBERSHIP*
Trainee
Affiliate
Associate Member
Member (MRCA)
Associate Fellow
Fellow *ad eundem* (FRCA)
Fellow (FRCA)
Honorary Fellow (FRCA)

*QUALIFICATION/EXAMINATIONS*
FRCA Examinations

*DESIGNATORY LETTERS*
MRCA, FRCA

## THE ROYAL COLLEGE OF PATHOLOGISTS

2 Carlton House Terrace
London SW1Y 5AF
Tel: 020 7451 6700
E-mail: info@rcpath.org
Website: www.rcpath.org

The College aims to advance the science and practice of pathology, to provide public education, to promote research in pathology and to disseminate the results.

*MEMBERSHIP*
Affiliate Member
Associate
Diplomate Member (DipRCPath)
Fellow (FRCPath)

*QUALIFICATION/EXAMINATIONS*
Training programmes are approved for all pathology specialities and sub-specialities. The exact examination arrangements vary for each speciality but they will all involve a Part 1 and a Part 2 which include, inter alia, written, practical and oral components. In addition the College offers a Diploma in Cytopathology, a Diploma in Dermatopathology and a Diploma in Forensic Pathology. Further details may be obtained from the Examinations Department or the College's website.

*DESIGNATORY LETTERS*
DipRCPath, FRCPath

## THE ROYAL COLLEGE OF PHYSICIANS AND SURGEONS OF GLASGOW

232–242 St Vincent Street
Glasgow G2 5RJ
Tel: 0141 2216072
Fax: 0141 2211804
E-mail: exams@rcpsg.ac.uk
Website: www.rcpsg.ac.uk

The Royal College of Physicians and Surgeons of Glasgow (RCPSG) welcomes professionals from a diverse range of disciplines. At present, our collegiate body includes Physicians, Surgeons, professionals in Dentistry, Travel Medicine, Podiatric Medicine and other professions allied to medicine. The College aims to provide career support to our membership through education, training, professional development, examinations and assessment, whilst acting as a charity and leading voice on health issues in order to set the highest standards of health care.

*MEMBERSHIP*
Member MRCPS(Glasg)/ MFDS RCPS(Glasg)/ MRCS(Glasg)/ MRCS(ENT)(Glasg)/ MFTM RCPS(Glasg)/ MFPM RCPS(Glasg)
Fellow FRCP(Glasg)/ FRCS(Glasg)/ FDS RCPS(Glasg)/ FFTM RCPS(Glasg)/ FFPM RCPS(Glasg)
Associate Member
Affiliate Member
Associate in Training
Introductory Member

*QUALIFICATION/EXAMINATIONS*
Diploma in Child Health (DCH)
Diploma in Dermatology (Dip Derm)
Diploma in Geriatric Medicine (DGM)
Diploma in Otolaryngology – Head and Neck Surgey (DOHNS)
Diploma in Travel Medicine (DipTravMed)
Diploma of Membership of the Royal Colleges of Physicians of the United Kingdom (MRCP(UK)) (see MRCP(UK) website)
Diploma of Membership of the Royal College of Surgeons (MRCS(Glasg))
Diploma of Membership of the Royal College of Surgeons (MRCS(ENT)(Glasg))
Diploma of Membership of the Faculty of Dental Surgery (MFDS RCPS(Glasg))
Diploma of Membership in (dental specialty) (M(dental specialty) RCPS(Glasg)

Diploma of Membership of the Faculty of Travel Medicine (MFTM RCPS(Glasg))
Diploma of Membership of the Faculty of Podiatric Medicine (MFPM RCPS(Glasg))
Diploma of Fellowship of the Royal College of Physicians and Surgeons of Glasgow in Ophthalmology (FRCS(Glasg))

Diploma of Fellowship of the Royal College of Physicians and Surgeons of Glasgow (FDS (dental specialty)RCPS(Glasg))
Diploma of Fellowship of the Royal College of Physicians and Surgeons of Glasgow (FRCSGlasg (surgical specialty))
Diploma of Fellowship of the Faculty of Travel Medicine (FFTM RCPS(Glasg))
Diploma of Fellowship of the Faculty of Podiatric Medicine (FFPM RCPS(Glasg))

*DESIGNATORY LETTERS*
MFDS RCPS(Glasg), MFTM RCPS(Glasg), MRCP(UK), MRCS(Glasg), MRCS(ENT)(Glasg), MRCPS(Glasg), MFPM RCPS(Glasg), M(dental specialty) RCPSG(Glasg)/ FRCP(Glasg)/ FRCS(Glasg)/ FRCSGlasg(surgical specialty)/ FDS RCPS(Glasg)/ FRCS(Urol)(Glasg), FFTM RCPS(Glasg)

## THE ROYAL COLLEGE OF PHYSICIANS OF EDINBURGH

9 Queen Street
Edinburgh EH2 1JQ
Tel: 01312 257324
E-mail: l.tedford@rcpe.ac.uk
Website: www.rcpe.ac.uk

The RCPE promotes the highest standards in internal medicine internationally. Along with our sister Colleges in Glasgow and London we oversee the Member of the Royal College of Physicians (MRCP(UK)) examination enabling doctors to enter higher specialist training, leading eventually to a Certificate of Completion of Specialist Training (CCST).

*MEMBERSHIP*
Student + Foundation
Associate
Collegiate Member (MRCPE)
Fellow (FRCPE)

*QUALIFICATION/EXAMINATIONS*
MRCP(UK)
Specialty Certificate Examinations

*DESIGNATORY LETTERS*
MRCPE, FRCPE

## THE ROYAL COLLEGE OF PHYSICIANS OF LONDON

11 St Andrews Place
Regent's Park
London NW1 4LE
Tel: +44 (0)20 3075 1649
E-mail: via website
Website: www.rcplondon.ac.uk

The Royal College of Physicians of London offers a Diploma in Geriatric Medicine (DGM) Examination and a Diploma in Tropical Medicine and Hygiene, run in conjunction with the London School of Tropical Medicine and Hygiene.

*MEMBERSHIP*
The Royal College of Physicians of London runs the MRCP(UK) Examination which is the MRCP(UK) membership examination. As the examination is run in conjunction with two other Royal Colleges of Physicians, this examination and the membership qualification MRCP(UK) are listed in this directory

under ***The Federation of Royal Colleges of Physicians***

*QUALIFICATION/EXAMINATIONS*

**Diploma in Geriatric Medicine** The Diploma in Geriatric Medicine is designed to give recognition of competence in the provision of care of older people to General Practitioner vocational trainees, staff physicians and others working in non-consultant career posts in Departments of Geriatric Medicine, and other doctors with interests in or responsibilities for the care of older people.

The Diploma in Geriatric Medicine is available to all registered doctors. It is not primarily directed towards career geriatricians, but is generally to family doctors, psycho-geriatricians and indeed any doctor involved in the care of older people.

The Diploma in Geriatric Medicine is in two parts, the first of which is a written examination of multiple choice (best of 5) questions, lasting 2 hours and 30 minutes normally held twice a year at the Royal College of Physicians of London.

The second part is a Clinical Examination also held twice a year at various clinical centres in England and Wales. The clinical examination is a four-station standardized examination similar to an Objective Standard Clinical Examination (OSCE).

**Diploma in Tropical Medicine and Hygiene** The Diploma in Tropical Medicine and Hygiene is intended to test the knowledge required of physicians who wish to practise medicine effectively in developing countries.

Candidates for the Diploma in Tropical Medicine & Hygiene must hold a primary medical qualification recognized by the Royal College of Physicians of London.

The Royal College of Physicians of London will accept applications from candidates who are in the process of completing, or have completed within the last 5 years, the Tropical Medicine courses in London, Liverpool, Sheffield and Glasgow, which are recognized as appropriate training centres for the examination. The examination is held once a year over 2 days (unless required for a viva) and is conducted in the following sections: A **Practical Section** lasting 2 hours and 30 minutes consists of a mixture of microscopy specimens, including 20 'spot' questions that are set up on a microscope for identification. Other specimens require the candidate to use the microscopes themself. They are mainly parasitological and may include faecal, blood and haematological preparations together with some entomological specimens. A **Written Section** (3 hours and 20 minutes in total) consists of three papers. The **Clinical Paper** (1 hour) contains 18 compulsory questions. The first 16 are based on clinical pictures – usually of patients with abnormal physical signs; but occasionally laboratory slides, X-rays, or epidemiological data may be shown. There will be two or three questions on each, asking (for example) identification, diagnosis, further investigation, treatment etc. Each of these 16 questions is worth a maximum of 5 marks. The last 2 questions (17 and 18) are brief clinical cases, with 2 or 3 questions (again concentrating on diagnosis or differential diagnosis, investigation and treatment). The **Multiple Choice Question Paper** ( 1 hour and 20 minutes) consists of 40 multiple choice questions designed to test the knowledge of tropical medicine and hygiene over a wide area. The **Preventative Medicine Paper** (1 hour including 5 minutes reading time) consists of 10 questions of which the candidate must choose 5. Each question may have several parts, covering all aspects of preventative medicine and international community health in a tropical context. There is also an **Oral ('Viva') Examination** for borderline candidates. The examination is conducted by two examiners. The first part of the examination (10 minutes) is a discussion of an illustrated clinical case history, which candidates are allowed to study for 10 minutes before the examination. The second part of the examination (10 minutes) consists of more general questions.

## THE ROYAL COLLEGE OF PSYCHIATRISTS

17 Belgrave Square
London SW1X 8PG
Tel: 020 7235 2351
Fax: 020 7245 1231
E-mail: reception@rcpsych.ac.uk
Website: www.rcpsych.ac.uk

The RCPsych is the professional and educational body for psychiatrists in the UK and Ireland. We are committed to improving the understanding of psychiatry and mental health, and are at the forefront in setting and achieving the highest standards through education, training and research. We actively promote psychiatry as a career, and provide guidance and support to our members and associates.

*MEMBERSHIP*
Pre-Membership Psychiatric Trainee
New Associate
Affiliate
Specialist Associate
Member (MRCPsych)
Fellow (FRCPsych)
Honorary Fellow
International Associate

*QUALIFICATION/EXAMINATIONS*
MRCPsych qualifying exams

*DESIGNATORY LETTERS*
MRCPsych, FRCPsych

## THE ROYAL COLLEGE OF RADIOLOGISTS

63 Lincoln's Inn Fields
London WC2A 3JW
Tel: 020 7405 1282
E-mail: enquiries@rcr.ac.uk
Website: www.rcr.ac.uk

The RCR is a professional body representing over 8, 900 medical and dental practitioners worldwide that aims to advance the science and practice of clinical radiology and clinical oncology. We promote the highest standards of professional competence, undertake regular audits of training and practice, conduct examinations for Certificates and Diplomas, encourage CPD among our members, and provide information for the public.

*MEMBERSHIP*
Junior Member
Associate
Trainee
Member
Fellow (FRCR)
Honorary Member/Fellow (Hon MRCR/Hon FRCR)

*QUALIFICATION/EXAMINATIONS*
First FRCR Examination
Final FRCR Examination
Diploma in Dental and Maxillofacial Radiology (DDMFR)

*DESIGNATORY LETTERS*
FRCR, Hon MRCR, Hon FRCR

## THE ROYAL COLLEGE OF SURGEONS OF EDINBURGH

Nicolson Street
Edinburgh EH8 9DW
Tel: 0131 527 1600
Fax: 0131 557 6406
E-mail: mail@rcsed.ac.uk
Website: www.rcsed.ac.uk

The Royal College of Surgeons of Edinburgh, which dates from 1505, is dedicated to the maintenance and promotion of the highest standards of surgical practice, through education, training and rigorous examination, and its liaison with external medical bodies. Today, with more than 20, 000 Fellows and Members, we pride ourselves also on our innovation and adaptability.

*MEMBERSHIP*
Affiliate
Associate
Member (MRCSEd)
Fellow (FRCSEd)

*QUALIFICATION/EXAMINATIONS*
Please see the Royal College of Surgeons of Edinburgh website.

*DESIGNATORY LETTERS*
MRCSEd, FRCSEd

## THE ROYAL COLLEGE OF SURGEONS OF ENGLAND

35–43 Lincoln's Inn Fields
London WC2A 3PE
Tel: 020 7405 3474
E-mail: membership@rcseng.ac.uk
Website: www.rcseng.ac.uk

The Royal College of Surgeons of England is committed to enabling surgeons to achieve and maintain the highest standards of surgical practice and patient care. We examine trainees, supervise the training of and provide support and advice for surgeons, promote and support surgical research in the UK, and liaise with the DoH, health authorities, Trusts and hospitals in the UK and other medical and academic organizations worldwide.

*MEMBERSHIP*
Affiliate
Associate
Fellow *ad eundem*
Membership *ad eundem*
Specialty Membership

*QUALIFICATION/EXAMINATIONS*
Please see the Royal College of Surgeons of England website.

## THE WORSHIPFUL SOCIETY OF APOTHECARIES OF LONDON

Black Friars Lane
London EC4V 6EJ
Tel: 020 7236 1180
Fax: 020 7329 3177
E-mail: via website
Website: www.apothecaries.org

The Society of Apothecaries of London was incorporated by Royal Charter in 1617 and allowed to prepare and sell drugs for medicinal purposes, laying the foundations of the British pharmaceutical industry. Later, apothecaries were permitted to prescribe and dispense medicines, becoming the forerunners of today's GPs. Now the Society is primarily an examining body.

*QUALIFICATION/EXAMINATIONS*
PGDip in the Forensic and Clinical Aspects of Sexual Assault (DFCASA)
PGDip in Forensic Medical Sciences (DFMS)
PGDip in Genitourinary Medicine (Dip GU Med)
PGDip in the History of Medicine (DHMSA)
PGDip in HIV Medicine (Dip HIV Med)
PGDip in the Medical Care of Catastrophes (DMCC)
PGDip in Medical Jurisprudence (Pathology) (DMJ[Path])
PGDip in the Philosophy of Medicine (DPMSA)

# METALLURGY

## *Membership of Professional Institutions and Associations*

### INSTITUTE OF CORROSION

The Newton Building
St George's Avenue
Northampton NN2 6JB
Tel: 01604 893883
Fax: 01604 893878
E-mail: admin@icorr.org
Website: www.icorr.org

The Institute of Corrosion has since 1959 been serving the corrosion science, technology and engineering community in the fight against corrosion, which costs the UK around 4 per cent of GNP per annum. We promote the establishment and promotion of sound corrosion management practice, the advancement of cost-effective corrosion control measures, and a sustained effort to raise corrosion awareness at all stages of design, fabrication and operation.

*MEMBERSHIP*
Student Member
Ordinary Member
Technical Member (TICorr)
Professional Member (MICorr)
Engineering Technician (EngTech)
Incorporated Engineer (IEng)
Chartered Engineer (CEng)
Chartered Scientist (CSci)

*QUALIFICATION/EXAMINATIONS*
Cathodic Protection Technician (Level 1)
Senior Cathodic Protection Technician (Level 2)
Senior Cathodic Protection Engineer (Level 3)
Painting Inspector (ICorr Levels 1, 2 and 3)
Coating Inspector (ICorr Levels 1 and 2)

*DESIGNATORY LETTERS*
TICorr, MICorr, EngTech, IEng, CEng

## THE INSTITUTE OF METAL FINISHING

Exeter House
48 Holloway Head
Birmingham B1 1NQ
Tel: 01216 227387
Fax: 01216 666316
E-mail: exeterhouse@instituteofmetalfinishing.org
Website: www.uk-finishing.org.uk

The IMF, founded in 1925, provides a focus for surface engineering and finishing activities worldwide through the fulfilment of technical, educational and professional needs at all levels for individuals and companies involved in the coatings industry. We promote R&D within the industry and CPD for our members, cooperate with other institutes, and liaise with legislative bodies to influence decision-making.

*MEMBERSHIP*
Student
Affiliate
Associate (AssocIMF)
Technician (TechIMF)
Licentiate (LIMF)
Member (MIMF)
Fellow (FIMF)
Engineering Technician (EngTech)
Sustaining Member (company)

*QUALIFICATION/EXAMINATIONS*
Foundation Certificate
Technician Certificate
Advanced Technician Certificate

*DESIGNATORY LETTERS*
AssocIMF, TechIMF, LIMF, MIMF, FIMF, EngTech

# METEOROLOGY AND CLIMATOLOGY

## *Membership of Professional Institutions and Associations*

## MET OFFICE COLLEGE

Met Office
Fitzroy Road
Exeter
Devon EX1 3PB
Tel: 01392 885680
Fax: 01392 885681
E-mail: enquiries@metoffice.gov.uk
Website: www.metoffice.gov.uk

The Meteorological Office College is part of the Met Office and is located in Exeter, Devon. We provide meteorological training for our own staff and to meteorological services worldwide, as places become available on a fee-paying basis.

*QUALIFICATION/EXAMINATIONS*
Level 3 Diploma in Meteorological Observing (QCF)
Level 4 Certificate for a Meteorological Forecasting Technician (QCF)
Level 5 Diploma in Meteorological Forecasting (QCF)
Level 5 Award in Meteorological Briefing (QCF)
Level 5 Certificate in Meteorological Broadcasting (QCF)
Level 6 Diploma in Flood Forecasting (QCF)

## ROYAL METEOROLOGICAL SOCIETY

104 Oxford Road
Reading RG1 7LL
Tel: 0118 956 8500
Fax: 0118 956 8571
E-mail: info@rmets.org
Website: www.rmets.org

The RMetS is the learned and professional society for anyone whose profession or interests are connected with weather and climate. It administers the NVQs of the profession and is the accreditation body for the status of Chartered Meteorologist. Its principal aim is the advancement of the understanding of weather and climate for the benefit of everyone.

*MEMBERSHIP*
Student
Associate Fellow
Fellow (FRMetS)
Honorary Member
Chartered Meteorologist (CMet)
School Member
Corporate Member

*DESIGNATORY LETTERS*
FRMetS, CMet

# MICROSCOPY

## *Membership of Professional Institutions and Associations*

## THE ROYAL MICROSCOPICAL SOCIETY

37/38 St Clements
Oxford OX4 1AJ
Tel: 01865 254760
Fax: 01865 791237
E-mail: info@rms.org.uk
Website: www.rms.org.uk

The RMS, which dates from 1839, is an international scientific society dedicated to advancing the science of microscopy and the interests of its 1, 400 members, who range from individuals interested in microscopy to scientists and company members representing manufacturers and suppliers of microscopes, other equipment and services.

*MEMBERSHIP*
Ordinary Member
Fellow (FRMS)
Corporate Member

*DESIGNATORY LETTERS*
FRMS

# MUSEUM AND RELATED WORK

## *Membership of Professional Institutions and Associations*

### MUSEUMS ASSOCIATION

42 Clerkenwell Close
London EC1R 0AZ
Tel: 020 7566 7800
E-mail: info@museumsassociation.org
Website: www.museumsassociation.org

The MA is the oldest museums association in the world, set up in 1889 to guard the interests of museums and galleries. Today, we have 5, 200 individual members, 600 institutional members and 250 corporate members. Our aim is to enhance the value of museums to society by sharing knowledge, developing skills, inspiring innovation and providing leadership.

*MEMBERSHIP*
Student
Volunteer
Professional Member
Associate (AMA)
Corporate Member
Institutional Member

*DESIGNATORY LETTERS*
AMA

# MUSIC

## *Membership of Professional Institutions and Associations*

### ABRSM (ASSOCIATED BOARD OF THE ROYAL SCHOOLS OF MUSIC)

24 Portland Place
London W1B 1LU
Tel: 020 7636 5400
Fax: 020 7637 0234
E-mail: abrsm@abrsm.org
Website: www.abrsm.org

ABRSM's mission is to motivate musical achievement. We aim to support the development of learners and teachers in music education worldwide and to celebrate their achievements. We do this through authoritative and internationally recognized assessments, publications and professional development support for teachers, and through charitable donations.

*MEMBERSHIP*
Licentiate (LRSM)
Fellow (FRSM)

*QUALIFICATION/EXAMINATIONS*
Certificate of Teaching (CT ABRSM)
Diploma in Instrumental/Vocal Teaching (DipABRSM)
Diploma in Music Direction (DipABRSM)
Diploma in Music Performance (DipABRSM)

Please see the ABRSM website for details of other examinations and awards.

*DESIGNATORY LETTERS*
CT ABRSM, DipABRSM, LRSM, FRSM

## INCORPORATED SOCIETY OF MUSICIANS

10 Stratford Place
London WIC 1AA
Tel: 020 7629 4413
Fax: 020 7408 1538
E-mail: membership@ism.org
Website: www.ism.org

The ISM, a non-profit-making organization founded in 1882, is the UK's professional body for musicians. We promote the art of music and the interests of musicians through campaigns, support and practical advice. Members also receive our monthly in-house magazine, *Music Journal*, which includes news and information on CPD.

*MEMBERSHIP*
Student Member
Associate Member
Full Member
Corporate Member
Graduate Member

# MUSICAL INSTRUMENT TECHNOLOGY

## *Membership of Professional Institutions and Associations*

## INCORPORATED SOCIETY OF ORGAN BUILDERS

2 Monarch Drive
Oakwood
Derby DE21 2XW
Fax: 0870 139 3645
E-mail: secretary@isob.co.uk
Website: www.isob.co.uk/

The ISOB was founded in 1947 to advance the science and practice of organ building, to provide a central organization for organ builders, and to provide for the better definition and protection of the profession by a system of examinations and the issue of certificates and distinctions. We hold regular meetings and conferences around the UK and overseas.

*MEMBERSHIP*
Student Member
Ordinary Member (MISOB)
Associate Member (AISOB)
Fellow (FISOB)
Counsellor (CISOB)
Companion

*DESIGNATORY LETTERS*
MISOB, AISOB, FISOB, CISOB

## PIANOFORTE TUNERS' ASSOCIATION

PO Box 1312
Lightwater
Woking
Surrey GU18 5UB
Tel: 0845 602 8796
E-mail: secretary@pianotuner.org.uk
Website: www.pianotuner.org.uk

The PTA is a professional body committed to improving standards, and applicants for membership must pass a theoretical and practical examination to prove their ability as a qualified piano tuner or technician. We publish a regular newsletter and hold an Annual Convention and General Meeting in different towns around Britain, to which members and aspiring non-members are invited.

*MEMBERSHIP*
Student
Patron
Associate
Technician Member
Member
Subscriber

# NAVAL ARCHITECTURE

## *Membership of Professional Institutions and Associations*

## THE ROYAL INSTITUTION OF NAVAL ARCHITECTS

8-9 Northumberland Street
London WC2N 5DA
Tel: 020 7235 4622
Fax: 020 7259 5912
E-mail: membership@rina.org.uk
Website: www.rina.org.uk

The RINA is an internationally renowned professional institution whose members are involved at all levels in the design, construction, maintenance and operation of marine vessels and structures. Our members are widely represented in industry, universities and colleges, and maritime organizations in over 90 countries.

*MEMBERSHIP*
Student Member
Associate (AssocRINA)
Associate Member (AMRINA)
Member (MRINA)
Fellow (FRINA)

*DESIGNATORY LETTERS*
AssocRINA, AMRINA, MRINA. FRINA

# NAVIGATION, SEAMANSHIP AND MARINE QUALIFICATIONS

## *Membership of Professional Institutions and Associations*

## THE NAUTICAL INSTITUTE

202 Lambeth Road
London SE1 7LQ
Tel: 020 7928 1351
Fax: 020 7401 2817
E-mail: sec@nautinst.org
Website: www.nautinst.org

The Nautical Institute is the international representative body for maritime professionals involved in the control of sea-going ships with an interest in nautical matters. It provides a wide range of services to enhance the professional standing and knowledge of members who are drawn from all sectors of the maritime world.

*MEMBERSHIP*
Honorary Fellow
Fellow
Associate Fellow (AFNI)
Member (MNI)
Associate Member (AMNI)

*QUALIFICATION/EXAMINATIONS*
Harbour Master's Certificate
Pilotage Certificate
Command Diploma

*DESIGNATORY LETTERS*
AFNI, MNI, AMNI

## THE ROYAL INSTITUTE OF NAVIGATION

1 Kensington Gore
London SW7 2AT
Tel: 020 7591 3134
Fax: 020 7591 3131
E-mail: admin@rin.org.uk
Website: www.rin.org.uk

The RIN is a learned society with charitable status. Our aims are: to unite those with a professional or personal interest in any aspect of navigation in one unique body; to further the development of navigation in every sphere; and to increase public awareness of both the art and science of navigation, how it has shaped the past, how it impacts our world today, and how it will affect the future.

*MEMBERSHIP*
Junior Associate Member
Student
Associate
Member (MRIN)
Associate Fellow (AFRIN)
Fellow (FRIN)
Affiliate Club
Affiliate College or University
Corporate Member
Small Business

*DESIGNATORY LETTERS*
MRIN, AFRIN, FRIN

# NON-DESTRUCTIVE TESTING

## Membership of Professional Institutions and Associations

### THE BRITISH INSTITUTE OF NON-DESTRUCTIVE TESTING

Newton Building
St George's Avenue
Northampton NN2 6JB
Tel: 01604 89 3811
Fax: 01604 89 3861
E-mail: info@bindt.org
Website: www.bindt.org

The BINDT was formed in 1976 from the merger of the Society of Non-Destructive Examination (SONDE) and the Society of Industrial Radiology and Allied Methods of Non-Destructive Testing, later renamed the NDT Society of Great Britain (NDTS), both formed in 1954. Our aim is to promote and advance the science and practice of non-destructive testing, condition monitoring, diagnostic engineering and all other materials and quality testing disciplines.

*MEMBERSHIP*
Student Member
Affiliate
Practitioner Member (PInstNDT)
Graduate Member (GInstNDT)
Member (MInstNDT)
Fellow (FInstNDT)
Engineering Technician (EngTech)
Incorporated Engineer (IEng)
Chartered Engineer (CEng)
Licensed Engineering Practitioner
Associate Member (corporate)

*DESIGNATORY LETTERS*
PInstNDT, GInstNDT, MInstNDT, FInstNDT, EngTech, IEng, CEng

# NURSERY NURSING

## Membership of Professional Institutions and Associations

### COUNCIL FOR AWARDS IN CHILDREN'S CARE AND EDUCATION

Apex House
81 Camp Road
St Albans
Hertfordshire AL1 5GB
Tel: 0845 347 2123
Fax: 01727 818618
E-mail: info@cache.org.uk
Website: www.cache.org.uk

CACHE is an Awarding Body that designs courses and qualifications in the care and education of children and young people. Our courses, which are widely available, range from entry level to advanced qualifications for sector professionals. We regularly lobby the government and other agencies to raise the quality and professionalism of child care.

*QUALIFICATION/EXAMINATIONS*
Please see the CACHE website.

## THE SOCIETY OF NURSERY NURSING PRACTITIONERS

40 Archdale Road
East Dulwich
London SE22 9HJ
Tel: 0845 643 6832
Fax: 0845 643 6834
E-mail: info@snnp.org.uk
Website: www.snnp.org.uk

The Society is the only professional examining body in the field. Incorporated in 1991, it caters for the interests and aspirations of childminders, nursery nurses and all those who look after children and young people from birth to age 0-5. It also exists to raise the flagging professional image of nursery nurses.

*MEMBERSHIP*
Graduate (GSNNP)
Associate (ASNNP)
Fellow (FSNNP)

*QUALIFICATION/EXAMINATIONS*
The examinations in Early Childhood Studies are in three stages, namely: Certificate, Advanced Certificate and Diploma. The subjects for all the examinations are the same but the questions are set and marked at the appropriate level. The subjects are:
Care of the sick child and special needs
Data investigation and interpretation
Early childhood play and learning
First aid and safety
Legal aspects of child care, health and community care
Management in the Early Years (Diploma level)
Managing self evaluation reflection
Observation, assessment and the young child
Overview of growth and development
Practice in service in child care
Pregnancy, birth and child development
Preparing for employment with young children
Protecting children from abuse
Social and psychological development
Working with parents and young children
Course work on a topic selected by the student

*DESIGNATORY LETTERS*
GSNNP, ASNNP, FSNNP

# NURSING AND MIDWIFERY

## *Membership of Professional Institutions and Associations*

## THE NURSING & MIDWIFERY COUNCIL

23 Portland Place
London W1B 1PZ
Tel: 020 7333 9333
E-mail: UKenquiries@nmc-uk.org
Website: www.nmc-uk.org

We are the nursing and midwifery regulator for England, Wales, Scotland, Northern Ireland and the Islands. We exist to safeguard the health and well-being of the public.

# OCCUPATIONAL THERAPY

## *Membership of Professional Institutions and Associations*

### BRITISH ASSOCIATION OF OCCUPATIONAL THERAPISTS

106–114 Borough High Street
Southwark
London SE1 1LB
Tel: 020 7357 6480
Fax: 020 7450 2299
E-mail: membership@cot.co.uk
Website: www.cot.org.uk

The British Association and College of Occupational Therapists is the professional body for occupational therapy in the UK. The College has 29, 000 members and represents the profession nationally and internationally.

*MEMBERSHIP*
Student Member
Associate
Discounted Associate
Professional Member
Discounted Professional Member
Self-employed Member
Retired Member
Overseas Member

*QUALIFICATION/EXAMINATIONS*
BA (Hons)
PG Dip
MSc

*DESIGNATORY LETTERS*
MBAOT

# OPTICIANS (DISPENSING)

Dispensing opticians must be registered with the General Optical Council (GOC, 41 Harley Street, London W1G 8DJ; Tel: 020 7580 3898; e-mail: goc@optical.org; website: www.optical.org). The GOC publishes registers of all optometrists, dispensing opticians, student opticians and optical businesses that are qualified and fit to practise, train or carry on business (www.optical.org/en/utilities/online-registers.cfm).

Qualification takes three years in total, and can be completed by combining a distance learning course or day release while working as a trainee under the supervision of a qualified and GOC-registered optician. Alternatively students can do a two-year full-time course followed by one year of supervised practice with a qualified and registered optician. The GOC has approved training courses in dispensing optics at the following six institutions in the UK: Anglia Ruskin University, Association of British Dispensing Opticians (ABDO) College, Bradford College, City University, City and Islington College, and Glasgow Caledonian University. All routes are assessed by final ABDO examinations. On successful completion of training you must register with the GOC in order to practise in the UK. Once qualified, you will need to undertake a minimum amount of continuing education and training to remain on the register.

The approved training course for the contact lens specialty is run by ABDO College and City and Islington College. If you qualify as a dispensing optician and have worked in practice as a qualified dispensing optician for at least two years, the University of Bradford offers a career progression course that enables you to graduate with a degree in optometry in one calendar year (Tel: 01274 234290; e-mail: lifesciences-ug@bradford.ac.uk).

*ENTRY REQUIREMENTS*
You will normally need to have five GCSEs (or equivalent) at grades C or above, including English, maths and science. For mature and overseas students, alternative and vocational courses, admission requirements will vary and may be more flexible. For further details contact the admissions tutor at the university you wish to apply to.

## *Membership of Professional Institutions and Associations*

### ASSOCIATION OF BRITISH DISPENSING OPTICIANS

199 Gloucester Terrace
London W2 6LD
Tel: 020 7298 5100
E-mail: general@abdolondon.org.uk
Website: www.abdo.org.uk

---

The ABDO is the qualifying body for dispensing opticians in the UK. Our aims are to advance the science and art of dispensing optics, to further the education and training of dispensing opticians, and to support and promote the interests of the profession.

*MEMBERSHIP*
Student Member
Associate Member
Full Member
Fellow (FBDO)
Elder

*QUALIFICATION/EXAMINATIONS*
Certificate in Contact Lens Practice (Level 6)
Diploma in The Assessment & Management of Low Vision (Level 6)
Diploma in Ophthalmic Dispensing (Level 6)
Diploma in Advanced Contact Lens Practice (Level 7)
Diploma in Spectacle Lens Design (Level 7)

*DESIGNATORY LETTERS*
FBDO

### ASSOCIATION OF CONTACT LENS MANUFACTURERS

PO Box 735
Devizes
Wiltshire SN10 3TQ
Tel: 01380 860418
Fax: 01380 860863
E-mail: secgen@aclm.org.uk
Website: www.aclm.org.uk

---

The ACLM was founded in 1962 to publicize the work of UK contact lens manufacturers, to develop new products and to raise standards. Today we represent the manufacturers of the vast majority of prescription contact lenses and lens care products sold in the UK, and provide a cohesive voice for our members.

*MEMBERSHIP*
Member

# OPTOMETRY

Careers in optometry are overseen by the General Optical Council (41 Harley Street, London W1G 8DJ; e-mail: goc@optical.org; website: www.optical.org). You can study for an undergraduate optometry degree from one of nine GOC-approved institutions in the UK: Anglia Ruskin University, Aston University, the University of Bradford, Cardiff University, City University, Glasgow Caledonian University, Plymouth University, the University of Manchester and the University of Ulster.

*LENGTH OF COURSE*
Usually four years in total (five in Scotland): a full-time three-year (four-year in Scotland) degree course, followed by one year's salaried pre-registration training with a practice under the guidance of a GOC-registered optometrist. This includes a series of assessments, set by the College of Optometry, throughout the placement.

*ENTRY REQUIREMENTS*

You will normally need five GCSEs (or equivalent) at grade C or above, one of which should be English; often maths and physics or double science are also required. You will normally be required to have three A Level passes/approximately 320 UCAS tariff points from the following subjects: physics, biology, chemistry or mathematics. Requirements vary between universities, so be sure to check the university's prospectus and/or consult the relevant admission tutors.

## *Membership of Professional Institutions and Associations*

### ASSOCIATION OF OPTOMETRISTS

2 Woodbridge Street
London EC1R 0DG
Tel: 020 7549 2000
Fax: 020 7251 8315
E-mail: postbox@aop.org.uk
Website: www.aop.org.uk

The AOP serves its members by promoting and protecting them, providing them with relevant services, representing and supporting them, enhancing their professional and business effectiveness, and expanding the role of optometry in primary and secondary eyecare.

*MEMBERSHIP*

Student Member
Honorary Member
Dispensing Associate
Full Member

# ORTHOPTICS

## *Membership of Professional Institutions and Associations*

### BRITISH AND IRISH ORTHOPTIC SOCIETY

62 Wilson Street
London EC2A 2BU
Tel: 01353 66 55 41
E-mail: membership@orthoptics.org.uk
Website: www.orthoptics.org.uk

Orthoptists are AHPs, who diagnose and treat problems with visual development and binocular vision (how the eyes work together as a pair), and eye movement disorders. They are experts in childhood vision screening. Extended roles include stroke, glaucoma, reading difficulties, neurological disorders, low vision.

*MEMBERSHIP*

Student Members
Members

*QUALIFICATION/EXAMINATIONS*

Degrees in orthoptics are offered by Liverpool University (www.liv.ac.uk) and Sheffield University (www.sheffield.ac.uk)

# OSTEOPATHY AND NATUROPATHY

## *Membership of Professional Institutions and Associations*

### BRITISH OSTEOPATHIC ASSOCIATION

3 Park Terrace
Manor Road
Luton
Bedfordshire LU1 3HN
Tel: 01582 488455
Fax: 01582 481533
E-mail: boa@osteopathy.org
Website: www.osteopathy.org

The BOA was formed in 1998 as a result of the merger of the British Osteopathic Association, the Osteopathic Association of Great Britain and the Guild of Osteopaths. We provide opportunities for individual and professional development in osteopathic practice and promote the highest standards of osteopathic education and research.

*MEMBERSHIP*
Student Member
1st/2nd/3rd/4th Year Graduate Member
Full Member
Overseas Member

# PATENT AGENCY

## *Membership of Professional Institutions and Associations*

### THE CHARTERED INSTITUTE OF PATENT ATTORNEYS

95 Chancery Lane
London WC2A 1DT
Tel: 020 7405 9450
Fax: 020 7430 0471
E-mail: mail@cipa.org.uk
Website: www.cipa.org.uk

CIPA is the professional, training and examining body for patent attorneys in the UK. From 2010 the IP Regulation Board, an independent body within the CIPA, sets the standards for regulation of the profession. Trainees, all technical graduates, also study for the qualification to practise before the European Patent Office.

*MEMBERSHIP*
Student Member
Associate
Fellow
British Overseas Member
Foreign Member

*QUALIFICATION/EXAMINATIONS*
Qualifying examination for registration as a Patent Attorney

*DESIGNATORY LETTERS*
RPA, CPA

# PENSION MANAGEMENT

## Membership of Professional Institutions and Associations

### THE PENSIONS MANAGEMENT INSTITUTE

PMI House
4–10 Artillery Lane
London E1 7LS
Tel: 020 7247 1452
Fax: 020 7375 0603
E-mail: via website
Website: www.pensions-pmi.org.uk

The Pensions Management Institute is the professional body that promotes standards of excellence and lifetime learning for pensions professionals and trustees through its qualifications, membership and ongoing support services. For further details please visit our website.

*MEMBERSHIP*
Student membership
Certificate Membership
Diploma Membership
Associate Membership
Fellowship
Affiliate Membership
Trustee Group Membership

*QUALIFICATION/EXAMINATIONS*
Award in Pensions Essentials (APE)
Certificate in Pensions Essentials (CPE)
Certificate in Pension Calculations (CPC)
Certificate in Pensions Administration (CPA)
Diploma in Pensions Administration (DPA)
Retirement Provision Certificate (RPC)
Certificate in Pensions Automatic Enrolment (CPAE)
Diploma in Retirement Provision (DRP)
Diploma in Employee Benefits and Retirement Savings (DEBRS)
Diploma in International Employee Benefits (DipIEB)
Diploma in Regulated Retirement Advice (DRRA)
Advanced Diploma in Retirement Provision (ADRP)
Awards in Pensions Trusteeship (APT)

*DESIGNATORY LETTERS*
CertPMI, DipPMI, APMI, FPMI

# PERSONNEL MANAGEMENT

## Membership of Professional Institutions and Associations

### CHARTERED INSTITUTE OF PERSONNEL AND DEVELOPMENT

151 The Broadway
Wimbledon
London SW19 1JQ
Tel: +44(0)20 8612 6208
Fax: +44(0)20 8612 6201
E-mail: membershipenquiry@cipd.co.uk
Website: www.cipd.co.uk

The CIPD is the world's largest Chartered HR and development professional body. With 135, 000 members across 120 countries it supports and develops those responsible for the management and development of people within organisations.

*MEMBERSHIP*
Affiliate member
Student member
Associate member (Assoc CIPD)
Chartered Member (MCIPD)

Chartered Fellow (FCIPD)
Academic member
For further information see: www.cipd.co.uk/membership

*QUALIFICATION/EXAMINATIONS*
CIPD qualifications are available at three levels:
Level 3 Foundation
Level 5 Intermediate
Level 7 Advanced
In three different sizes:
Awards
Certificates
Diplomas
For more information and to find out where to study CIPD qualifications visit: www.cipd.co.uk/qualifications

*DESIGNATORY LETTERS*
Assoc CIPD, Chartered MCIPD, Chartered FCIPD, CCIPD

## THE INSTITUTE OF CONTINUING PROFESSIONAL DEVELOPMENT

Royal Institute of Chartered Surveyors
Parliament Square
London SW1P 3AD
Tel: 020 7695 1673
E-mail: info@cpdinstitute.org
Website: www.cpdinstitute.org

The Institute of Continuing Professional Development is part of the Continuing Professional Development Foundation, an educational charitable trust providing high-quality and broad-ranging CPD since 1981. We serve the public interest by helping to raise the effectiveness of professionals through the promotion of CPD as an important and integral element of lifelong learning.

*MEMBERSHIP*
Member (MInstCPD)
Fellow (FInstCPD)

*DESIGNATORY LETTERS*
MInstCPD, FInstCPD

## UK EMPLOYEE ASSISTANCE PROFESSIONALS ASSOCIATION

PO Box 7966
Wilson
Derby DE1 0XP
E-mail: info@eapa.org.uk
Website: www.eapa.org.uk

The UK Employee Assistance Professionals Association represents the interests of professionals concerned with employee assistance, psychological health and wellbeing in the UK. Members include external and internal EAP providers, purchasers, counsellors, consultants and trainers.

*MEMBERSHIP*
Individual Member
Associate Member
Organisational Member
Registered External or Internal Provider

# PHARMACY

## *Membership of Professional Institutions and Associations*

### GENERAL PHARMACEUTICAL COUNCIL

1 Lambeth High Street
London SE1 7JN
Tel: 020 7735 9141
Fax: 020 7735 7629
E-mail: enquiries@rpsgb.org
Website: www.pharmacyregulation.org

The RPSGB, which dates from 1841, is the professional body for pharmacists and pharmacy technicians in England, Scotland and Wales. Our primary objectives are to lead, regulate, develop and represent the profession. We promote advancement of the science and practice of pharmacy, and pharmaceutical education and knowledge, and liaise with government and other bodies in the interests of our members.

*MEMBERSHIP*
Pharmacy Technician
Pharmacist
Student

*DESIGNATORY LETTERS*
MRPharmS, FRPharmS

### THE PHARMACEUTICAL SOCIETY OF NORTHERN IRELAND

73 University Street
Belfast BT7 1HL
Tel: 028 9032 6927
Fax: 028 9043 9919
E-mail: info@psni.org.uk
Website: www.psni.org.uk

The Pharmaceutical Society of Northern Ireland, founded in 1925, is the regulatory and professional body for pharmacists in Northern Ireland. It maintains a register of more than 2, 000 pharmacists and over 500 pharmacy premises, and sets and promotes the standards for pharmacists' admission to and remaining on the register, thereby protecting public safety.

*MEMBERSHIP*
Trainee
Member

*QUALIFICATION/EXAMINATIONS*
Registration Examination

# PHOTOGRAPHY

## *Membership of Professional Institutions and Associations*

### ASSOCIATION OF PHOTOGRAPHERS (AOP)

21 Downham Road
London N1 5AA
Tel: 020 7739 6669
E-mail: info@aophoto.co.uk
Website: www.the-aop.org

The AOP was founded in 1968 to promote the highest standards throughout the industry and to improve the rights of all professional photographers based in the UK. Our membership currently comprises 1, 800 photographers and photographic assistants, and we are supported by photographers' agents, printers, and manufacturers and suppliers of photographic equipment.

*MEMBERSHIP*
Student Member
Assistant Member
Photographer (full) Member
Agent Member
College Member
Affiliated Company

### BRITISH INSTITUTE OF PROFESSIONAL PHOTOGRAPHY

The Coach House
The Firs, High Street
Whitchurch
Aylesbury
Buckinghamshire HP22 4SJ
Tel: 01296 642020
Fax: 01296 641553
E-mail: info@bipp.com
Website: www.bipp.com

The BIPP is the qualifying body for professional photographers in the UK. We provide support, training and qualifications for photographers across all types of photography, and organize a number of regional activities and events. A not-for-profit organization, we ensure that professional standards are met and maintained.

*MEMBERSHIP*
Open to full- or part-time professional photographers. Join as a Provisional member (maximum of 1 year) and work towards gaining a professional qualification. Student membership is also available.

*QUALIFICATION/EXAMINATIONS*
Three tiers of qualification:
Licentiateship (LBIPP)
Associateship (ABIPP)
Fellowship (FBIPP)
Full details of the qualifications criteria can be found at www.bipp.com

*DESIGNATORY LETTERS*
LBIPP, ABIPP, FBIPP

## MASTER PHOTOGRAPHERS ASSOCIATION

Jubilee House
1 Chancery Lane
Darlington
Co Durham DL1 5QP
Tel: 01325 356555
Fax: 01325 357813
E-mail: general@mpauk.com
Website: www.mpauk.com

The MPA was founded in 1952 and is now the UK's only organization for FT, qualified professional photographers. We have more than 2, 000 members, who enjoy a range of benefits, including education, qualifications, informative regional meetings, business building promotions and marketing support, and abide by the Association's Code of Conduct.

*MEMBERSHIP*
Licentiate (LMPA)
Associate (AMPA)
Fellow (FMPA)

*QUALIFICATION/EXAMINATIONS*
The Diploma in Photographic Practice (DipPP) is recognized by SkillSet, as a benchmark competence mapped to the Photo Imaging National Standards: it is available to all qualified members and is an assessment process of professional photographic business and personal skills.

*DESIGNATORY LETTERS*
LMPA, AMPA, FMPA, DipPP

## THE ROYAL PHOTOGRAPHIC SOCIETY

Fenton House
122 Wells Road
Bath BA2 3AH
Tel: 01225 325733
E-mail: reception@rps.org
Website: www.rps.org

The RPS, which dates from 1853, is an educational charity whose aim is to promote the art and science of photography. Membership is open to anyone and we provide information, training and advice, hold workshops on a variety of photographic topics and stage three major touring exhibitions, as well as a monthly exhibition of members' work at our headquarters in Bath.

*MEMBERSHIP*
Student Member
Member
Licentiate (LRPS)
Associate (ARPS)
Fellow (FRPS)

*QUALIFICATION/EXAMINATIONS*
Qualified Imaging Scientist and Licentiate (QIS LRPS)
Graduate Imaging Scientist and Associate (GIS ARPS)
Accredited Imaging Scientist and Associate (AIS ARPS)
Accredited Senior Imaging Scientist and Fellow (ASIS FRPS)

*DESIGNATORY LETTERS*
LRPS, ARPS, FRPS

# PHYSICS

## *Membership of Professional Institutions and Associations*

### INSTITUTE OF PHYSICS AND ENGINEERING IN MEDICINE

Fairmount House
230 Tadcaster Road
York YO24 1ES
Tel: 01904 610821
Fax: 01904 612279
E-mail: office@ipem.org.uk
Website: www.ipem.ac.uk

---

The IPEM is dedicated to bringing together physical science, engineering and clinical professionals in academia, healthcare services and industry to share knowledge, advance science and technology, and inform and educate the public, with the purpose of improving the understanding, detection and treatment of disease and the management of patients.

*MEMBERSHIP*
Student Member
Affiliate
Associate
Medical Member (MedMIPEM)
Medical Fellow (MedFIPEM)
Corporate Member (MIPEM)
Fellow (FIPEM)
International

*DESIGNATORY LETTERS*
MedMIPEM, MedFIPEM, IIPEM, MIPEM, FIPEM

### THE INSTITUTE OF PHYSICS

76 Portland Place
London W1B 1NT
Tel: 020 7470 4800
Fax: 020 7470 4848
E-mail: physics@iop.org
Website: www.iop.org

---

The IOP is a scientific charity devoted to increasing the practice, understanding and application of physics. We have a worldwide membership of over 36, 000 and are a leading communicator of physics-related science to all audiences, from specialists through to government and the general public. Our publishing company, IOP Publishing, is a world leader in scientific publishing and the electronic dissemination of physics.

*MEMBERSHIP*
Student Member
Affiliate
Associate Member (AMInstP)
Member (MInstP)
Fellow (FInstP)
Chartered Physicist (CPhys)
IOPi Member

*DESIGNATORY LETTERS*
AMInstP, MInstP, FInstP, CPhys

# PHYSIOTHERAPY

## *Membership of Professional Institutions and Associations*

### THE CHARTERED SOCIETY OF PHYSIOTHERAPY

14 Bedford Row
London WC1R 4ED
Tel: 0207 306 6666
E-mail: via website
Website: www.csp.org.uk

The CSP is the professional, educational and trade union body for the UK's 52, 000 chartered physiotherapists, physiotherapy students and assistants. In order to become a member of the CSP it is necessary to have undertaken a qualification recognized by the Health and Care Professions Council (HCPC) – see: www.hcpc-uk.org

*MEMBERSHIP*
Student Member
Associate
Member (MCSP)
Fellow (FCSP)

*DESIGNATORY LETTERS*
MCSP, FCSP

# PLUMBING

## *Membership of Professional Institutions and Associations*

### CHARTERED INSTITUTE OF PLUMBING AND HEATING ENGINEERING

64 Station Lane
Hornchurch
Essex RM12 6NB
Tel: 01708 472791
Fax: 01708 448987
E-mail: info@ciphe.org.uk
Website: www.ciphe.org.uk

The CIPHE, founded in 1906, is the professional body for the UK plumbing and heating industry. Our membership of around 12, 000 is made up of individuals from a wide range of backgrounds and includes consultants, specifiers, designers, public health engineers, lecturers, trainers, trainees and practitioners, as well as manufacturers and distributors.

*MEMBERSHIP*
Trainee
Affiliate
Companion (CompCIPHE)
Associate (ACIPHE)
Member (MCIPHE)
Fellow (FCIPHE)

*QUALIFICATION/EXAMINATIONS*
Apprentice, Journeyman and Master Plumber Certificate (awarded jointly with the Worshipful Company of Plumbers and the City & Guilds of London Institute)

*DESIGNATORY LETTERS*
CompCIPHE, ACIPHE, MCIPHE, FCIPHE

# PRINTING

## Membership of Professional Institutions and Associations

### PROSKILLS UK

Unit 24 East Central
127 Olympic Avenue
Milton Park
Abingdon
Oxfordshire OX14 4SA
Tel: 01235 833844
E-mail: info@proskills.co.uk
Website: www.proskills.co.uk

Proskills UK is the bridge between employers and government on skills and training. Employer-led representing key industries including: Building Products, Coatings, Furniture, Furnishings & Interiors, Glass & Related Industries, Health and Safety Paper, Printing and Wood industries, which make up a third of the UK manufacturing sector. We help to raise the profile of the sector, set the skills standards and qualifications and ensure that the skills and funding system delivers against the current and future needs of the industries.

*QUALIFICATION/EXAMINATIONS*
Please see the Proskills UK website.

### THE INSTITUTE OF PAPER, PRINTING AND PUBLISHING (IP3)

Claremont House
70–72 Alma Road
Windsor
Berks SL4 3EZ
Tel: 0870 330 8625
Fax: 0870 330 8615
E-mail: info@ip3.org.uk
Website: www.ip3.org.uk

IP3 is the professional body representing the interests of individuals within the paper, printing and publishing sector. It was formed in 2005 from the merger of the Institute of Paper, the Institute of Printing and the Institute of Publishing, and brought together more than 2, 000 members and a wealth of knowledge.

*MEMBERSHIP*
Student
Associate (AIP3)
Member (MIP3)
Fellow (FIP3)

*QUALIFICATION/EXAMINATIONS*
Certificate

*DESIGNATORY LETTERS*
AIP3, MIP3, FIP3

# PROFESSIONAL INVESTIGATION

## *Membership of Professional Institutions and Associations*

### THE INSTITUTE OF PROFESSIONAL INVESTIGATORS

Claremont House
70–72 Alma Road
Windsor
Berkshire SL4 3EZ
Tel: 0870 330 8622
Fax: 0870 330 8612
E-mail: admin@ipi.org.uk
Website: www.ipi.org.uk

The IPI was founded in 1976 as a professional body, catering primarily for the work and educational needs of professional investigators of all types and all specializations. We encourage members' CPD and require them to adhere to the Institute's strict code of ethics, and we promote the recognition of professional investigation as a profession by government, legislative bodies and the public.

*MEMBERSHIP*
Associate
Member (MIPI)
Student
Fellow (FIPI)

*QUALIFICATION/EXAMINATIONS*
The Institute provides an interactive online Foundation Course for students and others interested in becoming part of the investigative industry; this course also provides a refresher course for those who need to update their specialization and/or interest in other areas of investigative work.

*DESIGNATORY LETTERS*
MIPI, FIPI

# PSYCHOANALYSIS

## *Membership of Professional Institutions and Associations*

### THE BRITISH PSYCHOANALYTICAL SOCIETY

Byron House
112a Shirland Road
London W9 2EQ
Tel: 020 7563 5000
Fax: 020 7563 5001
E-mail: admin@iopa.org.uk
Website: www.psychoanalysis.org.uk

The British Psychoanalytical Society was founded in 1913 and now has 438 members and 46 candidates for membership. Our aims include: to support the development of psychoanalytical knowledge as a general theory of mind, to further the clinical and scientific standards of psychoanalysis, and to train high-quality psychoanalytical professionals in sufficient numbers to develop the profession.

*MEMBERSHIP*
Associate Member
Full Member
Fellow

# PSYCHOLOGY

## *Membership of Professional Institutions and Associations*

### BRITISH PSYCHOLOGICAL SOCIETY

St Andrews House
48 Princess Road East
Leicester LE1 7DR
Tel: 0116 254 9568
Fax: 0116 227 1314
E-mail: enquiries@bps.org.uk
Website: www.bps.org.uk

Psychology is the scientific study of people, the mind and behaviour. The British Psychological Society is the representative body for psychology and psychologists in the UK. We are responsible for the development, promotion and application of psychology for the public good.

*MEMBERSHIP*
Student Member
Graduate Member (MBPsS)
Associate Fellow (AFBPsS)
Fellow (FBPsS)
Honorary Fellow (HonFBPsS)
Affiliate
Chartered Membership (CPsychol)
Subscriber
e-Subscriber

*QUALIFICATION/EXAMINATIONS*
Qualification in Clinical Psychology (SoE)
Qualification in Educational Psychology (Scotland) (Stage 2)
Qualification in Forensic Psychology (Stage 2) (QFP)
Qualification in Clinical Neuropsychology (QiCN)
Qualification in Counselling Psychology (QCoP)
Qualification in Health Psychology (Stage 2)
Qualification in Occupational Psychology (QOccPsych)
Qualification in Sport & Exercise Psychology (QSEP)

*DESIGNATORY LETTERS*
MBPsS, AFBPsS, FBPsS, CPsychol, HonMBPsS, HonFBPsS, SoE

# PSYCHOTHERAPY

## *Membership of Professional Institutions and Associations*

### ASSOCIATION OF CHILD PSYCHOTHERAPISTS

120 West Heath Road
London NW3 7TU
Tel: 020 8458 1609
E-mail: admin@childpsychotherapy.org.uk
Website: www.childpsychotherapy.org.uk

The ACP is the main professional body for psychoanalytic child and adolescent psychotherapists in the UK. Our members work with children and young people as well as their parents, families and wider networks, treating a wide range of difficulties ranging from problems with sleeping and bedwetting to eating disorders, self-harm, depression and anxiety.

*MEMBERSHIP*
Member

## BRITISH ASSOCIATION FOR COUNSELLING AND PSYCHOTHERAPY

BACP House
15 St John's Business Park
Lutterworth
Leicestershire LE17 4HB
Tel: 01455 883300
Fax: 01455 550243
E-mail: bacp@bacp.co.uk
Website: www.bacp.co.uk

BACP is the largest and broadest body within the sector and participates in the development of counselling and psychotherapy at an international level. Our work with large and small organizations ranges from advising schools on how to set up a counselling service to assisting the NHS on service provision, working with voluntary agencies and supporting independent practitioners.

*MEMBERSHIP*
Individual Member
Registered Member (MBACP)
Senior Accredited Member (Snr Accred)
Student Member
Affiliate Member
Associate Member
Member (MBACP)
Accredited Member (MBACP Accred)
Fellow (FBACP)

*QUALIFICATION/EXAMINATIONS*
We run workshops for members and accredit individual counsellors/psychotherapists, supervisors, counselling services and training courses. For details see our website.

*DESIGNATORY LETTERS*
MBACP, MBACP (Accred), FBACP, Snr Accred

## BRITISH ASSOCIATION FOR THE PERSON CENTRED APPROACH

BAPCA
PO Box 143
Ross-on-Wye
Herefordshire HR9 9AH
Tel: 01989 763863
E-mail: via website
Website: www.bapca.org.uk

The BAPCA was founded in 1989 as a non-religious, non-profit-making organization with the aim of advancing education in Client-Centred Psychotherapy and Counselling and the Person-Centred Approach through its publications and website, and cooperation with other national and international organizations with similar goals.

*MEMBERSHIP*
Individual Member
Joint Member
International Member
Institutional Member

## BRITISH PSYCHOTHERAPY FOUNDATION

37 Mapesbury Road
London NW2 4HJ
Tel: 020 8452 9823
E-mail: mail@bap-psychotherapy.org
Website: www.bap-psychotherapy.org

The BAP is one of the longest established and largest independent providers of Jungian analytic and psychoanalytic psychotherapy for adults and children in the UK. We have been training psychoanalytic and Jungian psychotherapists for nearly 60 years, and our members work in the NHS, the corporate and voluntary sectors and as private practitioners.

*MEMBERSHIP*
Member

*QUALIFICATION/EXAMINATIONS*
Certificate/Diploma/MSc in Psychodynamics of Human Development (jointly with Birkbeck College, University of London)
DPsych in Child and Adolescent Psychotherapy (jointly with Birkbeck College, University of London)

## CAMBRIDGE COLLEGE OF HYPNOTHERAPY

7 Bold Street
Warrington WA1 1DN
Tel: 01925 659303
E-mail: info@thecch.com
Website: www.hypnotherapytraining.org.uk

The CCH offers training to become a professional hypnotherapist. The course is accredited by the NCH, HA, APHP, NGH and NRAH. No formal qualifications are required to enrol on the course. What is required is a willingness to learn, a sense of humour and a genuine compassion and liking for people from all paths in life. This can be a very rewarding new or second career or a supplement to your current work / lifestyle. In addition to the College Diploma, it is possible to gain the HPD (Hypnotherapy Practitioner Diploma) which is awarded by ncfe and also possible to gain a Diploma awarded by the National Guild of Hypnotists in the USA. The HPD is at NVQ level 4/5 and has transferable credits of 45 for a first year degree with the Open University.

*QUALIFICATION/EXAMINATIONS*
Intermediate Practitioner Certificate
Diploma in Therapeutic Hypnosis (DipTHP)

*DESIGNATORY LETTERS*
DipTHP

## NATIONAL COLLEGE OF HYPNOSIS AND PSYCHOTHERAPY

PO Box 5779
Loughborough
Leicestershire LE12 5ZF
Tel: 0845 257 8735
E-mail: enquiries@nchp.org.uk
Website: www.hypnotherapyuk.net

The NCHP is a not-for-profit organization founded in 1977 and now offers accredited hypnotherapy training, hypnosis training and psychotherapy training at weekends in Leeds, Leicester, Liverpool, London, Manchester, Newcastle, Oxford, Glasgow and South Wales. We also provide a programme of 1- and 2-day workshops and seminars, and (where appropriate) distance-learning courses.

*QUALIFICATION/EXAMINATIONS*
Foundation Course
Certificate in Hypno-Psychotherapy (CHP(NC))
Diploma in Hypno-Psychotherapy (DHP(NC))
Advanced Diploma in Hypno-Psychotherapy (ADHP(NC))

## NATIONAL COUNCIL OF PSYCHOTHERAPISTS

PO Box 541
Keighley BD21 9DS
Tel: 0800 170 1250
E-mail: info@thencp.org
Website: www.ncphq.co.uk

The National Council is a registering and accrediting body for psychotherapists, counsellors and coaches within the UK and also, through the International Council, the rest of the world.

Members can join the Council regardless of which discipline and where they completed their training.

*MEMBERSHIP*
Accredited Member (MNCP Accred)
Member (MNCP)
Fellow (FNCP)

*DESIGNATORY LETTERS*
ANCP, LNCP, MNCP, FNCP

## THE FOUNDATION FOR PSYCHOTHERAPY AND COUNSELLING

5 Maidstone Buildings Mews
72-76 Borough High Street
London SE1 1GN
Tel: 0207 378 7392
E-mail: membership@thefpc.org.uk
Website: www.thefoundation-uk.org

The Foundation for Psychotherapy and Counselling was formed during the 1970s as the graduate body of WPF Therapy (the largest charitable provider of counselling and psychotherapy in England) and now has some 700 fully trained and qualified members, most of whom are in private practice.

*MEMBERSHIP*
Member

## THE NATIONAL REGISTER OF HYPNOTHERAPISTS AND PSYCHOTHERAPISTS

1st Floor
18 Carr Road
Nelson
Lancashire BB9 7JS
Tel: 01282 716839
E-mail: admin@nrhp.co.uk
Website: www.nrhp.co.uk

NRHP (est 1985) – a professional association of qualified hypno-psychotherapists who trained with a UKCP-accredited training organisation. Members are required to adhere to a code of ethics and carry appropriate insurance. We publish a Directory of Practitioners and offer a public referral service via our website and office. Member of the UKCP.

*MEMBERSHIP*
Student
Associate 1 (NRHP(Assoc 1))
Associate 2 (NRHP(Assoc 2))
Associate 3 (NRHP(Assoc 3))
Full Member (MNRHP)
Fellow (FNRHP)

*DESIGNATORY LETTERS*
NRHP(Assoc 1), NRHP(Assoc 2), NRHP(Assoc 3), MNRHP, FNRHP

### UK COUNCIL FOR PSYCHOTHERAPY

2nd Floor Edward House
2 Wakley Street
London EC1V 7LT
Tel: 020 7014 9955
Fax: 020 7014 9977
E-mail: info@ukcp.org.uk
Website: www.psychotherapy.org.uk

The UK Council for Psychotherapy (UKCP) is recognised as the leading professional body for the education, training and accreditation of psychotherapists and psychotherapeutic counsellors. We represent 75 training and accrediting organisations and over 7, 500 individual therapists – working privately or in public health organisations – offering a wide variety of psychotherapeutic approaches or modalities. UKCP exists to uphold the highest standards in psychotherapy. Our national register of psychotherapists and psychotherapeutic counsellors lists those practitioner members who meet exacting standards and training requirements. As part of our commitment to protecting the public, we work to improve access to psychological therapies, to support and disseminate research, to improve standards and to respond effectively to complaints against our members.

# PURCHASING AND SUPPLY

## *Membership of Professional Institutions and Associations*

### THE CHARTERED INSTITUTE OF PURCHASING & SUPPLY

Easton House
Easton on the Hill
Stamford
Lincolnshire PE9 3NZ
Tel: 01780 756777
Fax: 01780 751610
E-mail: press@cips.org
Website: www.cips.org

The Chartered Institute of Purchasing & Supply (CIPS) is the world's largest procurement and supply professional organisation. It is the worldwide centre of excellence on purchasing and supply management issues. CIPS has a global community of 100, 000 in 150 different countries, including senior business people, high-ranking civil servants and leading academics. The activities of purchasing and supply chain professionals have a major impact on the profitability and efficiency of all types of organisation and CIPS offers corporate solutions packages to improve business profitability.

*MEMBERSHIP*
Student Member
Affiliate
Certificate Member
Diploma Member

Associate Member
Full Member (MCIPS)
Fellow (FCIPS)

*QUALIFICATION/EXAMINATIONS*
Please see website: www.cips.org

*DESIGNATORY LETTERS*
MCIPS, FCIPS

# QUALITY ASSURANCE

## *Membership of Professional Institutions and Associations*

### THE CHARTERED QUALITY INSTITUTE

2nd Floor North
Chancery Exchange
10 Furnival Street
London EC4A 1AB
Tel: 020 7245 6722
Fax: 020 7245 6788
E-mail: membership@thecqi.org
Website: www.thecqi.org

The CQI is the chartered body for quality management professionals. Established in 1919, we gained a Royal Charter in 2006 and became the CQI shortly afterwards. Our vision is to place quality at the heart of every organization; we promote the benefits of quality management to industry, disseminate quality knowledge and resources, provide qualifications and training, and assess quality competence.

*MEMBERSHIP*
Student
Associate Member (ACQI)
Practitioner (PCQI)
Member, Chartered Quality Professional (MCQI, CQP)
Fellow, Chartered Quality Professional (FCQI, CQP)
Company Member
Corporate Member

*QUALIFICATION/EXAMINATIONS*
Level 3 Certificate in Quality Management (QCF)
Level 5 Certificate in Systems Management (QCF)
Level 5 Certificate in Assuring Service & Product Quality (QCF)
Level 5 Certificate in Managing Supply Chain Quality (QCF)
Level 5 Certificate in Quality Improvement for Business (QCF)
Level 5 Certificate in Quality Management Systems Audit (QCF)
Level 5 Diploma in Quality Management (QCF)

*DESIGNATORY LETTERS*
MCQI, CQP; FCQI, CQP

# RADIOGRAPHY

## *Membership of Professional Institutions and Associations*

### THE SOCIETY OF RADIOGRAPHERS

207 Providence Square
Mill Street
London SE1 2EW
Tel: 020 7740 7200
Fax: 020 7740 7233
E-mail: via website
Website: www.sor.org

The Society of Radiographers, founded in 1920, represents diagnostic and therapeutic radiographers in the UK. Associated professionals working in medical imaging, radiation therapy and oncology are also welcome. It is responsible for their professional, educational, public and workplace interests. Together with the College of Radiographers, our charitable subsidiary, our efforts are directed towards education, research and other activities in support of the science and practice of radiography.

*MEMBERSHIP*
We have a range of membership options, including student, associate professional, healthcare support worker and assistant practitioner, retired and international membership options.

# RETAIL

## *Membership of Professional Institutions and Associations*

### IGD

Grange Lane
Letchmore Heath
Watford
Hertfordshire WD25 8GD
Tel: 01923 857141
Fax: 01923 852531
E-mail: askigd@igd.com
Website: www.igd.com

IGD (the Institute of Grocery Distribution) was formed in 1972 from the merger of the Institute of Chartered Grocers and the Institute of Food Distribution. We provide information and practical training to the industry and now have more than 700 corporate members, covering a broad spectrum of companies and organizations across the world.

*MEMBERSHIP*
Corporate Member

## INSTITUTE OF MASTERS OF WINE

24 Fitzroy Square
London W1T 6EP
Tel: 020 7383 9130
Fax: 020 7383 9139
E-mail: peter@mastersofwine.org
Website: www.mastersofwine.org

The Institute of Masters of Wine is a membership body that represents the interests of its members (Masters of Wine), administers the MW Examination, and runs an education programme in preparation for the examination. We also hold a number of events throughout the year, including seminars and tastings, master classes, discussions and, every 4 years, a symposium, most of which are open to the public.

*MEMBERSHIP*
Master of Wine (MW)

*QUALIFICATION/EXAMINATIONS*
Master of Wine Examination

*DESIGNATORY LETTERS*
MW

## MEAT TRAINING COUNCIL (MTC)

PO Box 6404
Leighton Buzzard
Bedfordshire LU7 6DX
Tel: 01525 371641
E-mail: mary.fisher@meattraining.org.uk
Website: www.meattraining.org.uk

The Meat Training Council is the independent voice of training in the red meat and poultry sector. MTC is a registered charity. MTC provide information about jobs and qualifications required to work in this sector of the food industry. We are the parent company of FDQ, a specialist food industry awarding organisation.

*QUALIFICATION/EXAMINATIONS*
Please see the Meat Training Council's website.

## THE BRITISH ANTIQUE DEALERS' ASSOCIATION

20 Rutland Gate
London SW7 1BD
Tel: 020 7589 4128
Fax: 020 7581 9083
E-mail: info@bada.org
Website: www.bada.org

BADA, which was founded in 1918, is the trade association for antique dealers in Britain. Our vetted members are elected for their high business standards and expertise, and adhere to a strict code of practice; we provide safeguards for members of the public who deal with our members, including independent arbitration if a dispute arises.

*MEMBERSHIP*
Member

## THE GUILD OF ARCHITECTURAL IRONMONGERS

BPF House
6 Bath Place
Rivington Street
London EC2A 3JE
Tel: 0207 033 2480
Fax: 0207 033 2486
E-mail: info@gai.org.uk
Website: www.gai.org.uk

The GAI represents the interests of architectural ironmongers and manufacturers of architectural ironmongery. We develop, promote and protect standards of integrity and excellence, and encourage academic study relating to the industry, operating an Institute for individual members to facilitate their continuous professional development. We liaise with various bodies on matters affecting the industry.

*MEMBERSHIP*
Affiliate Member
Associate Member
Full Member
Registered Architectural Ironmonger (Reg AI)

*QUALIFICATION/EXAMINATIONS*
The GAI provides a 3-year incremental training programme. Students are examined each year and must pass each year in turn before progressing to the next. A Certificate is awarded to successful students each year, culminating in the GAI Diploma (Dip GAI) on successful completion of year 3.

*DESIGNATORY LETTERS*
Reg AI

## THE INSTITUTE OF BUILDERS MERCHANTS

1180 Elliot Court
Coventry Business Park
Herald Avenue
Coventry CV5 6UB
Tel: 01767 650662
E-mail: admin@iobm.co.uk
Website: www.iobm.co.uk

To improve through seminars and website articles, the technical and general knowledge of persons engaged in builders' merchants; to verify management training courses with providers; to acknowledge personal achievements and award diplomas, certificates and other distinctions; to encourage the need for knowledge, integrity and efficiency in the builders' merchants industry.

*MEMBERSHIP*
Student
Associate
Member
Fellow
Corporate Supporter

*QUALIFICATION/EXAMINATIONS*
University Degree
The Institute of Builders Merchants Business Studies Course
The Builders Merchants Federation Diploma in Merchanting
Higher National Certificate (HNC) in Business Studies
Higher National Diploma (HND) in Business Studies
NVQ Level 4
Company management programmes as approved by the Board of Governors

## THE SOCIETY OF SHOE FITTERS

c/o The Anchorage
28 Admirals Walk
Hingham
Norfolk NR9 4JL
Tel: 01953 851171
Fax: 01953 851190
E-mail: secretary@shoefitters-uk.org
Website: www.shoefitters-uk.org

The Society of Shoe Fitters is a not-for-profit organization started in 1959, set up to assist the trade and public. We disseminate shoe fitting/footwear knowledge to the trade via courses and examination, and assist the public free of charge with shoe fitting advice via our website, leaflets and helpline.

*MEMBERSHIP*
Student Member
Associate Member
Member (MSSF)
Fellow (FSSF)
Associate Member (corporate membership)

*QUALIFICATION/EXAMINATIONS*
One-day on-site courses – certificate only
Five- or ten-month course leading to membership qualification
Entrance Examination and Entrance Application for experienced shoe fitters leading to qualification

*DESIGNATORY LETTERS*
MSSF, FSSF

# SECURITY

## *Membership of Professional Institutions and Associations*

## THE SECURITY INSTITUTE

1 The Courtyard
Caldecote
Warwickshire CV10 0AS
E-mail: info@security-institute.org
Website: www.security-institute.org

The Security Institute promotes professionalism in the security world and encourages a proper understanding of the value of the security function by management. The Institute manages the Register of Chartered Security Professionals – the ultimate standard for practitioners. Institute membership is recognized as an employment prerequisite by many companies and government departments.

*MEMBERSHIP*
Affiliate/Student
Graduate
Associate (ASyI)
Member (MSyI)
Fellow (FSyI)
Chartered Security Professional (CSyP)

*QUALIFICATION/EXAMINATIONS*
Certificate in Security Management
Diploma in Security Management

*DESIGNATORY LETTERS*
ASyI, MSyI, FSyI, CSyP

# SOCIAL WORK AND PROBATION

*SOCIAL WORK*

The role of the Health and Care Professions Council (HCPC) is to protect the health and wellbeing of those using or needing the services of registrants. It does this by developing and monitoring strategy and policy for the HCPC, and ensuring that the organization fulfils its functions under the Health and Social Work Professions Order 2001. The Council consists of 20 members appointed by the Appointments Commission on behalf of the Privy Council. Four statutory committees have been set up to establish and monitor standards of education and training and to deal with fitness to practise issues. In addition, the Council has established four non-statutory committees to provide it with advice and guidance on specific issues.

The HCPC accredits universities that offer social work qualifications at both qualifying and post-qualifying levels, and quality-assures all social work courses. Professional qualifying training for social workers in the United Kingdom is a degree in social work. To find HCPC-approved degree courses visit www.hcpc-uk.org/education/programmes/register

For further details, contact The Health and Care Professions Council, Park House, 184 Kennington Park Road, London SE11 4BU; Tel: 0845 300 6184; Fax: 020 7820 9684; e-mail: registrations@hcpc-uk.org; website: www.hcpc-uk.org

For information about social work training in Scotland, contact Scottish Social Services Council, Compass House, 11 Riverside Drive, Dundee DD1 4NY; Tel: 0845 6030 891; e-mail: enquiries@sssc.uk.com; website: www.sssc.uk.com

For information about social work training in Wales, contact Care Council for Wales, South Gate House, Wood Street, Cardiff CF10 1EW; Tel: 0300 3033 444; e-mail: info@ccwales.org.uk; website: www.ccwales.org.uk

For information about social work training in Northern Ireland, contact Northern Ireland Social Care Council, 7th Floor, Millennium House, 19–25 Great Victoria Street, Belfast BT2 7AQ; Tel: 028 9041 7600; e-mail: info@niscc.hscni.net; website: www.niscc.info

## *Membership of Professional Institutions and Associations*

### THE BRITISH ASSOCIATION OF SOCIAL WORKERS

16 Kent Street
Birmingham B5 6RD
Tel: 0121 6223911
Fax: 0121 6224860
E-mail: membership@basw.co.uk
Website: www.basw.co.uk

---

The BASW is the largest professional association representing social work and social workers in the UK. Whether you are qualified or not, experienced or just entering the profession, we are here to help, support, advise and campaign on your behalf.

*MEMBERSHIP*

Student Member
Affiliate
Member (4 categories)
Retired Member
Overseas Member

# SOCIOLOGY

## *Membership of Professional Institutions and Associations*

### BRITISH SOCIOLOGICAL ASSOCIATION

Bailey Suite, Palatine House
Belmont Business Park
Belmont
Durham DH1 1TW
Tel: 0191 383 0839
Fax: 0191 383 0782
E-mail: enquiries@britsoc.org.uk
Website: www.britsoc.co.uk

The BSA was founded in 1951 to promote sociology in the UK. Our members include researchers, teachers, students and practitioners in a variety of fields. We provide a network of communication to all who are concerned with the promotion and use of sociology and sociological research.

# SPEECH AND LANGUAGE THERAPY

## *Membership of Professional Institutions and Associations*

### ROYAL COLLEGE OF SPEECH AND LANGUAGE THERAPISTS

2 White Hart Yard
London SE1 1NX
Tel: 020 7378 1200
E-mail: info@rcslt.org
Website: www.rcslt.org

The RCSLT is the professional body for speech and language therapists and support workers. We set, promote and maintain high standards in education, clinical practice and ethical conduct. Our national campaigning work aims to improve services for people with speech, language, communication and swallowing needs and to influence health, education and social care policies.

*MEMBERSHIP*
Student Member
Newly Qualified Member
Full Member
Fellow (FRCSLT)
Honorary Fellow (Hon FRCSLT)

*DESIGNATORY LETTERS*
FRCSLT, Hon FRCSLT

# SPORTS SCIENCE

## *Membership of Professional Institutions and Associations*

### LONDON SCHOOL OF SPORTS MASSAGE

28 Station Parade
Willesden Green
London NW2 4NX
Tel: 020 8452 8855
Fax: 020 8452 4524
E-mail: via website
Website: www.lssm.com

---

The LSSM, founded in 1989, was the first to provide specialist training in Sport & Remedial Massage. We offer vocational training for those who want to develop a professional career in massage therapy and were instrumental in setting up the Institute of Sport & Remedial Massage (ISRM), which is the professional body promoting our needs and aspirations as clinical therapists.

*MEMBERSHIP*
Member

*QUALIFICATION/EXAMINATIONS*
Introductory Massage Workshop
Professional Diploma in Clinical Sport & Remedial Massage Therapy (BTEC Level 5)

# STATISTICS

## *Membership of Professional Institutions and Associations*

### THE ROYAL STATISTICAL SOCIETY

12 Errol Street
London EC1Y 8LX
Tel: 020 7638 8998
E-mail: rss@rss.org.uk
Website: www.rss.org.uk

---

The RSS is the learned society and professional body for statistics and statisticians in the UK. We have over 7, 000 members worldwide, and are active in a wide range of areas both directly and indirectly relating to the study and application of statistics.

*MEMBERSHIP*
Student Member
Fellow
Affiliate
Graduate Statistician (GradStat)
Chartered Statistician (CStat)

*QUALIFICATION/EXAMINATIONS*
Ordinary Certificate in Statistics
Higher Certificate in Statistics
Graduate Diploma in Statistics

*DESIGNATORY LETTERS*
GradStat, CStat

# STOCKBROKING AND SECURITIES

## *Membership of Professional Institutions and Associations*

## CFA SOCIETY OF THE UK

2nd Floor
135 Canon Street
London EC4N 5BP
Tel: 020 7280 9620
Fax: 020 7280 9636
E-mail: info@cfauk.org
Website: www.cfauk.org

The CFA Society of the UK was formerly the UK Society of Investment Professionals (UKSIP) and was renamed in 2007. Our aim is to promote the development of the investment profession in the UK through the promotion of the highest standards of ethical behaviour and the provision of education, professional development, information, career support and advocacy to our members.

*MEMBERSHIP*
IMC Member
Candidate Member
Affiliate Member
Regular Member

*QUALIFICATION/EXAMINATIONS*
Investment Management Certificate (IMC)

## THE CHARTERED INSTITUTE FOR SECURITIES & INVESTMENT

8 Eastcheap
London EC3M 1AE
Tel: 020 7645 0600
E-mail: customersupport@cisi.org
Website: www.cisi.org.uk

The Chartered Institute for Securities & Investment is the largest professional body for practitioners in stockbroking, derivatives markets, investment management, corporate finance, operations and related activities, having over 44, 000 members.

*MEMBERSHIP*
Student Member
Affiliate
Associate (ACSI)
Member (MCSI)
Chartered Member (Ch. MCSI)
Fellow (FCSI)
Chartered Fellow (Ch. FCSI)

*QUALIFICATION/EXAMINATIONS*
Introduction to Investment
Islamic Finance Qualification
IT in Investment Operations
Risk in Financial Services
Combating Financial Crime
Global Financial Compliance
Investment Operations Certificate (IOC) also known as Investment Administration Qualification (IAQ)
Certificate in Corporate Finance
Certificate in Investments
Certificate in Private Client Investment Advice & Management
International Certificate in Wealth Management
Investment Advice Diploma
Advanced Certificate in Global Securities Operations
Advanced Certificate in Operational Risk
Diploma in Investment Compliance
Diploma in Investment Operations
CISI Diploma
CISI Masters in Wealth Management
Fundamentals of Financial Services
International Introduction to Investment
Diploma in Finance, Risk & Investment
Certificate in Finance Risk & Decision Making

Certificate for Introduction to Securities & Investment
Level 3 Certificate in Investment Management
Level 3 International Certificate in Investment Management
Level 4 Certificate in Investment Management

*DESIGNATORY LETTERS*
ACSI, MCSI, Ch. MCSI, FCSI, Ch.FCSI

# SURGICAL, DENTAL AND CARDIOLOGICAL TECHNICIANS

## *Membership of Professional Institutions and Associations*

### THE BRITISH INSTITUTE OF DENTAL AND SURGICAL TECHNOLOGISTS

4 Thompson Green
Shipley
West Yorkshire BD17 7PR
Tel: 0115 9683 182
E-mail: via website
Website: www.bidst.org

---

The BIDST has been established for over 70 years and exists to provide a vehicle for the continuing education of technicians within the spheres of dental and surgical technology. It is our aim to make membership of the Institute an aspiration for all technicians, raising standards and portraying an image of professionalism which professional technicians deserve.

*MEMBERSHIP*
Affiliate (Overseas)
Affiliate (DCP)
Affiliate (Student)
Associate
Member
Fellow
Corporate Member

*DESIGNATORY LETTERS*
LBIDST, FBIDST

# SURVEYING

## *Membership of Professional Institutions and Associations*

### ASSOCIATION OF BUILDING ENGINEERS

Lutyens House
Billing Brook Road
Weston Favell
Northampton NN3 8NW
Tel: 01604 404121
E-mail: building.engineers@abe.org.uk
Website: www.abe.org.uk

---

The ABE is the professional body for those specializing in the technology of building and the management processes by which buildings are designed, constructed, renewed and maintained. Our objectives are to promote and advance the planning, design, construction, maintenance and repair of the built environment; to maintain a high standard of professional practice; and to encourage cooperation between professionals.

*MEMBERSHIP*
Student

Technician
Training Affiliate
Academic Affiliate
Associate Member (ABEng)
Graduate Member (GradBEng)
Corporate Member (MBEng)
Corporate Fellow (FBEng)
Honorary Fellow (HonFBEng)

*QUALIFICATION/EXAMINATIONS*
ABBE Level 3 NVQ Diploma in Town Planning Technical Support (QCF)
ABBE Level 3 NVQ Diploma in Conservation Technical Support (QCF)
ABBE Level 3 NVQ Diploma in Building Control Technical Support (QCF)
ABBE Level 6 NVQ Diploma in Building Control (QCF)
ABBE Level 6 NVQ Diploma in Town Planning (QCF)
Edexcel Level 3 NVQ Diploma in Construction Site Supervision (Construction) (QCF)
Edexcel Level 3 NVQ Diploma in Construction Contracting Operations (QCF)
Edexcel Level 6 NVQ Diploma in Construction Contracting Operations (QCF)
Edexcel Level 6 NVQ Diploma in Construction Site Management (Construction) (QCF)
Edexcel Level 6 NVQ Diploma in Senior Site Inspection (QCF)
Edexcel Level 6 NVQ Diploma in Built Environment Design Management (QCF)
Edexcel Level 7 NVQ Diploma in Built Environment Design and Consultancy Practice (QCF)
Edexcel Level 7 NVQ Diploma in Construction Senior Management (QCF)

*DESIGNATORY LETTERS*
ABEng, GradBEng, MBEng, FBEng

# SWIMMING INSTRUCTION

## *Membership of Professional Institutions and Associations*

### THE SWIMMING TEACHERS' ASSOCIATION

Anchor House
Birch Street
Walsall
West Midlands WS2 8HZ
Tel: 01922 645097
Fax: 01922 720628
E-mail: sta@sta.co.uk
Website: www.sta.co.uk

The STA is dedicated to the preservation of human life by the teaching of swimming, lifesaving and survival techniques to as many people as possible, both in the UK and internationally. We offer a range of specialist training programmes and qualifications, which are used in more than 25 countries worldwide, and liaise with other organizations concerned with swimming teaching and water safety.

*MEMBERSHIP*
Junior Member
Associate Member (ASTA)
Qualified Member (MSTA)
Corporate Member

*QUALIFICATION/EXAMINATIONS*
STA Level 2 Award in Swimming Teaching (QCF)
STA Level 2 Certificate in Swimming Teaching (QCF)
STA Level 1 Award for Pool to Open Water Swimming Coaching (QCF)
STA Level 2 Award for Open Water Swimming Coaching (QCF)
STA Level 2 Award in Aquatic Teaching – People with Disabilities (QCF)
STA Level 2 Award in Aquatic Teaching – Baby & Pre-School (QCF)
STA Level 1 Award in Pool Emergency Procedures (QCF)
STA Level 2 Award for Pool Responder (QCF)
STA Level 2 Award for Pool Lifeguard (QCF)

STA Level 2 Award in Emergency First Aid at Work (QCF)
STA Level 2 Award in Paediatric First Aid (QCF)
STA Level 2 Award in Activity First Aid (QCF)
STA Level 2 Award in Swimming Pool Water Testing (QCF)
STA Level 2 Award in Swimming Pool Water Treatment (QCF)
STA Level 3 Award in Pool Plant Operations (QCF)
STA Level 3 Award in Preparing to Teach in the Lifelong Learning Sector (QCF)
STA Level 4 Award in Preparing to Teach in the Lifelong Learning Sector (QCF)
STA Professional Award in Teaching Swimming at SCQF Level 6
STA Professional Certificate in Teaching Swimming
STA Professional Award in Aquatic Teaching – Baby and Pre-School at SCQF Level 6
STA Professional Award in Pool Emergency Procedures at SCQF Level 6
STA Professional Award for Pool Responder at SCQF Level 7
STA Professional Award for Pool Lifeguard at SCQF Level 7
STA Award in Emergency First Aid at Work at SCQF Level 5
STA Award in First Aid at Work at SCQF Level 6

*DESIGNATORY LETTERS*
ASTA, MSTA

# TAXATION

## *Membership of Professional Institutions and Associations*

### SOCIETY OF TRUST & ESTATE PRACTITIONERS

Artillery House (South)
11–19 Artillery Row
London SW1P 1RT
Tel: +44 (0)20 7340 0500
Fax: +44 (0)20 7340 0501
E-mail: step@step.org
Website: www.step.org

The Society of Trust and Estate Practitioners (STEP) is the worldwide professional association for practitioners dealing with family inheritance and succession planning. The Society helps to improve public understanding of the issues families face in this area and promotes education and high professional standards among its members.

*MEMBERSHIP*
Full members of STEP are the most experienced and senior practitioners in the field of trusts and estates.

*QUALIFICATION/EXAMINATIONS*
STEP Diplomas and Certificates are recognised as essential qualifications and TEPs are sought after by employers. A portfolio of courses has been designed to enhance your career, including the STEP Diploma for England & Wales (Trusts and Estates), STEP Diploma for Ireland, STEP Diploma for Scotland, STEP Diploma in International Trust Management and the STEP Diploma for Accountants & Tax Practitioners. The Certificate series includes the STEP Advanced Certificate in Family Business Advising, the STEP Certificate for Financial Services (Trusts and Estate Planning) and many more.

*DESIGNATORY LETTERS*
STEP

## THE ASSOCIATION OF TAXATION TECHNICIANS

1st Floor
Artillery House
11–19 Artillery Row
London SW1P 1RT
Tel: 020 7340 0551
E-mail: info@att.org.uk
Website: www.att.org.uk

The ATT was founded in 1989 in recognition of the increasing demand for tax services and the development of tax practice as a professional activity in its own right. Our primary aim is to provide an appropriate qualification for individuals who undertake such work, and we now have more than 10, 500 members, affiliates and registered students.

*MEMBERSHIP*
Member

*QUALIFICATION/EXAMINATIONS*
Certificate of Competency

*DESIGNATORY LETTERS*
ATT

## THE CHARTERED INSTITUTE OF TAXATION

First Floor
11–19 Artillery Row
London SW1P 1RT
Tel: 020 7340 0550
E-mail: via website
Website: www.tax.org.uk

The CIOT, which dates from 1930, is the professional body for Chartered Tax Advisers and has 14, 300 members. Our aims are to promote education in and the study of the administration and practice of taxation, and to achieve a better, more efficient, tax system for all affected by it – taxpayers, advisers and the authorities.

*MEMBERSHIP*
Member (CTA)

*QUALIFICATION/EXAMINATIONS*
Chartered Tax Adviser (CTA) examination
Advanced Diploma in International Taxation (ADIT)
VAT Compliance Diploma (VCD) (offered by the Institute of Indirect Taxation)

*DESIGNATORY LETTERS*
CTA, ATII, FTII

# TAXI DRIVERS

### *Membership of Professional Institutions and Associations*

## TAXI DRIVERS (LONDON)

Cab drivers and cab proprietors in the Metropolitan Police District and City of London are licensed by an Assistant Commissioner of the Metropolitan Police, through the Public Carriage Office at 15 Penton Street, Islington N1 9PU. A cab driver's licence is valid for 3 years and a cab proprietor's licence for 1 year.

# TEACHING/EDUCATION

## Initial qualifications in the UK

**Qualified Teacher Status**

To obtain a teaching appointment as a qualified teacher in maintained schools in England and Wales, it is necessary to have Qualified Teacher Status (QTS). To be qualified, teachers must have satisfactorily completed an approved course of initial teacher training (ITT), and to be able to teach in maintained schools in England must have successfully completed their induction period (there are similar arrangements for teaching in Scotland, Wales and Northern Ireland).

**Teacher training courses**

Initial teacher training courses in England and Wales are provided by accredited training providers mainly through university departments of education. Courses available include Bachelor of Arts or Bachelor of Science with QTS, Bachelor of Education (BEd) for undergraduates, and Postgraduate Certificates of Education (PGCEs) for graduates.

Undergraduate training courses generally take three or four years full time, or four to six years part time. However, if you have undergraduate credits from previous study you may be able to complete a course in two years. A PGCE generally lasts one year full time, or up to two years part time.

There are also some employment-based routes into teaching. The School Direct Programme allows schools to recruit trainees with the expectation that they will go on to work in the school or group of schools in which they have been trained, though there is no guarantee of employment. There are more than 100 schools offering places. Courses generally last for one year full time.

School Direct offers two separate training options: the School Direct Training Programme and the School Direct Training Programme (salaried). The School Direct Training Programme (salaried) is open to graduates with three or more years' career experience. Trainees will be employed as unqualified teachers with a salary subsidized by The National College for Teaching and Leadership. Trainees on a School Direct course will have to pay tuition fees to cover the cost of the course, but home and EU trainees will be eligible for a tuition fee loan to cover these costs. For more information, see The National College for Teaching and Leadership, School Direct (www.education.gov.uk).

School-centred initial teacher training (SCITT) is training in a school environment for those with a UK degree or an equivalent qualification. SCITT programmes are designed and delivered by groups of neighbouring schools and colleges; they are usually full time for one year. Taught by experienced, practising teachers, and often tailored towards local teaching needs, all SCITT courses lead to QTS. Many, though not all, will also award you a PGCE validated by a higher education institution. There are consortia of schools and colleges running SCITT courses all over England. These groups provide all kinds of SCITT, covering primary, middle years and the full range of secondary subjects. Application for SCITT courses is usually through the Graduate Teacher Training Registry (www.gttr.ac.uk), although some SCITT providers require direct applications.

Teach First offers a two-year Leadership Development Programme for those interested in an employment-based route into teaching. Teach First enables graduates to spend two years working in secondary and primary schools in low-income communities while earning a full-time salary. It offers the programme in ten regions: East Midlands, Kent and Medway, Greater London, North East, North West, South Coast, South West, West Midlands, Wales (South) and Yorkshire and the Humber. A PGCE is awarded on completion of the course.

The qualification of Professional Graduate Diploma in Education (PGDE) is a one-year postgraduate degree course leading to registration as a primary or secondary school teacher in Scotland (see www.teachinginscotland.com). Alternatively it is possible to undertake a four-year undergraduate degree course in education. In Scotland there are eight universities that offer teacher training courses: University of Aberdeen, University of Dundee, University of Edinburgh, University of Stirling, University of Glasgow, University of Strathclyde, University of the West of Scotland and the Open University in Scotland. For more information on how to apply for a teaching course in Scotland contact Graduate Teacher Training Registry (GTTR), Tel: 0871 468 0469, www.gttr.ac.uk; and Universities and Colleges Admissions System (UCAS), Tel: 0871 468 0468, www.ucas.com

GTCW is responsible for the notification of award of QTS in Wales, on behalf of the Welsh Government. The main ways to gain QTS in Wales are completion of a course of teacher training at an accredited institution in Wales (see www.teachertrainingcymru.org/home) or completion of employment-based training under the Graduate Teacher Programme (GTP). GTP programmes in Wales are managed and delivered by three regional centres of teacher training and education on behalf of the Welsh Government. Their contact details can be found at www.teachertrainingcymru.org/node/4

The Postgraduate Certificate of Education course, approved by the Department of Education Northern Ireland, or a four-year BEd (Hons) course, leads to recognition as a schoolteacher in Northern Ireland (see www.deni.gov.uk).

**Qualifications for admission to training**

Higher education institutions offering undergraduate ITT courses will set admissions criteria, typically two good A levels (or equivalent qualifications). Entrants to PGCE and other graduate training courses will require a relevant UK Bachelor's degree or a recognized equivalent and be expected to demonstrate a standard equivalent to GCSE grade C in English and mathematics, and additionally a standard equivalent to GCSE grade C in a science subject for those wishing to train to teach primary school children. Trainees who have undertaken their initial teacher training in England must pass professional skills tests in numeracy and literacy before starting the course. These tests cover core skills that teachers need in their jobs and QTS cannot be awarded until they are passed. If you are undertaking initial teacher training in Wales, you are not required to complete the skills tests in order to be awarded QTS.

**The National College for Teaching and Leadership**

The National College for Teaching and Leadership is the executive agency of the Department for Education (DfE). It is the body responsible for ITT in England and the award of QTS. It has two key aims: improving the quality of the education workforce; and helping schools to help each other to improve. There is no requirement to register with The National College for Teaching and Leadership and no registration fee. For information about the College, visit www.education.gov.uk

Visit www.education.gov.uk/teachregister or call 0800 389 2500 for queries relating to becoming a teacher, initial teacher training, recruitment opportunities or provision of relevant training.

**General Teaching Councils**

General Teaching Councils exist in Wales (GTCW), Scotland (GTCS) and Northern Ireland (GTCNI). These councils hold registers of qualified teachers and also act as disciplinary bodies. You can find out more from their respective websites: GTCW: www.gtcw.org.uk; GTCS: www.gtcs.org.uk; GTCNI: www.gtcni.org.uk

**Applications**

Applications for undergraduate courses are made through UCAS and postgraduate applications through the Graduate Teacher Training Registry (GTTR). You cannot apply for courses in Northern Ireland through GTTR, but must visit the Department for Education in Northern Ireland's website for information about these courses (www.deni.gov.uk). You can find out more about training to teach from the following websites: GTTR: www.gttr.ac.uk; UCAS: www.ucas.ac.uk; The National College for Teaching and Leadership: www.education.gov.uk/get-into-teaching

# TECHNICAL COMMUNICATIONS

## *Membership of Professional Institutions and Associations*

### THE INSTITUTE OF SCIENTIFIC AND TECHNICAL COMMUNICATORS (ISTC LTD)

Airport House
Purley Way
Croydon CR0 0XZ
Tel: 020 8253 4506
Fax: 020 8253 4510
E-mail: istc@istc.org.uk
Website: www.istc.org.uk

The ISTC is a non-profit-making organization and the largest UK body representing professional communicators and information designers. Our aims include improving standards of scientific and technical communication, promoting scientific and technical communication as a career, supporting our members, and consulting, cooperating and collaborating with other bodies that share our ideals.

*MEMBERSHIP*
Student
Associate
Junior
Member (MISTC)
Fellow (FISTC)
Business Affiliate

*DESIGNATORY LETTERS*
MISTC, FISTC

# TEXTILES

## *Membership of Professional Institutions and Associations*

### THE TEXTILE INSTITUTE

1st Floor St James' Buildings
79 Oxford Street
Manchester M1 6FQ
Tel: 0161 2371188
Fax: 0161 2361991
E-mail: tiihq@textileinst.org.uk
Website: www.textileinstitute.org

The Textile Institute covers all disciplines – from technology and production to design, development and marketing – relating to fibres, fabrics, clothing, footwear, and interior and technical textiles.

*MEMBERSHIP*
Student
Individual
Licentiate (LTI)
Associate (CText ATI)
Fellow (CText FTI)
Companion
Honorary Fellow
Corporate

*DESIGNATORY LETTERS*
LTI, CText ATI, CText FTI

# TIMBER TECHNOLOGY

## *Membership of Professional Institutions and Associations*

### WOOD TECHNOLOGY SOCIETY

The Boilerhouse
Springfield Business Park
Caunt Road
Grantham
Lincs NG31 7FZ
Tel: 01476-513880
Fax: 01476-513899
E-mail: emily.drury@iom3.org
Website: www.iom3.org/content/wood-technology

The Wood Technology Society (IWSc – a Division of the Institute of Materials, Minerals and Mining), formerly the Institute of Wood Science, is the professional body for the timber and allied industries. We promote and encourage a better understanding of timber, wood-based materials and associated timber processes, and are the UK examining body, awarding qualifications at Foundation, Certificate and Diploma level.

*MEMBERSHIP*
Student Member
Affiliate Member
Technician (EngTech)
Fellow (FIMMM)
Professional Member (MIMMM)
Graduate (Grad IMMM)
Corporate Member

*QUALIFICATION/EXAMINATIONS*
Level 2 Award in Timber and Panel Products (QCF)
Certificate
Diploma

*DESIGNATORY LETTERS*
TIWSc, LIWSc, MIWSc, FIWSc

# TOWN AND COUNTRY PLANNING

## *Membership of Professional Institutions and Associations*

### ROYAL TOWN PLANNING INSTITUTE

41 Botolph Lane
London EC3R 8DL
Tel: 020 7929 9494
E-mail: membership@rtpi.org.uk
Website: www.rtpi.org.uk

The RTPI is the largest professional institute for planners in Europe, with over 22, 000 members. As well as promoting spatial planning, we develop and shape policy affecting the built environment, work to raise professional standards and support members through continuous education, training and development.

*MEMBERSHIP*
Student Member
Licentiate Member
Associate Member
Legal Associate Member (LARTPI)
Technical Member (TechRTPI)
Retired Member
Chartered Member (MRTPI)

*QUALIFICATION/EXAMINATIONS*
Please see www.rtpi.org.uk/item/178/23/5/3 for a list of accredited training providers

*DESIGNATORY LETTERS*
LARTPI, TechRTPI, HonMRTPI, MRTPI, FRTPI

# TRADING STANDARDS

## Membership of Professional Institutions and Associations

### THE TRADING STANDARDS INSTITUTE

1 Sylvan Court
Sylvan Way
Southfields Business Park
Basildon
Essex SS15 6TH
Tel: 0845 608 9400
Fax: 0845 608 9425
E-mail: institute@tsi.org.uk
Website: www.tradingstandards.gov.uk

The TSI, formed in 1881, is a not-for-profit membership association representing trading standards professionals in both the public and private sectors in the UK and overseas. TSI encourages honest enterprise and business, and helps safeguard the economic, environmental, health and social well-being of consumers.

*MEMBERSHIP*
Student Member
Affiliate Member
Associate Member (ATSI)
Full Member (MTSI)
Fellow (FTSI)
Corporate Affiliate
International

*QUALIFICATION/EXAMINATIONS*
The Trading Standards Qualification Framework consists of:
Certificate of Competence
Foundation Certificate in Consumer Affairs and Trading Standards
Core Skills Certificate in Consumer Affairs and Trading Standards
Module Certificate in Consumer Affairs and Trading Standards
Diploma in Consumer Affairs and Trading Standards
Higher Diploma in Consumer Affairs and Trading Standards

*DESIGNATORY LETTERS*
ATSI, MTSI, FTSI

# TRANSPORT

## Membership of Professional Institutions and Associations

### INSTITUTE OF TRANSPORT ADMINISTRATION

The Old Studio
25 Greenfield Road
Westoning
Bedfordshire MK45 5JD
Tel: 01525 634940
Fax: 01525 750016
E-mail: director@iota.org.uk
Website: www.iota.org.uk

The primary aim of IoTA is to broaden and improve the knowledge, skills and experience of its members in the practice of efficient road, rail, air and sea transport. We are one of the few professional bodies still recognized within the terms of the Road Traffic 1968 (Statutory Instrument 78), wherein it is permitted to proffer qualified opinion as to the professional competence of its members. Established in

1944, the Institute continues to set new benchmark standards for the industry; promoting a policy of Experience Teaches.

*MEMBERSHIP*
Student (StInstTA)
Associate (AInstTA)
Honorary Member
Associate Member (AMInstTA)
Member (MInstTA)
Fellow (FInstTA)
Patron Scheme for Companies

*DESIGNATORY LETTERS*
StInstTA, AInstTA, AMInstTA, MInstTA, FInstTA

## THE INSTITUTE OF TRAFFIC ACCIDENT INVESTIGATORS

Column House
London Road
Shrewsbury
Shropshire SY2 6NN
Tel: 08456 212066
Fax: 08456 212077
E-mail: gensec@itai.org
Website: www.itai.org

The Institute provides a means of communication, education, representation and regulation in the field of Traffic Accident Investigation. Our main aim is to provide a forum for spreading knowledge and enhancing expertise among those engaged in the discipline. Members include police officers, lecturers in higher education and private practitioners.

*MEMBERSHIP*
Affiliate
Associate (AITAI)
Member (MITAI)

*DESIGNATORY LETTERS*
AITAI, MITAI

# TRAVEL AND TOURISM

## *Membership of Professional Institutions and Associations*

## CONFEDERATION OF TOURISM AND HOSPITALITY

37 Duke Street
London W1U 1LN
Tel: 020 7258 9850
Fax: 020 7258 9869
E-mail: info@cthawards.com
Website: www.cthawards.com

The Confederation of Tourism and Hospitality is an awarding body approved by Ofqual, and registered on the QCA's National Qualifications Framework. We were established in 1982 to provide recognized standards of management and vocational training appropriate to the needs of the hotel and travel industries, via our syllabuses, examinations and awards.

*MEMBERSHIP*
Student Member
Professional Member (MCTH)
Honorary Fellow (FCTH)

*QUALIFICATION/EXAMINATIONS*
Level 2 Diploma in English Communication Skills (QCF)
Level 3 Diploma in Communication and Research Skills (QCF)

Level 3 Diploma in Tourism and Hospitality (QCF)
Level 4 Diploma in Hospitality Management (QCF)
Level 4 Diploma in Tourism Management (QCF)
Level 5 Diploma in Hospitality Management (QCF)
Level 5 Diploma in Tourism Management (QCF)
Level 6 Diploma in Hospitality and Tourism Management (QCF)
Level 7 Diploma in Hospitality and Tourism Management (QCF)

*DESIGNATORY LETTERS*
MCTH, FCTH

## INSTITUTE OF TRAVEL AND TOURISM

PO Box 217
Ware
Hertfordshire SG12 8WY
Tel: 0844 4995 653
Fax: 0844 4995 654
E-mail: enquiries@itt.co.uk
Website: www.itt.co.uk

The ITT, founded in 1956, is a professional membership body for individuals employed in the travel and tourism industry. We provide support and guidance for our members throughout their career and offer them CPD and training to maintain standards for the benefit of the industry as a whole.

*MEMBERSHIP*
Student Member
Introductory Member
Affiliate Member
Member
Member (MInstTT)
Fellow
Fellow (FInstTT)
University/College Member
Group Member
Corporate Member
Retired Member

*DESIGNATORY LETTERS*
MInstTT, FInstTT

## THE TOURISM MANAGEMENT INSTITUTE

c/o Hon Secretary, Dr Cathy Guthrie, FTMI, FTS
18 Cuninghill Avenue
Inverurie
Aberdeenshire AB51 3TZ
Tel: 01467 620769
E-mail: secretary@tmi.org.uk
Website: www.tmi.org.uk

Part of the Tourism Society, TMI is the professional body for tourism destination managers. Its network of 250+ members shares information via website, conferences, e-mails and newsletters. Committed to excellence, the TMI CPD programme aims to support destination management professionals through its events, Knowledge Bank and course recognition scheme.

*MEMBERSHIP*
Student
Associate (ATMI)
Member (MTMI)
Fellow (FTMI)

*DESIGNATORY LETTERS*
ATMI, MTMI, FTMI

## THE TOURISM SOCIETY

Queens House
55-56 Lincoln's Inn Fields
London WC2A 3BH
Tel: 020 7269 9693
Fax: 020 7404 2465
E-mail: admin@tourismsociety.org
Website: www.tourismsociety.org

The Tourism Society, founded in 1977, is the professional membership body for people working in all sectors of tourism. We strive to drive up standards of professionalism and act as an advocate of tourism to the government and the public and private sectors, and liaise with other tourism professionals worldwide. We also provide advice, support and networking opportunities to our 1, 200 or so members.

*MEMBERSHIP*
Student
Full Member (MTS)
Fellow (FTS)
Overseas/Retired Member
Group Member
Corporate Member
Graduate

*DESIGNATORY LETTERS*
MTS, FTS

# VETERINARY SCIENCE

## *Membership of Professional Institutions and Associations*

## BRITISH VETERINARY ASSOCIATION

7 Mansfield Street
London W1G 9NQ
Tel: 020 7636 6541
Fax: 020 7908 6349
E-mail: bvahq@bva.co.uk
Website: www.bva.co.uk

The BVA is the representative body for the veterinary profession in the UK and has more than 11, 500 members. We promote and support the interests of our members and the animals under their care, liaise with the government and are the leading provider of veterinary information to the media and general public.

*MEMBERSHIP*
Student Member
Associate Member
Full Member
Overseas Member

## SOCIETY OF PRACTISING VETERINARY SURGEONS

The Governor's House
Cape Road
Warwick CV34 5DJ
Tel: 01926 410454
Fax: 01926 411350
E-mail: office@spvs.org.uk
Website: www.spvs.org.uk

The SPVS was founded in 1933 with the aim of promoting the interests of veterinary surgeons in private practice. We are a non-territorial division of the British Veterinary Association. Our remit is to advise on all aspects of managing the business of a clinical veterinary practice, and we hold one-day, weekend and week-long courses and an annual congress.

*MEMBERSHIP*
Student Member
Graduate Member
Practice Member
Retired Member

## THE ROYAL COLLEGE OF VETERINARY SURGEONS

Belgravia House
62–64 Horseferry Road
London SW1P 2AF
Tel: 020 7222 2001
Fax: 020 7222 2004
E-mail: info@rcvs.org.uk
Website: www.rcvs.org.uk

The RCVS is the regulatory body for veterinary surgeons in the UK. Its role is to safeguard the health and welfare of animals committed to veterinary care, through the regulation of the educational, ethical and clinical standards of the veterinary profession, and to act as an impartial source of informed opinion on relevant veterinary issues.

*MEMBERSHIP*
Member (MRCVS)
Fellow (FRCVS)

*QUALIFICATION/EXAMINATIONS*
Certificate in Advanced Veterinary Practice (CertAVP)
RCVS Specialist
Diploma in Advanced Veterinary Nursing
Diploma of Fellowship (FRCVS)

*DESIGNATORY LETTERS*
MRCVS, FRCVS

# WASTES MANAGEMENT

## Membership of Professional Institutions and Associations

### CHARTERED INSTITUTION OF WASTES MANAGEMENT

9 Saxon Court
St Peter's Gardens
Marefair
Northampton NN1 1SX
Tel: 01604 620426
Fax: 01604 621339
E-mail: membership@ciwm.co.uk
Website: www.ciwm.co.uk

The CIWM represents more than 6, 000 waste management professionals – predominantly in the UK but also overseas. We promote education, training and research in the scientific, technical and practical aspects of waste management for the safeguarding of the environment, and set and strive to maintain high standards for individuals working in the waste management industry.

*MEMBERSHIP*
Student Member
Technician Member (TechMCIWM)
Associate Member (AssocMCIWM)
Graduate Member (GradMCIWM)
Licentiate (LCIWM)
Member (MCIWM)
Fellow (FCIWM)
Affiliated Organization

*QUALIFICATION/EXAMINATIONS*
CIWM Training Services specializes in developing and providing waste management training for individuals and organizations. Each year we organize more than 70 courses. For details see the website.

*DESIGNATORY LETTERS*
TechMCIWM, AssocMCIWM, GradMCIWM, LCIWM, MCIWM, FCIWM

# WATCH AND CLOCK MAKING AND REPAIRING

## Membership of Professional Institutions and Associations

### THE BRITISH HOROLOGICAL INSTITUTE LIMITED

Upton Hall
Upton
Newark
Nottinghamshire NG23 5TE
Tel: 01636 813795
Fax: 01636 812258
E-mail: via website
Website: www.bhi.co.uk

The BHI, which was formed in 1858 to promote horology, is a professional body with about 3, 000 members worldwide. We provide education and specialist training, set recognized standards of excellence in workmanship and professional conduct, and support our members in their work, making, repairing and servicing clocks and watches.

*MEMBERSHIP*
Associate
Member (MBHI)
Fellow (FBHI)

*QUALIFICATION/EXAMINATIONS*
Diploma in Clock and Watch Servicing (Level 3)

Diploma in the Servicing and Repair of Clocks / Watches (Level 4)
Diploma in the Repair, Restoration and Conservation of Clocks / Watches

*DESIGNATORY LETTERS*
MBHI, FBHI

# WELDING

## *Membership of Professional Institutions and Associations*

### THE WELDING INSTITUTE

Granta Park
Great Abington
Cambridge CB21 6AL
Tel: 01223 899000
E-mail: professional@twi.co.uk
Website: www.twiprofessional.com

The Welding Institute is the engineering institution for welding and joining professionals. We are committed to promoting the importance of welding/materials joining technology, given its importance as a key industrial technology governing the reliability and safety of many products, and to the advancement of education, training and CPD for our members.

*MEMBERSHIP*
Graduate (GradWeldI)
Technician (TechWeldI)
Senior Associate (SenAWeldI)
Incorporated Member (IncMWeldI)
Member (MWeldI)
Senior Member (SenMWeldI)
Fellow (FWeldI)
Honorary Fellow (HonFWeldI)
Engineering Technician (EngTech)
Incorporated Engineer (IEng)
Chartered Engineer (CEng)

*DESIGNATORY LETTERS*
GradWeldI, TechWeldI, SenAWeldI, IncMWeldI, MWeldI, SenMWeldI, FWeldI, HonFWeldI, EngTech, IEng, CEng

# WELFARE

## *Membership of Professional Institutions and Associations*

### INSTITUTE OF WELFARE

PO Box 5570
Stourbridge DY8 9BA
Tel: 0800 0 32 37 25
E-mail: info@instituteofwelfare.co.uk
Website: www.instituteofwelfare.co.uk

The Institute of Welfare was founded in 1945 and exists to promote the highest possible standards in the delivery of welfare to those who need it. We make representations to government, undertake research on welfare issues, encourage and facilitate the exchange of information, and provide opportunities for those engaged in welfare work to pursue CPD.

*MEMBERSHIP*
Affiliate Member
Member (MIW)
Fellow (FIW)
Companion (CIW)

*DESIGNATORY LETTERS*
MIW, FIW, CIW

# Part 6

# Bodies Accrediting Independent Institutions

# THE BRITISH ACCREDITATION COUNCIL FOR INDEPENDENT FURTHER AND HIGHER EDUCATION (BAC)

BAC is a registered charity that was established in 1984 to act as the national accrediting body for independent further and higher education. It is independent of both government and of the colleges it accredits.

A college that is accredited by BAC undergoes a thorough inspection every four years, with an interim visit after two years. Until 2000, BAC accreditation was only available to colleges in the United Kingdom, but there are now accredited colleges in 11 countries around the world: Bulgaria, the Czech Republic, Germany, Greece, Hungary, India, Lebanon, Mauritius, Singapore, South Africa and Switzerland. At present BAC accredits or approves 286 colleges in the United Kingdom and 24 overseas. Lists of accredited colleges are published each year; full details can be viewed on the BAC website.

BAC has a close relationship with the accreditation scheme operated by Accreditation UK (in the field of English as a Foreign Language) and is an affiliate of ENQA, the European Association for Quality Assurance in Higher Education. It maintains close links with all the major bodies concerned with the maintenance of standards in British education, including The British Council, Open and Distance Learning Quality Council (ODL QC), the Council of Validating Universities (CVU), National Recognition Information Centre (UK NARIC), GuildHE, UK Council for International Student Affairs (UKCISA) and the Joint Council for Qualifications (JCQ).

Accreditation by BAC is recognized by the UK Border Agency (UKBA) of the Home Office as a qualifying requirement for institutions to enrol visa students.

Further details of the work of the BAC and a current list of accredited institutions may be obtained from The Chief Executive, BAC, Fleet House, 5th Floor, 8–12 New Bridge Street, London EC4V 6AL; Tel: 0300 330 1400; Fax: 0300 330 1401; e-mail: info@the-bac.org; website: www.the-bac.org

# THE BRITISH COUNCIL

The British Council runs the Accreditation UK scheme in partnership with English UK for the inspection and accreditation of organizations that provide courses in English as a Foreign Language (EFL) in Britain. One of its aims is to promote accredited UK English Language Teaching (ELT) through the British Council's network of overseas offices.

Under the terms of the scheme, institutions are inspected rigorously every four years in the areas of management, resources and environment, teaching and learning, and welfare and student services. The scheme also includes a system of random spot-checking. The management and policy of the scheme are conducted by an independent board while a separate independent committee reviews inspectors' reports.

The majority of recognized schools are also members of English UK, which insists on British Council accreditation as a criterion for membership. In addition, all English UK members, of which there are around 450, are required to abide by the Association's Code of Practice and Regulations. English UK exists to raise the high standards of its members even further through conferences, training courses and publications. The association also represents the interests of members and students to government bodies, and promotes international student mobility through membership of the UK Border Agency User Panel.

Further information on the Accreditation UK scheme may be obtained from the Accreditation Unit, British Council, Bridgewater House, 58 Whitworth Street, Manchester M1 6BB; Tel: 0161 957 7692; e-mail: accreditation.unit@britishcouncil.org; website: www.britishcouncil.org/accreditation

Further information on English UK may be obtained from English UK, 219 St John Street, London EC1V 4LY; Tel: 020 7608 7960; Fax: 020 7608 7961; e-mail: info@englishuk.com; website: www.englishuk.com

## THE OPEN AND DISTANCE LEARNING QUALITY COUNCIL (ODLQC)

ODLQC was established in 1968 as the Council for the Accreditation of Correspondence Colleges, a joint initiative of the then Labour government and representatives of the sector. It is the principal accrediting body for a wide variety of providers of open and distance learning (ODL) in the UK, from commercial colleges to professional and public-sector institutions. Now independent, it nevertheless continues to have the informal support of government. ODLQC promotes quality by:

- establishing standards of education and training in ODL;
- recognizing good quality provision, wherever it occurs;
- supporting and protecting the interests of learners;
- encouraging the improvement of existing methods and the development of new ones;
- linking ODL with other forms of education and training;
- promoting wider recognition of the value of ODL.

Accreditation includes a rigorous assessment of educational provision, covering materials, tutorial support, publicity, contractual arrangements with learners and general administrative procedures, each of which is measured against the Council's published benchmark standards. If accredited, the provider is monitored on a regular basis and reassessed at least once every three years.

The Council promotes those colleges that it accredits, which are by definition quality providers of ODL, and acts as honest broker in matching accredited colleges to potential markets. A list of accredited providers is included on the Council's website: www.odlqc.org.uk. The Council also seeks to protect the interests of learners by promoting the importance of accreditation, and by offering advice and support directly to learners. At the same time, knowledge of good practice is disseminated more widely, and quality encouraged wherever ODL occurs.

The Council consists of members drawn from professional and public bodies involved in education, as well as representatives of accredited providers, and has strong links with other bodies in the sector, both in the UK and abroad.

All enquiries should be addressed to ODLQC, 79 Barnfield Wood Road, Beckenham, Kent BR3 6ST; website: www.odlqc.org.uk

# THE COUNCIL FOR INDEPENDENT EDUCATION (CIFE)

CIFE was founded in 1973 to promote strict adherence by independent sixth-form and tutorial colleges to the highest standards of academic and professional integrity and to provide an inspection service for these colleges. All member colleges must be accredited by the British Accreditation Council for Independent Further and Higher Education (BAC), and/or the Independent Schools Inspectorate (ISI). CIFE colleges all undergo regular inspection by the Department for Education. Candidate membership is available for up to three years for colleges that are seeking BAC or ISI accreditation and otherwise satisfy CIFE's exacting membership criteria. All colleges must also abide by stringent codes of conduct and practice; the character and presentation of their published exam results are subject to regulation, and the accuracy of the information must be validated by BAC as academic auditor to CIFE. Full members are subject to re-inspection by their accrediting bodies. There are 18 colleges in full or candidate membership of CIFE at present, spread throughout England but with concentrations in London, Oxford and Cambridge.

CIFE colleges offer a wide range of GCSE, A and AS level courses. In addition, some CIFE colleges offer English language tuition for students from overseas, and degree-level tuition. A number of the colleges offer summer holiday academic courses, and most of them also provide A level and GCSE revision courses during the Christmas and/or Easter holidays. Further information on CIFE may be obtained from the CIFE website: www.cife.org.uk; Tel: 020 8767 8666; e-mail: enquiries@cife.org.uk

# Part 7

# Study Associations and the 'Learned Societies'

Study associations consist of people who wish to increase their knowledge of a particular subject or range of subjects; they may be professionals or amateurs. Some associations consist almost entirely of specialists (eg the Royal Statistical Society); others (eg the Royal Geographical Society and the Zoological Society of London) have a more general membership. The learned societies usually have two grades of membership: fellows and members. Some also admit group members (such as schools or libraries), known as corporate members, and junior associate, corresponding and overseas members, who pay lower subscriptions. Some also elect honorary fellows or members. The members of some societies may use designatory letters, but this does not mean that the holder is 'qualified' in the same sense as a doctor or a chartered accountant.

Membership of some learned societies is by election, and is commonly accepted as distinguishing the candidate by admission to an exclusive group. Candidates may be selected in respect of pre-eminence in their subject or in the public service. The chief associations of this type are the Royal Society (founded in 1660 and granted Royal Charters in 1662 and 1663), the Royal Academy of Arts (founded in 1768) and the British Academy (granted the Royal Charter in 1902).

The Royal Society (www.royalsociety.org) was established to improve 'natural knowledge' and is mainly concerned with pure and applied science and technology. Election to Fellowship (FRS) is regarded as one of the highest distinctions. The society elects Fellows, Foreign Members, Royal Fellows and Honorary Fellows. The Royal Academy (www.royalacademy.org.uk) was established to cultivate and improve the arts of painting, sculpture and architecture. There are two main grades of membership: Academicians (RA), including Senior Academicians, and Associates (ARA); there are also a small number of Honorary Academicians. The British Academy (www.britac.ac.uk) is the UK's national academy for the humanities and the social sciences. It is the counterpart to the Royal Society that exists to serve the natural sciences. The Academy has Fellows (FBA), Corresponding Fellows and a small number of Honorary Fellows.

A list of learned societies and study associations can be found below.

## OCCUPATIONAL ASSOCIATIONS

The occupational associations do not qualify practitioners but organize them. Some coordinate the activities of specialists and others promote the individual and collective interests of professionals working in a wider area. Both types also seek to safeguard the public interest and to offer an educational service to their members. The latter type of association is especially numerous among teachers (eg the National Union of Teachers (NUT), the Educational Institute of Scotland (EIS), NASWUT (the National Association of Schoolmasters/Union of Women Teachers) and the National Association of Head Teachers (NAHT)), and is represented in the medical profession by the British Medical Association.

## LIST OF STUDY ASSOCIATIONS AND LEARNED SOCIETIES

This list largely excludes qualifying bodies, which are covered in Part 5. The date on the left is that of foundation or adoption of title.

## Agriculture and related subjects

1926 Agricultural Economics Society
1952 British Agricultural History Society
1945 British Grassland Society
1944 British Society of Animal Science
1947 British Society of Soil Science
1921 Commonwealth Forestry Association
1927 Herb Society of Great Britain
1925 Institute of Chartered Foresters
1938 Institution of Agricultural Engineers
1947 International Fertiliser Society
1839 Royal Agricultural Society of England
1882 Royal Forestry Society of England, Wales and N Ireland
1784 Royal Highland and Agricultural Society of Scotland
1804 Royal Horticultural Society
1854 Royal Scottish Forestry Society
1904 Royal Welsh Agricultural Society
1943 Society of Dairy Technology
1945 The Soil Association

## Anthropology and related subjects

1963 African Studies Association of the UK
1979 Association for the Study of Modern and Contemporary France
1982 Association for the Study of Modern Italy
1946 Association of Social Anthropologists of the UK and Commonwealth
1985 British Association for Irish Studies
1974 British Association for Japanese Studies
1972 British Association for South Asian Studies
1961 British Institute of Persian Studies
1973 British Society for Middle Eastern Studies
1981 European Association for Jewish Studies
1878 Folklore Society
1943 Hispanic and Luso Brazilian Council
1974 International Association for the Study of German Politics
1972 Japan Foundation
1891 Japan Society
1843 Royal Anthropological Institute of Great Britain and Ireland
1823 Royal Asiatic Society of Great Britain and Ireland
1868 Royal Commonwealth Society
1901 Royal Society for Asian Affairs
1936 Saltire Society
1977 Society for Caribbean Studies
1964 Society for Latin American Studies
1969 Society for Libyan Studies
1983 Society for the Promotion of Byzantine Studies
1879 Society for the Promotion of Hellenic Studies
1910 Society for the Promotion of Roman Studies
1969 University Association for Contemporary European Studies
1892 Viking Society for Northern Research

## Archaeology and related subjects

1924 Ancient Monuments Society
1979 Association for Environmental Archaeology
1843 British Archaeological Association
1996 British Epigraphy Society
1948 British Institute at Ankara
1846 Cambrian Archaeological Association
1944 Council for British Archaeology
1838 Eccleriological Society
1882 Egypt Exploration Society
1855 London and Middlesex Archaeological Society
1865 Palestine Exploration Fund
1908 Prehistoric Society
1843 Royal Archaeological Institute
1967 Society for Post-Medieval Archaeology

## Art and Design

| | |
|---|---|
| 1974 | Association of Art Historians |
| 1910 | Contemporary Art Society |
| 1915 | Design and Industries Association |
| 1950 | International Institute for Conservation of Historic and Artistic Works |
| 1888 | National Society for Education in Art and Design |
| 1899 | Pastel Society |
| 1768 | Royal Academy of Arts |
| 1814 | Royal Birmingham Society of Artists |
| 1883 | Royal Institute of Oil-Painters |
| 1831 | Royal Institute of Painters in Watercolours |
| 1826 | Royal Scottish Academy of Art and Architecture |
| 1754 | Royal Society for the Encouragement of Arts, Manufactures and Commerce |
| 1904 | Royal Society of British Sculptors |
| 1904 | Royal Society of Marine Artists |
| 1895 | Royal Society of Miniature Painters, Sculptors and Gravers |
| 1884 | Royal Society of Painter/Printmakers |
| 1891 | Royal Society of Portrait Painters |
| 1804 | Royal Watercolours Society |
| 1919 | Society of Graphic Fine Art |
| 1952 | Society of Portrait Sculptors |
| 1952 | United Society of Artists |
| 1955 | William Morris Society |

## Biology and related subjects

| | |
|---|---|
| 1936 | Association for the Study of Animal Behaviour |
| 1904 | Association of Applied Biologists |
| 1968 | Biomedical Engineering Society |
| 1836 | Botanical Society of Scotland |
| 1836 | Botanical Society of the British Isles |
| 1896 | British Bryological Society |
| 1929 | Freshwater Biological Association |
| 1889 | Marine Biological Association |
| 1833 | Royal Entomological Society |
| 1931 | Society for Applied Microbiology |
| 1911 | The Biochemical Society |
| 1913 | The British Ecological Society |
| 1896 | The British Mycological Society |
| 1858 | The British Ornithologists' Union |
| 1959 | The British Society for Cell Biology |
| 1933 | The British Trust for Ornithology |
| 1937 | The Systematics Association |
| 1826 | Zoological Society of London |

## Chemistry

| | |
|---|---|
| 1918 | Oil and Colour Chemists' Association |
| 1980 | Royal Society of Chemistry |
| 1881 | Society of Chemical Industry |
| 1897 | Society of Leather Technologists and Chemists |

## Economics, Statistics and related subjects

| | |
|---|---|
| 1992 | Association of Business Schools |
| 1927 | Economic History Society |
| 2003 | Economic Research Institute of Northern Ireland |
| 1955 | Institute of Economic Affairs |
| 1902 | Royal Economic Society |
| 1834 | Royal Statistical Society |
| 1897 | Scottish Economic Society |

## Engineering and related subjects

| | |
|---|---|
| 1847 | Architectural Association |
| 1966 | Concrete Society |
| 1946 | Faculty of Building |
| 1978 | Institute of Concrete Technology |
| 1997 | Institute of Ergonomics and Human Factors |
| 1976 | Royal Academy of Engineering |
| 1866 | Royal Aeronautical Society |

1916 Royal Incorporation of Architects in Scotland
1860 Royal Institution of Naval Architects
1916 Society of Automotive Engineers
1958 Society of Environmental Engineers
2003 The Energy Institute
1899 Town and Country Planning Association

## Geography, Geology and related subjects

1963 British Cartographic Society
1949 British Geotechnical Society
1940 British Society of Rheology
1968 Council for Environmental Education
1923 English Place-Name Society
1931 Gemmological Association of Great Britain
1893 Geographical Association
1807 Geological Society of London
1858 Geologists Association
1846 Hakluyt Society
1971 Institution of Environmental Sciences
1876 Mineralogical Society of Great Britain and Ireland
1847 Palaeontographical Society
1957 Paleontological Association
1830 Royal Geographical Society
1997 Royal Institute of Navigation
1884 Royal Scottish Geographical Society

## History and related subjects

1902 British Academy
1952 British Agricultural History Society
1888 British Record Society
1932 British Records Association
1947 British Society for the History of Science
1988 Centre for Metropolitan History
1864 Early English Texts Society
1964 Furniture History Society
1869 Harleian Society
1885 Huguenot Society of Great Britain and Ireland
1961 Institute of Heraldic and Genealogical Studies
1921 Institute of Historical Research
1893 Jewish Historical Society of England
1964 London Record Society
2000 Museums, Libraries and Archives Council
1920 Newcomen Society for the Study of the History of Engineering and Technology
1921 Oriental Ceramic Society
1868 Royal Historical Society
1836 Royal Numismatic Society
1869 Royal Philatelic Society, London
1953 Scottish Genealogy Society
1886 Scottish History Society
1897 Scottish Record Society
1976 Social History Society
1921 Society for Army Historical Research
1910 Society for Nautical Research
1967 Society for Renaissance Studies
1970 Society for the Social History of Medicine
1707 Society of Antiquaries of London
1780 Society of Antiquaries of Scotland
1956 Society of Architectural Historians in Great Britain
1947 Society of Archivists
1911 Society of Genealogists
1906 The Historical Association
1958 Victorian Society

## Languages

1883 Alliance Française
1891 An Comunn Gaidhealach
1981 Association for French Language Studies
1932 Association for German Studies in Great Britain and Ireland
1990 Association for Language Learning
1910 Chartered Institute of Linguists
1991 Instituto Cervantes

| | |
|---|---|
| 1964 | National Association for the Teaching of English |
| 2003 | National Centre for Languages |
| 1993 | University Council of Modern Languages |
| 1988 | Women in German Studies |

## Law

| | |
|---|---|
| 1958 | British Institute of International and Comparative Law |
| 1972 | Intellectual Property Bar Association |
| 1922 | Law Society of Northern Ireland |
| 1949 | Law Society of Scotland |
| 1920 | Royal Institute of International Affairs |
| 1965 | Scottish Law Commission |
| 1887 | Selden Society |

## Literature and Arts

| | |
|---|---|
| 1959 | Academi – Yr Academi Gymreig |
| 1973 | Alliance of Literary Societies |
| 1969 | Art Libraries Society |
| 1970 | Association for Scottish Literary Studies |
| 1989 | Association of Independent Libraries |
| 1892 | Bibliographical Society |
| 1992 | British Association for Information and Library Education and Research |
| 1975 | British Comparative Literature Association |
| 1933 | British Film Institute |
| 1960 | British Society of Aesthetics |
| 1893 | Bronte Society |
| 1949 | Cambridge Bibliographical Society |
| 1935 | Charles Lamb Society |
| 1904 | Classical Association |
| 1902 | Dickens Fellowship |
| 1890 | Edinburgh Bibliographical Society |
| 1906 | English Association |
| 1886 | Francis Bacon Society Inc |
| 1960 | H. G. Wells Society |
| 1997 | Historical Novel Society |
| 1973 | Joseph Conrad Society |
| 1997 | Leeds Philosophical and Literary Society |
| 1906 | Malone Society |
| 1781 | Manchester Literary and Philosophical Society |
| 1995 | Philip Larkin Society |
| 1842 | Philological Society |
| 1909 | Poetry Society |
| 1820 | Royal Society of Literature |
| 1884 | Society of Authors |
| 2004 | Society of College, National and University Libraries |
| 1984 | Standing Conference for the Arts and Social Sciences |
| 1968 | Thomas Hardy Society |

## Management

| | |
|---|---|
| 1986 | British Academy of Management |

## Mathematics and Physics

| | |
|---|---|
| 1924 | Astronomical Society of Edinburgh |
| 1890 | British Astronomical Association |
| 1966 | British Biophysical Society |
| 1927 | British Institute of Radiology |
| 1933 | British Interplanetary Society |
| 1930 | Institution of Electronics |
| 1871 | Mathematical Association |
| 1820 | Royal Astronomical Society |
| 1850 | Royal Meteorological Society |

## Medicine (including Psychology)

1887 Anatomical Society of GB and Ireland
1957 Association for Child and Adolescent Mental Health
1957 Association for the Study of Medical Education
1932 Association of Anaesthetists of GB and Ireland
1933 Association of British Neurologists
1953 Association of Clinical Biochemistry
1927 Association of Clinical Pathologists
1920 Association of Surgeons of GB and Ireland
1959 British Academy for Forensic Science
2003 British Association for Sexual Health and HIV
1977 British Association of Clinical Anatomists
1950 British Association of Forensic Medicine
1962 British Association of Oral Surgeons
1943 British Association of Otolaryngologists
1954 British Association of Paediatric Surgeons
1973 British Association of Surgical Oncology
1945 British Association of Urological Surgeons
1934 British Diabetic Association
1948 British Geriatrics Society
1832 British Medical Association
1950 British Neuropathological Society
1953 British Occupational Hygiene Society
1965 British Orthodontic Society
1918 British Orthopaedic Association
1925 British Osteopathic Association
1913 British Psychoanalytical Society
1901 British Psychological Society
1948 British Society for Allergy and Clinical Immunology
1962 British Society for Clinical Cytology
1937 British Society of Gastroenterology
1960 British Society for Haematology
1947 British Society for Research on Ageing
1945 British Thoracic Society
1947 Ergonomics Society
1946 Experimental Psychology Society
1950 Faculty of Homeopathy
1959 Forensic Science Society
1819 Hunterian Society
1969 Institute of Occupational Medicine
1964 Institute of Pharmacy Management
1773 Medical Society of London
1901 Medico-Legal Society
1941 Nutrition Society
1906 Pathological Society of Great Britain and Ireland
1875 Royal Environmental Health Institute of Scotland
1734 Royal Medical Society
1931 Royal Pharmaceutical Society of Great Britain
2008 Royal Society for Public Health
1805 Royal Society of Medicine
1907 Royal Society of Tropical Medicine and Hygiene
1946 Society for Endocrinology
1950 Society for Reproduction and Fertility
1884 Society for the Study of Addiction
1926 Society of British Neurological Surgeons

## Music

1977 Alkan Society
1979 British Music Society
1971 Chopin Society
1932 English Folk Dance and Song Society
1882 Incorporated Society of Musicians
1888 Plainsong and Medieval Music Society
1874 Royal Musical Association
1955 Welsh Music Guild

## Philosophy

1880 Aristotelian Society
2003 British Philosophical Association
1984 British Society for the History of Philosophy
1819 Cambridge Philosophical Society

1990 Friedrich Nietzsche Society
1979 Hegel Society of Great Britain
1781 Manchester Literary and Philosophical Society
1913 Philosophical Society of England
1925 Royal Institute of Philosophy
1802 Royal Philosophical Society of Glasgow

## Politics

1975 British International Studies Association
1951 David Davies Memorial Institute of International Studies
1884 Electoral Reform Society
1945 Federal Trust for Education and Research
1987 Institute of Welsh Affairs
1974 International Association for the Study of German Politics
1950 Political Studies Association
1868 Royal Commonwealth Society
1920 Royal Institute of International Affairs

## Science general

1924 Association for Informational Management
1831 British Science Association
1956 British Society for the History of Science
1960 British Society for the Philosophy of Science
1799 Royal Institution of Great Britain
1660 Royal Society
1783 Royal Society of Edinburgh

## Theology and Religious Studies

1908 Baptist Historical Society
1954 British Association for the Study of Religions
1904 Canterbury and York Society
1904 Catholic Record Society
1961 Ecclesiastical History Society
1981 European Association for Jewish Studies
1903 Friends Historical Society
1972 United Reformed Church History Society
1893 Wesley Historical Society

# General Index

Note: In addition to the abbreviations listed at the beginning of the book, the following are used throughout the index; FE – Further Education; HE – Higher Education. Universities are listed under locations eg: Aberdeen, University of